Christ in Egypt

The Horus-Jesus Connection

D.M. Murdock

Stellar House Publishing
www.stellarhousepublishing.com

ALSO BY D.M. MURDOCK a.k.a. ACHARYA S

The Christ Conspiracy: The Greatest Story Ever Sold
Suns of God: Krishna, Buddha and Christ Unveiled
Who Was Jesus? Fingerprints of The Christ

Library of Congress Cataloging in Publication Data
Murdock, D.M./Acharya S
 Christ in Egypt: The Horus-Jesus Connection.
 1. Jesus Christ—Historicity 2. Christianity—Origin
Includes bibliographical references and index
ISBN: 0-9799631-1-7
ISBN13: 978-0-9799631-1-7

Design and layout by D.M. Murdock.
Cover art by JimJupiterDesign.com adapted from:
Left: Statue of Isis suckling Horus, from the Gregorian Egyptian
Museum in the Vatican, Italy
Right: Statue of Virgin Mary suckling Baby Jesus, Venice, Italy.

Table of Contents

Mediterranean Sea

Canaan

Jerusalem

Rosetta

Alexandria

Buto
Sais

Tharu

The "Way of Horus"

Lake Mareotis

Busiris

Bubastis

Heliopolis/On

Giza
Saqqara

Memphis

Sinai

Lower
Egypt

Nile

Oxyrhynchus

Hermopolis

Amarna

Nag Hammadi

Abydos

Dendera

Deir el Bahari
Valley of the Kings
Valley of the Queens

Thebes
Karnak
Luxor

Red Sea

Esne

Hierakonpolis

Edfu

Upper
Egypt

Kom Ombo/Ombos

Elephantine
Aswan

Philae

Nabta

Abu Simbel

Kush

Nubian Desert

Napata

Jebel Barkal

Meroe

© D.M. Murdock & Stellar House Publishing.

Preface

"So there grew, during those first centuries of Christianity, a whole literature of the Hermetic sort in which the symbols, interpreted in the orthodox Christian tradition as historical, were being read in a proper mythological sense. And these then began to link the Christian myth to pagan analogues. The Gnostics, for instance, were in that boat. But the orthodox Christians insisted on the historicity of all these events."

Joseph Campbell, *An Open Life* (77)

Over a century ago, renowned British Egyptologist Sir Dr. E.A. Wallis Budge (1857-1934), a Keeper of the Egyptian and Assyrian Antiquities at the British Museum, as well as a confessed Christian, remarked that a study tracing the "influence of ancient Egyptian religious beliefs and mythology on Christianity" would "fill a comparatively large volume."[1] Since Dr. Budge's time, for a variety of reasons, including the seemingly irreconcilable academic gap between historians and theologians, no one has taken up the call to produce such a volume—until now.

This book is the result of decades of study of the world's religions and mythologies, focusing on comparative religion with the intention of showing from where Christianity in particular likely devised many of its most cherished beliefs. My previous books on the subjects of comparative religion, mythology and Christian origins include: *The Christ Conspiracy: The Greatest Story Ever Sold*; *Suns of God: Krishna, Buddha and Christ Unveiled*; and *Who Was Jesus? Fingerprints of The Christ*. I continue this ongoing investigation with the fascinating land of the pharaohs not only because that nation was extremely influential in the world into which Christianity was born, but also because it possesses so much material preserved from the centuries of destruction—much of it quite deliberate—that it is to Egypt we may look for solid, primary-source proof of our premise.

It should be noted, however, that I did not originally set out to prove a thesis established *a priori* but that, having been engaged in this field for so many years and, having been raised a Christian and knowing that faith very well, I have been struck over the decades by the profound and relevant resemblances between it and pre-Christian and non-Christian religions, and it has become clear that Egypt was the fount of much of this religious and spiritual knowledge.

In this groundbreaking effort, I have used the latest and best technology to search far and wide through a massive amount of material across several languages, beginning with the ancient primary sources and extending into the modern era. In order to demonstrate a solid case, I have been compelled to do extensive and

---

[1] Budge, *GE*, I, xvi.

exhaustive research in the pertinent ancient languages, such as Egyptian, Hebrew, Greek, Latin and Coptic, while I have also utilized authorities in modern languages such as German and French.

Not only have I provided much important and interesting information directly addressing the striking comparisons between the Egyptian and Christian religions, but also I have exposed on several occasions various biases, censorship and other behaviors that have impacted mainstream knowledge over the centuries, allowing for certain revelations to come to light in English here possibly for the first time in history.

In order to set the stage for the various premises of each chapter, I have included quotations at the beginnings thereof, at times both modern and ancient. After thus providing a summary of the premise, in each chapter I delve into the appropriate *primary sources* to whatever extent possible. In my analysis of the ancient Egyptian texts, I consulted and cross-referenced as many translations as I could find, and I attempted to defer to the most modern renditions as often as possible. All of this work was accomplished as truly independent scholarship, without funding from any group, organization or institution, as has been the case with all of my past endeavors as well.

The result is that *Christ in Egypt: The Horus-Jesus Connection* comprises nearly 600 pages with almost 2,400 footnotes and citations from more than 900 books, journals and assorted other sources from experts in germane fields of study from different time periods beginning in antiquity up to the most modern Egyptologists, in order to create a consensus of opinion since the topic is so contentious. In this regard, brief biographical material is also included for many of these authorities, so that readers may be assured of the individual's credentials. The broad scope of these sources dating from thousands of years ago to the most modern research means there can be no dismissive argument based on either a lack of primary sources or because the authorities cited are "outdated."

Yet, for all this erudition, I have hopefully succeeded in making *Christ in Egypt* as readily accessible to the average reader as possible, so that the book can be enjoyed by all who wish to know the hidden history of the origins of religious ideology. Some of the material may strike some readers as difficult and/or tedious, but I hope it will be understood that, in consideration of the controversial nature of this issue, it was necessary to be as thorough as possible. This book is therefore not meant to be a "quick read." Rather, it is intended as a reference book providing knowledge for years to come.

In comparison to other literature on the subject, the present book might be considered the most complete and scientific study of the Egyptian influence on Christianity ever produced in English. Each major contention and many minor ones have been carefully cited with an eye to as exacting accuracy as is possible, and every effort has been made to doublecheck particularly controversial facts. My intent has always been to restore the proper milieu of the eras in question, resurrecting cultures that have been the object of disinformation and disdain. In creating this opus, I experienced great delight at a number of significant features that came to light, and I offer this unusual but intriguing research in the spirit in which it was intended: To wit, to demonstrate that mankind's most cherished and fervently held religious beliefs are rooted firmly in *human* creation based on natural phenomena, without the need for supernatural genesis but nonetheless extraordinarily marvelous and meaningful.

D.M. Murdock
aka Acharya S
February 2009

Introduction

"Out of Egypt have I called my son."

The Gospel of Matthew (2:15)

"For what is now called the Christian religion existed of old and was never absent from the beginning of the human race until Christ came in the flesh. Then true religion which already existed began to be called Christian."

Saint Augustine, *Retractiones* (1:13)

"The Religion proclaimed by him to All Nations was neither New nor Strange."

Bishop Eusebius, *The History of the Church* (2:4)

"Christianity represents the last term of [the] invasion of oriental ideas into the West. It did not fall like a thunderbolt in the midst of a surprised and alarmed old world. It had its period of incubation, and, while it was seeking the definitive form of its dogmas, the problems for which it was pursuing the solutions preoccupied the thoughts in Greece, in Asia, in Egypt. There were in the air stray ideas that combined themselves in all sorts of proportions."[1]

Dr. Louis Ménard, *Hermes Trismégiste* (ix)

"There can be no doubt that the oldest Egyptian writings contain some vestiges of primeval faith. Egyptians in very remote areas believed in the immortality of man, with reward or punishment in the future state. They believed in the existence of good and evil powers in this life, and were not without a sense of personal responsibility..."

Rev. Dr. W.H. Rule, *The Horus Myth and Its Relation to Christianity* (66)

Over the centuries, it has been the contention of numerous scholars and researchers of comparative religion and mythology that one of the major influences on the Christian faith was that of ancient Egypt. Although we today may find the ancient Egyptian religion bizarre and amusing, with all its peculiarities, including gods and goddesses in the forms of many kinds of animals, the truth is that the Egyptians themselves took their faith *very* seriously, so much so that, as with religions of today, murder in its name was not unknown. One need only look to the cautionary tale of the notorious monotheistic pharaoh Amenhotep IV, aka Akhenaten, for an example of how sincerely the Egyptians and their priesthoods upheld their religion. Indeed, many Egyptians—and especially their priests—were as devout in their own religion as are the most pious among us today. And this faith was not isolated or fleeting: The Egyptian religion was

---

[1] Translation mine. The original French of Ménard is: "Le christianisme représente le dernier terme de cette invasion des idées orientales en Occident. Il n'est pas tombé comme un coup de foudre au milieu du vieux monde surpris et effaré. Il a eu sa période d'incubation, et, pendant qu'il cherchait la forme définitive de ses dogmes, les problèmes dont il poursuivait la solution préoccupaient aussi les esprits en Grèce, en Asie, en Égypte. Il y avait dans l'air des idées errantes qui se combinaient en toute sorte de proportions." (Ménard, ix-x.)

exceedingly widespread and possessed an antiquity unparalleled in the known world at the time. As the Greek historian Herodotus (c. 484-c. 425 BCE[1]) wrote in his *Histories* (2.37) almost 2,500 years ago, the Egyptians were "religious to excess, beyond any other nation in the world."[2] Concurring with this assessment, renowned Egyptologist Dr. Jan Assman (b. 1938), a professor of Egyptology at the University of Konstanz, remarks:

> In ancient Egypt, mortuary religion was not simply one area of cultural praxis, among others, such as the cult of the gods, economy, law, politics, literature, and so forth. Rather, in this case, we are dealing with a center of cultural consciousness, one that radiated out into many—we might almost say, into all—others areas of ancient Egyptian culture.[3]

In *Egyptian Religion*, Egyptologist Dr. Siegfried Morenz (1914-1970), a director of the Institute of Egyptology at the University of Leipzig, likewise describes religion as the "matrix of culture" and "womb of culture," especially as found in Egypt.[4]

Over its vast life of several millennia, hundreds of millions of people engaged in the Egyptian religion, with its major themes and motifs well known and highly respected. In fact, it has been estimated that some 500 million Egyptians were mummified during the time of the pharaohs, indicating there were at least *half a billion followers* of the Egyptian religion during that era.[5] Hence, any competing faith would be hard-pressed to overturn this deep and abiding reverence for the Egyptian religion and its gods, and would need to incorporate as much of the Egyptian mythos and ritual into itself as was possible. The fact is that such devoutly religious people do not easily and

---

[1] In dating notations, "c." means "circa" or "around," while "b." is the abbreviation for "born" and "d." means "died." The abbreviation "fl." means "flourished," representing the time during which a ruler was in power or any other individual was active in his/her occupation. "BCE" is equivalent to "BC" and means "Before the Common Era," while "CE" equals "AD" but means "Common Era."

[2] Herodotus/de Selincourt, 99.

[3] Assman, *DSAE*, 2-3.

[4] Morenz, 13.

[5] See "The Pyramids and the Cities of the Pharaohs." This figure apparently comes from calculations done by Egyptologist Dr. George R. Gliddon (1809-1875) as follows: "Let us call the period of mummification 3,000 years, which would be greatly below the mark. The average population of Egypt during the time probably amounted to five millions, which died off every generation of thirty-three years. We have, then, by a simple process of calculation, 450 millions of mummies for the 3,000 years; but as the time was probably more than 3,000 years, the number of mummies might be estimated in round numbers at five hundred millions." (Gliddon, 73.) This mindboggling number of half a billion appears impossible at first; however, it works out to only 167,000 or so people dying per year over a period of 3,000 years, so it is in reality rather plausible. It should be kept in mind that not all Egyptians could afford to be mummified by human methods; many of the poorer classes would bury their dead at the edge of the desert in order to allow for natural mummification to occur. (Redford, 233.) Nevertheless, one may reasonably presume that even the poorest of the deceased were afforded some sort of burial ritual.

readily abandon their religion and god(s)—do fervent Christians, for instance, give up their god without a fight?

Also, much of the disparagement of the Egyptian gods and religion emanates from the Christian Church fathers of the second century and onwards, such as the particularly snide Clement of Alexandria (c. 150-211/216 AD/CE), in a transparent play to usurp the others' deities with their own faith, which was, in reality, no less ridiculous overall.[1] This behavior is unwarranted, in light of what we know today about the Egyptian religion, which, largely because of these prejudicial efforts, was almost lost to us forever. Fortunately, a number of individuals over the centuries were able to overcome these prejudices to see for themselves what the Egyptian religion truly represented—and they did so often at great risk, as there was a concerted effort by the Church to censor this information. This type of abuse continues to this day, with those who dare to suggest that Christianity is not original but basically constitutes a reworking of old faiths subjected to all sorts of derision and ridicule, as well as irrational and impossible demands for evidence of an obvious fact, when, in upholding their own religious beliefs, these same detractors require little or no evidence at all. As independent philosopher N.W. Barker says, "If there were valid scientific evidence in support of the supernatural religious claims, *faith* would not be the main requirement."

Despite the disparagement and dismissal, the reality remains that the many Egyptian myths and rituals, including numerous gods and goddesses, prayers and hymns, were not obscure and ignored but were known by millions of people over a long period of time. *These hallowed Egyptian motifs included the sacredness of the cross, the virgin mother who gave birth to the divine son, a godman who taught on Earth, led 12 followers, healed the sick, and raised the dead, and who was murdered, buried and resurrected, etc.* Although they were often deemed "mysteries," a number of these important concepts were undoubtedly in the minds of many people by the time the Christian religion appeared in the same areas of the Mediterranean. As pointed out by renowned Swiss Egyptologist Dr. Erik Hornung (b. 1933), a professor emeritus of Egyptology at the University of Basel, the Egyptian mysteries were not necessarily secrets but were carried out in public, such as the annual passion play of the god Osiris.[2] As Dr. Morenz also points out, "The participation of large masses of the population was necessary at the so-called mysteries..."[3] These *mysteries* were particularly known to those responsible for the creation of religion, the priests, who actively studied and imitated

---

[1] For more on the problems with Christianity, see my book *Who Was Jesus? Fingerprints of The Christ.*
[2] Hornung, *SLE*, 13.
[3] Morenz, 90.

Peter's Basilica in Rome stands an obelisk moved from Egypt by Emperor Caligula (12-41 AD/CE), who placed it in his circus, after which it was later transported during the 16th century AD/CE to the Piazza San Pietro,[1] eventually serving as the gnomon of a sundial.

In the end, the lack of artifacts and primary sources thus reflects the criminal destruction on the part of the devout. In this same regard, Christian writers also mutilated the works of ancient authors, both Christian and non-Christian. Much destruction of ancient culture has likewise occurred during the many wars, including both World Wars, which greatly affected Christian civilization.

Included in the "sources" debate is the constant dunning for credentials, along with the notion that only those with the highest qualifications in the most salient fields are able to give any truthful or educated opinion on a subject. In reality, such is not necessarily the case, with many non-specialists often capable of putting forth erudite and accurate views. Moreover, in shoring up their faith, fervent believers frequently require no credentials at all. Nevertheless, again, in order to satisfy this request for credentials, every effort has been taken here to provide commentary from highly credentialed scholars in relevant fields.

In any event, amid the rubble of the past destroyed remains enough primary-source material to show sufficiently that there is little original or "historical" about Christianity. This claim regarding primary sources ranks as especially true in Egypt, where the material could not be completely obliterated, as no matter how mightily the utter annihilation of evidence was attempted, there simply existed too much, despite the destruction ages before by grave robbers and other vandals. In addition to trashing texts and mutilating monuments, Christians even stuccoed over the hieroglyphs in order to remove them from sight, because they could not chip them away. However, this behavior had the effect of *preserving* the hieroglyphs for us to work with now, and scientists and scholars have only had serious access to the Egyptian culture over the past couple of centuries. Indeed, not so long ago even the massive Great Pyramid was partially buried in sand, while the Sphinx was covered up to its neck.

The ancient texts in which many of the aspects and myths of the Egyptian religion can be found date back millennia, with estimates varying from more than 4,000 to 7,000 years ago.[2] Precise dates for the oldest Egyptian texts are difficult to ascertain: For example, the Pyramid Texts—claimed to be the "world's oldest religious literature"[3]—are conservatively dated to at least 4,000 years ago and

---

[1] Tronzo, 19, 26ff; Jokilehto, 36.

[2] Allen, J., *AEPT*, 1.

[3] This contention is up for debate, as Indian scholars assert that the portions of the Rig Veda are many thousands of years old, while Sumerian writings are also considered the "oldest literature in history," with some Sumerian religious texts dating to perhaps as much as 4,000 years ago. The Sumerian script purportedly preceded the Egyptian

are said to be the basis for what became the Book of the Dead (c. 1600 BCE).[1] Yet, parts of the Book of the Dead or "BD"—the *Egyptian Bible,* as many have styled it—have been dated to at least 7,000 years ago as well, based on the chronology provided by the Egyptians themselves, who asserted these portions to have been so old as to have been lost by the time of the First Dynasty (c. 3100 to c. 2890 BCE).[2]

In any case, beginning at least 4,000 years ago the Pyramid Texts (c. 2350 BCE) were inscribed all over Egyptian pyramids, eventually to adorn the many tombs, both royal and non-royal, as well as "sarcophagi, coffins, canopic chests, papyri, stelae, and other funerary monuments..."[3] These texts continued in one form or another into the common era, some embodied into the more famous Book of the Dead and other writings such as on mummy wrappings that included portions of the BD.[4]

Beginning in the First Intermediate Period (2181-2041 BCE),[5] the mortuary literature began to be written on coffins as well, constituting the "Coffin Texts." The Coffin Texts represent a mass of "magical and liturgical spells"[6] inspired by the Pyramid Texts that were written on the coffins of wealthy but non-royal individuals. However, the Coffin Texts ranks as "far less coherent than the Pyramid Texts, for they lack a unifying point of view."[7] Numbering over 1,000, these texts constitute a result of the "[f]ear of death and longing for eternal life [that] have been brewed in a sorcerer's cauldron from which they emerge as magic incantations of the most phrenetic sort."[8] The Coffin Texts are important in that they allowed for the spread of the ideas within the Pyramid Texts, along with much material newly introduced, demonstrating not only longevity for the PT but also that the religion changed, as well as that it became pervasive and well known by even the common people.

Working with the Egyptian material is quite satisfying overall, since so much of it escaped destruction—again, much of which was deliberate. With a little teasing here and there, the secrets of the Egyptian religion yield themselves up beautifully, providing excellent

---

hieroglyphs as we have them, although earlier forms of writing do appear in Egypt as well, dating to almost as early as the Sumerian, both over 5,000 years ago. (Hornung, *SLE,* 11.) Davies and Friedman, however, relate that "recent discoveries at Abydos have shown that the Egyptians had an advanced system of writing even earlier than the Mesopotamians, some 150 years before Narmer." (Davies, V., 36.)

[1] Hornung, *VK,* 8.
[2] Bonwick, 188-189. The numbering used here for the chapters/spells of the Book of the Dead follows the convention of "BD 1," "BD 2," etc. (See, e.g., Griffiths, *DV,* 214.)
[3] Allen, J., *AEPT,* 1.
[4] Gatty, 35.
[5] Brier, 12.
[6] *The Oxford History of Ancient Egypt,* 115.
[7] Lichtheim, 131.
[8] Lichtheim, 131.

primary-source data for our major contentions concerning the relationship to Christianity. Indeed, regarding the Egyptian mortuary literature, or "Books of the Netherworld," Dr. Hornung remarks:

> Their purpose was to provide the king with a systematic description of the world beyond death, one that followed the path of the sun after sunset through the twelve hours of the night.... Private tombs and sarcophagi of the Late Period were also decorated with copies of these works, and *it is not improbable that even early Christian texts were influenced by ideas and images from the New Kingdom religious books.*[1]

Thus, by the words of a major modern Egyptologist, we are encouraged to look for "ideas and images from the New Kingdom religious books" that may have influenced "early Christian texts!"

Speaking of sources, it often appears necessary to repeat that searching encyclopedias will not yield adequate results when it comes to deep research, particularly since until lately most of the encyclopedias in English were written and edited by Christians who would hardly be keen on including obvious parallels to Christ in their various entries on gods and men.[2] Moreover, flipping through encyclopedias will not make an expert of anyone; thus, caution is required when reading hasty rebuttals from fervent believers—such commentaries tend to be inadequate, representing a cursory scan by those who are rarely experts. Such interpretations may sound impressive at first to the untrained eye; however, with serious, time-consuming research digging into long-forgotten and buried archives, most if not all of these shallow encyclopedia-rebuttals can be put to rest, as demonstrated in this present work.

Egyptian Language Translations

The most important and obvious place we may turn in our quest for data regarding the Egyptian religion is to the ancient Egyptian texts, monuments and other artifacts, including, of course, the fabled hieroglyphs, the ancient script used to describe, among other things, the many sacred concepts. In discussing the translations of these hieroglyphs, it should be kept in mind that, while some antiquated "religious" language is frequently used, there is in general not as

---

[1] Hornung, *VK*, 9. (Emph. added.)

[2] Encyclopedias provide for some consensus of opinion and a valuable starting point for research. In such generally short entries, of course, only a small portion of a subject can be addressed, and encyclopedias thus tend to be sanitized of controversial material. Older encyclopedias may contain material that has been omitted not because it is erroneous but because it is not popular with mainstream authorities. Some encyclopedias are simply better, regardless of their age, particularly in consideration of "timeless" subjects such as religious ideology. One such example is the renowned *Encyclopaedia Britannica* of 1911, which is still considered to be exemplary. Another is the *Catholic Encyclopedia*, which, although in some entries a century old, remains highly valuable not only because, other than in places where faith does not permit, it tends to be fairly accurate, but also because of its many admissions against interest.

much room for interpretation as some might aver, and the common renderings by older scholars such as Sir Dr. E.A. Wallis Budge and devout Catholic Sir Peter Le Page Renouf (1822-1897), the previous Keeper at the British Museum, tend to be fairly faithful and accurate for the most part.[1] Of course, various more modern translations represent improvements in certain areas and often may be preferable. We know this assertion concerning interpretation to be true in part because these scholars were using the keys provided by the famous Rosetta Stone (196 BCE), which included not only the Egyptian hieroglyphic and demotic scripts but also Greek, the main language along with Coptic that allowed for the Egyptian to be translated at last. The Greek language is very specific and readily translated into English, usually with little interpretation necessary. Hence, we can be relatively certain that the English renderings of the Egyptian hieroglyphs using the decoding provided by the ancient Greek translations are relatively accurate and generally require little interpretation, although at times some is necessary. Regarding the ability of modern scholars to read the Egyptian hieroglyphs, professor of Egyptology at Brown University Dr. James P. Allen (b. 1945) concludes:

> Since Champollion's time, Egyptologists have continually refined our knowledge of ancient Egyptian writing, words, and grammar. Except for the most obscure words, hieroglyphic texts can be read today almost as easily as those of any other known language.[2]

---

[1] I am aware of the debate concerning Budge's voluminous work, a controversy that some have suggested represents a form of rivalry not uncommon in the academic world or in the world at large. I personally have found nothing egregious about Budge's discussion of the Egyptian religion, although I cannot vouch for everything in his hieroglyphic dictionaries, for instance, which are considered outdated in their system of transliteration (Allen, J., *AEPT*, 13). Nor can Budge be criticized for venturing what turned out to be certain flawed dates of pharaohs and texts; in consideration of the more limited knowledge of those particular subjects at the time, in general Budge did very well in his estimations, especially in view of the mass of material this pioneer sifted through. The fact remains that Budge was extremely talented linguistically, as well as extraordinarily well educated and experienced as to Egyptian antiquities, culture, religion and language. He also knew his own Christian faith very well, as evidenced by his remarks thereupon. I therefore provide Budge's assessment of Egyptian religion, including some linguistic interpretation, but no subject that would become "obsolete" within the decades since his passing. Moreover, in comparing the older and newer editions of Egyptian texts, I am not convinced that the latter are always superior in terms of translation. In fact, some more modern renditions seem stilted in their rigid adherence to academic sterility in the interest of purported precision, possibly lacking the potential spirit and potent spirituality intended by the text. In various instances, it is probable that *Budge is unpalatable to some because he repeatedly compared the Egyptian and Christian religions and stated that an investigation of the former's influences upon the latter would fill "a comparatively large volume!"* (*GE*, I, xvi.) In any event, the more modern translations are quite honorable overall and are referenced here as well whenever possible.
[2] Allen, J., *ME*, 9.

Thus, we can be reasonably assured when reading the various translations that we are faced with the essential intention of the writers of the original texts. In order to provide a consensus, in this present work I have used translations of not only Sirs Budge and Renouf but also several others, such as Dr. James Allen, Dr. Thomas George Allen, Dr. Samuel Birch, Dr. James Breasted, Dr. Heinrich Brugsch-Bey, Dr. Hellmut Brunner, Dr. Raymond Faulkner, Dr. John Gwyn Griffiths, Dr. Tom Hare, Dr. Richard Hooker, Dr. Samuel Mercer, Dr. William Murnane and Neil Parker.

Even though some of the renditions may seem "outdated" because they use the archaic English pronouns "thou," "thy," "thee" and "thine," there was a method to the madness of these translators beyond simply attempting to emulate biblical verbiage: In Egyptian, like so many other languages, including French and Spanish, there were different forms for the word "you" and "yours," etc., one formal and one informal. Where the Egyptian word for "you" was formal, addressing a god or higher up, the term was translated as "thou," "thee," etc. In more modern translations this salient distinction has become lost by the uniform rendering as "you," "your" and so on. Although the modern language is more accessible, particularly to non-native speakers of English, in some instances the older form is preferable, as it reveals the sense of reverence indicated by the original Egyptian, also providing a better comparison with the equal but not exceeding reverence with which biblical figures, including God, are held.

When comparing translations, it is also important to keep in mind that various translators at times used different editions of the ancient texts, some of which possessed alterations and emendations. A study of the Egyptian texts themselves is thus eye-opening for a variety of reasons, including not only the content but also the differences from text to text over the centuries, with mistakes creeping in, transpositions changing meaning and interchangeability of characters, among other discrepancies. A careful comparison of editions reveals these discrepancies, which are at times meaningful, such that there is some leeway in the interpretation, as reflected in the translator's notes, for example, in several places in the Coffin Texts rendered by Dr. Raymond O. Faulkner (1894-1982), a professor of Egyptian language at University College London.[1] Moreover, Faulkner's notes regarding a number of Coffin Texts demonstrate that there are certain times when the writings are incomprehensible and therefore impossible to interpret in any fashion. In other words, there is at times uncertainty even with the best of translations.

---

[1] Faulkner is also forthcoming in his footnotes about disagreements between Egyptologists on various details, validating that there is not always a set-in-stone consensus by experts in any given field, as we know from many ongoing scientific debates.

In the long run, however, the painstaking work of the translators of the Rosetta Stone, Jean-François Champollion (1790-1832) and Dr. Thomas Young (1773-1829), as well as the diligent labor of many others using a wealth of texts since then, to establish an accurate understanding of the Egyptian culture, including and especially the religion, were successful enough for us to reconstruct a fairly reliable picture of what the Egyptians believed about this world and the next.

God, Man or Myth?

A major source of confusion within the field of religion has occurred because there has existed a tendency over the centuries to make gods into men and men into gods. It is therefore imperative that we develop our skills for discernment as to what is historical and what is mythical. In the case of the Egyptian gods, all of the major deities have been mythical, not historical, despite the stories that place them into history and claim they were "real people" at some point.[1] Let us take for example the Egyptian god Osiris, upon whose "life" so much of the gospel tale appears to have been based. Was Osiris ever a "real person?" Concerning Osiris, Budge remarks:

> ...we can see that in very primitive times Osiris passed through many forms, and that his attributes were changed as the result of the development of the minds of the Egyptians and the natural modification of their religious views. Osiris, as we know him, was a compound of many gods, and his cult represented a blending of numerous nature cults, many of them being very ancient.[2]

Nevertheless, even in ancient times the story of Osiris included his advent on what seems to be Earth, and, as related by historians Herodotus and Diodorus Siculus (c. 90-27 BCE) beginning centuries prior to the common era, *many* people have believed Osiris was a real person, as they have with numerous other gods and goddesses worldwide for thousands of years. Even in the modern era we find statements such as, "That Osiris was actually an ancient divine king who reigned in the Delta is now generally agreed among Egyptologists...."[3] Yet, as Renouf says, "It must be remembered...that many of the geographical localities named in the Book of the Dead have their counterparts in the Egyptian heaven."[4] In reality, Osiris is in large part a sun god, and, although there may have been real people by the same name, the figure in the myths was never a human being who lived on Earth. The tales that assert Osiris to have traveled here and there saving and civilizing humanity in fact refer to the

---

[1] One of the relatively few actual instances of what is called "euhemerism" or "evemerism"—making a human into a god or goddess, also deemed "apotheosis"—apparently occurred with the Egyptian architect Imhotep, who evidently lived during the Third Dynasty (c. 2687-2668 BCE). (Redford, 79.)
[2] Budge, *OER*, I, 18.
[3] Hornblower, *Man*, vol. 37, 155.
[4] Renouf, *EBD*, 6.

Introduction

spread of his *cult* or religion.[1] The same phenomenon may be claimed as concerns the tales of other gods and goddesses having supposedly walked the Earth, extending even to the story of Jesus Christ.

The tendency to make the gods into real people dates back into ancient times and was developed most notoriously by the Greek writer Euhemerus or Evemeros (c. 330/320-c. 260 BCE), who argued that the gods and goddesses of the day had been real people of old, such as kings, queens and other heroes and legendary figures. This thesis developed by Euhemerus may be called "euhemerism," "evemerism"[2] or the "evemerist position," defined as follows:

> Evemerism represents the perspective that many of the gods and goddesses of antiquity had been real people, such as kings, queens and other heroes and legendary figures, to whose biographies were later added extraordinary and/or supernatural attributes.

While such a development has happened as concerns a relative handful of individuals, the fact will remain that the majority of popular deities have constituted *mythical* entities who never were real people but who often largely represented natural and astronomical phenomena.

In his long treatise in volume V of the *Moralia* entitled "Isis and Osiris," Greek writer Plutarch (46-120 AD/CE) positively fumed while discussing the theories of Euhemerus/Evemeros. In his criticisms, Plutarch (23, 360A) harshly remarked:

> I hesitate, lest this be the moving of things immovable and not only "warring against the long years of time," as Simonides has it, but warring, too, against "many a nation and race of men" who are possessed by a feeling of piety towards these gods, and thus we should not stop short of transplanting such names from the heavens to the earth, and eliminating and dissipating the reverence and faith implanted in nearly all mankind at birth, opening wide the great doors to the godless throng, degrading things divine to the human level, and giving a splendid licence to *the deceitful utterances of Euhemerus of Messenê, who of himself drew up copies of an incredible and non-existent mythology, and spread atheism over the whole inhabited earth by obliterating the gods of our belief and converting them all alike into names of generals, admirals, and kings*, who, forsooth, lived in very ancient times and are recorded in inscriptions written in golden letters at Panchon, which no foreigner and no Greek had ever happened to meet with, save only Euhemerus....[3]

---

[1] The term "cult" is often used in a derogatory manner. In this present work, however, it is meant in its first, anthropological meaning of "a particular system of religious worship, esp. with reference to its rites and ceremonies."

[2] The Greek spelling is Εὐήμερος, with an upsilon or "u." Because of pronunciation difficulties, I prefer the transliteration of "Evemeros" and "Evemerism," with a "v," as is done with the term εὐάγγελος, for example, which is transliterated in such words as "evangelism" but which is also spelled in Greek with an "u." Moreover, in modern Greek the combination of "eu" is pronounced "ev" or "ef," as in ευχαριστῶ, pronounced "evhareesto."

[3] Plutarch/Babbitt, 56-57. (Emph. added.)

As we can see, Plutarch accused Euhemerus of spreading "atheism over the whole inhabited earth." Plutarch's sentiment is well founded that reducing to human exploits the glorious cosmic dramas of the Egyptian gods and others constitutes a degradation of "things divine to the human level." In this regard, no such tendencies will appear in this present work, as we are convinced that these deities represent mythical and fabulous entities, and that, if there were any human beings named Osiris, Isis and Horus, it is not *their* story being told within Egyptian religion. The same contention may be made of individuals who happened to have been named "Yeshua," "Joshua" or "Jesus" during the first century of the common era—they may indeed have been real people and historical individuals, but it is not *their* story being told in the gospels. In fact, the most scientific and valid evidence points to an origin for Jesus Christ as mythical and fabulous as that of the Egyptian, Greek and Roman gods of the same general era and area. Moreover, in the end the evidence also demonstrates a strong connection between these various mythical entities, including and especially the gods of Egypt and the Jewish godman of Christianity.

In this regard, when the mythological layers of the gospel story are removed, there remains no core to the onion, no "real person" to point to as found in the evemerist position. To put it another way, a composite of 20 people, whether mythical, historical or both, is no one. This perspective can be called "mythicism" or the "mythicist position," which is defined as:

> Mythicism represents the perspective that many gods, goddesses and other heroes and legendary figures said to possess extraordinary and/or supernatural attributes are not "real people" but are in fact mythological characters. Along with this view comes the recognition that many of these figures personify or symbolize natural phenomena, such as the sun, moon, stars, planets, constellations, etc., constituting what is called "astromythology" or "astrotheology." As a major example of the mythicist position, it is determined that various biblical characters such as Adam and Eve, Satan, Noah, Abraham, Moses, Joshua, King David, Solomon and Jesus Christ, among other entities, in reality represent mythological figures along the same lines as the Egyptian, Sumerian, Phoenician, Indian, Greek, Roman and other godmen, who are all presently accepted as myths, rather than historical figures.

It should be kept in mind throughout this work that when we talk about "myth," we are not dismissing something necessarily as being "false." While it may be true that a myth never occurred in history, as a third-dimensional reality, myth nevertheless can be very profound and possess much meaning. As explained by Dr. Vincent Arieh Tobin, a professor of Classics at Saint Mary's University:

> ...Myth is a means of sacred revelation, a method of communication that functions through symbolic expression and has its own inner

logic—a logic belonging to a realm of the mystical and metaphysical rather than to that of reason and rationality.[1]

As may have been gathered from the important work of renowned mythologist Joseph Campbell (1904-1987), rather than serving as something "fabricated" that needs to be dismissed, mythology possesses a vital role in culture worldwide. Hence, myth has a very real purpose and meaning, which is in reality depreciated when removed from its context and placed into "history."

Who Is Gerald Massey?

In exploring the various Egyptian influences upon the Christian religion, one name frequently encountered is that of lay Egyptologist Gerald Massey (1828-1907). Born in abject poverty in England, Gerald Massey was almost entirely self-taught; yet, he was able to write and lecture about several subjects with tremendous erudition and authority. Despite his lack of formal education, Massey could read several languages, including not only English but also French, Latin, Greek and evidently Hebrew and Egyptian to a certain degree.

Massey was fortunate enough to live during an exciting time when Egyptology was in its heyday, with the discovery in 1799 of the Rosetta Stone and the subsequent decipherment of hieroglyphs in 1822 by Champollion. This monumental development allowed for the exposure to light of the fascinating Egyptian culture and religion, meaning that before that time no one could adequately read the Egyptian texts, which Massey ended up spending a considerable portion of his life studying and interpreting, and relatively little was known about the religion, for which Massey possessed a keen sense of comprehension.

In his detailed and careful analysis of the Egyptian religion, the pioneer Massey extensively utilized the Egyptian Book of the Dead—which was termed "The Ritual" by Champollion, a convention followed by Massey and others but since abandoned[2]—as well as several other ancient Egyptian sources, including the Pyramid Texts and assorted other funeral texts and stele. Massey quite evidently understood the Egyptian spirituality and was able to present it in a highly sound and scientific manner.

In these intensive and meticulous efforts, Massey studied the work of the best minds of the time—all towering figures within Egyptology, especially during Massey's era, when most of them were alive and some were familiar with his work. These celebrated authorities in Egyptology whose works Massey studied and utilized included: Sir Dr. Budge; Dr. Brugsch-Bey; Jean-François

---

[1] Redford, 239.
[2] Renouf (xviii) objects that the *Book* does *not* constitute a "ritual" per se. Rather, it is, according to the British Museum's T.G.H. James, a "compilation of spells, prayers and incantations." In any event, this term "Ritual" will be used here occasionally along with the "Book of the Dead" and the abbreviation "BD."

Champollion; Dr. Eugene Lefébure; Dr. Karl Richard Lepsius; Sir Dr. Gaston Maspero; Dr. Henri Edouard Naville; Sir Dr. William Flinders Petrie; Dr. Thomas Joseph Pettigrew; Sir Renouf; le vicomte de Rougé; Dr. Samuel Sharpe; and Sir Dr. John Gardner Wilkinson, among many other scholars in a wide variety of fields. As other examples, Massey also used the work of Sir Dr. J. Norman Lockyer, the physicist and royal English astronomer who was friends with Budge and knew Egypt well, along with that of Dr. Charles Piazzi Smyth, royal Scottish astronomer and professor of Astronomy at the University of Edinburgh. Massey further studied the work of Reverend Dr. Archibald Sayce, professor of Comparative Philology at Oxford, as well as that of famous mythologist Sir Dr. James George Frazer, although he did not agree with their conclusions. He likewise cited the work of Francois Lenormant, professor of Archaeology at the National Library of France, as well as that of comparative theologian and Oxford professor Dr. Max Müller, philosopher and Jesus biographer Dr. Ernest Renan, and Christian monuments expert Rev. Dr. John Patterson Lundy.

Gerald Massey was very influenced by the work of Dr. Samuel Birch (1813-1885), archaeologist, Egyptologist and Keeper of the Department of Oriental Antiquities in the British Museum. The creator of the first alphabetically arranged Egyptian dictionary, Dr. Birch also was the founder of the prestigious and influential Society of Biblical Archaeology, to which belonged many other notables in the fields of archaeology, Assyriology, Egyptology and so on.[1] Much of this eye-opening work on comparative religion, in fact, emanated from this august body of erudite and credentialed individuals. Birch held many other titles and honors, including from Cambridge and Oxford Universities. His numerous influential works on Egypt, including the first English translation of the Book of the Dead, were cited for decades in scholarly publications.

In the "Introduction" to his book *The Natural Genesis*, Gerald Massey writes:

> The German Egyptologist, Herr Pietschmann...reviewed the "Book of the Beginnings"... The writer has taken the precaution all through of getting his fundamental facts in Egyptology verified by one of the

---

[1] Begun by Dr. Birch, Sir Joseph Bonomi and W.R. Cooper in 1870, the Society of Biblical Archaeology had over 400 members by 1877, with many more to come in the 30+ years of the organization's existence. The list of distinguished members included James Bonwick, St. Chad Boscawen, Dr. Heinrich Brugsch-Bey, Sir Dr. E.A. Wallis Budge, Ernest de Bunsen, F.C. Burkitt, Dr. A. Henry Layard, Dr. M. Eugene Lefébure, Francois Lenormant, Rev. Dr. J.B. Lightfoot, Dr. Gaston Maspero, Dr. Edouard Naville, Sir W.M. Flinders Petrie, Dr. W. Pleyte, Sir Henry C. Rawlinson, Sir Peter Le Page Renouf, Rev. A.H. Sayce, William Sloane, Henry Villiers Stuart and Dr. W.D. Whitney. While there was a relative handful of "Lady Members," it appears that initially not a single one held any degrees or positions of importance, or presented any papers at any time, although a few women made it into the later main list of members.

foremost of living authorities, Dr. Samuel Birch, to whom he returns his heartiest acknowledgements.[1]

Dr. Richard Pietschmann was a professor of Egyptology at the University of Göttingen, an impressive "peer reviewer" for one of Massey's early works on Egypt. By verifying his "fundamental facts" with Birch, Massey appears to be saying that his work was also reviewed by Birch, with whom he enjoyed a personal relationship expressed in his letters. Indeed, following this statement in *The Natural Genesis*, in his "Retort" to various attacks he endured, Massey remarked:

> As I also say in my preface [to *The Natural Genesis*] I took the precaution of consulting Dr. Samuel Birch for many years after he had offered, in his own words, to "*keep me straight*" as to my facts, obtainable from Egyptian records. He answered my questions, gave me his advice, discussed variant renderings, read whatever proofs I sent him, and corrected me where he saw I was wrong.[2]

It is evident from these remarks that a significant portion of Massey's work was "peer reviewed" by the eminent Dr. Samuel Birch, a remarkable development that should be factored into the assessment of Massey's work. With such developments, it becomes evident that it is not the quality of Massey's work at issue, since it is obviously sound, but that his conclusions as to the nonhistoricity and unoriginality of the Christian religion do not sit well with his detractors. This latter fact is critically important to bear in mind when studying Massey's works, especially since he largely discovered and developed parallels between the Egyptian and Christian religions, crucial data that may have otherwise been left to lie fallow based on occupational considerations by the vested-interested professionals upon whose work Massey relied.

Massey was likewise personally friendly with Sir Lockyer (1836-1920), as well as Dr. Birch's protégé Assyriologist Dr. Theophilus Goldridge Pinches (1856-1934). Naturally, among these various scholars of his era, Massey also had his critics, including, apparently, the devout Roman Catholic Renouf, who evidently was a mysterious anonymous Egyptologist who spewed calumny and vitriol at Massey, essentially calling him a lunatic. That Massey was so well known as to draw such attention and ire speaks to his efficacy, rather than his incompetence. As he himself said in his retort to such vituperation, "*Such damnation is dirt cheap! Also, the time has passed for denunciation to be mistaken for disproof.*"[3] In his "Retort," Massey also made the following observation, which readers of this present work might wish to keep in mind as well: "I had already warned my readers that they must expect little help from those Egyptologists and

---

[1] Massey, *NG*, viii.
[2] Massey, *GML*, 251.
[3] Massey, *GML*, 250.

Assyriologists who are bibliolaters first and scholars afterwards. Bibliolatry puts out the eye of scholarship or causes confirmed strabismus," the latter term referring to a vision disorder. "Bibliolatry," of course, refers to "Bible worship," while "bibliolaters" are "Bible worshippers."

In his scholarly works on Egypt, in addition to the available Egyptian sources, Gerald Massey utilized numerous other ancient texts, including Judeo-Christian writings such as the Bible, as well as those of early Church fathers such as Justin Martyr, Irenaeus, Clement of Alexandria, Tertullian, Hippolytus, Eusebius, Epiphanius and Jerome. Massey also cited non-Christian, Jewish and Gnostic writers such as Herodotus, Philo, Pausanias and Valentinus, along with writings such as the Talmud and the Hindu Puranas. Having taught himself to read not only English but also several other languages including Egyptian hieroglyphs as well as Sanskrit, providing an extensive comparison between these two languages, Massey scrutinized and interpreted the texts and monuments for himself, such as the Book of the Dead, as well as the famous zodiacs in the Temple of Dendera and the "Nativity Scene" at the Temple of Luxor, texts and images that predated the "Christian era" by centuries to millennia.[1] Regarding his abilities with the hieroglyphs, Massey states:

> ...although I am able to read the hieroglyphics, nothing offered to you is based on my translation. I work too warily for that! The transcription and literal renderings of the hieroglyphic texts herein employed are by scholars of indisputable authority. There is no loophole of escape that way.[2]

Thus, while Massey did read hieroglyphs and therefore worked with *primary sources*, knowing the contentiousness of the subject, he purposely did not rely on his own translations and interpretations but consulted repeatedly with "scholars of indisputable authority," in other words, those previously mentioned, including Dr. Samuel Birch, with whom Massey conferred personally on much of his work.

Massey was not only skilled at interpreting the Egyptian data in a highly intelligent and unusual manner, but, having been raised a Protestant Christian compelled to memorize whole sections of the Bible, he was also quite knowledgeable about the scriptures and was able to see the numerous and significant correlations between the Christian and Egyptian religions, or the "mythos and ritual," as he styled them.

Gerald Massey appears to have possessed an understanding of the spirituality and *astrotheology* being conveyed by the Egyptians

---

[1] The term "Christian era" is misleading, as such a time varied widely depending on the area. For example, the country of Lithuania did not become Christian until the 14th century; hence, the "Christian era" did not occur there until then.
[2] Massey, *GML*, 1.

more profound than most who have worked on the subject. As was possibly the case with the Egyptian masses to a large extent, the astronomical or *astrotheological* meanings behind Christianity have been lost on the majority of its adherents. Concerning this "astronomical mythology,"[1] Lockyer, the founder of the respected journal *Nature*, remarks:

> Naville rightly pointed out how vital the study of mythology becomes with regard to the advancement of any kind of knowledge of the thoughts and actions of the ancient Egyptians. Mythology, as Bunsen said, is one of the poles of the existence of every nation; hence it will be well not to neglect the opportunity thus afforded of studying the astronomical basis of one of the best-known myths.[2]

Dr. Henri Edouard Naville (1844-1926) and Dr. Christian C.J. Baron von Bunsen (1791-1860) were well-known Egyptologists, the former Swiss and the latter German. If mythology is "one of the poles of the existence of *every nation*," we might rightly ask, where is the *Jewish mythology*, if not in the Bible, with its supernatural claims and bizarre tales? Isn't the gospel tale simply more of the same "god on Earth" mythology of the past?

In any event, the case demonstrating that "astrotheology"—the reverence for the sun, moon, stars, planets and other natural phenomena—has been the main motivating factor behind major religious myths and rituals the world over can be found in my book *Suns of God: Krishna, Buddha and Christ Unveiled*. This fact of an astrotheological foundation for major religious and spiritual concepts—so brilliantly discerned by Gerald Massey, who was far ahead of his time—is being demonstrated on a regular basis by numerous archaeological discoveries around the world.

Although Budge also has been the subject of certain criticism, in part perhaps because, like Massey, he found many parallels between Christianity and the Egyptian religion, he too had a fine grasp of the spirituality within the latter faith, and expressed it in spiritual terms usually reserved—in a culturally biased move—for the Bible. Dr. James Allen likewise possesses an exceptional understanding of the Egyptian spirituality and *astrotheology*, remarking upon it throughout his important works on the Pyramid Texts and Egyptian language. Regarding Egyptian nature worship, in *Middle Egyptian*, Allen states:

---

[1] The phrase "astronomical mythology" has been shortened to "astromythology," a term often used to describe what would also be called "astro*theology*." Although today we know it as mythology, ancient religion is represented better by the word "astrotheology," in depicting how the ancients themselves perceived their faith, which constituted true *theology* in the same sense used today to describe current religions.
[2] Lockyer, *DA*, 148.

Just as there are hundreds of recognizable elements and forces in nature, so too there were hundreds of Egyptian gods. The most important, of course, are the greatest phenomena.[1]

In *The Ancient Egyptian Pyramid Texts*, Allen also says: "The Sun was the original and daily source of all life: his appearance at the creation and at every sunrise thereafter made life possible in the world."[2]

The astronomical science of the ancient Egyptians is likewise prominently displayed in the ancient astronomical papyri found at Oxyrhynchus, Egypt, dating from the first century BCE to the sixth AD/CE. Regarding these astronomical texts from Oxyrhynchus, Dr. Alexander Jones, a professor of Classics at the University of Toronto, remarks:

> The fragments tend to be of three kinds: horoscopes, numerical tables, and prose texts. Horoscopes record the positions of the sun, moon, planets, and ascendant point of the ecliptic computed for the birthdate of a person, who is often named. Positions of the heavenly bodies also appear in many of the tables ("almanacs"), computed now for not an arbitrary given date but for a succession of dates at regular intervals or determined by some other astronomical criterion.... the prose texts are also by and large concerned with knowing the positions of the sun, moon, and planets and the disposition of the heavens at specific times, or the dates and circumstances of such conspicuous phenomena as eclipses and the alternating appearances and disappearances of the planets. In contrast to the modern conception of Greek astronomy as a theoretical enterprise, the papyri portray a science that was overwhelmingly directed towards prediction....
>
> The papyrus horoscopes give an indication of the range of dates during which astrology flourished, from the earliest horoscope, a demotic ostracon cast for a native born in 38 B.C., to the latest..., for a native born in A.D. 508.[3]

From early times, the Egyptians were keen observers of natural phenomena, including the movements and characteristics of celestial bodies, not only engaging in astronomical and astrological efforts, but, most importantly, developing an intensely *astrotheological* religion.

Indeed, rather than constituting alien and incomprehensible concepts, the Egyptian gods are reflective of these natural phenomena, the "greatest" of which would be the cycles and

---

[1] Allen, J., *ME*, 44.
[2] Allen, J., *AEPT*, 8.
[3] Jones, 4-5. Regarding the individuals named in the horoscopes, Dr. Jones states, "The only recognizably Christian 'natives' among the horoscopes from Oxyrhynchus are the Anup of *P. Oxy.* 2060 and the Theodoros of 4275, who were born in A.D. 478 and 508 respectively." (Jones, 8) It appears the Egyptian name "Anup" may have been fairly common, possibly reflecting the popularity of the god called "Anubis" in Greek, well into the common era.

Introduction

characteristics of the sun, moon, planets, stars and so o
demonstrated repeatedly by Gerald Massey, for one, to reveal the ᴜ ᴜ.
meaning behind not only the Egyptian but also the Christian religion.

Over the decades, much has been made about the numerous
correlations determined by Gerald Massey between Horus and Jesus
as well as other characters in the Egyptian and Christian religions.
Independently of Massey, however, many others also noted these
numerous and profound correlations between the two faiths, with
Budge, as we have seen, definitively stating that a treatise on the
Egyptian religion's influence on Christianity would fill a
"comparatively large volume."[1] A professed Christian, Budge was so
convinced of the important correspondences between the two faiths
that *he believed the Egyptian religion had been fulfilled in Christianity.*

In 1877, William R. Cooper (1843-1878), a young lawyer and
Egyptologist who was a co-founder and the Secretary of Dr. Birch's
influential Society of Biblical Archaeology,[2] as well as a Fellow and
Member of the Royal Astronomical Society, published a work entitled
The Horus Myth in Its Relation to Christianity, in which he highlighted
many germane correspondences between the myth of the Egyptian
god Horus and Christianity. So many were these correspondences,
including in numerous physical artifacts, that Cooper termed them
"the Horus Christian class."[3] From his constant apologies and
declarations of devotion to the Christian faith, it is evident that
Cooper was disturbed by his findings and hoped not to run afoul of
the authorities who might censure him or worse. Indeed, at that time
"blasphemy" laws in England were not only on the books—as they
still were until 2008—but they were actually being used, ensnaring
Rev. Dr. Robert Taylor (1784–1844), for example, who was
imprisoned twice in Britain a half century previously for revealing
Christianity to be based on previous religions and mythologies.

Unfortunately, William Cooper died at the early age of 35, but his
valuable works on Egypt—and its relationship to the Bible and
Christianity—were issued *years before* Gerald Massey published his
famous writings on the same subject. Thus, the claim of
correspondences between the Egyptian and Christian religions did
not originate with Gerald Massey at all, and a significant number of
the previous writers on the subject were well respected *Christians.*
Moreover, in analyzing Cooper's assessment that "the works of art,
the ideas, the expressions, and the heresies of the first four centuries
of the Christian era cannot be well studied without a right
comprehension of the nature and influence of the Horus myth," in
Isis and the Ancient World, Egyptologist and University of London
professor Dr. Reginald E. Witt (1903-1980) remarked that Cooper's

---

[1] Budge, *GE,* I, xvi
[2] *Transactions of the Society of Biblical Archaeology (TSBA),* V, iii, v.
[3] Cooper, *HM,* 49.

"words are still true" and then added that we must also look to the goddess Isis for clues about "emergent Christianity's struggle."[1] Dr. Witt's comments indicate that behind the scenes within academia there persists knowledge of the Egypto-Christian connection, in bits and pieces among certain scholars.

This latter inference may be surprising in consideration of the fact that such scholarship is not readily forthcoming from the modern halls of academia. However, it is important to keep in mind that there are a number of mitigating factors involved in what is approved and current within scholarship in any given subject. First and foremost is what may be expedient to the goal of the institution in which the subject may be taught, its motivations and financial considerations. Next, over the past several decades, scholars have become increasingly specialized, and they may not be aware of various oversights and biases preventing them from putting forth the data as explicated by Witt. The colored perspective of Christian scholars, modern or otherwise, is well known, but secular scholars or those of other religions likewise possess biases. In this regard, the late great Dr. Cyrus H. Gordon (1908-2001), a chairman of the Department of Near Eastern Studies at Brandeis University and a director of the Center for Ebla Research at New York University, remarked that "we absorb attitudes as well as subject matter in the learning process. Moreover the attitudes tend to determine what we see, and what we fail to see, in the subject matter."[2] Hence, it is very likely that the material found in treatises such as this present work is not widely known because it is not a focus of professional scholars.

Adding to this academic blind spot are deliberately induced biases such as described by Hornung regarding the attitude towards Egyptian religion following the famed discovery of King Tutankhamun's tomb in 1922. After discussing the unbridled "Egyptomania" that followed Napoleon's opening up Egypt to the West, which culminated in "Tut Fever," Hornung refers to the "next generation" of Egyptologists being "deterred" by noted Egyptian philologist Adolf Erman, who denigrated the Egyptian cosmology as "philistine." Concerning this disdainful attitude of professional Egyptologists, in *The Valley of the Kings* Hornung remarks:

> The intellectual treasures of the Valley, already remarked on by Champollion and Maspero, were thus buried beneath the debris of

---

[1] Witt, 279.

[2] Gordon, C., 11-12. A highly credentialed authority in the field of biblical archaeology, Gordon's own groundbreaking work was dismissed and ridiculed, until significant aspects of it became the mainstream perspective. When asked shortly before his passing at 87 by Biblical Archaeology Review's Herschel Shanks about Gordon's take on how his views were first resisted and then came to be accepted as true, the wise scholar humorously responded to the effect, "I outlived all my critics." Gordon's experience perfectly exemplifies how new theories are initially resisted and then finally accepted as reality—and how preconceived notions and biases continually oppress potential truths.

prejudice, incomprehension, and the extension of modern values and ways of thought; strenuous efforts to free them once again for contemplation were required.[1]

The prejudices of professional Egyptologists remained intact until the end of the 1930s, when Western scholarship began to return to its previous appreciative mentality.

Massey's impressive role in "Egyptomania" during the 19th to early 20th century is likewise verified by Hornung in *The Secret Lore of Egypt*, in which he remarks that "Gerald Massey also exerted a great deal of influence in esoteric circles with his book *Ancient Egypt: The Light of the World....*"[2]

In regard to higher education, Gerald Massey had the distinct disadvantage of having been born into crippling poverty that gripped him for most of his life, such that higher education and degrees were not easily available to him in Dickensian England of the 19th century, in which he was forced into manual labor as a child. This sad fact, of course, leaves him open to the charge of not possessing the proper credentials to analyze the data accurately—an argument that at times constitutes little more than the logical fallacy of "appeal to authority." While credentials can certainly be helpful because they may provide proper scientific training for any given subject, there are many instances where even "properly credentialed" individuals are in gross error in their perception of the data, and there are also numerous examples of individuals who, without any of the "correct" bona fides, have been able to work with the information in a brilliant and superior manner. As one example, the young British architect and amateur linguist Michael Ventris (1922-1956) possessed no formal higher credentials in the relevant field; yet, succeeding where all others had failed —including some of the most highly credentialed individuals of the time—Ventris deciphered the ancient Cretan script of Linear B. In the subject of Egyptology, another example would be that of Dr. Thomas Young, a talented linguist and giant of Egyptology, having helped decipher the Egyptian language and hieroglyphs by way of the Rosetta Stone; yet, Young was a *physician*, not a formally trained Egyptologist.[3] Although Champollion is the more famous, not a few Egyptologists have placed Young ahead of the French scholar in their analysis of who contributed the most to the field of the day. As can be seen from these and many other examples, possessing a pristine pedigree is not always necessary for important

---

[1] Hornung, *VK*, 19.

[2] Hornung, *SLE*, 174. Hornung calls Massey a "theosophist." However, according to Massey biographer David Shaw, although Massey knew about the Theosophists, there is no evidence he ever considered himself one of them. In fact, various of Massey's remarks indicate that he did not support the Theosophists, such as: "I am opposed to all man-made mystery, and all kinds of false belief." (Massey, *GML*, 248.)

[3] Dr. Young was widely ridiculed for his theory that light rays "interfere with each other"; yet, this "undulatory theory" was later accepted as scientific fact. (Clayden, 61.)

discoveries, breakthroughs and hypotheses. In any event, as we have seen, Massey took the precaution of having his work reviewed by eminent Egyptologists of his day.

Those who insist that Gerald Massey's work has been "debunked" or "refuted" have rarely read it. Although certain aspects of Massey's voluminous work may be considered speculative, as is the case with practically every scholar's work, it can be honestly stated that most of his analysis is not only brilliantly insightful but appears to be sound, based on what was popular religiously and mythologically prior to the Christian era, sometimes centuries and many times millennia before the period in question. This information, of course, is not amenable to Christian claims of veracity and uniqueness; hence, fervent believers and especially their leaders do not enjoy knowing or hearing about it. Regardless of what details of Massey's may have been lacking in total accuracy, the facts will remain that major aspects of the Christian myth and ritual can be found in the preceding pre-Christian religions and mythologies of the "known world." Moreover, the earlier characters such as Horus, Osiris, Isis, Hercules, Krishna and many other gods and goddesses cannot be deemed any more mythical or any less historical than Jesus, as the evidence for their existence on Earth is as, if not more, abundant and convincing than that of Jesus Christ.

Although we do not find meritable the severe criticisms regarding Gerald Massey—many of which appear driven by a desire to make the gospel story historical, no matter how much truth and facts are bent—this present analysis of the claims regarding the correspondences between the Egyptian and Christian religions is not dependent on Massey's work for the most part. Only a small portion of his exegesis will be cited, in places where extrapolation of the texts has been necessary in order to unearth the correspondences hinted at by Budge and other experts on the Egyptian religion.

For example, when one studies the pioneering work of Dr. Lockyer, who scientifically demonstrated various astronomical properties and alignments of Egyptian myths and architecture, one can readily understand how Massey would find astrotheological correlations within Christianity, as, combining the opinions of Lockyer and others,[1] with those of Budge and others, who definitively

---

[1] Lockyer's work was fundamental to the developing field of archaeoastronomy, as well as astrotheology. Yet, naturally, there have been debates as to its accuracy. Indeed, the reaction of other scientists to Lockyer's archaeoastronomy thesis of megalithic alignments was typical of how scholarship progresses in a faltering manner when new ideas are proposed. Lockyer's logical conclusions regarding the sophistication of ancient man's knowledge of the natural world were uncomfortable to those who had settled on interpretations of the ancient world based on the Bible and, subsequently, Darwin. The ancients, it was opined, were primitives, even though they could build something as spectacular as the Great Pyramid or Stonehenge. As such, common wisdom said, they could not have possessed the knowledge found within archaeoastronomy and astrotheology. This bias led to several decades of ignoring the

stated that the Egyptian religion was a major influence on Christianity, we are left with the following logical conclusion:

- If the myths of Osiris, Isis, Horus and Set, etc., are largely astronomical in nature; and
- If Christianity is highly influenced by—and is a fulfillment of—the Egyptian religion in significant part; then
- Christianity too must represent astronomical myth or *astrotheology.*

With such an impression in mind, someone with a passion may go on a quest such as Massey's to find these correspondences between the Egyptian and Christian religions, as well as the true astrotheological underpinnings of Christianity. Furthermore, many of Massey's most important contentions can be verified and demonstrated utilizing the primary sources of Egyptian texts and monuments—in other words, the parallels are real and significant.

Timeline of Destruction

Addressing why we have not seen a large effort among scholars to point to Egypt for Christian genesis, historian Dr. Richard A. Gabriel states, "That historians have overlooked the Egyptian origins of Christianity leaving the subject to the concern of theologians is not terribly surprising."[1] He next recounts the violent overthrow of the Egyptian religion by the Christian mobs during the fourth century. This destruction of the Egyptian faith included the outlawing of hieroglyphs to express it. Gabriel tersely recounts this disturbing history:

> In 356 C.E. Constantius II ordered the Egyptian temples of Isis-Osiris closed and forbade the use of Egyptian hieroglyphics as a religious language. In 380 C.E. Emperor Theodosius declared Christianity to be the official Roman state religion, and all pagan cults were thereafter forbidden. These edicts were devastating to Egyptian culture and religion, both of which had been preserved over millennia through the Egyptian language and the writing systems of Egyptian priests. In 391 C.E., the Patriarch of Alexandria, Theophilus, summoned the monks to arms and turned them against the city of Memphis and the great shrine of Serapis, the *Serapeum*, the main temple of the Osiran-Isis religion. The attack was akin to

---

astronomical alignments of megalithic structures worldwide, until the door was blasted open again principally by the work of Drs. Gerald S. Hawkins and Alexander Thom. They too were resisted; yet, it is now commonly accepted that wherever archaeologists find ancient megalithic ruins, they will also likely discover astronomical alignments, largely associated with religion, which yields more evidence of the ancient astrotheological faith. This case serves to illustrate a number of points about censorship and why we have not known before much of the information found in this present work. (For more on this debate, see the works of Dr. Clive L.N. Ruggles, e.g., *APBI*, 6ff.) Regardless of any measurements or other details Lockyer may have gotten wrong, the fact will remain that his insight into ancient ruins possessing astronomical alignments has been proved correct numerous times over the past century.
[1] Gabriel, *JE*, 3.

ering the destruction of the Vatican. Egyptian priests were _____ssacred in their shrines and in the streets. The ferocity of the violence consumed priests, followers, and the Egyptian intellectual elite of Alexandria, Memphis and the other cities of Egypt who were murdered and their temples and libraries destroyed. The institutional structure of Egyptian religion, then more than four millennia old, was demolished in less than two decades.[1]

Reading through this horrendous destruction, and knowing the cultural climate of our day, in which the Christian faith appears to be losing ground to secularism and a swelling Islam, one might wonder if Christianity is now suffering a global "mummy's curse."

The Art of Mythmaking

In order to understand the many important correlations between the Egyptian and Christian religions and how they have been framed in popular media, as well as in my books *The Christ Conspiracy* and *Suns of God*, we need to remember that these common motifs in the Egyptian religion do not necessarily emerge in story form, as they appear in the gospel tale, which itself, we contend, is a patchwork of motifs, myths, sayings and rituals found in pre-Christian religion. It also needs to be kept in mind that *the information concerning these previous myths, rituals and symbols was not written down in one neat, ancient encyclopedia but is found widespread around the Mediterranean and elsewhere.* Many of the elements of the tale, however, could have existed within the walls of the massive Library of Alexandria, Egypt, where undoubtedly much of the most serious work in creating Christianity, the gospel story and the character of Jesus Christ was committed.

Regarding how diverse elements of myths become unified into one narrative—the very act used by encyclopedists to create their entries—Egyptologist Dr. Ogden Goelet, a professor of Egyptian language and culture at New York and Columbia Universities, states:

> ...Myths, or stories about the gods, were seldom gathered into narrative passages of any length. In most cases when a book on ancient Egypt mentions a myth about a certain deity, what is actually meant is a series of facts and events which modern scholars have been able to compile from a wide variety of sources.... Although we probably know more about the legends concerning Osiris than about any other god, even this myth is essentially a scholarly reconstruction from many texts. Like most such reconstructions, it is occasionally uncertain which elements belong to which version of the myth.[2]

This lack of a comprehensive narrative is also related by renowned Welsh professor of Classics and Egyptology Dr. John Gwyn Griffiths (1911-2004): "The early religious texts of Ancient Egypt do

---

[1] Gabriel, *JE*, 4.
[2] Faulkner, *EBD*, 149.

not present long passages of coherent mythology."[1] Dr. Griffiths further clarifies that Egyptian myths evolved into a more concrete account:

> What emerges clearly from a study of the Horus-myth and the Osiris-myth is that although they appear in the Pyramid Texts as a composite story they were not originally so.[2]

The difficulty of discerning one particular myth for the Egyptian god Osiris, for example, is remarked upon by Dr. Thomas Hare (b. 1952), a professor of Comparative Literature at Princeton University:

> But even in looking for "the" legend of Osiris, we are misled: to assume the priority of "a" legend of Osiris over a web of narratives, prayers, topographies, and etymologies in which he is known in Egyptian texts already shrouds and mummifies the king. And if the voices of the Egyptians themselves are hard to make out, we must sharpen our intent upon them all the more, and recall that they had been utterly mute until 170 years ago. The faint and heavily accented murmur we can now discern is itself no small wonder.[3]

As we can see, even with the abundant, currently available primary sources there is no one place to find a unified myth. Indeed, there exists no single, unified myth, although there are basics repeated in many places, such that we can draw a general outline, to which we need to append varying details—such constitutes the very definition of myth.

Like the scholars of Egyptian myth who must create a narrative by piecing together bits of "biographical" material, it is our contention that the creators of the gospel tale likewise picked various themes and motifs from pre-Christian religions and myths, including and especially the Egyptian, and wove them together, using also the Jewish scriptures, to produce a unique version of the "mythos and ritual." In other words, the creators of the Christ myth did not simply take an already formed story, scratch out the name of Osiris or Horus, and replace it with Jesus. They chose their motifs carefully, out of the most popular religious symbols, myths and rituals, making sure they fit to some degree with the Jewish "messianic scriptures," as they are termed, and created a new story that hundreds of millions since have been led to believe really and truly took place in history. Over the centuries, those who have clearly seen this development have asserted that this history is a fallacy imposed upon long pre-existing myths and rituals that have been reworked to result in the gospel story. In other words, we are convinced that "Jesus Christ" may well be a *fictional character* created out of older myths, rituals and symbols.

---

[1] Griffiths, *OOHC*, 1.
[2] Griffiths, *OOHC*, 14.
[3] Hare, 11.

It needs to be emphasized that we are not claiming that anyone took an ancient encyclopedia entry of the myth of Osiris and/or Horus, erased their names and simply inserted "Jesus." Mythmaking is never that simple. When we assert that the myths of older cultures were taken and reworked, we are stating that many factors were involved, including the politics of the day and, in this case, the intertwining of Jewish scriptures and thought, which put a decidedly unique twist on the older myths. Such is always the case with mythmaking, as it is utilized to integrate another perspective of reality, in other words, that of an individual, cult, tribe, nation or other group. New myths are always unique; otherwise, they would not be new! Yet, evidence demonstrates that they *are* myths, and that they were based on older precedents, as opposed to representing a "divine revelation" straight from God. Moreover, it becomes clear that even if the parallels and correspondences are not exact, as they would not be when a unique version of them has been created, the essential *concepts* did in fact exist in pre-Christian religion and were in reality utilized by the creators of Christianity.

While reading this present work, it is important also to recall these various caveats and points, including that what we ourselves are attempting to convey is that to the ancients these diverse themes, motifs and concepts shared by the pre-Christian and Christian religions were all important and very much in the front of their minds, such that they could not be overlooked or ignored when priests went about to create a new, empire-unifying religion that came to be called Christianity.

In writing this book about such a contentious subject that invokes such passion, it is my fervent hope to impart a clearer and more comprehensive sense of the ancient world, as well as an appreciation for the beauty and brilliance thereof, including and especially its religious and spiritual traditions, as can be discerned from the example of "Christ in Egypt." With these facts at hand, as well as that there is no one concrete source for the complete story as found in the New Testament, but that there are many scattered sources used by the priesthood which created this tale, and that reconstructing their deeds can be very difficult, let us proceed through a scientific analysis of "the Horus-Jesus connection."

Columns at Philae, Egypt, defaced by Coptic Christians.

Horus, Sun of God

"Now when the ancient Egyptians, awestruck and wondering, turned their eyes to the heavens, they concluded that two gods, the sun and the moon, were primeval and eternal: they called the former Osiris, the latter Isis...."

Diodorus Siculus, *The Antiquities of Egypt* (14)

"There are some who without reservation assert that Osiris is the Sun and is called the Dog-star (Sirius) by the Greeks...and there are those who declare that Isis is none other than the Moon; for this reason it is said that the statues of Isis that bear horns are imitations of the crescent moon, and in her dark garments are shown the concealments and the obscurations in which she in her yearning pursues the Sun..."[1]

Plutarch, "Isis and Osiris," *Moralia* (V, 52, 372D)

"Ruling over the universe by day, the Sun was identified with Horus, the god of kingship; at sunset he was seen as Atum, the oldest of all gods. The Sun's daily movement through the sky was viewed as a journey from birth to death, and his rebirth at dawn was made possible through Osiris, the force of new life....

"...In the middle of the night the Sun merged with Osiris's body; through this union, the Sun received the power of new life while Osiris was reborn in the Sun."

Dr. James P. Allen, *The Ancient Egyptian Pyramid Texts* (8)

"In Osiris the Christian Egyptians found the prototype of Christ, and in the pictures and statues of Isis suckling her son Horus, they perceived the prototype of the Virgin Mary and her Child. Never did Christianity find elsewhere in the world a people whose minds were so thoroughly well prepared to receive its doctrines as the Egyptians."

Dr. E.A. Wallis Budge, *Egyptian Ideas of the Future Life* (48)

Over the millennia, one of the most pervasive and greatest forms of religious devotion has revolved around the celestial bodies and forces of nature, including the sun, moon, stars, constellations and planets, as well as earth, wind, water and so on. This natural system of worship found globally has been represented in large part by what is deemed "astrotheology," which involves the science of *archaeoastronomy*,[2] and upon which have been built entire cultures,

---

[1] Plutarch/Babbitt, 129.

[2] The relatively new science of archaeoastronomy is defined as "the branch of archaeology that deals with the apparent use by prehistoric civilizations of astronomical techniques to establish the seasons or the cycle of the year, esp. as evidenced in the construction of megaliths and other ritual structures." (*Random House Unabridged Dictionary*, 2006.)
This definition has only recently become necessary because the idea of the ancients astronomically aligning their buildings has become acceptable mainly in past four decades or so. This example illustrates how scholarship and knowledge can be held back for various reasons—indeed, we can see that this archaeoastronomical knowledge was completely lost to the point where we did not even know our ancestors possessed

including architecture, art, laws, literature, medicine, myths, philosophy, politics, science, time-keeping and other artifacts. The astronomical observations that led to the astrotheology of the ancients are described by royal astronomer Lockyer, who was one of the first modern scholars to analyze many of them:

> There is no doubt that if we are justified in assuming that the stars were first observed, the next thing that would strike the early astronomers would be the regularity of the annual movement of the sun; the critical times of the sun's movements as related either to their agriculture, or their festivals, or to the year; the equinoxes and the solstices, would soon have revealed themselves to these early observers, if for no other reason than they were connected in some way or other with some of the important conditions of their environment.[1]

The ubiquitous ancient astrotheological religion is likewise discussed by Griffiths in his article concerning the "Solar Cycle":

> That the Sun and other heavenly objects should have universally affected human thought is a natural result of life on Earth; and the frequent evidence of their impact on religious thought is also beyond question. A clear example occurs in the *Deuteronomy* warning (perhaps of the seventh century BCE) against the worship of the Sun, Moon, and stars (4.19). Since a prohibition presupposes a practice, we may assume that some Israelites knew of or even indulged in such worship, as did several neighboring peoples.[2]

As one of these neighboring peoples and oldest advanced civilizations, with roots going back thousands of years, Egypt too developed a sophisticated system of worship and governance that incorporated practically every natural force and entity which humans of the time and place could possibly perceive and conceive. Again, the result constitutes a highly astrotheological religion, as found abundantly in the Egyptian religion and mortuary literature, exemplified further by a Coffin Text spell (CT Sp. 991): "I am that god who rises in the East and sets in the West..."[3] Regarding the Egyptian faith, Lockyer concludes: "In Egypt, then, as India, the pantheon was astronomical and, to a very large extent, solar in origin."[4]

The Loving, Immortal Father-Mother Sun

In his book *The Sun: Symbol of Power and Life*, a fascinating study of the sun worship worldwide dating back many millennia and continuing to the present, UNESCO Goodwill Ambassador Dr. Madanjeet Singh (b. 1924) remarks of Egypt:

---

it. Yet, here it is being revealed as factual and actual. The same can be said for a number of the other germane motifs and details in the present work.
[1] Lockyer, *DA*, 61.
[2] Redford, 255.
[3] Faulkner, *AECT*, III, 99.
[4] Lockyer, *DA*, 39.

The solar theology of the Old Kingdom taught that the sun brought into being the entire universe—including gods, the earth, and all living things—at the moment of Creation.[1]

Concerning this solar religion in Egypt, Hornung concurs:

Since the late Old Kingdom the sun god had been worshipped under various names as the most important deity and as the creator and sustainer of all creatures and things.[2]

Demonstrating the supreme reverence for the solar orb by the Egyptians, especially during certain periods such as Amarna (14th cent. BCE) and earlier in the New Kingdom (16th-11th cents. BCE), the sun's sacred epithets included:

Perfect of Form, Divine God, Ruler of all gods, Ruler, Chief of the gods, King of Eternity, Lord of Everlastingness, King of heaven, Universal Lord, Primeval One, Unique God, Greatest of greats, Ruler of rulers, Self-Created, Creator, Great Illuminator, Lord of Life, Lord of the gods, Great God, Lord of men, Father of the gods, Lord of all, God, Father of humankind.[3]

The Great God Sun is also "father and mother for those who put him in their hearts,"[4] as well as both father and mother of mankind in general, as expressed in the sun hymns from the New Kingdom: "Mother of the earth, father of humankind, who illuminates the earth with his love."[5] Obviously, Christianity is not unique in these many divine epithets or in its traditional concept that "God is love." The Egyptian faith demonstrates itself to be full of the same type of grace, glory, beauty and love considered to represent the best of human religion, including Christianity.

The Egyptian attitude towards the sun is expressed in the following sun hymn, as an example of the reverence developed during the reign of pharaoh Akhenaten (d. c. 1336 BCE) in particular:

You are the light, which rises for humankind;
the sun, which brings clarity,
so that gods and humans be recognised and distinguished
when you reveal yourself.
Every face lives from seeing your beauty,
all seed germinates when touched by your rays,
and there is no-one who can live without you.
You lead everyone, because they have a duty to their work.
You have given form to their life, by becoming visible.[6]

Another sun hymn eloquently invokes the beautiful and timeless Lord of creation:

You appear beautiful,

---

[1] Singh, 323.
[2] Hornung, *CGAE*, 54.
[3] Adapted from Assman, *ESRNK*, 105-106, 116, 117.
[4] Assman, *ESRNK*, 118.
[5] Assman, *ESRNK*, 84.
[6] Assman, *ESRNK*, 78.

You living sun, lord of Endless Time,
are sparkling, beautiful and strong,
Love of you is great and powerful.
Your rays touch every face...
Your radiant skin animates hearts.
You have filled the Two Lands with love of yourself.[1]

The sun at midday is addressed in a hymn with the highest esteem:

You are beautiful, powerful and shining
You are high over every land
Your rays, they embrace the lands of the earth as far as the end of your whole creation
As Re you penetrate to its limits
And subject them to your beloved son
You are remote, but your rays are on earth
You are in their face, but your movement is not known.[2]

There are many concepts here evoking a typical religious sentiment and paralleling Christianity, even in detail, such as addressing the god's "beloved son," an epithet adopted much later for Jesus. In reality, right from the beginning of the Pyramid Texts appears an obvious comparison to the gospel story: At PT 1/T 5, the sky goddess Nut, speaking from *heaven* regarding the deceased, who assumes the role of Osiris, remarks, "...This is my son, my first born...this is my beloved, with whom I have been satisfied."[3] Compare this scripture with that found at Matthew 3:17: "and lo, a voice from heaven, saying, 'This is my beloved Son, with whom I am well pleased.'"[4] This "son of God," as we have seen and will continue to see, is also the "sun of God."[5]

As in Christianity, within the Egyptian solar religion the sun god's power is illustrated by the divine qualities of omnipresence, omnipotence and omniscience, typically defining *the* god of the cosmos within monotheism. For example, demonstrating his omnipresence, the God Sun is contained in everything, as in the "Great Hymn," which addresses the sun as "you create millions of incarnations from yourself, the One."[6] In a section about the god "Re-Horakhty," Dr. Assman entitles a selection of hymns, "Omnipresence of the Light: God-Filled World." This material reflecting omnipresence,

---

[1] Assman, *ESRNK*, 94.
[2] Assman, *ESRNK*, 96.
[3] Mercer, 20. See James Allen's translation of T 5b: "Teti is my son, whom I caused to be born...he is the one I have desired and with whom I have become content." (Allen, J., *AEPT*, 67.) Because Nut is a female, the utterance/hymn refers to her "womb" or "belly." A copyist rewriting the scripture to revolve around a male deity would naturally remove such instances of femininity.
[4] Revised Standard Version (RSV).
[5] This statement, while factual, is not dependent on the naturally arising play-on-words involving "son" and "sun." In other words, the claim is not being made that the two terms are cognates.
[6] Assman, *ESRNK*, 95.

omnipotence and omniscience includes scriptures such as: "Every way is full of your light"; "Are you not the leader on all ways?"; and "There are no limits to the field of his vision and no place hidden to his ka."[1] The *ka* is defined by James Allen as the "force of conscious life."[2] In any event, the power of the sun is so strong as to impart omniscience in its worshippers—called in the texts the "sun-folks"[3]— as highlighted in this line from a sun hymn: "The morning sun, which enables one to know all things."[4]

This concept of the "omniscience of light" is part of the "new solar theology" in which "the unattainably distant sun comes palpably near to earth creatures," providing "the idea of the simultaneous remoteness and proximity of god...."[5] The German scholar next says:

> The idea of the proximity of god arises not from the sensual experience of light, but from the transcendental idea of a divine omniscience and omnipresence, in which god is right next to the heart "that turns to him."[6]

As we can see, the Egyptian concept of God here is highly reminiscent of that found in Judeo-Christianity. The Egyptian God Sun is also depicted as hearing "the prayers of all who call him" and coming "from far away in a moment to those who call him."[7] Further demonstrating "his" personal nature, the god has a "face on all sides for those he loves," much like Indian deities with multiple faces and eyes, as well as the depiction of the Christian god as the all-knowing, loving father, with whom one has a personal relationship.

Creator of "all that exists"[8] and an "artist" in creation, the sun is also the "lord of endless time."[9] The sun is likewise called the "unique shepherd, who protects his flock, who leads millions with his light,"[10] much like the later Lord Jesus, the Good Shepherd and Light of the World. Also like the Christian Lord, in whom one must believe to gain eternal salvation, the God Sun "gives life only to those he loves..."[11]

Highlighted in these texts as well is the sun's role as "cosmic god," "savior," "helper of the oppressed" and "judge,"[12] once again like the biblical god. In the sun myths compiled by Assman appear so many correspondences between the Egyptian and Judeo-Christian concepts of God that space would not permit us to list them all here.[13]

---

[1] Assman, *ESRNK*, 76.
[2] Allen, J., *AEPT*, 434.
[3] Faulkner, *AECT*, I, 242.
[4] Assman, *ESRNK*, 78.
[5] Assman, *ESRNK*, 199.
[6] Assman, *ESRNK*, 200.
[7] Assman, *ESRNK*, 200.
[8] Assman, *ESRNK*, 86, 92.
[9] Assman, *ESRNK*, 85.
[10] Assman, *ESRNK*, 86. See also Assman, *ESRNK*, 198.
[11] Assman, *ESRNK*, 117.
[12] Assman, *ESRNK*, 156ff, 198ff, 201ff.
[13] See, e.g., Assman, *ESRNK*, 170, 172-173, 177 and throughout that work.

This conclusion is particularly true concerning the sun hymns of the Amarna period, during the "monotheistic" era of Akhenaten.

As we can tell by the ebullience of the speaker in many chapters/spells and hymns, the sun in its many permutations was the epitome of divinity to the average Egyptian, who may have heard such words as found in the funereal/mortuary literature that comprised the BD on a number of occasions during his or her lifetime, whenever someone close passed away.

In this regard, throughout the history of Egyptian religion, the great cosmic and celestial entities rate as venerated symbols of the everlasting life so highly prized within Egyptian religion, including and especially the sun. As James Allen relates:

> This vision of daily death and rebirth lay behind the ancient Egyptian concept of the afterlife. Like the Sun, each person's ba [soul] was seen as passing through the night of death before coming to life again with the sunrise.[1]

In addition, the desired state of deathlessness was associated with the rebirth of the (other) stars as well as the sun:

> Not only the Sun-gods, but the stars, were supposed to travel in boats across the firmament from one horizon to the other. The under-world was the abode of the dead; and daily the sun, and the stars which set, died on passing to the regions of the west, or Amenti, below the western horizon, to be born again on the eastern horizon on the morrow. In this we have the germ of the Egyptian idea of immortality.[2]

As we can see, the God Sun "dies" and is "born again" or "resurrected," many centuries to millennia before the common era. Elucidating further the profoundly astrotheological Egyptian religion, tying in celestial phenomena with an afterlife, Hornung states:

> In the Pyramid Texts of the third millennium B.C.E., the orientation toward a celestial afterlife led to intense concern with stars; in these texts, the king is a star in the sky among the gods... But in this oldest corpus of texts the solar afterlife is fundamentally more important than the stellar, and soon thereafter, emphasis shifted to the netherworld, where the sun was the only heavenly body to play a predominant role, assisting the dead in acquiring renewed life by means of its nightly journey.[3]

In his book *Ancient Egyptian Coffin Texts*, in a note to CT Sp. 152, a description of "those who are in the sunshine" being released, Faulkner remarks, "Apparently the dead ascend to the sky at sunset, having previously gone forth from the tomb into the day to deal with enemies..."[4]

---

[1] Allen, J., *AEPT*, 8.
[2] Lockyer, *DA*, 35.
[3] Hornung, *SLE*, 26.
[4] Faulkner, *AECT*, I, 131.

The overall solar salvation evoked in the Egyptian religion is described by Egyptologists Dr. Vivian Davies, a keeper of the Egyptian Antiquities at the British Museum, and Dr. Renée Friedman, a curator also at the British Museum, thus:

> To the Egyptians, creation was not a single, isolated event but an ongoing cycle of renewal to be repeated daily with the rising of the sun, as the sun god emerged anew from the mound of creation victorious over the demons of the netherworld who sought to destroy him each night.[1]

In the sacred literature of Egypt, the sun is all-important, repeatedly invoked, beseeched and prayed to as facilitating the beneficent passage of the soul into the afterlife. In fact, it is evident from the ancient texts that there is no greater purifying power than the sun, and its function in faith of Egypt was supreme. As Assman says, "The life-giving effect of sunlight is clear and is expressed hundreds of times in the texts."[2]

Regarding the sun's path, its role in immortality, and the god Osiris, Allen also says:

> The Sun's daily movement through the sky was viewed as a journey from birth to death, and his rebirth at dawn was made possible through Osiris, the force of new life.[3]

In reality, the sun was thus so singularly significant that its own cycles were closely tied with *the salvation of the human soul*, thousands of years before the common era.

Further illustrating the importance of the sun in Egyptian thought, after discussing the pharaoh Akhenaten's "Hymns to the Sun," Dr. Hare remarks:

> The sun is seen as the vital force that maintains the multitude of natural phenomena; it is as well the original motive for life in all animate beings. The sun shapes the infant in its mother's womb, the sun creates semen in the father. In a particularly observant and artful passage, the sun is depicted as breathing life into an egg, to enliven the chick before it breaks forth from the shell...[4]

This solar breath of life pervades the Egyptian obsession with "cheating death," as the solar imagery throughout the extensive ancient Egyptian funereal and mortuary literature is clear and persistent, with the deceased in his efforts to attain resurrection and immortality continuously likened to the sun in its daily battle with the darkness of night. As Faulkner remarks, "The deceased is compared with the sun, which is renewed nightly to rise next day."[5] In this regard, Renouf remarks that "all the forms assumed in the

---

[1] Davies, V., 154.
[2] Assman, *ESRNK*, 81.
[3] Allen, J., *ME*, 8.
[4] Hare, 193.
[5] Faulkner, *AECT*, I, 52.

Book of the Dead by the deceased are well known forms of the Sun-god."[1] Indeed, the original, ancient title of the BD, "Going Forth by Day," demonstrates the hopes of immortality tied in with the sun's daily resurrection from its nightly death.

In demonstrating the pervasiveness of religious awe in Egyptian life, Dr. Amanda-Alice Maravelia of Russian Academy of Sciences Centre for Egyptological Studies discusses the Egyptian perception of the widely used sculpting material faience as a "manifestation of the color of the sky and light itself..."[2] Dr. Maravelia next says, "The ancient Egyptians connected faience with the resurrection of the sun from the Netherworld and the bright light that followed, which was essentially for the well-being of a 'justified' deceased person in the afterlife."[3] The blue-green color of faience was symbolic also of Osiris, who is frequently depicted with green skin, representing life, as in the color of thriving foliage. Osiris's role as "vegetation god" is demonstrated at CT Sp. 317:115: "I am the Nile-god, Lord of Waters, who brings vegetation..."[4] It is possible therefore that Osiris as the "force of life" symbolized the very act of the foliage turning from brown to green representing the resurrection or imbuement of Osiris into the world. In this case, Osiris could be said to be representative of photosynthesis, an action that may indeed have seemed miraculous and supernatural to the ancients. It is further possible that desert dwellers seeing a lush and green *oasis* may have believed it too exemplified the existence of Osiris in the world.

In this same regard, many amulets depicting the scarab beetle are made of this material for its Osirian symbolism. Concerning scarabs, Maravelia remarks:

> ...They were used in the symbolic context of the regenerating sun...connected with the heart of the deceased..., which would save him and allow him to become...triumphant and resurrected like the morning sun.[5]

As we can see, the reverence for the sun and its *resurrection* in the morning was all important to the Egyptians, representing the hope for humanity to attain to eternal life. This identification of the deceased with the solar life-renewal is evidenced throughout the mortuary literature, such as the Pyramid Texts, Coffin Texts and the Book of the Dead.

The Deceased as Osiris

One of the main copies of the Book of the Dead is the Papyrus of Ani, designed to facilitate the passage of the deceased scribe by that name, and estimated to have been composed around 1250 BCE. As an

---

[1] Renouf, *EBD*, 141-142.
[2] Maravelia, *JNES*, 82.
[3] Maravelia, *JNES*, 82.
[4] Faulkner, *AECT*, I, 241.
[5] Maravelia, *JNES*, 86.

example of how much Egypt's spirituality was tied into the sun, chapter or spell 15 of the BD constitutes a long prayer or hymn to the divine solar orb, said in the voice of the deceased to ensure his passage into the afterlife as an immortal soul. The profound reverence for the sun is highly evident in this chapter, in which the speaker repeatedly addresses the sun—or "Re," also transliterated as "Ra"—including in several rubrics (titles of different sections) such as: "*Worship of Re when he rises in the horizon until the occurrence of his setting in life.*"[1] In another section of BD 15 appears the following expression of veneration for the sun, Re/Ra:

> *Worship of Re when he rises in the eastern horizon of the sky, when those who are in his following are joyful.*

> O Sun-disk, Lord of the sunbeams, who shines forth from the horizon every day: may you shine in the face of Ani, for *he worships you* in the morning, he propitiates you in the evening. May the soul of Ani go up with you to the sky...

> The Osiris Ani says when he honors his lord, the Lord of Eternity:

> Hail to you, Horakhty, Khepri the self-created! How beautiful is your shining forth from the horizon when you illumine the Two Lands with your rays! All the gods are in joy when they see you as king of the sky...[2]

In his translation of the Papyrus of Ani, Faulkner thus refers to the deceased as "the Osiris Ani,"[3] identifying him with the god Osiris, the "Lord of Eternity," elsewhere deemed "Lord of Resurrections,"[4] two epithets essentially describing the role of the much later Lord Jesus. In this regard, Sir Dr. James George Frazer (1854-1941) states that "every man after death was identified with Osiris and bore his name."[5] In multiple Pyramid Texts as well, the deceased is named as Osiris, the father of Horus, as at PT 600:1657a/N 359: "this king is Osiris."[6] Concerning the Pyramid Texts, Egyptologist Dr. Ann Macy

---

[1] Faulkner, *EBD*, pl. 18. It should be kept in mind that, although "Re" or "Ra" is used to designate the proper name of the sun god, the term in Egyptian simply means "sun"; thus, in some instances, James Allen, for one, differentiates between "the sun" and the name of the god by capitalizing the latter as "the Sun." (Allen, J., *AEPT*, 14.)

[2] Faulkner, *EBD*, pl. 20; Allen, T., *BD*, 12; Bunsen/Birch, 167; Budge, *EBD* (1967), 246.

[3] Faulkner, *EBD*, pl. 11, etc.

[4] Renouf, *EBD*, 118; Allen, T., *BD*, 56. Faulkner's translation seems contrived in order to steer away from this uncomplicated concept of "Lord of Resurrections." (Faulkner, *EBD*, 106) Birch's rendering certainly implies divine resurrection commanded by the God of Light, the sun: "I am the Yesterday, the Morning, the Light at its birth the second time... Lord of mankind seen in all his rays, the Conductor coming forth from the darkness." (Bunsen/Birch, 206.)

[5] Frazer, *AAO*, 217.

[6] Redford, 305; Allen, J., *AEPT*, 269; Mercer, 254. As concerns the numbering used here for the Pyramid Texts, references are to the "PT" system devised by Dr. Kurt Sethe in *Die altägyptischen Pyramidentexte* and utilized by Drs. Samuel Mercer and Raymond Faulkner in their translations, as well as to the numbering employed by James Allen, whose work *The Ancient Egyptian Pyramid Texts* should be consulted for purposes of

Roth of Howard University says, "The king is identified throughout as the god Osiris, and the speaker acts as his son Horus."[1] In this same regard, Hornung remarks that "the deceased appears as Osiris, the suffering, murdered, and resurrected ruler-god, husband and brother of Isis."[2] Again, Hornung says that "the fact of death makes the king himself an 'Osiris'; he bears this name as a title of honor."[3] Indeed, Morenz adds that "the entire ritual complex of Osirian burial, including mummification itself...enabled the dead to become Osiris."[4]

Regarding the epithet "the Osiris," Egyptologist Dr. Adolph Erman (1854-1937), a professor of Egyptology at the University of Berlin and director of the Egyptian Museum at Berlin, remarks, "From the time of the Middle Empire the deceased is addressed directly as the *Osiris N. N.*, as if he were that god himself..."[5] In his description of Osiris, Dr. William J. Murnane (d. 2000), a professor of History and adjunct professor with the Institute of Egyptian Art and Archaeology at the University of Memphis, relates, "Dead individuals were identified with him (as 'The Osiris NN') in the orthodox religion..."[6] Following the ancient convention, throughout his translation of the Book of the Dead, Renouf likewise refers to the deceased as "the Osiris" or "the Osiris *N*," the latter of which is favored by Goelet and Assman, while Budge uses "the Osiris Nu" and "Osiris Ani."[7] Professor of Egyptology and Oriental History at the University of Chicago, Dr. James H. Breasted (1865-1935) discusses the kings Unis and Pepi I as "Osiris," and also calls the deceased "this Osiris."[8] He likewise states, "In the earliest versions of the Book of the Dead...the deceased says of himself: 'I am Osiris, I have come forth as thou...'"[9] In his translation of the Book of the Dead, Dr. T. George Allen prefers simply "Osiris N.,

---

cross-referencing the variously numbered texts. I have taken the liberty of combining the Utterance/PT numbers with the "*Pyr.*" line numbers, separated by a colon. Footnotes indicate the pages in Mercer and Faulkner, as well as Allen for the equivalent verse. Allen's translation substitutes the name of the subject of the spell/papyrus, such as "Unis" or "Pepi," rather than the "N." or "Osiris" of Mercer and Faulkner. Regarding the Coffin Texts, I have chosen to follow Lesko in numbering each *spell* using the "CT Sp." designation. (See, e.g., Lesko, 39.) As concerns the numbering of passages in other ancient works, I have generally converted Roman numerals to Indian/Arabic numerals and separated books from chapters, and chapters from verses, with a period.

[1] Redford, 149.
[2] Hornung, *VK*, 25.
[3] Hornung, *VK*, 115.
[4] Morenz, 55.
[5] Erman, 308.
[6] Murnane, 283.
[7] Renouf, *EBD*, 10, 22; Wilson, 391, etc.; Budge, *BD* (1899), 182; Faulkner, *EBD*, 154; Assman, *DSAE*, 152.
[8] Breasted, *DRTAE*, 19.
[9] Breasted, *DRTAE*, 22-23. Breasted further relates the deceased as saying, "I live as 'Grain.' I grow as 'Grain.'" Osiris also represented fertility and growth of nature, as brought out by Frazer.

while in *The Origin of Osiris and His Cult*, Griffiths settles on the term "Osiris-King."[1]

This experience of being the "Osiris NN" was not limited to royalty, however, as the introduction of the voluminous Coffin Texts "eliminated the royal exclusivity of the Pyramid Texts, putting the texts at the disposal of all deceased persons and thus making the enjoyment of the afterlife something that all could attain..."[2] Now, Hornung continues, "*every* deceased person was an Osiris NN,"[3] and Morenz says that "in that course of time all the Egyptian dead were mummified and became Osiris..."[4] Thus, the deceased in the Coffin Texts also represents Osiris, as at CT Sp. 47,[5] and the interchangeability of the deceased with Osiris—and Horus—is likewise illustrated at CT Sp. 215, in which the speaker states: "...he [Osiris] says: He is his son, he is his heir; He is Horus, and I am he."[6] In a spell (CT Sp. 227) entitled, "Becoming the Counterpart of Osiris," the deceased says: "I indeed am Osiris, I indeed am the Lord of All, I am the Radiant One, the brother of the Radiant Lady..."[7] Again, in the same spell, the deceased states, "I indeed am Osiris... I am Horus the Elder... I am Anubis..."[8] As noted, the number of deceased followers of the Egyptian religion has been estimated at a half a billion—that would mean hundreds of millions of Osirises!

Moreover, as Griffiths relates, the deceased shares not only the name of the god but also his *experiences*:

> The King is frequently addressed as *Osiris Wenis* [Unis], *Osiris Pepi* and so on; but the relation is also made clear, especially with regard to the benefits accruing from the identification, by an equation of the King's experiences with those of Osiris.[9]

This fact of the deceased being "the Osiris" in both name and deed ranks as highly important and needs to be recalled throughout this present work, as the subject becomes part of the composite Osirian myth evidently utilized in the later Christian effort.

As can be seen, the deceased is not only Osiris but also many other gods, including Horus, a fact that demonstrates these characters' interchangeability. Concerning the important chapter or spell 64—one of the oldest in the text—Budge states:

> The formulae which constitute the Chapter are of a highly mystical character, and the recital of them gave to the deceased the power to

---

[1] Griffiths, *OOHC*, 18, et al.
[2] Hornung, *AEBA*, 9.
[3] Hornung, *AEBA*, 9. (Emph. added.)
[4] Morenz, 195.
[5] Faulkner, *AECT*, I, 42.
[6] Faulkner, *AECT*, I, 171.
[7] Faulkner, *AECT*, I, 179.
[8] Faulkner, *AECT*, I, 179.
[9] Griffiths, *OOHC*, 45.

identify himself with all the great gods, and to make use of all their attributes as he pleased for his own benefit.[1]

The deceased is identified as Osiris, who is reborn as the figure of "Horakhty," mentioned in BD 15 and elsewhere, representing "Horus of the Two Horizons," which refers to the sunrise and sunset. "Horakhty" or "Harakhte" is a combination of "Her/Har/Horus" with "Akhte/Akthy," defined by Hornung as, "'He of the horizon'; an epithet of Horus as a solar deity."[2] In other words, "Herakhty"—another variant spelling—is "Horus as the morning sun,"[3] referred to by Morenz as "the sun-god Harakhti."[4] (The morning sun is also the "beetle" Khepri, who reproduces himself at dawn.)

Of Mysteries and Myths

A millennium and a half or so after the Book of the Dead was first compiled, the Greek historian Herodotus (2.42) discussed major Egyptian deities, such as Osiris and Isis, who, during the historian's time, were "worshipped by everyone throughout Egypt," demonstrating the continued massive popularity of the Egyptian religion.[5] Herodotus (2.47) further related that the Egyptians equated Osiris with the Greek god Dionysus, stating, "The only deities to whom the Egyptians consider it proper to sacrifice pigs are Dionysus and the Moon."[6] Regarding these deities, Herodotus editor Marincola notes: "Dionysus is Osiris, the Moon (Selene) is Isis."[7] Herodotus (2.144, 156) also identified Horus as the Greek *sun god* Apollo.[8] This identification of the hawk-headed Horus with Apollo rates as appropriate, as the latter had been associated with the *hawk* centuries before in *The Odyssey* (15.526) by Homer (9th cent.?), who styled the bird "Apollo's swift messenger."[9] Beyond these mentions in his long treatise on Egypt, Herodotus does not spell out any comprehensive myths of Osiris, Isis and Horus. Nevertheless, in book 2, chapter 61, the Greek historian appears to imply that there are *mysteries* of Osiris that he cannot relate,[10] which may refer to assorted myths, motifs and rituals not readily disclosed to the masses. Later in his book (2.171), while discussing the lake near Athena's temple at Sais, Herodotus clearly raises the mysteries, disclaiming that he will not address them further:

---

[1] Budge, *BD* (1899), cxxxii.
[2] Hornung, *AEBA*, 153.
[3] Armour, 28.
[4] Morenz, 63.
[5] Herodotus/Waterfield, 112.
[6] Herodotus/de Selincourt, 104.
[7] Herodotus/de Selincourt, 563.
[8] Herodotus/de Selincourt, 139, 145.
[9] Homer, 51. The phrase in the original Greek is "...κιρκος, Απολλωνος ταχυς αγγελος..." The Greek word for "messenger" here is *angel*.
[10] Herodotus/de Selincourt, 108, 564.

It is on this lake that the Egyptians act by night in what they call their Mysteries the Passion of that being whose name I will not speak. All the details of these performances are known to me, but—I will say no more.[1]

Indeed, mysteries are often raised in the Egyptian texts: For example, in the Coffin Texts we find mention of "the private matters of the god...in the secret places" (CT Sp. 1099).[2] Also in the Coffin Texts, opening the windows on "the Ennead" or nine principal gods will allow the Osiris to "see the mysteries which are in them..."[3] The mysteries are also mentioned in numerous places in the Book of the Dead, such as at BD 168, discussing the "gods of the tenth cavern in the Netherworld, who cry aloud and whose mysteries are holy."[4] Around 1360 BCE, Amenhotep/Amenhotpe "son of Hapu" referred in an inscription to his own association with the mysteries of "the transfigurations of Thoth."[5] The "true names" of Egyptian gods likewise represented secrets or hidden "mysteries."[6]

As part of the mysteries appear sacred texts comprising hymns to the sun, categorized by Assman as one of three groups of such writings: "*Texts of an esoteric body of knowledge.*"[7] Included in these sacred sun hymns were the "standard texts" that were "not secret or esoteric." As the German scholar continues, "The sun cult must have had an exoteric side that enabled the lay person to participate in it."[8] In his analysis of the sun hymns from the New Kingdom, Assman sifted through some 500 texts, reflecting the abundance of such sacred writings concerning the Egyptian solar religion. In a chapter entitled, "The Mysteries of the Sun Cult," in describing the "tripartite form" of the New Kingdom solar cult, the professor remarks that the first part comprises "a closely guarded secret cosmology, depicted in royal tombs as 'underworld books' for the use of the king in the afterlife."[9] The second part constitutes a "set of hymns located in countless non-royal tombs, which praise the solar journey in its polytheistic form," while the third form is a "sort of monotheism that regards the sun as the natural manifestation of the uniqueness of god..."[10] Some of these mysteries were likely carried out in sacred areas such as crypts, an indication of a "secret cult."[11] Despite the precautions to preserve them as secrets or mysteries, the hymns of

[1] Herodotus/de Selincourt, 149.
[2] Faulkner, *AECT*, III, 154.
[3] Faulkner, *AECT*, I, 56.
[4] Faulkner, 126. See also chapters/spells 1, 78, 94, 101, 137A, 169, 180. (Faulkner, pls. 5, 26 and pp. 109, 112, 119, 128, 132.)
[5] Hornung, *SLE*, 5.
[6] Morenz, 21-22.
[7] Assman, *ESRNK*, 7.
[8] Assman, *ESRNK*, 8.
[9] Assman, *ESRNK*, 16.
[10] Assman, *ESRNK*, 16.
[11] Assman, *ESRNK*, 147.

the secret sun cult "did find their way out of this cult into the wider non-priestly circles of the population."[1]

One of the priestly commentators who may have passed along mysteries and secrets was an Egyptian priest of the sun god Re at Heliopolis named Manetho (3rd cent. BCE), who wrote in Greek about the Egyptian gods. Since his works have all been lost or destroyed, we must rely on the descriptions thereof by other ancient writers, including Plutarch (28, 362A) and the Jewish historian of the first century AD/CE, Josephus (*Apion* 1.16, et al.), the latter of whom informs us that Manetho claimed to have based his work on "Egyptian records," such as oral traditions, "priestly writings" and other documents.[2] In his histories, Manetho styled the gods by their Greek names, also equating Horus with Apollo, for example.[3] Over the centuries, it has been claimed that Manetho was an adept and expert in the Egyptian mysteries. Indeed, Manetho is called by the Christian monk George Syncellus (9th cent. AD/CE) the "High Priest and Scribe of the Mysteries of the Temple,"[4] while Plutarch too related that the Egyptian was the high priest of the mysteries as Heliopolis. Hence, the destruction of his work may have been committed in order to hide these mysteries and their use in the later Christian effort. It may well be that Manetho's work was utilized centuries later by the Assyrian philosopher Iamblichus (c. 245-c. 325 AD/CE), in his extensive discourse on *The Mysteries*,[5] in which the mystic says about Osiris's center of worship, "The mysteries in Abydos are never disclosed" (VI.7) [6]

During the first century BCE, the Greek writer Diodorus Siculus likewise related that Osiris was the sun and Isis the moon, remarking that the god was called "many-eyed" because of his rays. In *The Antiquities of Egypt* (1.11), Diodorus further comments, "Some of the early Greek mythologists call Osiris 'Dionysus' and also, changing the word slightly, 'Sirius'...."[7] Diodorus (1.13) also addresses the five intercalary days added to the end of the old 360-day calendar and identified as the birthdays of the gods "Osiris and Isis, Typhon [Set], Apollo [Horus], and Aphrodite [Nephthys]."[8] In the same book and chapter, the historian further associates Isis with the Greek goddess Demeter or Ceres, the virgin earth mother who gave birth to

---

[1] Assman, *ESRNK*, 17.
[2] Verbrugghe, 103; Josephus/Whiston, 612. The numbering system for Josephus used here includes both the English (book, chapter, paragraph) and the Greek (book, verse), depending on the length of the passage in question.
[3] Verbrugghe, 99.
[4] Bunsen/Birch, 224.
[5] Iamblichus/Clarke, xxxviii.
[6] Iamblichus/Clarke, 289.
[7] Diodorus/Murphy, 14.
[8] Diodorus/Murphy, 18.

Persephone or Kore.[1] Lending greater antiquity to Diodorus's assertions, Catholic Church historian Eusebius (c. 260-c. 341 AD/CE) indicated that in chapters 11-13 the Sicilian historian was essentially summarizing the work of Manetho.[2] Giving further credence to Herodotus's comments about Egyptian mysteries, Diodorus (1.20, 23) also refers several times to "sacred rites," "mysteries" and "mystical rites" in association with Egyptian gods, including and especially Osiris and Isis.[3] In fact, after describing inscriptions on two ancient stelae in "Nysa of Arabia" that supposedly marked the deities' graves, Diodorus (1.27) comments:

> They say that only this much of the writing on the columns is legible and that the rest, the larger part, has been effaced by time. Be that as it may, most writers disagree over the burial place of the two gods. This is because the real facts in the case were handed down in secret tradition by the Egyptian priests, who cared neither to share the truth with the populace, nor to incur the retribution threatened for any who should reveal the mysteries of these gods to the vulgar.[4]

In many locations, the penalty for divulging the mysteries was death, so it is obvious why the Egyptian priests and initiates would shy away from doing so. While these secret rites changed from place to place and era to era, some of the characteristics, myths, motifs, symbols and rituals discussed in this present work undoubtedly constituted *Egyptian* mysteries not to be revealed to the vulgar masses, which is one reason they are not tidily laid out in an ancient encyclopedia—a point that needs to be emphasized. Paradoxically, at times what are termed "mysteries" are nevertheless made public during festivals that reenacted myths, for instance.[5] Throughout this book, however, it needs to be kept in mind that both phenomena occurred at once, as they do to this day within Christianity as well, which possesses both esoteric and exoteric mysteries.

In any event, the path to a unified myth leads to Greek historian Plutarch, who also refers to the "divine mysteries" (τα θεια) and "Mysteries" (τα οργια, οι μυστικοι) on a number of occasions (*Iside*, 3, 352A; *Obs. Or.*, 13, 417A; 14, 417B).[6] In creating his famous treatise on "Isis and Osiris"—in which he recounted the composite myth of the most popular Egyptian gods of the time, stating that Osiris was the sun and Isis the moon—Plutarch was himself evidently compelled to pull together characteristics from numerous sources, including papyri and inscriptions, from a wide era. Thus, prior to Plutarch's time it appears there existed few comprehensive sources for the

---

[1] Diodorus/Murphy, 18. See *The New Schaff-Herzog Encyclopedia of Religious Knowledge* (*NSHERK*), 212.
[2] Diodorus/Murphy, 18.
[3] Diodorus/Murphy, 25, 28.
[4] Diodorus/Murphy, 34.
[5] Hornung, *SLE*, 13.
[6] Plutarch/Babbitt, 11, 157,

various myths surrounding these deities. Because Christianity was unknown to Plutarch, he naturally would not have factored it into his analysis by couching his narrative of the myth in Christian terms. We, however, are very aware of the gospel story, as well as the assertion that it too was based largely on the Egyptian mythos and ritual. Hence, in our comparisons we will summarize the Egyptian influence on Christianity in terms of how its successor and borrower—the Christian myth—itself reworked the Egyptian myths and rituals into a composite tale.

Who Is Horus?

Many of the salient and fascinating parallels between the Christian and Egyptian religions revolve in particular around the highly important god Horus, son of the famed god Osiris and goddess Isis, who, again, were said by Herodotus (2.42) five centuries before the common era to be "worshipped by everyone throughout Egypt."[1] The significance of Horus, or "Heru" in the Egyptian, cannot be overestimated, for a variety of reasons, including that he was the morning sun and often the speaker in the mortuary literature, as well as the priest conducting the afterlife rituals, along with the living pharaoh/king, as we shall see. As the great healer who himself is resurrected from the dead, Horus was likewise the patient him or herself in the Egyptian healing rituals, meaning that wherever the Isiac cult was present, so too was Horus, especially in times of healing. Moreover, Horus's worship was not only widespread but also long-lived, spanning from the earliest times of Egyptian religion, well into the common era. As Egyptologist Dr. Edmund S. Meltzer remarks:

> Horus is one of the earliest attested of the major ancient Egyptian deities, becoming known to us at least as early as the late Predynastic period (Naqada III/Dynasty 0); he was still prominent in the latest temples of the Greco-Roman period, especially at Philae and Edfu, as well as in the Old Coptic and Greco-Egyptian ritual-power, or magical, texts.[2]

The Predynastic period began prior to 5,000 years ago, and Horus's reverence continued for centuries into the common era. Hence, the Egyptian god's worship had been in existence at least 3,000 years before Christ purportedly lived. By the time Christianity was created, Horus's cult was widespread around the Mediterranean, such as in Greece, and he was one of the most popular gods of the Roman Empire.

In reality, a number of the mythical motifs regarding Horus and other Egyptian deities startlingly resemble characteristics and events attributed to Jesus Christ, indicating that the gospel story is neither

---

[1] Herodotus/Waterfield, 112.
[2] Redford, 165.

original nor historical. As may have been expected, many of these correspondences are not widely and neatly found in encyclopedia entries and textbooks, so they have often been dismissed without adequate study and with extreme prejudice. In my previous work, *The Christ Conspiracy*, I presented various aspects of the Horus myth out of the hundreds brought to light by Gerald Massey and others. Some of these comparisons are as follows:

- Horus was born on "December 25th" (winter solstice) in a manger.
- He was of royal descent, and his mother was the "virgin Isis-Mery."
- Horus's birth was announced by a star in the East and attended by three "wise men."
- At age 12, he was a child teacher in the Temple, and at 30, he was baptized.
- Horus was baptized by "Anup the Baptizer," who was decapitated.
- The Egyptian god had 12 companions, helpers or disciples.
- Horus performed miracles, exorcised demons and raised Osiris from the dead.
- The god walked on water.
- Horus was "crucified" between two "thieves."
- He (or Osiris) was buried for three days in a tomb and resurrected.
- Horus/Osiris was also the "Way, the Truth, the Life," "Messiah," the "Son of Man," the "Good Shepherd," the "Lamb of God," the "Word made flesh," the "Word of Truth," etc.
- Horus's personal epithet was "Iusa," the "ever-becoming son" of the Father. He was called "Holy Child," as well as "the Anointed One," while Osiris was the *KRST*.
- Horus battled with the "evil one," Set/Seth.
- Horus was to reign for one thousand years.[1]

---

[1] See Acharya, *CC*, 115. Various of these parallels were popularized in the official version of the internet movie "ZEITGEIST," released in 2007, the Companion Guide for which was the basis of this present work. The pertinent part of that movie by Peter Joseph is as follows: "This is Horus. He is the Sun God of Egypt of around 3000 BC. He is the sun anthropomorphized, and his life is a series of allegorical myths involving the sun's movement in the sky. From the ancient hieroglyphs in Egypt, we know much about this solar messiah. For instance, Horus, being the sun, or the light, had an enemy known as Set, and Set was the personification of the darkness or night. And, metaphorically speaking, every morning Horus would win the battle against Set—while in the evening, Set would conquer Horus and send him into the underworld. It is important to note that 'dark vs. light' or 'good vs. evil' is one of the most ubiquitous mythological dualities ever known and is still expressed on many levels to this day.

"Broadly speaking, the story of Horus is as follows: Horus was born on December 25th of the virgin Isis-Meri. His birth was accompanied by a star in the east, which in turn, three kings followed to locate and adore the new-born savior. At the age of 12, he was a prodigal child teacher, and at the age of 30 he was baptized by a figure known as Anup and thus began his ministry. Horus had 12 disciples he traveled about with, performing miracles such as healing the sick and walking on water. Horus was known

As we can see, these features of the Horus myth are virtually identical to major elements in the story of Jesus Christ, as found in the New Testament and in Christian tradition. When reading this synopsis of the Horus myth, one needs to keep in mind that it is our contention that snippets of the myths of various gods—the "essential parts of the myth," as Cooper puts it—were pulled out of context and woven together to create the gospel story. Again, one does not find the Horus myth as above outlined in an ancient Egyptian encyclopedia, such that the creators of the Jesus story merely scratched out the Egyptian names and inserted the Christian ones. Those who have been attempting to explain the creation of the Christ myth have been compelled to back-engineer the story in order to analyze its components and concepts. In other words, in explaining the various mythical motifs used in the gospel story, some have recounted the tale utilizing the original god or gods, in a gospel-like manner in order to express those components.

Hence, although the myth of Horus, for example, was not told in this condensed manner, such storytelling is useful to convey quickly and readily that the germane aspects of the Christian myth and ritual *were* found in Egypt, long predating the common era. Such is how mythmaking is accomplished, and those who created the *Christian myth* out of bits and pieces of pre-Christian writings and rituals engaged in the same process as well. As we have seen, this type of synopsis constitutes the same manner by which scholars create narratives of myths for encyclopedia entries and textbooks—another point that cannot be overemphasized. Also, as noted, this process of summarization did in fact occur to some extent with the Egyptian myths, as they were congealed and formalized over a period of centuries to millennia. In other words, the stories of Osiris, Isis and Horus, for example, were increasingly woven into a narrative over the centuries, as we have seen in the works of Plutarch, for example.

Since so many claims of Egyptian influence on Christianity thus involve the god Horus (and/or his father/brother, Osiris), investigating his identity becomes critical to our quest. Mainstream sources often list Horus only as a "sky god" with a hawk or falcon's head, the eyes of whom are correctly related as representing the sun and moon. We have already seen, however, that Horus of the Horizon or Horakhty is a solar deity and the morning sun, part of the combined Re-Horakhty, whose name Egyptologist Dr. Rudolf Anthes renders, "Re, the heavenly Horus of the horizon in which he appears as the sun."[1] Indeed, the fact of Horus himself symbolizing the sun was understood centuries prior to the common era by ancient writers

---

by many gestural names such as The Truth, The Light, God's Anointed Son, The Good Shepherd, The Lamb of God, and many others. After being betrayed by Typhon [Set], Horus was 'crucified,' buried for 3 days, and thus, resurrected."
[1] Anthes, 181.

such as Herodotus, Manetho and Diodorus, who equated him with
the sun god Apollo. In the text *The Hieroglyphica*, attributed to the
aptly named Horapollo (5th century AD/CE), one of the last priests of
the Egyptian religion, the author equates Horus with the sun and
states (1.17) that "the Sun is called Horus because he has power over
the Hours."[1] Like Homer in *The Odyssey* describing the bird as
"Apollo's swift messenger," Horapollo too discusses the hawk as a
symbol of the sun: "And since the sun is the lord of sight, they draw
him sometimes in the shape of a hawk."[2]

Also depicted in the shape of a hawk is the main sun god Re/Ra,
with whom Horus is likewise identified. In this regard, there exist
hieroglyphs not only for the combined solar god Horus-Ra but also
that could represent either Horus *or* Ra, including one of a hawk
inside a sun disc, demonstrating the interchangeability of these two
gods, as well as Horus's unquestionably solar nature. Adding to this
solar identity is Horus's epithet as "son of Ra" as well.[3] Indeed, in
many Coffin Texts, Horus is called "first-born of Re."[4]

Discussing this sacred merger, in his opus, *History of Egypt*,
renowned Egyptologist Sir Dr. Gaston Maspero (1846-1916), a head
of the Antiquities Service at Cairo and the original developer and
director of the Cairo Museum, remarks:

> Horus the Sun, and Râ, the Sun-God of Heliopolis, had so permeated
> each other that none could say where the one began and the other
> ended. One by one all the functions of Râ had been usurped by
> Horus, and all the designations of Horus had been appropriated by
> Râ. The sun was styled Harmakhûîti [Harmakhis], the Horus of the
> two mountains—that is, the Horus who comes forth from the
> mountain of the east in the morning, and retires at evening into the
> mountain of the west; or Hartimâ, Horus the Pikeman, that Horus
> whose lance spears the hippopotamus or the serpent of the celestial
> river; or Harnûbi, the Golden Horus, the great golden sparrow-hawk
> with mottled plumage, who puts all other birds to flight; and these
> titles were indifferently applied to each of the feudal gods who
> represented the sun.[5]

And again Dr. Maspero states:

> When the celestial Horus was confounded with Râ, and became the
> sun..., he naturally also became the sun of the two horizons, the sun
> by day, and the sun by night.[6]

Regarding Horus's solar role, as well as the Egyptian custom of
naming, personifying and deifying different aspects of the sun, along
with rolling them together as one, James Allen remarks:

---

[1] Boas, 16.
[2] Boas, 46.
[3] Brier, 60, 61.
[4] See, e.g., CT Sp. 1104, 1105, 1110, 1114 and 1175. (Faulkner, *AECT*, III, 159, 161, 162, 187.)
[5] Maspero, *DC*, 100.
[6] Maspero, *HE*, I, 197.

> The sun...can be seen not only as the physical source of heat and light (Re) but also as the governing force of nature (Horus), whose appearance at dawn from the Akhet makes all life possible—a perception embodied in the combined god Re-Harakhti (Re, Horus of the Akhet). The tendency to syncretism is visible in all periods of Egyptian history.[1]

Horus therefore represents the sun as the governor of nature, the "Lord of lords," as it were. The "Akhet" is the "region between the day and night skies," or the horizons, into which the sun sets and rises, before and after entering the *Duat, Djat, Dat* or Tuat, the nightly "netherworld."[2] As can be seen, Horus at the dawn is so important as to make "all life possible," much like Jesus, who is the source of eternal life. Indeed, Horus himself is "universal and eternal."[3]

In ancient Egyptian writings such as the Pyramid Texts, in which he is called the "Lord of the Sky,"[4] along with other solar epithets such as "He Whose Face is Seen," "He Whose Hair is Parted," and "He Whose Two Plumes are Long,"[5] Horus's function as a sun god or aspect of the sun is repeatedly emphasized, although this singularly pertinent fact is seldom found in encyclopedias and textbooks, leaving us to wonder why he would be thus diminished.

In the Coffin Texts as well is Horus's role as (morning) sun god made clear, such as in the following elegantly rendered scripture from CT Sp. 255:

> ...I will appear as Horus who ascends in gold from upon the lips of the horizon...[6]

In CT Sp. 326, Horus is even called "Lord of the sunlight."[7] Concerning Horus's solar nature, James Allen also relates:

> Horus was the power of kingship. To the Egyptians this was as much a force of nature as those embodied in the other gods. It was manifest in two natural phenomena: the sun, the most powerful force in nature; and the pharaoh, the most powerful force in human society. Horus's role as the king of nature is probably the origin of his name: *hrw* seems to mean "the one above" or "the one far off"... This is apparently a reference to the sun, which is "above" and "far off" in the sky, like the falcon with which Horus is regularly associated...[8]

Thus, again, Horus symbolizes the ruling-power aspect of the sun, the "King of kings," much like Jesus. Even Horus's very name may signify the sun, and the hawk or falcon, by which he is

---

[1] Allen, J., *ME*, 44.
[2] Allen, J., *ME*, 21; Griffiths, *OOHC*, 9.
[3] Anthes, 178.
[4] Allen, T., *HPT*, 17.
[5] Allen, J., *AEPT*, 432.
[6] Faulkner, *AECT*, I, 196.
[7] Faulkner, *AECT*, I, 253.
[8] Allen, J., *ME*, 144.

identified, likewise represents a solar symbol by virtue of how high it flies. In summary, Dr. Meltzer remarks, "Horus the falcon was predominantly a sky god *and* a sun god."[1]

Furthermore, regarding the Horus epithets in the Pyramid Texts from Saqqara/Sakkara, Allen states that the "solar element in Horus clearly predominates," while the "less common epithets of Horus are likewise largely celestial, as is his habitat."[2] Therefore, in his many epithets, attributes and deeds, Horus ranks as *astrotheological* overall.

The Many Horuses

Over the millennia during which the Egyptian religion was popular, there appeared a number of Horuses or *Horus epithets*, one of whom, Horus the Elder, also called Heru-Ur or Haroeris, was the *brother* of Osiris and Isis, and two of whom were named as the *son(s)* of Osiris and Isis. In addition, there are several other Horuses or Horus epithets. For example, we have already seen the epithets of "Horakhty" or "Harmakhis," i.e., Horus of the "rising and setting sun"[3]; and "Hartimâ," the latter being a sort of "fisher," as he spears the "serpent of the celestial river." In *The Manners and Customs of the Ancient Egyptians*, Sir Dr. John G. Wilkinson (1797-1875), the "Father of British Egyptology," describes the various Horuses and demonstrates the solar nature of the epithet previously seen as "Harnûbi": "Her-Nub [*Hr nbw*], 'the Golden Horus,' is primarily the god of the morning sun, manifesting himself in the golden glory of the dawn."[4]

Understandably, these many Horuses have been confused in both ancient and modern times. As Budge relates:

> Heru or Horus, the sun-god, was originally a totally distinct god from Horus, the son of Osiris and Isis, but from the earliest times it seems that the two gods were confounded, and that the attributes of the one were ascribed to the other; the fight which Horus the sun-god waged against night and darkness was also at a very early period identified with the combat between Horus, the son of Isis, and his brother Set.[5]

Regarding the confounding of supposedly different Horuses, Dutch Egyptologist Dr. Henri Frankfort (1897-1954) adds:

> It is therefore a mistake to separate "Horus, the Great God, Lord of Heaven," from "Horus, son of Osiris," or to explain their identity as due to syncretism in comparatively late times. The two gods "Horus"

---

[1] Redford, 166. (Emph. added.)
[2] Allen, T., *HPT*, 11-12.
[3] Maspero, *GCM*, 4. Other transliterations of Harmakhis are Harmachis, Hormachis and Hor-m-akhu. Horakty/Harakhte and Harmakhis/Harmachis are essentially the same epithet, both meaning "Horus of the Akhet." (Bleeker, *HR*, 59.)
[4] Wilkinson, J., *MCAE*, III, 29.
[5] Budge, *TBD*, cxiv-cxv.

whose titles we have set side by side are, in reality, one and the same. Their identity is also confirmed by an important pyramid text which addresses the king as follows: "Thou art Horus, son of Osiris, the eldest god, son of Hathor."[1]

Adding to these opinions as to the many Horuses, Meltzer states:

Egyptologists...often speak of distinct, sometimes originally distinct, Horuses or Horus-gods. Combinations, identifications, and differentiations were, however, possible for Horus, and they are complementary rather than antithetical. A judicious examination of the various Horuses and the sources relating to them supports the possibility that the roles in question are closely interrelated, and so they may be understood as different aspects, or facets, of the same divine persona.[2]

Hence, the different Horuses could be considered "facets of the same divine persona." In his dissertation on *Horus in the Pyramid Texts*, Egyptologist Dr. Thomas George Allen of the Oriental Institute at the University of Chicago therefore discusses the "group of Horuses" as one entity.[3] As we can see, in constructing a composite myth about Horus, we have many entities, qualities, characteristics and aspects from which to choose.

The Horus-King: "Son of the Sun"

In addition his other "facets," Horus as the living king is another important aspect within the Egyptian religion, and the god's solar role was also expressed in the adoption of the important "Horus names" by kings and pharaohs. In this regard, Cooper remarks:

The Egyptian kings, who by a magnificently conceived political fiction were themselves incarnations of the Deity, generally assumed also the name and offices of Horus the Sun in one of their two cartouches, which was called the Horus title, and which was, in fact, their proper name. This cartouche was always preceded by the hieroglyphics signifying Son of the Sun...[4]

In the same vein and demonstrating the connection again between Horus and Re, Egyptologist Dr. Robert Brier (b. 1943), a senior research fellow at Long Island University, states: "Six of the Fifth Dynasty's nine pharaohs incorporate Ra in their names, and all follow them with, the phrase 'Son of the Sun.'"[5] As we have seen, Horus too was called the "son of Re," i.e., the "son of the sun." This epithet is important to remember, as it is claimed that throughout the ages numerous luminaries belonged to a group or groups by the same title, "Sons of the Sun."

---

[1] Frankfort, 41.
[2] Redford 165.
[3] Allen, T., *HPT*, 10.
[4] Cooper, *HM*, 8.
[5] Brier, 10.

During a long period of Egyptian history—in fact, "throughout the existence of Pharaonic Egypt"[1]—the king or pharaoh, the son of the sun, was thus identified as Horus and was given a "Horus name." In this regard, Dr. Rudolf Anthes (1896-1985), a curator of the Egyptian Section at the University of Pennsylvania Museum, says that "the denotation 'Horus' introduced the name of virtually every king since the beginning of the First Dynasty."[2] And Dr. Frankfort remarks:

> Each king, at death, becomes Osiris..., just as each king, in life, appears "on the throne of Horus"; each king *is* Horus...[3]

Indeed, as related by Dr. Murnane, Horus is "the primary divine identity of the pharaoh."[4] The solid connection between Horus and the Egyptian king is explained further by Frankfort:

> It is well in keeping with the theory of kingship, which is set forth in the Memphite Theology and which remained valid throughout the existence of Pharaonic Egypt, that the king is commonly referred to as Horus. Sometimes the name is qualified—"Horus who is in the castle"—but *there is no doubt that the divinity of Pharaoh was specifically conceived as sharing of essentials with the god Horus...*[5]

Frankfort also states: "Pharaoh, then, is an incarnation of Horus the Great(est) God, Lord of Heaven."[6] Hornung likewise describes the close relationship between the king/pharaoh, Horus and Osiris: "The extensive textual evidence of the Middle and New kingdoms suggests that at his accession Pharaoh took on the role of Horus, and at his death he took on the role of Osiris, adopting the attributes of these gods without being identical with them."[7] As separate entities, the three are obviously not identical or even necessarily equal; however, the king certainly shares in Osiris's and Horus's attributes and epithets.

Moreover, like the deceased as Osiris, the king is called in the texts the "Horus NN,"[8] the "NN," of course, standing for the pharaoh's name. The *deceased* king is likened to Horus in the Coffin Texts as well, as at CT Sp. 53, in which the Osiris is exhorted to "see your beauty, having appeared as Horus..."[9] Despite any distinctions, so sound is this identification of the king with Horus that, when the ruler died an official would declare, "The Falcon has flown up to heaven," reflecting "the role of the king as a manifestation of Horus."[10]

[1] Frankfort, 36.
[2] Anthes, 185.
[3] Frankfort, 32.
[4] Murnane, 280.
[5] Frankfort, 36. (Emph. added.)
[6] Frankfort, 40.
[7] Hornung, *CGAE*, 192.
[8] Morenz, 34.
[9] Faulkner, *AECT*, I, 52.
[10] Hornung, *VK*, 40.

The equation of Horus with the king in Egypt is extremely old, dating to some 5,000 years ago, based on its appearance on a famous artifact called the Narmer Palette, from the dawn of Egypt as a political entity.[1] Also, in a later hymn to Osiris in the temple of Isis at site of Philae, "the king is Horus himself,"[2] demonstrating that this tradition continued well into the Ptolemaic period. This long-lived association is so complete that the term "Horus-king" has been utilized to describe the pharaohs.[3]

In addition, because of his role as father of Horus, Osiris could likewise be deemed the father of the pharaoh or king as well: "Osiris [is] the father of the mythical son Horus...at the same time, he is also father of the living king, the living Horus..."[4]

Horus—and Osiris—as the king represents one of the main purposes of the Egyptian religion: "...it was the king's transition from Horus into Osiris which confirmed his existence as an eternal being."[5] In reality, as Dr. Anthes says, "The deceased king, according to the Pyramid Texts, is sometimes Osiris...and sometimes Horus..."[6]

As an example of how the king may be endowed with Horus's attributes, Dr. Louis V. Žabkar (1914-1994), a professor of Egyptology at Brandeis University, mentions "Ptolemy II, who, as a living Horus, is associated with 'his mother' Isis and participates in her triumph over Seth."[7]

These germane facts need to be kept in mind throughout this exploration in order for us to maintain a clear picture of the importance of this god, as well as to understand how characteristics and experiences of the king/pharaoh could be perceived as those of "Horus," possibly used in the later Christian mythmaking effort.

Priest as Horus

As noted, the officiating priest at a funeral would likewise impersonate Horus, a fact that adds to the "confounding" of Horuses. As Griffiths remarks, "One of the officiating priests, probably the *sem*-priest, assumes the role of Horus, the Beloved Son of Osiris..."[8] To reiterate, per T. George Allen, *"The king is here regularly called Osiris,"*[9] and the priest's services for the deceased "symbolized those of Horus for his father Osiris."[10] In other words, Horus is the priest resurrecting the deceased as his father, Osiris; hence, the speaker in

---

[1] Hare, 20.
[2] Žabkar, 25, 63. See also Žabkar for a hymn to Isis in which she addresses Ptolemy as "my son, Horus, my beloved..." (Žabkar, 42.)
[3] Luckert, 64, et al.
[4] Žabkar, 37.
[5] Anthes, 180.
[6] Anthes, 192.
[7] Žabkar, 60.
[8] Griffiths, *OOHC*, 26.
[9] Allen, T., *HPT*, 13. (Emph. added.)
[10] Allen, T., *HPT*, 13.

the Pyramid Texts is frequently Horus as well. In the Coffin Texts too, at CT Sp. 45, for example, the priest speaks as Horus, while the speaker at CT Sp. 46 referring to "Followers of the Lord of the Horizon" is also the *deceased* as Horus.[1] Again, we find in CT Sp. 62 that the speaker is the Horus-priest,[2] and so on, through almost 1,200 spells, in many of which Horus serves as priest.

Regarding the role of Horus (or the priest) in various Pyramid Texts, Allen further remarks:

> ... Horus is...called upon to aid the dead king, not only by such offices as the myth assigned him on behalf of Osiris, but in many purely solar connections, especially noticeable in the sections on purification, ascent, deification, and rule.[3]

Thus, Horus serves a godly and priestly role in assisting the deceased to become the risen Osiris, providing *purification*, for example, which is a *solar* attribute. It is important to note that the term "purify" can also connote "baptize,"[4] meaning that, like Jesus, who at Matthew 3:11 is said to baptize with the Holy Spirit and with fire, Horus not only purifies also *baptizes*, a subject explored in detail later.

In yet another aspect of the merging of entities, such as gods with each other or, here, gods with humans, Allen states that "the deceased king's own person" was "often identified with Horus" and "became identified likewise with the magic Horus-eye."[5] The Horus eye "was further identified with the sun, and, like Horus himself, endowed with human form."[6] *The fact of the king and priest both being identified with and as Horus constitutes yet another extremely germane fact that needs to be kept in mind, as do the solar attributes of Horus.* These facts of syncretism represent another reason we do not find various attributes of "Horus" in encyclopedia entries, as they may be ascribed to "different" Horuses. Nonetheless, these attributes are relevant to the investigation of what was influential upon Christianity, because they were held to be "sacred" and part of Egyptian religion to be copied and emulated.

"Amen-Ra-Osiris-Horus"

Adding to this mythical mélange, we have seen that Horus is essentially solar in nature, having even been identified with the main Egyptian sun god Re/Ra, as well as the Greek sun god Apollo, along with possessing many solar attributes, including as the morning and rising sun, born again each day. In his *Guide* to the Egyptian rooms

---

[1] Faulkner, *AECT*, I, 39, 41, 42.

[2] Faulkner, *AECT*, I, 58.

[3] Allen, T., *HPT*, 13. For "purification" by Horus, see Pyramid Texts PT 268:372a-d/W 175, PT 323:519a-b/T 8, PT 606:168-1685/M 336, etc.

[4] See, e.g., *American Heritage Dictionary* (4th ed.), "baptize," no. 2.

[5] Allen, T., *HPT*, 13.

[6] Allen, T., *HPT*, 13.

at the British Museum, Budge summarizes the Egyptian solar mythology, revealing that the many separate personas are all aspects of the one sun:

> The Sun has countless names, Ptah, Tmu, Ra, Horus, Khnemu, Sebek, Amen, etc.; and some of them, such as Osiris and Seker, are names of the Sun after he has set, or, in mythological language, has died and been buried.... All gods, as such, were absolutely equal in their might and in their divinity; but, mythologically, Osiris might be said to be slain by his brother Set, the personification of Night, who, in his turn, was overthrown by Horus (the rising sun), the heir of Osiris.[1]

Confirming this observation, Hornung states that "in the New Kingdom, Amun, Ptah, Osiris, Khnum, and most of the other great gods and even goddesses of Egypt can be understood as solar deities."[2] In discussing the multiple faces of the sun god, Griffiths notes a comparison to Christianity:

> A text of the Ramesside era...refers to the triple positions of these gods during the course of day: "I am Khepri in the morning, Re in the afternoon, Atum in the evening." Three forms or modes of the sun god are implied—an example, thus of a modalistic trinity, comparable to the later Christian concept.[3]

This "trinity" or triad is one of a number with Egyptian deities, as we will continue to see here. Another such Egyptian triad/trinity appears on a papyrus from the 19th Dynasty (1292-1182 BCE) called the "Leiden Hymn to Amun":

> All gods are three:
>
> Amun, Re, and Ptah, who have no equal.
> He who hides his *names* as Amun,
> he is Re in *appearance*,
> his *body* is Ptah.[4]

Regarding the Egyptian and Christian trinities and scriptural parallels, Morenz is prompted to conclude, "The multifarious links between Egypt and Judaeo-Christian scriptures and trinitarian theology can already be traced with some degree of plausibility."[5] In his discussion of "Egyptian trinities," as he terms them, Morenz includes a section addressing the idea of "unity in plurality."[6] The German scholar also points out that a "trinity" can likewise be created out of the "primordial One" and "the first pair of gods to be begotten."[7] Regarding the motif of the trinity, Morenz further states:

---

[1] Budge, *AGFSR*, 2-3.
[2] Hornung, *CGAE*, 55.
[3] Redford, 256. See also Morenz, 145.
[4] Assman, *SGAE*, 8; Johnson, P., 86; Kamil, 148.
[5] Morenz, 257.
[6] Morenz, 142ff.
[7] Morenz, 145.

...thus three gods are combined and treated as a single being, addressed in the singular. In this way the spiritual force of Egyptian religion shows a direct link with Christian theology.[1]

Various of these "triplets" or other groupings often symbolize aspects of the one sun, as likewise described by Hornung in his definition of "Sun god":

Many Egyptian gods can be the sun god, especially *Re, Atum, Amun,* and manifestations of *Horus.* Even *Osiris* appears as the night form of the sun god in the New Kingdom. It is often not defined which particular sun god is meant in a given instance.[2]

Hornung also cites the text the "Litany of Re, first inscribed in tombs around 1500 B.C., which invokes the sun god, as in a litany, in 'all his forms.'"[3] He further explains that, while these forms are specific to the underworld, "part of the pantheon...is thus turned into a set of differentiated manifestations of a single sun god."[4] Hornung next describes this "Great Litany" as a text "wherein the sun god is invoked seventy-five times in various names and forms..."[5] The various forms of Re in this text include the deities Atum, Tefnut, Geb/Seb, Nut, Isis, Nephthys, Horus, Nun and many others.[6] So fused are these manifestations of the sun god—these individual gods, as they were—that "Litany of Ra" translator Dr. Naville was led to declare:

The importance of this text consists in this, that it gives us an idea of the esoteric doctrine of the Egyptian priests, which was clearly pantheistic, and which certainly differed from the polytheistic worship of the common people.[7]

While Hornung evinces that the Egyptian religion could never be pantheistic, as it did not view the entirety of creation as divine,[8] Naville is undoubtedly correct that the Egyptian priesthood explored concepts within its esoteric mysteries that differed from what was taught exoterically, as Hornung himself addresses in *The Secret Lore of Egypt.* Moreover, the pantheism evident in Egypt is expressed by Morenz thus: "...Egyptian society, and the individuals who comprise it, cannot escape from God, but encounter him everywhere."[9] Here Morenz is compelled to speak of God in "Christian" terminology, giving the concept a monotheistic interpretation as well.[10]

---

[1] Morenz, 255.
[2] Hornung, *CGAE*, 283.
[3] Hornung, *CGAE*, 283.
[4] Hornung, *CGAE*, 56.
[5] Hornung, *AEBA*, 137.
[6] *Records of the Past*, VIII, 368ff.
[7] *ROTP*, VIII, 104.
[8] Hornung, *CGAE*, 128.
[9] Morenz, 5.
[10] Various arguments can be dismissed with the apology that we are "reading Christian theology" into something, succumbing to what is termed *interpretatio christiana.* The distinctions made by theologians suffer the opposite, as they attempt to drive whatever

Regarding the confusion between gods within Egyptian mythology in general, Brigham Young University professor Dr. Hugh W. Nibley (1910-2005) states:

> Over a century ago Edouard Naville observed "that there is nothing harder than to recognize the distinctive marks of each individual deity" in an Egyptian picture, for while "every divinity has specific emblems which are like ideograms of his particular qualities," these are swapped around with a total indifference toward the individual gods, the distinctions between them having become almost expunged by the process of equating, equalizing, interpenetrating, as names, forms, powers all become confused in a common basic nature which is the mark of the Egyptian gods.[1]

In discussing the Book of the Dead, the same phenomenon is explained by Renouf:

> In reading this and almost every chapter of the Book of the Dead, it is absolutely necessary to bear in mind that different divine names do not necessarily imply different personalities. A name expresses but one attribute of a person or thing, and one person having several attributes may have several names. It is not implied in this chapter that the Sun is the Nile or the Inundation, but that the same invisible force which is manifested in the solar phenomena is that which produces the inundation; He is the Inundator. But he has many other names and titles.

> In this chapter [64], as in others before it, the speaker at one time talks in terms identifying him with some divinity, and at another as a simple mortal petitioning some favour.[2]

In the Book of the Dead, the deceased is made to take a variety of roles, demonstrating the interchangeability of the characters in these recitations, utterances or spells. For example, in BD 69, the dead king is made to say, "...I am Horus the Elder on the Day of Accession, I am Anubis of Sepa, I am the Lord of All, I am Osiris."[3] The unity of divine and mortal personalities is also recognizable in the Coffin Texts, as at CT Sp. 485, in which the deceased says, "...I am Horus and Thoth, I am Osiris and Atum."[4] In this regard, the fusion of the deceased and the many deities—not a few of whom possess solar

---

wedge they can between Pagan and Christian religious concepts. These efforts are at times disingenuous, however, as apologists perceive Pagan myths through their own Christian minds, consistently interpreting the myths as if the ancients had viewed them as one-time "historical" events, for example, when in fact they are cyclical, revolving around nature, and thus change over time. Moreover, one could make the argument in the reverse for the early Christian effort constituting the result of Judaism manifested through an *interpretatio pagana*.

[1] Nibley, "All the Court's a Stage."
[2] Renouf, *EBD*, 122.
[3] Faulkner, *EBD*, 107; Allen, T., *BD*, 63; Bunsen/Birch, 212; Budge, *BD* (1899), cxxxiv. Birch renders this part regarding Horus as, "The Osiris is the elder Horus, the rising Sun."
[4] Faulkner, *AECT*, II, 130.

attributes—also needs to be kept in mind as we attempt to outline the Egyptian mythos and ritual.

As another example of the tendency towards syncretism, in addition to Horus-Ra is the sun god Amen—"the hidden god"—combined with the sun god Re/Ra as "Amen-Ra," etc., reflecting their interchangeability. "Osiris-Ra" or "Ra-Osiris" is yet another dual god addressed in the texts.[1] So interchangeable are Osiris and Horus that there is even a hybrid god Osiris-Horus or Asar-Heru.[2] Indeed, the two are so close that one sees discussion of the "Horus-Osiris king," referring to the pharaoh, who is both Osiris and his son, such as by Anthes, who repeatedly refers to "Horus-Osiris" as a single entity.[3]

In any event, as the sun progresses through the day and night, "he" becomes a number of characters—or changes his epithets and characteristics, as it were, as he merges with other gods—beginning with the rising sun, Horus, who at noon becomes Re, who at sunset becomes Tmu or Atum, who at midnight becomes Osiris, who becomes Horus at sunrise, and so on. As Hornung says, "...in his role as the sun god Re, Horus is 'tomorrow,' whereas Osiris is 'yesterday'..."[4] Archaeologist and Egyptologist Dr. Karol Myśliwiec, director of the Polish Academy of Science, also describes Atum's role as a sun god: "Atum's solar associations are with the sunset and the nightly journey of the sun, when he appears with a ram's head or, sometimes, as a tired old man walking with a stick."[5] At some point, these gods are in effect all one, as are their adversaries.

Polytheistic Monotheism/Monism?

Many of the gods in the Egyptian pantheon fuse together in the syncretism previously discussed, for the reason, it has been averred, that the Egyptian mysteries long ago taught monotheism, with one overarching god whose numerous "members"—assorted gods and goddesses—expanded and merged with each other. Concerning this development, Assman remarks that "most polytheisms known to the history of religion are complex in the sense that they reckon—or better, live—with a divine realm beyond which there is a 'god' or 'highest being' who created the world and its deities."[6] Although it is widely believed that monotheism was essentially introduced by the pharaoh Akhenaten/Amenhotep IV (d. c. 1334 BCE), the consensus of earlier Egyptologists was that monotheism and polytheism existed "side by side" at least as early as the 5th Dynasty, around 2500 BCE.[7] We would venture that such concepts may have been devised much

---

[1] Budge, *BD* (1899), 91.
[2] Budge, *HVBD*, 60. See also Campbell, *IAHN*, 142.
[3] Anthes, 177, 178, 182, 192.
[4] Hornung, *CGAE*, 154.
[5] Redford, 25.
[6] Assman, *SGAE*, 11.
[7] Budge, *EBD* (1967), xciii.

earlier in humankind's long history, possibly tens of thousands of years previously. In any case, regarding the confusion and confounding of gods, following his famous brother, Champollion-Figeac was prompted to write, "The Egyptian religion is a pure monotheism, which manifested itself externally by a symbolic polytheism."[1] Yet, whether or not Egyptian religion was essentially monotheistic has been the subject of much debate.

Concerning the sacred fusion of Egyptian gods, James Allen comments:

> Although the Egyptians recognized most natural and social phenomena as separate divine forces, they also realized that many of these were interrelated and could also be understood as *different aspects of a single divine force*. That realization is expressed in the practice known as "syncretism," the combining of several gods into one.[2]

As is the case in other religions and mythologies, such as the Indian, the Egyptian faith at times has appeared to represent a sort of "polytheistic monotheism" or "polytheistic monism" that ascribes divinity to a vast proportion of creation, while maintaining the cosmos to be one. Hence, in the Egyptian texts we find prayers to one god or goddess that include the names or epithets of many other gods or goddesses.

As concerns the debate as to whether or not the structure could be deemed "monotheistic," Hornung asserts that "one must note that Egyptian religion, which retained its plurality of gods to the end, never became a monotheistic faith, even in its most 'philosophically' tinged utterances."[3] In recounting this debate, in *The Gods of Egypt*, Dr. Claude Traunecker of Université des Sciences Humaines de Strasbourg remarks:

> In 1971, Erik Hornung published a definitive work on the divine world of Egypt, and it has enjoyed a rather large consensus. Since 1975, Jan Assman, a specialist in solar hymns, has published a series of studies in which he has relaunched the debate concerning the apparent contradiction between a largely polytheistic divine realm and the concept of a single deity...[4]

The cases for the varying perspectives will not be rehashed here.[5] Despite any finer points of understanding, the Egyptian religion was no more monolithic than is the Indian, in which basically anything goes, from monotheism to polytheism.[6] The determination of which

---

[1] Budge, *EBD* (1967), xcii. See also Budge, *FFGAE*, 52.

[2] Allen, J., *ME*, 44. (Emph. added.)

[3] Hornung, *CGAE*, 53.

[4] Traunecker, 11.

[5] For an extensive discussion of this debate as to the status of monotheism in Egypt, see Hornung's *Conceptions of God in Ancient Egypt*, 17ff. See also Traunecker's *The Gods of Egypt*.

[6] From the earliest Pyramid Texts, the Egyptian religion at that point would seem to be decidedly polytheistic. See Hornung, *CGAE*, 24.

came first, polytheism or monotheism, does not concern us here, although it is wise to keep in mind that the multiplicity of deities frequently resolve to the One, especially as concerns an original creator. For example, the Coffin Texts repeatedly refer to the "primeval god" or the "Primeval One," who is "superior to the primeval gods" (CT Sp. 39)[1] and who is "older than the gods" (CT Sp. 317).[2]

This spiritual oneness is also exemplified in CT Sp. 858, in which Osiris is invoked to "take your son" and "put him within yourself."[3] And at CT Sp. 949, the speaker says, "I know you, I know your names, I live as you, I come into being as you...."[4] Concerning the concept of oneness within the Egyptian faith, Assman remarks, "Time and again the Egyptian sources predicate the oneness/singleness/uniqueness of a god."[5] Indeed, the great God Sun is "the One Alone with many arms."[6]

As Dr. Traunecker also states, "Rare are deities who make do with having a single function, and many are those who declare themselves to have been the Sole One at the first moment of creation."[7] This contention for the multiplicity of function and interchangeability of roles will be understood more so for the Egyptian religion than for, say, the Greek or the Roman, with their distinct deities and well developed myths.

In *Conceptions of God in Ancient Egypt*, Hornung discusses Egyptian syncretism, remarking:

> ...The natures of the individual gods are not clearly demarcated, so that aspects of one god can be identical with those of another. Here we encounter a phenomenon that is of the greatest importance for Egyptian religion and its deities: "syncretism."[8]

Hornung continues with a thorough attempt to establish a distinction between the Egyptian religion and syncretism, by delineating "identification" and "inhabitation" of gods, with a hybrid god such as Amun-Re indicating not that they are one but that Amun is "inhabiting" Re or vice versa: "the degree of intimacy and the duration of the combination vary from case to case."[9] For all the laborious distinctions, however, we are left with important instances of identification and syncretism to the point where disentanglement is futile, and undesirable. As Hornung further comments:

> ...in his daily descent into the realm of the dead the sun god Re must also become "Osiris," for he dies and appears in the underworld as a

---

[1] Faulkner, *AECT*, I, 31.
[2] Faulkner, *AECT*, I, 241.
[3] Faulkner, *AECT*, III, 37.
[4] Faulkner, *AECT*, III, 86.
[5] Assman, *ESRNK*, 134.
[6] Assman, *ESRNK*, 153.
[7] Traunecker, ix.
[8] Hornung, *CGAE*, 91.
[9] Hornung, *CGAE*, 91.

"corpse." But in this case the Egyptians imagine that there is a true union. Unlike the rest of the deceased, Re does not assume the title "Osiris"; instead he incorporates the ruler of the dead into his own being so profoundly that both have one body and can "speak with one mouth." Osiris does indeed seem to be absorbed into Re, and becomes the night sun, which awakens the underworld dwellers from the sleep of death.[1]

The remark concerning "the Egyptians" imagining a "true union" is salient, in that despite all the theological banter, what the *average* Egyptian perceived of his or her religion is significant in regard to what any creators of a *new religion* would wish to incorporate to gain adherents. In the long run, the simpler understanding would win out among the masses, as it does also with Hornung, as in his definition of "Sun god" previously provided. Thus, the average Egyptian would see true union and believe that Osiris was "absorbed" into Re and had *become the night sun*, to be born again or resurrected as his son, Horus, the morning sun. Moreover, in his definition of "Re," Hornung himself must fall back on syncretism to explain the sun god's pervasive and all-encompassing role by declaring that Re "is combined syncretistically with many other gods..."[2]

Thus, in discussing the myths and characteristics of Osiris or Horus, for example, we could reasonably ascribe to one qualities of the other. The same can be said of the attributes of other gods, as well as those of the Horus-king and Horus-priest, all of which could be attached to the god himself in a description of his mythical "life."

A Fluid Faith

When analyzing Egyptian myths, in addition to knowing about the syncretism of deities, it is important to realize that, because they *are* myths, there will often be different versions of any particular story or motif. Such is the case with the myths surrounding Osiris, Isis and Horus, as well as many other Egyptian gods going back thousands of years, as is to be expected in consideration of all the interchangeability.

The lack of uniformity in myths is remarked upon by Dr. Robert A. Armour, a professor emeritus at Virginia Commonwealth University:

> We cannot expect to find unity in a mythology that spanned over three thousand years. Moreover, there were many cult-centers, each with its own gods, such as Heliopolis, Memphis, Elephantine, Thebes. As each of these centers enjoyed its period of political ascendancy, it assimilated its own theology with some of the others in order to achieve dominance. This process brought many of the myths into general accord but left others in a state of conflict which was never resolved.[3]

---

[1] Hornung, *CGAE*, 96.
[2] Hornung, *CGAE*, 281.
[3] Armour, 14.

Concerning the fluid state of the Egyptian religion, G.D. Hornblower asserts:

> To clear the ground, it must be understood that Egyptian religion does not consist of one connected logical system but is composed of a series of cults which have been roughly synthesized to fit, more or less harmoniously, into a general national system; the synthesis was incomplete and led to endless contradictions and anomalies, some of them quite startlingly, as all Egyptologists know.[1]

Anthes concurs with this assessment:

> It is in accordance with the prominent feature of Egyptian religion that mythological concepts are very often contradictory.[2]

As one important example of how myths change over the centuries, regarding Plutarch's identification of Isis with the moon, Dr. Diana Delia White, a professor of History at Rhode Island College, remarks, "As Isis' associations in the pharaonic period were purely solar, her metamorphosis into a preeminent lunar deity among Greeks and Romans is quite extraordinary."[3] Indeed, in addition to her many other roles, including her later characterization as the moon, Isis was considered a sun goddess as well.[4] This example ranks as another of many demonstrating how myths change to incorporate cultural exchange as well as further observations of natural phenomena.

It can thus be stated that the Egyptian concepts of God and divinity were not set in stone but changed and mutated over the thousands of years. Even today our own concepts of God and religion are fractured into as many pieces as there are people, and the Egyptian faith over a period of thousands of years was also perceived and conceived by many millions of minds. It is a fact that there was a great deal of evolution and change in Egyptian religion, particularly as it came into contact with other cultures. It is equally true that Christianity has altered and transmuted as it has come under numerous influences from around the known world. Indeed, it can be asserted to a large degree of certainty that Christianity is a remake of earlier religions, mythologies and spiritual traditions, especially the Egyptian.

The Moon and Morning Star

When studying Egyptian religion and mythology, it should be noted that its deities are not "simply" sun gods but symbolize a wide variety of elements, qualities or aspects of life as well. These various gods or epithets represent not only the physical sun but also its disk, light and heat, as well as the cosmic power behind it. Although

---

[1] Hornblower, *Man*, vol. 37, 153.
[2] Anthes, 174.
[3] Clarysse, 540.
[4] Žabkar, 63.

Osiris, for example, is largely a sun god, the ancients also recognized that the sun's light is reflected in the moon, a symbol of Isis, who gives birth to Horus, the "reincarnation" of his father, as the "light of the world." As another example, regarding the lunar nature of the Egyptian god Thoth or Tehuti, as well as the soli-lunar characteristics of Egyptian myth in general, Renouf remarks:

> It must be sufficient here to say that Thoth is a personification of the moon, and that the relations of solar and lunar phenomena are the sources of a great deal of Egyptian mythology.[1]

Thoth's soli-lunar nature is also made clear in the Coffin Texts, as at CT Sp. 1092, in which the god is said to be "chosen as Lord of the Morning,"[2] along with CT Sp. 1096, which says, "This is Thoth who is the sky; the Eye of Horus is on his hands in the Mansion of the Moon,"[3] and in which a variant names the god "Moon-Thoth."[4]

In this regard, Osiris was both solar and lunar, as related by Anthes: "...later texts assure a close connection between Osiris and the moon..."[5] Osiris is also the god of the star Sirius, of the river Nile, of water in general, of fertility, and of the resurrection and afterlife, these latter two precisely as was said of the later, Jewish rendition, Jesus Christ. In addition, like Jesus, who is identified in the biblical book of Revelation (22:16) as the "morning star"—one of many astrotheological themes in Christianity—so too is the Osiris equated in the Coffin Texts with the Morning Star, as at CT Sp. 722: "...for N is the Morning Star, N is the beautiful $w3$-star of gold which went up alone from the horizon..."[6] Also, in the Pyramid Texts (PT 519:1207a) appears "Horus of the Duat" called the "morning star."[7] In the Book of the Dead (BD 109), the speaker says: "I know the Powers of the East: Horus of the Solar Mount, the Calf in presence of the God, and the Star of Dawn."[8] Here Renouf translates the hieroglyph for "Horakhty" as "Horus of the Solar Mount," who is the "sun-calf," as well as the "Star of Dawn" or *morning star*. These "powers of the east" constitute the "Souls of the Easterners."[9] The "morning star" identity of Horus is remarked upon by Egyptologist Dr. László Kákosy (d. 2003) in *Egyptian Religion: The Last Thousand Years*:

> The astral associations of Horus are of ancient origin. The composite celestial deity in the Pyramid Texts who is addressed as "god of the morning, Horus of the netherworld" and has "four contented faces"

---

[1] Renouf, *EBD*, 18.
[2] Faulkner, *AECT*, III, 151.
[3] Faulkner, *AECT*, III, 152.
[4] Faulkner, *AECT*, III, 153.
[5] Anthes, 187.
[6] Faulkner, *AECT*, II, 274.
[7] Allen, T., *HPT*, 37; Mercer, 200; Faulkner, *AEPT*, 192. James Allen (P 467) renders the phrase "Morning god, Horus of the Duat..." (Allen, J., *AEPT*, 160.)
[8] Renouf, *EBD*, 182.
[9] Faulkner, *EBD*, 113. Dr. T. George Allen calls the "powers of the east" the "eastern souls," which are "Re-Harakhte." (Allen, T., *BD*, 86.)

can perhaps be identified with Venus. The cosmic character of Horus was again emphasized in the New Kingdom and the Late Period, when he was associated with more planets.[1]

Regarding Horus's multifold nature, Anthes concludes, "The heavenly Horus was a star as well as the sun, and perhaps also the moon."[2]

Horus thus represents a multiplicity of gods and possesses a wide variety of attributes, including various astrotheological characteristics. Moreover, we may recognize here a seed for the strange imagery found elsewhere in the bizarre biblical book of Revelation, in which we find not only the morning star or Venus but also the four "beasts," who at one point all say, "Amen."[3] (Rev 5:14)

Horus is Osiris Reborn

The "confounding" of deities so abundant within Egyptian religion constitutes not an error but may be deliberate since, as stated, the myths and characteristics of gods and goddesses frequently blend into and overlap each other. The interchangeability of Osiris and Horus, for example, becomes evident on a daily basis, as the night sun Osiris at dawn *becomes* Horus, as we have already seen. Regarding Osiris's transformation into Horus, James Allen states:

> Within Nut's womb, he embodied the force through which the Sun received the power of new life, to appear at dawn as *Osiris reborn in his own son*, the god Horus.[4]

Indeed, Horus is the living god, the earthly incarnation of the father, precisely as was said of Christ and God the Father. Adding to this understanding of Osiris's renewal as Horus, as well as their relationship to the king/pharaoh, Griffiths states:

> Horus as the living Pharaoh and his father Osiris as the dead Pharaoh: these are the basic elements in the royal funerary cult. Osiris *per se* is the king of the domain of the dead, so the dead Pharaoh is naturally regarded as aspiring to sovereignty in the afterworld in the form of Osiris. At the same time the royal burial rites adumbrate [foreshadow] the birth of a new Horus in the son who succeeds the deceased...[5]

Concerning this interchangeability, Anthes remarks:

> Since Horus was the living king and Osiris the deceased one, the slaying of Osiris was strictly speaking the slaying of Horus, who in consequence of his being slain, became Osiris.[6]

Once again, we have the king identified as both Osiris and Horus, as well as Horus and Osiris identified with each other, leading to a

[1] Clarysse, 134.
[2] Anthes, 171, 185-186.
[3] For the astrotheological meaning of Revelation, see *The Christ Conspiracy*, 265-273.
[4] Allen, J., *AEPT*, 9. (Emph. added.)
[5] Griffiths, *OOHC*, 3.
[6] Anthes, 200.

blending of personas and attributes. In such a climate, for the purpose of easily and quickly describing important aspects of the Egyptian religion—especially as they concern correspondences with Christianity—certain sources have therefore combined at times the various Horuses with each other and with Osiris, along with other appropriate entities, such as other deities, as well as kings/pharaohs, priests and patients, relating the data in a composite and comprehensive narrative.

We further contend that this very same confounding was done by the creators of Christianity when they took over elements of the Egyptian religion and rolled them into one encompassing myth called the gospel story. In essence, when studying this situation, the scenario that reveals itself is that the creators of the gospel story in large part appear to have been scouring the vast Library of Alexandria in Egypt, as well as collections elsewhere, such as at Antioch and Rome, and picking out various aspects of pre-Christian religions to combine with Jewish scriptures in their creation of a cohesive Christian mythical tale that was set fallaciously into history and presented as a "true story."

As is abundantly clear, the sun in the Egyptian religion symbolized life, purification, salvation, resurrection and immortality, among many other important qualities, such as omniscience, omnipresence and omnipotence. Indeed, in Egypt over a period of thousands of years, the sun in all its permutations constituted a symbol of the *divine*, and was beseeched as such in countless prayers and invocations, directed at not just the solar disk or orb itself but also as the unseen power behind it, as well as its heat, light and all its various aspects and movements through the heavens.

Many of the major and most beloved deities in the Egyptian pantheon symbolized aspects or epithets of the life-giving, sacred sun, including the very important god Horus, who represents the renewal of the nightly "solar life force," Osiris, as the solar orb passes through the treacherous darkness of the underworldly Duat. If the parallels between Horus and Jesus are real and accurate to a sufficient extent, meaning the claims are true that there is significant Egyptian influence on Christianity, it is reasonable and scientific to suggest that the story of Jesus Christ—which is *highly implausible* as "history"—ranks largely as a rehash of the mythos of the ancient, exceedingly revered sun god.

"Figures praying, accompanied by a star," reflecting the
astrotheological Egyptian religion.
(Wilkinson, *The Manners and Customs of the Egyptians*, III, 48)

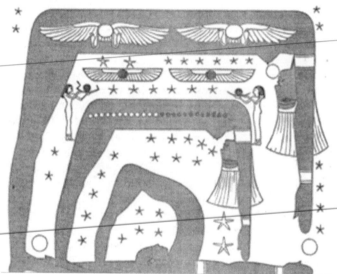

"Pe, or the heaven, with the sun and stars. The figure beneath is
Seb."
(Wilkinson, *The Manners and Customs of the Ancient Egyptians*, III,
206)

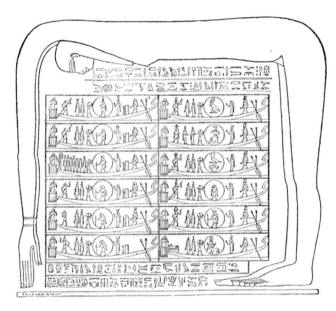

"The Twelve Stages in the Life of the Sun and Its Twelve Forms
Throughout the Day."
(Maspero, *The Dawn of Civilization*, 89)

"The Sun Springing from an Opening Lotus Flower in the Form of
the Child Horus."
(Maspero, *History of Egypt*, I, 193)

Horus or Rā in his disk.

Hieroglyph representing either Horus or Ra in his Sun Disk.
(Budge, *An Egyptian Hieroglyphic Dictionary*, cxiv)

Isis and Nephthys attending the composite god Re-Osiris.
(Hornung, *The Valley of the Kings*, 129)

Ȧsȧr Ḥeru   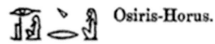   **Osiris-Horus.**

Hieroglyph for hybrid god Osiris-Horus
(Budge, *A Hieroglyphic Vocabulary to the Book of the Dead*, 60)

Horus versus Set

"The Christian Trinity ousted the old triads of gods, Osiris and Horus were represented by our Lord Jesus Christ, Isis by the Virgin Mary, Set the god of evil by Diabolus [Satan]...and the various Companies of the Gods by the Archangels, and so on."

Sir Dr. E.A. Wallis Budge, *Egyptian Tales and Romances* (12)

"The god Seth, called Typhon by the Greek writers, was the Satan of later Egyptian mythology. He was the personification of the evil in the world, just as Osiris was the personification of the good."

Dr. Philip Van Ness Myers, *Ancient History* (38)

"Horus is presented in manifold aspects in Egyptian mythology. Mainly as the vindicator of the principle of Good; as the avenger of his father, Osiris, who succumbed temporarily in his struggle against Evil embodied in the god Set, who corresponds to our Satan. Set was represented as a beast with long pointed ears and erect tail, and may perhaps be the origin of the popular representations of Satan, the ears having come to be regarded as horns."

Rev. Henry Windsor Villiers Stuart, *Egypt After the War* (191)

Despite the common misconception that the ancients as a whole were primitive, many cultures of old were in reality highly sophisticated, as evidenced not only by their impressive architectural accomplishments such as the massive ruins around the world, but also by other artifacts such as political organization, language development and philosophical achievement. One of these advanced cultures was that of Egypt, which created along with its magnificent edifices such as the Great Pyramid and the Temple complex at Luxor/Karnak both a sophisticated cosmology and an elegant writing system in which to express it. When we examine the religious and mythological beliefs of the Egyptians, in fact, we discover there is little theological they did not consider and incorporate into their faith that we possess in modern religions today. In other words, the Egyptians in particular not only were highly spiritual but also either originated or developed many of the cosmological and theological concepts found in current popular religions, such as the afterlife, immortality, heaven, deity, soul and so on. As has been seen, one of the main religions in which we find much Egyptian influence is Christianity, in both its myths and rituals. Like many other faiths, the Egyptian and Christian religions share a strong overall theme of good versus evil and light versus dark. In the case of the Egyptian religion, good and evil were manifested in several gods, including and especially Horus and Set, while their Christian counterparts are Jesus and Satan.

As we explore the original Egyptian mythos and ritual upon which much of Christianity was evidently founded, it needs to be kept in mind that the gods Osiris and Horus in particular were frequently interchangeable and combined, as in "I and the Father are one." (Jn 10:30) In fact, as part of the mythos, Osiris was "re-born under the form of Horus," as previously noted. This particular development exists in significant part because these figures are largely sun gods, and when one sun god "dies," as occurred with Osiris daily, monthly and annually, another replaces and *becomes* him, as happens with Horus taking the place of his father. Like Osiris's many followers, whose prayers included a request to *become* "the Osiris" in the afterlife, so too does Horus *become* his father after Osiris's demise, which is caused by the sun god's enemy, the serpent of the night and Prince of Darkness, Set. Concerning Horus battling Set, Dr. Badrya Serry, director of the Antiquities Museum at the Bibliotheca Alexandrina in Egypt, says:

> It is known that the child Harpocrates struggled with his uncle Seth to revenge his father...and attain victory upon him. Since he overcame the powers of darkness (Seth) [he was] likened to the Greek hero Heracles who battled the powers of evilness.[1]

To reiterate, as is the case with myths around the world, the story of Osiris was not neatly laid out in an entry in an ancient encyclopedia, but, rather, appears in bits and pieces in primary sources such as the Pyramid Texts, Coffin Texts and the Book of the Dead, which were compiled and altered over a period of centuries, beginning possibly up to 7,000 years ago. Nevertheless, nearly 2,000 years ago Plutarch did tell the myth of Osiris, Isis and Horus in some detail and in a fairly cohesive manner as a story, as we have seen.

In the commonly known depiction of his death, the good god Osiris is killed by his evil brother Set, who first encloses the god in a container or "ark" and later dismembers him into 14 pieces, scattering the parts around Egypt.[2] In the version by Plutarch, Osiris's wife-sister, Isis, finds most of the pieces, except the god's phallus, and eventually Osiris is resurrected and emerges from the "other world" to instruct his son Horus to battle and defeat "Typhon" (19, 358B), the Greek name for the god Set or *Seth*.[3]

Concerning the conflict between Osiris and Set, Budge remarks, "Details of the engagement are wanting, but the Pyramid Texts state that the body of Osiris was hurled to the ground by Set at a place called Netat, which seems to have been near Abydos."[4] The Pyramid Texts, in fact, contain another, *older* version of Osiris's death, in

---

[1] Goyon, 121.
[2] Diodorus relates that the pieces numbered 26. However, Murphy notes that, as the god became more popular, so too did his parts, eventually numbering 42 for each of the Egyptian nomes. This increase occurred as each priesthood wished to claim a relic for its own "tomb of Osiris," reflecting the enormous relics industry that continues to this day with countless bogus artifacts of the Christian faith. (For more, see *The Christ Conspiracy, Suns of God* and *Who Was Jesus?*)
[3] Plutarch/Babbitt, 47.
[4] Budge, *LEG*, xlix.

which he was said to have been *drowned* by Set.[1] According to a later magical papyrus, this drowning took place in the "water of the underworld."[2] This aspect of the myth is interesting in light of the fact that in Greek mythology the sun god Helios was said to have been drowned in the river Eridanus or "*Jordan*," in which Jesus was likewise said to have been baptized or dunked.[3]

The earliest versions of Osiris's passion[4] depict Set simply as slaying the god, without the ark and the dismemberment, while later sources attach 72 villainous helpers to assist in Set's murderous crime against Osiris.[5] The story of Osiris being entombed in a tree and found by Isis at the city of Byblos in Phoenicia, also related by Plutarch (15, 357A), is later than the one in which his parts are simply tossed around Egypt.[6] The Byblos tale may have been added by the Egyptians after 1500 BCE in order to explain the similar myth of the god Adonis-Tammuz in that part of the Near East.[7] In any event, the different versions of Osiris's death illustrate how myths vary and are not set in stone, an important point that needs to be kept in mind.

The Astrotheology of the Passion

Although appearing bizarre and incomprehensible, the story of Osiris's death possesses, like so many other myths, underlying *astrotheological* meaning that makes sense and teaches some of the important workings of the natural world. As Plutarch (13, 356E-D) relates, Osiris was entombed in the ark on the 17th day of the month of Athyr, "when the sun passes through Scorpion [sic]," and in the 28th year of either his reign or his life.[8] Coincidentally, the 17th of Athyr is equivalent to the same day that the equally mythical biblical character Noah was said to have been shut up in *his* ark, the Hebrew patriarch too having been identified as a sun god or solar hero.[9] The

---

[1] Griffiths, *OOHC*, 9. The drowning is alluded to in PT 33:24d/N 125, PT 364:615d/T 196, PT 423:766d/P 7. (Mercer, 25, 124, 145; Allen, J., *AEPT*, 255, 80, 101.)
[2] Griffiths, *OOHC*, 9.
[3] According to Cooper, in Egyptian the Jordan was called "Iu-Ru-Ta-Na." (Cooper, *AAD*, 259.) This name is evidently the same term—Iurutana, Iarutana or Eri-tana—for the constellation of the river Eridanus. (Massey, *BB*, 1, 192; *AELW*, I, 293.)
[4] The term "passion" refers to the sufferings of the god and does not belong exclusively to the Christian faith, despite the biases and oversights of dictionaries, as well as the claims of Christian apologists. Osiris's sufferings have been referred to as a "passion" by numerous writers for a century or more, including by Dr. Franz Cumont, who related: "Since the time of the twelfth dynasty, and probably much earlier, there had been held at Abydos and elsewhere a sacred performance similar to the mysteries of our Middle Ages, in which the events of Osiris's passion and resurrection were reproduced." (Cumont, *OORP*, 98.)
[5] Gray, 114.
[6] Plutarch/Babbitt, 39; Gray, 114.
[7] Gray, 120.
[8] Plutarch/Babbitt, 37.
[9] See my book *The Christ Conspiracy*, 238.

at Osiris was 28 when he suffered his passion is also ...esting, in light of the fact that Jesus was likewise said to have been around 28-30 when he began his ministry, depending on the source. Indeed, one early Christian tradition also places Christ's *passion* at when he was "only twenty eight, and one-quarter years of life,"[1] quite possibly in imitation of the Osiris myth.

In the solar myth, the enclosure in the ark during the zodiacal sign of Scorpio (October 24-November 22) symbolizes the weakening of the sun as it approaches the winter solstice. The number 28 is likewise astrotheological and represents the days of an average or mean monthly lunation, after which the soli-lunar god Osiris is torn into 14 pieces—the number 14 signifying the days of the moon's waning per month—and then resurrected, as the moon waxes again. As Plutarch (42, 367E) remarks, "The Egyptians have a legend that the end of Osiris's life came on the seventeenth of the month, on which day it is quite evident to the eye that the period of the full moon is over."[2]

Again in chapter 42 (368A), Plutarch further explains the astrotheological meaning of the Osiris myth:

> Some say that the years of Osiris's life, others that the years of his reign, were twenty-eight; for that is the number of the moon's illuminations, and in that number of days does she complete her cycle. The wood which they cut on the occasions called the "burials of Osiris" they fashion into a crescent-shaped coffer because of the fact that the moon, when it comes near the sun, becomes crescent-shaped and disappears from our sight. The dismemberment of Osiris into fourteen parts they refer allegorically to the days of the waning of that satellite from the time of the full moon to the new moon....[3]

Regarding this tale, astronomer Dr. Edwin C. Krupp, the director of the Griffith Observatory in Los Angeles, remarks:

> The numbers are significant. Although the moon completes its phases in 29½ days, the number 28 was used symbolically for this interval....

> The 14 pieces of the body of Osiris sound like the 14 days of the waning, or "dying" moon, and on the main ceiling of the Dendera temple are inscriptions and pictorial reliefs that leave no doubt. In one panel, an eye, installed in a disk, is transported in a boat. The eye, we know, was a symbol of the sun or moon. Thoth, the ibis-headed scribe god of wisdom and knowledge, pilots the barge. Thoth was closely associated with the moon and counted the days and seasons. The text for this panel refers to the period after the full moon, and 14 gods accompany the eye in the disk.[4]

---

[1] *CE*, "Christmas,." III, 726.
[2] Plutarch/Babbitt, 103.
[3] Plutarch/Babbitt, 103.
[4] Krupp, 18.

The "age" when Osiris dies thus symbolizes the "lunar mansions," as "celebrated" in the Book of the Dead as "twenty-eight."[1]

In addition, the 72 "co-conspirators" in the later version of the Osiris myth likewise possess astrotheological meaning, representing the 72 *dodecans*, or divisions of the circle of the zodiac into 5 degrees each. Interestingly, in the gospel story (Lk 10:1) Jesus is depicted with either 70 or 72 "disciples," the number 70 often symbolizing the dodecans as well. Modern translations of Luke 10:1 such as the NLT, NIV and ESV prefer the number as 72, as do modern apologists, referring to them as "the Seventy Two."

Furthermore, the drowning of Osiris in the "river" Eridanus evidently signifies the god's passage through the well-known *constellation* of the same name. The subsequent avenging of Osiris's murder by his son(s) Horus also constitutes an astrotheological motif. In the myth as presented by Plutarch (18, 358A), Horus the first son of Osiris and Isis is already alive before Typhon/Set tears Osiris's body into 14 pieces.[2] Indeed, Osiris is depicted by Plutarch as later coming from "the other world" to train this Horus to battle Set. At a certain point, the other, newborn Horus becomes the avenger of his father's death by killing Set, the god of catastrophe, pestilence and darkness.

The battle between Horus and Set is mentioned in many places in Egyptian texts, in which the dynamic duo is called, among other things, the "Two Combatants" or "Two Contestants," as well as the "Divine Pair."[3] The story of this conflict includes various details such as Horus's association with Re, his sometime father, in attempting to destroy Set, as well as numerous other characters such as the blacksmiths on Horus's side and the vast army of "bad guys" with Set. Some of these particulars signify astrotheological elements added as the science of astronomy became more sophisticated. In addition to the example of the 72 dodecans, Horus's battle with Set as depicted in the inscriptions at the relatively late site of Edfu includes him slaying Set's monsters, the crocodile and hippopotamus, which symbolize two of the "circumpolar stars" that are "washed out" or removed from sight when the sun's rays appear on the horizon.[4] With or without the details, of course, the contention between Horus and Set ultimately represents the battle of good versus evil and light versus dark, once more displaying astrotheological meaning.

Who is Set?

One of the five children of Geb or Seb, the earth-god, and Nut, the sky-goddess, the notorious Egyptian god Set is described in BD 17 as

---

[1] Bonwick, 175.
[2] Plutarch/Babbitt, 45.
[3] Allen, J., *AEPT*, 42; Mercer, 76; Renouf, *EBD*, 140.
[4] Lockyer, *DA*, 151.

"that god who steals souls, who laps up corruption, who lives on what is putrid, who is in charge of darkness, who is immersed in gloom, of whom those who are among the languid ones are afraid."[1] As the one "who is in charge of darkness," Set "comes to carry off the light."[2] In this regard, the life-destroying adversary in the Coffin Texts (CT Sp. 49), for example, is named as the "Evil One who is in darkness."[3]

Regarding Set's role, James Lewis Spence (1874-1955) remarks, "As the days began to shorten and the nights to lengthen it was thought that he stole the light from the sun-god."[4] Hence, Set is a *thief in the night* who robs Osiris/Horus of his strength and life. As the monster that prevents the sun from shining, Set also symbolizes storm clouds:

> This battle may likewise be found in the sky by day when storm-clouds darken the face of the sun, so that the myth of the serpent and the solar deity Re merges into the old story of the conflict between Horus and Seth. Thus the serpent becomes more and more identical with Seth, as being an additional manifestation of the wicked god who later is said to have fought against Horus in the form of other water monsters as well, such as the hippopotamus and the crocodile. This confusion of 'Apop and Seth, however, does not take place until after the Eighteenth Dynasty.[5]

In the papyrus of the scribe Nesi-Amsu (c. 305 BCE) from Thebes, in a section entitled "The Book of Overthrowing of Apepi" appear the "enemies of Ra" called *Sebau, Qettu* and *Sheta,* written with some variant of 𓏏 and translated also as "devils," "enemies," "fiends," "foes," "rebels" and "sinners."[6] About these characters, Renouf remarks: "The *sebau* are the enemies of the sun, either as Ra or Osiris. I believe that under this mythological name the dark clouds are personified."[7] Thus, we discover yet more personified entities with astrotheological meaning. These Sebau are also equivalent to the conspirators or "Sami" of the Set myth, which, we have seen, represent the 72 dodecans. The sebau/sami, et al., are equatable with "sinners" in the Christian mythos.[8]

Set/Seth's identification with Re/Ra's enemy Apepi/Apophis can be further seen in the depiction of the Judgment Hall in the tomb of Ramesses VI, in which Osiris's adversary is portrayed as a pig, representing "both Seth and Apophis."[9] Prior to his identification with the monster Apophis, enemy of the sun god Re, Set was not always

---

[1] Faulkner, *EBD*, pl 10; Allen, T., *BD*, 31.
[2] Bonwick, 133.
[3] Faulkner, *AECT*, I, 46.
[4] Spence, *AEML*, 100.
[5] Gray, 107.
[6] Gardiner's A14A, Z3; Budge, *OHPNA*, 425, 522, etc.; Faulkner, *EBD*, pl. 5.
[7] Renouf, *EBD*, 6.
[8] Massey, *EBD*, 110.
[9] Hornung, *VK*, 159.

considered "evil" but was worshipped as a divine being, evidenced by the pharaonic choice of the name "Seti" or "Sety." In this regard, Griffiths remarks:

> Only in the Greco-Roman period does [Seth] achieve in Seth-Typhon a kind of satanic persona in the Greek papyri; and even then it is not Satanism in the full Iranian sense of a creator of evil beings.[1]

At a certain point, Set or *Seth* thus became demonized and was abandoned as a king-name:

> The last king bearing Seth's name belongs to the Twentieth Dynasty, about 1200 B.C. The interesting evolution of this god into a Satan is due to the influence of the Babylonian myth of Tiamat.[2]

It has also been claimed that, like the mythical Babylonian monster Tiamat, Set himself was originally a *Semitic* god imported into Egypt,[3] an interesting assertion in light of the contention that Set is equivalent to *Satan*, the word "Satan" being related to the Hebrew or Semitic term *shaytan*, meaning "adversary" and later adopted into Christianity. Regarding Set/Seth, James Bonwick, a member of Dr. Birch's prestigious Society of Biblical Archaeology ("SBA"), states:

> [French Egyptologist and SBA member] Pleyte has no doubt about Set being the *El* or *Elohim* of the East, and the same as Baal. Finding that curious passage in the book of Numbers about the destruction of the sons of Seth, he says, "It is probable that the Septuagint meant by the 'Sons of Seth,' the people who rendered homage to the god Seth (Set), the same divinity who was adored in Egypt by the Palestino-Asiatic tribes."[4]

Concerning the "children of Seth" at Numbers 24:17, Dr. Samuel Sharpe (1799-1881), an Egyptologist and translator of the Bible, relates, "Seth is an Egyptian name for Satan, and by the children of Seth, the Samaritans seem meant."[5] Moreover, mythologist Dr. Louis Herbert Gray (1875–1955), a professor at the University of Nebraska, calls Seth "the general patron of Asiatics and of warriors,"[6] and Rev. Dr. Sayce writes:

> Set or Sut became for the later Egyptians the impersonation of evil. He was identified with Apophis, the serpent of wickedness, against whom the sun-god wages perpetual war; and his name was erased from the monuments on which it was engraved. But all this was because Set was the god and the representative of the Asiatic invaders who had conquered Egypt, and aroused in the Egyptian mind a feeling of bitter animosity towards themselves.[7]

---

[1] Redford, 253.
[2] Gray, 392.
[3] Bonwick, 130.
[4] Bonwick, 135.
[5] Sharpe, 28.
[6] Gray, 155.
[7] Sayce, 162.

Therefore, it would appear that the Egyptian god Set was originally one of the Semitic Elohim, the plural gods worshipped by the Israelites.[1]

Set as Satan

As we have seen, the villain in the myth revolving around the sun god Re is named Apophis, Apop, Apap, Apep or Apepi, all variants of the same word. Like the myth of Horus versus Set, Re battles on a daily basis the "great serpent" of the night sky, Apophis, defeating him at dawn. Indeed, Apophis is the "devourer" and the "fiend of darkness."[2] Regarding the serpent motif, SBA member Rev. Henry Windsor Villiers Stuart states:

> ...It is remarkable that Satan—our evil principle—is spoken of also as the Great Serpent, and like Apop is represented as chained in the bottomless pit.[3]

Another transliterated *Egyptian* title for the destructive and fiendish serpent is "*Sata*," as found in Budge's translation of the Papyrus of Nu, which reads:

> I am the serpent Sata whose years are many. I die and I am born again each day. I am the serpent Sata which dwelleth in the uttermost parts of the earth. I die, and I am born again, and I renew myself, and I grow young each day.[4]

Thus, even Set/Sata dies and is resurrected on a regular basis.

In his *Egyptian Hieroglyphic Dictionary*, using the same transliteration Budge calls Sata the "serpent-fiend in the Tuat."[5] The Tuat or Duat is defined as "a very ancient name for the land of the dead, and of the Other World."[6] The "land of the dead" and "other world" also signify the "cave," "tomb" or "underworld" of the nightly terrain through which Osiris (or Re) must pass daily, to be born again at sunrise as his son, Horus.[7] This journey is described in the ancient Egyptian book "Amduat" or "Am Tuat," as summarized by Budge:

> When the Sun-god set in the west in the evening he was obliged to travel through the Tuat to the eastern sky, in order to rise again on this earth the following day.[8]

---

[1] See "The Myth of Hebrew Monotheism" in *The Christ Conspiracy*.
[2] Spence, 13.
[3] Stuart, 345.
[4] Budge, *BD* (1899), 278.
[5] Budge, *EHD*, I, 640.
[6] Budge, *EHD*, II, 871-872.
[7] See Murray, *LAE*, 50-51: "Great and mighty is the river of the sky, flowing across the heavens and through the Duat, the world of night and of thick darkness, and on that river floats the Boat of Ra.... Slowly goes the Boat of Ra, passing through the Duat, to regions of thick darkness, of horror and dismay, where the dead have their habitations, and Apep lies in wait for the coming of Ra."
[8] Budge, *AIAEL*, 245.

Thus, Apophis/Sata is the same as the monster Typhon/Set battled every day by Horus. In other words, all of these names—*Apap, Apep, Apepi, Apop, Apophis, Seth, Set, Sut, Sutu, Sata*—represent epithets for the same god or phenomenon: Both "the Arch-Enemy of Osiris, and the personification of Evil,"[1] as well as "the Arch-fiend and great Enemy of Ra."[2] Hence, it can be truthfully stated that Set is *Satan*, and the battle between Jesus and Satan—Light versus Darkness—represents a formulaic rehash of the far more ancient contention between Horus and Set. Indeed, if Set is Satan, then Osiris/Horus is Jesus, as has been maintained for centuries for this and many other reasons.

Naturally, this identification of Set/Seth with Satan was made by early Christians, including and especially the Egyptians or Copts. In a similar vein, Dr. Claas Jouco Bleeker (1898-1983), a professor of Religious History at the University of Amsterdam, states: "It can be proved that a number of Gnostic conceptions go back to ancient Egyptian religious thoughts...."[3]

Adding to this assertion, Dr. Wilson B. Bishai (d. 2008), a professor emeritus of Arabic for the Department of Near Eastern Languages and Civilizations at Harvard University, remarks:

> A very plausible story of ancient Egypt that fitted very well into the Biblical record of creation was the legend of the rebellion of *Seth* against *Horus*. *Seth*, a synonym of hatred and disobedience in Egyptian mythology, caused all sorts of troubles to befall man in revenge for his banishment by *Horus* and the rest of the Egyptian Ennead. In the minds of the early Egyptian Christians, Satan, as a parallel to *Seth*, became the rebel and the enemy of man, who began to lurk in ambush in order to drag him (man) into disobedience.[4]

In discussing the perception of Seth in Egyptian texts, Dr. Bleeker further relates:

> It is true that Seth is condemned and punished, but his evil power is not broken forever. That is the theme of another number of well-known texts which paint Seth as a sort of Satan figure.[5]

We also learn from Griffiths that eventually Set/Seth is "treated as a kind of Satan, especially in the Greek magical papyri."[6] So close is this correlation that the editors of *Mythology: Myths, Legends and Fantasies* comment, "The Egyptian name for Seth, *Sutekh*, may have evolved into the word Satan."[7]

---

[1] Budge, *LOLM*, liii.
[2] Budge, *LEG*, xlii.
[3] Bishai, 128.
[4] Bishai, 128.
[5] Bleeker, *HT*, 136.
[6] Plutarch/Griffiths, 389.
[7] Parker, Janet, 297.

Like Satan, Set rebels against his divine birth. Also like Satan, who in the Old Testament/Tanakh is merely "the Adversary," rather than the personification of Absolute Evil that he became in the New Testament, Set/Seth was not always considered absolutely evil. Like Yahweh, God of the Old Testament, who was the orchestrator of both good *and* evil, Set is represented as the "twin" of Horus, half of the dual god who is a single being: Horus-Set.[1] Yet, Set is also a separate entity who becomes locked in an eternal struggle with his alter ego and enemy, Horus, and, again, at a certain point the "old thunder-god" Set became "the representative of all evil" and "a real Satan."[2]

Like Satan, Set/Seth too had his devoted followers, possibly equivalent to the "sons of Seth" recorded in the Old Testament and generally thought to refer to the descendants of Adam's third son Seth. Like Adam's other son Cain, who kills his brother Abel, Seth/Set is depicted as murdering *his* brother Osiris. And like other characters in the Old Testament, such as Abraham and Moses, in the "patriarch" Seth we seem to have yet another instance of an ancient tribal god demoted to human status.[3]

In addition, as does Satan with Jesus (Rev 12:1-5), Set attempts to kill Horus,[4] with Set representing the "god of the desert," while Jesus is tempted in the desert by Satan. Furthermore, like Satan, who has a forked tail, Set too is depicted with a forked tail. In fact, Set's portrayal with bizarre ears and an anteater-like snout makes him appear creepy and demonic:

> Seth was identified with an animal that had the body of an elongated jackal or greyhound; a long neck; a thin, curved snout; rectangular, upraised ears; and a stiff, forked tale. Seth was often portrayed with a human body and the head of this beast.[5]

Set is the serpent of the night, the Prince of Darkness and other qualities in line with Satan, while Horus is the "sun of righteousness" and the Prince of Light, much like Christ. As we have seen and will continue to see, there are many such correspondences between the myth of Osiris/Horus and that of Jesus. In the end, the tale of Jesus versus Satan, we contend, is equally astrotheological and mythical as the prototypical epic drama of Osiris/Horus versus Set. This readily

---

[1] Budge, *FFGAE*, 375. In the Pyramid Texts and elsewhere, as another one of the gods born on the five intercalary or epagomenal days completing the 365-day year, Horus the Elder is also said to be, like Set, the son of Geb or *Seb*—the earth god and "father of the gods"—just as Jesus was the son of Jo-*seph*, the earthly father of God.
[2] Gray, 109.
[3] Adding to this contention of Egyptian culture influencing that of Judea, Israel and Palestine, the name "Moses" is "probably of Egyptian origin." (*NSHERK*, VIII, 24.)
[4] The scriptures in the biblical book of Revelation (12:1-5) discuss the "male child" or "man-child" who will "rule all the nations with a rod of iron..." (RSV). Although there has been some debate as to the identity of this "male child," as Pastor Chuck Smith says, "Most scholars agree that the 'man child' is Jesus Christ." (*Blue Letter Bible*, "Commentaries.")
[5] *WBE*, 321.

discerned Egyptian precedent for a "Christian" concept is noteworthy, as it easily demonstrates the apparent influence of Egyptian religion upon Christianity.

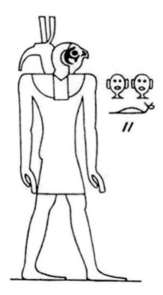

"Horus and Seth united in a single being, the god 'with the two faces,' from the Amduat."
(Hornung, *The Valley of the Kings*, 115)

"Horus spearing Apap, or Apôphis."
(Wilkinson, *The Manners and Customs of the Ancient Egyptians*, III, 155)

Born on December 25th

"As the annual rebirth of the sun's light, the winter solstice was important in most parts of the world. In fact, the Romans already had an ancient winter festival whose seven days bracketed the solstice.... Choosing the birth of Christ as December 25 successfully integrated long-standing popular traditions with the imagery of a new religion, and the theme of renewal is still part of Christmas."

Dr. Edwin C. Krupp, *Echoes of the Ancient Skies* (81)

"The well-known solar feast...of Natalis Invicti, celebrated on 25 December, has a strong claim on the responsibility for our December date [for Christ's Nativity]."

"Christmas," *Catholic Encyclopedia* (III, 727)

"...every year the temples of Horus presented to worshipers, in mid-winter (or about December 25th), a scenic model of the birth of Horus. He was represented as a babe born in a stable, his mother Isis standing by. Just in the same way is the birth of Christ dramatized today in every Roman Catholic church in the world on December 25th. The Roman writer Macrobius makes the same statement about the representation of the birth of Horus in the temples...and adds that the young god was a symbol of the rebirth of the sun at that date. The fact is, at all events, beyond question. We are brought to the very threshold of Christianity. The whole world by the year 1 A.D. was familiar with the Egyptian statues or pictures of Isis with the divine babe Horus in her arms."[1]

Joseph McCabe, *The Story of Religious Controversy* (169)

"The symbol of the savior-child was the eye of the sun newly born every year at the winter solstice."

Dr. Bojana Mojsov, *Osiris: Death and Afterlife of a God* (13)

Although many people remain unaware of the real meaning behind "Christmas," one of the better-known correspondences between pre-Christian religion and Christianity has been the celebration of the god's birth on the 25th of December.[2] Nevertheless, it has been argued that this comparison is erroneous because Jesus Christ was *not* born on December 25th, an assertion in itself that would come as a surprise to many, since up until just a few years ago only a miniscule percentage of people knew such a fact. Indeed, over

---

[1] McCabe says that this display is related in an "early Christian work, the 'Paschal Chronicle' (Migne ed. xcii, col. 385)." However, a close scrutiny of that text does not reveal this particular contention in certain details, such as the winter-solstice birthday or the specific name of Horus. Nevertheless and quite importantly, as addressed below, *the passage does discuss the Egyptian virgin-born savior in a manger centuries before the common era.*

[2] The use of the English phrase "December 25th" does not imply that this date was written as such in ancient times. Neither the name nor the calendar involved is relevant, as what is important is that this time of the year represented the *winter solstice*, however it may be called.

the many centuries since the holiday was implemented by Christian authorities, *hundreds of millions of people* have celebrated Jesus's birthday on December 25th, or *Christmas*, so named after *Christ*. Moreover, hundreds of millions continue to celebrate the 25th of December as the birth of Jesus Christ, completely oblivious to the notion that this date does not represent the "real" birthday of the Jewish son of God.[1] Lest "Christmas" eventually end up being acknowledged widely as the birthday not of the Jewish messiah but of the *sun*, it needs to be immortalized that for hundreds of years that day *was* celebrated as the birthday of Jesus Christ. In this regard, a century ago Dr. K.A. Heinrich Kellner, a professor of Catholic Theology at the University of Bonn stated concerning "Christmas, or the feast of our Lord's birth," that the "whole Church, and all the sects, agree in observing the 25th December as this date."[2] This type of proclamation came in America only after a hard-fought battle for nearly a century in which certain fundamentalist Christian groups strenuously objected to December 25th for Christ's birthday, specifically because the date was too Pagan, before "Christmas" became an official federal holiday in 1870.[3] Although it took a long time for "Christmas" to catch on, it was not particularly long before the real significance of the date—i.e., the winter solstice—had been completely severed to the point where very few people were aware of its existence. So it was for the bulk of humanity up until recently, largely because of the efforts to educate about the true meaning of "Christmas" as the winter solstice.

In actuality, it would be highly refreshing for the facts regarding the *true* meaning of Christmas to be known around the world: To wit, "Christmas"—or the *winter solstice*—represents the birth of the *sun god* dating back thousands of years. In other words, as Christian apologists who claim Christ was not born on December 25th must agree, Jesus is *not* the "reason for the season," which is precisely the point of this discussion. In addition, since it is our contention that the character in the gospels called "Jesus Christ" is mythical, it is quite futile to argue that December 25th is not the "real" date of his birthday, since myths do not have "real birthdays." The truth is that, as is typical of *myths*, Christ's birthday from the earliest times of his conception has been variously placed, on a myriad of dates such as: January 5th, January 6th, March 25th, March 28th, April 19th, April 20th, May 20th, August 21st, November 17th and November 19th.[4] Many

---

[1] In 2007, the U.S. House of Representatives passed HR 847, officially declaring December 25th to be the birthday of the Lord and Savior Jesus Christ: "Whereas on December 25 of each calendar year, American Christians observe Christmas, the holiday celebrating the birth of their savior, Jesus Christ..."
[2] Kellner, 127.
[3] See Nissenbaum, *The Battle for Christmas*. See also Stathis, "CRS Report for Congress: Federal Holidays: Evolution and Application."
[4] Acharya, *SOG*, 231.

if not all of these dates are, like December 25th, mythological and astrotheological, representing milestones in the cycles of the sun, moon, planets and so on.

Concerning the origins of the *solar holiday* of December 25th vis-à-vis Christianity, the authoritative *Catholic Encyclopedia* ("Christmas") states:

> The earliest rapprochement of the births of Christ and the sun is in [the writings of Church father] Cyprian [200-258]..."O, how wonderfully acted Providence that on that day on which that Sun was born...Christ should be born."

> In the fourth century, Chrysostom...says:... "But Our Lord, too, is born in the month of December...the eighth before the calends of January [25 December]..., But they call it the 'Birthday of the Unconquered'. Who indeed is so unconquered as Our Lord...? Or, if they say that it is the birthday of the Sun, He is the Sun of Justice."[1]

As we can see from these revealing remarks, the birth of Christ at the winter solstice has been asserted since as early as the 3rd century. Moreover, the reason for this birthdate is clearly given: This date represents *"the birthday of the Sun!"* This longstanding birthday of the "Unconquered Sun" or *Sol Invictus* was formally instituted in the Roman Empire after Emperor Aurelian (214/5-275 AD/CE) introduced a new state cult in 274 AD/CE, constructing a temple to Sol Invictus at Rome to commemorate his victory over "the East": "The Sol worshiped there seems to have been the Ba'al of Palmyra combined with other Oriental sun gods..."[2] The temple was commemorated on December 25th in the year 274, the day of the "rebirth of the sun."

Regarding Christ's birth and the establishment of Christmas, Christian apologist Thomas Thorburn relates:

> The earliest church commemorated it at various times from September to March, until in 354 A.D. Pope Julius I assimilated the festival with that of the birth of Mithra (December 25), in order to facilitate the more complete Christianisation of the empire.[3]

Thus, Christ's birth at the winter solstice was not formalized until the fourth century—and this fact demonstrates a *deliberate contrivance by Christian officials to usurp other religions*, as we contend the entire Christian religion was specifically created by *human beings* to do.

It should be kept in mind also that this December 25th date was related to the Nativity of John the Baptist at the *summer solstice*, or June 24th, per the Catholic calendar of festivals. The placement of Christmas and St. John's Day as six months apart is based on *biblical* scripture at Luke 1:24-27, in which the Baptist's mother was

---

[1] *CE*, III, 727.
[2] Richardson, 363.
[3] Thorburn, 33.

have conceived six months before the Virgin Mary did likewise. The astrotheological nature of this tale is evidenced further at John 3:30, in which the Baptist is made to say mysteriously in reference to Christ: "He must increase, but I must decrease." While this peculiar statement would make little sense if applied to human beings, it may provide a clue that the gospel writers in fact knew that they were discussing the winter and summer sun as it moved from solstice to solstice.

Prior to its celebration as the birthday of Jesus Christ, the 25th of December/winter solstice was claimed as the nativity for a number of other gods and godmen, including the Perso-Roman god Mithra. As another version of the solar hero, the Greek god Dionysus too was asserted to have been born at the winter solstice, when his followers held a wild celebration in his and the sun god Apollo's honor.[1] This winter-solstice birth may also have come with Dionysus's identification with the Egyptian god Osiris, since, as Plutarch states (35, 364E), "Osiris is identical with Dionysus."[2] Concerning winter-solstice "Feasts and Festivals," the *Encyclopedia Britannica* reports, "The common people in China have a similar custom on the arrival of the winter solstice..."[3] The EB also names several other cultures as having winter celebrations, including the Mexicans and Peruvians. Even the lunar Jews had their winter holiday, or "Feast of the Dedication," as mentioned at John 10:22. The winter solstice in Latin is called *bruma*, serving as one source of the Roman celebration called "the Brumalia."[4]

Of course, the Romans were famed for their lengthy winter festival of Saturnalia, which ended on the first day of the solstice, after which another celebration was held. In this regard, in his analysis of the Egyptian zodiac, Dr. William Mure (1799-1860), a lord-rector of Glasgow University,[5] provides a "curious passage" from the works of the Emperor Julian (331-363 AD/CE), who reinstated Pagan worship—and possibly paid for it with his life:

> Immediately after the completion of the month of Saturn (December), we celebrate magnificent games to the sun, called the feast of the Invincible Sun, in which it is not permitted to introduce any of those unseemly though necessary rites, which belong to the previous month; but the Saturnalia being at an end, the feast of the Sun comes next in succession; nor was it the intention of the ancients, that this solemnity should be fixed to the very day on which the god

---

[1] Thomson, 481; Sophocles/D'Ooge, 136fn.
[2] Plutarch/Babbitt, 85.
[3] *Enc. Brit.*, X, 220.
[4] The dates of the Brumalia, a Bacchic or Dionysian festival, have been reckoned as March 12th and September 18th. However, Bell relates that "there are others who say that the Brumalia was a religious festival, celebrated on the day of the winter solstice." This confusion evidently comes from two different terms as the basis for "Brumalia," one referring to the "shortest day" and the other to Bacchus/Dionysus. (Bell, 141)
[5] Anderson, W., 222.

passes the tropic, but to that on which his return from south to north first becomes perceptible to all; for they knew not yet the nice mode of observation, afterwards discovered by the Chaldees and Egyptians, and perfected by Hipparchus and Ptolemy.[1]

In this passage, Julian discusses the festival of the winter solstice, not necessarily on the first day when the sun "passes the tropic," in other words, December 21/22nd, but when the sun was visibly moving north again, i.e., the 25th. Julian's remarks confirm that the winter solstice was observed in ancient times not only by the famed astrologers the Chaldeans, but also by the Egyptians. As we can see, the celebration at the winter solstice represents an ancient tradition in many parts of the world,[2] with the evidence revealing that Egypt possessed this annual celebration concerning the sun god as well.

There appears to be much confusion regarding the dates of December 21st, 22nd and 25th. The fact is that *all* of them represent the time of the winter solstice, which *begins* at midnight on the 21st— equivalent to the morning of the 22nd—and *ends* at midnight on the 24th, the morning of December 25th. To summarize, in the solar myth the "death" of the "old sun" occurs as the days decrease in length towards the winter solstice—the word "solstice" meaning "sun stands still"—as for three days the sun appears not to be moving south or north. Hence, it was considered "dead" in the "tomb" or "cave," and did not "return to life" until three days later, at midnight on December 24th, when it began its northerly journey again. Therefore, the ancients said the sun was born, reborn or resurrected on December 25th.

Ancient and Modern Voices

It has been the frequent contention of writers since antiquity that, like many other cultures, the Egyptians too celebrated the birth of the sun at the winter solstice, a logical conclusion, considering the reverence with which the sun was held in Egypt. Concerning this cycle in Egypt, in "Isis and Osiris" (65, 378C), **Plutarch remarked that Horus the Child—or "Harpocrates," his Greek name—was "born about the winter solstice, unfinished and infant-like..."**[3] This term "Harpocrates" is a Greek word, which in the original Egyptian is "Her-pa-chruti" or "Heru-pa-Chrat," etc., meaning "the

---

[1] Mure, 90-91, citing "Orat. iv. p. 156 Ed. Spannh." The standard story of Julian's death may have been a cover for an assassination by Christians, some of whom had previously attempted to murder the emperor. Following Julian's death, Christian writers such as John Malalas (Chronicle 13.25) claimed that Christ himself had sent "St. Mercurius" (the god Mercury?) to slaughter the Emperor, thereby essentially taking responsibility for the murder. It is therefore possible that Julian was felled not by a Persian arrow but by one from his own soldiers.

[2] A more in-depth study of the subject is provided in my book *Suns of God*.

[3] King, C.W., *PM*, 56. See Plutarch/Babbitt, 153.

morning sun."[1] This fact of Plutarch stating that Horus was born on "December 25th" is vitally important to keep in mind, because there has been much denial and censorship of it.

Adding to this highly noteworthy assertion are some fascinating remarks by Church father Epiphanius (c. 310-403 AD/CE) in his *Panarion adversus Haereses* (51, 22.4-11):

> "...Christ was born on the eighth before the Ides of January, thirteen days after the winter solstice and the increase of the light and the day." Greeks, I mean the idolaters, celebrate this day on the eighth before the Kalends of January, which Romans call Saturnalia, Egyptians Cronia, and Alexandrians, Cicellia.... For this division between the signs of the zodiac, which is a solstice, comes on the eighth before the Kalends of January, and the day begins to lengthen because the light is receiving its increase....[2]

The "Ides of January" occurred on the 13th of the month, counting back eight days from which, Epiphanius elucidates (51, 24.1), places Christ's birthday on January 6th—which just happens also to be a "birthday" of Osiris centuries before Christianity was created.[3] Epiphanius quotes the "Syrian sage Ephrem" as explaining (away) this date as the "beginning of the increase of the light" with the addition of the 13 days based on Christ and his 12 disciples, rather than for the reason of emulating Osiris's birth. The "Calends of January," of course, is the first of that month, with the eighth day before falling on "Christmas Eve."

In this intriguing passage from Epiphanius appear two names for Egyptian winter-solstice celebrations, "Cronia" and "Cicellia," both Greek terms, the latter of which is mysterious but was found also on

---

[1] Budge, *Mummy* (1894), 271-272.

[2] Epiphanius/Williams, 50. Talley's translation of the pertinent passage is as follows: "...Christ was born on 8 before the Ides of January, 13 days after the winter solstice and the increasing of the day and of the light. This day is celebrated by the Hellenes, i.e,. by the idolaters, on 8 before the Kalends of January, called among the Romans 'Saturnalia,' among the Egyptians 'Kronia,' among the Alexandrians 'Kikellia.' This is the day on which the change takes place, i.e., the solstice, and the day begins to grow, the light receiving an increase." (Talley, 104.) Dr. Rahner's translation is thus: "...Christ was born on the eighth day before the Ides of January, thirteen days after the winter solstice from whence onward the light and the days begin to grow longer. On this day, i.e. on the eight day before the Calends of January, the Greeks—I mean, the idolaters—celebrate a feast that the Romans call Saturnalia, the Egyptians Cronia and the Alexandrines Cicellia. The reason is that the eighth day before the Calends of January forms a dividing-line, for on it occurs the solstice; the day begins to lengthen again and the sun shines longer and with increasing strength until the eight day before the Ides of January, viz., until the day of Christ's nativity..." (Rahner, 137.) The fact that there are various editions demonstrates that they are translations of a real passage found in another language, in this case Greek. This point needs to be emphasized because of the massive tampering and literary fraud that has been committed over the centuries. In addition, Epiphanius's works traditionally have not been made readily available in English or other languages, perhaps because his chronicle of Christian origins contradicts the received Church history. (See Mead, *DJL*, 389-391.)

[3] Rahner, 139.

the tablet of Canopus.[1] The Cronia festival is named for the god Cronus or Kronos, who is called "Saturnus" in Latin. The association of Cronia or Kronia with Saturnalia is also verified by a papyrus fragment found at Oxyrhynchus (I 122.4), dating to the late third or early fourth century and constituting a portion of a letter from "one Gaianus to a legionary prefect," in which appears a brief mention of "the day of the Kronia," referring to the Saturnalia.[2]

Regarding the festival of Kronia, in "A New Greek Calendar and Festivals of the Sun," classicist Dr. Stefan Weinstock (1901-1971) states:

> Accordingly, if we find that at the end of the year the period of 24th November-24th December is called Kronia and celebrated at night, this was not done because [the god] Kronos, banned by Zeus to the Underworld, lives in the dark, but because it was a celebration of the dark period of the year, Helios having descended to the Underworld and having assumed there the name of Kronos.[3]

Kronia thus ended with the sun's ascent from the underworld, representing its "birthday" on December 25th. Concerning the Kikellia and other such "Christmas" celebrations, Dr. Kellner remarks:

> ...the Kikellia was kept at Alexandria on the 25th December, in Bostra and Pella, a festival of local observance, and in Rome, the Saturnalia began on the 17th December and lasted until the 23rd. It was only natural that the winter solstice should give rise to a festival, and find its place marked in the Calendar of Feasts. Indeed, in the Roman Calendar of much later date—that of Philocalus—the 25th December is marked as the birth-day of the unconquerable Sun-God....[4]

Per Birch, the Egyptian term for Cicellia, Kykellia or Kikellia is *Kaaubek*,[5] with this fact of possessing an Egyptian name obviously serving as an indication that the festival did indeed exist in Egypt. These Kikellia—Κικηλλια being a *plural* term in the Greek—are "celebrated in the month of Choiach before the procession (Periplus) of Osiris,"[6] as written on the stela from Canopus. This famous tablet was discovered in the Eastern Delta in 1886 and contains a decree in both Egyptian hieroglyphs and demotic, as well as Greek, written in 239 BCE as a record of religious festivals created for the deceased "Queen of Virgins," Berenice, wife of Ptolemy III. The decree also established the most accurate calendar of the ancient world, which served as the basis of the Alexandrian calendar introduced by Caesar Augustus (63 BCE-14 AD/CE) in 25 BCE.[7] The Greek word for

---

[1] Wilkinson, J., *MCAE*, III, 377.
[2] Haase, 3088.
[3] Weinstock, 41.
[4] Kellner, 150-151.
[5] *ROTP*, VIII, 89.
[6] Budge, *DMC*, 177; Mahaffy, 117.
[7] Budge, *DMC*, 10-13. The wandering or "vague" Egyptian calendar was reformed by Augustus, producing the "Alexandrian calendar," meaning that the two calendars were

_~cession," περιπλους, can also be translated as "sailing round" or "second course," a term indicative of a _rebirth_ of sorts, when applied to an animate object such as Osiris. This nautical term is appropriate since Osiris is depicted as being shut up in his _ark_, and the sun's journey is portrayed as taking place in a boat or "bark." Thus, in the Kikellia we possess a winter-solstice festival representing the marking of the increase of the day and sun's light, along with the "second course" or restoration/rebirth of Osiris.

Epiphanius's discussion of the Kikellia or winter-solstice festival continues with him relating that the celebration took place at the large Egyptian city of Alexandria "at the so-called Virgin's shrine." Railing against "those who guilefully preside over the cult of idols" and who "in many places deceitfully celebrate a very great festival on the very night of the Epiphany" (51, 22.8), Epiphanius next describes this festival as follows (51, 22.9-10):

> First, at Alexandria, in the Coreum, as they call it; it is a very large temple, the shrine of Core. They stay up all night singing hymns to the idol with a flute accompaniment. And when they have concluded their nightlong vigil torchbearers descend into an underground shrine after cockcrow...and bring up a wooden image which is seated naked <on> a litter. It has a sign of the cross inlaid with gold on its forehead, two other such signs, [one] on each hand, and two other signs, [one] actually [on each of] its two knees—altogether five signs with a gold impress. And they carry the image itself seven times round the innermost shrine with flutes, tambourines and hymns, hold a feast, and take it back down to its place underground. And when you ask them what this mystery means they reply that today at this hour Core—that is, the virgin—gave birth to Aeo.[1]

Here we find a Pagan sacred icon with a _cross_ on its forehead, like that made by Catholic priests on the heads of Christian worshippers. We also discover this sacred image constitutes the divine son of the holy virgin mother within _Paganism_! This Pagan _virgin mother_ was styled Core or Kore, meaning "maiden," as another name for the Greek nature goddess Persephone, who descended each year into the underworld, to return at springtime, bringing life back with her. This descent into the underworld and the resurrection to life are echoed in a number of myths, including that of Jesus, a subject treated more fully later in this present work. Kore's son Aeo or Aion is called "the eternal," whose birth from a virgin constitutes a _mystery_, presumably ages prior to the common era. The fact that the virgin-birth motif represents a mystery explains why it is currently not widely known to have existed long before the purported advent of Jesus Christ and his

---

in harmony that year, in terms of the same dates appearing for the same day. After that, they diverged one day for every four years. (Evans, 19) The new year of the Alexandrian calendar began when the sun was in Virgo; thus, it could justly be said that the year was "born of a virgin."

[1] Epiphanius/Williams, 51.

alleged virgin birth, because evidently it was written down frequently, and where even rarely it *was* memorialized, many references may have been destroyed or hidden. In this regard, it is our contention that Christianity constitutes little more than the mysteries turned inside out and broadcast openly. Moreover, the fact that there was a "very large temple" at Alexandria devoted to the worship of the virgin mother, even named after her, is indication of her worship as both widespread and ancient.

This same event of the Pagan virgin-goddess giving birth to the divine son was celebrated also by Arabs at the ancient site of Petra in Jordan, as likewise recounted by Epiphanius (51, 22.11):

> This also goes on in the city of Petra, in the idolatrous temple there. (Petra is the capital city of Arabia, the scriptural Edom.) They praise the virgin with hymns in the Arab language and call her Chaamu— that is, Core, or virgin—in Arabic. And the child who is born of her they call Dusares, that is, "only son of the Lord." And this is also done that night in the city of Elusa, as it is there in Petra, and in Alexandria.[1]

Regarding Epiphanius's account, in a chapter entitled "The Virgin Birth," Joseph Campbell writes:

> We learn from the fourth-century saint and churchman Epiphanius (ca. 315-402), for example, of an annual festival observed in Alexandria on January 6, the date assigned to the Epiphany and (originally) the Nativity of Christ, and to his Baptism as well. The pagan occasion was in celebration of the birth of the year-god Aion to the virgin goddess Kore, a Hellenized transformation of Isis.[2]

As we have seen from Diodorus, in pre-Christian times Isis was also identified with the Greek goddess Demeter, Kore's mother, who, like her daughter, was likewise perceived to be a virgin.

According to Rev. Dr. Hugo Rahner (1900-1968), a dean of the Faculty of Catholic Theology at the University of Innsbruck, by the time of Epiphanius this "year-god" Aion was "beginning to be regarded as identical with Helios and Helios with Dionysus..."[3] Dr. Rahner also discusses the ages of the sun, as related by the Roman philosopher and writer Macrobius (395-423 AD/CE) concerning Dionysus. Thus, in Aion—the "only begotten son of God"—we possess a sun god born of a virgin who is in turn identified with the goddess Isis. Interestingly enough, as Griffiths relates, "Osiris was sometimes identified with Aion,"[4] which is fitting since Osiris's other alter ego, Dionysus, is likewise "identical" with Aion.

To summarize this very significant testimony: In Epiphanius's writings appear important details about the Alexandrian festival celebrating the winter solstice, when the days and sun's light begin to

---

[1] Epiphanius/Williams, 51.
[2] Campbell, *TMI*, 34.
[3] Rahner, 139.
[4] Redford, 307.

increase, and culminating with an image being carried forth of a child with a golden cross who was born at that time of a virgin! Nowhere does Epiphanius apparently attempt to claim that this widely celebrated non-Christian virgin birth at "Christmas" had been copied *from* Christianity, leaving us to conclude that any borrowing occurred in the opposite direction.

The pertinent parts of Epiphanius concerning the winter solstice celebrations in Egypt, with the festival at that time of the virgin Kore giving birth to Aion, as well as the same virgin-birth celebration taking place among the Arabs at Petra, are cited in the Williams translation to be in Heresy 51 at section 22.3-11.[1] However—in a twist worthy of a mystery/thriller—in the Migne edition, which contains the "original" Greek alongside with a Latin translation, *these crucial sections are entirely missing.*[2] In fact, the Migne text does not resume until 22.19, with a discussion of Christ's birth in the 42nd year of Augustus's reign, completely lacking all mention of Egypt, the winter solstice and the Pagan virgin birth. The Williams translation uses Holl's original Greek text found in *Die griechischen christlichen Schriftsteller der ersten drei Jahrhunderte*, the source of which is the Codex Marcianus, a manuscript ("MS") from the 10th century. This passage in Epiphanius can also be found in the Dindorf edition (ii, p. 482), which likewise uses the Codex Marcianus. Previously published editions and translations lacking this critical passage were evidently based on a "severely censured and bowdlerized fourteenth century MS [manuscript]."[3]

Hence, in the Epiphanius passage we possess a case of deliberate and egregious censorship of an ancient author's work apparently for the specific purpose of preventing information damaging to the Christian tradition from being known. We contend that there have occurred *many* such instances of censorship concerning numerous correspondences between Christianity and pre-Christian religion, which is another reason why, if some of these important "mysteries" were nonetheless well known in ancient times, they are not today. This particular example of textual tampering removed not only the reference to the Pagan winter-solstice celebrations in Egypt and Greece but also Epiphanius's discussion of the Pagan *virgin birth* associated with it. Thus, in one fell swoop references to two highly important parallels between Christianity and Egyptian religion were obliterated from the historical record. We can only wonder what else has been suppressed in the same manner, and we can see from erroneous and fallacious commentaries in popular publications and

---

[1] Epiphanius/Williams, 50-51.
[2] Migne, 927-930.
[3] Mead, *TGH*, 160. "To bowdlerize" means to expurgate or remove parts of, named after Thomas Bowdler, who notoriously edited Shakespeare's work.

forums, as well as mainstream education, that the effect censorship has been thorough.

Fortunately, the earlier manuscript of Epiphanius survived, and we also possess the testimony of Plutarch, as well as that of the writer Macrobius in the fourth century, to verify the facts concerning the Egyptian winter-solstice festival. In his *Saturnalia* (1.18:10), Macrobius likewise reported on the annual Egyptian "Christmas" celebration:

> ...at the winter solstice the sun would seem to be a little child, like that which the Egyptians bring forth from a shrine on an appointed day, since the day is then at its shortest and the god is accordingly shown as a tiny infant.[1]

In *The Origins of the Liturgical Year*, Rev. Dr. Thomas Talley, a professor at the General Theological Seminary, discusses the Macrobius passage and remarks:

> This similarity to Epiphanius' description is heightened further by the scholion of Cosmas of Jerusalem [d. 760? AD/CE] on Gregory Nazianzen [329-389 AD/CE], which described the Hellenes [Greeks] as celebrating a festival on the winter solstice with the festal shout, "the virgin has brought forth, the light grows," and the Calendar of Antiochus, which places beside the entry for December 25 the remark, "birth of the sun, the light increases," although it notes the occurrence of the solstice itself on December 22.[2]

The "Calendar of Antiochus" refers to that of a resident of Athens about 200 AD/CE in which, as stated, December 25ᵗʰ is named as the "sun's birthday" or the "birthday of Helios."[3] In this regard, Dr. Weinstock states:

> ...In Egypt and in Greece the terms of human life were applied to the Sun. It was thought to be a child at its rise in the morning, an adult at its culmination and an old man at its setting. The same view was applied to its annual course: child at the winter solstice, youth in the spring, adult in the summer, and old man in the autumn. Thus the course of the Sun in its lifetime, and we should expect that states of this "life" were marked in the calendars, from the time that they became solar calendars. Yet in Greek calendars, corresponding entries were missing until Boll published in 1910 the Calendar of Antiochus which contains the entry to 25ᵗʰ December Ἡλίου γενέθλιον· αυξει φως [Birth of the Sun: the light increases], and lends strong support to the famous entry of Philocalus...: "N(atalis) Invicti." This emergence of the "birthday" of the Sun caused much sensation and some controversy because of its obvious relevance to the Christian tradition concerning Christmas and Epiphany.[4]

---

[1] Macrobius/Davies, 129. The original Latin of this paragraph in Macrobius is: "...ut parvulus videatur hiemali solstitio, qualem Aegyptii proferunt ex adyto die certa, quod tunc brevissimo die veluti parvus et infans videatur..." (Rahner, 140.)
[2] Talley, 107.
[3] See Beck, 57.
[4] Weinstock, 41.

Philocalus is the creator of a calendar or chronography, in the year 354 AD/CE of which appears a notation on "December 25th as the *Dies Natalis Invicti.*"[1] Moreover, as we can see from Weinstock's remarks, the correspondence between the "birth of the sun" and Christmas was not lost on the various scholars who published and studied the Calendar of Antiochus. The increase of the light on December 25th makes sense, as that day represents the *end* of the solstice, which begins on the 21st/22nd. Concerning the "birthday of the Sun on 25th December," Weinstock continues:

> In the preceding night the Egyptians carried from a sanctuary the image of a new-born child, the Sun, and shouted that "the Virgin has born," and that the light is increasing...[2]

Weinstock concludes, "The full calendar seems to have recorded, in addition to other festivals, phases in the 'life' of the Sun in a way similar to that in which the calendar of our days records the phases in the life of Christ."[3]

As we can see, the ancient winter-solstice festival is well attested, including by yet another fairly early *Christian* source (Cosmas of Jerusalem or Gregory Nazianzen), complete with *the virgin bringing forth*, independent of Christianity and representing *the birth of the sun*. Needless to say, this astrotheological point cannot be overemphasized.

As to the antiquity of the Egyptian winter-solstice, virgin- or solar-birth drama depicted by Plutarch, Epiphanius and Macrobius, Professor Orlando P. Schmidt makes some interesting contentions regarding the king Amenemhet or Amenemhat I (c. 1991/1985-c. 1962/1956 BCE), styled in Greek "Amenemes" or "Ammenemes," founder of the 12th Dynasty:

> Now, as the sun of the Sothiac year reached the winter solstice in the seventeenth year of the reign of King Amenemes I, he assumed the title of Nem-mestu, meaning "Re-born," in commemoration of his birth as Harpokrates.[4]

Thus, according to Schmidt the birth of "Harpocrates" at the winter solstice apparently dates back almost 2,000 years prior to the common era, a tradition evidently verified by Plutarch.

The epithet "Nem-mestu" represents the king's "Horus name" and means "repeater of births," "repetition of births" or "reborn." Regarding this title, Budge says:

> ..."nem mestu," i.e., "repeater of births," the allusion being to the idea that the king was like the Sun-god Re who was reborn daily;

---

[1] Halsberghe, 144.
[2] Weinstock, 42.
[3] Weinstock, 42.
[4] Schmidt, 19. The Sothiac or Sothic year is "the Egyptian year of 365 days and 6 hours, as distinguished from the Egyptian vague year, which contained 365 days."

this title became a great favorite with the kings of the XIIth [12th] Dynasty.[1]

Budge thus verifies that this particular Horus name was indeed popular in the dynasty in question. Intriguingly, according to Budge the Egyptian word for winter solstice is *nen*, which would make a Horus name of "*Nen*-mestu" equivalent to "born of the winter solstice." The Egyptian word for "birth" is also transliterated as *mesut*[2] and *mswt*,[3] while Amenemhet's full Horus name was "Horus, the born again."[4]

In any case, the Horus name "repeaters of births" as a reflection of the sun god's daily birth, apparently dates back thousands of years in Egypt, and the significance of the winter solstice in Egypt, as well as its perception as the birthday of the sun god, seems evident.

On the subject of Plutarch and Harpocrates, in his *Egyptian Book of the Dead*, Budge remarks:

> The curious legend which Plutarch relates concerning Harpocrates and the cause of his lameness is probably based upon the passage in the history of Osiris and Isis given in a hymn to Osiris of the XVIIIth [18th] Dynasty.[5]

Here we discover that Harpocrates or "Horus the Child" as the weak or lame sun evidently dates to an Osirian hymn written during the period of 1534-1292 BCE. Budge never seems to return to this "curious legend," apparently coming from chapter 19 of Plutarch (358E), which mentions Horus as the weak and lame son of Isis but omits the pertinent part about him representing *the sun being born at the winter solstice*, as in chapter 65.[6] In any event, we have confirmation of the antiquity of Horus being depicted as "lame," as Plutarch relates, and of a *Horus* name reflecting the sun being born on a daily basis.

Concerning the Osirian myth presented in Plutarch, in *Egyptian Ideas of the Future*, Budge further comments: "When we examine this story by the light of the results of hieroglyphic decipherment, we find that a large portion of it is substantiated by Egyptian texts..."[7] The British scholar proceeds to name many of the most significant details from Plutarch as having been verified by hieroglyphs, including in inscriptions, papyri and so on. In neither the *Book of the Dead* nor *Egyptian Ideas* does Budge describe the assertion in chapter 65 of Plutarch connecting Harpocrates to the winter solstice. Perhaps as a professed Christian, Budge did not wish to reproduce these

---

[1] Budge, *EUGPB*, 190.
[2] Budge, *AERBB*, 434.
[3] Allen, J., *ME*, 103.
[4] Renouf, *Life-Work*, 195.
[5] Budge, *EBD* (1967), cxv-cxvi.
[6] In chapter 19 (358E), Plutarch remarks of Isis that she "became the mother of Harpocrates, untimely born and weak in his lower limbs." (Plutarch/Babbitt, 49.)
[7] Budge, *EITFL*, 35.

noteworthy remarks concerning the "Christmas" birth of the Egyptian sun god. As can be seen from the debacle with Epiphanius's work, censorship of this exact sort occurred in important instances. Furthermore, from comments by various writers of Budge's era, it appears there was a debate as to whether or not to accept the "opinions of the Greek" (Plutarch) with regard to Harpocrates's nature as the sun born at the winter solstice. Hence, he could hardly have been oblivious to the debate or its subject. In consideration of all factors, including the various ancient testimonies and all the evidence of the importance of the winter solstice in Egyptian culture, much more of which we shall soon see, one must ask whether or not this argument over the "correctness" of Plutarch in his assertions regarding this figure—a debate continued by apologists today—has been based on scientific reasoning or on *religious prejudice*, representing an intentional suppression and censorship of pertinent data. As a demonstration of how thorough has been this censorship and lack of common sense, when contacted about Horus's birth at the winter solstice, an individual at Budge's old haunt, the Egyptian Department at the British Museum, pronounced the assertion to be "a fantasy!" The facts, however, prove to the contrary.

If the bulk of Plutarch's summary of the myth of Osiris, Isis and Horus is sustainable through Egyptian writings, as Budge himself states, can we not reasonably assume that this winter-solstice birth of Horus would be accurate as well? If Horus was not born at the winter solstice, why does Plutarch state that he was, in his form as Harpocrates or Horus the Child? In *The Dictionary of Deities and Demons in the Bible*, the Christian editors remark, "Harpokrates was very popular in the Graeco-Roman period."[1] Therefore, the myths and attributes of the "Horuses" in general would likely be well known. Indeed, *DDDB* further notes, "The birth of Horus is a well-known mythological theme..."[2] In such an environment, with a popular god whose birth was well known, Plutarch could hardly fabricate something so important and obvious without being caught in a noticeable lie! In reality, other than religious prejudice there is no reason whatsoever to cast such an aspersion on this respected historian's account of Horus being born at the winter solstice or on December 25th. Indeed, if Harpocrates symbolizes the sun born again *every* morning—as we have seen abundantly—would he not also be the sun born in the morning of the winter solstice? To suggest otherwise would seem to be preposterous—yet another point that needs to be emphasized. **It is obvious that Horus, as the *morning sun* born *every* day, was also born on "December 25th" or the winter solstice.**

---

[1] van der Toorn, 427.
[2] van der Toorn, 354.

Moreover, why would Macrobius's account of an Egyptian *festival* of apparent antiquity that specifically celebrated the birth of the baby sun at the winter solstice likewise not be valid? Why would the Christian father Epiphanius actually give not one but *two* names for Egyptian winter-solstice celebrations also of apparent antiquity, as well as—testifying against Christian interest—providing an account of a *Pagan virgin birth*, if these contentions were not true? Why did the Christian writer Cosmas of Jerusalem repeat this claim concerning a virgin bringing forth at the winter solstice—was he lying? Would the Egyptians—who were so keenly aware of astronomy, solar mythology and astrotheology—truly be completely oblivious to, or deliberately unaffected by, the revered status of the sun at the winter solstice? Certainly the Egyptians were highly conscious of the all-important solstices, could they possibly fail to integrate them into their solar religion? The Egyptians were very devoted to marking the rebirth of the sun on a daily basis, as part of their religion in regard to the deceased being equivalent to "the Osiris." In fact, they would have had to go out of their way *not* to celebrate the birth of the sun on the day of the winter solstice. As we shall see, therefore, the assertions of the ancient writers are well founded, as there exists a mountain of evidence that the Egyptians knew well and revered the winter solstice, as *the birth of the sun god*, thousands of years ago.

Hieroglyphic Evidence

In the same manner demonstrated by Budge regarding the bulk of Plutarch's important observations about the Egyptian religion, we can in fact find validation of the Greek historian's assertion regarding the winter solstice as the birth of the sun god in ancient hieroglyphs, as well as many other artifacts indicative of the importance to the Egyptians of that time of year, such as calendars, monuments, clocks, myths and festivals, which we will be exploring here in that order.

In consideration of the evident significance of the winter solstice in Egypt, it might be surprising that in all of Budge's voluminous works there appears to be only one mention of a hieroglyph for the winter solstice, were it not for the fact that the British Egyptologist seems to have been averse to discussing the solstice. In *An Egyptian Hieroglyphic Dictionary*, Budge cites this one winter-solstice hieroglyph as appearing in the work of the German Egyptologist Dr. Heinrich ("Henry") Brugsch-Bey (1827-1894), who studied Egyptian inscriptions for 30 years while sponsored by the Egyptian government, and who was a director of the Egyptian Museum at Berlin. The impression given by this scarcity of the winter solstice in the works of Budge, arguably the most prolific and famous Egyptologist, is that the subject was of little interest to the Egyptians themselves—and this attitude appears to have been carried into more modern times, as there is a dearth of information on this subject in English.

Yet, in *Thesaurus Inscriptionum Aegyptiacarum*, which is composed of handdrawn hieroglyphs and difficult-to-read, handwritten German, we find that Dr. Brugsch spends considerable time on a fascinating discussion of the history of the winter solstice in Egypt from at least 1650 BCE, up to the Greco-Roman period concerning the sites of Edfu and Esne under the Ptolemies (325-30 BCE). In this opus, Brugsch provides a number of individual hieroglyphs symbolizing the winter solstice, as well as various *groups* of hieroglyphs that also describe that time of year. It is evident from Brugsch's extensive and absorbing discussion that, despite its minimization in popular publications in English, *the winter solstice was highly significant in ancient Egypt beginning thousands of years before and continuing into the common era.*

As Brugsch explains, the Egyptians not only abundantly recorded and revered the time of the winter solstice, they also created a number of hieroglyphs to depict it, including the image mentioned by Budge, which turns out to be the goddess-sisters Isis and Nephthys with the solar disc floating above their hands over a life-giving *ankh*—the looped Egyptian cross—as the sun's rays extend down to the cross symbol.[1] This image of the sun between Isis and Nephthys, which is sometimes depicted without the ankh, is described in an inscription at Edfu regarding Ptolemy VII (fl. 145 BCE?) and applied to the winter solstice, translated as: "The sun coming out of the sky-ocean into the hands of the siblings Isis and Nephthys."[2] This image very much looks like the *sun being born,* which is sensible, since, again, Harpocrates, the morning sun, was born *every* day, including at the winter solstice.

Another image depicting the winter solstice portrays a star next to the Horus hawk/falcon with a sun symbol on the right. Brugsch declares that the Horus falcon image is newer than the Isis-Nephthys glyph, which in fact dates back to the time of Ramses III (fl. c. 1186-1155 BCE) in the 20th Dynasty.[3] Moreover, in a series of hieroglyphs in the Rhind Papyrus (c. 1650 BCE), the sun of the winter solstice is depicted as "the little sun in his boat in the sea" (in other words, the "sky-ocean").[4] Brugsch names the date for the voyage of the little sun in his boat as "26. Choiak"—December 22nd, in the Alexandrian calendar.[5]

---

[1] Budge, *EHD*, 351.
[2] Brugsch, *TIA*, II, 427.
[3] Brugsch, *TIA*, II, 409.
[4] Brugsch, *TIA*, II, 409.
[5] Brugsch also discusses the confusing state of calendars in ancient Egypt, including the Canopic (238 BCE), the Alexandrian/Coptic (c. 25 BCE), the Julian (45 BCE) and that of Eudoxus of Cnidus (c. 395/390-342/337 BCE). (Brugsch, *TIA*, II, 442, 444, 445.)

In some inscriptions the single hieroglyphic symbols representing the winter solstice—which can also refer to *morning*—are further appended by hieroglyphs such as *neter* or "god" in order to emphasize that the winter solstice is meant.[1] Since "morning" was clearly considered in ancient Egypt to be the time of the new birth of the "little sun," it is logical to conclude that using the same symbol for the winter solstice indicates it too represents *the birth of the little sun*, as has been the perception in other cultures and as was related of Egypt as well by ancient authors such as Plutarch, Epiphanius and Macrobius.

As another example of a sign for "winter solstice," in his book on hieroglyphs (2.3), Horapollo depicts a symbol that represents two feet, "joined, and walking," signifying "the path of the sun in the winter solstice."[2] The fact that there are a number of hieroglyphs meaning "winter solstice" indicates both that the Egyptians were well aware of that time of the year and that they attached importance to it.

In any event, the facts that Horus is considered the sun born in the morning *every day* and that it is *Horus* who is depicted in the later winter-solstice glyph, signify that it was *Horus* who was born at the winter solstice, precisely as Plutarch relates. These winter-solstice hieroglyphs *unquestionably* pre-date the common era by centuries to millennia. All of these factors combined provide solid evidence that the winter solstice in Egypt was not only widely recognized but also viewed as *the birthday of the new sun*, which in turn was "Horus the Child" or Harpocrates, the very popular god during the Greco-Roman period whose birth was well known.

Calendrical Considerations

Further evidence of the importance of the winter solstice in Egypt can be found in the Egyptian calendar itself, emphasizing the various solar milestones, including the solstices, which were *personified as gods*.[3] The personification of the winter solstice is the god "Ap-uat,"[4] also transliterated as *Wepwawet*, who is "identical with Osiris."[5] Thus, Osiris too would represent the winter solstice, making this time of year evidently highly significant to the Egyptians. The personified solstices were deemed "Opener of the Ways," a title apparently reflecting in part their role as the beginning of the Egyptian New Year.

---

[1] Brugsch, *TIA*, II, 410. See also Assman: "...the sun child 'on the arms of Isis and Nephthys' is the typical morning icon, which appears in Ptolemaic epigraphy as a hieroglyph for *dw3w* 'morning.'" (Assman, *ESRNK*, 45.) Žabkar also provides the text from a hymn to Isis from Philae in which appears the morning hieroglyph of Isis and Nephthys with the sun between them floating above an ankh. (Žabkar, 57.)

[2] Sharpe, 30.

[3] The Egyptian calendar, it should be noted, is doubly important, because, as Morenz says, it "forms the basis for our own calendar." (Morenz, 8.)

[4] Budge, *GE*, 264.

[5] Renouf, *EBD*, 99.

Indeed, in Egypt the summer solstice, which was personified by the god Anubis as "Opener of the Ways," was "paramount, for it heralded the rise of the Nile."[1] As Herodotus states, the Nile began to overflow around the *summer solstice*—specifically named as such by him (1.19). The Greek historian further remarks that the river continues to rise for about 100 days, at which point it levels off and then starts to drop again, remaining low throughout winter.[2] This life-giving time was so vital to the Egyptians that at periods over the millennia they opened the new year with the summer inundation of the Nile.

During other periods, the year may have begun at the *winter* solstice, which would provide further evidence that such a time was considered the "birth of the sun," as in so many other cultures and indicated not only by Plutarch but also by hieroglyphs dating to at least 3,600 years ago.[3] Adding weight to this contention of the Egyptian New Year beginning at the winter solstice is the fact that, at the alleged instigation of the legendary Roman king Numa Pompilius or Pompilio (8th cent. BCE), the Roman Civil Year too began at the winter solstice.[4] As concerns the Egyptian winter-solstice new year, in *Horae Aegyptiacae: Or, the Chronology of Ancient Egypt, Discovered from Astronomical and Hieroglyphic Records Upon Its Monuments,* Egyptologist and professor of Archaeology Dr. Reginald Stuart Poole (1832-1895), another Keeper at the British Museum, states:

> "The Season of the Waters," in the ancient nomenclature, plainly shows that the Tropical Year to which that nomenclature was originally applied commenced at the winter solstice, and not at, nor near, either of the equinoxes, or the summer solstice...
>
> Thus we find that the true period of the commencement of "the Season of the Inundation" was one month before the autumnal equinox; and the end, at the winter solstice; and, consequently, that the Tropical Year anciently in use among the Egyptians commenced at the winter solstice, when all things in Egypt begin anew.[5]

Confirming Dr. Poole's assertions, Willem Zitman remarks:

---

[1] Lockyer, *DA*, 57.

[2] Herodotus/de Selincourt, 92-93.

[3] Concerning the solstices and the calendar, Depuydt remarks, "Two other astronomical phenomena have been postulated as the beginnings of a calendar. Again, no indisputable evidence exists and it is not clear how the corresponding calendars would be organized. These phenomena are the winter solstice (cf. Seth 1919-20: 39) and the summer solstice (cf. Leitz 1989: 24-25). In fact, there is no unambiguous evidence that these two phenomena were at all recorded before the Late Period, when such sophistication could be due to Greek or Babylonian influence...." (Depuydt, 16.) While the solstices may not have been unambiguously recorded in writing until the Late Period (664-323 BCE), as we see here there is plenty of evidence that they *were* noted and incorporated into many other aspects of Egyptian life long before then.

[4] *Edinburgh Encyclopedia*, 407.

[5] Poole, 4-5.

An ancient Egypt source informs us that the Egyptian year originally commenced around the winter solstice. According to the "adjustable calendar," the beginning of the First Dynasty should consequently be set at around 3518 BCE. Between 3518 and 3514 BCE, their New Year's Day—known to the Egyptians as I Achet 1—fell on January 16ᵗʰ or 17ᵗʰ (Julian calendar), the day of the winter solstice....

During the reign of Thutmosis III [fl. 1479-1425 BCE], this winter solstice from times beyond recall was apparently still observed as a commemorative day on which festivities were held—and considered a cause for rejoicing. Even during the Graeco-Roman period, this commemorative festival was still celebrated in the temples at Edfu and Esna.[1]

Zitman also asserts that the "birth and installation of Kingship" occurred on the winter solstice and that this event is mentioned in texts in the temples at Edfu and Esna.[2] His thesis emphasizes the winter solstice as the marker for the very beginning of the institution of Kingship in Egypt, in other words, the First Dynasty (c. 3100-2890 BCE).[3] In this regard, the commemoration of the winter solstice in Egypt would date to at least 5,000 years ago. The winter-solstice year-opening is likewise verified by Brugsch, as the time of the "little sun,"[4] a logical period for the beginning of a year. Brugsch further explains that in Dendera the new year was celebrated as the "day of the birth of the sun disc" and the reappearance or "rising up" of Isis-Sothis,[5] the latter epithet representing the star Sirius. In discussing the day of the sun disc's birthday, *Brugsch is actually translating a group of hieroglyphs*, demonstrating once more that this concept very much existed in pre-Christian Egypt.

Because it was lacking the additional quarter day of the true solar year, the ancient Egyptian calendar was "adjustable," also called "wandering" and "vague," such that it differed one day for every four (4) years. If the "New Year" was celebrated on the same day and month, say, 1 Akhet/Thoth, over a span of at least 1,460 years (365 days x 4 years)—the time it takes for the wandering calendar to make its way back to the beginning—during that period the New Year would eventually fall on *every* day of the year, including *both* solstices and equinoxes.

As a result of the wandering calendar, the opening of the year at the winter solstice occurred again just decades before the common era, at which time, as another example of Egyptian astronomical

---

[1] Zitman, 28-30; citing Brugsch's *Thesaurus Inscriptionum Aegyptiacarum*, II, 525. (This citation refers to the reprint in 1968; the original of 1883 is contained in one volume.)
[2] Zitman, 30.
[3] Zitman, 95. It is generally agreed that the First Dynasty began around 3100 BCE, with the period prior to that representing the Pre- and Proto-Dynastic eras. Zitman appears to be proposing an alternative dating for the First Dynasty.
[4] Brugsch, *TIA*, II, 408.
[5] Brugsch, *TIA*, II, 417: "Tag der Geburt der Sonnenscheibe."

knowledge and the particular importance of the winter solstice, in 46
BCE famed Alexandrian astronomer Sosigenes created a new solar
calendar for Julius Caesar (100-44 BCE), called the Julian Calendar:
"The new system, depending wholly on the sun, would naturally have
commenced with the winter solstice."[1] This new system was followed
by the creation of the Alexandrian calendar by Augustus around 25
BCE.

Regarding the calendrical confusion, in his extensive study *Civil
Calendar and Lunar Calendar in Ancient Egypt*, Dr. Leo Depuydt (b.
1957), associate professor of Egyptology at Brown University,
remarks:

> Some sense of the level of controversy can be derived from the fact
> that, on the basis of the same evidence, eminent authorities have
> postulated, in addition to the civil calendar, calendars based on the
> star Sirius, the brightest in the sky, on the star Canopus, the second
> brightest, on the winter solstice, and on the summer solstice. This
> proliferation of postulated calendars is characteristic of the study of
> ancient Egypt as compared to that of other ancient Mediterranean
> civilizations.[2]

In any event, as is becoming obvious, the Egyptians were well
aware of the winter solstice, which they evidently identified with
various gods at some point and which during certain eras and in
various places opened the Egyptian year.

Monumental Alignments

In our quest, we have examined ancient testimony and
hieroglyphic evidence that the winter solstice in Egypt represented
the "birth of the little sun," as well as the beginning of the new
calendar year, as is sensible in a solar culture. Much evidence for the
reverence of the winter solstice in Egypt may also be found in the
construction of ancient monuments and edifices. Concerning the
annual landmarks of the solstices and equinoxes as recorded in
monuments, astronomer Lockyer remarks:

> Did the ancients know anything about these solstices and these
> equinoxes? That is one of the questions which we have to discuss.
> Dealing with the monumental evidence in Egypt alone, the answer is
> absolutely overwhelming.[3]

As we have seen over the past several decades, there are in fact
many Egyptian sites that possess astronomical alignments, dating
back to the earliest times, as at the site of Nabta (c. 7,000-3,000 BCE)
and extending into the common era, including, among others,
temples in the Upper Nile valley with "some astronomical
alignments," especially "upon the winter solstice sun."[4]

[1] Froude, 425.
[2] Depuydt, 10.
[3] *Nature*, XLIV, 10.
[4] Ruggles, *AA*, 146.

Lockyer was one of the earliest to describe the astronomical alignments of various monuments and buildings in Egypt, beginning with the temple enclosure at Karnak near Luxor. Calling the temple of Amun-Ra at Karnak the "finest Egyptian solar temple" and "the most majestic ruin in the world,"[1] the royal astronomer dated its foundation to 3700 BCE, using astronomical measurements, a date that has been rejected because of a lack of archaeological or textual confirmation.[2] Encompassing twice the area covered by St. Peter's in Rome, the complex at Karnak comprised "two temples in the same line back to back, the chief one facing the sunset at the summer solstice, the other probably the sunrise at the winter solstice."[3] Concerning the smaller temple of Re-Horakhty, Lockyer states:

> The amplitude of the point to which the axis of the small temple points is 26° S. of E., exactly the position of sunrise at the winter solstice.

> There is more evidence of this kind....[4]

Although some of Lockyer's conclusions were in error, including the alignment at the summer solstice by the main temple, other of his assertions were validated by archaeoastronomer Dr. Gerald S. Hawkins (1928-2003), a chairman of the Astronomy Department at Boston University, "whose studies indicated that the solar chamber of Ra-Hor-Akhty, high in the major temple, had a window looking toward the winter solstice sunrise."[5] As further related by Dr. David H. Kelley, a professor emeritus of Archaeology at the University of Calgary, a "smaller temple of Ra-Hor-Akhty to the southeast was also aligned to the winter solstice sunrise (noted by Lockyer and confirmed by Hawkins)."[6] As Kelley also says, Amun-Re's temple was clearly "oriented to the winter solstice sunrise."[7]

These contentions are confirmed by Dr. Clive L.N. Ruggles, professor emeritus of Archaeoastronomy at the University of Leicester:

> The central axis of the Great Temple of Amun-Ra is aligned toward winter solstice sunrise. The main enclosure at Karnak also contains several other temples with solstitial orientations.[8]

This fact is also verified by Krupp, who clarifies that "the main axis of the great temple of Amun-Re coincided with the direction of

---

[1] Lockyer, *DA*, 99.
[2] Lockyer, *DA*, 119. The negative reaction to Lockyer discussed earlier was based both on his status as an "outsider" and on his "extravagant dates and fast-and-loose mythology," again preventing serious study of archaeoastronomy until decades later with Drs. Gerald Hawkins and Alexander Thom. (Ruggles, *RS*, 477.)
[3] Lockyer, *DA*, 102.
[4] *Nature*, XLIV, 57. See also Ruggles, *RS*, 476.
[5] Kelley, 268.
[6] Kelley, 268; Ruggles, *RS*, 479.
[7] Kelley, 268.
[8] Ruggles, *AA*, 145.

winter solstice sunrise during the eighteenth and nineteenth dynasties."[1]

As more evidence of the winter-solstice alignments, the colossal statues of the pharaoh Amenhotep/Amenophis III (c. 1390-c. 1352 BCE) on the plain of Thebes were oriented to watch "for the rising of the sun at the winter solstice,"[2] while Amenhotep's now-lost temple nearby possessed "a series of Sed festival reliefs, and opened to the winter solstice sunrise."[3]

While the main temple at Abu Simbel is not aligned with the winter solstice, a small "chapel" of Re-Horakhty at the complex, built by Ramesses II from around 1284 to 1264 BCE, "faces the winter solstice sunrise."[4]

Adding to this list is the female pharaoh Hatshepsut's famous temple, as related by Krupp:

> Winter solstice sunrise alignment was also found at the solar sanctuary in Hatshepsut's mortuary temple at Deir el-Bahri, and these sanctuaries were linked with the Egyptian beliefs about the passage of Re through the netherworld and the transformation of the soul of the deceased pharaoh.[5]

In the *Encyclopedia of the Archaeology of Ancient Egypt* ("*EAAE*") appears a discussion of the small temple at Aghurmi in the Siwa Oasis. This building possesses a window in the west wall of the sanctuary that connects with an opposite window, producing a light-shaft which illuminates the "god's barge naos in the center of the sanctuary." *EAAE* then states:

> The fact that Onuris and Tefnut are represented right next to this window and the mythology connected with these two gods suggest that occurrence of this event to have coincided with the winter solstice.[6]

The myth of the god Onuris, *Ini hri-t* or Anhur, an epithet meaning, "He who brings the one that was far away"[7] or "he who brings back the Eye of the Sun," and the goddess Tefnut, identified with Mekhit and Sekhmet, all daughters of Re, apparently symbolizes the northerly return of the sun after the winter solstice. Onuris is identified with the god Shu, "the uplifter," who along with his sister Tefnut represent the two eyes of Horus. Tefnut's disappearance "caused the absence of light," while her "return indicated the victory

[1] Ruggles, *RS*, 479.
[2] *Nature*, Suppl. (1891), 57; Lockyer, *DA*, 79; Ruggles, *RS*, 483.
[3] Ruggles, *RS*, 482.
[4] Ruggles, 483, 484. The temple complex at Abu Simbel was moved in 1968 by UNESCO in order to preserve it from the flooding caused by the Aswan Dam. The monuments were, however, reconstructed at a higher attitude with the "exact same relationship to each other and to the sun."
[5] Krupp, xii.
[6] *EAAE*, 742.
[7] Boylan, 35.

of light over darkness and was a signal for rejoicing."[1] This myth further demonstrates the importance of the winter solstice within Egyptian religion.

The idea of the winter solstice representing resurrection, rebirth and renewal is conveyed largely by these monumental alignments as well. Concerning the "High Room of the Sun and Sokar chapel" of Thutmose/Tuthmosis III's "Festival Hall," Krupp remarks:

> Hawkins embraced Barguet's interpretation of the High Room of the Sun and saw in its orientation an allusion to the annual renewal of the sun at the winter solstice—another kind of defeat for darkness and chaos. This idea of cosmic restoration is a central theme in Egyptian religion and belief.[2]

The fact that at least two temples of Re-Horakhty, those at the important sites of Karnak and Abu Simbel,[3] were aligned to the winter solstice provides evidence for the contention that the Egyptians celebrated *Horus* as being born at that time thousands of years ago.[4]

In any event, the various aligned temples were thus logically used to keep time:

> We may conclude that there was some purpose of utility to be served, and the solar temples could have been used undoubtedly, among other things, for determining the exact length of the solar year.[5]

These alignments provided for a very dramatic experience as well, especially at the moment when the sun's rays penetrate the temple during this time of the year:

> We should have a "manifestation of Ra" with a vengeance during the brief time the white flood of sunlight fell on it...[6]

Hence, we find not only testimony, hieroglyphs and calendars but also multiple astronomical alignments in monuments, as well as myths, proving that the ancient Egyptians highly valued the winter solstice. In reality, according to Brugsch the winter solstice was so important to the Egyptians, as a period of *rebirth* and *renewal*, that they timed the restoration of their temples (as at Esne) to coincide with it.[7] In fact, when discussing the rebuilding and restoration of the temple at Esne planned according to the period of the winter solstice, Brugsch specifically calls this time "the rebirth of the sun at the time of the winter solstice." The language could not be clearer: The Egyptians celebrated the birth of the "little sun" at the winter solstice,

---

[1] Armour, 34.
[2] Ruggles, *RS*, 483.
[3] See Ruggles, *RS*, 476, 484.
[4] See Krupp: "Similar open-air sanctuaries dedicated to Re-Horakhty are known at other New Kingdom mortuary temples. In general they face south-east, but they have not been examined in detail." (Ruggles, *RS*, 492.)
[5] Lockyer, *DA*, 110.
[6] Lockyer, *DA*, 111.
[7] Brugsch, *TIA*, II, 419.

so, in fact, that, again, they planned their all-important storations around this day.[1]

Clockworks

In addition to monumental alignments, we discover a number of ancient Egyptian water clocks, such as at Karnak, designed to measure the winter and summer solstices.[2] Indeed, that the Egyptians were keen measurers of time may be seen in an inscription from the tomb of the Karnak clock's creator, a "certain official" named Amenemhet who was buried "near the top of the hill of Sheikh Abd el-Gurna in Western Thebes." This very ancient inscription describes the measurements of the "longest night of wintertime" and the "shortest night of summertime," i.e., the winter and summer solstices respectively. This inscription also refers to Egyptian sacred literature as "the books of the divine word,"[3] demonstrating the reverence with which these texts were held, no less than the holy books of today.[4] The official in question dedicated his clock to Amenhotep I (fl. c. 1526-c. 1506 BCE), who reigned in the 18th Dynasty, revealing once again how far back in Egypt stretched this knowledge of and esteem for the solstices. We would wager that such knowledge and reverence in fact goes back much farther.

In *Ancient Egyptian Science*, professor of Historical Studies Dr. Marshall Clagett (1916-2005) depicts another ancient Egyptian clock used to measure the equinoxes and solstices:

> The first (and indeed only) Egyptian technical description of an ancient Egyptian shadow clock is found in an inscription in the cenotaph of Seti I (ca. 1306-1290 [BCE])...[5]

Dr. Clagett also describes an Egyptian sundial from Luxor that apparently dates to the Greco-Roman period and that possesses marks to measure, among other things, the winter solstice.[6]

Thus, in Egyptian time keeping we find artifacts measuring the winter solstice dating back over three thousand years, until shortly before the common era.

Winter Solstice Celebrations

Associated with the hieroglyphs, calendars, buildings, myths and clocks were celebrations and festivals, not a few of which in Egypt

---

[1] Brugsch, *TIA*, II, 419: "Die Wiedergeburt der Sonne zur Zeit der Winterwende..."
[2] So closely have the Egyptian gods been associated with time that it has been repeatedly claimed that the name Horus has been brought forth into English in the word "hours." In his translation of Diodorus, Edwin Murphy—who is not prone to fantasy—remarks, "Horus was also said to have first divided the day into *hours*, which still reflect his name." (Diodorus/Murphy, 32, footnote 51.)
[3] Clagett, 69-70.
[4] In CT Sp. 405 also appears reference to the "Book of the Divine Words." (Faulkner, *AECT*, II, 56.)
[5] Clagett, 84, 86-87.
[6] Clagett, 96-97.

revolved around the winter solstice, as we have seen from Plutarch, Epiphanius and Macrobius, among others. In addition to the Kronia and Kikellia festivals already discussed, we find another example of an Egyptian winter-solstice celebration in the inscription from Khnumhotep II's tomb at Beni Hassan (12th Dynasty, c. 1820 BCE), in which the winter solstice is referred to as "the feast of little heat."[1] Such would be an appropriate designation, especially in Egypt, which does not suffer the severe winters of northern Europe, for instance, where the winter solstice could be called "the time of intense cold!" From this inscription we know for a fact that there existed a winter-solstice festival in Egypt almost 4,000 years ago, in addition to the commemoration that evidently occurred at the beginning of the First Dynasty, some 5,000 years ago. In CT Sp. 623, the Osiris remarks upon "those happy monthly festivals of yours of the summer, of the inundation season and of the winter."[2] As have seen, the Egyptian winter-solstice festivals apparently occurred well into the common era as well.

Festivals of Osiris

According to a lengthy inscription at the Temple of Hathor at Dendera, which was created during the Ptolemaic era (325-30 BCE), a "festival of Osiris" was celebrated from the 12th to the 30th of the Egyptian month of Choiach/Choiak/Coiak/Khoiak/Koiak, ending with Osiris being laid in the "holy sepulchre." Osiris is next shown being resurrected in an image, about which Frazer remarks, "The resurrection of the god could hardly be portrayed more graphically."[3] While Frazer, abiding by his "vegetation-god" thesis, sees in this scenario an occasion for sowing grain, with Osiris the "lord of the resurrections" of the grain, it could not have escaped the notice of those who carried out the festival or portrayed it in the inscription that it coincided with the winter solstice, which is when the second half of the month of Koiak fell during this period. Indeed, regarding the "Osiris rites commonly called 'mysteries' and the Festival of Khoiakh which immediately followed them," renowned Egyptologist Sir Dr. Alan H. Gardiner (1879-1963) remarks that "they are intimately connected in the first place with the death and burial of Osiris and the rising up of Horus in his stead..."[4]

The month of Koiak corresponding to December also can be found in the later Alexandrian and Coptic calendars, which are essentially the same. In *Calendrical Calculations* by professors of Computer Science at Tel Aviv University and University of Illinois, respectively, Drs Nachum Dershowitz and Edward M. Reingold state: "The

---

[1] Brugsch, *AHUEP*, 171.
[2] Faulkner, *AECT*, II, 207.
[3] Frazer, *AAO*, 261.
[4] Hornblower, *Man*, vol. 37, 153.

Christian Copts, modern descendants of the Pharaonic Egyptians, use a calendar based on the ancient Egyptian solar calendar...but with leap years."[1] Drs. Dershowitz and Reingold further remark that "the Copts celebrate Christmas on Koiak 29 (which is always either December 25 or 26 on the Julian calendar)..."[2] Adding to this observation, the 15th of Koiak in the wandering calendar was calculated by scientist Dr. Otto E. Neugebauer (1899-1990), a professor of Mathematics at Brown University, to have fallen on the winter solstice around 70 BCE,[3] fitting in with the decades in the latter part of the Ptolemaic era and meaning that the month of Koiak during the first century before the common era also fell in December according to the old Egyptian calendar as well.

The celebration of Osiris's restoration, resurrection or rebirth in the Dendera inscription resembles the Kikellia from the Canopus stela and as mentioned by Epiphanius, representing the *periplus* or "second course" of the god. We also saw that the Kikellia were said to be celebrating the god's *birth* from the *virgin mother*, the former identified as the sun god and the latter as Kore, who in Egypt was equivalent with Isis.

In *The Sacred Tradition in Ancient Egypt*, Rosemary Clark describes what is apparently the same festival of Osiris during the time of the winter solstice:

> As the winter solstice denotes the literal decline of solar light, festivals celebrated at this time are connected with the renewal of the life force. One of these festivals was the annual raising of the Djed pillar of Asar [Osiris] at his great temple at Busiris in Lower Egypt. This was a symbolic restoration of the Neter's [God's] life, an event which followed a ritual reenactment of an episode in the great Osirian mythos, The Contendings of Heru [Horus] and Set. It took place, according to ancient records, on the 30th of Choiach, a time coinciding with the end of the Nile's inundation over the land. In our calendar the festival begins on December 10 and culminates at the winter solstice (December 22).[4]

The djed pillar—also called a "Tet," "Tat" or "Tau"—is a very ancient "cult icon of Osiris" that was "erected in a rite symbolizing Osiris's revivification after death."[5] The raising of the djed pillar at the sacred city of Busiris is mentioned in BD 18 and elsewhere.[6]

Adding to the idea of the restoration or *rebirth* of Osiris at the winter solstice, according to Nibley the winter solstice in Egypt was

---

[1] Dershowitz, 73.
[2] Dershowitz, 77.
[3] Evans, 21.
[4] Clark, 131.
[5] Allen, J., *AEPT*, 428.
[6] Allen, T., *BD*, 32; Faulkner, *EBD*, pl. 12; Bunsen/Birch, 180. Birch translates the pertinent part as "setting up the Tat in Tattu," the latter being the Egyptian name for Busiris.

called the "Day of the Great Coming Forth," as found in the Leiden Papyrus (T32, 4/22), which addresses Osiris thus:

> "You establish yourself in the land at the feast of the Fixing of Times, on the Day of the Great Coming Forth [*tr.t*, the first day of the winter, the solstice]."[1]

Furthermore, the "restoration of Osiris" at the winter solstice—which would essentially constitute *his rebirth in Horus*—is also related by Plutarch (52, 372C):

> Moreover, at the time of the winter solstice they lead the cow seven times around the temple of the Sun and this circumambulation is called the Seeking for Osiris, since the Goddess in the winter-time yearns for water; so many times do they go around, because in the seventh month the Sun completes the transition from the winter solstice to the summer solstice. It is said also that Horus, the son of Isis, offered sacrifice to the Sun first of all on the fourth day of the month, as is written in the records entitled the Birthdays of Horus.[2]

Although here Plutarch discusses Osiris's water aspect, logic would indicate that the god's *solar* nature was also being sought at the winter solstice, when the sun is viewed as "weakening," "dying" or otherwise diminishing, in line with the shortest day of the year. Elsewhere, in fact, Plutarch (39, 366D-E) specifically states that one of the reasons for mourning Osiris was "the day's growing shorter than the night."[3]

In addition, this "Seeking for Osiris" at the winter solstice is deemed by the conservative *Encyclopedia Britannica* as one of the Egyptians' "most characteristic celebrations":

> Among those most characteristic celebrations of the Egyptians were those which took place at the αφανισμος [aphanismos] or disappearance of Osiris in October or November, at the search for his remains, and their discovery about the winter solstice...[4]

The discovery of Osiris's remains at the winter solstice essentially means that he was "born again" at that time, since he was thereafter resuscitated.

Regarding this important time of the year, Dr. Mure remarks:

> Osiris dead is, as we have seen, Osiris at the winter solstice, when the Nile was nearly at the lowest, and when, as we have shown in our account of that season, Harpocrates was born.[5]

Because Horus and Osiris were one and interchangeable, the new sun replacing the old, it could be stated truthfully that the "restoration" of Osiris at the winter solstice represents the "new birth" of Horus, as does every other day of the year. Hence, again we find

---

[1] Nibley, 466-556. Citing Stricker, B.H., *De egyptische mysteriën* Pap. Leiden T 32 (vervolg), 21. (Note in brackets is Nibley's.)
[2] Plutarch/Babbitt, 127.
[3] Plutarch/Babbitt, 94.
[4] *Enc. Brit.*, 221.
[5] Mure, 137.

Horus being born on "December 25th," the "Day of the Great Coming Forth."[1] In this regard, Brugsch asserts that certain Gnostics claimed *the Egyptians actually called the winter solstice by the name of* "*Harpokrates*," i.e., Horus the child,[2] which verifies once again the identification of Horus as the born-again sun at the winter solstice.

The winter-solstice motif is also indicated in the story related by Plutarch of Osiris being shut up in his ark *during the sign of Scorpio*, the "backbiter," who robs the sun of its strength as the solar orb nears the death of winter. In one myth describing the death of *Horus*, the god is killed by Set as a *scorpion*, a motif that would likewise symbolize the same theme, indicating once more the interchangeability of the sun gods. In fact, the winter solstice was considered a time to drive away Set through a ritual in which "an ass was slain, and a model of the serpent-fiend was hewn in pieces."[3] Thus, we possess an Egyptian solar myth of the darkness being vanquished at the solstice.

Obviously, it would be fascinating to inspect the ancient "records entitled the Birthdays of Horus" to which Plutarch refers in his comments about the "Seeking for Osiris." It is possible that any such records—if they were actually written down—could be found in the Library of Alexandria, which unfortunately was destroyed, taking with it a vast amount of human culture and knowledge, including many of these mysteries and secrets. Again, when we hear the clamor for "primary sources," we are reminded of this massive destruction of ancient culture, often by religious fanatics trying to prevent the truth from becoming known.

Dual Birthdays of Horus

In the same vein as Plutarch, and quite possibly discussing the same text, in his treatise on the *dual birthdays of Horus*—one at the vernal equinox and the other at the winter solstice—Massey refers to "the Egyptian Book of the Divine Birth":

> The double birth of Horus at the two times, or the birth of the babe in the winter solstice and the rebirth as the adult in the Easter equinox is acknowledged in the Egyptian Book of the Divine Birth. The celebration of the Nativity at the solstice is referred to in the calendar of Edfu, and it is said that "everything is performed which is ordained" in the "Book of the Divine Birth."[4]

The text that Massey cites was also evidently mentioned by Austrian professor Dr. J. Krall:

> On the 6th of Pachons...the solstice is then celebrated. The Uza-eye is then filled, a mythical act which we have in another place referred to

---

[1] Again, December 25th represents the *end* of the three-day "sun stands still" period, thus still remaining a part of the winter solstice.
[2] Brugsch, *TIA*, II, 419.
[3] Budge, *GE* (1904), 248.
[4] Massey, *AE*, 572.

the celebration of the solstice, and "everything is performed which is ordained" in the book "on the Divine birth."[1]

The solstice celebrated on the 6th of Pachons is that of the summer, once again demonstrating the significance of that time of year. The "Uza-eye" being filled apparently refers to the Eye of the Sun (Re and/or Horus) approaching its culminating strength at the summer solstice.

Of course, the mere existence of a book "on the Divine Birth" discussing a celebration of the winter solstice is in itself a strong indication that this time of the year was indeed considered in Egypt to be the birth of the sun, as is logical and reasonable to assume in any event, since, again, *every day* was the birth of the sun!

Festival of Ptah

According to Lockyer, Dr. Krall also discusses an inscription discovered at both Edfu and Esne "which seems to have astronomical significance." This inscription describes a feast day during the period of "1. Phamenoth" called the "Festival of the suspension of the sky by Ptah" or the "Feast of the suspension of the sky."[2] Krall clarifies these festivals as being "connected with the celebration of the Winter Solstice, and the filling of the Uza-eye..." He then continues:

> Perhaps the old year, which the Egyptians introduced into the Nile valley at the time of their immigration, and which had only 360 days, commenced at the Winter Solstice. Thus we should have in the "festival of the suspension of the sky" by the ancient god Ptah— venerated as creator of the world—a remnant of the time when the Winter Solstice...marked the beginning of the year, and also the creation.[3]

As we have seen on the good authority of Drs. Poole and Brugsch, the Egyptian year at one point did begin with the winter solstice, which makes sense because of the wandering calendar as well.

In addition, the god Ptah is the very ancient Father-Creator figure who, in "suspending the sky," resembles other Egyptian deities such as Isis, Horus and Shu with arms outstretched in the "vault of heaven," as well as the Greek god Atlas supporting the world on his shoulders, and various renderings of the Christian Father and Son holding up the heavens.

Feast of Sokar

The father-god Ptah represents one of a pre-Christian "trinity in unity" constituting the hybrid god Ptah-Sokar-Osiris. Sokar, also written as Sokaris and Seker, is perceived as a distinct god, but he is also a form of Osiris, said to represent the sun god in his

---

[1] Lockyer, *DA*, 284-285.
[2] Lockyer, *DA*, 284.
[3] Lockyer, *DA*, 284.

"underworld" role, enabling the sun "to complete its course during the night and to be reborn in the morning."[1] Concerning these gods, Maravelia remarks, "The syncretism of Sokar and Osiris, evident from the Middle Kingdom on, associated both deities as tutelary lords of the dead and dispensers of the resurrection in the Netherworld."[2] The god Sokar as the "reborn sun" was conceived at least 3,400 years ago, as related by Dr. Hawkins:

> In Kherouef's tomb, circa 1400 B.C., it says, "The doors of the underworld are open, O Sokaris, sun in the sky. O reborn one, you are seen brilliant on the horizon and you give back Egypt her beauty each time the sky is pierced with rays..."[3]

Regarding the "feast of Sokar," Maravelia also states, "The festival of Sokar was celebrated with considerable pomp, probably rivaling the festival of Opet; it was the continuity of the cult of the divine king connected with the resurrection of the god."[4] Furthermore, it was claimed that Osiris died during the feast of Sokar, in other words, around the winter solstice.[5] Regarding this feast, Wilkinson remarks:

> At the festival of the god his bark was borne in solemn procession round the walls of the temple of Sokaris.... The festival was connected with the winter solstice, with the "little sun," as the Egyptians called it at that time. In the Ptolemaic period it fell on the morning of the 26th of Khoiak (22nd December), while in earlier times it would seem to have been held in the evening....[6]

In a papyrus fragment of a calendar from the Hibeh collection (27), evidently created at Sais and dating to circa 301-240 BCE, the 26th of Koiak is deemed the "Festival of Osiris."[7] This "festival of Osiris" was said to last four days, beginning on the 26th of Koiak and ending on the 29th of Koiak (Canopus Inscr. 1. 51). This four-day period evidently constitutes the same span in Plutarch when Isis is mourning for Osiris. Concerning this festival, Egyptologist Dr. Bernard P. Grenfell (1869-1926), a professor of Papyrology at Oxford, remarks, "At Esneh the feast of Sokar, the Memphite god of the dead,

---

[1] Redford, 338.
[2] Maravelia, *JNES*, 86.
[3] Hawkins, 210.
[4] Maravelia, *JNES*, 92.
[5] Johnston, 247.
[6] Wilkinson, J., *MCAE*, III, 135. See also Riel: "Und wie das Fest der Sonnenwende, so fällt auch das Fest der Winterwende im Festkalender von Esne auf denselben Tag, wie im Alexandrinischen Jahre. Dieses Winterwendefest hat Brugsch eingehend besprochen und bis zur Evidenz erwiesen, nicht nur, dass das Festkalender von Esne am 26. Choiak vorkommende Sokarfest das Fest der Winterwende ist, sondern auch, dass dasselbe Fest im Rhind-Papyrus (aus dem 21. Jahre des Augustus) ebenfalls auf den 26. Choiak gesezt ist... Der 26. Choiak ist aber nach Ptoelmäus der Tag der Winterwende des Alexandrinischen Jahres, dessen Sommerwende auf den 1. Epiphi fällt. Sommer- und Winterwende treten hiermit als Zeugen ein, dass sich der Festkalender von Esne auf das Alexandrinische Jahr bezieht." (Riel, 341.)
[7] Grenfell, 144.

identified with Osiris in later times, also took place on Choiak 26."[1] Brugsch likewise discusses the fest of Sokar, which was held on the 26th of Koiak, equivalent to December 22nd in the Julian calendar and December 25th in the calendar of Eudoxus (410/408-355/347 BCE).[2] In the temple of Dendera, Brugsch relates, we find a description of the 26th of Koiak—December 22nd also in the Alexandrian calendar— as representing the day of the winter solstice and of the "Rising of Osiris as the sun and moon."[3]

Brugsch further states that the winter-solstice festival—along with the Sokar fest—on the 26th of Koiak was proved to have existed during the period of the Alexandrian calendar, i.e., just before the common era.[4] This fact, of course, means that we possess mention of winter-solstice celebrations in Egyptian records dating from at least 20 centuries before the common era, right up to the time of Christ's alleged advent and, in fact, well into the common era. In reality, the winter-solstice celebration was so important that King Ptolemy VII Neos Dionysos (81-55 BCE) is depicted as pulling a ceremonial sled as part of a solemn procession on that date.[5] Brugsch describes the sled drawn by Ptolemy VII as representing the "Exodus of Sokar," with an image on the sled—sitting on top of an *ark*, as in the "ark of the Covenant" and as in the boat or bark of the "little sun"—resembling a baby hawk or falcon, with the sun disc on his head.[6] The image at Edfu being pulled by Ptolemy is unquestionably that of Sokar, whose "barque represents solar triumphs and is set on a sledge."[7]

Moreover, this great festival of Sokar during Koiak, in which the falcon-headed sun god is carried out of the temple, was thought to help the pharaoh succeed in the annual restorative digging of the canals that had been destroyed by the Nile flooding. As such, the festival evidently occurred at least as early as the Old Kingdom (3rd millennium BCE).[8] One thing is clear: The festival of Sokar was very popular, especially during the New Kingdom and into Ptolemaic times. Thus, many thousands of Egyptians over a period of millennia must have been aware of the sun's birth at the winter solstice.

Could this image of the pharaoh bringing out the baby sun at the winter solstice reflect the ritual described by Macrobius? If so, we possess a clear pre-Christian validation that Macrobius was correct— and this image would tend to verify Plutarch's description as well,

---

[1] Grenfell, 153.
[2] Brugsch, *TIA*, II, 442, 444, 445.
[3] Brugsch, *TIA*, II, 426: "...der Aufgang des Osiris..."
[4] Brugsch, *TIA*, II, 416.
[5] Brugsch, *TIA*, II, 416. See figs on pp. 378-379.
[6] The use of an "ark" in which to carry the deity was quite common in ancient Egypt, rendering the similar Hebrew ark far from unusual and certainly not exceptional in purportedly possessing magical powers of any sort. See "Ark" in *Smith's Bible Dictionary*, 156.
[7] Dunn, J., "Sokar, an Egyptian God of the Underworld."
[8] Dunn, J., "Sokar."

although Plutarch names the god brought out as Harpocrates or "Horus the Child." In consideration of the fact that both Sokar and Horus are sun gods, both are identified with Osiris, both are represented as hawks or falcons as well as the "little sun" or "baby sun," and that the Egyptians associated Horus with Sokar,[1] it would seem again that Plutarch too is correct. Moreover, like Horus, one of Sokar's major roles is that of the *resurrected Osiris*; hence, the baby sun as a hawk/falcon emerges at the winter solstice as the resurrected Osiris. Thus, we can state once more that the Egyptian sun god dies and is reborn at the winter solstice, precisely as we find in other cultures.

Festivals of Isis

As further evidence of the importance of the winter solstice to the Egyptians, in a text from the fourth century BCE called "The Festival Songs of Isis and Nephthys," we find reference to the "Festival of the Two 'Terti," which is the term for Isis and Nephthys "in their character of protectors of the deceased..."[2] In a footnote by Budge, we discover that this festival took place from December 25th to the 29th.[3] Again, the winter solstice is described in an inscription from King Ptolemy VII as "the sun disc coming out of the sky-ocean into the hands of the siblings Isis and Nephthys,"[4] and this festival reminds one of the hieroglyph symbolizing the winter solstice with the two goddesses holding the sun above an ankh, apparently restoring the dead orb to life. Adding to this notion, in his description of Nephthys, Hornung mentions that she is "often depicted together with Isis, either mourning Osiris or keeping the sun disk in motion,"[5] which seems to describe the winter-solstice hieroglyph and its evident life-giving meaning.

Another example of an Egyptian celebration associated with the winter solstice appears in the writings of the Greek astronomer and mathematician Geminos/Geminus (1st cent. BCE?), who claimed that the Greeks of his day had erroneously asserted the Festival of Isis, or "the *Isia*," to have occurred on the winter solstice, but that it had so happened at that time over 120 years prior to the change in the

---

[1] Pyramid text T 196 (PT 364:620b-c): "Horus has lifted you up in his identity of the Sokar-boat and will bear you in your identity of Sokar." (Allen, J., *AEPT*, 81.) At M 375 (PT 610:1712a, c), "Horus says he will akhify his father...as Sokar..." (Allen, J., *AEPT*, 232.) Thus, Sokar is identified with the "akhified" Osiris. The *akh* is the process whereby the deceased's *ba* (soul) is reunited with the *ka* (spiritual body) to produce eternal life. (Allen, J., *AEPT*, 425.) In describing the image of the birth of Horus in the Hall of Ptah (A.17) at Abydos, John Anthony West explains Sokar as "symbolizing Horus-immanent-in-Osiris..." (West, J., *TKAE*, 387.)

[2] Budge, *OHPN*, 398.

[3] Budge, *OHPN*, 398.

[4] Brugsch, *TIA*, II, 427.

[5] Hornung, *AEBA*, 154.

calendar.[1] Adding to this assertion, the *Encyclopedia Britannica* evinces that during certain eras the festival of Isis was indeed celebrated at the winter solstice.[2] In any event, in Geminos we possess yet another testimony that at some point prior to the common era the Egyptians were indeed celebrating at the time of the winter solstice.

Knowing all these facts, it is logical and rational to assume that Geminos, Plutarch, Epiphanius and Macrobius were not in error in their reports about the Egyptian winter-solstice festivals. If Geminos and Epiphanius are right that such winter-solstice celebrations occurred, and if Macrobius is correct in his assertions that the Egyptians brought out an image of the baby sun at that time, we have no credible, scientific reason to dismiss Plutarch's statement regarding Harpocrates/Horus the Child being this baby sun born at the winter solstice, especially since many of his contentions can be verified by the hieroglyphs, as stated by Budge, as well as by the evidence provided by Brugsch. The fact that Harpocrates, the *morning sun*, was born *every* day constitutes proof that Horus was likewise born at the winter solstice. In addition, Egyptian festivities placed Osiris's death and rebirth as Sokar at the winter solstice as well, the newborn sun likewise symbolized as a baby hawk or falcon, as we would expect Horus the Child to be represented.

In *On Mankind: Their Origin and Destiny*, Arthur Thomson summarizes the story of the baby sun at the winter solstice, who was born of a *virgin mother*, specifically as applied to Horus and Isis:

> The Egyptians did in fact celebrate at the winter solstice the birth of the son of Isis (Plut. De Iside), and the delivery of the goddess who had brought this young child into the world, feeble and weak, and in the midst of the darkest night. This child, according to Macrobius, was the god of light, Apollo, or the sun, painted with his head shorn of his beaming hair, his head shaved, and with only a single hair left. By this, says Macrobius, the dimness of the light at the winter solstice, and the shortness of the days as well as the darkness of the deep cave in which this god seemed to be born, and from which he issued forth to rise in the direction of the northern hemisphere and the summer solstice, in which he reassumed his dominion and his glory, was indicated...
>
> It was this child of whom the virgin Isis called herself the mother in the inscription over her temple at Sais (Plut. De Iside) which contained the words, "The fruit which I have begotten is the sun." (Procl. in Tim. p. 30). This Isis of Sais has been correctly assumed by Plutarch to be the chaste Minerva, who, without fearing to lose her name of virgin, nevertheless says of herself that she is the mother of the sun.... She is the Virgin of the constellations, who is called by

---

[1] Mure, 88. Neugebauer placed Geminos in the first century AD/CE, while Jones argued for a date of the first century BCE, which currently constitutes scholarly consensus. (See Evans, 21-22.)
[2] *Encyc. Brit. Supp.*, 50.

Eratosthenes, a learned Alexandrian (Eratosthen. cap. vii.), Ceres or Isis; that Isis who opened the year, and presided over the birth of the new solar revolution, and of the god of day—in a word, of her in whose arms we shall soon see the symbolic child.[1]

From all of the abundant evidence, it is apparent that the winter solstice was a highly important time and included the theme of the baby in a manger born on December 25th for centuries in Egypt long prior to the creation of Christianity and that, as we shall see further demonstrated, the solar babe's mother was deemed a "virgin," precisely as was said of Christ's mother.

As concerns the possible age of the Egyptian winter solstice celebration, continuing one very ancient tradition, modern Egyptians still observe a festival around the vernal equinox called "Sham el-Nessim," or "Shamo," which traditionally occurs in April and resembles the Western holiday of Easter. This festival may be reflected by Plutarch's remarks in chapter 43 of "Isis and Osiris" (368C), in which he discusses a celebration at the new moon in the month of Phamenoth called "Osiris's coming to the Moon," which the historian says "marks the beginning of spring."[2] Since this spring festival of Shamo is estimated to date to at least 4,500 years ago, it would be reasonable to assert that comparable winter-solstice celebrations may approach that age in Egypt as well. Indeed, the evidence indicates the winter solstice in Egypt was recognized at least 5,000 years ago, from the very beginning of Egyptian pharaonic history, extending well into the common era.

Christian Sun Worship?

The fact that the highly important winter-solstice solar festival was not added to the Christ myth until centuries after the purported advent of Jesus does not make the connection any less significant or him any less of a solar hero himself. Concerning this solar celebration and the obvious correlation to Jesus Christ, Kellner states:

> Since on the 21st December the sun reaches its lowest point, and then begins once more to rise higher in the heavens, man, in his simplicity, marked the day on which this change in the sun became perceptible as the new birth or birth-day of the sun, the invincible Sun-God. What was more natural for the Christians of that age than to connect this obvious natural event with the thought of the nativity of Him who is the Light of the World! Even if the Holy Scriptures had not suggested this idea, it must have presented itself to the Christian mind. The comparison of Christ with the sun, and of His work with the victory of light over darkness, frequently appears in the writings of the Fathers. St. Cyprian spoke of Christ as the true sun (*sol verus*). St. Ambrose says precisely, "He is our new sun (*Hic sol novus*

---

[1] Thomson, 468-469.
[2] Plutarch/Babbitt, 105-106.

noster)." Similar figures are employed by Gregory of Nazianzus, Zeon of Verona, Leo the Great, Gregory the Great, etc.[1]

As we have seen from Luke 1:24-27 and John 3:30, it would appear that the "Holy Scriptures" in fact *may* have suggested this idea!

In reality, so common was the contention of *Christians worshipping the sun* that Church fathers such as Tertullian (c. 155-230 AD/CE) and Augustine (354-430 AD/CE) were compelled to compose refutations of the claim. In *Ad Nationes* (1.13), Tertullian writes:

> The Charge of Worshipping the Sun Met by a Retort.
>
> ...Others, with greater regard to good manners, it must be confessed, suppose that the sun is the god of the Christians, because it is a well-known fact that we pray towards the east, or because we make Sunday a day of festivity. What then? Do you do less than this? Do not many among you, with an affectation of sometimes worshipping the heavenly bodies likewise, move your lips in the direction of the sunrise?

Once more, in his *Apology* (16), Tertullian addresses what appears to be a widespread insight that he surprisingly asserts comes from those with "more information" and "greater verisimilitude," or *truth*:

> ...Others, again, certainly with more information and greater verisimilitude, believe that the sun is our god. We shall be counted Persians perhaps, though we do not worship the orb of day painted on a piece of linen cloth, having himself everywhere in his own disk. The idea no doubt has originated from our being known to turn to the east in prayer. But you, many of you, also under pretence sometimes of worshipping the heavenly bodies, move your lips in the direction of the sunrise.

In addition to turning to the east for prayer, early Christians oriented their churches to the sun, a practice that continued into more modern times in some places:

> All our churches are more or less oriented, which is a remnant of old sun-worship. Any church that is properly built today will have its axis pointing to the rising of the sun on the Saint's Day, i.e., a church dedicated to St. John ought not to be parallel to a church dedicated to St. Peter.... Certainly in the early centuries the churches were all oriented to the sun, so the light fell on the altar through the eastern doors at sunrise.[2]

Adding to this knowledge, archaeoastronomer Dr. Ruggles remarks:

> Christian churches generally point eastwards. Liturgical traditions dating from medieval times associate the direction east—the rising

---

[1] Kellner, 151.
[2] Lockyer, *DA*, 95-96.

place of the heavenly bodies and particularly of the sun—with the resurrection of Christ and the dawning of the "day of eternity" for righteous souls.[1]

As can be seen, the association of Christ's resurrection with the sunrise is little different from the same theme of Osiris being resurrected in Horus as the morning sun.

Demonstrating his astrotheological knowledge, Ruggles also comments:

> It is no coincidence...that the date of Christ's nativity was fixed as December 25, the date the Romans believed to be the winter solstice, and which had been established by Aurelian in C.E. 274 as the feast of the birth of the unconquered sun (Natalis Solis Invicti). Neither is it any coincidence that the Christian holy day is named Sunday.[2]

Interestingly, in the Coffin Texts (CT Sp. 196, 207) appear references to the "festival of the seventh day,"[3] instantly reminding one of the Jewish sabbath and the Christian Sunday. Not only is the Sun's day also the Lord's day, but from early times Christ himself was depicted with his face "shining as the sun" (Mt 17:2), as "the light of the world" (Jn 8:12) and "a light from heaven, above the brightness of the sun" (Acts 26:13). Lord Jesus was also called by a number of solar epithets, such as "Sun of Righteousness" (Mal 4:2), "the true sun," "our sun" and the "Sun of the Resurrection."[4] This latter epithet, which sounds very Egyptian, especially as concerns Osiris, was given to Christ by *Clement of Alexandria,* for one.[5] Furthermore, in the late second century Bishop Theophilus of Antioch ("Autolychus," 2.15) specifically stated that the sun is a "type of God," thereby imbuing it with divine qualities and essentially identifying it with Christ, who is likewise a "type of God."

Moreover, the statement in the New Testament book of Revelation (3:14) that Jesus is *"the* Amen" gives another important clue as to his true identity. In the Bible "amen" is αμην in Greek and אמן in Hebrew—who is *"the* Amen?" Although its definition is given differently in biblical translations, typically represented as signifying "so be it," *the Amen* has been suggested to reflect Ammon, Amon, Amun or Amen, meaning "hidden," and representing an old Egyptian god who eventually took on many solar attributes, essentially constituting a sun god, but also symbolizing the "hidden" power behind the sun. Amen/Amun became so powerful that in the Middle Kingdom (2040-1650 BCE) and onward he was deemed "the ultimate

[1] Ruggles, *AA*, 96.
[2] Ruggles, *AA*, 270.
[3] Faulkner, *AECT*, I, 161, 168.
[4] See Gregory Thaumaturgus, "Oration and Panegyric Addressed to Origen"; Augustine, "Tractates on the Gospel of John" (19).
[5] Clement, *Exhortation to the Heathen,* 9.

creator of the world."[1] It is therefore easy to see why Christ would be identified with the Egyptian god as *the* Amen.

The contentions of Christian sun worship based on these various factors continued well into the fifth century, as St. Augustine also was forced to address them in his *Tractates on the Gospel of John* (34), protesting:

> Let us not suppose that the Lord Jesus Christ is this sun which we see rising from the east, setting in the west; to whose course succeeds night, whose rays are obscured by a cloud, which removes from place to place by a set motion: the Lord Christ is not such a thing as this. The Lord Christ is not the sun that was made, but He by whom the sun was made. For "all things were made by Him, and without Him was nothing made."[2]

Although Augustine doth evidently protest too much in attempting to delineate Christ from the physical sun, the fact remains that this distinction is precisely the same as was said of Amen, Re, Osiris and other sun gods or epithets of the sun and/or creators of the solar disc, which was distinguished by the epithet "Aten."

There are in reality numerous astrotheological characteristics within Christianity, many of which can be found not only here but also in my books *The Christ Conspiracy* and *Suns of God*. Indeed, it is apparent from the massive amount of evidence provided here and elsewhere that the figure of "Jesus Christ" constitutes in large part a sun god based on the older solar heroes, including and especially those of Egypt such as Osiris and Horus. It is likely that anyone who wished to turn the popular and powerful sun god into a Jewish messiah, as we contend was done, would not immediately attach anything so obvious as the most well-known solar festival—the birth of the sun god himself—to the myth they were attempting to propagate as "history." The fact that this celebration eventually was added to the expanding Christian mythology indicates: 1. The powers that be had some inkling as to what they were dealing with, i.e., a solar myth; and 2. No birthday of Jesus was previously celebrated to any significant degree. Again, the December 25th date is in reality one of *many* birthdays for Christ proposed by the various Church fathers and Christian authorities over the centuries.[3] In the end, the December 25th birthday represents the birth not of the Jewish messiah but of the *sun*.

From the abundant evidence provided by ancient testimony, hieroglyphs, calendars, monuments, myths, clocks and festivals, it is clear that the Egyptians celebrated at the winter solstice ("December 25th") the restoration, resurrection, renewal or rebirth of the sun in

---

[1] Allen, J., *AEPT*, 425.
[2] Augustine/Dods, 443.
[3] Acharya, *SOG*, 231ff.

one form or another, including as Re, Osiris, Sokar or Horus, at many points in their history from some 5,000 years ago into the common era. It is also apparent from the censorship of various texts over the centuries that there have been serious and prolonged attempts to hide these salient facts.

nen ![hieroglyph], Thes. 408, Wört. 1621, the winter solstice.

Isis and Nephthys holding the baby Sun over the Life-Giving Ankh, representing the Winter Solstice.
(Budge, *An Egyptian Hieroglyphic Dictionary*, 351)

Ptah-Sokar-Osiris and the Ark carrying the baby Sokar
(Wilkinson, *The Manners and Customs of the Ancient Egyptians*, III, 18)

Ark of Horus at Edfu.
(Hancock, *Heaven's Mirror*)

Pharaoh Akhenaton and his wife Nefertiri worshipping the Sun.

"Irish monks raising hands in the ancient Egyptian manner of paying homage to the sun. Cave-chapel of St. Columbanus, St. Peter's Basilica, Vatican City."
(Singh, *The Sun*, 116)

"A second-century polychrome mosaic of the sun god Helios in the pagan tomb, discovered in 1574 beneath St. Peter's Basilica in the Vatican, is now known as Cristo Sole."
(Singh, *The Sun*, 119)

The Virgin Isis-Mery

"…at the last, when [Osiris's] cult disappeared before the religion of the Man Christ, the Egyptians who embraced Christianity found that the moral system of the old cult and that of the new religion were so similar, and the promises of resurrection and immortality in each so much alike, that they transferred their allegiance from Osiris to Jesus of Nazareth without difficulty. Moreover, **Isis and the child Horus were straightway identified with Mary the Virgin and her Son**, and in the apocryphal literature of the first few centuries which followed the evangelization of Egypt, several of the legends about Isis and her sorrowful wanderings were made to centre round the Mother of Christ. *Certain of the attributes of the sister goddesses of Isis were also ascribed to her, and, like the goddess Neith of Sais, she was declared to possess perpetual virginity.* Certain of the Egyptian Christian Fathers gave to the Virgin the title 'Theotokos,' or 'Mother of God,' forgetting, apparently, that it was an exact translation of *neter mut*, a very old and common title of Isis."

> Dr. E.A. Wallis Budge, *The Gods of Egypt* (I, xv-xvi)

"…Horus was not the only sun-god recognised by the Egyptians. His own father Osiris, the Savior (of whom Horus was a re-incarnation), was born—also at the winter solstice—of an immaculate virgin, the goddess Neith, who, like Isis, the mother of Horus, was known by the titles of Mother of God, Immaculate Virgin, Queen of Heaven, Star of the Sea, The Morning Star, The Intercessor."

> William Williamson, *The Great Law: A Study of Religious Origins* (26)

"The miraculous birth of Jesus could be viewed as analogous to that of Horus, whom Isis conceived posthumously from Osiris, and Mary was closely connected with Isis by many other shared characteristics."

> Dr. Erik Hornung, *The Secret Lore of Egypt* (75)

"The Egyptian goddess who was equally 'the Great Virgin' (*hwnt*) and 'Mother of the God' was the object of the very same praise bestowed upon her successor [Mary, Virgin Mother of Jesus]."

> Dr. R.E. Witt, *Isis in the Ancient World* (273)

Over the centuries, a number of individuals have brought to light the obvious correspondences between the Christian Mother of Jesus, the Virgin Mary, and the Egyptian Mother of Horus, the great goddess Isis, as well as the commonality of the miraculous births of their respective offspring, who were both fathered by a god and mothered by an eternal virgin. The similarities between Horus and Jesus's mothers, including both their state of purity and their names, along with these gods' nativities, render the Christian savior's divine birth commonplace and mundane.

As concerns the parallels between Mary and Isis, in *The Egyptian Revival*, Dr. James S. Curl, a professor emeritus at the Queen's University of Belfast, remarks:

...the resemblances between Isis and the Virgin Mary are far too close and numerous to be accidental. There can, in fact, be no question that the Isiac cult was a profound influence on other religions, not least Christianity. As Dr. Witt has noted, the more we probe the mysterious cult of the goddess Isis, the greater that goddess appears in historical terms: Isis was a familiar deity in the cosmopolitan cities of Rome and Alexandria, in the towns of Pompeii and Herculaneum, in the city-states of the Hellenistic period (c. 323-end of the first century BC) in Asia Minor, and throughout Gaul, whilst there was an important Isiac temple in Roman Londinium. She cannot be ignored or wished out of existence, nor can it be assumed that one day in the fifth century of our era she simply vanished from the hearts and minds of men....

...[Isis] was the sacred embodiment of motherhood, yet was known as the Great Virgin, an apparent contradiction that will be familiar to Christians.[1]

Beginning four to five centuries before the common era, the influential gods of the Isiac cult became widespread around the Mediterranean, with Isis emerging as one of the most popular deities at Rome by the first century BCE.[2] As Hornung says, "The beginnings of the 'Isis mission,' as it has been called, can be placed no later than the fourth century B.C.E."[3]

As she traveled around, Isis's form became influenced by the native religious thought, particularly by the Greek, thus becoming "Hellenized." Concerning this development, Morenz states:

In this Grecianized form, Isis penetrated to the furthermore extremities of the Greek and Roman world. As is known, she is to be found in the Danubian lands, in the province of Germania, and even as far north as Hadrian's Wall in Britain.[4]

From Rome, Isis worship spread throughout other parts of the Empire, including Europe and Libya. As Hornung further recounts:

The spread of the cult of Isis began in the fourth century B.C.E. That was when...a temple was founded at Piraeus and another circa 300 at Eretria; others followed on the islands of Delos, Rhodes, Cos, Samos, Lesbos, and Cyprus, and also at Ephesus. At Athens, the cult of Isis lasted until the fourth century C.E. In the western Mediterranean, Sicily was first to have an Isis cult, followed in the second century B.C.E. by the Italian mainland, in particular Pompeii; at this time, Pozzuoli already had a Serapeum of its own. The cult of Isis is attested at Rome as early as Sulla (88-78 B.C.E.), and Isis sanctuaries were gradually established in nearly all provinces of the Roman empire. In particular, it spread via river valleys that were important trade routes, such as the Rhone valley in Gaul, and in Germany, the Rhine valley as far as Cologne. It eventually reached

---

[1] Curl, 12-13.
[2] Budge, *LOLM*, lvii-lviii.
[3] Hornung, *SLE*, 64.
[4] Morenz, 249.

rthwest Holland and England (there was an Iseum in London and a Serapeum in York), and Hungary in the northeast; additionally, it spread to north Africa and Spain.[1]

By the time of the common era, Isis was perhaps the most important deity of the Roman Empire, and, as such, her influence cannot be overstated. Concerning her popularity during the Greco-Roman period, Serry states, "The goddess Isis strongly dominated the religious awareness."[2] Isis's millions of worshippers would no more simply forget her than would the devotees of the Virgin Mary today, without a very powerful and concerted effort to usurp her worship by setting up a competing cult, which is precisely what happened with Christianity.

Concerning the rise of Isis worship, Dr. Delia White relates that the "successful spread of the Isis-Sarapis-Harpokrates cult throughout the Mediterranean vastly increased Isis' importance in the lives of many individuals."[3] As we have already seen, Harpokrates/Harpocrates or "Horus the Child" was a popular god who, obviously, was revered along with his mother as her worship flourished throughout the Roman Empire. Regarding Harpocrates during the Greco-Roman period, Serry states, "His cult spread in Greece and Italy and even reached India. His portraits were a favorite artistic subject for the Ptolemaic and Roman artists."[4] Horus's importance into the common era is indicated as well by a "Horus stela that was set up next to a statue of Isis-Fortuna on the Esquiline Hill" in Rome, with others found "in places such as Byblos, Meroe, and Axum."[5] This Roman stela was one of many Egyptian monuments, including pyramids, which were set up all around the Empire.

At this point in history, the many worshippers of the Egyptian religion around the vast territory of the Roman Empire may have perceived reality in the following manner:

> ...The resurrection of Osiris taught them to believe in the resurrection of the dead, the conception and birth of Horus, preached the doctrine of life arising out of death, the triumph of Horus over Set symbolized the ultimate victory of good over evil, and the sorrows of Isis and her tender mother-love touched all hearts.[6]

From this summary of what the followers of Egyptian religion were taught to believe, we are immediately struck by the profound similarities to Christianity. Concerning this "preparation for Christianity," as apologists over the centuries have disingenuously

---

[1] Hornung, *SLE*, 67.
[2] Goyon, 118.
[3] Clarysse, 550.
[4] Goyon, 121.
[5] Hornung, *SLE*, 68.
[6] Budge, *LOLM*, lviii.

deemed the "uncanny" resemblance between the Egyptian religion and their own faith, Budge states:

> ...the knowledge of the ancient Egyptian religion which we now possess fully justifies the assertions that the rapid growth and progress of Christianity in Egypt were due mainly to the fact that *the new religion*, which was preached there by Saint Mark and his immediate followers, *in all its essentials so closely resembled that which was the outcome of the worship of Osiris, Isis and Horus* that popular opposition was entirely disarmed. In certain places in the south of Egypt, e.g., Philae, the worship of Osiris and Isis maintained its own until the beginning of the fifth century of our era, though this was in reality due to the support which it received from the Nubians, but, speaking generally, at this period in all other parts of Egypt Mary the Virgin and Christ had taken the places of Isis and Horus, and the "God-mother" or "mother of the god," was no longer Isis but Mary whom the Monophysites styled θεοτοκος ["Mother of God"].[1]

Far from being unique to Christianity, the title "Mother of God" was utilized in the Egyptian religion ages before the purported existence of the Virgin Mary, to whom the epithet was a relatively late addition:

> The Egyptian goddess was described by the Egyptians as Mother of God (*Mwt ntr*); this appellation is reprised by the Christians concerning Mary...the first example appearing with Origen in the first quarter of the third century.[2]

In her temple at Philae appear many Ptolemaic-era "hymns to Isis" dating back centuries prior to the common era that include numerous epithets of the goddess, such as not only "Mother of God" or "God's Mother," but also "the Great" and "Giver of Life."[3] Isis was also called "Lady of Heaven, Earth, and the Netherworld," because, according to this theology, she was their creator.[4] Indeed, in demonstrating her function as the creator god, it was said that Isis "brought the world into existence 'through what her heart conceived and her hands created.'"[5] As part of this role of creator, the goddess declares in an aretalogy at Philae, "I regulated the course of the sun and the moon,"[6] much like the biblical god, as at Psalm 74:16 and 8:3.

Regarding the apparent takeover of the Egyptian religion by Christianity, as concerns Isis and Horus in particular, Budge further remarks:

---

[1] Budge, *TGE*, 220-221. (Emph. added.)
[2] Leclant, 44. (My translation from the French.)
[3] Žabkar, 22, etc.
[4] Žabkar, 53.
[5] Žabkar, 53.
[6] Žabkar, 140.

And the bulk of the masses in Egypt and Nubia who professed Christianity transferred to Mary the Virgin the attributes of Isis the Everlasting Mother, and to the Babe Jesus those of Horus.[1]

And once more Budge says, "When the Egyptians embraced Christianity they saw nothing strange in identifying [Isis] with the Virgin Mary, and her son Horus with the Babe Christ."[2] Validating Budge's impression, Hornung also comments on the similarities between Isis and Mary, as well as Jesus and Horus:

> There was an obvious analogy between the Horus child and the baby Jesus and the care they received from their sacred mothers; long before Christianity, Isis had borne the epithet "mother of the god."[3]

As can be seen from these candid remarks by some of the world's foremost experts on Egyptian culture, there is much good reason to make both an Isis-Mary and a Horus-Jesus connection.

Since Isis was one of the most popular deities of the Roman Empire by the time of Christ's alleged advent, many instances of borrowing are probable, including not only iconography but also numerous attributes, such as Isis's virgin-mother status and epithets. As one obvious example of borrowing, there are numerous pre-Christian images of Isis and Horus in the "Madonna and Child" pose precisely as echoed later in depictions of the Virgin Mary and baby Jesus.[4] Thus, it has been asserted by not a few people, quite logically, that the Christian iconography is based directly upon this extremely popular Egyptian image. Concerning this development, Witt states: "The historians of ecclesiastical pictorial art need to bear in mind that the holy pair of Mother and Son had been in vogue for many centuries in the temples of Egypt before the genius of Christendom developed fresh treatments of an age-old subject."[5]

The Beloved Mother of God

In addition to the Egyptian "Madonna and Child" imagery prefiguring its Christian counterpart by centuries to millennia, the Egyptian and Christian Divine Mothers even share the same name, with Jesus's mother named "Mary," of course, while Horus's mother possessed the epithet of "Meri," or "*Mery*," as the Egyptian word 𓄟𓇋𓇋 or 𓄟𓂋𓇋𓇋[6] is transliterated by several scholars, including

---

[1] Budge, *OER*, II, 306.
[2] Budge, *ASH*, 181.
[3] Hornung, *SLE*, 60.
[4] For pre-Christian images of the "Madonna and Child," see my books *The Christ Conspiracy* and *Suns of God.*
[5] Witt, 217.
[6] There are some 2,000 hieroglyphic symbols used over the millennia by Egyptian scribes. Many of these have been categorized by Sir Dr. Alan H. Gardiner, producing "Gardiner's Sign List."

Egyptologists Drs. W.M. Flinders Petrie and Erik Hornung.[1] In addition to the fact that there have been pre-Christian goddesses named "Mari," such as on the Greek island of Cyprus,[2] as well as in the Middle East,[3] in India,[4] and among the Basques,[5] this epithet of "Meri" or "Mery" in Egyptian simply means "beloved," "desired,"[6] "delight"[7] "loving,"[8] "lover"[9] and the "loving one,"[10] and we would thus expect it to have been applied many times in some form or another to the highly esteemed, loving mother Isis during the long history of her reverence by millions of people around the Mediterranean.

Demonstrating that the appellation "Mary" is not unique to the Jewish Mother of God, the important sacred epithet *meri/mery/mry* was attached to numerous figures in ancient Egypt, such as deities, kings, priests, government officials and others. Even Egypt itself is called *Ta-Meri* or *t3 mry*—"beloved land."[11] As stated by Dr. Denise M. Doxey of the Boston Museum of Fine Arts, "Among the most common epithets found in the Middle Kingdom inscriptions are those introduced by a form of the verb *mri*, 'love,'"[12] which is defined also as "want," "wish" and "desire."[13] So important was love or *mrwt* to the Egyptians that they regarded it as "the means by which one achieved a venerated state in the afterlife."[14]

Before the New Kingdom, the bestowal of "divine love" occurred by a "superior" deity upon a human, a subordination that extended down the chain of authority, passed from gods to royals, from royals to non-royal officials, from officials to their wives and relatives, etc.[15] In this regard, Doxey further relates:

> [Egyptologist] W.K. Simpson has studied the concept of divine love, asserting that prior to the New Kingdom, love was always bestowed by a superior upon a subordinate. Simpson's view is certainly correct with regard to the love of gods. During the Middle Kingdom, humans

---

[1] Petrie, 139; Hornung, *VK*, 149, 172. James Allen uses the modern transliteration of *mry* (Allen, J., *ME*, 356, etc.), while Faulkner prefers *mri*. (Faulkner, *CDME*, 111.) Although in Egyptian writing vowels were not used, this transliteration is soundly based, as the term for "beloved" in Coptic is *merit*, essentially the same word. (Lambdin, 57, 240; Good, 51; Budge, *EHD*, 310.) For the *mry* hieroglyphs, see, e.g., Allen, J., *ME*, 33, 42; Budge, *EHRB*, 428.
[2] Graves, 326.
[3] Clifton, 26.
[4] *Gazetteer of the Bombay Presidency*, 308.
[5] Gimbutas, 173.
[6] Allen, J., *AEPT*, 97, 170, etc. In his translation of various Pyramid Texts, Allen prefers "desired" to "beloved."
[7] Faulkner, *CDME*, 111.
[8] Budge, *EHRB*, 429.
[9] Budge, *EHD*, I, 310.
[10] Allen, J., *ME*, 326.
[11] Budge, *AHE*, 306; Labrique, 206.
[12] Doxey, 131.
[13] Faulkner, *CDME*, 92.
[14] Doxey, 131.
[15] Doxey, 131, 132, 136.

always receive divine love; they are never described as "loving" a god.[1]

On some occasions, such as when the king was "beloved by the people," such love or *mri* could apparently be "reciprocated between superiors and subordinates" as well.[2] The clarification of the Middle and New Kingdoms indicates that this custom changed during the New Kingdom, with the use of the *mry* epithet becoming increasingly popular even as applied to deities. It is evident that, especially after the Hellenization of the Ptolemaic and Greco-Roman periods, various Egyptian deities became the *objects* of "divine love" and were themselves invoked as "beloved" or *Mery*. In reality, this ability to bestow *mry* upon even the "chief of all gods" is demonstrated as early as the New Kingdom in a hymn from the Papyrus Kairo CG 58038 (Boulaq 17), parts of which may date to the late Middle Kingdom,[3] such as the 18th Dynasty (1550-1292 BCE), and in which we find the combined god Amun-Re praised as "the good god beloved."[4] Indeed, at P. Boulaq 17, 3.4, we find Amun-Re deemed *Mry*, as part of the epithet "Beloved of the Upper Egyptian and Lower Egyptian Crowns."[5] Amun-Re is also called "beloved" in Budge's rendering of the Book of the Dead created for the Egyptian princess and priestess Nesi-Khonsu (c. 1070-945 BCE).[6]

Concerning the pairing of "Mery" with deities, Doxey comments, "*Mry*, followed by the name of a god or goddess, is the second most common form of epithet referring to deities..."[7] Along with the most common epithet, "venerated by" (*imȝh(y) hr*), these terms represent part of "offering formulas"[8] seen as "referring to deities."[9] In fact, there are various "offering formulas" that end each line with the epithet Meri,[10] making the word highly noticeable. Moreover, when Doxey speaks of the *mry* epithet, she discusses it as "referring to superiors, gods, esteemed ancestors and elder family members."[11] In other words, although technically an epithet may be applied to a king, it nevertheless constitutes a *reference* to the deity as well, a subtlety that needs to be kept in mind when examining the possibility of this epithet's influence on Christianity.

---

[1] Doxey, 132.
[2] Doxey, 192.
[3] Assman, *SGAE*, 195.
[4] *TSBA*, II, 253.
[5] Luiselli, 10: "Geliebter der oberägyptischen und der unterägyptischen Krone." See also the hieroglyphs on p. 56.
[6] Budge, *BD* (1899), 653.
[7] Doxey, 132.
[8] Doxey, 83.
[9] Doxey, 83.
[10] Budge, *CECFM*, 74.
[11] Doxey, 187.

Loved by the Gods

Qualifying its recipient as "beloved" of one god or another, the epithet of Meri/Mery was commonly applied to Egyptian kings and authorities, such as Meri-ab-taui, Meri-Amen-setep, Meri-Aten, Meri-ka-Ra, Meri-mes, Meri-neter and so on.[1] At the Abydos temple, Seti I is called "Mer-n-Ptah," as well as "Mer-Sokar," "Mer-Horus" and "Mery-Osiris."[2] Some of these royal epithets represent "Horus names," while Horus himself is called "beloved"—in other words, *mery*—in the Book of the Dead and elsewhere.[3]

In any event, the epithets "served to link the official" to the "divine and royal superiors" named therein.[4] In this way, many gods had attached to their names the word *meri/mery*, such as Ra-Meri or Mery-Re and Amun-Mery or Meri-Amen, meaning "beloved of Re" and "beloved of Amen," respectively. The combination of the word Mery with the god's name, i.e., Amun, therefore, constitutes an epithet itself, which is distinctly set apart in cartouches sometimes containing only the very simple symbols of the god's name and *mry*. In the case of Meri-Ra, the cartouche merely contains the minimal symbols for the two words in the order of r^c and *mry*: ⊙ ⚊ ⎰⎰ or *Re-Mery*.[5] Furthermore, the symbol for "Mery" in a cartouche may also be the even simpler ⚊,[6] meaning that it can be inserted easily into a hieroglyph, especially a cartouche containing a name. In a chart sampling some Middle Kingdom sites, Doxey lists the following deities, among others, as being "named with mry/mrrw": Anuket, Hathor, Hekat, Heqaib, Horus, Khnum, Ptah-Sokar, Satet, Sekhet, Sopedu, Tayet, Thoth and Wepwawet.[7] The list of deities with the epithet Mery attached to their names also includes: Amun, Maat,[8] Onuris, Amun-Re, Isis, Tefnut, Shu,[9] Atum/Atmu, Montu-Re,[10] Ptah,[11] etc.

In addition to nuances of meaning, the order of the epithet can be switched, as we have already seen with Meri-Ra being also Re-Mery, as in Pepi I's Horus name.[12] In this regard, James Allen relates that "when the king is called the 'beloved' of a god, the god's name is often put first..."[13] In *Middle Egyptian*, Allen further explains:

---

[1] Budge, *BKE*, 243.
[2] Brand, 173.
[3] See, e.g., BD 9 and BD 99. (Faulkner, *EBD*, pl. 18, p. 110; Allen, T., *BD*, 78.)
[4] Doxey, 131.
[5] Budge, *BD* (2003), 600, 22. These hieroglyphs are numbered N5, U7, M17 and M17 in Gardiner's list.
[6] N36 in Gardiner's.
[7] Doxey, 133-134.
[8] Török, *KK*, 201, 203, etc.
[9] Török, *IOW*, 63.
[10] Török, *IOW*, 64.
[11] Budge, *AHE*, 40.
[12] See Budge, *BD* (2003), 600.
[13] Allen, J., *ME*, 42.

Kings are often described as "beloved" of a particular god by means
of the perfective relative form ⳥𓏭 *mry* with the god's name as subject
(often in honorary transposition)...[1]

As other examples of honorary transposition, Dr. Mark Collier, a
senior lecturer in Egyptology at the University of Liverpool, and Dr.
William Manley, a professor of Egyptology at the University of
Glasgow, show Egyptian phrases with the god's name first, such as
"Amun Mery."[2]

As further evidence of this honorary transposition, in which the
god's name appears first in a cartouche, several pharaohs and
Roman Emperors had as part of their names "Auset Meri"[3] and "Ast
Meri"[4]—*Isis Mery*. As one instance of a beloved dignitary, the mother
of the "high official" Het-hert-sa or Sa-Hathor (c. 1922-1878 BCE) was
named "Ast-meri" or *Isis Meri*.[5] The pharaoh Thekeleth/Takeleth/
Takeloth/Takelot II (837-813) was also called "Amen-meri Auset-
Meri."[6] In addition, the cartouche of Caesar Augustus (63 BCE-14
AD/CE) likewise contained the epithet "Ptah Auset-Meri" or "Ptah and
Isis Beloved,"[7] just before the common era. This *mry* popularity would
mean that when someone was called "beloved of Isis" Egyptian
speakers would essentially hear "Mery Isis" or "Isis Mery."

Merry Deities

As an important development over the centuries, Isis's son,
Horus, is said frequently to be "beloved," revealing once more that
deities were included in those who received this epithet of *mry*,
especially in the case of "subordinate" gods and goddesses. Indeed,
under entries in his hieroglyphic dictionary for *Merr* (𓏠𓏭𓏤) and
meri (𓏠𓏭𓏭𓏤), meaning "beloved one," Budge notes the terms
represent "a title of several gods,"[8] as distinguished by the final
symbol/determinative of a male god.[9]

In reality, one of Horus's common titles in the Book of the Dead
(e.g., BD 18) is *Se-meri-f*: "the Beloved Son,"[10] precisely as was said of
Jesus. In the Coffin Texts, Horus is also called "beloved," as at CT Sp.

[1] Allen, J., *ME*, 356.
[2] Collier, 33.
[3] Budge, *Mummy* (1994), 102ff.; Brugsch, *EUP*, xxv.
[4] Budge, *BKE*, II, 159.
[5] Budge, *GEG*, 41.
[6] Budge, *AGTSER*, 206.
[7] Budge, *CH*, 211.
[8] Budge, *EHD*, 310.
[9] The determinative symbol here is A41 in Gardiner's list.
[10] Renouf, *EBD*, 51, 54; Griffiths, *OOHC*, 26. In his translation of chapter 18, Faulkner
relates that the "Horus priest" is referred to as the "Son-Whom-He-Loves Priest."
(Faulkner, *EBD*, pl. 12.) The pertinent symbols here are ⳤ ⳨ (U7 and D21). See also
BD 9, BD 73, BD 78, BD 81 and BD 151. (Budge, *BD* (1899), 57; Budge, *EBD* (1967),
235, 321; Budge, *EHD*, 310; Bunsen/Birch, 166, 215, 221; Faulkner, *EBD*, pls. 18, 26,
33.)

251, where the deceased is deemed, "beloved of my father,"[1] and at CT Sp. 397, in which Horus is "one beloved of my father, whom my father greatly loves."[2] In CT Sp. 784, the deceased is likewise "our son, our beloved."[3] In an inscription regarding one of the Greek rulers of Egypt, the Ptolemies, we find a reference to "Horus, son of Isis, beloved," the word for "beloved" being *meri/mery*.[4] In the hymns at Philae appears a lively dialogue between Isis and the king, in which the goddess is depicted as addressing the ruler as "my son, Horus, my beloved."[5] In the later Greek magical papyri, Horus continues to be deemed "your beloved son."[6]

The important god Osiris too is labeled with the Mery epithet, as in CT Sp. 404 and 405, where Osiris is called the "Well-beloved."[7] In CT Sp. 104, we find a deity labeled as the "Beloved" or "Well-beloved," using the term *mry*, about which Faulkner notes, "The 'Beloved' may be Osiris."[8] In a hymn to Osiris at Philae the god is deemed "beloved of his father..."[9] As another example, BD 69 refers to "the Osiris" as the son of "Nu" and as "her beloved."[10] Osiris has also "come out beloved" at BD 127.[11] In the fifth staircase or portal of BD 148, the speaker says, "...I am the Sun or Osiris the beloved..."[12] In another hymn to Osiris, the god is addressed as "thou gracious one who are beloved..."[13] Moreover, Osiris provides an example of a god clearly loved by *subordinate humans* during the Middle Kingdom, as at CT Sp. 317, in which the speaker identifies himself as the "Nile-god, *whom men love*..."[14]

Isis the Loving and Loved

As we have seen, the epithet Mery Isis or Isis Mery was commonly applied to important dignitaries from an early age into the Greco-Roman era. Anyone who was said to be "loved by Isis" would thus

---

[1] Faulkner, *AECT*, I, 195.
[2] Faulkner, *AECT*, II, 24.
[3] Faulkner, *AECT*, II, 307.
[4] Budge, *AHE*, 210.
[5] Žabkar, 88.
[6] Betz, 328.
[7] Faulkner, *AECT*, II, 48, 51, 54.
[8] Faulkner, *AECT*, I, 101.
[9] Žabkar, 34.
[10] Bunsen/Birch, 212. Faulkner translates the pertinent phrase not as "her beloved" but as "at her desire," providing another definition of *mri*: "to desire." (Faulkner, *EBD*, 107; Faulkner, *CDME*, 111.) In this case, the term rendered as an epithet by Birch is interpreted as a noun by Faulkner, providing another example of how interpretation is at times important and how the Egyptian writing in some instances—particularly with epithets, which may be transposed—is not always set in stone as concerns translations.
[11] Faulkner, *EBD*, 117.
[12] Bunsen/Birch, 300. Faulkner's spell 148 differs from that in Birch.
[13] Budge, *EBD* (1967), lii.
[14] Faulkner, *AECT*, I, 241. (Emph. added.)

carry the epithet "Meri n Iset," "Merniset," "Mer Ast" or "Meri Iset,"[1] etc., by which the title *mry* in connection with Isis would be frequently invoked. The epithet "Mery Isis" or "Isis Mery" might be understood by the Egyptians as referring to the subject, often a king, as not only "beloved of Isis," but also "loved by Isis"[2] or "whom Isis loves."[3] Additionally, wherever Isis was deemed "loving," she would likewise be called *Mer.*[4] As James Allen relates, the Egyptian word *mr* also means "the loving one."[5] In her hymns at Philae, Isis is said to be "great of love,"[6] and "Isis the loving," i.e., "Mery," emerges in a relief also at Philae regarding the evemerized princess Arsinoë, in the phrase *nrt mry(t)*, which Dr. Žabkar translates as "the goddess who loves..."[7] It is apparent from their fervor that Isis's devoted followers felt and evoked love for their *beloved* goddess. From the evidence, it also appears that the bestowal of the epithet of Mery upon Isis may have been emphasized as part of the Hellenization during the Greco-Roman period, leading into the common era.

The association of Isis with the epithet Mery or Mer can also be demonstrated by the fact that she and her sister-goddess Nephthys were called the two "Merti" or "Mertae," as all these terms begin with the same Egyptian symbols: ⳿⳽.[8] Indeed, these etymological connections provide an interesting thesis concerning the Mary and Martha of the New Testament as well:

> Mary is the Egyptian Meri, in its plural form Merti, in Latin Mertae, in Hebrew and German Martha, in Italian Marta.... All irrefutable evidence that the Gospels were merely a re-script of ancient Egyptian literature.[9]

The term "Merti" in reference to "the primeval gods and goddesses" is in fact a plural word beginning with the same signs as Mery.[10] As Renouf remarks, "Merta...is the name given to the goddess pair Isis and Nephthys."[11] While the Egyptian word in BD 58, for example, is *mrti/mrty* or *mrt*, Faulkner labels this pair as the "two Songstress-serpents."[12] "Merti" means "two eyes" as well, and one of Horus's epithets is "Harmerti" or "Horus of the Two Eyes."[13] His

---

[1] Dunand, *Le culte*, 39.
[2] Hölbl, 155.
[3] For examples of epithets translated as "whom Isis loves," see Cotter, 197; Budge, *SA*, lii; Reed, 337; and Griffith, 121.
[4] Egyptian grammar is complicated and is not a subject to be covered here. See Collier, James Allen, et al., for more information.
[5] Allen, J., *ME*, 326.
[6] Žabkar, 153.
[7] Žabkar, 177, 89.
[8] Collier, 109. (Gardiner's U7, D21.)
[9] *Freethinker*, 158.
[10] Budge, *EHD*, I, 310; Renouf, *EBD*, 13.
[11] Renouf, *EBD*, 113.
[12] Faulkner, *EBD*, pl. 16.
[13] Leitz, 787.

father too was named "Osiris Mrty"[1] or *Osiris Merty*. Indeed, concerning the "Merty" addressed in CT Sp. 103, Faulkner notes that it is a "male deity."[2] In the Coptic, the plural of *merit* is ⲙⲉⲣⲁⲧⲉ or *merate*,[3] a word that with two letters transposed would be *mertae*.

Concerning the use of Mery to describe deities, in the *Proceedings* of Birch's Society of Biblical Archaeology, Egyptologist Dr. Alfred Wiedemann (1856-1936), a professor of Oriental Languages at the University of Bonn, states:

> The Egyptian word Meri means, very generally, "the loving or the beloved," and serves in this sense as a title of goddesses, and is as often used as a proper name... [4]

The ever-important Isis was in fact one of these goddesses known by the title of *Meri/Mery*, especially a few centuries before and into the common era. That goddesses were beloved or *mery* is obvious from an enigmatic spell (BD 141) that invokes "the Goddess greatly beloved with red hair"[5] or "Her who is greatly beloved, the red-haired..."[6] Birch renders this phrase "the Greatly beloved, red-haired [Mystical Cow]."[7] The "red of hair," as Faulkner translates the epithet, represents "the Much Beloved," referring to cows,[8] who are undoubtedly representative of Hathor, another "mistress of the gods"[9] and sometime mother of Horus.[10]

In this regard, Massey refers several times to "Hathor-Meri or Isis." After relating that in BD 17 "Osiris-Ani is found in Annu with the hair of Isis spread over him," Massey further states that elsewhere "the hair is assigned to Hathor—one of whose names is Meri."[11] He also discusses "Hathor, who is Meri, the beloved by name in the Ritual,"[12] while, in examining the various Marys in the New Testament, further remarking:

> The Egyptian goddess *Meri* is a form of Hathor.... The name of *Meri* denotes love, the beloved. Hathor=Meri was the Egyptian goddess of

[1] Lloyd, A., 89.
[2] Faulkner, *AECT*, I, 101.
[3] Plumley, 13.
[4] *PSBA*, XI, 272.
[5] Budge, *BD* (1899), 430.
[6] Faulkner, *EBD*, 120.
[7] Bunsen/Birch, 275.
[8] Faulkner, *EBD*, pl. 35.
[9] Lesko, 126.
[10] See, e.g., CT Sp. 331, in which the speaker is Hathor "who brings her Horus and who proclaims her Horus..." (Faulkner, *AECT*, I, 225.) In CT Sp. 334, the speaker is identified as the son of both Isis and Hathor. (Faulkner, *AECT*, I, 257-258.) See also Žabkar regarding Hymn VII to Isis at Philae: "In the same relief of the lintel of Room I, Hathor, too, appears in the role of the mother of the living king, which probably goes back to an early tradition in which Hathor was the mother of Horus." (Žabkar, 132.)
[11] Massey, *AELW*, II, 846.
[12] Massey, *AELW*, II, 844.

love; and the Virgin Mary is, or was, worshipped by the Kypriotes under the name of Aphroditissa.[1]

Massey again says: "To this day the sycamore-fig of Hathor, one of whose characters and names is Meri...is pointed to at Maturea as the tree of Mary and her child."[2] In addition, in numerous of the various hymns inscribed at Dendera appears the phrase "beloved of Hathor"—*mry Ht-ḥr* or "Mery Hathor"—including as concerns Horus, who is also called *mry Ḥr-s3-3st*[3] or "Mery Horus son of Isis." In her chart entitled, "Deities Named with *mry/mrrw*," Doxey lists Hathor as receiving the epithet in nine inscriptions found at the Middle Kingdom sites of Beni Hassan, Serabit el Khâdim and the West Nubian Desert alone.[4] Hathor is, in fact, "frequently named in the epithets of women throughout Egypt,"[5] and hers is a name commonly associated with Mery.

Increasingly in the Greco-Roman period onward, Hathor is also associated or identified with Isis, as Isis-Hathor,[6] who had her temple at Dendera[7] and who was identified with the Greek goddess of *love*, Aphrodite,[8] as was purportedly also the Virgin Mary on the Greek island of Cyprus, not far from Egypt.[9] Isis is thus strongly associated with love, which is *mri* in Egyptian. Moreover, shortly before the common era, Isis had "completely assimilated" Hathor,[10] presumably absorbing her epithets as well.

As examples of the increasing use of "beloved," "loving" or "lover" as an epithet for Isis during the Greco-Roman period, in *The Isis-*

---

[1] Massey, *NG*, II, 461-462.
[2] Massey, *NG*, I, 375.
[3] Cauville, 120.
[4] Doxey, 133.
[5] Doxey, 84.
[6] Heyob, 49; Meyboom, 35, 38, 59, 60, 78, etc.
[7] Meyboom, 59.
[8] Heyob, 49.
[9] Dr. Hauben argues that the "Panayia Aphroditissa"—a Greek title of the Virgin Mary based on the ancient worship of Aphrodite—is a myth that lacks the evidence of historical continuity between the cults of the Greek goddess and Jewish Mother of God. In attempting to delineate Mary from Aphrodite, Hauben nevertheless states: "It is a commonly accepted fact that more or less similar patterns underlie the popular cults of old Mother Goddesses like Aphrodite and Isis, and that of the Christian Virgin Mary in more recent times." (Janssen, 281ff.) If Isis, Aphrodite and Mary are linked by underlying similar patterns, combined with intriguing archaeological remains—in this case a chapel built in the 12th to 14th centuries AD/CE adjoining the site of a sanctuary dedicated to Aphrodite temple (Janssen, 282)—it is certainly logical to examine for historical continuity. Our quest may be satisfied by the work of Dr. Emilia D. Vassiliou of University College London in surveying the "continuity of worship of Aphrodite at Paleopaphos from the Bronze Age to classical antiquity, and its later tradition in Christian churches in the area (one of them named Our Lady Aphroditissa)," as published in a peer-reviewed journal. (Tsetskhladze, 432, citing Muskett.) In this article, Vassiliou remarks: "Another example of the long-standing influence of Aphrodite worship can be found in the district of Paphos, where the ruins of an orthodox church are dedicated to Our Lady Aphroditissa..." (Muskett, 75.)
[10] Witt, 124.

Book (Metamorphoses, Book XI), Griffiths discusses an inscription from Thessalonica, Greece, in which "Osiris is said to 'make the beloved Isis rejoice'..."[1] In a Greek magical papyrus (PGM IV.2785-2890), the moon goddess Selene—the Greek equivalent of Isis who is combined at times as "Isis-Selene,"[2] a "very popular figure" in the Roman Empire[3]—is invoked as "O beloved mistress."[4] In the common era, Plutarch (2, 351E) termed Isis "wise and wisdom-loving" or "lover of wisdom,"[5] the Greek word being φιλόσοφος or *philosophos*, serving as an epithet. By the time of the Latin writer Lucius Apuleius (c. 123/125-180 AD/CE), Isis was the "All-Loving Mother,"[6] a name that would also bestow upon her the *meri* epithet in Egyptian.

In consideration of the popularity of the *mry* epithet and its prominence in cartouches, it would be understandable for non-native Egyptian-speaking followers of the religion to be struck by the association of Mery with various gods and goddesses, including the much loved Isis, and to view the term as an epithet of the deity him or herself. This increasing association during the Greco-Roman period would explain the epithet's presence in Greek texts representing "beloved Isis," as well as how Isis eventually morphed into *Mary*. The non-native speakers who were responsible for the creation of Christianity would likely not be interested in any finer points of Egyptian grammar—some of which evidently had not been adhered to strictly for several centuries—but would merely emulate the longstanding epithet of divine love *mry* in determining the name of their heroine.

The question of whether or not Isis herself was the recipient of divine love is addressed briefly by Žabkar, who raises the Greek phrase by which she is called in a papyrus at Oxyrhynchus (1380): αγαπην Θεων, meaning "the love of the gods"[7] and thereby reflecting the development of labeling her *Mery*. In his discussion of this subject, Žabkar states:

> As to the possible meaning of the phrase "the love of the gods" as "beloved by the gods," implying that Isis herself is the object of divine love, one recalls that in Hymn V at Philae the goddess is said to be "beloved of the Great Horus"...[8]

We have seen that by the Greco-Roman period Isis was esteemed as "beloved" and "loving" in Greek. From the hymns in her temple at Philae, we discover that in the Ptolemaic period Isis was definitely deemed *Mery* in Egyptian as well, such as in Hymn V, in which Isis is

---

[1] Griffiths, *IB*, 350.
[2] Turcan, 161.
[3] Brenk, 766.
[4] Betz, 90.
[5] Witt, 22; Plutarch/Babbitt, 9.
[6] Witt, 130ff, 133. See also Fairservis, 171.
[7] Žabkar, 154.
[8] Žabkar, 154.

called "beloved"—*Mry(t)*—twice, using the single hieroglyph ⌐.[1] In one stanza of this hymn, Isis is labeled, "The female Horus, beloved of the Great Horus," while in another she is the "daughter of Re, beloved of his very heart."[2] In Hymn IV, found in Room X above the main text, Isis is called "the Great, God's mother, Lady of Philae, Lady of Heaven, Mistress of all gods, the beloved, giving life like Re..."[3] In the transliteration, therefore, appears the word *mry(t)*.[4] Again, in a hymn in Room VII, Isis is labeled "Beloved of Re"—*Mry(t) Rˁ*— as she is also in Hymn VIII, using the same hieroglyph as in Hymn V.[5]

In the transliteration *Mry(t)* or *merit*, the feminine suffix "t" is used to emphasize that it is Isis who is the subject of the epithet: She herself is the beloved. However, the final "t" was eventually unwritten and unspoken, as Wiedemann relates: "In later times the pronunciation of the *t* was dropped..."[6] We are told by Serge Rosmorduc from Université Paris VIII that leaving the final "t" in a word silent began occurring as early as the Middle Kingdom and that by the Late Kingdom, "it was no longer useful to write it." In the original Egyptian passage, therefore, appears no "t," which is why the transliteration places the letter in parentheses. In the end, it is evident that Isis was simply called by the epithet of *Mery*.

Whether she was deemed "Isis the Beloved" or "Isis the Loving," the goddess was nevertheless associated frequently with the epithet of *mry*, as Mery Isis/Isis Mery. An individual in Egypt may have heard or read the epithet "Mery Isis" or "Isis Mery" many times, regardless of whether it was applied to a mortal or to the goddess herself. Since "beloved of Isis," *mry ꜣst*, or "Mery Isis/Isis Mery," was a common epithet, anyone wanting to usurp Isis's power would likely wish to incorporate this popular "loving" title.

In addition, the title of "beloved" lasted long into the common era, and the word *merit* appears over 50 times in the Coptic translation of the New Testament.[7] Jesus himself is called "beloved" or *Merit* in the Coptic NT, as at Matthew 3:17, 17:5; Mark 1:11, 9:7; and Luke 3:22.[8] In the Gnostic texts, it is *Mary Magdalene* who is repeatedly referred to as "the beloved" and "the beloved disciple," likely reflecting her role as one aspect of the "triple goddess," also identified with Isis. From all of the evidence, it is clear that early Christians made the

---

[1] Žabkar, 57. (Gardiner's N36.)
[2] Žabkar, 58.
[3] Žabkar, 51.
[4] Žabkar, 168.
[5] Žabkar, 90, 118, 119.
[6] Wiedemann, *RAE*, 16.
[7] Metzger, *LWOF*, 8.
[8] Horner, I, 18, 146, 286; II, 40. The word in the references from the Northern Dialect (Memphitic and Bohairic) is part of the compound ⲡⲁⲙⲉⲛⲣⲓⲧ, ⲡⲁ meaning "my." The word for "beloved one" in Coptic is generally ⲙⲉⲣⲓⲧ. (Plumley, 13.)

identification between the Egyptian Mother of God Mery and the Jewish Mother of God Mary.

Mery, Miriam and Mary

Naturally, the connection between Mery and Mary has been noted many times in the past and into the present. In the original Greek of the New Testament, the name for Jesus's mother is "Maria." However, one must ask why the name was shortened to "Mary"—was it because, centuries into the common era, Isis remained a *beloved* goddess dubbed "Mery?" When was Maria first called "Mary," and by what mechanism did this change occur? Early Christians noted the similarity between Maria and "mare" or "mari," meaning "sea" in Latin, as in "stella maris." Thus, it appears that Mary was called as such fairly early, certainly long before the time Isis worship had disappeared openly. In any event, it would be beyond "coincidence" that *an Egyptian virgin mother of God was evidently called Mery centuries before the Jewish virgin mother of God was likewise named.*

The accepted opinion concerning the origin of the name Mary is that it comes from the Hebrew "Miriam," which means "rebellion." However, as is frequently the case within the field of etymology, this point is debatable, since the New Testament Mary certainly does not epitomize "rebellion," in reality representing *utter submission* to God, and the epithet "beloved" would be much more suitable, especially in consideration of our discussion of "superiority" and "subordination."

In *Faiths of Man*, Major-General James G.R. Forlong (1824–1904) remarks in his entry about "Mary. Miriam": "As a Semitic name this has no true derivative, though it has been connected with Marah 'bitter.'"[1] Moreover, Forlong's editor notes, "As Egyptian, however, *Meri-amu* may mean 'mother's love,' and Miriam the sister of Moses, after whom Mary was called, has been thought to bear an Egyptian name."[2] In this same manner, under the entry "Virgin Mary," the *Catholic Encyclopedia* relates:

> Fr. von Hummelauer...mentions the possibility that miryam may be of Egyptian origin. Moses, Aaron, and their sister were born in Egypt.... hence, it is possible that their sister's name Mary was also of Egyptian origin....[3]

In an article in *The Contemporary Review* under the entry for "Miriam," Rev. Dr. William Robertson Smith (1846-1894), a professor at the University of Cambridge and editor for the *Encyclopedia Britannica*, ventures a derivation of the name as "probably the Egyptian Meri-(t)," meaning, "beloved, a woman's name..."[4] The same logical association of *Meri* and *Mary* is posited by Rev. Henry

---

[1] Forlong, 505.
[2] Forlong, 505.
[3] *CE*, XV, 464a.
[4] *TCR*, 362.

Tompkins in *Journal of the Transactions of the Victoria Institute*: "May not Miriam be one of the many Egyptian names beginning with Meri?"[1]

Thus, research has indicated that "Miriam" is "probably of Egyptian derivation," explaining that the name may be equivalent to *meri-amu* or to "*mer Amon (Amun),* 'beloved of Amon'..."[2] As also proposed in *Faith and Thought*, "Was the name of *Miriam* Egyptian— *Meri-Ammon*, "the Beloved of Ammon?"[3] In addition, the goddess name "Mari-amma" appears in Dravidian (Indian) mythology,[4] providing another mythical precedent for the Lady Mary or *Miriam*.

This obvious Mary-Mery connection has been duly noted and carried into the current scholarship as well. Under his entry of "Miriam," Dr. James Karl Hoffmeier, a professor of Old Testament and Ancient Near Eastern History and Archaeology at Trinity Evangelical Divinity School, states:

> ...The sister of Moses and a prophetess, like her brother, appears to have an Egyptian name. Although there are different linguistic explanations for the second *mem*, there is agreement that *mary* is the writing for the root *mry*, meaning "love" or "beloved," just as was proposed with Miriam's ancestor, Merari. This is behind the name Mary in the New Testament, and of course continues to be used in the twenty-first century. Alan Gardiner considered this to be one of several ancient Egyptian names that has survived into English.[5]

In his article in the *Journal of American Oriental Society* entitled "The Egyptian Origin of Some English Personal Names," Gardiner discusses the origins of certain biblical names:

> The majority of scholars...have settled down to the comfortable belief that Moses is really an Egyptian name.[6]

Gardiner further states, "The best argument in favour of the derivation of Mōsheh-Moses from the Egyptian Mōse is that there is no other derivation as good."[7] But, he also notes, "And, on due reflection, would it not be more scientific to admit that we have no satisfactory evidence for choosing any derivation at all?" He continues to aver that "at least as good a case can be made out for an Egyptian derivation of Miriam as has been made for Moses."[8] In presenting the case, Gardiner also refers to receiving "warm approval" for various of

---

[1] *JTVI*, 137.

[2] Thorburn, 9. Christian apologist Thorburn calls the theory "equally remote with that of Doctor Schmiedel from the one sought to be established by the mythicists."

[3] *FT*, 146.

[4] Hewitt, 31.

[5] Hoffmeier, 225, citing Alan H. Gardiner, "The Egyptian Origin of Some English Personal Names," *JAOS* 56 (1936): 194-196.

[6] Gardiner, *JAOS*, 192.

[7] Gardiner, *JAOS*, 194.

[8] Gardiner, *JAOS*, 194.

his theses,[1] as well as that the Egyptian derivation of the biblical name Potiphera is admitted by "all sensible scholars."[2]

In his discussion of the Egyptian derivation of the name Miriam, which is alleged to be the origin of "Mary," Gardiner says:

> No Egyptian personal names are commoner than what the hieroglyphs write as *Mry* or the masculine and as *Mryt* for the feminine, meaning either "The-beloved" absolutely or "The-beloved" as shortening of some theophorous name like *Imn-mryt* (doubtless to be read *Mryt-Imn*) "The-beloved-of-Amūn." At some time or other *Mryt* was doubtless vocalized Marye, since we have in Coptic a well-authenticated perfect passive particle from another verb... [3]

In a note addressing the order of the epithet *Imn-mryt* or Amun-Meryt, Gardiner says that "[d]ivine names were often written *honoris causa* in front of words which they followed in actual speech."[4] In other words, here is another instance of honorary transposition. Again, Gardiner remarks:

> ...It seems impossible not to think of the Egyptian goddesses and priestesses who were called *Mrt*, i.e., in all probability Marye "the-beloved..."[5]

Gardiner's remarks reveal that it is often scholarly consensus based on serious study, as opposed to a pristine "smoking gun" artifact, that determines an accepted fact. Such educated speculation constitutes, in reality, the reason for scholarly, peer-reviewed journal articles in the first place. In this same manner, Gardiner presents his convincing and "comfortable" case that Mary is Miriam is Mery, revealing that the Mrt-Mery-Marye-Mary connection constitutes a scientifically sound thesis.[6]

In the end, the assertion that "Isis was never called Mery" remains unsustainable and erroneous, as not only was the Great Lady much *beloved* by many millions of people over a period of centuries to millennia but also, as we have seen, she was most

---

[1] Gardiner, *JAOS*, 193.
[2] Gardiner, *JAOS*, 194.
[3] Gardiner, *JAOS*, 195.
[4] Gardiner, *JAOS*, 195.
[5] Gardiner, *JAOS*, 196.
[6] Nevertheless, after essentially proving that Moses and Mary are of Egyptian origin, Gardiner does an about-face in the last sentence that debunks the thesis, claiming that the Egyptian origin of the names Moses and Miriam are "extremely doubtful" and leaving us to wonder about a possible fear of backlash, as has happened to so many others. (Gardiner, *JAOS*, 197.) Knowing how the censorship gears have ground scholars down, we may logically suspect an agenda of not wishing to offend religious sensibilities. Obviously, we believe that Gardiner demonstrated satisfactorily scientific arguments to *prove* the thesis that the derivation of Mary is the Egyptian Mery. Adapting Gardiner's own words concerning the name biblical Phineas obviously being Egyptian, it would "demand an excessive skepticism to reject" the etymology of Mary from Mery. (Gardiner, *JAOS*, 192.) It is apparent from Dr. Hoffmeier's comments that he too has chosen to ignore Gardiner's disclaimer.

definitely labeled many times during that period with the epithet of *Mery* in the Egyptian, centuries prior to the common era.

Perpetual Virginity

The assertion that Horus's mother was called "Mery" is sound and important, as is the claim that, like her Christian counterpart, the Egyptian Mother of God was deemed an "immaculate virgin."[1] As we have already seen, Church father Epiphanius related that the Egyptians did indeed celebrate a *virgin mother*, although in his account these were Greek followers of the goddess Kore at Alexandria. This information was evidently too threatening to the Church, however, such that it was expurgated from at least one edition of Epiphanius's work. Nevertheless, this virgin mother, says Campbell, is a "Hellenized transformation of Isis," and, during the first century BCE, Diodorus equated Isis with Demeter, Kore's *virgin mother*.[2] Like Diodorus, the poet Apuleius likewise identified Isis with Demeter in his famous work *The Golden Ass* (11.2).[3] As we have also seen, Cosmas of Jerusalem speaks of the same festival as Epiphanius, with "Hellenes" (Greeks) shouting that "the virgin has brought forth, the light grows."[4] Combining these and other testimonies with the fact of various goddesses such as Isis being called "virgin" in ancient Egyptian texts, and it is obvious that in Egypt existed pre-Christian precedents of the virgin mother.

The Paschal Chronicle

Another Christian source for the theme of *the Egyptian virgin-mother goddess and her babe in a manger* is the Chronicon Paschale or Paschal Chronicle, also known as the Chronicle of *Alexandria*, compiled beginning in the third century AD/CE and ending in the sixth to seventh centuries. In *The Origin of All Religious Worship*, French Abbé Charles Francois Dupuis (1742-1809), a professor at the Collège de France, describes the Chronicon:

...the author of the Chronicle of Alexandria...expresses himself in the following words: "The Egyptians have consecrated up to this day the child-birth of a virgin and the nativity of her son, who is exposed in a 'crib' to the adoration of the people. King Ptolemy, having asked the reason of this custom, he was answered that it was a mystery, taught by a respectable prophet to their fathers."[5]

Also verifying these assertions, Arthur Thomson states:

The Chronicle of Alexandria has preserved the tradition of the practice of exhibiting the sun on the supposed day of his birth as a

---

[1] See also Acharya, *SOG*, 200-201.
[2] Diodorus/Murphy, 31.
[3] Apuleius/Adlington, 336.
[4] Talley, 107; Machen, 346, citing "Cosmas Hierosolymitanus, *in carm. Greg. Naz.*, in Migne, *Patrologiae cursus completus*, series Graeca prior, xxxviii, col. 464."
[5] Dupuis, 237.

new-born infant as being held sacred in the mysteries of Egypt... "Up to the present time Egypt has held sacred the delivery of a virgin and the birth of her son, who is exposed in a cradle to the adoration of the people. King Ptolemy having asked the reason of this practice, the Egyptians told him that it was a mystery taught to their ancestors by a venerable prophet."[1]

The original Greek of the Chronicon Paschale first discusses the Hebrew prophet Jeremiah and then the motif of the virgin mother and divine babe in a manger:

Οὗτος ὁ Ἰερεμίας σημεῖον ἔδωκεν τοῖς ἱερεῦσιν Αἰγύπτου ὅτι δεῖ σεισθῆναι τὰ εἴδωλα αὐτῶν καὶ συμπεσεῖν διὰ σωτῆρος παιδὸς ἐκ παρθένου γενομένου, ἐν φάτνῃ δὲ κειμένου. Διὸ καὶ ἕως νῦν θεοποιοῦσιν παρθένον λοχὸν καὶ βρέφος ἐν φάτνῃ τιθέντες προσκυνοῦσιν.[2]

This passage is translated quite literally by me thus:

This Jeremiah gave a sign to the Egyptian priests that their idols would be shaken, and it would come to pass by a child-savior born from a virgin, lying in a manger. Therefore, for some time now they deify a virgin child-bearer and worship a newborn child placed in a manger.

"This Jeremiah," of course, refers to the biblical prophet, who supposedly lived in the seventh century BCE. It seems that the Chronicle author(s) was attempting to explain why the Egyptians worshipped a virgin-mother and her babe in a manger centuries *before* the Christian era, when Christ's identical circumstances were supposed to be unique. However, Isis and Horus were revered long before even the time of Jeremiah, and the evidence points to the motif of the virgin-mother and babe predating the common era and being usurped by the creators of the Christ myth.

As noted previously, the Chronicle author next relates that after "King Ptolemy" inquired as to the reason for this tradition, he was informed it was a *mystery* handed down by a "holy prophet" to "their forefathers." Hence, we possess a Christian account admitting that

---

[1] Thomson, 481. Citing the "*Chronicum Alexandrinum*" (366) as his source, Thomson provides the original Greek, which does indeed say what it is alleged to relate, the pertinent word here being *parthenos* or "virgin": "Εως νυν Αιγυπτιοι θεοποιουσιν Παρθενον λοχον και ΒρεΦος εν Φατνη τιθεντες προσκυνουσιν. Και Πτολεμαιω τω Βασιλει την αιτιαν πυνθανομενω ελεγον, οτι παραδοτον εστι μυστηριον υπο οσιου Προφητου τοις πατρασιν ημων παραδοθεν." This citation refers to an edition published in the 17th century that is evidently slightly different than the one provided in the text here.

[2] *Chronicon Paschale* in Migne, "Documenta Catholica Omnia," lines 02465-02466. The pertinent passage can be found in Migne's *Patrologia Graeca*, xcii, or "PG92," at column 385, section 157. The Latin as found in Migne (col. 386) is: "Hic Jeremias signum dedit Ægyptiis sacerdotibus, quo futurum praedixit ut eorum idola concuterentur et conciderent per Salvatorem purem ex Virgine natum, et in prasepi jacentem. Quapropter etiamnum ut deam colunt virginem puerperam, et infantem in praesepi adorant. Ptolemæo autem regi causam sciscitanti, responderunt se accepisse arcanum istud ab sancto propheta patribus suis traditum."

this Egyptian tradition and *mystery* of the virgin-born divine son in a manger dates to at least a century before the common era, with the Chronicle author's apology regarding Jeremiah pushing it centuries farther back! It is clear from his remarks, including the comment that this tradition had been going on for "some time now," that the Chronicle author believed it to be many centuries old by his time. Indeed, if the tradition did in fact emanate from Jeremiah's time, by the final Chronicle author's era, it would be over 1,000 years old.

To emphasize, this part about Ptolemy and the mysteries is important for a couple of reasons: Firstly, it means that this custom of bringing forth the newborn sun of the virgin mother dated back at least to the time of the Ptolemies, centuries prior to the common era; and secondly, the custom being a *mystery* indicates it was not necessarily stressed to the masses, such that we do not find it recorded in numerous sources from the pertinent period. Nevertheless, as we have seen here the virgin-mother motif constituted an important religious concept well known enough in antiquity to those movers and shakers who create religions, i.e., the priesthoods, which in Egypt and elsewhere included the rulers themselves.

In addition, the "manger" or "crib" aspect of the solar hero's birth is reflected in the Book of the Dead: In chapter 69, the speaker identifies himself as several of the gods—such as Osiris, Horus and Anubis—once again demonstrating their interchangeability, and reference here is made to the "cradle of Osiris," which Renouf identifies as "where Osiris renews his birth."[1] Osiris's "renewed birth," of course, would be his son Horus.

Son of Neith

Combining all of these factors, including Plutarch and Macrobius, we receive the impression of *Horus* being the son of the *virgin mother* celebrated in Egypt centuries before the common era. Moreover, the assertion that Horus's mother was a virgin can likewise be found in BD 66, in which the deceased identifies himself as Horus and says: "I know that I have been conceived by Sechit and that I am born of Neith."[2] Birch renders the pertinent part, "I know that I was begotten [said] by Pasht, brought forth [said] by Neith. I am Horus..."[3] Budge's translation of the same passage is as follows: "I was conceived by the goddess Sekhet, and the goddess Neith gave birth to me. I am Horus..."[4]

---

[1] Renouf, *EBD*, 131-132. Faulkner calls it the "birth-stool of Osiris" and Sir Budge terms it the "birth-chamber." (Faulkner, *EBD*, 108; Budge, *BD* (1899), 235.) The "birth-stool" of Osiris is also mentioned at CT Sp. 286. (Faulkner, *AECT*, I, 214.)

[2] Renouf, *EBD*, 128.

[3] Bunsen/Birch, 210.

[4] Budge, *BD* (1898); (1899) 228. This chapter appears in the Theban recension and is missing from the Papyrus of Ani. Faulkner's translation of the relevant part of ch. 66 is

Sechit, Sekhet or Sekhmet is the wife of Ptah and mother of the god Atum, representing the "second personage of the Memphis triad,"[1] one of the Egyptian "holy trinities." Identified with the goddess Hathor,[2] who in turn is identified with Isis, Sekhet represents another form of the Dawn goddess.[3] Not surprisingly, in the mythology of other cultures, such as the Indian and Greek, appears the same theme of the personified and deified Dawn giving birth to the sun, as *the inviolable or virgin mother*.[4] While "Pasht" is a different goddess from Sechit, she is equivalent to the goddess Bubastis, who is identified with the Greek goddess Artemis or the Roman Diana,[5] famed for being a *virgin* goddess.

In this ancient text the Egyptian Book of the Dead, we also possess an identification of the mother of Horus as the goddess Neith, who in turn is represented as a virgin mother from thousands of years prior to the common era. In fact, certain scholarship provides for estimates of the pre-historic Neith's worship dating back some 7,000 years.[6] In his analysis of archaic creation stories, anthropologist Dr. Wim van Binsbergen (b. 1947), chairman of the Foundations of Intercultural Philosophy at Erasmus University, discusses the Egyptian Neith tale as an example of "female parthenogenetic cosmogenesis."[7] In other words, Neith is a virgin-mother goddess—and, per Dr. van Binsbergen's study, such parthenogenesis or *virgin birth* constitutes a common cosmogonic theme dating to at least as early as the Neolithic period, some 5,000 to 8,000 years ago.

---

as follows: "I know that I was conceived by Sekhmet and borne by Satis. I am Horus." (Faulkner, *EBD*, 107.) Satis is a relatively obscure goddess of Elephantine, who was "associated with Khnum" (Faulkner, *EBD*, 175). Faulkner's reasoning for identifying the hieroglyph as Satis, as opposed to Neith, as found in the other translations, is unclear, although it may have to do with the former's status as a fertility goddess. Neith, of course, is also a fertility goddess, serving as the "Mother of the gods." The hieroglyph in question depicts a goddess with the Deshret crown on her head and a loom or shuttle next to her, an image traditionally symbolic of Neith. (See Wilkinson, J., *MCAE*, III, 42 and Allen, J., *ME*, 440.) Allen cites this symbol as Gardiner's R24: ⋈. The Deshret crown represents *Lower* Egypt, whereas Satis is from *Upper* Egypt. Perhaps Faulkner supposed the shuttle symbol in question to be a bow, representing Satis. In any event, Neith too is symbolized by a bow, although not in this particular hieroglyph. Even if it were of Satis, she is identified with Isis, so the passage in the BD would remain somewhat appropriate to our analysis. However, the goddess in question appears to be *Neith*, not Satis, which is logical if we factor in the relationship between Nut, Osiris's mother, and Horus, brother of Osiris, likewise born of Nut, who, it has been suggested, was identified with Neith. Hence, in this case Neith/Nut would be Horus's mother, as in the BD.

[1] Wilkinson, J., *MCAE*, III, 39.
[2] Lockyer, *DA*, 211.
[3] Lockyer, *DA*, 31.
[4] See Acharya, *SOG*, 178, 180, 182, 199, 202, 205, 214, 222.
[5] Rawlinson, *HH*, 103.
[6] Bonwick, 114.
[7] van Binsbergen, 35.

Another example of a virgin mother who predated Christianity by millennia is the goddess Anat or Anath, popular in the Middle East from Ugaritic times into the Roman era. Anat/Anath is called the "Mother of Gods" and the "wetnurse of the gods"; yet, in the epic of Keret, she is deemed the "Virgin Anat"[1]: "Although she is regarded as the mother of gods, the most common epithet at Ugarit is batulat, *Virgin* or *Maiden*,"[2] a term related to the Hebrew word *bethulah*.[3] As stated by Dr. Barbara S. Lesko of the Department of Egyptology at Brown University, "Indeed, Anath is often referred to as a virgin."[4] According to Dr. Karel van der Toorn (b. 1956), President of the University of Amsterdam, who along with Drs. Bob Becking and Pieter W. van der Horst of the University of Utrecht edited the *Dictionary of Deities and Demons in the Bible*, the "predominant view among scholars is that the Ugaritic texts present Anat as a 'fertility goddess' who is the consort of Baal. It is also stated that she is the mother of Baal's offspring."[5]

In Egypt, we find a similar role as that of Anat representing the virgin as well as a wetnurse: The Egyptian word *renen-t* or *rnnt* (⊂ ⎯ ⎯ ◦) means "wetnurse,"[6] for one. However, changing the determinative—the symbol placed at the end of the word imparting further meaning—creates other words such as "a girl, virgin, young woman,"[7] similar to the Hebrew term *almah*. With different determinatives, *rnnt* can also mean Amun[8] and "the nurse-goddess."[9] That the Egyptians valued virginity is indicated also by the word "Nefrit," *nefer-t* or *nfrt* (𓄤 ⎯ ◦ 𓁐), which means "the good, or beautiful, goddess, the virgin-goddess,"[10] as well as "virgin."[11] Avoiding the word "virgin," Faulkner renders the same Egyptian term as "fair woman."[12]

---

[1] van der Toorn, 37, 177.
[2] Ellison, "Anat, Mother of Gods."
[3] Botterweck, 340.
[4] Lesko, 47.
[5] van der Toorn, 36. However, these authors proceed to relate recent controversy as to Anat's procreative and sexual role, a debate that may be motivated in part at least by a tendency to question inferences of a pre-Christian virgin mother. Concerning the "virgin" epithet of the Ugaritic goddess Anat, *btlt*, which is cognate with the Hebrew *bethulah* (Botterweck, 340), Bergman-Ringgren state, "However, it is not entirely clear what this means. Obviously Anat is not a virgin in the modern sense of the word, since she has sexual intercourse repeatedly." (Botterweck, 339-340) Nevertheless, the "born-again virgin" *mystery* is clear, and once we understand it, we can see that the ancients did indeed mean that the goddess regained her *physical* virginity, in a manner of speaking.
[6] Faulkner, *CDME*, 150. (Gardiner's D21, N35, N35, X1)
[7] Budge, *EHD*, 426.
[8] Budge, *EHD*, 426.
[9] Faulkner, *CDME*, 151; Budge, *EHD*, 426.
[10] Budge, *EHD*, 371.
[11] Budge, *EHD*, 372.
[12] Faulkner, *CDME*, 132. A search across many books dealing with Egyptian hieroglyphs, including dictionaries, reveals a trend avoiding reference to the term "virgin," which nevertheless existed in the Egyptian language. Indeed, there is little

In any case, Anat was likewise worshipped in Egypt and may have been identified with the goddess Neith, which would be appropriate in consideration of her role as Virgin Mother.[1] In Egyptian, Neith is "NT," also transliterated as "Nat" or "Net," and she has further been identified as and/or with the goddess Nut, Nout or Mut, mother of Osiris and *Horus the Elder* (Haroeris).[2]

Concerning Nut, James Allen remarks:

> As the sky itself, the goddess Nut was not merely the surface across which the sun traveled by day but also the Sun's mother. The solar god was thought to gestate at night within her womb and to be born at dawn from between her thighs.[3]

Hence, in the sky-goddess Nut we possess yet another mother of the sun god, the traditional role of the dawn goddess as well, whom, we have noted, was considered "inviolable" and "virginal." Indeed, Osiris and Horus's mother, Nut, has likewise been asserted to have been a virgin, also remaining "inviolable," as related by Dr. Schmidt:

> Thus we find *Seb*, the father, *Nut*, the virgin, and Osiris, the son, in the Pyramid texts, just as we afterwards find *Amen*, the father, Muth, the mother, and Chons, the son...
>
> Virgo, who now lends her name to this sign of the zodiac, is the heavenly Nut, the virgin mother of Osiris, who was called the "perfect one" and "the ancient one," and symbolized light and goodness, concord or harmony, peace and happiness. This virgin, the "great mother," the "queen of heaven," the "inscrutable Neith, whose veil no mortal could lift and live," had such a hold on the minds of the inhabitants of Lower Egypt, that the Theban notions of Amen, Muth, and Chons were never able to supplant it.[4]

Whether or not Neith and Nut are associated, as is so common with Egyptian deities, if Nut is also an inviolable and virginal entity, then her sons Osiris and Horus both would be deemed "born of a virgin."

Another virgin was the "Mother goddess of all Egypt," Muth or Mut, who was represented by a vulture and whose name means simply "Mother," an epithet applied to other goddesses as well. Interestingly, the vulture is "a symbol of parthenogenesis,"[5]

---

doubt that what Faulkner defines as "fair woman" refers to a *virgin*. Considering the importance of virginity to Egyptians, it seems curious that this word is so difficult to find in the dictionaries. It is possible this trend is based on religious sensitivities raised earlier when previous scholars such as Budge were more forthright regarding this terminology, which treads too near Christian doctrine. For the same reason, it seems, the phrase "virgin birth" is avoided and "parthenogenesis" substituted in its place.

[1] Rawlin, *HH*, 446.

[2] Both are called "Mother of the Gods," among other shared attributes, leading to a confounding in ancient times as well. In a long analysis, Morris evinces that Neith is Asenath, who in turn is Nut: "In the above I have stated that Nut is Neith." (Morris, 88-92.)

[3] Allen, J., *AEPT*, 9.

[4] Schmidt, 52-53.

[5] West, *TKAE*, 70.

_ussed by Church father Origen (*Contr. Cels.*, 1.37),[1] and the .rgin vulture bringing forth" may have constituted part of the mysteries.[2] Concerning the mother goddess, Budge relates that "in late times [Mut] was said to possess, like Neith, the power of parthenogenesis"[3]—in other words, *virgin birth.*

Regarding the important and ancient goddess Neith, from whom in the Book of the Dead Horus is said to have been born, Budge also states:

> And the priests of the goddess Net (Neith) of Sais...held the view that she was self-begotten and self-produced, that she was the mother of the Sun-god, and at the same time a perpetual virgin-goddess.[4]

Under the entry for the goddess "Net," Budge gives her Greek name, Νηιθ—Neith—and then defines the term as "a self-produced perpetually virgin-goddess, who gave birth to the Sun-god..."[5] Moreover, in a series of admissions concerning *Isis*, sincere Christian Budge further remarks:

> ...it is clear that early Christians bestowed some of her attributes upon the Virgin Mary. There is little doubt that in her character of the loving and protecting mother she appealed strongly to the imagination of all the Eastern peoples among whom her cult came, and that the pictures and sculptures wherein she is represented in the act of suckling her child Horus formed the foundation for the Christian figures and paintings of the Madonna and Child. Several of the incidents of the wanderings of the Virgin with the Child in Egypt as recorded in the Apocryphal Gospels reflect scenes in the life of Isis as described in the texts found on the Metternich Stele, and *many of the attributes of Isis, the God-mother, the mother of Horus, and of Neith, the goddess of Sais, are identical with those of Mary the Mother of Christ.* The writers of the Apocryphal Gospels intended to pay additional honour to Mary the Virgin by ascribing to her the attributes which up to the time of the advent of Christianity they had regarded as the peculiar property of Isis and Neith and other great indigenous goddesses, and if the parallels between the mythology history of Isis and Horus and the history of Mary and the Child be considered, *it is difficult to see how they could possibly avoid perceiving in the teachings of Christianity reflections of the best and most spiritual doctrines of the Egyptian religion.* **The doctrine of partheno-genesis was well known in Egypt in connexion with the goddess Neith of Sais centuries before the birth of Christ;** and the belief in the conception of Horus by Isis through the power given her by Thoth, the Intelligence or Mind of the God of the universe, and in the resurrection of the body and of everlasting life, is coeval with the beginnings of history in Egypt. We may note too in passing the probability that many of the heresies of the early Christian Church in

[1] Origen/Chadwick, 36.
[2] White, 108.
[3] Budge, *EHD*, I, 295.
[4] Budge, *ASH*, 168-169.
[5] Budge, *EHD*, 399.

Egypt were caused by the survival of ideas and beliefs connected with the old native gods which the converts to Christianity wished to adapt to their new creed.[1]

Essentially Budge is indicating that much of the Christian religion and tradition is related to the Egyptian religion, including *direct lifts* of attributes from Egyptian goddesses later ascribed to the Virgin Mary. Like Dr. van Binsbergen, Budge states definitively that parthenogenesis—again, *virgin birth*—was known in Egypt *centuries prior to the common era*, specifically in regard to the goddess Neith.

Bonwick likewise states, "Neith or Nout is neither more nor less than the *Great Mother*, and yet the *Immaculate Virgin*, or female god, from whose bosom all things has [sic] proceeded."[2] And once more, Budge says, "She was the Virgin-mother of the Sun-god, and the 'Mother-goddess' of the Western Delta."[3]

In *History of the Egyptian Religion*, Dr. Cornelius P. Tiele (1830-1902), a professor of the History of Religions at the University of Leiden, likewise comments on the virginity of Neith:

> ...Neith is distinguished...by being a virgin goddess. This is expressed in the words inscribed on her temple, "My garment no one has lifted up," which is immediately followed by, "The fruit that I have borne is the sun." She is thus the virgin mother of the sun...[4]

In *Religious Systems of the World*, Dr. Tiele also refers to "Isis the virgin."[5] As Neith gives birth to the sun god Re (and Horus), so too does Isis bring forth the sun god Horus. In reality, Isis is a later form of Neith, and the two are combined as "Isis-Neith" or "Neith-Isis."[6] Budge states that Neith was "identified with Hathor and Isis,"[7] while in *Egypt's Place in Universal History* Drs. C.C.J. Baron Bunsen and Birch include a section entitled "Isis as Neith," demonstrating the association as well.[8] Concerning this identification of Isis with Neith, whose virginal status long prior to the common era has been attested by a number of sources, Bonwick likewise says of Isis: "She is seen to assume the role of Neith."[9]

The goddess Neith was celebrated at the Egyptian site of Sais, where she had a temple, also dedicated to her alter-ego Isis. Budge further discloses that "at Sais there were several chambers in which the 'Mysteries' of the ancient Virgin Mother-goddess Neith were celebrated."[10] Hence, once more we discover *mysteries* associated

---

[1] Budge, *GE*, II, 220. (Emph. added.)
[2] Bonwick, 115.
[3] Budge, *FFGAE*, 59.
[4] Tiele, *CHEMR*, 204.
[5] *RSW*, 214.
[6] Temporini, 950; Zitman, 192; de Vos, 75.
[7] Budge, *FFGAE*, 59.
[8] Bunsen/Birch, 418-419.
[9] Bonwick, 113.
[10] Budge, *FFGAE*, 25.

with a virgin mother, this time possibly dating back thousands of years prior to the common era.

According to Plutarch (9, 354C), "In Saïs the statue of Athena, whom they believe to be Isis, bore the mysterious inscription: 'I am all that has been, and is, and shall be, and my robe no mortal has yet uncovered.'"[1] As indicated, this writing at Sais finished with the sentence, "The fruit I have produced is the sun." Regarding the Saitic inscription, Thomson states:

> Proclus, who, as well as Plutarch, has given the inscription over the temple of the Virgin of Sais, the mother of the sun, whom they both say is identical with Minerva [Athena], speaking of the seat of this goddess in the heavens, gives her two places—the one near Aries, or the equinoctial Lamb, whose form the god of light assumes in spring, and other in the celestial Virgin, or in the sign which presides at her birth (Procl. in Tim. p. 43); so that it appears that Isis, the mother of the sun, to whom the temple at Sais was dedicated, was the same that Eratosthenes places in the constellation Virgo, which opened that year. The symbolic representation of the year itself was a woman called Isis, according to Horapollo (vol. I. cap. iii.). It was in honour of this same virgin, the image of the pure and luminous substance, that the celebrated feast of lights (on which Candlemas, or the feast of Lights of the Purification, is founded) and was celebrated.[2]

In his *Commentary on Plato's Timaeus*, Greek neoplatonist Proclus (c. 412-485 AD/CE) discusses the city of Sais, the founding goddess of which is Neith, whom he likewise says the Egyptians equate with the Greek goddess Athena.[3] In this regard, Dr. Robert Turcan, a professor of Roman History at the Sorbonne, remarks that "Isis-Neith of Sais was an armed goddess likened to Pallas [Athena]."[4]

Proclus's rendering in Greek of the inscription at Sais (21E) is:

τα οντα και τα εσομενα και τα γεγονοτα εγω ειμι. τον εμον χιτωνα ουδεις απεκαλυψεν. ον εγω καρπον ετεκον, ηλιος εγενετο.[5]

My very literal translation of this inscription is as follows:

The present and the future and the past, I am. My undergarment no one has uncovered. The fruit I brought forth, the sun came into being.

Regarding the meaning of the statement about no one uncovering Neith's garment, Wm. Emmette Coleman concludes:

> The point is this: Does the expression, "lifting the garment"...of Neith refer to her perpetual virginity or to her inscrutability? There is not a shadow of doubt that it refers to the former, and I am confident that every Egyptologist in the world will so decide.[6]

---

[1] Plutarch/Babbitt, 25.
[2] Thomson, 468-469.
[3] Diehl, I, 97.
[4] Turcan, 90.
[5] Diehl, I, 98.
[6] *Miscellaneous Notes and Queries*, X, 66.

The general interpretation of this inscription is that Neith, one of the most important deities of the Egyptian pantheon, is not only the "Alpha and Omega," so to speak, but also the *inviolate* begetter of the sun, the Immaculate Virgin *and* Great Mother. Validating this contention, Dr. John D. Ray, a professor of Egyptology at Cambridge, comments:

> In Sais in the Delta...there was a virgin goddess who gave birth to the sun at the beginning of time by some form of parthenogenesis.[1]

In addition, in the texts of Esna/Esne appears a hymn to Neith, the "creator of all that exists," which "celebrates the goddess of Sais as an androgynous, primeval, and creator deity, the divine mother of Re..."[2] As the androgynous and primeval creator, the goddess reproduces *parthenogenically.*

The fact of her ancient association with the famous Greek goddess Athena—herself a chaste and pristine virgin, as indicated by the name of her temple at Athens, the *Parthenon*—confirms Neith's esteemed virginal status.[3] Nevertheless, Athena—the *Parthenos*—too is considered "the mother by Hephaistos of Apollo Patroos" as well as the "mother of Erechtheus by Hephaistos but a virgin."[4] Moreover, as professor emeritus at the University of Clermont-Ferrand Dr. Paul Faure asserts, "At Athens, on the Acropolis, the virgin Athena was the mother of Erichtonius," referring to the king of Athens.[5] The discussion of Athena as the mother of Apollo appears in *On the Nature of the Gods* (III, 22, 23) by Cicero (106-43 BCE)[6]: Since Athena's main sanctuary was called the *Parthenon*, it is obvious that her *virginity* was highly prized; yet, in this *pre-Christian* source, she is also named as the *mother* of the sun god. Moreover, Athena/Minerva was considered to be a deity of the sea,[7] which would give her the epithet of *mare* in Latin.

Among other astrotheological attributes, scholars have found in Neith a representation of both the winter solstice and the summer solstice, as well as the sun itself,[8] as was Isis also deemed the sun goddess. The suggestion that Neith—who gives birth to the sun—likewise symbolizes the winter solstice adds to the tradition that the solar Horus was born on that day, as he was on every other day,

---

[1] Ray, 63.

[2] Žabkar, 113.

[3] The names "Athena" and "Neith" may be related, as the former essentially represents a transposition of the latter, with the letter "a" on either end.

[4] Price, T., 204. Price calls this attribution of motherhood of Apollo Patroos to the virginal Athena a "late tradition," but it is certainly pre-Christian, found in the works of Cicero, for example.

[5] Bonnefoy, *REM*, 33, 41, 90.

[6] Cicero/Brooks, 183-184.

[7] Raphals, 217.

[8] Bonwick, 117.

since in the Book of the Dead Horus says he is born of Neith, further validating the inscription at Sais.

Interestingly, Budge cites both Neith and Isis as among the goddesses who are "names of the Sky, especially at sun-rise and sun-set."[1] That fact would make of Neith also a dawn goddess, and once more the identification of Neith with Isis is indicated. Again, in the myths of other cultures, the "inviolable begetter of the sun" is the dawn, personified as a chaste goddess. Concerning Isis, Budge remarks, "As a nature goddess she is seen standing in the boat of the sun, and she was probably the deity of the dawn."[2] Budge also says, "Isis was the dawn, and Horus her son by Osiris was the sun in his full strength."[3] Lockyer concurs: "*Isis* represents the Dawn and the Twighlight; she prepares the way for the Sun-god."[4] As we have seen from James Allen, this role is precisely the same as that of Nut, mother of Osiris and Horus.

As yet another example of an Egyptian virgin mother of Horus, in describing how PT 466 and 467 make a "clear distinction" between two of the Horuses, Bleeker discusses the "sky-god Horus" who was the son of *Hathor*, remarking:

> It is characteristic of the position of Hathor in the Egyptian pantheon that there is no mention of a father, as is the case with Horus, son of Osiris and Isis. Hathor's motherhood is therefore conceived of as parthenogenesis or as being purely symbolical.[5]

As the "Primeval" (CT Sp. 331),[6] Hathor may also be said to reproduce parthenogenetically, including as the mother of Horus. In this regard, concerning the epithet "Horus who issued from Gold," Faulkner notes at CT Sp. 362 that "the Gold" is "the well-known epithet of Hathor, whose son Ihy is sometimes equated with the young Horus."[7] After discussing the birth of various sons of Hathor, including Ihy and Harsomtus ("Horus who unites the Two Lands"), Bleeker further states, "Even in the latter days of Egyptian culture and religion Hathor retained her independence and virginity. In this respect she can more aptly be compared with Athene, who remained parthenos even though sometimes called mother, than with Aphrodite."[8] As noted, Hathor is identified with Isis, as Isis-Hathor.

"Isis, the Pure Star of Lovers"

In the debate concerning the influence of the Egyptian religion upon Christianity, it is claimed that, because in one version of the

[1] Budge, *AGFSER*, 2.
[2] Budge, *EBD* (1967), cxiv.
[3] Budge, *DN*, 139.
[4] Lockyer, *DA*, 29. 31
[5] Bleeker, *HT*, 62-63.
[6] Faulkner, *AECT*, I, 255.
[7] Faulkner, *AECT*, II, 5.
[8] Bleeker, *HT*, 63, 65.

myth Isis impregnates herself with Osiris's severed phallus, she cannot be considered a "virgin." In our analysis, it needs to be kept in mind that, in the tale related by Plutarch, we are discussing *astrotheological motifs* revolving around the sun and moon, not set-in-stone biographies of real people with the relevant body parts. Moreover, concerning the story by Diodorus and Plutarch of Isis inseminating herself with Osiris's replaced phallus, Assman says, "The Egyptian texts, which seldom mention this scene, know nothing of this detail."[1] Hence, this aspect represents a later addition to the myth, as it is absent from the earlier texts. In later times, we find the image of a "bird labeled 'Isis'...atop the phallus, receiving his seed for the conception of Horus" in reliefs from the temple to Osiris at Abydos.[2] In a similar image from Dendera, Isis as the bird merely hovers above Osiris's body—minus the phallus—in order to become pregnant with Horus.[3] Therefore, while some of these images show Osiris with an erect phallus, others do not. Indeed, as it turns out, there are different versions of the myth, and Isis, as we have already seen, has been deemed a "perpetual virgin" regardless of the manner of her impregnation.

According to Assman, the *locus classicus* or first mention of the impregnation of Isis occurs in the Pyramid Text 366:632a-633b/T 198, which is essentially the same as PT 593:1636a-b/M206 and which is translated by the German Egyptologist thus: "Isis comes to you, rejoicing for love of you, that her seed might issue into her, it being sharp as Sothis. Horus, the sharp one, who comes forth from you in his name 'Horus, who is in Sothis'..."[4] In his translation of T 198, James Allen includes the word "phallus," noting that it comes from the word "sit,"[5] while, like Assman, Egyptologist and theologian Dr. Samuel A.B. Mercer (1879-1969) omits the word "phallus." With the inclusion of the inundation-heralding star Sirius/Sothis in this utterance, the impression is given from the text that it is a description of the Nile (Osiris) overflowing its banks, spreading its "seed" on the land (Isis) in order to create Horus.[6] In this instance, the "phallus" is evidently the star Sirius itself. In this myth, then, we are also not discussing *sexual intercourse* in the human sense, and Isis's soil remains "virginal" or renewed each year, like the *perpetual virginity* of Neith previously discussed.

Moreover, there are different versions of the death of Osiris, in one of which Isis cannot find his phallus, such that she must "resort to parthenogenesis in order to conceive and bring forth Horus," as

[1] Assman, *DSAE*, 25.
[2] Hare, 120.
[3] Budge, *OFLER*, 80.
[4] Assman, *DSAE*, 25.
[5] Allen, J., *AEPT*, 81, 95.
[6] Mercer, 251.

Dr. Curl states.[1] Thus, differing myths led to a variety of beliefs regarding Isis's pregnancy: One evidently later version has Isis using Osiris's phallus, while in others, "Horus's birth was the result of parthenogenesis," as related also by Dr. Bettina L. Knapp, a professor emerita at Hunter College.[2]

Indeed, in his eye-opening comparison of Isis with the Virgin Mary, Budge states that in the Osirian myth it is by "spells, incantations, magical names and words of power" provided to Isis by Thoth that the goddess conceives Horus:

> By means of them Isis drew seed into herself from Osiris after his death, and conceived Horus... By these spells she, assisted by her son Horus and by Anubis, the divine physician, reconstituted and revivified the body of Osiris, and thus created her son Horus, and recreated Osiris.[3]

In addition, like Jesus, the "Alpha and Omega" who was claimed to have existed from the beginning of time, it was said that "Horus was born of Isis 'before Isis came into being',"[4] such that the goddess certainly did not have a chance to impregnate herself with a phallus! As illustrated here again, the virgin birth is a cosmic mystery.

In his summary of *Frühes Christentum im Orient* by German theologian Dr. Johannes Leipoldt (1880-1965), French Egyptologist Dr. Jean Leclant (b. 1920) remarks:

> Bien que Mère d'Horus, Isis est parfois qualifiée de Vierge, tout comme Marie...

> Although the Mother of Horus, Isis is sometimes described as "Virgin," like Marie...[5]

Indeed, the original German of Leipoldt further relates:

> Not only do Isis and Mary share the title "Mother of God." Isis is also known as virgin, although giving life to a son.[6]

After stating that, despite being the mother of Horus, there were times when Isis was depicted as a Virgin, just like Mary, Leclant continues: "The history of Marie and that of Isis have other common points..."[7] He then proceeds to name a number of these correspondences. Leclant further states, "The influence of the personality of Isis on Christianity is understandable better when one knows the trend of the Isiac cult in the Greco-Roman world."[8]

---

[1] Curl, 15.
[2] Knapp, 243.
[3] Budge, *LOLM*, lii.
[4] Hornung, *CGAE*, 151.
[5] Leclant, 44. (English translation mine.)
[6] Leipoldt, 36: "Nicht nur den Titel 'Mutter Gottes' tragen Isis und Maria gemeinsam. Auch Isis wird Jungfrau genannt, obwohl sie einem Sohne das Leben schenkt." (English translation mine.)
[7] Leclant, 44. (English translation mine.)
[8] Leclant, 44. (English translation mine.)

Addressing Leipoldt as "J.L.," Leclant resumes:

> Christianity has borrowed from ancient Egypt certain religious concepts like psychostasia or judgment of the deceased upon his arrival in the afterlife... But above all, one can consider that the personality of the Madonna borrows much from that of Isis...to the point that J.L. speaks of *Isis-Marie*...[1]

Confirming this notion, the Russian classicist Dr. Thaddeus von Zielinski (1859-1944), a professor at the University of St. Petersburg, referred to Isis as the "prototypical Virgin, the 'Virgin of the World.'"[2]

In *Pan du Désert*, in describing a Greek inscription mentioning the name "Parthenios" along with Isis, French archaeologist André Bernand, a professor at Ain Chams University, states: "It is possible that Parthenios is a name chosen according to the cult of Isis, the prototype of the virgin-mother."[3]

Furthermore, the director of l'Institut d'Histoire des Christianismes Orientaux at the Collège de France, Dr. Michel Tardieu, comments that one of the Egyptian magical "formulas of constraint" from the "cryptogram...preserved in the library of the University of Michigan (=PGM 57)," which evidently dates to the early second century AD/CE and which invokes Isis as a "pure virgin."[4] There are many other such instances of scholarship in other languages discussing Isis and/or Isis-Neith as a *virgin*.[5]

Indeed, in describing the birth of Harpokrates at the winter solstice, Brugsch calls his mother the "Jungfrau Isis-Ceres,"[6] *Jungfrau* meaning in German "young woman" or "virgin," much like the Hebrew *almah*. As we have seen, the Greek goddess Ceres or Demeter was considered a virgin as well and was identified with Isis by Diodorus Siculus in the first century before the common era.

Regarding the Egyptian words for "virgin," the editors of the *Theological Dictionary of the Old Testament*, including Dr. G. Johannes Botterweck (1917-1981), a professor of Old Testament and Catholic Theology at the University of Bonn, remark:

> 1. *Egypt.* The Egyptian words for "girl, virgin," are *'dd.t, rnn.t,* and especially *ḥwn.t.* This last word is already attested in the Pyramid Texts, including the expression, "the girl in the eye," i.e., the pupil. It means "girl, virgin," in a general sense, but can also denote the

---

[1] Leclant, 44: "Le christianisme a emprunté à l'Egypte ancienne certaines conceptions religieuses comme la psychostasie, ou jugement du défunt à son arrivée dans l'au-delà... Mais surtout, on peut considérer que la personalité de la Madone emprunte beaucoup a celle d'Isis...au point que J.L. parle d'Isis-Marie....." (English translation mine. Emph. added.)

[2] Dieterich, 359.

[3] Bernand, 204: "Il est possible que Parthénios soit un nom choisi en fonction du culte d'Isis, prototype de la vierge-mère."

[4] Bonnefoy, *GEM*, 254.

[5] See also Beauregard, who refers to "Neith-Isis, la 'Vierge génératrice...'" (Beauregard, 174.)

[6] von/de Bunsen, *DPT*, 293.

young marriageable woman in particular. The Pyramid Texts speak of "the great virgin" (*hwn.t wr.t*) three times (682c, 728a, 2002a, cf. 809c); she is anonymous, appears as the protectress of the king, and is explicitly called his mother once (809c). It is interesting that Isis is addressed as *hwn.t* in a sarcophagus oracle that deals with her mysterious pregnancy. In a text in the Abydos Temple of Seti I, Isis herself declares: "I am the great virgin." In the Legend of the Birth of Hatshepsut, Queen Ahmose is characteristically presented to Amon as a virgin (*hwn.t*) ... In this context it is to be observed that her husband is called a "young child," which apparently means that the young king was not able to consummate the marriage; thus the queen, although married, is a virgin. Therefore, the sole fatherhood of Amon cannot be doubted....

In the Late Period in particular, goddesses are frequently called "(beautiful) virgins," especially Hathor, Isis, and Nephthys. As a virgin, Hathor also has virgins that wait on her. It is well known that the wives of Amon in Thebes lived in celibacy as consecrated to this god alone. A Ptolemaic papyrus gives an account of cultically motivated virginity. It is expressly said of the two women who played the roles of Isis and Nephthys as mourners that they should be women of a pure body, whose wombs had not been opened. Summarizing, it can be stated that *hwn.t* is not used to denote biological virginity, but rather youthful vigor and potential motherhood. However, there are important points of contact in the Egyptian texts and representative art with the Hellenistic idea of *Isis parthénos* and the virginity of the mother-goddess.[1]

Here we discover in a Christian publication that the Egyptian goddesses Isis, Hathor and Nephthys were commonly called "virgin" in the Late Period (665-323 BCE), meaning that the concept was abundant in worshippers' minds a few centuries before the common era. As concerns the "Great Virgin" in the Pyramid Texts, the average reader might not realize this fact from reading the various translations, which tend to render the particular term *hwn.t* not as "virgin" but as "girl," "damsel" or the increasingly obscure "lass." For example, Mercer translates PT 389:682c as, "N. is the great mistress (or, damsel)," while PT 412:728a and PT 675:2002a are rendered "the great damsel."[2] Beinlich has *hwn.t* as meaning "Mädchen," which is one German rendering of the English word "virgin,"[3] as in the case of the Virgin Mary, who is called "Mädchen Maria" in German, although the phrase "Jungfrau Maria" is more common. In any event, it is evident that both terms can mean "virgin" in precisely the same manner in which the Virgin Mary is considered.

Furthermore, we also discover that at PT 438:809c this "great virgin" is likewise deemed a "mother," clearly a common motif, as further indicated by the *Theological Dictionary* in its use of the phrase

---

[1] Botterweck, 338-339.
[2] Mercer, 133, 140, 297.
[3] Schemann, 525.

"the virginity of the mother-goddess." Additionally, the "mother" here is that of the king, whom we have seen is identified with Horus. As we shall also see, the king's mother is *Isis*, here represented as the "Great Virgin." We also discover that Horus's mother does in fact declare herself in the temple of Abydos the "Great Virgin."

The Ptolemaic papyrus raised here is evidently the Bremner-Rhind Papyrus (4th cent. BCE), in which appears the "ritual of the Two Kites" with instructions that include "two women pure in body, virgins...their names inscribed on their upper arms, namely Isis and Nephthys," as related by Dr. Paul F. O'Rourke from the Department of Classical and Ancient Middle Eastern Art at the Brooklyn Museum of Art.[1] Concerning this text and ritual, Dr. O'Rourke further states that the two virginal women "take on active roles as the sisters of Osiris..."[2] This identification of the two virginal women—specifically emphasized as *pure of body*—as Isis and Nephthys indicates the goddesses themselves were considered by the Egyptians to be spotless virgins as well, regardless of their motherhood status.

Apparently, in order to explain how these various goddesses can remain virgins after becoming mothers, Botterweck, et al., conclude that the virginity indicated by *hwn.t* is not virginity at all, a distinction seemingly forced that would be unnecessary if the mythological and astrotheological nature of the stories were understood, and this *perpetual virginity* comprehended as a *mystery*, as it is within Christianity.[3] Indeed, Jesus's mother, Mary, was said to be a perpetual virgin, explaining why she could give birth yet remain virginal, virtually the same as these other virgin mothers discussed here.

Moreover, the average believer in the Egyptian religion doubtlessly did not engage in the hair-splitting by either the Egyptian priesthood or the modern theologian as concerns the true meaning of *parthenos*, *hwn.t* and "virgin." It is likely that these many millions would have perceived the virginity of the Egyptian goddess in much the same way as occurs with the average modern believer in the perpetual virginity of Mary. In this regard, it is interesting to note that the very word used in the New Testament (e.g., Lk 2:7) to describe Mary giving birth to Jesus—τίκτω, which means, "bring forth, bear; beget"[4]—is likewise used to depict Isis-Neith's begetting of the sun as at Sais, as well as by Plutarch (38, 366C) to portray Isis bearing Horus.

Despite the attempt at redefining the word "virgin," we nonetheless discover from the *Theological Dictionary* that "there are important points of contact" between the Egyptian Isis and the Hellenized Isis—who is called *Isis parthenos*, or "Isis the virgin"—as

---

[1] Redford, 114.
[2] Redford, 114.
[3] See, e.g., Neumann, C., 198, etc.
[4] Plutarch/Babbitt, 92-93; *OCGD*, 320.

well as "the virginity of the mother-goddess," these concepts obviously serving as very real archetypes. From all of these conclusions, it would thus seem that the idea of parthenogenesis or *virgin birth* by Egyptian goddesses—specifically those giving birth to a Horus—has been well known among scholars for quite some time.

The Virginal Mystery

Regardless of the manner of her impregnation, Isis has been asserted to remain a *virgin*, calling herself the "Great Virgin" and identified in ancient times with virgin goddesses such as Neith, Athena and Kore. We have seen that the Egyptians allegedly told Ptolemy that the tradition of bringing out a virgin-born savior was a "mystery." Another related mystery was the doctrine of "perpetual virginity" or "born-again virginity," so to speak, despite the female's status as wife and mother, as discussed by the Jewish philosopher Caius Julius Philo of Alexandria (c. 20 BCE-c. 50 AD/CE) in his treatise "On the Cherubim" (XIV, 49-50).[1] In this essay, which appears in the very time and place germane to our discussion, Philo speaks of God as the "husband of Wisdom"—in other words, the female entity *Sophia*, who has been identified with Isis—and then talks about the virtues of virginity, demonstrating the mystery that allows for a "woman" (one who has known man) to become a virgin once again. Indeed, it was believed by both Philo and early Christians that a woman could *regain* her virginity "through mystical union with God," a stance based on Jewish scripture as at Jeremiah 3:4,[2] which Yonge translates as, "Hast thou not called me as thy house, and thy father, and the husband of thy virginity?"[3] Following his discussion in "On the Cherubim" (XIV, 48) in which he first quotes Jeremiah 3:4, Philo remarks:

> For the association of men, with a view to the procreation of children, makes virgins women. But when God begins to associate with the soul, he makes that which was previously woman now again virgin.[4]

The first chapter of Jeremiah 3, in fact, discusses a "woman"—allegory for the land—who has played harlot and engaged in "whoredoms." The solution to her "pollution" is the scriptural appeal to God: "My father, the author of my virginity." (Jer 3:4) The Hebrew word translated here as "virginity" is נְעֻר—*na'uwr*—which *Strong's Exhaustive Concordance of the Bible* (H5271) defines as "youth, early life," while the Septuagint renders the term as παρθενίας—*parthenias*, obviously related to parthenos and indeed meaning "virginity." Jerome's Latin Vulgate translation of the pertinent word in Jeremiah follows suit with *virginitatis*, which also means "virginity."

---

[1] Philo/Yonge, 85.
[2] Conybeare, 305.
[3] Philo/Yonge, 85.
[4] Philo/Yonge, 85.

From his discussion of the Jeremiah passage almost 2,000 years ago, it is evident that Philo too believed the pertinent word *na'uwr* to refer to *virginity*. Indeed, this scripture was interpreted by Philo and others, apparently, to mean that purification "through mystical union with God" could restore a woman's virginity. **In essence, a God-focused woman can become a "born-again virgin."**

In discussing the biblical story of the barren, aged wife of the Hebrew patriarch Abraham, Philo remarks that God "will not converse with Sarah before all the habits, such as other women have, have left her, and till she has returned into the class of pure virgins."[1] Thus, even though Sarah has obviously engaged in intercourse, she becomes a "born-again virgin" by virtue of her piety. This reasoning was probably also used by Christians maintaining that, even though Jesus is depicted in the New Testament as having siblings (Mt 12:46, 13:55; Mk 3:32; Lk 8:19; Jn 2:12), his mother was considered a "perpetual virgin." Of course, other excuses were proffered as well, such as that these were not really Jesus's "brothers and sisters" but his cousins instead or Joseph's children by his "first wife." Yet, in certain scriptures (Mt 1:24, 25; Lk 2:7) it is implied that after Jesus was born Mary and Joseph engaged in intercourse, so Mary could not possibly be considered a "virgin," regardless of whether or not she gave birth, unless by this same mystical method as outlined by Philo and as applicable to other divine mothers as well centuries before the common era.[2] In the Greek world, this divine "born-again virgin" status was attained "by means of a bath in a sacred river," as in the case of the goddess Hera, wife of Zeus and mother of many.[3] Hence, in this mystery we may also find the answer to the dichotomy of goddesses who give birth, yet remain "virgins."

As we can see, this *Jewish* writer was retroactively making *Jewish* heroes the products of *virgin births*. And Philo's work appeared *before* Christianity was founded. There is no evidence whatsoever that Philo had any knowledge of Christ, Christians or Christianity, but there is sufficient evidence that the creators of Christianity used Philo's works in their efforts. Why would Philo do such a thing? Is it because there were so many virgin-born Pagan gods and heroes with whom to compete? Is this not a clear instance of doctrine being created to compete with another religion, and would we not be wise to suspect that Christianity constitutes but more of the same?

---

[1] Philo/Yonge, 85.
[2] The goddesses who give birth to a number of children yet remain pure, chaste and "virginal" include Krishna's mother, Devaki. (See "Krishna, Born of a Virgin?" in my book *Suns of God: Krishna, Buddha and Christ Unveiled*.)
[3] Price, T., 203.

In addition to the renewal of virginity, the virgin birth itself is also one of "the sacred mysteries" repeatedly discussed by Philo,[1] comprising the "mystic union of the soul as female with God as male."[2] Oxford University professor of Theology Dr. Frederick C. Conybeare (1856-1924) comments that "Philo believed that it was possible for women under exceptional circumstances to conceive and bring forth δια του θεου [through the god] and without human husband."[3] Thus, Philo revealed the notion of a miraculous or virgin birth to have been a *mystery*, which is likely one reason we do not find it blasted all over the place in ancient writings, although the concept was surely known to many people over the centuries and millennia.

Isis, Mary and Virgo

As we have seen, the holy mysteries of the virgin birth and virginity restoration/perpetuation existed not only among the Greeks and Jews but also in Egypt, concerning both Neith and Isis, among others. The identification of Isis with the Virgin, in fact, is further made in an ancient Greek text called *The Katasterismoi*, or *Catasterismi*, allegedly written by the astronomer Eratosthenes (276-194 BCE), who was for some 50 years the head librarian of the massive Library of Alexandria.[4] Although the original of this text has been lost, an "epitome" credited to Eratosthenes in ancient times has been attributed by modern scholars to an anonymous "Pseudo-Eratosthenes" of the 1st to 2nd centuries AD/CE.[5] In this book, the title of which translates as "Placing Among the Stars," appear discussions of the signs of the zodiac. In his essay on the zodiacal sign of Virgo (ch. 9), under the heading of "Parthenos," the author includes the goddess Isis, among others, such as Demeter, Atagartis and Tyche, as *identified with and as the constellation of the Virgin.*[6] In *Star Myths of the Greeks and Romans*, Dr. Theony Condos of the American University of Armenia translates the pertinent passage from the chapter "Virgo" by Pseudo-Eratosthenes thus:

> Hesiod in the Theogony says this figure is Dike, the daughter of Zeus [Dios] and Themis... Some say it is Demeter because of the sheaf of grain she holds, others say it is Isis, others Atagartis, others Tyche...and for that reason they represent her as headless.[7]

---

[1] See, e.g., *De Fuga et Inventione*, XVI (Philo/Yonge, 328); *Quod A Deo Mittantur Somnia*, XIV (Philo/Yonge, 372).
[2] Conybeare, 304.
[3] Conybeare, 304.
[4] Condos, 17.
[5] Condos, 18-19.
[6] Eratosthenes, 244-245. The original Greek reads: "Παρθένος. Ταύτην Ἡσιοδος εν Θεογονία ειρηκε θυγατέρα Διος Θέμιδος...οἱ μεν γαρ αυτήν φασιν ειναι Δήμητραν δια το εχειν στάχυν, οι δε Ισιν, οι δε Αταργάτιν, οι δε Τύχην..."
[7] Condos, 205.

The Virgin Isis-Mery

The headlessness of the goddess/constellation is interes consideration of the story that Isis too was at some point decapitated.[1] Thus, in ancient times Isis was identified with the constellation of Virgo, the *Virgin*. In fact, as we know well, much of the myth surrounding Osiris, Isis and Horus is indeed astrological or astrotheological. Hence, in the myth of Isis and Horus appears the theme of the constellation of the Virgin giving birth to the baby sun at the winter solstice, long before the Christian era and likely serving as one source for the nativity story of Jesus Christ.

The fact that the Virgin Mary herself is associated with the constellation of Virgo becomes evident from the placement of her "ascension into heaven," called the "Assumption of the Virgin Mary," on August 15th, representing one of the four greatest religious festivals in France, for one.[2] Christians believe that this date reflects the time when the mortal Mary ascended or was assumed into heaven. However, the fixation on this date of the supposedly mortal Mary's assumption is quite obviously a reflection of an ancient observance of the assumption of the constellation of Virgo during the time when the sun god "absorbs the celestial virgin in his fiery course, and she disappears in the midst of the luminous rays and the glory of her son."[3] Concerning this event, Sir Rev. Jacob Youde William Lloyd (1816-1887) relates:

> The Roman Calendar of Columella (*Col.* lii, cap. ii, p. 429) marks the death or disappearance of Virgo on the thirteenth day before the Kalends of September, that is, on the 15th of August; and on this day the ancient Greeks and Romans fix the Assumption of Astraea, who is the same as Isis. At the end of three weeks or thereabouts, the Calendar notes the birth of the virgin Isis, or her release from the solar rays. On the third day before the Ides, that is the 8th of September, it says the middle of Virgo rises, so that the same constellation, which is born on the 8th of September, presides at midnight on the 25th of December over the birth of the sun...[4]

The ancient Roman calendar of Columella dates to around 65 AD/CE and does indeed discuss the assumption of the constellation of Virgo, on the precise date centuries later ascribed to Mary's assumption in the Christian mythos.[5] The Greek goddess Astraea was a daughter of Zeus who, after her ascension into heaven, became Virgo.

---

[1] Griffiths, *OOHC*, 104; Redford, 111, 355.
[2] Levillain, 124.
[3] Lloyd, II, 360.
[4] Lloyd, II, 360-361.
[5] The original Latin is as follows: "XIII Kal. Sept. Sol in Virginem transitum facit. Hoc et sequenti die tempestatem significat, interdum et tonat. Hoc eodem die Fidis occidit.... III Kal. Sept. Vmeri Virginis exoriuntur, Etesiae desinunt flare et interdum hiemat." (Columella, XI, 58; Lundström edition, 1902-1917.)

Other Virgin Mothers

As previously demonstrated, Neith and Isis are not the only pre-Christian and non-Christian virgin mothers, and their offspring are not the sole products of a virgin or miraculous birth. In yet another instance of an Egyptian virgin birth, the bull god Apis was said to be born from a virgin cow,[1] with Apis identified with Osiris and Hathor also a virgin "cow mother." Even the sun god Re/Ra is depicted in the texts as being a product of "virgin birth," being self-created: "I am Rē͑ who came into being of himself..."[2] Speaking of Re and parthenogenesis, Dr. David Adams Leeming, a professor emeritus at the University of Connecticut, says, "The sun god Re was the father of certain Egyptian pharaohs, whose virgin mothers conceived through contact with the 'breath' of heavenly fire."[3]

Regarding the virgin birth, Dr. Leeming further comments:

> The point would seem to be that, in the context of myth and religion, the term *virgin birth* is rightly applied to any miraculous conception and birth. That is, whether or not the mother is technically a virgin is of secondary importance to the fact that she conceives and/or gives birth by some means other than the ordinary. The virgin birth story is ultimately not the story of a physiological quirk; it is the story of divinity entering the human experience by the only doorway available to it.[4]

Leeming continues with an extensive survey of *virgin births* worldwide that are quite independent of Christianity.

Concerning the commonality of the pre-Christian divine birth, Dr. Conybeare remarks:

> The idea of a woman being made pregnant by the impact of light is common in ancient thought. Thus Plutarch, De Iside 368 D, speaks of Isis as being filled and impregnated by the Sun... The legend of Danae conceiving by Zeus through a shower of gold is similar.[5]

Indeed, Plutarch (43, 368D) does specifically state that Isis, the moon, is impregnated by the *sun*, which he has elsewhere identified as Osiris:

> For this reason they also call the Moon the mother of the world, and they think that she has a nature both male and female, as *she is receptive and made pregnant by the Sun*....[6]

The Greek myth of the virgin Danae being impregnated by Zeus as a "golden shower"—essentially sunlight, which could be deemed the "breath of heavenly fire"—and giving birth to the divine son, Perseus, is referred to by the Christian apologist Justin Martyr (100-

---

[1] Taylor, J.H., 251; *Enc. Brit.*, II, 173.
[2] Faulkner, *AECT*, I, 244.
[3] Leeming, 273.
[4] Leeming, 273.
[5] Conybeare, 242.
[6] Plutarch/Babbitt, 105. (Emph. added.)

165 AD/CE), in his comparison of Christianity with pre-Christian myth. In *Dialogue with Trypho* (66), in his defense of Christ's virgin birth, Justin says:

> ...in the fables of those who are called Greeks, it is written that Perseus was begotten of Danae, who was a virgin; he who was called among Zeus having descended on her in the form of a golden shower.[1]

In chapter 22 of his *First Apology*, Justin reiterates the comparison between Christ's birth and that of Perseus:

> And if we even affirm that He was born of a virgin, accept this in common with what you accept of Perseus.[2]

In this same regard, ancient skeptic Celsus (2nd cent. AD/CE) remarked; "Clearly the Christians have used the myths of the Danae

---

[1] Roberts, A., *ANF*, I, 231. In *The Virgin Birth*, evangelist Rev. Dr. John Gresham Machen (1881-1937) asserts that, while Justin himself uses the term "virgin," it does not appear in the original Pagan stories of divine and miraculous births. Machen also objects that the comparison is inapt, because the Pagan gods such as Zeus were full of "lust," while the Christian God impassively causes Christ's conception. In the first place, the Greek word παρθένος/*parthenos* appears hundreds of times in pre-Christian texts, such as in the works of Homer, Hesiod, Aeschylus, Sophocles, Aristophanes, Euripides, Xenophon and Plato, in reference to various deities, among others. It is apparent that the term "virgin" *was* used in ancient texts, many of which have not come down to us either at all or without tampering. Indeed, we have seen that Epiphanius's work in which he discusses the *virgin birth* of "Aion" was mutilated in at least one edition, leading us to wonder both why and whether or not such censorship has happened with other works from antiquity. It is thus possible, perhaps even *probable*, that Justin knew of such texts with the pertinent word for "virgin" in them— why else would he raise the subject, when it constituted an admission against the originality and uniqueness of Jesus's virgin birth? If the Pagan "virgin birth" was not the same or was a plagiarism based on Christian doctrine, why wouldn't Martyr point out that fact? But he never does, and logically we may conclude that the Pagan divine birth of Perseus, e.g., was indeed *virginal* and that it was *not* taken from Christianity. Also, we do know that the virginity of goddesses *and* gods was a subject of great interest to the Pagans, as not only were Athena, Artemis and Apollo called *parthenos*— "virgin"—but so too was Zeus, despite having impregnated so many. Per Robert Graves: "Thus the Orphic hymn celebrates Zeus as both Father and Eternal Virgin." (Graves, R., 361.) Furthermore, we have seen from Philo, writing around 25 AD/CE, that the *virgin birth* was a mystery, one that he surely did not just make up on the spot but was relating as a very old tradition that undoubtedly preceded the common era. In his discussion, Philo definitely uses the term *parthenos*, many times in fact, although not in the context of a goddess *per se*.

As to Machen's second objection, even in the dispassionate account of Mary's impregnation by *God the Father*—and if it is not *he* who is fecundating Mary, then Jesus cannot be deemed his "son"—we find an *imposition* by the all-powerful God upon an innocent little girl traditionally depicted as *12 years old* when she became pregnant! It is difficult to see how these two acts are very different and how the Christian conception of the son of God is morally superior to the Pagan conception of the son of God. Instead of causing such trouble for a little girl—whose character was assailed because of it, according to the tale—would it not be more sensible for God simply to have manifested himself fully grown? Why the silly game, unbecoming of a dignified deity? And why not manifest now and set the record straight once and for all?

[2] Roberts, A., *ANF*, I, 170.

and the Melanippe, or of the Auge and the Antiope in fabricating the story of Jesus' virgin birth."[1]

In chapter 54 of the same Apology, Justin basically accuses the "heathens" of plagiarizing the Old Testament "prophecy" at Isaiah 7:14:

> ...And when they heard it said by the other prophet Isaiah, that He should be born of a virgin, and by His own means ascend into heaven, they pretended that Perseus was spoken of.[2]

This scripture at Isaiah 7:14 refers to a "maiden" giving birth to one named "God is with us" or Emmanuel who has been interpreted in Christian tradition to be a "virgin," i.e., Mary, bringing forth Jesus. Indeed, the author of the gospel of Matthew (1:23) copies this passage in the Septuagint verbatim. Furthermore, the argument about the "prophecy" at Isaiah 7:14 is specious, because the original Hebrew term for "maiden" is *almah*, which means "young woman" but not necessarily a virgin. As noted, the Hebrew term for "virgin" is *bethulah*. This example provides an important instance where facts have been twisted by fervent Christian proselytizers in attempts to validate their faith.

In Trypho (70), Justin comes up with the infamous Christian excuse for the existence of these various themes in pre-Christian mythology—"the devil got there first!":

> "...And when I hear, Trypho," said I, "that Perseus was begotten of a virgin, I understand that the deceiving serpent counterfeited also this."[3]

Thus, as we can see, in order to explain the presence of the virgin birth in so-called Pagan mythology, Justin, along with other Church fathers, argued both that the Pagans plagiarized the Old Testament and that the devil, knowing Christ would be born of a virgin, planted the idea in the heads of the pre-Christians. Nowhere does this early Church father suggest that the Pagans plagiarized *from* Christianity, and it is quite evident that the virgin-birth motif is *pre-Christian* and therefore neither unique nor any more "historical" with Christianity than these other, *mythical* nativities. Of course, centuries later the author of the Paschal Chronicle came up with a different but more sophisticated excuse for the pre-Christian virgin birth of the divine savior as having been "prophesied" by Jeremiah and imitated out of piety before it happened.

In *The Virgin Goddess: Studies in the Pagan and Christian Roots of Mariology*, Dr. Stephen Benko, a professor of Religion and Philosophy at Temple University and a professed Christian, discusses the apocryphal text regarding Christ's childhood called the *Protevangelium*. In his analysis of this Christian text, Dr. Benko

---

[1] Celsus/Hoffman, 56.
[2] Roberts, A., *ANF*, I, 181.
[3] Roberts, A., *ANF*, I, 234.

suggests that the author was influenced by the widespread cult of the Phrygian goddess Cybele, concluding, "Apparently the author's aim was to elevate Mary to the level of the great virgin-mother goddesses of the Greco-Roman world."[1] Like Binsbergen's matter-of-fact statements regarding parthenogenesis, Benko's comments indicate that the existence of pre-Christian, virgin-mother goddesses and their influence upon Christianity represents a foregone conclusion within the world of academia. Indeed, in *A Feminist Companion to Mariology*, Dr. John W. Van den Hengel, Dean of the Faculty of Theology at St. Paul University, Ottawa, remarks: "Few theologians doubt, in the words of Stephen Benko, that the development of early doctrines concerning Mary is 'rooted in popular piety that was motivated by pagan precedents, more precisely by the worship of Cybele.'"[2]

As we have seen, the Greek goddess Hera, wife of the amorous Zeus, was said to restore her virginity each year by bathing in a river. In *Virgin Mother Crone*, Donna Wilshire states that Hera "*is specifically said to have conceived Her children parthenogenically.*"[3] Regarding Hera, Wilshire further states that "'Parthenia' is one of Her titles that translates as 'Virgin,' meaning 'belonging to Herself,'..."[4] Dr. Theodora Hadzisteliou Price likewise asserts that such mother goddesses as Hera and Athena were called "Parthenos," with Hera annually bathing to renew her virginity.[5]

In this regard, Dr. Price also says in her analysis of the ancient Greek nursing deities that the "concept of virgin-birth of Gods and heroes is very common."[6] In reality, the Greeks "would not accept a new god unless he was born by the visitation of God to a virgin."[7] In her study of the "nursing goddess," or *Kourotrophos*, Price also says that "it is not surprising that the Kourotrophos, originally the Goddess of fertility of plants, animals and men, is in many cases a virgin and mother."[8]

As another example of a virgin-born Greek hero, Conybeare relates that the famous Greek mystic Plato (428/427-348/347 BCE), upon whose work significant aspects of Christianity appear to have been founded, was also thought to have been the product of a virgin birth:

---

[1] Benko, 202.

[2] Levine, 134. The devout Christian Benko offers the apology that, despite the obvious "borrowing" by Christians of these "pagan precedents," this fact "means only that Christianity is firmly anchored in the historical process; it does not mean that Christianity reverted to an earlier, primitive state of paganism." (Benko, 205.) However, what this fact *does* mean is that *Christianity did indeed borrow cherished doctrines and that it is therefore not a "divine revelation."*

[3] Wilshire, 32.

[4] Wilshire, 32.

[5] Price, T., 203.

[6] Price, T., 202.

[7] Price, T., 203.

[8] Price, T., 203.

...Plato was himself believed to have been a born of a virgin mother, who conceived him by the god Apollo. Such a myth grew up quite naturally about Plato...[1]

Indeed, in his apology for Christ's nativity, Origen (*Contra Celsus* 1.37) raises the issue of Plato's purported virgin birth from the union of his mother and the god Apollo,[2] as does Jerome in his *Against Jovinianus* (*Adv. Jov.* 1.42).[3]

In the same regard, Forlong states:

The legend of virgin birth was at least as old as the 2nd century A.C. among Christians; but Buddha, Zoroaster, Plato, Alexander, and even Tartar emperors and Pharaohs, were called the children of virgins by some god, as well as Christ.[4]

In *Heroes and Heroines of Fiction*, William S. Walsh likewise discusses the virgin-birth motif found in the non-Christian world:

Virgin-mothers. Long before the time of Christ, parthenogenesis, or reproduction by a virgin, was as familiar to ancient Greek, Egyptian and Oriental legend as it is to modern biology. ...Buddha was only one of many Oriental heroes whose mother was a virgin. The Egyptian Horus was conceived by Isis without the direct intervention of a male. Isis has been identified with the Greek Demeter, and Demeter also was a virgin, even when she bore a child, Persephone or Proserpine.[5]

As we have seen, the Greek earth mother Demeter/Ceres, who gave birth to the season goddess Persephone/Kore, was also said to be a virgin, equated with Virgo by Pseudo-Eratosthenes, for one, as well as with Isis by Diodorus. As Theodora Price likewise states, "Demeter, the mother par excellence of the Greek religion, who gave birth to Kore, perhaps to Iakchos, even to Artemis according to one tradition...is also a virgin."[6] Regarding the virginal status of Demeter, in its entry on the "Virgin Birth," the authoritative Christian publication *The New Schaff-Herzog Encyclopedia of Religious Knowledge* reports:

Nowhere, perhaps, has comparative religion discovered a more impressive instance of virgin birth than in the Eleusinian Mysteries. The supreme moment of the solemn celebration of these rites was marked by the marriage of the sacred mother and the birth of the sacred child. The mother was Brimo, a maiden, a goddess of the underworld, the Thessalian Kore or Demeter, the goddess of the fruits of the cultivated earth.... Thus at the very heart and culmination of the ceremonies at this sacred shrine in ancient

---

[1] Conybeare, 317.
[2] Origen/Chadwick, 36.
[3] Schaff, VI, 380-381.
[4] Forlong, 505.
[5] Walsh, 344.
[6] Price, T., 204.

Greece, centuries before its appearance in the Septuagint, the dogma had been created, "A virgin shall conceive and shall bear a son."[1]

As we have also seen, Epiphanius asserted that Kore herself was the virgin mother of the sun, brought out at the winter solstice. Also, the presence of the virgin-mother theme in the Septuagint or Greek Old Testament at Isaiah 7:14 might prove the motif's pre-Christian existence, if it were certain the relevant texts from the Septuagint ("LXX") had actually been translated *before* the creation of the Christ character. Indeed, despite Christian tradition that the entire LXX was created centuries before the common era, there remains a debate about whether or not the Greek books of the prophets were forged well into the common era to conform to Christian doctrine and demonstrate it to be "biblical." If it is contended that the book of Isaiah was translated into Greek along with the Torah two to three centuries before the common era—with the term *parthenos* to describe the mother—we therefore possess a *pre-Christian* mention of the virgin birth that could have been used as a *blueprint* for Christ's nativity. If, however, it is admitted that this part of the LXX was translated *after* Christ's purported advent, then we have a clearcut instance of dishonesty and forgery on the part of early Christians, as has been the case with the many forged or "apocryphal" Christian gospels, letters and so on.[2]

Not only does this entry from Schaff-Herzog validate the claim that there were other, pre-Christian virgin births, but it also supports the contention that this motif of parthenogenesis constituted a *mystery*, part of the famous Eleusinian Mysteries, for example. Indeed, concerning the "double goddess of Eleusis," the site of the Eleusinian Mysteries, Dr. Faure relates that she is "both virgin and mother" who gives birth to "the child she conceived by the supreme god..."[3]

This fact of the virgin birth representing a mystery was also verified by Philo, long before the virgin birth of Jesus Christ could be found in the historical/literary record, and, we contend, is one of the reasons it is not widely known today, although it was well enough acknowledged in ancient times. In the same manner, Isis likewise possessed her mysteries, evidently including her own perpetual virginity.

In our analysis of the divine, miraculous and virgin birth, we could become involved into a long digression concerning the terms *virgo* and *virgo intacta*, but, despite the quibbling, we would still need to establish that the *average worshipper* likewise perceived these theological subtleties. Indeed, the discussion becomes moot when we

---

[1] *NSHERK*, 212.
[2] For more on the subject, see my book *The Christ Conspiracy*.
[3] Bonnefoy, *REM*, 33.

ıis propensity towards renewed or "born again" virginity, as
ıe mysteries.

Mary is Mery Redux?

The similarities between the Egyptian and Christian mothers of
God do not end with their names or perpetual virginity. Like the
Virgin Mary turned away from an inn while with child, the pregnant
Isis too is refused a "night's lodging."[1] Also like Mary, who flees with
the baby Jesus into Egypt to escape the tyrant Herod, Isis must flee
with the baby Horus to another part of Egypt to escape the tyrant
Set.[2]

Like Jesus, Isis is imbued with the ability to raise the dead, first
resurrecting Osiris, and then, after Set as a scorpion stings the baby
Horus to death, resurrecting her son as well.[3] Isis is also depicted as
the healing deity, likewise saving the life of the sun god Re, when he
too was poisoned.[4] Of Isis's healing abilities, Budge remarks, "The
great Codices of the Book of the Dead written under the XVIIIth [18th]
dynasty prove that the blood of Isis was believed to possess great
magical protective powers."[5] Thus, Isis's magical blood is like that of
Christ, which is perceived by Christians to heal and wash away their
sins. In addition, as Christians do with the Virgin Mary, Isis's female
worshippers petitioned her to make them fertile and able to
conceive.[6] Isis's titles were many, including many similar epithets to
those of Mary: "Divine Lady," "Greatest of gods and goddesses,"
"Queen of the gods," "Lady of heaven," "Holy one of heaven," "Great
goddess of the Other World," "Mother of Horus," "Mother of the God,"
"Lady of Life," "Lady of joy and gladness" and "Queen of heaven."[7]

As we have seen, Budge was one of the first to address and
develop extensively the correspondences between Mary and Isis,
while many others have balked at the task, for various reasons.
Indeed, of the transparent usurpation of the Egyptian religion by
Christians, the British Egyptologist boldly concludes:

> **It has often been said and written that the cult of Isis and Horus
> and the worship of Mary the Virgin and the Child are one and
> the same thing...**[8]

With all these facts in mind, the insistence that Christianity
sprang up in a vacuum as a unique and new "divine revelation"
appears unsustainable, to say the least.

---

[1] Budge, *LOLM*, liii-liiii.
[2] Budge, *LOLM*, liii-liiii.
[3] Budge, *LOLM*, liiii.
[4] Budge, *LOLM*, liiii.
[5] Budge, *LOLM*, liv.
[6] Budge, *LOLM*, lv.
[7] Budge, *LOLM*, lv-lvi.
[8] Budge, *LOLM*, lix. (Emph. added.)

The Virgin Isis-Mery

Nevertheless, Budge, a pious Christian, attempts to delin... two cults, based on the contention that Mary was not a goddess but a "real person." However, we think the apologist does protest too much and that it is obvious the Christian *myth* was designed to take over the Egyptian one, with the *mythical* Virgin Mary composed in order to usurp the highly popular Isis.

Oddly, in the face of his protests Budge continues to make strong comparisons between Isis and Mary, even relating that, according to early Christian belief, Mary too had "raised the dead and worked other miracles," a contention that continues to this day by her devoted believers, who flock to such places as Lourdes and Medjugorje, to petition the Virgin for healing. And the parallels persist:

> Osiris, more than Horus, resembles Jesus in respect of His murder by the Jews. Isis bewailed Osiris in the shrines of Egypt, as Mary bewailed her Son at Golgotha. The seven scorpion-goddesses who attended Isis seem to have their counterpart in the seven maidens who were associated with Mary in weaving the Veil of the Temple....[1]

At this point, Budge tries again to differentiate the two stories, all the while assuming the Judeo-Christian tale to be "historical." In reality, the differences are slim and to be expected if Jewish priests were merely weaving Egyptian myths together with their own scriptures, which is precisely what we contend was done in the creation of the Christ and Virgin Mary characters, as well as Christianity as a whole. These peculiar attributes of Mary are not found in the canonical gospels, it should be noted, but come from the apocryphal or "hidden" texts concerning her alleged life.

As yet another example of how the Egyptian religion was copied to become "Christian revelation" emerges a "little work" of magical writings called the "Lefafa Sedek," or "Bandlet of Righteousness." In the Lefafa Sedek, the Christian author claims the booklet constitutes a "divine revelation" dictated to Jesus and passed along firstly to the Virgin Mary and then to the archangel Michael, who revealed its contents to the apostles. Concerning this book, Budge remarks, "The Lefafa Sedek is constructed on the same plan as the Egyptian Book of the Dead, and is a veritable Ethiopian Book of the Dead. But the author, who was a Christian, substitutes God for Ra, Christ for Thoth, and the Virgin Mary for Isis."[2]

Like the Book of the Dead, this *Christian* booklet "Bandlet of Righteousness" was written on strips of linen and wrapped around dead bodies. Thus, we possess a cut-and-dry case of Christians copying the Egyptian religion, which, again, we assert was done with the gospel story itself and many other aspects of Christianity.

---

[1] Budge, *LOLM*, lix-lx.
[2] Budge, *AS*, 195-196.

This changeover from the Egyptian to the Christian religion occurred within the Gnostic movement as well:

> The Egyptian Gnostics rejected many of the pagan cults of the early dynastic Egyptians, but they regarded Ra, Horus and Harpokrates [Horus the Child] as forms of their "One God of heaven," and they connected Isis with the Virgin Mary, Osiris and Serapis with Christ...[1]

In fact, when we include the apocryphal and Gnostic texts in our investigation, we develop an even longer list of parallels between the Egyptian and Christian religions that would require another volume.

Fortunately, like Budge not everyone has been afraid of making the Mary-Isis connection, as the correspondence between the two was recognized not only during the 19th to early 20th centuries but also long into the latter era as well. For example, regarding the work of Egyptologist Dr. R.E. Witt, who died in 1980, Curl comments, "Dr. Witt is particularly illuminating on the merging of Isis with the Blessed Virgin Mary."[2] Indeed, concerning Isis and Mary, in *Isis in the Ancient World*, Witt states:

> In Hopfner's invaluable collection of the literary sources, Isis needs more pages of the Index than any other name. A brief glance at her attributes as there listed reveals her sharing titles with the Blessed Virgin whom Catholic Christianity has ever revered as Mother of God. Some of these resemblances may be set aside as [sic] once as commonplace. Yet so many are the parallels that an unprejudiced mind must be struck with the thought that cumulatively the portraits are alike. Indeed, one of the standard encyclopedias of classical mythology specifically deals with "Isis identified with the Virgin Mary."
>
> Let us observe a few of the resemblances. Isis and Osiris, as we have so often seen, are mythologically interfused. In the language of the Roman Church the Blessed Virgin Mary is "sister and spouse of God: sister of Christ." Christian writers identify Sarapis with Joseph and then make Isis "wife of Joseph." Like her heathen forebear the Catholic Madonna wears a diadem. She too is linked with agricultural fertility...[3]

Witt continues with a long list of comparisons between Mary and not only Isis but also other goddesses, such as Juno and Minerva. The list of parallels, in fact, goes on for several pages and includes

---

[1] Budge, *AS*, 203.

[2] Curl, 66.

[3] Witt, 272. "Hopfner's invaluable collection of literary sources" refers to Theodor Hopfner's *Fontes Historiae Religionis Aegyptiacae*, Bonn, 1922. The remark by Witt asserting early Christian identification of the Old Testament Joseph with the Egyptian god Serapis is verified by Theodore Foster, who says, "Serapis, no less than Apis, was regarded by some early Christian writers as a symbol of the Patriarch Joseph." (Foster, 182.) Foster also relates that Serapis was the "sun in Hades," an important factoid in consideration of the story of Christ's descent into the underworld. There are many other similarities between Joseph, Serapis and Christ. (See my book *Who Was Jesus?* for a Joseph-Jesus comparison.)

both the Christian and Egyptian figures being at once "the Great Virgin" and "Mother of God."[1] Witt further remarks:

> Convincing examples can be found of the influence on Christian iconography of the figure of Horus/Harpocrates, both in his mother's company and on his own. The most obvious parallels appear when we compare the ways in which the sacred Mother and Child of Egypt are portrayed and the types of the Theotokos/Madonna together with the infant Jesus in Byzantine and Italian ecclesiastical art...[2]

Witt proceeds to name several pieces of art demonstrating the obvious link between the earlier Egyptian gods and the later Christian characters. In this regard, the connection between the Egyptian goddess and the Jewish virgin is so strong that Leipoldt described them as one syncretistic entity called "Isis-Marie." From all the evidence so far presented, it may be truthfully asserted that the Christian "Virgin Mother of God" concept represents a *mythical* construct based in large part on the Egyptian religion, as does much else of the Christian religion and tradition, including many other aspects of Isis found in the myth of Mary.

The Nativity Scene at the Temple of Luxor

As an example of the pre-Christian divine birth, in the temple of Amun at the site of Luxor appears a series of scenes depicting the nativity of the king/pharaoh of the 18th Dynasty (c. 1570-1293 BCE), Amenhotep/Amenhotpe or Amenophis III, who reigned during the 14th century BCE. The precise nature of these scenes has been the subject of much debate since they were first analyzed by Western scholars in the 19th century, beginning most prominently with Champollion. In consideration of the magnitude of the Luxor-Karnak temple complex, it is apparent that Amenhotep III was a highly noteworthy king to have been figured there so abundantly. In fact, Amenhotep III is so important that he is called the initiator of the "new concept" of "a divine living king."[3] Among other divine epithets, Amenhotep III is also called "The Good God" and "Son of Re."[4] Indeed, so strong was the association of Amenhotep/Amenhotpe III with Re/Ra that the king deemed himself "the dazzling sun."[5] As stated by Egyptologist Dr. David P. Silverman, curator at the Egyptian Section of the University of Pennsylvania, in the temple of Luxor Amenhotep III is equated with the "dazzling disk of the sun,"[6] giving greater signification to the solar disk or *Aten*, an innovation that undoubtedly led his son, Amenhotep IV, to become the notorious "heretic" pharaoh Akhenaten/Ikhnaton. Also indicating his

---

[1] Witt, 273.
[2] Witt, 216-217.
[3] Silverman, 12.
[4] Silverman, 14.
[5] Redford, 327.
[6] Silverman, 29.

e, Breasted refers to the king's nativity images and
ariptions as "representing Amenhotep III's supernatural birth and
his coronation by the gods..."[1]

Regarding the Egyptian birth scenes overall, as well as the status
of the pharaohs of the time, Breasted further comments:

> It is evident that the priests of Heliopolis had become so powerful
> that they had succeeded in seating this Solar line of kings upon the
> throne of the Pharaohs. From now on the state fiction was
> maintained that the Pharaoh was the physical son of the Sun-god by
> an earthly mother, and in later days we find the successive incidents
> of the Sun-god's terrestrial amour sculptured on the walls of the
> temples. It has been preserved in two buildings of the Eighteenth
> Dynasty, the temple of Luxor and that of Der el-Bahri.[2]

The Egyptian nativity must thus be considered to represent a
divine birth no less significant or real to the Egyptians than the much
later Christian nativity is to Christians. In factoring the potential
influence of the Luxor nativity scene on the religious psyche of the
centuries prior to the common era, it needs to be kept in mind that
the pharaoh Amenhotep/Amenophis III has been labeled "extremely
vain," having commissioned over 1,000 portraits of himself to appear
in monuments during his lifetime. Having his birth cycle at such a
significant site as Luxor gave Amenhotep greater notoriety than many
other rulers, and it is likely his story was highly influential upon later
versions of birth narratives. Indeed, it is obvious that the individual
featured on the walls of the temple of Luxor, a massive and expensive
edifice, was no minor figure, such that it would not surprise us if his
birth drama were reenacted as a "cult play" on a regular basis, much
like the nativity story of Jesus. As archaeologist Dr. Dieter Arnold of
the Metropolitan Museum of Art relates, the Luxor temple was the
"location for the annual celebration of the divine birth of the king and
the awarding to him of the divine *ka*,"[3] the "double" and "life force"
that accounts for the difference between a living person and a dead
body. The fact that there was an annual celebration of the
miraculous birth of the divine Egyptian king is, of course, striking,
presenting one of several correlations to the Christian nativity.

The nativity scenes at Luxor were not the first to have been
created, as similar depictions existed earlier concerning the birth of
the female pharaoh Hatshepsut (15th century BCE) in her temple at
Deir el Bahari. Nativity scenes were also commonly used in "the
Mamisi of the later periods,"[4] *mamisi* or *mammisis* constituting "birth
rooms" or "birth houses." As explained by Dr. Eric H. Cline, chairman
of the Department of Classical and Semitic Languages and Literature
at George Washington University, "The worship of the child born of

---

[1] Breasted, *ARE*, II, 334.
[2] Breasted, *DRTAE*, 15-16.
[3] Arnold, 135.
[4] O'Connor, 72.

divine parents finds an ultimate expression in the 'birth houses,' or *mammisis*, of the Greco-Roman period."[1] After bringing up the "so-called Birth House" near the temple of Hathor at Dendera, Karl Baedeker remarks:

> Similar "Birth Houses" were erected besides all large temples of the Ptolemaic period. They were dedicated to the worship of the sons of the two deities revered in the main temple, in the present case to Har-sem-tewe or Ehy, son of Horus of Edfu and Hathor. This "Birth House" was built by Augustus and some of its reliefs were added by Trajan and Hadrian....[2]

This fact means that these birth scenes or "nativity templates," so to speak, were popular and in the minds of Egyptians beginning at least 3,400 years ago and continuing into the second century of the common era, with its eventual creation of Christianity, which, as we shall see, evidently took yet another page out of the Egyptian holy book. Moreover, as Dr. Arnold says, "Birth houses started as way stations or processional stations entered by the procession of gods performing the mysteries attendant on the birth of the divine child."[3] It is important to note not only that the divine birth was reenacted as a play annually but also that there were *mysteries* attached to its celebration. Indeed, it is quite possible if not probable that this celebration of the birth of the divine child surrounded by mysteries was along the lines of, if not the same as, that discussed by Epiphanius, Macrobius, the Chronicle author(s) and Cosmas— previously mentioned concerning the baby sun god brought out in the manger, the god identified by Plutarch as *Horus*.

As Frankfort observes, the connection of the divine child at Luxor and Deir el Bahari to the sun god is undoubted. In his extensive discussion of the birth of the female pharaoh Hatshepsut, Breasted states, "Beginning with the Fourth Dynasty, every Egyptian king might bear the title, *"Son of Re,"* the sun-god.[4] Regarding the Egyptian royal birth dramas and the title "son of Re, Breasted further remarks that "in its strictest sense the title indicated that the king was immediately and physically the offspring of the god and a mortal mother..."[5] Breasted also calls these birth scenes a "stereotyped form" and comments that "both Hatshepsut and Amenhotep III used almost identically the same scenes in their birth reliefs..."[6] The imagery itself may be essentially the same in both the Hatshepsut and Amenhotep scenes, and some of the same language is used in both inscriptions. However, even though they have been haphazardly mixed at times, the inscriptions of these two pharaohs' birth cycles are "substantially

---

[1] Cline, 173.
[2] Baedeker, 223.
[3] Arnold, 33.
[4] Breasted, *ARE*, II, 75.
[5] Breasted, *ARE*, II, 76.
[6] Breasted, *ARE*, II, 76fn.

different," according to Dr. Murnane, a director of the Great Hypostyle Hall Project at the Karnak Temple in Luxor.[1]

In any event, the same gods do appear in both the Hatshepsut and Amenhotep birth narratives, the father god being Amon, Amun or Amen, who is the "successor of Re" in divine kingship paternity. In addition, Amun is not just any god but one of the oldest and most revered—in fact, he is the creator of the world and *father* of the gods, who was given the attributes of many of the other deities. His temple precinct at the combined Luxor-Karnak sites was not only massive but also extremely long-lived, constructed over a period of some 2,000 years by a multitude of pharaohs and possessing some 80,000 employees during a certain point around 1200 BCE.[2]

Another "divine son of Amun" was Alexander the Great (356-323 BCE), possibly enjoying the same nativity template as Hatshepsut and Amenhotep, which makes sense in consideration of his relationship to Luxor in particular, where he ordered the temple sanctuary to be rebuilt. During his sojourn in Egypt, Alexander was established as a typical pharaoh, receiving honors as "Horus," along with a "Horus name." Thus, in Alexander we possess a divine birth with a major god as father a few centuries prior to the common era, with its similar claims of a Jewish son of God. In Alexander, in fact, emerges a tale about a "divine child" who became the prominent founder of the very city in which we contend much of Christianity was created, meaning that many thousands of people over the centuries had heard this famous birth tale, such that it may well have been in the minds of those who composed the gospel story, lending further credence to the suggestion that the Egyptian divine-birth template itself was used by them as well.

The Amenhotep Birth Cycle

At Luxor, the pertinent scenes regarding Amenhotep III's birth appear in the temple of Amun "in the first chamber on the east of the holy of holies, on the west wall."[3] In *The Nile: Notes for Travellers in Egypt*, Budge provides a synopsis of the Luxor panels:

First or *Lowest Row.* 1. Khnemu [Khnum, Kneph], seated opposite Isis, fashioning the body of the young king and his *ka* or double upon a potter's wheel; he predicts that the child shall be king of Egypt. 2. Amen and Khnemu holding converse. 3. Amen and Mut-em-ua [Mutemuia or Ahmose], wife of Thothmes IV., and mother of Amenophis III., holding converse in the presence of the goddess Selq, or Serq [Selkit], and Neith. In the text the god Amen declares that he had taken the form of the husband of Mut-em-ua and that he is the father of the child who is to be born. 4. Amen and Thothmes IV. 5. Mut-em-ua being embraced by the goddess Isis in the presence of

[1] Murnane, 22.
[2] "The Pyramids and the Cities of the Pharaohs."
[3] Breasted, *ARE*, II, 334.

Amen. *Second* or *Middle Row.* 1. Thoth telling the queen that Amen has given her a son. 2. The queen being great with child, is being sustained by Khnemu and Isis, who make her to breathe "life." 3. The child is born in the presence of Thoueris, the goddess of children, and Bes, the driver away of evil spirits from the bed of birth. 4. Isis offering the child to Amen, who addresses him as "son of the Sun." 5. The child Amenophis III, seated on the knees of Amen, whilst his destiny is being decreed in the presence of Isis or Hathor; Mut offers to him a palm branch, at the end of which is the emblem of festivals. Amen declares that he will give him "millions of years, like the Sun." *Third* or *Top Row.* 1. The queen seated on the bed of birth, and the child being suckled by Hathor in the form of cow. 2. The seven Hathors (?) and two goddesses. 3 The Niles of the South and North purifying the child. 4. Horus presenting the king and his *ka* to Amen. 5. The gods Khnemu and Anubis. 6. The king and his *ka* seated and also standing before Amen. 7. Amenophis seated on his throne....[1]

For our present analysis we will explore only a few of these images in any depth, especially scene 3 in row 1, in which we find the god Amun "holding converse" with the virgin queen—it is presumably at this point that the queen conceives the divine child. According to Budge, in row 1, scene 5, Isis embraces the queen, representing a sort of "annunciation"; while, in the first scene of the next row, the god Thoth—the divine messenger—announces to the queen that she will bear a divine "son of God" who is also the "son of the Sun." Adding to this description are details provided by Baedeker in his guidebook on Egypt, including that, in the hotly debated panel 3 of the first row, Amun and the queen are depicted as "seated on the hieroglyph for 'sky' and supported by the goddesses Selkit [Selq] and Neith..."[2]

In the various analyses of these famous images, we find them in a different order at times, such as Budge stating that the god Khnum appeared first, pre-fashioning the god-king and his *ka* before the sacred marriage and conception takes place, while others put the panel afterwards. The important ram-headed god Khnum, Khnemu or Kneph is called the "creator of the gods," among other epithets, and is equivalent to the "holy spirit," in Christian terminology.

Also, while Budge places the embrace by Isis (Hathor) *after* the "converse" by Amun and the queen, according to Breasted the "annunciation" to the *virgin* queen that she is going to be impregnated by a god occurs *before* the conception, with the goddess "informing the queen of what is to befall her."[3] Confirming Breasted's order, Murnane also tells us that, rather than starting with Khnum, the very first scene in the Luxor birth narrative represents the god Amun-Re watching as the "King's Chief Wife," MUTEMWIA, is

[1] Budge, *NNTE*, 579-580.
[2] "Luxor—Temple of Luxor—Birth Room."
[3] Breasted, *ARE*, II, 79.

embraced by the goddess Hathor.[1] In other words, again, there is an apparent transmission to the queen that Amun-Re would fecundate her, constituting an annunciation *before* the conception.

In addition to the varying order, we also discover commentary on the birth scenes only from the second row up, excluding the first row altogether, possibly because the latter had not yet been reproduced for study and/or was largely still unknown to European Egyptologists of the time.[2] These analyses begin with the scene of Thoth announcing to the queen, leaving the impression of a "miraculous conception" such as allegedly occurred in the Christian narrative, with the archangel Gabriel announcing to the Virgin Mary that she will give birth, a scene called the "Annunciation."

The Birth of Pharaoh Hatshepsut

In describing the birth narrative of *Hatshepsut* at Deir el Bahari, Assyriologist Dr. Leonard William King (1869-1919), also a Keeper of the Egyptian Department at the British Museum, states:

> ...Amen's first act is to summon the great gods in council, in order to announce to them the future birth of the great princess. Of the twelve gods who attend, the first is Menthu, a form of the Sun-God and closely associated with Amen. But the second deity is Atum, the great god of Heliopolis, and he is followed by his cycle of deities... The subsequent scenes exhibit the Egyptian's literal interpretation of the myth, which necessitates the god's bodily presence and personal participation. Thoth mentions to Amen the name of queen Aahmes as the future mother of her husband, Aa-kheper-ka-Ra (Thothmes I), sitting with Ahmes and giving her the Ankh, or sign of Life, which she receives in her hand and inhales through her nostrils. God and queen are seated on thrones above a couch, and are supported by two goddesses. After leaving the queen, Amen calls on Khnum or Khnemu, the horned ram-headed god, who in texts of all periods is referred to as the 'builder' of gods and men; and he instructs him to create the body of his future daughter and that of her *Ka*, or 'double', which would be united to her from birth.

> ...When Amenophis III copied Hatshepsut's sculptures for his own series at Luxor, he assigned this duty [the ankh to the nostril] to the greater goddess Hathor, perhaps the most powerful of the cosmic goddesses and the mother of the world.... Monsieur Naville points out the extraordinary resemblance in detail which Hatshepsut's myth of divine paternity bears to the Greek legend of Zeus and Alkmene...[3]

Here the gods are sitting in council, being *12* in number, a significant development indicating a very ancient instance of a divinity associated with "the Twelve"—as in the story of Jesus—and demonstrating that, like the Greeks and Romans, the Egyptians

---

[1] Murnane, 22; Brunner, "Szene I L," Tafel 1.
[2] See, e.g., the analysis by Count Ferdinand de Lesseps (1804-1895), 204.
[3] King, L., 15-107.

possessed a circle of 12 gods.[1] Skipping ahead, in par.
Breasted's analysis of the same Hatshepsut cycle, Hathor ¡
the divine child to Amun, who responds that the child is "his b᷊ᵥved"
and that he will reign "upon the Horus-throne forever."[2]

As noted by Dr. King, Naville observed the "extraordinary
resemblance" between the Egyptian birth narrative and that of the
Greek Son of God, Heracles/Hercules. It should be further noted that
Hercules's mother, Alcmene, was said to be a *virgin* before she
miraculously conceived through divine intervention.[3]

As we can see, the order of the scenes in the Hatshepsut cycle is
different from that of the Amenhotep narrative. This point of varying
order is important to emphasize, in that the Luxor birth template fits
more with that of Christ's birth narrative and its pre-conception
"Annunciation." Also, this situation shows that if the creators of the
Christian narrative wanted to change the order of any template they
might be using, they had precedent in the creators of the Luxor cycle
and, of course, were free to do so in any event.

The Egyptian birth narrative incorporates much beyond what is
portrayed in the Christian nativity. Of course, the obvious
correspondences between the Egyptian narratives and the story of
Christ include: A god essentially fecundating a mortal woman; an
announcement of the conception; an adoration of the divine child by
a number of personages; a pronouncement of the divine child as the
god's "beloved"; and the declaration that this *son of God* would reign
forever. These correlations in themselves rank as enough evidence
that the Christian divine-birth narrative is neither original nor
unique.

The Christ Connection

When it comes to older scholarship, we discover a distinct trend
of writers who had little problem seeing correspondences between the
Egyptian nativity narrative and that of Jesus Christ. For example,
Gerald Massey's summary of the *Luxor* images and inscriptions
appears in his book *The Historical Jesus and The Mythical Christ*:

> We shall find that the gospel history was "*written before*" from
> beginning to end. The story of the divine Annunciation, the
> miraculous Conception (or incarnation), the Birth, and the Adoration
> of the Messianic child, had already been engraved in hieroglyphics
> and represented in four consecutive scenes upon the innermost walls
> of the holy of holies in the temple of Luxor which was built by
> Amenhept III., a Pharaoh of the eighteenth dynasty. In these the

---

[1] Dr. Brunner names the 12 gods in the first scene of *Hatshepsut's* narrative as: Osiris,
Isis, Horus, Nephthys, Seth, Hathor, Month [Menthu or Mont], Atum, Shu, Tefnut, Geb
and Nut. (Brunner, 15.) Brunner presents the German rendering of "Shu" as "Schu."
The god "Month," Brunner relates, is "der Herr von Theben"—the Lord of Thebes.
[2] Breasted, *ARE*, II, 84.
[3] Smith, R., 27.

maiden queen Mut-em-Ua, the mother of Amenhept, her future child,
impersonates the virgin mother who bore without the fatherhood, the
mother as the solar boat, the mother of the Only One...

The first scene on the left hand shows the god Taht [Thoth], the
lunar Mercury, the divine Word or Logos, in the act of hailing the
virgin queen, announcing to her that she is to give birth to the
coming son. In the next scene the god Kneph (in conjunction with
Hathor) gives life to her. This is the Holy Ghost or Spirit that causes
conception; Kneph being the spirit. Impregnation and conception are
made apparent in the virgin's fuller form. Next the mother is seated
on the midwife's stool, and the child is supported in the hands of one
of the nurses. The fourth scene is that of the adoration. Here the
child is enthroned, receiving homage from the gods and gifts from
men. Behind the deity Kneph, on the right *three* men are kneeling
and offering gifts with the right hand and life with the left. The child
thus announced, incarnated, born, and worshipped was the
Pharaonic representative of the Aten sun, the *Adon of Syria*, and
Hebrew Adonai, the child-Christ of the Aten cult, the miraculous
conception of the ever-virgin mother personated by Mut-em-Ua.[1]

In *Gerald Massey's Lectures* appears a shorter essay by the same
title that is slightly different but largely consistent.[2] The book version
differs from the lecture version in a few instances, however, that
indicate the former to have been written after the latter. For example,
in the book version, Massey replaces the 18th Dynasty for the 17th,
the former being the correct date. In addition, he substitutes the term
"miraculous" for "immaculate" when describing the conception and
removes the words "magi" and "spirits" as descriptions of the three
individuals in the "adoration" scene. These latter changes indicate
that Massey's work may have been criticized for using Christian
terminology. Yet, it is surprising that no one appears to have taken
him to task for not including the first row panel of the birth scene,
such that he would be sure to incorporate it in his later analysis, if
such had been known to him. It is possible, therefore, that this scene
had not been copied and widely distributed from Egypt yet and was
not known to European scholars of the day.

Massey ends the lecture edition of his description thus:

These scenes, which were mythical in Egypt, have been copied or
reproduced as historical in the Canonical Gospels, where they stand
like four corner-stones to the Historic Structure, and prove that the
foundations are mythical.[3]

Massey describes the scenes in his other works as well, including
Ancient Egypt: The Light of the World, in which, regarding the panel
with Taht/Thoth "announcing" to the "virgin queen" that she is "to
give birth to the coming son," he adds, "That is, to bring forth the

---

[1] Massey, *HJMC*, 32-33. This material is also included in Massey's *The Natural
Genesis*, 398-399.
[2] Massey, *GML*, 4ff.
[3] Massey, *GML*, 5.

royal Repa in the character of Horus or Aten, the divine heir."[1] Thus, the divine child is identified with Horus, as we would expect, since both are the king. From Massey's interpretation of the scenes we can see a number of important correspondences to Christianity.

The depiction of the Luxor scene in terms of its relationship to Christianity emanates not originally from Massey but earlier from Dr. Samuel Sharpe, who presents the last two panels and then makes some surprising remarks:

> In this picture we have the Annunciation, the Conception, the Birth, and the Adoration, as described in the First and Second Chapters of Luke's Gospel; and as we have historical assurance that the chapters in Matthew's Gospel which contain the Miraculous Birth of Jesus are an after addition not in the earliest manuscripts, it seems probable that these two poetical chapters in Luke may also be unhistorical, and be borrowed from the Egyptian accounts of the miraculous birth of their kings.[2]

Like Dr. Sharpe, we would do well to suspect that the miraculous nativity scene in the gospels is no more "historical" than that of the Egyptian pharaohs. In fact, as we have seen and will continue to see, there is good reason to believe that, despite any differences, the gospel birth narrative was in reality a continuation of this old and ongoing Egyptian nativity tradition.

Egyptologist Sayce evidently concurred with some of Sharpe's conclusions:

> Yet more striking is the belief in the virgin-birth of the god Pharaoh, which goes back at least to the time of the Eighteenth Dynasty. On the western wall of one of the chambers in the southern portion of the temple of Luxor, Champollion first noticed that the birth of Amon-hotep III. is portrayed. The inscriptions and scenes which describe it have since been copied, and we learn from them that he had no human father; Amon himself descended from heaven and became the father of the future king. His mother was still a virgin when the god of Thebes "incarnated himself," so that she might "behold him in his divine form."[3]

The learned Dr. Sayce's notes indicate that he had before him the inscriptions and was translating them himself. In discussing the age of this *virgin-birth* concept, Sayce raises the nativity of *Hatshepsut* and remarks:

> How much further back in Egyptian history the belief may go we do not know: the kings of the Fifth and Sixth Dynasties called themselves sons of the sun-god, and the Theban monarchs whose virgin-mothers were wedded to Amon, incarnate in the flesh, did but work out the old conception in a more detailed and definite way.[4]

---

[1] Massey, *AELW*, II, 757.
[2] Sharpe, *EMEC*, 19. (Emph. added.)
[3] Sayce, *RAE*, 249.
[4] Sayce, *RAE*, 250.

Citing Sayce, *The New Schaff-Herzog Encyclopedia*—again, a respected *Christian* publication—relates: "The birth of Amenophis III. of Egypt is described on the walls of the temple of Luxor as from a virgin and the god of Thebes, in other words, Ammon-Ra..."[1] Thus, in Sayce's work we possess a qualified authority using primary sources and interpreting them to represent the birth of the sun god and his proxy on Earth, the pharaoh, from a *virgin mother* and a god as father, a concept dating to very ancient times. The remarks about Amen/Amun being "incarnate in the flesh" and "working out the old conception in a more detailed and definite way" indicate Sayce also had before him the first-row panel, with Amun the queen sitting on a platform facing each other.

Naturally, the pronouncements of Drs. Sharpe and Sayce were met with all sorts of "skepticism" because of their implication of the unoriginality of the Christian nativity scene. It is interesting, however, that such profound skepticism rarely seems to be applied to the improbable divine birth of *Jesus Christ*, while impossible standards of proof for the existence of the virgin-birth motif within *Paganism* are often demanded.

The God-King as Horus

Like Massey, Ernest Busenbark describes the Luxor scenes in much the same way and also identifies the divine child with Horus.[2] In *Christianity Before Christ*, Dr. John Jackson associates the god-king with Horus and his mother with Isis. This association is not without merit and precedent, since, as we have already seen, the living king was considered to be Horus on Earth, and Horus's birth was extremely significant in Egyptian religion, especially in later times, closer to the common era. Since Hatshepsut is not a queen but a pharaoh herself, she too is equated with Horus, Hare relates, "...Hatshepsut also made the same claims to being Horus and to being the son of Re that we find in all the standard pharaonic titularies."[3] Moreover, both the pharaoh and Horus are thus the "son of the Sun."

In the original birth legend of the "falcon god," it is Amun and *Hathor*, sometimes called "Mut," which simply means "Mother," who parent the divine child,[4] explaining their presence in the Luxor imagery. In fact, at Luxor there existed a very ancient sun-god festival involving the union of Hathor with the sun god, producing the "divine son," as related by Dr. Erich Neumann:

> The figure of the virgin bride of God has an analogy in the Luxor festival, where the royal priestess of Hathor joins herself, in an age-

---

[1] *NSHERK*, XII, 210.
[2] Busenbark, 117-118.
[3] Hare, 136.
[4] Ellis, 16.

old predynastic ritual, to the sun-god for the production of the divine son. Later in patriarchal times, this role was taken over by the king, representing the sun-god.[1]

The sun god in this case must be the hybrid Amun-Re. Indeed, regarding the temple of Luxor, Budge says that "it formed an important part of the sacred buildings of Thebes, which were dedicated to the Theban triad of Amen-Ra, Mut, and Khonsu..."[2] In the later mythology, it is *Osiris* and *Isis* who beget the falcon god, i.e., *Horus*. Indeed, Khonsu was one of the many gods with whom Horus was identified. As Meltzer remarks: "Horus was combined, syncretized, and closely associated with deities other than the sun god Re, notably (but not exclusively) Min, Sopdu, Khonsu, and Montu."[3] As a "divine child" within the various Egyptian triads, Khonsu is also connected to the god Shu, who is likewise identified with Horus.[4]

In his description of "scene 12" at Luxor (Budge's row 3, scenes 1 and 2), in which the queen appears with the goddess Selkis behind her and two goddesses in front, Murnane states that these personages "each suckle a figure of the child, Horus NEBMAATRE,"[5] revealing the babe's *Horus* name. There are also a couple of (Hathor) cows under the bed, and four times is invoked the wish for the baby to "sit on the Horus throne." Murnane describes scene 13 thus:

> *Two fecundity figures are shown, one bearing symbols of life, the other carrying the infant king and his Ka—the latter carrying on his head a serekh inscribed with the king's Horus name*: The Horus, Mighty Bull "Who Appears in Maat."[6]

These "fecundity figures" (the two Niles) are guiding the baby and his *ka* into the "birth house of Horus and Seth" to be purified.[7] This paragraph with the inscription of the Horus name upon the forehead of the divine child's *ka* is noteworthy in consideration of the assertion that the birth narrative has "nothing to do with Horus." As we can clearly see, the baby in this scene is the proxy of Horus, as are all living Egyptian kings or pharaohs. Again, Horus is "the primary divine identity of the pharaoh."[8] Indeed, the *serekh* upon the *ka*'s head is described by Murnane as the hieroglyphic "palace façade" that "encloses the first of the king's 'great names,' which defines him as a *manifestation of Horus*."[9] Therefore, identifying the baby in this birth narrative as Horus does not constitute an error—and this

---

[1] Neumann, E., 135.
[2] Budge, *NNTE*, 575.
[3] Redford, 167.
[4] Redford, 186.
[5] Murnane, 25.
[6] Murnane, 25.
[7] Murnane, 26.
[8] Murnane, 280.
[9] Murnane, 283. (Emph. added.)

situation of the miraculous birth of a god and son of God could not have escaped the notice of those who ostensibly imitated the Egyptian divine-birth narrative in creating the Christian one.

Identifying the mother as "Isis" is also not erroneous but would be logical, since she is Horus's mother. Concerning the role of the king as Horus and his mother as Isis, Hornung describes a scene in the burial chamber of Tuthmosis III of "a stylized tree offering its breast to the pharaoh," underneath which is the inscription: "He sucks [on the breast of] his mother Isis."[1] The "Royal Mother Isis," Hornung continues, is the pharaoh's "real mother." The Swiss Egyptologist further remarks upon the fact that Tuthmosis thus "had an Isis as his earthly mother," while "[a]t the same time, the king as Horus on earth is able to return to his heavenly mother Isis..."[2] Hornung also relates that the king, like Horus, is "the loyal son born to Isis...."[3]

Moreover, in various of the hymns to Isis in her temple at Philae, built beginning centuries before the common era, appear references by the king to his "mother" Isis, identifying the Ptolemy who is the hymn's subject as the "beloved son" of the goddess.[4] As Žabkar relates:

> Thus Isis, mother of Horus, is also mother of the king, not only because she addresses him as "my beloved son," or "my son, Horus, my beloved," but because his royal function and character are coextensive with those of Horus, her son, who long ago had become the mythical prototype of the Egyptian king, with whom the Ptolemies tended to identify themselves.[5]

In discussing the "Egyptian royal rites," Griffiths also relates that the king's mother is Isis:

> ...In the coronation rites, attention is naturally focused on the new king, who is equated with Horus, but since Isis is the mother of Horus (in his forms as Horus the Child and Horus the Elder), she figures in the retrospective aspect of such rites, as indeed does Osiris as his father.[6]

Therefore, the divine child is essentially *Horus*, while his mother is identified with *Isis*, a perpetual virgin, taking the place of Mut, who, as we have seen, was said in later times to be a *virgin mother*. In addition, the confounding of Isis and Hathor—resulting in the composite goddess Isis-Hathor[7]—lends further weight to this identification, particularly since it is *Hathor* who is depicted in the divine-birth narrative as nursing the divine Horus-king's *kas*, as in scene 12 at Luxor. As Meltzer says concerning Horus's genealogy,

---

[1] Hornung, *VK*, 55.
[2] Hornung, *VK*, 55.
[3] Hornung, *VK*, 118.
[4] Žabkar, 23.
[5] Žabkar, 25, 31.
[6] Redford, 170.
[7] Hornung, *SLE*, 38.

"The full picture is more complex: Hathor (herself identified with Isis) also appears as the mother of Horus...".[1] Indeed, the name "Hathor" means "House of Horus," about which Griffiths remarks that "perhaps house here refers to the celestial domain of the falcon god... But her early claims to be the mother of Horus may more probably be implied."[2] As Egyptologist Delia White remarks, "Scenes of Hathor suckling Horus continued to be carved on temple walls down into the New Kingdom period."[3]

In this regard, the images in the nativity scenes are said to represent not only a king and queen but also a god and goddess, specifically Horus and Isis, who is a *virgin mother*. Hence, when we are debating the nature of certain aspects of the nativity scenes, we must keep in mind that we are addressing *mythology*, not set-in-stone biography or history. We have already seen that Horus's mother was unquestionably considered the "Great Virgin" in pre-Christian times. It would also follow that, despite any sexual innuendo, the queen too retains her "perpetual virginity" after conceiving and giving birth to the Horus-king, especially when the pharaoh's mother is at times identified with Isis.

Furthermore, concerning the nativity scene at Luxor, Dr. Wiedemann states, "There is a similar scene in a temple of Dendera, dating from about the time of Trajan and representing the birth of the Sun god."[4] From the imagery at Dendera of Bes holding Harpocrates on his shoulder, it would appear that this sun god being born is *Horus*, in a scene from the second century AD/CE, around the time when Christianity truly began to be formulated. Thus, we have a continual line of divine births of Horus-kings from over 1400 years before the common era until the second century into it—a long-lived motif of obvious notoriety, particularly in consideration of the popularity of Harpocrates previously discussed.

"Soft-Core Porn?"

In his extensive and frequently cited study of the birth scenes of the Egyptian pharaohs, *Die Geburt des Gottkönigs*, Egyptologist Dr. Hellmut Brunner (1913-1997), a professor of Theology, Archaeology and Egyptology at the University of Tübingen, presents the scenes at *Luxor* in the following order:

1. Hathor, in the middle, embraces the queen on the left, with Amun on the right.
2. Amun is on the right, with another figure on the left (the god Thoth? King Thothmes IV?).
3. Amun, on the left, turns back and looks at Thoth, who is holding scrolls.

---

[1] Redford, 166.
[2] Redford, 170.
[3] Clarysse, 544.
[4] Wiedemann, 164.

4. The queen is sitting on the left, Amun on the right, of the platform being supported by the two goddesses. Amun is holding an ankh to the queen's nostril.
5. Khnum is on the left, with Amun on the right.
6. Khnum on the right fashioning the king and his *ka*, with Hathor on the left holding an ankh or cross of life.
7. Thoth announces to the queen.
8. Khnum is on the left and Hathor on the right of the queen, Hathor holding an ankh to her nostril, while Khnum holds one to the back of her head.
9. The queen is sitting on a couch surrounded by five figures on the left and four on the right, one in a group of three holding the baby. Below this couch appear 10 beings, while underneath them are three Anubis figures, three Horuses and the deities Thoueris/Taurt and Bes.
10. Hathor presents the divine child to Amun.
11. Amun is on the right in a throne, holding the baby, with Hathor in the middle saluting and another figure (Mut?) on the left.
12. In this scene several *kas* are being held and/or nursed by a number of figures.
13. The divine child and his *ka* are being carried by the two Niles.
14. Horus presents the divine child and his *ka* to Amun.
15. Once again the divine child and his *ka* are presented to a company of gods and others.

In his brief analysis of the scenes as portrayed by Dr. Brunner, historian Richard Carrier interprets Brunner's German translation of the inscriptions of scene or panel 4 (Budge's first row, scene 3), to depict a "risque" portrayal of "very real sex" between Amun and the queen:

> The inscription in Panel 4...describes the god Amun jumping into bed with the human Queen on her wedding night (or at any rate before she consummates her marriage with the human King) disguised as her husband. But she recognizes the smell of a god, so he reveals himself, then "enters her" (sic). The narrative then gets a bit risque—the god burning with lust, queen begging to be embraced, there's kissing going on, Amun's buddy Thoth stands by the bed to watch, and after Amun "does everything he wished with her" she and Amun engage in some divine pillow talk, and so on. At one point the queen exclaims amazement at "how large" Amun's "organ of love" is, and she is "jubilant" when he thrusts it into her. Ah, I lament the death of pagan religion. It's [sic] stories are so much more fun! At any rate, the couple relax after "getting it on," and the god tells her in bed that she is impregnated and will bear his son, Amenophis. To be more exact, the Queen inadvertently chooses the name by telling Amun she loves him, which is what "Amenophis" means.

Despite the giddy "Penthouse Forum" interpretation presented here, there is no mention by Budge, Breasted or Sayce, et al., that the *Luxor* inscriptions reveal the god "jumping into bed" or engaging in "very real sex," with the queen discussing the size of Amun's "organ of love," or that he specifically "thrusts it into her." Nor is the expression "getting it on" to be found in any rendition of the scene. Budge delicately describes the god and queen merely as "holding converse," while Rev. Dr. James Baikie (1866-1931) elegantly opines that the mother is impregnated by the *ankh*, "the divine breath of life, which is held to her nose."[1] Neither of these scholars indicates anything sexual about the scene, the implications of which represent the greatest matter of debate about these birth scenes. Like Baikie, Busenbark asserts that the virgin's impregnation occurs with the holding of the ankhs or "crosses of life" to the head and nostrils. Dr. Jackson recounts the scene with "Kneph" (Khnum) and Hathor holding crosses/ankhs to the "head and nostrils" of the virgin queen, after which she becomes "mystically impregnated."[2] Indeed, the activity of Khnum/Kneph putting the ankh to the queen's nostril to impart life constitutes another sort of conception, mystically and spiritually—a significant concept that is not tremendously different from that found within Christianity and that has been claimed as a predecessor for the Christian nativity motif of the Holy Spirit fecundating the Virgin Mary. In his description of Amenhotep's "birth room," Andrew Humphreys avers the conception occurs through the fingertips of the god and queen sitting on the bed/sky, remarking, "You can even see the moment of conception when the fingers of the god touch those of the queen and 'his dew filled her body', according to the accompanying hieroglyphic caption."[3] Nor does Egyptologist Dr. Karol Myśliwiec give any inkling of "risque sex" in his brief description of the Luxor scenes in *Eighteenth Dynasty Before the Amarna Period*, even though he cites the 1964 edition of Brunner's book in his bibliography, specifically as a source of his information regarding the birth scenes.[4] Other analyses that contain slightly erotic language such as Breasted and Frazer's concern the *Hatshepsut* inscription, not the Luxor one.[5] In any event, as may be obvious, there exists a debate as to when and how the conception/impregnation occurs.

Moreover, where Carrier sees "pillow talk," in the *image* the god and the queen are seated on a platform floating above two goddesses. The pair is therefore not lying down on a bed, as is the impression given by the phrase "pillow talk." In describing the image of the fourth scene, Brunner's German simply relates what we can see: Amun and the queen are discreetly sitting on a "bed," which is simply a platform being held by two goddesses.[6] Again, this "bed" or *platform* is said to be indicated by the hieroglyph for "sky," while Murnane calls it the "vault of heaven." Describing this scene as "the god Amun

---

[1] Baikie, 418-419, as also in Monderson, 165.
[2] Jackson, *MGC*, 124.
[3] Humphreys, 211.
[4] Myśliwiec, 10, vii.
[5] See Frazer, *GB*, II, 131-132
[6] Brunner, 35, 36-37.

jumping into bed with the human Queen" seems to be unnecessarily sexual, even when we factor in the inscription.

For the inscription of this "bed" scene, Carrier refers us to page 42, et seq., of Brunner, upon which we find two main paragraphs in German relating the words spoken by Amun and the queen as reflected in the hieroglyphs surrounding the image. Carrier states this is where the "very real sex" and "soft-core porn" come in. However, in "skimming" Brunner's text, as he puts it, Carrier has mistakenly dealt with the substantially different *Hatshepsut* text (Brunner's "IV D"), demonstrating an egregious error in garbling the cycles, when in fact we are specifically interested in the *Luxor* narrative (IV L). Indeed, the *Luxor* inscription is lacking two important passages found in the Hatshepsut text that could be considered "erotic" but hardly constitute "soft-core porn": "he gave his heart to her" *("er gab sein Herz zu ihr hin")* (IV D a) and "she kissed him" *("[sie] küßte [ihn]")* (IV D d).[1] In the Luxor inscription, there is no kissing or giving of the heart.

This last point is particularly important because there exists another debate as to what the phrase "he gave his heart to her" means in the *Hatshepsut* inscription that accompanies the "bed" scene. Hare's translation of the pertinent *Hatshepsut* passage (IV D a) is as follows:

> Amun...found her asleep deep in the interior of her palace. She awoke at the scent of God and smiled upon His Majesty. He came up to her at once, and He was filled with passion for her, and He gave His heart into her, and He gave unto her His form as god to see. And when He had come before her, she rejoiced at His perfection. The love of Him penetrated her body. The palace was pervaded with the scent of God and every breath was fragrant with Punt.[2]

In his book cleverly titled *ReMembering Osiris*, one of Hare's main purposes is to explore glossed-over sexuality in Egyptian hieroglyphs. Yet, he only mentions the Hatshepsut narrative in order to demonstrate *male dominance*, and his translation of the pertinent passage indicates no overt sexuality, other than noting that "the expression 'gave his heart into her' represents a slight alteration of the direct translation of the Egyptian *rdj jb=f r=s*, which, if translated as 'gave his heart to her' might erroneously evoke the romantic associations of that English expression without the daring sexual significance the phrase had in Egyptian."[3] Hare does not clarify further but cites "Müller, 'Die Zeugung durch das Herz,'" an article the full title of which translates into English as "Procreation through the Heart in Religion and Medicine of Egypt." The germane point here is that Hare does not use the narrative as an object lesson for his

---

[1] Brunner, 43, 44.
[2] Hare, 135. Murnane explains that Punt is cited because one of its "chief exports" was incense.
[3] Hare, 275.

thesis of erotic understanding of Egyptian hieroglyphs, which he surely would have done, had the scene truly represented "soft-core porn."

While Hare sees the text describing Amun "giving his heart to her" as implying sex, Brunner explains the term "heart" (*Herz*) as "seat of being."[1] Brunner adds that the sentence could also signify, "He exposed to her his secret,"[2] apparently referring to the revelation of his Godhood in the next phrase. Indeed, *Brunner specifically disagrees with the sexual interpretation of "heart,"* stating that this part when Amun gives his heart to the queen appears too early in the narrative to indicate conception.[3] In Brunner's opinion, the recognition of the god by the queen—"*er ließ sie ihn sehen in seinen Gottesgestalt,*" the Egyptian of which Hare renders as "He gave unto her His form as a god to see"—comes *before* the conception. In fact, Brunner recounts the opinions of several others debating whether or not true sexual intercourse (*Zeugungsakt*) is meant in the narrative.[4] Indeed, if there is a debate as to whether or not "he gave his heart to her" refers to the conception—and Brunner nevertheless says that it does *not*—there could not be any clear reference as to when exactly the queen *was* impregnated and hence no graphic description of sexual intercourse. In any event, this phrase about the heart does not even appear in the *Luxor* inscription, so the point is moot, and there occurs one less place to look for erotic intention.

Since we are concerned in reality with the *Luxor* narrative, let us look at the first paragraph of Brunner's German translation of the inscription in scene 4 (IV L a), in which we find the words of Amun, followed by a description of the initial part of the scene:

> Er fand sie, wie sie ruhte im Innersten ihres Palastes. Sie erwachte wegen des Gottesduftes, sie lachte Seiner Majestät entgegen. Er ging sogleich zu ihr, er entbrannte in Liebe zu ihr; er ließ sie ihn sehen in seiner Gottesgestalt, nachdem er vor sie gekommen war, so daß sie jubelte beim Anblick seiner Vollkommenheit; seine Liebe, (sie) ging ein in ihren Leib. Der Palast war überflutet (mit) Gottesduft, und alle seine Gerüche waren (solche) aus Punt.[5]

My translation of Brunner's German is as follows:

> He found her, as she rested in the interior of her palace. She awoke because of the god's scent, and she laughed at His Majesty. He went immediately to her, he was passionately in love with her; he let her see him in his Godliness, after he had come in front of her, so that she rejoiced at the sight of his perfection; his love (it) went into her

---

[1] Brunner, 51: "Hier ist die Rede vom Herzen als dem Sitz des Wessen, des geheimen Kernes der Person."
[2] Brunner, 51: "Er offenbarte ihr sein Geheimnis."
[3] See Brunner, 52.
[4] Brunner, 53.
[5] Brunner, 45.

body. The palace was flooded with God-scent, and all his aromas were (such) out of Punt!

Murnane directly translates the *Egyptian* of the same scene from Luxor:

> It was resting in the interior of the palace that he found her. At the god's scent she awoke, and she laughed in front of his Person. He went to her at once, for he lusted after her. He caused her to see him in his godly shape after he had come right up to her, so that she rejoiced at seeing his beauty. Love of him coursed through her limbs, and the palace was flooded <with> the god's scent: all his smells were those of Punt![1]

As we can see, the phrase "he gave his heart to her" is missing, because it was not present in the *Luxor* narrative. Moreover, what Brunner renders "he was passionately in love with her," Murnane translates as "he lusted after her"; in this regard, Brunner's interpretation is actually *less sexy* than Murnane's. While there is the word "lusted" and a bit of passion on the part of the queen, there is no mention of Amun's phallus or anything else to give the impression of the "soft-core porn" we encounter in the Carrier interpretation. In fact, again, Murnane's rendition is so tame that it is not a *bed* upon which the two lovers are seated but the *"vault of heaven."* Also, the phrase "his love went into her body" does not necessarily mean, as Carrier (or Brunner) apparently believes it does, that he "thrust his organ into her," particularly in consideration of Murnane's translation of the Egyptian as, "Love of him coursed through her limbs." Naturally, the word "love" could also indicate *romance*, rather than "organ of love." In fact, the Egyptian word for love here is ≈⌣◠ *mert*, which, as we have seen, refers to "divine love."

In addition, when Carrier is relating the words of the queen, he is likewise apparently referring to the section of the *Hatshepsut* inscription Brunner labels "IV D b," the text of which is substantially different from the *Luxor* inscription. One phrase in this part of the *Hatshepsut* inscription for which Brunner uses the German term "umfangen," meaning "embrace," might indicate intercourse.[2] In his translation of the *Hatshepsut* birth narrative, Frankfort states that the god "went to her immediately; then he had intercourse with her..."[3] Other writers likewise use the word "intercourse" to describe what went on between Amun and the queen Ahmose, *Hatshepsut's* mother, while still others call it "interview."[4] However, again, whereas the term rendered by Brunner as *"umfangen"* might indicate "intercourse," *this phrase is not in the Luxor inscription.*

---

[1] Murnane, 23.
[2] Brunner, 43.
[3] Frankfort, 44-45.
[4] See Matthews, V., 52; Wren, 37.

Brunner's German rendition of the queen's words in the *Luxor* inscription (IV L b) is as follows:

"Wie groß since doch deine Bas! Wie vollkommen ist diese [deine]...! Wie [verborgen] sind die Pläne, die du durchführst! Wie zufrieden ist dein Herz über meine Majestät! Dein Duft ist in allen meinen Gliedern!", nachdem die Majestät dieses Gottes alles, was er wollte, mit ihr getan hatte.[1]

In *Near Eastern Religious Texts Relating to the Old Testament*, theologian and Bible scholar Dr. Walter Beyerlin, in collaboration with Brunner, provides an English translation of the same Luxor passage as follows:

"How great is your power! How perfect is your...! How hidden are the plans which you make! How contented is your heart at my majesty! Your breath is in all my limbs," after the majesty of this god has done with me all that he willed...[2]

In Dr. Beyerlin's book, he and Brunner further remark that these birth narratives represent the "most detailed version of the account of the election by God of the bringer of salvation."[3] Beyerlin also says, "It is probable that the myth was recorded of every Egyptian king." He further refers to corresponding biblical citations, mostly from the Old Testament, noting, "Marginal reference may be made to points of contact with the birth narratives in the gospel of Luke,"[4] a correlation also contended by Sharpe. Here Beyerlin, with Brunner, is clearly aware that there *is* a correspondence to both Old and New Testament scripture.

Indeed, in his own work on the births of the god-kings, Brunner briefly indicates his own awareness of the Christian connection to the ubiquitous Egyptian birth narrative in at least three places,[5] including in the *concluding paragraph*, with a brief statement that "careful examination" is required in regard to any relationship to the New Testament.[6] Brunner also cites other studies such as "Pharao und Jesus also Söhne Gottes," or "Pharaoh and Jesus as Sons of God," once again demonstrating his knowledge that there exists an important discussion concerning a relationship to the Christian nativity. The fact that Brunner ends his important monograph with this cautious discussion is an indication that he believes there is significant merit to the subject and that it may have been on his mind throughout the entire analysis.

Continuing with the Luxor text, Murnane's direct translation of the Egyptian inscription for the queen's words is thus:

---

[1] Brunner, 46. See also Breasted, *ARE*, II, 80fn.
[2] Beyerlin, *NERTROT*, 30.
[3] Beyerlin, *NERTROT*, 29-30.
[4] Beyerlin, *NERTROT*, 30.
[5] Brunner, 29, 81, 215.
[6] Brunner, 215.

"How great, indeed, is your power! How beautiful is [everything] which you have [done]. How hidden are the plans which you have made. How satisfied is your heart at my Person! Your fragrance is throughout all my body." After this, (i.e.), the Person of this God's doing all that he wanted with her.[1]

The term *Bas* in the first sentence of the Egyptian represents the plural of *ba*, which is generally translated as "soul" and which in this case apparently refers to the souls of the kings, as defined by Murnane: "The Bas of a locality are assumed to be the divinized ancient kings of those places."[2] Like Beyerlin, Murnane renders this passage as the queen exclaiming, "How great is your *power!*" This is the only phrase in which the queen is depicted as shouting about the size of something, and, unless the *Bas* are to be misinterpreted as such, her cry is not about the god's "organ of love."

The phrase describing "the majesty of this god" doing or having done "what he wanted with her" implies sexual activity in both German and English. Yet, of course, the term "Majestät" in German decidedly refers to the god as *king* and is not a sexual innuendo for his member. Hence, we remain at a loss as to where exactly the queen is exclaiming about the large size of the god's "organ of love."

Other than the word "lusted" in the first paragraph, there is nothing *overtly* sexual in Murnane's translation from the Egyptian of the relevant parts of the *Luxor* inscription. The queen is not "begging to be embraced," nor is there any kissing going on.[3] Also, according to Murnane, in the third scene at Luxor—*before* the conception scene—Amun-Re "bids farewell" to Thoth on his journey to the king's palace, while in the fourth and critical scene the god and the queen are sitting alone "upon the vault of heaven, supported by the goddesses Selkis and Neith."[4] It is difficult to see how "Amun's buddy" Thoth therefore appears as a leering voyeur at the conception scene, as Carrier claims.

The hieroglyphs themselves in the Amenhotep inscription do contain two phallic symbols; however, one of these clearly is part of a term meaning "husband,"[5] and the phallus signs (Gardiner's D52 and D53) are often used to indicate maleness, rather than sexual intercourse. In consideration of the fact that there are Egyptian representations of men and gods with erect phalluses ("ithyphallic"), indicating that the Egyptians felt no compunction to avoid "pornographic" imagery, the question remains, why the delicacy of the birth narrative *images*, which do not indicate any sort of sexuality at all? The figure of Amun holding an ankh to the nostril, imparting

---

[1] Murnane, 23.
[2] Murnane, 278.
[3] Again, the kissing only occurs in one line at "IV D d" of the Hatshepsut text. (Brunner, 44.)
[4] Murnane, 22.
[5] See Hare, 109.

life, appears elsewhere outside of the Luxor nativity cycle. Hence, it may be that, viewing the delicate scene alone, the average Egyptian—and Alexandrian Jew who was involved in the creation of Christianity—not being able to read the hieroglyphs, was not aware of any sexual innuendo in the narrative.

Concerning the scenes at both Luxor and Deir el-Bahari, Morenz does make the following statement: "God, in the guise of the pharaoh, is shown approaching the woman thus blessed. The images and the text depict the scene with a fine delicacy, yet dwell frankly upon the act of sexual union."[1] He does not elaborate, but his assessment is likely based on what we have already examined here, which is not particularly conclusive as "frankly dwelling upon sexual union" as concerns the *Luxor* text, which, again, is of particular interest to us. Moreover, the fact that Morenz goes on to differentiate between the Egyptian nativity scene and that of the Christian birth narrative indicates that the subject was on his mind and that the parallel is at least superficially evident enough to cause him to comment.

In her description of the birth narrative, in *Feasts of Light* Normandi Ellis eloquently bridges the pronounced gap between the writers of the Victorian and Playboy eras, with a decidedly feminine but inclusive take on the birth scenes at Luxor:

> The feast of The Conception of Horus celebrates the Queen Mother as the mortal embodiment of the divine Great Mother. In the birth chapel at the Temple of Luxor we find a delicate rendering of the immaculate conception of pharaoh Amenhotep III as the embodiment of Horus. Well before conception, the divine child's birth is preordained. On his potter's wheel, the god Khnum already shapes the twin images of the pharaoh and his *ka*, or "divine double." The spiritual contract has been struck between Khnum and the High God, in this case, Amun.

> Actual conception occurs in heaven. On earth the god Amun inhabits the body of the pharaoh's father; but in this spiritual portrait, the god Amun and Queen Mutemuia, the mortal mother of Amenhotep III, sit close together atop a hieroglyph depicting the sky. Their knees touch, their hands clasp, their eyes meet. Tenderly, Amun lifts his hand to touch Mutemuia's face, as if he were offering her the heady perfume of a lotus blossom. Held aloft by two goddesses, Serket and Neith, who act as heavenly angels, the feet of the divine couple never touch the ground. The images resonate with stories of the Christ Child's immaculate conception, the angelic messengers to Mary and Joseph, and the white dove that represents the descent of the Holy Spirit which stirs the seed in the womb of the Virgin Mary. Pregnancy and potentiality always being in the realm of the spirit....

> This same scene appears throughout Egypt—in the birth chapel of Queen Hatshepsut at Deir el-Bahri, in the birth house of Nectanebo at Dendera, and at both birth houses of Trajan at Philae and Edfu. In the Greek versions of the story, the divine spiritual partner is usually

---

[1] Morenz, 36.

depicted as Hathor, rather than the queen; the father is sometimes depicted as Horus. The Hierogamos always takes place between the divine beings of heaven, who use the physical bodies of the royal couple, so to speak, to conceive and create the heroic, divine son on earth.[1]

In Ellis's view the scene depicts the "conception of *Horus*," with whom the god-king is identified and whose "*actual conception occurs in heaven*," producing an "*immaculate conception*." The sacred bride is the "Great Mother," who, in the ancient world as in the Christian era, was undoubtedly viewed as "the Virgin" as well, serving in Egypt as the goddess Isis. Furthermore, following the order of Budge, Ellis declares that the "divine child's birth is preordained," or *announced*, as it were. In her analysis, Ellis is not loath to make a comparison between the Egyptian nativity and that of Christ. Ellis also notes the ubiquitousness of the birth narrative right up to and into the common era.

Furthermore, where Carrier sees "very real sex" and "risque" romping with a smelly god, Ellis perceives the *Hierogamos*—the "sacred marriage"—as "tender and sweet":

> The tenderness and sweetness of the Hierogamos, say the ancient texts, permeated the royal bedroom, even the whole palace, with the fragrance of ambrosia, the scent of the gods.[2]

Likewise depicting the panel somewhat more gracefully, John Anthony West describes this scene at Luxor as a portrayal of "'theogamy', the king born of the Neters—that is to say, the mystical creation through the Word, which is the 'Virgin' birth or Immaculate Conception..."[3]

In *A Guide to the Antiquities of Upper Egypt*, Sir Arthur E.P. Weigall (1880-1933), a director-general of Upper Egypt, Department of Antiquities, likewise calls the scenes at Deir el-Bahari the "immaculate conception and birth of Queen Hatshepsut."[4]

Also regarding Hatshepsut's birth cycle, in *Egyptian Temples* Dr. Margaret A. Murray (1863-1963) remarks, "...on the lower half of this [back] wall are scenes and inscriptions recording the immaculate conception and divine birth of the queen."[5] Dr. Murray was a well-regarded Egyptologist at the University College of London who taught the Egyptian language to Dr. Faulkner, whose *Concise Dictionary of Middle Egyptian* remains one of the most important works on the subject.

Declaring the pertinent scene 4 as being "handled with great delicacy," Dr. Barry J. Kemp, a Reader in Egyptology at the University of Cambridge and Field Director of the excavations at el-Amarna by

---

[1] Ellis, 127.
[2] Ellis, 127.
[3] West, J, *SS*, 158.
[4] Weigall, *AGAUE*, 266.
[5] Murray, *ET*, 124.

the Egypt Exploration Society, provides a translation of the first part of the *Luxor* inscription that includes the sentence, "He was aroused by her,"[1] in the same place rendered as "lusted after" by Murnane and "passionately in love" by Brunner. Dr. Kemp does not provide us with a translation of the queen's response but states that it was a "brief speech of joy." Kemp does, however, include an image of the scene, under which he writes:

> ...An immaculate conception; the god Amun (*upper right*) impregnates Queen Mutemwia (*upper left*), wife of Tuthmosis IV and mother of the future god-king Amenhetep III. Beneath them sit the goddesses Selket (*left*) and Neith (*right*). A scene from the divine birth cycle at Luxor temple... After H. Brunner, *Die Geburt des Gottskönigs*, Wiesbaden, 1964...[2]

Thus, Kemp's professional observation, based on his reading of Brunner, is that the *Luxor* scene represents an *immaculate conception*—his words.

The "Immaculate Conception" and "Virgin Birth?"

It is further claimed that the phrase "immaculate conception"— used, as we have seen, by Sir Weigall, Dr. Murray and Dr. Kemp, among others—is inappropriate, as it refers *only* to the Christian Mother of God, the Virgin Mary. While it is true that the phrase "immaculate conception" is in English and was invented only within the last four to five centuries, the question remains whether or not the **concept** behind it existed in ancient times and is applicable to the divine births of pre-Christian deities, royalty and heroes. As it is widely understood, the term merely means that the subject of the conception was created "without original sin," original sin being that which taints humanity from the moment it is conceived. The question then arises as to whether or not the ancient Egyptians perceived conception (or sex) in itself as inherently sinful. If so, we need to establish the conception of the pharaohs as being considered "sinful"; otherwise, their conception too must be deemed "immaculate." Moreover, if there is no original sin, *all* conceptions could be argued to be "immaculate."

Because of all the purported sexiness, there remains also a question as to whether or not the divine-birth scene at Luxor and elsewhere in Egypt constituted a "virgin birth" long before the common era, suggested by Drs. Sharpe and Sayce, as well as Massey, et al. It seems to be agreed by all parties that the queen in this image is a virgin *before* her impregnation, which occurs after her "converse" with the god Amun in the form of her husband. From all of the emphasis on "virginity" within the Egyptian religion—with Neith and Isis, as we have seen, said to remain "perpetual virgins" even

---

[1] Kemp, 198.
[2] Kemp, 199.

after they become mothers—it would be surprising *not* to find this motif within the divine-birth cycle of kings.

In this regard, however, in his brief comparison between the Christian and Egyptian birth narratives Carrier further asserts Brunner to comment that "there is no sex in the former and Mary remains a virgin, whereas in the Egyptian cycle, as the inscription makes unmistakably clear, the Queen definitely loses her virginity." Unfortunately, in several instances in his article, Carrier does not cite his contentions, and it is therefore difficult to follow his conclusions. Because of this lack of citation, we are left with the impression that Carrier has misinterpreted Brunner's remarks concerning the virginal state of both the Egyptian queen and the Jewish maiden prior to conception.[1] In fact, the intention of Brunner's discussion here appears to be to emphasize not that the inscription makes the lack of virginity in the fecundated queen "unmistakably clear" but that both women were *married virgins* before conception. This remark of Brunner's is important because what he does plainly state is that the Egyptian queen was a *virgin* before Amun approached her.[2]

As we have seen, over the decades there has been a debate not only as to what parts of this scene of the narrative are to be taken sexually, if at all, but also as to when exactly the conception takes place, as Brunner relates.[3] How, then, are we sure that there was any kind of intercourse remotely resembling that of a human being, especially when we are discussing a *mythical event?*

Furthermore, if all this eroticism were so obvious, one would think that it would be noticed by Rev. Sayce—*a devout Christian minister*—whose oversight in pointing out this difference between the Egyptian and Christian nativity narratives would seem baffling, since he undoubtedly believed the Luxor depiction to be of a *virgin birth*, which he specifically deemed it. Yet, if the sexual innuendo were so blatant, its omission from the interpretations of all these others' depictions of the scenes, from the earliest times to the present, would constitute a prime example of how scholars hold back data for a variety of reasons—verifying our contention that much pertinent information is hidden from the eyes of the masses.

In any event, even if we accept that there is an unseen romp in the hay in the Luxor scene—although, again, we can tell from the debate that the point of conception is not agreed upon, thereby

---

[1] "In unserem Zusammenhang soll diese Aussage des Thoth besagen, daß der König die Ehe mit seiner Gemahlin noch nicht habe vollziehen können, so daß die alleinige Vaterschaft des Gottes nicht bezweifelt werden kann; die Königin ist also, obwohl verheiratet, Jungfrau. Bis zur Jungfrauengeburt ist zwar noch ein weiter Schritt; es bleibt bemerkenswert, daß die frühchristliche Überlieferung, um die Jungfrauschaft der ebenfalls verheirateten Maria zu retten, zum Ausweg eines Gatten greift, der im Gegenteil zu alt zum Vollzug der Ehe ist." (Brunner, 29)

[2] Brunner also mentions the queen's virginity on page 191.

[3] Brunner, 53.

indicating no clearcut description of intercourse—so too in one version of the myth did the impregnation of Isis involve using Osiris's phallus. Yet, as we have seen, Isis remains a virgin. Moreover, this scenario of the god Amun approaching the *sleeping* queen[1] and impregnating her reminds one also of the Greek myths in which the god Zeus visits several mortal women, such as Danae and Leto, producing half-mortal heroic offspring. In those myths, despite this visitation that left the woman pregnant, in the case of Danae especially, she remains a "virgin." In reality, even with all of his paramours Zeus himself is called *parthenos*—"virgin."[2] In the end, if in the myth of Osiris, Isis and Horus, Isis remains a perpetual virgin, and if the pharaonic divine birth constitutes a reenactment of this trio, or a combination of mythical trios, then the queen also would remain a virgin, despite any erotic exploits.

In emulating this divine-birth scenario—which was so widely known as to be applied to the founder of Alexandria yet constituted an acknowledged mystery right into the common era—it would be a simple matter for the stoic Christian creators to *omit* any erotic aspects of the nativity template and continue with the common, archetypal birth narrative. If the creators of the Luxor scenes felt no difficulty in leaving out a number of phrases that might be considered erotic, it should not surprise us if the creators of Christianity did likewise. This insight of sanitization may in fact be behind the past analyses that omitted the first row of the scenes, because *the Christians themselves evidently did likewise* when they copied the Egyptian birth narrative. If the creators of Christianity merely lopped off the first row when copying the Egyptian birth narrative, they would start with the "messenger of the gods" (angel) announcing to the virgin queen that she was to give birth to the divine son, etc., precisely as we see in the nativity story of Jesus Christ. Again, the removal of the eroticism from this scene—as would be sensible for a group of ascetics and matter-denigrating Gnostics, for instance—would simply render this scene as the Virgin being fecundated by the Father God, which is what happens in the Christian tradition as well, with an innocent 12-year-old subjected to the will of God in her impregnation.

Further Parallels to the Gospel Story

Adding to this fact of the removal by the Amenhotep template-creators of various phrases from the Hatshepsut cycle, the imitators of the Hatshepsut narrative altered the *order* of the scenes at Luxor for their own purposes as well. Indeed, the order differs from birth narrative to birth narrative and authority to authority. In the Luxor panels, according to the order of Brunner and Murnane, the narrative

---

[1] West, M.L., 459.
[2] Graves, R., 361.

opens with the goddess Isis/Hathor embracing the queen and telling her Amun is about to give her a child, representing an *annunciation.* As we can see, if we are discussing the *Luxor* narrative and not erroneously that of Hatshepsut, the order of an annunciation before the conception is accurate and applicable in our comparison between the Egyptian and Christian religions. Yet, again, even if the Luxor panels clearly reveal a pre-conception annunciation, the Christian copyists could have simply left off the themes found in the first row of the Egyptian nativity template and proceeded from there, likewise presenting the scene with Thoth, the Word, announcing the conception to the queen.

As concerns other panels, the god Khnum finds his counterpart in the Bible as both the "Holy Spirit" and the creator of mankind, as the "potter" fashioning the *ka* and breathing life into the king, while the biblical God is specifically called "our potter" at Isaiah 64:8 and elsewhere, and is depicted at Genesis 2:7 breathing life into the first man, Adam.

Concerning the scenes with multiple deities, again, in creating the Christian narrative from the archetypical template—which need not necessarily have come directly from Luxor, as it was obviously common enough to have been perhaps even closer to home in both time and location, say, in a book or two at the Library of Alexandria— it would be critical to omit these distinctly Egyptian and polytheistic scenes. Their omission from the gospel tale, however, does not mean that the Egyptian divine-birth template was not used in the creation of the Christian myth.

Other highly Egyptian elements, such as the cow-goddess Hathor nursing the baby, as well as the discussion of the *ka*, would certainly not be included in the Christian myth, which, in the end, would simply represent the birth-narrative template stripped of all of its "erotic" and Egyptian elements. The creation of the Christian birth narrative, therefore, regardless of the differences, would simply be one more of the same priestly manufacture as had been tried and found true for many centuries.

The "Magi" Presenting Gifts?

In the panel labeled scene 9 by Brunner and Murnane appear a number of individuals, including, on the second level below the queen, a group of figures on the right holding up ankhs. In the earlier modern renditions of this image—which were engravings, not photos, based on the badly damaged walls at Luxor—these three figures were all drawn with human heads, thereby striking one as a set of three *men* who were obviously dignitaries of some sort, appearing at the divine child's birth, and offering him gifts. It is these three figures whom Massey calls "kings" or "magi," using terminology from the New Testament in order to provide a point of comparison possibly indicating where the Christian motif comes from. In Brunner's rendition, however, the third "king" bearing a gift is depicted with a ram's head and appears to be Khnum, who, combined with a crocodile-headed god (Sobek?) in front of the three, makes a grouping of four figures, two gods and two humans.[1]

Remarking upon the scene in which the figures present the newly born divine child with gifts, Earl Doherty first comments upon the terminology used by Massey and others, including the present author, in calling these figures "magis," and then says:

> The basic common parallel is there in the Adoration of the child, with dignitaries offering gifts. How apologists can get so excited over these minor distinctions is beyond my understanding. (I suppose when straws are all you have to grasp at, they have to do.)

In labeling these characters "magi" Massey was using a convention to convey the parallel to the scene as found in the gospel story. Surely he did not mean that the term "magi" was inscribed on the wall. Even so, the knowledge of Persian words in Egypt may not be so strange in consideration of the suggestion that Amenhotep III may have been a relative of the Indo-Persian Mitanni, who possessed a kingdom in northern Turkey and with whose royalty he enjoyed a relatively cordial relationship. Indeed, one of Amenhotep's wives was a Mitanni princess.[2] This fact of interchange between Egypt and a kingdom that was Indian in many of its essentials, including several deities, as early as the 14th century BCE, is important to keep in mind when discussing the exchange of religious ideas within the areas in which Christianity principally developed. Certainly, Indian religion and mythology are the source of a significant amount of Western religion and mythology, including the Greek and Roman, dating back many centuries before the common era.[3]

In any case, since in the gospel story the "king" and "wise men" are not numbered as three, Doherty's point about the comparison between dignitaries offering gifts to the babe in the adoration scene is well taken. Because we do not need *three* kings but any number will do to make this comparison, and because there are clearly a number of important figures offering gifts to the newborn babe, we remain justified in making the correlation between the Egyptian and Christian adoration scenes.

Also, there is another grouping of *three* adoring the divine babe (also scene 9), and, as we shall see, the motif of the "Three Kings" at the divine birth is pre-Christian and unhistorical, appearing elsewhere in Egyptian mythology.

Regardless of the order of the scenes, or the terminology used to describe elements thereof, the fact remains that at the Temple of Luxor is depicted the conception upon a virgin by the highly

---

[1] See Brunner, 91-92.
[2] Gordon, C., 67.
[3] For more on the subject, see my books *The Christ Conspiracy* and *Suns of God.*

important father god, Amun, to produce a divine son. As we have seen, Amun's divine child in this birth cycle is the "bringer of salvation," and this myth of the miraculous birth of the divine savior likely was "recorded of every Egyptian king," making it highly noticeable long before the Christ figure was ever conceived.

The Luxor nativity scene represents the birth sequence of an obviously very important god-king, as it was depicted in one of the most famous Egyptian sites that endured for some 2,000 years. Egypt, it should be kept in mind, was a mere stone's throw from the Israelite homeland, with a well-trodden "Horus road," called in the ancient texts the "Ways of Horus" or "Way of Horus," linking the two nations and possessing numerous Egyptian artifacts, including a massive, long-lived fort and Horus temple at the site of Tharu, for instance. Moreover, at the time when Christianity was formulated, there were an estimated 1 million Jews, Hebrews, Samaritans and other Israelitish people in Egypt, making up approximately one-half of the important and influential city of Alexandria. The question is, with all the evident influence from the Egyptian religion upon Christianity that we have seen so far—and will continue to see abundantly—were the creators of the Christian myth aware of this highly significant birth scene from this significant temple site in Egypt? If not, these scenes were widespread enough right up to and into the common era—could the creators of Christianity really have been oblivious to these images and the stories of royal divine births they depict?

Indeed, the point is not necessarily that the Alexandrian creators of Christianity used *this* particular narrative but that there were plenty of miraculous-birth templates ages prior to the common era, rendering Jesus's own nativity all too mundane, rather than representing a unique "historical" and "supernatural" event that proves his divinity above and beyond all others. With such a widespread precedent, could we honestly believe that the Christian nativity scene constituted something new and startling?

In the end, when all the evidence is weighed, from a mother named "Mery" who was a perpetual virgin and who shares many other attributes with the mother of Jesus, to the prominent presence of a divine-birth narrative with several germane similarities to the Christian nativity, it turns out that Horus, like Jesus, is the son of a virgin mother, laid in a manger and brought out for a yearly celebration, eons before the Christian era. In the end, rolling all of these qualities and myths into one, we can therefore honestly say that the Egyptian son of God, Horus, was born on December 25th of the Virgin Mother Isis-Mery.

CHAPTER LXVI.

[From the Papyrus of Åmen-em-ḥeb (Naville, *Todtenbuch*, Bd. I, Bl. 78).]

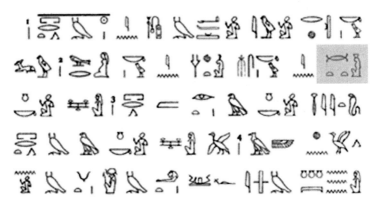

Book of the Dead, Chapter/Spell 66
Hieroglyph for "Neith" highlighted
(Budge, *Book of the Dead* (1898), 148)

Isis hovering over Osiris, conceiving Horus.
(Budge, *On the Future Life: Egyptian Religion*, 80)

Isis suckling Horus
(Wilkinson, *The Manners and Customs of the Ancient Egyptians*, III,
112)

Isis suckling Horus, with Crosses of Life to her Nostril and Back,
From the Temple of Isis at Philae.

Nativity Scene of Amenhotep III at Luxor, Panel 4.
(Brunner, *Die Geburt Des Gottkönigs*, pl. 4)

"King of the gods" Amun-Re "gives life to the nostril of the hawk,"
the Pharaoh.
(Wilkinson, *The Manners and Customs of the Ancient Egyptians*, III,
46)

The Star in the East and Three Kings

"Osiris's coming was announced by Three Wise Men: the three stars Mintaka, Anilam, and Alnitak in the belt of Orion, which point directly to Osiris's star in the east, Sirius (Sothis), significator of his birth."

Barbara Walker, *The Women's Encyclopedia of Myths and Secrets* (749)

"The soul or *sahou* of Osiris was said to have dwelt in Orion. The *Belt* of three stars, the middle one being of especial interest, could not fail to win attention. But everything in the stellar field pales before the brilliancy of Sirius, the dog-star."

James Bonwick, *Egyptian Belief and Modern Thought* (325)

"Sothis was the harbinger of the annual inundation of the Nile through her appearance with the rising sun at the time when the inundation was due to begin. The bright star would therefore naturally become, together with the conjoined constellation of Orion, the sign and symbol of new vegetation which the Year then beginning would infallibly bring with it."

Dr. John Gwyn Griffiths, *The Origins of Osiris and His Cult* (157)

Much has been made of the gospel account of the "star in the east" followed by "wise men" from afar, claimed to have heralded the birth of the newborn savior of the world. Over the centuries, various supposedly scientific theories have been put forth concerning this purported phenomenon that turn out to be all for naught, because this theme reveals itself to be an old *mythical* motif. In actuality, many ancient gods, kings and heroes were said to have been born under a "bright star" or some other sort of celestial sign, indicating their greatness and role as "savior" as well. Despite protests to the contrary, this heavenly theme is obviously *astrological* and *astrotheological* in nature, dating back centuries to millennia prior to the common era. Indeed, like so many other religious and mythological correspondences, the "bright star" and the "three kings" represent motifs that long predate Christianity and are found within Egyptian religion, symbolizing the star Sirius as well as those of the constellation called Orion, along with their relationship to Osiris, Isis and Horus.

In the gospel story, Jesus's birth is signaled by a bright star and a visit from wise men or *magi*, as they are termed in the New Testament, representing *Persian astrologers* following the star. Despite the stellar brilliance and obviousness, this tracking was apparently not a simple act, since these "wise men" are depicted as nevertheless illogically becoming hopelessly lost and must ask

Christ's enemy King Herod for assistance.[1] Herod points the wise men in the right direction, but he too evidently becomes so discombobulated that, instead of following his own instructions to find Jesus, he needs to slaughter all of the children in the village, a heinous act that can be found nowhere in the historical record and would be rather deplorable for the all-powerful God/Jesus to allow in order to save his own neck. In any event, although in the gospels these magi are not numbered, their gifts *are* counted as *three*, and over the centuries tradition has set them at three as well. Hence, the familiar tale is that Jesus's birth was accompanied by a "star in the east" and "three wise men." These three wise men were also said to be "kings," as in the popular Christmas song, "We Three Kings." At a certain point the three kings were given names, Caspar, Melchior and Balthasar, and the mythmaking continued.

Coincidentally, there happen to be three very conspicuous stars in the "belt" of the constellation of Orion that are also called the "Three Kings." Moreover, as French philosopher Simone Weil (1909-1943), herself a Christian, remarked, "The Christians named the three stars of Orion *the Magi*,"[2] revealing esoteric knowledge of *Christian astrotheology*, regardless of when it was first adopted. In addition, one of the brightest stars in the sky is that of Sirius, which, along with Orion, was a favorite of the Egyptian priesthood for thousands of years, keen observers of the skies as they were, and well aware of astronomical phenomena. Not a few people have thus equated this bright star and these wise men in Christian tradition with these revered celestial bodies within Egyptian and other mythologies.

Concerning the "Three Kings" who supposedly appeared in the gospel drama, S.C. Gould states:

> THE "THREE KINGS" OR ORION.... The kings referred to are generally believed to be the "three shepherd-kings" who are said to have followed the Star of Bethlehem at the Nativity of Jesus the Christ. Their names are given as Caspar, Melchior, and Balthasar; while the names of the "three star-kings" are Alnitak, Anilam, and Mintaka. These three stars always point to the Pleiades or Seven Stars on one side, and to Sirius or the Dog-Star on the other side.[3]

In reality, rather than representing a "historical" event surrounding the birth of a superhuman Jewish messiah and divine Son of God, the stellar appearance at the coming of the savior can be

---

[1] Murdock, *WWJ*, 185fn: "The word for the 'wise men' in the biblical Greek is μαγοι—*magoi* or *maji*—which, per Strong's Concordance (G3097), means: '1b) the oriental wise men (*astrologers*) who, having discovered by the rising of a remarkable star that the Messiah had just been born, came to Jerusalem to worship him.'" (Emph. added.) See *Who Was Jesus?* for further discussion of the illogicalness of the gospel story.

[2] Weil, 474. (Emph. added.)

[3] Gould, 37.

n the myths of Egypt, particularly concerning Osiris, Isis and Horus.

A Sirius Star

The coming of Osiris—the *savior* of Egypt—was associated with the "Star in the East" because the Egyptians recognized that the rising of Sirius with the sun, or "heliacally," occurred around the summer solstice, the time of the Nile flooding. This discussion of Sirius provides an example of how the astrotheology of the ancient world may be hidden beneath poetic but oblique language: For instance, in CT Sp. 567 appears a reference to the star Sirius or Sothis, who "speaks to me in her good time."[1] Reading this passage, few might guess that this ambiguous language is likely referring to the "regular heliacal rising of the star."[2] In any event, life along the Nile was highly dependent upon the inundation associated with the heliacal rising of Sirius, a flood deified as Osiris, who was said to be "born" at that time. Concerning this event, Frazer relates:

> And the sign of the rising waters on earth was accompanied by a sign in heaven. For in the early days of Egyptian history, some three or four thousand years before the beginning of our era, the splendid star of Sirius, the brightest of all fixed stars, appeared at dawn in the east just before sunrise about the time of the summer solstice, when the Nile begins to rise. The Egyptians called it Sothis, and regarded it as the star of Isis, just as Babylonians deemed the planet Venus the star of Astarte. To both peoples apparently the brilliant luminary in the morning sky seemed the goddess of life and love come to mourn her departed lover or spouse and to wake him from the dead. Hence the rising of Sirius marked the beginning of the sacred Egyptian year, and was regularly celebrated by a festival which did not shift with the shifting official year.[3]

Thus, this important association of Sirius—"Sothis" in the Greek and "Sepdet" or "Sopdet" in the Egyptian[4]—with the life-giving Nile flood began some 5,000 to 6,000 years ago. *Hence, the "Star in the East" heralded the birth of the Egyptian Messiah thousands of years before the Christian era.* This annual birth of Osiris was also a *resurrection*, as the goddess Sopdet "woke him from the dead." In addition, whereas the planet Venus was considered the "morning star" in the Middle East and elsewhere, in Egypt *Sirius* was also designated as the morning star. Furthermore, that there was a "shifting official year" needs to be kept in mind, as it explains a number of the difficulties and discrepancies encountered in the Egyptian calendar, or *calendars*, as we have seen.

---

[1] Faulkner, *AECT*, II, 95.
[2] Faulkner, *AECT*, II, 97.
[3] Frazer, *AAO*, 34-35.
[4] Mojsov, xv.

As part of the changing Egyptian calendar, five epagomenal days were eventually added to the old calendar of 360 days, the first of these five constituting Osiris's birthday, while his brother Horus ("the Elder") was born the next day. This period came to represent the beginning of the "Egyptian sacred year." Therefore, it could be said that, with Sirius preceding the inundation and new year, *the star in the east announced the births of both Osiris and Horus.*

Regarding the role of Sirius/Sothis in Egyptian mythology, in *The Ancient Egyptian Pyramid Texts*, James Allen states:

> Sothis (*spdt* "Sharp"). The morning star, Sirius, seen by the Egyptians as a goddess. In Egypt the star disappears below the horizon once a year for a period of some seventy days; its reappearance in midsummer marked the beginning of the annual inundation and the Egyptian year. The star's rising was also seen as a harbinger of the sunrise and therefore associated with Horus in his solar aspect, occasionally specified as Horus in Sothis (*hrw jmj spdt*), Sothic Horus (*hrw spdtj*), or Sharp Horus (*hrw spd*).[1]

Thus, sometime around the middle of April, Sirius could no longer be seen on the horizon, until its reemergence at the summer solstice, starting a new cycle. As noted, Sirius is identified with Isis: "Sirius, the herald of flooding of the Nile, was the star of the goddess Isis, consort to the great god Osiris, who was represented by the constellation of Orion."[2] Indeed, in CT Sp. 837 appears the epithet "Osiris as Orion..."[3]

In the Egyptian writings, Osiris is linked with Sirius/Sothis on many occasions: For example, the deceased as "the Osiris" is "the brother of the moon, he is the child of the star Sothis, he revolves in heaven like Osiris and Sothis, and he rises in his place like a star."[4] According to another legend, the Osiris "becomes like the morning star, near his sister Sothis." There he "lived in the form of the star Sothis."[5] Osiris is like Sothis, which is his sister, usually identified as Isis, but sometimes also as Hathor.[6] In one Pyramid Text (PT 263:341c/W 173), the Osiris's sister is Sothis, while one of his female relatives, either his sister or his mother, is the "morning star."[7] At another point (PT 509:1123b) the morning star is the Osiris's "guide,"[8] indicating Sirius rising with the sun in the morning at the summer solstice, signaling the arrival of the god as the life-renewing

---

[1] Allen, J., *AEPT*, 441.
[2] Wilson, R., 16.
[3] Faulkner, *AECT*, III, 24.
[4] Budge, *EBD* (1967), lxxiii.
[5] Budge, *EBD* (1967), cv.
[6] Lockyer, *DA*, 196, 210.
[7] Allen, J., *AEPT*, 48; Faulkner, *AEPT*, 72; Mercer, 86. Faulkner renders the pertinent hieroglyph "sister," while Allen translates it as "female sibling," and Mercer prefers "mother." (See also Mercer, 88, 89.) As Faulkner relates, "Sothis appears as both sister and mother." (Faulkner, *AECT*, II, 299.)
[8] Mercer, 192; Faulkner, *AEPT*, 184.

Nile. At PT 593:1636a/M 206, Sirius's announcement of Osiris is also discussed in terms of the god spreading his "seed" or "semen" upon Isis in order to create Horus, an event representing the Nile overflowing its banks and bringing fecundating waters to the ever-renewing virgin soil. *Once more, Horus's birth is announced by a bright star.* At PT 569:1437a/P 508, the deceased also was essentially identified with Sothis, such that the star's "birth" itself would be prevented from happening if the Osiris were not allowed into heaven.[1] Moreover, as Jesus in the biblical Book of Revelation (22:16) is the morning star, so too in the Pyramid Texts (PT 676:2014b/N 411) is Osiris the "morning star,"[2] as is Horus, previously noted.

In addition, PT 593:1636b/M 206 states: "Horus the pointed has come forth from thee, in his name of 'Horus who was in Sothis.'"[3] "Horus in Sothis," therefore, refers to when the sun rises with Sirius. *Again, in ancient texts we find the birth of Horus the sun associated with the star in the east.*

In BD 65, the deceased, as Horus, pleads, "May I rise up, a Babe [from between] the knees of Sothis, when they close together."[4] Regarding this passage, Renouf remarks, "The knees of a goddess are frequently mentioned in connection with the birth of a divinity. Here the Babe is mentioned (cf. opening of Chapter 42), and the closing of the knees."[5] The word Renouf translates as "rise up" also means "live." In BD 42, Renouf identifies "the Babe" as the "rising sun," while the speaker repeatedly calls himself "Horus."[6] Hence, the Babe—Horus—asks to be born from Sothis, representing both Sirius and Isis. Indeed, in BD 101, Horus is said to "reside in Sothis,"[7] once more representing Sirius's rising with the sun. *Thus, yet again, Horus is said to be born as the sun rises in conjunction with the star in the east.*

The bright star in the east was associated not only with Isis, Osiris, Horus and Hathor but also with the god Anubis, the "Dog-Headed," an epithet of Sirius as well.[8] In her analysis of the myth of the Bright Star and Three Wise Men, mythologist Barbara Walker states:

> The star of Anubis was Sothis (Sirius), the Eye of the Dog, in Greek, *Canopis.* Sirius is the star forming the "eye" of Canis Major, the Great Dog. It is the brightest star in the sky. Egyptians believed it held the soul of Osiris, whose rebirth coincided with the rising of the

[1] Mercer, 229; Allen, J., *AEPT*, 176; Faulkner, *AEPT*, 222.
[2] Mercer, 221; Faulkner, *AEPT*, 290; Allen, J., AEPT, 277. Allen renders the relevant phrase the "a star, the morning god."
[3] Mercer, 251; Allen, J., *AEPT*, 217; Faulkner, *AEPT*, 244.
[4] Renouf, *EBD*, 128. See Allen, T., *BD*, 60. Faulkner only includes what Allen labels "Spell Naville 65." (Faulkner, *EBD*, 107)
[5] Renouf, *EBD*, 128.
[6] Renouf, *EBD*, 95; Allen, T., *BD*, 48; Faulkner, *EBD*, 105.
[7] Renouf, *EBD*, 172; Allen, T., *BD*, 83; Faulkner, *EBD*, 112.
[8] Bonwick, 314.

Nile flood, when his star rose in the east. "Three wise men" pointed the way to the newborn Savior: the three stars in Orion's belt, which form a line pointing to Sirius.[1]

Regarding Sirius as Canis Major, Bonwick remarks, "This heavenly dog barked a warning for the people to shift to higher ground, and to have their canals and ditches ready for the overflow of the Nile."[2] Griffiths concurs that "the inundation of the Nile was often connected by the Egyptians with the heliacal rising of the star Sothis (the Dog Star, Sirius), seen in the constellation of Orion."[3] To summarize, the three wise men serve as pointers for the star in the east, which in turn announces the savior of Egypt.

Orion and the Three Kings

As important as Sirius was to life in Egypt, associated with the renewal of the land around the Nile and thus memorialized in Egyptian religion and mythology, so too did the constellation of Orion figure prominently in Egyptian culture. In fact, it was observed that, as the rising of Sirius signaled the beginning of the summer solstice and its life-giving inundation of the Nile, the rising of Orion, with its three distinct stars acting as a pointer, signified the *end* of the flooding, towards the winter solstice: "The Nile flood...its coming and going heralded by the stars of Sirius and Orion, was without parallel."[4] Explaining the correlation between Sirius and Orion, Egyptologist Dr. Bojana Mojsov comments:

> Both Sirius and Orion were related to the Nile flood. The ascent of Sirius during the third week in June heralded the beginning of the Nile's steady rise. By August in Upper Egypt, and September in the north, the river swelled to its full capacity. Then, stars from the constellation of Orion emerged in the night sky after being invisible for seventy days. At this time, the river began to abate. By November, it was back in its bed.[5]

The ascent of Orion could not have failed to impress its observers: "The heliacal rising of Orion occurs before that of Sirius, so, star by star, Osiris was revealed by this most magnificent of constellations straddling the celestial equator."[6]

The name for Orion in the Egyptian is *Sahou, Sahu, Saah* or *Sah*, mentioned several times in the Book of the Dead, but more frequently in the Pyramid Texts (e.g., PT 274:408c/W 180b), in which "he" is called the "father of the gods,"[7] among other epithets. PT 442:819c-822b/P 38 demonstrates that Orion is identified with Osiris:

---

[1] Walker, 242.
[2] Bonwick, 313.
[3] Redford, 256.
[4] Mojsov, 35.
[5] Mojsov, 6.
[6] Wilson, R., 16.
[7] Faulkner, *AEPT*, 82; Mercer, 94; Allen, J., *AEPT*, 52.

"Look, he is come as Orion," (they say). "Look, Osiris is come as Orion..." The sky shall conceive you with Orion, the morning-star shall give you birth with Orion. Live! Live, as the gods have commanded you live. With Orion in the eastern arm of the sky shall you go up, with Orion in the western arm of the sky shall you go down. Sothis, whose places are clean, is the third of you two: she is the one who will lead you...[1]

In this passage Osiris is Orion, which in turn is a marker for the soul's journey, as led by Sothis/Sirius. The command by the Horus-priest for the Osiris to "live, live as the gods have commanded you to live" demonstrates the main purpose of the funerary/mortuary literature in *resurrecting the deceased*.

Concerning the relationship between Orion, Sirius and the Egyptian deities, Dr. Mojsov further states:

The constellation of Orion was linked with Osiris: "He has come as Orion. Osiris has come as Orion," proclaim the Pyramid Texts. Sirius and Orion, Isis and Osiris, inseparable in heaven as on earth, heralded the inundation and the rebirth of life. Their appearance in the sky was a measure of time and a portent of great magnitude. In historic times, both occasions were always marked by celebrations.[2]

As we can see, the annual emergence of both Sirius and Orion were closely noted and commemorated, meaning that these celestial events factored significantly in the minds of possibly millions of Egyptians for thousands of years. Moreover, the "rebirth of life" in Osiris—*his resurrection on Earth*—constitutes an *annual event*, in the Nile's flooding.

Regarding Orion's role in Egyptian religion and mythology, Krupp recounts:

The pharaoh also makes another celestial journey: to Orion. This constellation is a symbol of the soul's rebirth because Orion stood for Osiris and the great cycle of birth, life, death, and resurrection.[3]

Again, Orion is associated with the *resurrection* or *rebirth* of Osiris. Orion was so important in Egypt that the Great Pyramid was aligned to it, as also related by Krupp:

Meanwhile, the stars in Orion's belt, the objective of the south shaft, were among the decans, the stars whose rising or transits marked the hours of the night throughout the Egyptian year. Orion, of course, was Osiris, who presided over the resurrection of souls.[4]

As noted, within the constellation of Orion, "the Hunter," are three bright stars said to make up his "belt." Concerning these stars, in *The Geography of the Heavens* renowned Christian astronomer Elijah Hinsdale Burritt (1794-1838) remarks:

[1] Allen, J., *AEPT*, 107; Faulkner, *AEPT*, 147; Mercer, 153. See Griffiths, *OOHC*, 13.
[2] Mojsov, 7.
[3] Krupp, 101.
[4] Krupp, 105.

They are sometimes denominated the *Three Kings,* because they point out the Hyades and Pleiades on one side, and Sirius, or the Dog-star, on the other. In Job they are called the *Bands of Orion...*[1]

The biblical Book of Job (38:32) also contains reference to the *Mazzaroth,* or "zodiac," and demonstrates significant astronomical knowledge, an important fact in consideration of the contention that, centuries later, the Jewish priesthood rehashed the Egyptian astrotheology in its "midrashic" or *fictitious* account of Jesus Christ. Additionally, in the biblical text of Amos (5:8) appears a reference to him "that maketh the seven stars and Orion," the latter being the Pleiades, of course. (KJV) Interestingly, one of the stars in Orion is name *Meissa,* meaning "shining one" in Arabic,[2] "moonlike" in Hindi and the "one who is coming forth" in Hebrew,[3] as in the concept of the *Messiah.* Regarding the "magi" or Chaldean priests, Dean of Canterbury Dr. Frederic William Farrar (1831–1903) remarks, "That the Jews and their Rabbis had borrowed many astrological notions from the Chaldaeans, and that they connected these notions with the advent of the Messiah, is certain."[4]

As noted, the three highly visible "king-stars" of the splendid constellation of Orion are named Mintaka, Aniltak and Anilam or Alnilam, the latter of which means "string of pearls," while the former two signify "belt."[5] The statement in the Egyptian texts that Sothis "leads Orion" thus constitutes the motif of *the bright star followed by these three "kings,"* which have also been called the "three kings of the soothsayers,"[6] a title that may indicate the antiquity of this royal appellation.

Furthermore, while Isis was identified with Sirius/Sothis, according to Plutarch (21, 359D) "the soul of Horus is called Orion,"[7] essentially equating Horus with Osiris. Hence, the three "king-stars" following the bright star represent both Osiris and Horus, to the point, in fact, that they are pertinent to the birth of the solar savior at the winter solstice as well as the summer solstice in the inundation of the Nile.

Indeed, the bright star Sirius rose with the sun at the summer solstice, signaling the birth of Osiris as the Nile inundation and the birth of Horus as the daily solar orb. In winter, the Three Kings in the belt of Orion pointed to Sirius at night before the annual birth of the sun, which, as we have seen, is also Horus.

---

[1] Burritt, 57.
[2] O'Meara, 85.
[3] See Bullinger, 127.
[4] Farrar, 29fn.
[5] Van Zyl, 2.
[6] Whitney, 297.
[7] Plutarch/Babbitt, 53.

Regarding the Three Kings and the Star in the East at the winter solstice or "December 25th," philosopher Edward Carpenter (1844-1929) states:

> Go out next Christmas Evening, and at midnight you will see the brightest of the fixed stars, Sirius blazing in the southern sky—not however due south from you, but somewhat to the left of the Meridian line. Some three thousand years ago (owing to the Precession of the Equinoxes) that star at the winter solstice did not stand at midnight where you now see it, but almost exactly on the meridian line. The coming of Sirius therefore to the meridian at midnight became the sign and assurance of the Sun having reached the very lowest point of his course, and therefore having arrived at the moment of his re-birth.[1]

The appearance of the three stars in a line with Sirius occurred in the night sky over Egypt thousands of years ago, pointing to the horizon as the new sun was born at the winter solstice. *Thus, it could be asserted that the three kings trailing the bright star announced the birth of the savior at the winter solstice in Egypt, ages prior to the same event purportedly taking place in Judea.*

To these themes, Gerald Massey adds:

> The birthplace of the *"coming one"* as it passed from sign to sign was indicated by the typical *"star in the east,"* and the Star in the East will afford undeniable data for showing the mythical and celestial origin of the gospel history. When the divine child is born, the wise men or magi declare that they have seen his star in the east. The wise men are identified as the Three Kings of other legends who are not to be derived from the canonical gospels.... When the birthplace was in the sign of the Bull, the Star in the East that arose to announce the birth of the babe was Orion, which is therefore called the star of Horus. *That was once the star of the three kings*; for the *"three kings"* is still a name of three stars in Orion's belt; and in the hieroglyphs a three-looped string is a symbol of *Sahu*, i.e., the constellation Orion. Orion was the star of the Three Kings which rose to show the time and place of birth in heaven some 6,000 years ago, when the vernal equinox was in the sign of the Bull...[2]

In Plato's *Second Letter/Epistle II* (2.312E)—predating the common era by centuries, if genuine—we find a discussion of the "Three Kings," who are identified by Latin writer Amelius (3rd cent.) with the Neoplatonic "three Intellects and Demiurges," as well as with "the three whom Orpheus celebrates under the names of Phanes, Ouranos, and Cronus."[3] Since Orion is speculated to be derived etymologically from the Akkadian *Uru-Anna*,[4] is it possible that "Ouranos" is also a cognate? In any event, in this Platonic example we possess "Three Kings" who are astrotheological, as in the Orion

---

[1] Carpenter, 29.
[2] Massey, *HJMC*, 12-13.
[3] Turner, 387; Wilkinson, *SSMCAE*, 190.
[4] Livo, 56.

mythos and possibly serving as a foreshadowing of the motif within Christianity.

That the Egyptians were well aware not only of the constellation of Orion as a whole but also the three very bright stars in its belt is demonstrated by the fact that the hieroglyph for Orion represents a "three-looped string."[1] In the past decades, there has been an effort to link these three stars to the pyramids at Giza, representing their builders, traditionally held to be three kings of Egypt.[2] Could it be that in ancient times the Egyptians themselves likewise associated the pyramid builders with Orion's belt, to the point of naming the stellar group "the three kings?" Since the deceased king is Osiris, and Osiris is Orion, it is possible the connection was made at some point also in antiquity. In any event, by whatever name, the Egyptians were well aware of the three belt stars and incorporated them into their mythology as "heralds" of the great savior, as, apparently, did the Christians.

Stellar Commonality

As can be seen, the motif of the star in the east and the three "wise men" or "kings" as heralds of the savior of the world was in existence long before the common era. Indeed, this stellar motif regarding the savior's birth appears repeatedly in Egyptian religion and mythology, as it can also be found in the stories of many other gods and heroes at whose births appeared bright stars, comets and other portents, such as the Hindu god Krishna,[3] the Indian sage Buddha,[4] the Persian king Mithridates and the biblical patriarch Abraham.[5] As Dr. Farrar also states:

> Even the Greeks and Romans had always considered that the births and deaths of great men were symbolised by the appearance and disappearance of heavenly bodies...[6]

Even the Jews depicted their coming messiah as being astrotheologically heralded, as at Num 24:17: "a star shall come forth out of Jacob." (RSV) Naturally, over the centuries Jesus has been claimed to have been this "star out of Jacob." Hence, the motif must have been in the minds of many people—possibly many millions—long prior to the common era and continuing well into it.

By whatever number, and whether or not they constitute astrotheological symbols, the presentation of gifts to the divine child

---

[1] See Budge, *EHD*, I, 638, entry for "*Sah.*"

[2] See the "Orion Correlation Theory" championed by Robert Bauvall, et al. See Krupp's criticism of this theory. (Fagan, 250.)

[3] Bryant, *KAS*, 119. So common is the star at birth within Indian culture that there are various words in Sanskrit for "natal star." (*The Concise Sanskrit-English Dictionary*, 150.)

[4] Beal, 32-33; 42-43.

[5] Strauss, 173-174.

[6] Farrar, 30.

by dignitaries is made plain in the various nativities scenes of Egyptian royals already examined. Based on the evidence, the Christmas story of the birth of Jesus Christ as a savior being announced by the star in the east attended by three kings represents an old pre-Christian mythical motif redressed and presented as "history."

Right to Left:
"The Sons of Horus-Osiris in the Sky Near their Father Orion (called
'Osiris')."
(Gray, *Mythology of All Races*, XII, 112)
"Orion, Sothis and Two Horus-Planets Standing in Their Barks,
from the Astronomical Ceiling in the Tomb of Seti I."
(Maspero, *History of Egypt*, I, 127)

Hieroglyph for Orion or *Sah* with Three-Looped String and Star
(Budge, *Ancient Egyptian Hieroglyphic Dictionary*, 638)

Horus at the Ages of 12 and 30

"Horus was the son of Seb, his father on earth. Jesus is the son of Joseph, the father on earth. Horus was with his mother the Virgin until twelve years old, when he transformed into the beloved son of God as the only-begotten of the father in heaven. Jesus remained with his mother the Virgin up to the age of twelve years, when he left her to be about his father's business. From twelve to thirty years of age there is no record in the life of Horus. From twelve to thirty years of age there is no record in the life of Jesus. Horus at thirty years of age became adult in his baptism by Anup. Jesus at thirty years of age was made a man of in his baptism by John the Baptist."

Gerald Massey, *Ancient Egypt* (787)

In addition to all of the correlations we have previously seen, another comparison between the Egyptian and Christian religions concerns significant ages of Horus that correspond to those of Jesus, for example, 12 and 30. In the gospel story it is claimed that, at the age of 12, Jesus wowed the temple elders with his precocious knowledge and wisdom. (Lk 2:42-46) Another age significant to Christ is "about 30 years," when he supposedly was baptized and started his ministry (Lk 3:22-23), dying within a year to three afterwards, depending on which conflicting gospel account one chooses to believe. Like those of Jesus, these same "ages" of 12 and 30 in the life of Horus—recalling, of course, that we are dealing with *myths*, not real people who actually *had* lives—correspond to the differences between the child and adult Horuses, naturally, but they also possess both ritual and *astrotheological* meaning as well.

It is odd that in the authorized (and sanitized) version of the gospel tale—claimed to be a *biography* of Jesus Christ—no mention is made of his early childhood or of his life between the ages of 12 and 30, when he allegedly began his ministry. Many attempts have been made to pad out this biography, with rumors of Christ's adolescence and early adulthood spent in India, Egypt or Great Britain, and with tales of his childhood recorded in apocryphal texts such as the Infancy Gospel of Thomas, which depicts a nasty and vicious boy Jesus who strikes children dead and causes people to go blind.[1] By the standards of a historian, however, none of these efforts at creating a biography has proved scientifically successful or satisfying. Needless to say, it is beyond peculiar that while no officially sanctioned biography of these "early years" of Jesus exists, in its stead emerges a dreadful account of a cruel, young magician.

It is further disturbing that none of Jesus's alleged immediate followers—two of whom purportedly wrote the gospels accepted as "canonical"—felt any interest in the earthly life of the alleged Lord of the universe prior to his ministry. Indeed, in the gospels we are given a miniscule biographical detail that supposedly casts Christ as a

---

[1] *The Lost Books of the Bible*, 61.

"carpenter." The word for "carpenter," however, appears only *once* in the gospels in connection with Jesus (Mk 6:3), and this term does not necessarily indicate a carpenter *per se*. Indeed, the definition of the Greek word used to describe Jesus's occupation, *tekton*, means not only carpenter but also craftsman, metalworker, builder, artisan, poet, etc.[1] Far from being a set-in-stone biographical fact that Jesus was a carpenter—an erroneous assumption that has made it nonetheless into many movies replete with fictional details—even in ancient times his occupation was variously depicted, such as the legend that Christ was a dyer of fabrics.[2] One would think that the biographers of God's only begotten Son would have more to say about this significant part of his supposed life on Earth. Not only is this one word the only information we possess indicating Christ's earthly vocation as a "carpenter," but there is not a hint of this occupation anywhere else in Jesus's supposed speeches, in which he speaks in parables mostly of "building," as in *masonry*, rather than anything in carpentry-related terms. Also, in Plato's philosophy, the creator of the cosmos was said to be the *tekton* or "builder," as in "Grand Architect of the Universe."[3] In this regard, in the Book of the Dead (BD 166), the god Ptah, equated by the Greeks with the forger god Hephaistos, is called the "Master Craftsman,"[4] a title also applied to the "High-Priest of Ptah at Memphis."[5] Moreover, at 1 Cor 3:10, the apostle Paul labels himself the *sophos architekton* or "wise masterbuilder." Oddly enough, in modern Greek *tekton* means not carpenter or even stonemason but *freemason*,[6] as in the secretive brotherhood supposedly behind much of the world's shenanigans, including in the field of religion. In any event, it would seem that Jesus as *tekton* represents yet another borrowed mythical motif designed to make him appear to be God, in competition with Pagan divinities.

Another interesting factoid that ties Christ to Egypt through masonry appears at Matthew 21:42, Mark 12:10 and Luke 20:17, in which Jesus discusses "scriptures," i.e., from the Old Testament, concerning the "stone which the builders rejected," further qualified as "the head of the corner..." (KJV) The word for "stone" here in the original Greek is *lithos*, which can refer to "stone" or "building stone," among others.[7] The "head of the corner" would be a cornerstone, of course. Indeed, 1 Peter 2:6 cites this passage in the gospels, after the author also quotes "scripture," i.e., a passage from the OT,

---

[1] Strong's G5045.

[2] Donehoo, 116.

[3] Pérez-Gómez, 115. See Plato's *Politicus* (Burnet, 259, section e, line 8); *Cratylus*, lines 11-12 and the *Timaeus*.

[4] Budge, *BD* (2003), 321.

[5] Faulkner, *EBD*, 174.

[6] *Collins Contemporary Greek Dictionary*, 168, 311; *Oxford Dictionary of Modern Greek*, 189.

[7] Strong's G3037.

specifically Isaiah 28:16. That scripture, in fact, discusses the Lord
GOD "laying in Zion" a "stone, a tested stone, a precious
cornerstone..." (RSV) The assumption is, of course, that Jesus is that
very "precious cornerstone." The author of Ephesians 2:20 states it
outright: "...Jesus Christ himself being the chief corner [stone]." (KJV)
Here and in 1 Peter, the term in Greek for "cornerstone" or "chief
corner" is ακρογωνιαος[1] or *akrogoniaios*, literally meaning "high
corner," which sounds like something at the peak of a pyramid or the
"capstone." The cornerstone is one of four in a square building, but
the "head" of the cornerstones could also be the peak of the pyramid.
While the "head of the corner" is ambiguous as to whether or not it is
a "chief cornerstone," it would be safe to assume that Jesus Christ is
indeed the "chief cornerstone" or peak of a pyramid, rather than one
of the four cornerstones at its base. In any event, this scripture is
singularly peculiar applied to a *human being*, even one claimed to be
God, but it would be logical if the creators of the story were part of a
builders guild attempting to depict their mythical figurehead as *the*
god of the cosmos.

In any event, the lack of an early background for Jesus tends to
verify the notion that *the original Christ was not a historical personage
but a mythical Gnostic concept*, as Docetic Gnosticism claimed that,
rather than having been born, Jesus emerged fully blown out of the
ethers as an adult phantasm. These facts add to the mythical air
surrounding the story of Jesus Christ, and we are left with the
impression that the tale as found in the New Testament and
elsewhere ranks as largely if not entirely *fictional*, based mainly on
the myths of other, preceding cultures from around the
Mediterranean and beyond. Indeed, as part of this widespread
mythology—which includes a number of *mysteries*—emerge the
notable ages of 12 and 30.

In *The Historical Jesus and the Mythical Christ*, Gerald Massey
describes the significance of these ages in Egypt:

> Jesus and Horus at 12 and at 30 years of Age.
>
> The first Horus was the child, who always remained a child. In Egypt
> the boy or girl wore the Horus-lock of childhood until twelve years of
> age. Thus childhood ended about the twelfth year. But although
> adultship was then entered upon by the *Sherau* ["adult son"], and
> the transformation of the boy into manhood began, the *full adultship
> was not attained until thirty years of age....* The god up to twelve
> years was Horus the son of Isis, the mother's child. The virile Horus,
> the adult of thirty years, was representative of the Fatherhood, and
> this Horus is the anointed son of Osiris. These two characters of
> Horus the child and Horus the adult of thirty years are reproduced in
> the two phases to which the life of Jesus is limited in the gospels.[2]

---

[1] Strong's G204.
[2] Massey, *HJMC*, 56-57.

The rite of passage at 12 years old may have constituted one of the *mysteries* that were not necessarily to be divulged to the masses, the remnants of which can be found in the Jewish *mitzvah* rituals. The Bar Mitzvah—which may have its roots in Egypt, as do other Jewish rituals, including circumcision[1]—celebrates the 13th birthday of the boy, who at this point is considered a man. Thus, the boy at twelve years remains a child but not after that point. The female version of the ritual, the Bat Mitzvah, occurs when the girl turns *twelve*, the difference based on the perception of when puberty begins. In addition, in some areas the Catholic Communion has also been set to be given at the age of 12.[2] Regarding the Egyptian ritual and its migration into Christianity, Massey comments: "So was it with the gnostic Jesus. The long lock of Horus, the sign of childhood, was worn by him until he attained the age of twelve years, when he was changed into a man."[3]

In BD 18, the speaker discusses the "Great Hoeing in Tattu," to which Renouf appends a note referring to a little child with the sidelock who is supposed to "scatter the seed in the field of Osiris."[4] Per the previous discussion, the upper age limit of Horus in this passage would be 12, at which point it could be said he is "working in his Father's house," as was claimed of Jesus as well when *he* was 12.

In the Egyptian story of Khamuas/Khamois found on Papyrus DCIV of the British Museum appears an interesting tale about *Sa-Asar, Si-Osiris* or *Senosiris*—the "son of Osiris"—who "grew rapidly in wisdom and knowledge of magic." The tale continues: "When Si-Osiris was twelve years old he was wiser than the wisest of the scribes."[5] This story includes fantastical elements—such as a visit to the underworld—that indicate it is not historical but may well revolve around *Horus, son of Osiris.* Thus, in Egypt we find a similar tale as in the gospel about the "son of God" who is 12 years old and is precocious in intelligence and knowledge, besting the elders and scribes.[6]

In addition to these facts of Egyptian age-related traditions exist astrotheological meanings for the 12 and 30. In the first place, Horus

---

[1] Brier, 69, 74.
[2] Villien, 365.
[3] Massey, *AELW*, I, 245.
[4] Renouf, *EBD*, 57. Faulkner calls this the "hacking up of the earth of Busiris." (Faulkner, *EBD*, pl. 14.) T. George Allen renders the "hoeing" as the "great earth-fertilizing," clarifying that it refers to the blood soaking created by Horus's battle against Set and his thugs. (Allen, T., *BD*, 33.)
[5] *Folk-Lore*, 498.
[6] The earliest date for papyrus DCIV is 46-47 AD/CE, as it is written on the back of official documents created at that time. Since there is absolutely no evidence for the existence at that time of the gospel of Luke, in which this story concerning Christ is contained—in fact there is no real scientific evidence for the existence of Luke's gospel as we have it until the end of the *second century*—if the pertinent story regarding Senosiris also dates to that early time, it would serve as clear indication that the gospel story was borrowed from it and not the other way around.

was commonly viewed as the rising sun, during which time, it could be said, "He dwelt on earth as mortal Horus in the house of Seb (earth) until he was twelve years of age."[1] In the solar mythos, the "age" of 12 refers to the sun at high noon, the twelfth hour of the day, when the "God Sun" is doing his "heavenly father's work" in the "temple" or "tabernacle" of the "most high." In the Egyptian myth, the child Horus—the rising sun—becomes Re at the "age" of 12 noon, when he moves into his "Father's house," in other words, that of Re and/or Osiris, who are interchangeable, as we have seen.[2] Indeed, while the sun gods or solar epithets are interchangeable in and of themselves, in certain texts, as we have seen, Re is specifically named as Horus's father;[3] hence, the relationship here is doubly appropriate. The fact of Horus attaining so quickly to such maturity certainly may impress his elders, the older suns, as he literally *becomes* them. To put it another way, Horus is the sun from the time it arrives on the horizon until 12 noon, at which point he becomes Re, the father of the gods and the "father of Horus" as well.[4] *It could thus be said that Horus does his father's work in the temple at the age of 12.*

In *The Dawn of Astronomy*, Lockyer describes this process of Horus becoming Re at the hour or "age" of 12:

> We have the form of Harpocrates at its rising, the child sun-god being generally represented by the figure of a hawk. When in human form, we notice the presence of a side lock of hair. The god Ra symbolises, it is said, the sun in his noontide strength; while for the time of sunset we have various names, chiefly Osiris, Tum, or Atmu, the dying sun represented by a mummy and typifying old age. The hours of the day were also personified, the twelve changes during the twelve hours being mythically connected with the sun's daily movement across the sky.[5]

The various "phases" of the sun's journey were given different personalities, while remaining one entity. Hence, Horus the Child wears the side lock until 12 noon when he becomes the adult Re.

The 12/30 motif further represents, of course, the 12 signs of the zodiac dividing the circle into sections of 30 degrees each, as well as the 12 months of the year of 30 days each, the latter concept noted in the fifth century BCE by Herodotus (2.4) regarding Egypt:

---

[1] Massey, *AELW*, I, 527. As concerns this "earthly father," Geb or *Seb*, it should be recalled that another of his sons was *Horus, brother* of Osiris. It seems to be another "coincidence" that Jesus's "earthly father" was named "Io-Seph," from the root words "Ya" and "Saf" in Hebrew. (Strong's H3254.) "Ya" is YHWH, the Jewish name for God, while "saf" means "add," "increase" or "do again." As Set is also Seth, could Seb have been rendered Sebh or *Seph*?

[2] Budge, *EBD* (1967), 30. See, e.g., BD 17.

[3] See, also Budge, *FFGAE*, 473.

[4] Brier, 60, 61.

[5] Lockyer, *DA*, 25.

The Egyptians...were the first to discover the solar year, and to portion out its course into twelve parts. They obtained this knowledge from the stars.... (To my mind they contrive their year much more cleverly than the Greeks, for these last every other year intercalate a whole month, but the Egyptians, dividing the year into twelve months of thirty days each, add every year a space of five days besides...)[1]

Herodotus goes on to state that the Egyptians "first brought into use the names of the twelve gods, which the Greeks adopted from them," possibly associating these gods with the months.

Moreover, when Osiris dies at 28—around the same age legend holds Jesus begins his ministry, not too long after which he too dies violently—the number represents the days in a lunation, the end of which signals the death of the soli-lunar god. Again, the "30" also constitutes the number of days in a month. In either event, this number would signify the movement of the sun into another month or sign, representing a sort of death and rebirth, much like the death and resurrection of Jesus around the age of 30. As Massey says, "Horus as the man of thirty years is initiated in the final mystery of the resurrection. So was it with the gnostic Jesus."[2]

The Sed Festival

Like Jesus, not only is Osiris associated with the "age" of "about 30," but so too is Horus in a very concrete, enduring and blatant fashion, in addition to obvious solar mythology and astrotheology. In this regard, in ancient Egypt there existed a celebration called the "Sed festival," which typically was supposed to take place every 30 years, yet which evidently also had been celebrated in 12-year intervals, once again demonstrating a 12/30 formula. As James Allen relates, the Sed Festival was "traditionally celebrated in the thirtieth year of a king's reign, designed to renew his vitality and power."[3] Indeed, Hornung calls it "the royal ceremony of rejuvenation."[4] The Sed Festival is very old, evidently dating to over 5,000 years ago based on a representation of it on the mace-heads of the Egyptian king Narmer.[5]

In *The Death of Gods in Ancient Egypt*, Jane Sellers further explains the purpose of the Sed Festival: "The Sed Festival is believed to have been celebrated by the ruling Pharaoh to commemorate the anniversary of his coronation and often, but not always, occurred in the thirtieth year of his rule."[6] Sellers further describes an inscription found at a temple at Bubastis regarding the goddess Bast: "She gives

---

[1] Herodotus/Rawlinson, 3-4.
[2] Massey, *AELW*, I, 245.
[3] Allen, J., *AEPT*, 440.
[4] Hornung, *VK*, 35.
[5] *Enc. Brit.*, IX, 66; Frazer, *GB*, III, 154.
[6] Sellers, 165.

Sed-Festivals of twelve years each."[1] In "The Egyptian Sed-Festival Rites," Egyptologist Dr. Eric P. Uphill (b. 1929) concludes, "The reference to twelve-year festivals is very interesting and bears out [Egyptologist Alexandre] Moret's doubts as to the exclusiveness of the thirty year period."[2]

Records indicate that the Sed festival took place not necessarily in the 30th year of the king or pharaoh's rule but at various other times as well: "...Prof. Petrie does point out and prove the astronomical reference to Sed, as a festival occurring regularly at periods of thirty years, and not in the thirtieth year of a king's reign..."[3] Frankfort concurs in showing that the Sed festival did not occur every thirty years of the reign of the king, but adds, nevertheless, that in the text of the Rosetta Stone the festival remains associated with a 30-year period:

> The Rosetta Stone, which calls the king κυριος τριακονταετηριδων ["lord of the 30-year festival"], proves the existence of a tradition connecting the festival with a thirty-year period... [4]

The Sed is also called the "pre-eminent festival of divine kingship,"[5] the "great festival of thirty years," and the "king's ceremonial."[6] The celebration was apparently often associated with Horus: At the Sed festival of the king Osorkon, for example, it was proclaimed, "Horus appears,"[7] reflecting the identification of the ruler with the god. Indeed, from the texts it is obvious that the living king/pharaoh *is* Horus, as previously demonstrated.

The astronomical theories regarding the 30-year period celebrated by the Sed festival are summarized thus:

> According to one view, it was based on the observation of Saturn's period of revolution round the sun, which is, roughly speaking, thirty years, or, more exactly, twenty-nine years and one hundred and seventy-four days. According to another view, the thirty years' period had reference to Sirius, the star of Isis. We have seen that on account of the vague character of the old Egyptian year the heliacal rising of Sirius shifted its place gradually through every month of the calendar.[8]

The shifting of the heliacal rising of Sirius or Sothis through every month was a result of the wandering or vague Egyptian year, one such cycle of 1460 years called a "Sothic year." The celebration of

---

[1] Sellers, 176.
[2] Uphill, 380.
[3] *PSBA*, XXIII, 225.
[4] Frankfort, 366.
[5] Wilkinson, T., 212.
[6] Frankfort, 79.
[7] Sellers, 177.
[8] Frazer, *GB*, III, 152.

"Saturn's return" represents a "renewal of kingship"[1] and *a type of rebirth, renewal or resurrection of Horus at 30 years.*

Also, the Sed festival appears to be associated with a water-purification rite "connected to the *hst* vase," which involved "the water libation as an offering, water in general and Nile water as the source of life and guarantor of fertility in particular."[2] In this regard, Kemp discusses an enormous T-shaped basin for "pure ritual water" dug evidently as part of the Sed festival at the site of Malkata.[3] This fact of a water-purification associated with the 30-year renewal of the Horus-king is important to keep in mind, as it constitutes a kind of *baptism* at that "age."

Concerning the Sed festival and its relationship to "Osiris" (Horus) and the number 30, in *The Paganism in Our Christianity,* Egyptologist and Christian apologist Sir Arthur Weigall concludes:

> At this festival the Pharaoh was made manifest as an incarnation of Osiris, and hence there may have been some tradition that Osiris was incarnated or chosen to be Lord of mankind exactly thirty years before he attained his earthly throne as Pharaoh. ...the idea perhaps passed thus into Christian minds that the manifestation of Jesus at His baptism occurred, like a Pharaoh's *Sed*-festival, exactly thirty years after His divine appointment, or birth in this case...[4]

Because the king/pharaoh becomes "the Osiris" upon his death, it is obvious why he would be identified with the god, although it is more appropriate for the *living* king/pharaoh to be called *Horus.* Thus, it would be *Horus* as the subject of the Egyptian tradition. In any event, the correlation between the Egyptian and Christian religions vis-à-vis the renewal or "baptism" at 30 was not lost on Weigall. As Horus is the savior reborn as an adult at 30, it could be said that he begins his "ministry" at this time, as was likewise said of Jesus.

In this important Sed festival there exists significant emphasis on boundaries and limits as well, with markers set up to outline a "ritual field," as Cambridge Egyptologist Dr. Toby A.H. Wilkinson remarks:

> At Saqqara these markers are arranged in pairs; on other Early Dynastic representations, such as the Narmer macehead and the ebony label of Den, they appear in sets of three. Oriented on a north-south axis, they clearly symbolise the territorial limits of the king's realm, the "field" between them representing the whole of Egypt... Clad in the tight-fitting Sed-festival robe, wearing the red, white or double crown, and carrying a flail in one hand and baton-like object in the other, the king ran or strode between the two sets of markers, reasserting his claim to the land of Egypt.[5]

---

[1] Frankfort, 366.
[2] Török, 246.
[3] Kemp, 277.
[4] Weigall, *POC*, 250.
[5] Wilkinson, T., 214.

This focus on boundary-marking needs to be kept in mind, as the Greek word for "boundary" or "limit" is *Horos*, pronounced the same as the Greek word for Horus, which is transliterated also as *Horos*—a fact that did not escape the notice of ancient writers, evidently including the later Gnostics of Alexandria when they went about creating their Judeo-Greco-Egyptian amalgamation of religions. Indeed, it is obvious from his epithet "of the Two Horizons" that Horus represented *boundaries*, such that a connection between Horos the god and Horos the boundary would be evident and logical. In any event, this grandiose 30-year festival with its symbolic life-renewal, "baptism" and marking of royal boundaries must have been well known to the Egyptian people beginning many centuries prior and continuing right up to the common era.

With constant Sed festivals celebrating the king/pharaoh as Horus representing the "lord of the 30-year period," it seems obvious that the god was thoroughly associated in the minds of Egyptians with an "age" of 30 years, so much so that anyone attempting to usurp this old and well-established religion would need to emphasize this essential rite-of-passage age as well. The same can be said of the important "age" of 12 as applied to Horus as well.

The Gnostic Horos

The fact that the "ages" of 12 and 30 in the Egyptian mythology and astrotheology are significant is evidenced by the focus on these numbers within the peculiar religion of Gnosticism, particularly as found at Alexandria. Regarding the origins of Gnosticism, Gnostic text expert Jean Doresse relates:

> There have been broadly two hypotheses about the origin of Gnosticism. Many historians have thought that this religion was merely a heresy that arose and developed within Christianity; but this theory has the defect of being hardly compatible with the facts—such as, for example, the existence of a Gnostic sect like that of the Mandeans with their essentially anti-Christian attitude. That is why other historians, seeing that there are some myths of characteristically Gnostic content which were equally well developed in both Judaism and Islam, have supposed that these various doctrines were all derived from the same stock of myth and imagery inherited from some identical source before the beginning of our era. To find this source they have looked to Egypt, to Babylonia and Persia, sometimes even to India.[1]

In other words, the evidence reveals a form of Gnosticism independent of Christianity that utilized myths from Egypt, Babylon, Persia and India. Regarding the presence of both Egyptian and *Jewish* themes within Gnosticism, Doresse remarks:

> We were able to note, in our survey of the authentic Gnostic writings (particularly in the case of the *Pistis-Sophia*), that Biblical elements

[1] Doresse, 110.

were associated with several Egyptian figures, some of
beings; but there was also, for instance, that fantastic open
heavens through which the Saviour and his disciples b
ships of the sun and the moon, which belongs to a mystic conception
inherited from the most ancient Pharaonic beliefs... One can clearly
discern, in all this magical, alchemical, astrological literature, a
competition between two rival currents of thought, one Judaizing
and the other Egyptianizing.[1]

Hence, in Gnosticism we have an apparent link between the
Egyptian, Babylonian, Persian, Jewish and Indian cultures, with the
Jewish and Egyptian battling for dominance. It is to Egyptian
Gnosticism in particular that we must thus turn for our analysis of
the correspondences between Egyptian faith and Christianity, which
is evidently largely the result of the dynamics between the Jewish
and Egyptian religions.

The Gnostic-Christian movement that sprang up in Alexandria
was led by a man named Valentinus (d. 161 AD/CE?), a famous
Egyptian Gnostic-Christian leader educated in that city. The
Encyclopedia Britannica calls Valentinus the "most prominent leader
of the Gnostic movement," also relating that he was considered for a
long time to be a member of the "orthodox" church.[2] Indeed, labeling
Valentinus "a preacher of 30 gods," Bishop Cyril of Jerusalem (c.
315-c. 386) indignantly objected to the fact that the Alexandrian
leader was called a "Christian." Prior to his status as a Gnostic
"heretic," Valentinus was thus a fervent member of orthodox
Christianity, although, because the received Church history remains
rife with difficulties, including the lack of evidence for the existence of
an apostolic lineage—or even the apostles themselves—as well as
fraud and forgery, it is difficult to determine precisely what
"orthodox" meant at the time Valentinus was alive. In any event, the
evidence indicates that the Gnostic movement *preceded* orthodox
Christianity. It was the Gnostic movement that bridged between the
old mythology and the new "history," which, we contend, turns out to
be fiction. It was the Gnostic movement that popularized many of the
mysteries, although cloaking them still in bizarre and
incomprehensible language and concepts, and it is to the Gnostic
movement that we may look for inferences of correlations between
Paganism and Christianity. In this case, if we investigate Gnosticism
as it emanated out of Egypt, in particular Alexandria, we find an odd
but relatively clear indication of the relationship between the 12/30
and "Horus," which would represent the continuation of the ages-old
correspondences between these numbers and the god already
explored.

In order to sort out this messy mystery, we will need to examine
the second century, when most of the Christian efforts began to take

---

[1] Doresse, 106-107.
[2] *Enc. Brit.*, XXVII, 852.

shape and hold, with things really heating up at the end of that period. It was, in fact, during the latter half to last quarter of the *second century* that the New Testament canon came into existence. Around 180, early Church father Irenaeus, Bishop of Lyons, France (Lugdunum of Gaul)—who from his writings appears to have been initiated into Gnosticism—first compiled the four canonical gospels into the "New Covenant," as it was often called, and gave them the names of Gospel according to Matthew, Mark, Luke and John. *Until the end of the second century, there is no clear evidence that any of the four canonical gospels as we have them even existed.*[1]

At that point, Irenaeus had his hands full of "heresy," including Docetic denials that Christ had even come in the flesh—such individuals said by Joseph Campbell to be in "that boat" with those who "began to link the Christian myth to pagan analogues."[2] Among these groups of "heretics" Irenaeus took on were the followers of Valentinus, the Gnostic Valentinians. One of the Valentinian subsects was that of the Marcosians, followers of Marcus (fl. c. 175 AD/CE), a disciple of Valentinus. Not only did Valentinus possess a substantial following but so too did Marcus or *Mark* as he would be called in English.[3]

In any event, it seems that Irenaeus's protracted skirmish with the Marcosians, who evidently had settled near the bishop in Lyons, exposed the Church father to *Egyptian* doctrines, which he fought with a fury, even to the extent of developing his own Judaized Egyptian mythology to battle them. Such may be one of the reasons why Irenaeus is the principal defender—and, some say, *composer*—of the Gospel of John,[4] which is a highly Egyptian text. Hence, Irenaeus himself may not have made it to Egypt, but Egypt certainly came to him, and he was quite familiar with the doctrines of the Egyptian Gnostics, as well as, apparently, regular Egyptian mythology to a lesser degree.

As priests had done for millennia with many objects and elements, such as the sun, moon, stars, planets, wind, water, etc., the Gnostic effort focused on personifying various perceived powers

---

[1] See my book *Who Was Jesus?* for more on the subject of the late dating of the gospels.

[2] Campbell, *AOL*, 77.

[3] It is interesting that while the Valentinian Mark was said to have lived at Alexandria, Christian legend has Mark the evangelist going to Alexandria and founding the Church there. Since there is no evidence that the gospel story happened at the alleged time and that the writer of Mark had any part in it, we will need to look more closely to determine precisely who the players were. Another candidate for the Mark who founded the Church at Alexandria could be a supposed follower of the Gnostic-Christian "heretic" Marcion by the same name. (See *CE*, "Marcus," IX, 650.)

[4] See Reber. Oddly enough, although several writers, including Jerome and Irenaeus, state John's gospel was written *against* the Gnostic heretic Cerinthus, there were others who believed Cerinthus himself had composed it. (See, e.g., Epiphanius, *Adv. Haer.* 51.3.6)

and factors that influence life on Earth. In some ways, this Gnostic personification and reverence of natural bodies, elements and powers represent the *essence* of *astrotheology*. The personified and astrotheological ideology constituting the "Theory of the Marcosians" is described by Irenaeus in *Against Heresies* (4:17):

> ...They next reckon up ten powers in the following manner:—There are seven globular bodies, which they also call heavens; then that globular body which contains these, which also they name the eighth heaven; and in addition to these, the sun and moon. These, being ten in number, they declare to be types of the invisible Decad, which proceeded from Logos and Zoe. As to the Duodecad, it is indicated by the zodiacal circle, as it is called; for they affirm that the twelve signs do most manifestly shadow forth the Duodecad, the daughter of Anthropos and Ecclesia. And since the highest heaven, beating upon the very sphere [of the seventh heaven], has been linked with the most rapid precession of the whole system, as a check, and balancing that system with its own gravity, so that it completes a cycle from sign to sign in thirty years,—they say that this is an image of Horus, encircling their thirty-named mother. And then, again, as the moon travels through her allotted space of heaven in thirty days, they hold, that by these days she expresses the number of the thirty Æons. The sun also, who runs through his orbit in twelve months, and then returns to the same point in the circle, makes the Duodecad manifest by these twelve months; and the days, as being measured by the twelve hours, as a type of the invisible Duodecad. Moreover, they declare that the hour, which is the twelfth part of the day, is composed of thirty parts, in order to set forth the image of the Triacontad. Also the circumference of the zodiacal circle itself contains three hundred and sixty degrees (for each of its signs comprises thirty); and thus also they affirm, that by means of this circle an image is preserved of that connection which exists between the twelve and the thirty. Still further, asserting that the earth is divided into twelve zones...[1]

In this pithy paragraph from an important Church father we thus find "Horus," the 12 and the 30 all neatly connected, along with a mass of astrotheological ideation. For example, in this Valentinian/ Marcosian Gnostic system appear the "Seven Heavens," an old concept from other mythologies, including the Babylonian and Jewish.[2] "Zoe" is *life* personified, while the "Logos," or *Word* personified, heavily promoted as Jesus in the Gospel of John, originated long before the common era and was symbolized by *the sun*. In the 4th-5th centuries BCE, the Greek philosopher Plato essentially equated the sun with *reason*, another definition of "logos," saying that "reason cannot discern the things of the ideal world without the light of truth," the latter being that which emanates from the sun, ideas replicated in the works of Alexandrian-Jewish

---

[1] Roberts, A., *ANF*, I, 342.
[2] Collins, A., 21.

philosopher Philo.[1] In any event, Plato's point is that those who stumble around in darkness rely upon opinion, while those who are in the light use reason.

Furthermore, in "On Dreams" (*De Somniis*), ch. 15, Philo remarks of Moses's discussion of the sun in Genesis: "But according to the third signification, when he speaks of the sun, he means the divine word..." The "fourth signification of the sun," according to Philo, "is the God and ruler of the universe himself."[2] These astrotheological notions explained by a famed Jewish philosopher rank as highly significant.

Moreover, it is important to bear in mind that Philo is basically aligning Judaism with Greek thought dating back centuries before the common era, and that he was a very wealthy and influential individual whose voluminous books were widely distributed and read by many people, beginning within his lifetime. In addition, Philo lived and wrote *before* Christianity took root. Indeed, it is evident that, because of his widely distributed works covering numerous religious and spiritual concepts that are clearly present in the *later* Christian effort, Philo is a major key to unlocking Christian origins. Not only were Philo and his family wealthy, but they were also therefore naturally well connected: When the Roman politician and emperor-to-be Vespasian (9-79 AD/CE) visited Egypt, he was accompanied also by Philo's rich nephew, who was the prefect of Egypt at that time—in fact, this very wealthy nephew spent a significant amount of time with Vespasian and Titus, even serving as a commander during the Jewish war, in which Titus destroyed Jerusalem! This type of alliance was at the genesis of Christianity, as we shall see.

In any case, concerning the logos and the sun, John Fellows concludes, "Logos is the same as Osiris, the sun, considered as the Demiurgus, the maker of the world, under the direction of the Supreme Being."[3] Hence, we see a smooth transition developing between the logos, the sun, Osiris, Horus and Jesus.

The "highest heaven" in the Alexandrian Gnostic system as summarized by Irenaeus "completes a cycle from sign to sign in thirty years," which sounds like the period of the Sed festival, while "Duodecad" constitutes a body of 12, as in the zodiac and months of the year. "Anthropos" means "Man," as in the species, but stands for the "Supreme God" as well,[4] while "Ecclesia" is *Church* personified.

---

[1] *Penny Cyclopaedia*, 239. See *The Republic*, book 4, 508-509, etc. Plato translators Davies and Vaughan epitomize this part of *The Republic* by saying: "In the world of sense we have the sun, the eye, visible objects; answering to which, we have in the intellectual world, the Good, Reason [*Logos*], the Forms or archetypes of visi-objects or, in the language of Socrates, Ideas." (Davies, P., xxiv.) See my books *The Christ Conspiracy* and *Suns of God* for more on the origins of the Word/Logos. See also, Philo's "Who is the Heir of Divine Things" (53). (Philo/Yonge, 299.)

[2] Philo/Yonge, 372.

[3] Fellows, 333.

[4] Krause, 25.

The "thirty-named mother" who is also the moon doubtlessly represents the Gnostic rendition of Isis, called elsewhere "Sophia," or personified *Wisdom*. As Witt says regarding Isis, "She could be the personification of Wisdom (*Sophia*) and Philosophy."[1] In discussing the apocryphal biblical text the "Wisdom of Solomon," Mojsov opines that the author must be of the Alexandrian school of thought who "introduced Sophia or Wisdom as the intermediary between the god of the Old Testament and his people..."[2] Concerning Wisdom personified, Mojsov also states:

> The similarity of Sophia to Isis also points to an Egyptian inspiration.
> In Christianity, the role of Sophia was taken over by Mary.[3]

Like the "thirty names," the "Triacontad" or "Thirty," including as "Aeons"—a word typically meaning *ages*—symbolize days in the month. The "Twelve," of course, constitute the months of the year, the signs of the zodiac and the hours of the day and night each, a figure, naturally, is based on the equal length of day and night at the equinoxes. As we can see, in the Gnosticism of Alexandria, the 12/30 motif is abundant, as is its relationship to both "Isis" and "Horus," the latter of whom is also associated with Horos, as the Logos, by way of the solar significance of both.

Interestingly, elsewhere in *Against Heresies* (1:3.2), Irenaeus remarks upon the number twelve as the age of the Lord while teaching in the temple, equating it with the "Aeons," of which there are 12 and which have likewise been identified with the signs of the zodiac:

> The production, again, of the Duodecad of the Æons, is indicated by the fact that the Lord was *twelve* years of age when He disputed with the teachers of the law, and by the election of the apostles, for of these there were twelve.[4]

We can thus see also that the association of the "age" of 12 with a Gnostic and astrotheological concept occurred early in Christian history, even by such an orthodox Church father as Irenaeus. In Irenaeus's writings also occurs a rebuttal of those who had attempted to associate Jesus's baptism at 30 with the 30 Aeons, in a treatise entitled, "The thirty Æons are not typified by the fact that Christ was baptized in His thirtieth year: He did not suffer in the twelfth month after His baptism, but was more than fifty years old when He died." In this polemic, Irenaeus rails against these notions in language so Gnostic that it is apparent he himself received education and indoctrination in that peculiar and mysterious system. In this paragraph too we have a reflection of the 12/30 formula, as applied to Jesus in ancient times, such that the Church father needed to

---

[1] Witt, 20.
[2] Mojsov, 113.
[3] Mojsov, 113.
[4] Roberts, A., *ANF*, I, 319.

e also see that Irenaeus argues an age of "more than fifty" Jesus supposedly suffered his passion, contradicting the gospels and received Christian tradition but evidently interpreting the gospel of John (8:57), in which the evangelist places Jesus as "not yet fifty years old," to indicate that Jesus was *over* 50 at his death.

The word "Horus" in Irenaeus's discourse on the Marcosians, in which he relates that "they say that this is an image of Horus, encircling their thirty-named mother," is often translated as "Limit," after the Greek word *Horos* or Ὁρος. The term for the god Horus used by Plutarch (38, 366A) and other Greek writers was in fact Ὡρος—*Horos*.[1] While pronounced the same, the two words are spelled differently in Greek, the term for "limit" or "boundary" starting with the Greek letter omicron ("O"), while the Egyptian god's name begins with an omega ("Ω").[2]

Nevertheless, the word for "hour" or "*limited* time" is ὡρα—*hora*—beginning with an omega, which would indicate that all three terms are cognates, especially since Horus himself has been identified with time, having been said to be the originator of 12 *hours* or ὡρες/*hores* in the Greek, a word claimed by Horapollo to come from Horus's name.[3] Plutarch (38, 366A) also noted the correspondence between *Hora* and *Horus*, remarking: "The all-conserving and fostering Hora, that is the seasonable tempering of the surrounding air, is Horus..."[4] Plutarch's word "Hora" is the same as that above, referring to a time period as well as a season or climate. Furthermore, the past tense of the ancient Greek verb "to limit"—ὁριζω—is ὡρισα, with an omega, the same as in the name Horus.

As we have seen, the Horus-king was associated with "limits" and "boundaries" during the Sed festival, but he was also linked with these factors even in Egyptian mythology:

---

[1] Plutarch/Babbitt, 92.

[2] Regarding the pertinent sentence in Irenaeus's writing containing the word "Horus," the translator Rev. Dr. Alexander Roberts notes: "Such is the translation which Harvey, following the text preserved by Hippolytus, gives the above intricate and obscure sentence." (Roberts, A., *ANF*, I, 342.) In the 19th century, Rev. Wigan Harvey used the Church father Hippolytus's "recently discovered" *Philosophoumena*, which was in Greek and which, in the opinion of scholars, was superior to the "barbarous Latin" version of the same work. Hippolytus was purportedly a direct disciple of Irenaeus, and as such one may consider his rendition of his teacher's work to be relatively faithful. In addition, the notion that this germane sentence is "obscure" may indicate that it cannot be found in other editions, giving cause to wonder why, in consideration of its importance, and making one suspect tampering with the passage in previous editions. In the original Greek, however, Hippolytus too uses the word *Horos* with an omicron, rather than *Horos* with an omega. It seems to be a convention, nonetheless, of translating the word for "boundary" or "limit" as *Horus*, which is perhaps reflective of a Latinizing tendency, rather than an acknowledgement that Horos the Limit equals Horus the Egyptian god. In fact, the word Horos meaning "limit" was apparently frequently translated into both Latin and English as *Horus*.

[3] Diodorus/Murphy, 32, footnote 51.

[4] Plutarch/Babbit, 93.

A limit is posed to Seth, "the enemy of boundaries": sometimes his share is the sky and sometimes the sedge country or the papyrus country, and sometimes the red land. He has to be separated from Horus to prevent further disasters.[1]

Horus's nemesis, Set, the "enemy of boundaries," is to be limited—Set is the enemy of boundaries or *horos*, as is the word "boundary" in Greek. Horos also means "limit," which Set is to undergo. *Horos* himself is the dividing line that *separates* Set from him. In the sun hymns too we find an echo of the discussion of the limits of creation being "subjected to" Re's "beloved son": "As Re you penetrate to its limits, And subject them to your beloved son..."[2] Basically, this hymn says that Re penetrates the whole of creation to its limits, while Horus is "subjected to" either the sun's rays or creation's limits. In CT Sp. 1035, the "paths of Osiris" are "in the limit of the sky."[3] Also, in CT Sp. 1075, the speaker—apparently as Horus—proclaims," I am he who limited the flood, "[4] while in CT Sp. 1184 appears another reference to him "who limited the flood," in a context that indicates the speaker is identified with Horus.[5] Horus is thus "the Limiter." The Egyptian Horus myth full of *Horos* may well have served at least partially as a prototype for the Gnostic myth.

As we may have expected, according to Doresse, the Gnostic *Seth* also was "originally an Egyptian god."[6] Doresse further states:

> ...We can read, in Plutarch's treatise on *Isis and Osiris* (§§ 30-33 and 49-50), an exegesis of the mythical relations between Seth and Osiris, derived from sources which seem to have been quite authentically Egyptian, in which we find what is almost a Gnostic dualism.[7]

With all these facts, and with the previously determined knowledge and popularity of Horus, we have good reason to believe that the Alexandrian Gnostics deliberately based their system on Egyptian mythology, using the Greek terminology for the gods and, as notoriously fond of word-play, being well aware of the double meaning of the term *horos*. Indeed, it would appear that the Alexandrian Gnostics were likewise well aware of Plutarch's association of *hora* and Horus when they created the character of Horos, evidently based on both. *The Encyclopedia Britannica* lends credence to this hypothesis, stating: "A figure entirely peculiar to Valentinian Gnosticism is that of Horos (the Limiter). *The name is perhaps an echo of the Egyptian Horus.*"[8]

---

[1] te Velde, 63.
[2] Assman, *ESRNK*, 96.
[3] Faulkner, *AECT*, III, 132.
[4] Faulkner, *AECT*, III, 146.
[5] Faulkner, *AECT*, III, 189.
[6] Doresse, 104.
[7] Doresse, 104.
[8] *Enc. Brit.*, XXVII, 854. (Emph. added.)

In this regard, *A Dictionary of Christian Biography, Literature, Sects and Doctrines* defines "Horus" thus:

> HORUS (ὁρος). According to the doctrine of Valentinus, as described by Irenaeus...the youngest Aeon Sophia, in her passion to comprehend the Father of all, runs the danger of being absorbed into his essence, from which she is saved by coming into contact with the limiting power ὁρος, whose function it is to strengthen all things outside the ineffable Greatness, by confining each to its appointed place. According to this version Horus was a previously existing power; but according to another, and apparently a later account, Horus is an Aeon only generated on this occasion at the request of all the Aeons, who implored the Father to avert a danger that threatened to affect them all.[1]

In a lengthy entry consistently using the term *Horus*—while insisting that it had nothing to do with the Egyptian god, perhaps protesting too much—this dictionary goes on to explain that in the version by Church father Hippolytus (d. c. 236) the Aeon Horus is called by his "primary title," *Stauros*, meaning "cross." Hence, in ancient times—during the second century, precisely when Christianity was finding its footing—there existed in Egypt the concept of *Horus as the Cross* personified.

This same concept can be found in Tertullian's work *Against the Valentinians* (chap. 9):

> But when Sophia, straining after impossible aims, was disappointed of her hope, she is both overcome with difficulty, and racked with affection. Thus she was all but swallowed up by reason of the charm and toil (of her research), and dissolved into the remnant of his substance; nor would there have been any other alternative for her than perdition, if she had not by good luck fallen in with Horus (Limit). He too had considerable power. He is the foundation of the great universe, and, externally, the guardian thereof. To him they give the additional names of Crux (Cross), and Lytrotes (Redeemer,) and Carpistes (Emancipator).[2]

The antiquity of Horos and Stauros as *pre-Christian* philosophical concepts can be demonstrated by the discussion of them as "the

---

[1] Smith, W., 162.

[2] This rendition, published on the several websites, is attributed to "Dr. Roberts," but is not the same as the translation by Rev. Dr. Alexander Roberts as found in various print editions, such as Charles Scribner's Sons (1903). It is possible that this translation was by a different "Dr. Roberts," of course, using a different Greek or Latin text, although to my knowledge there is only one extant Latin edition and no Greek translation. The Latin edition in the *Corpus Cluniacense* uses the word *Horon* (Riley) often translated as either "Horos" or "Limit." A reference in Latin to the Egyptian god would have been *Horus*, while in the Greek—if such a manuscript existed—the determination would be made by whether or not the word began with an omega or an omicron. While the German of Kellner renders the pertinent word *Horos*, de Genoude prefers *Horus* for his French translation. In addition, the references to the *god* Horus in Church father Aristides's Greek writings are frequently translated into English and other languages, such as German, as *Horos*. (See Menzies, Seeberg.) As we can see, the terms are haphazardly and confusedly used in both ancient and modern times.

limit" and "the intersection" in Plato's *Timaeus* (35 A-36 D).[1] Doresse discusses this Platonic passage:

> ...Plato imagines the creation by the Demiurge of the circles of "the same" and of "the other"—i.e., of the celestial equator and of the ecliptic intersecting in the form of a cross. Taking over this notion, the Gnostics saw this imaginary cross, traced upon the celestial vault which is the utmost bound of our eyesight, as "the limit" separating the higher universe from the material world in which we are confined. A Christian interpretation of this idea, analogous to that which Valentinus develops, is already to be found in the *Apology* of St. Justin (I. 60) who puts it this way—"Plato with a cross upon the universe."[2]

Doresse calls the theme of the Cross and the Limit "one of the most classic Gnostic doctrines,"[3] reflecting the influence of the Alexandrian movement upon Gnosticism. This "Horos and the Cross" motif was evidently popular yet constituted a *mystery*, about which we shall see more later.

In discussing the random mix-up of Horos/Horus the Egyptian god and Horos/Horus the Gnostic Limit, the fact will remain that a speaker of Greek would hear virtually the same sound when either word was spoken. This fact could not have failed to be noticed—or, indeed, to be used in a deliberate contrivance—by the Greek-speaking creators of Valentinian Gnosticism. It could thus be asserted logically and reasonably that the Alexandrian Gnostic creation was intentionally based on the highly popular Egyptian religion and mythology.

The characteristics and epithets ascribed to "Horos the Limit" need to be kept in mind, as they appear to be reflective of more or less esoteric knowledge—*mysteries*—also associated with the Egyptian god Horus. Based on what we have already discovered concerning the motifs from Egyptian religion evidently copied into Christianity, we have reason to suspect that there are more, including the determination of the god *Horus* as the "foundation of the great universe," as well as his association or identification with the *Cross*. Other epithets such as "Redeemer" or Emancipator" would likewise be appropriate for Horus the sun god. Furthermore, by the way in which Sophia is demoted and usurped in her power by Horos, it would appear that this Gnostic effort was also meant to denigrate Isis and the Goddess in general by promoting a *male* divinity in her stead, i.e., Horos/Horus.

The identification of the Egyptian myth with the Valentinian one is plainly laid out by Dr. Michel Tardieu, director of l'Institut d'Histoire des Christianismes Orientaux at the Collège de France:

---

[1] Doresse, 28.
[2] Doresse, 28.
[3] Doresse, 60.

The Egyptian myth in its Greek reinterpretation of the wanderings and tears of Isis, who is searching for her twin brother and lover Osiris (Plutarch, *Moralia*, 356a-358b), served as the starting point for the Valentinian myth of the wanderings and tears of Sophia, abandoned to the sorrows of this world, "a supplicant to the Father," because she has lost the unity of her origin and suffers from love of her twin... The child of Isis, Horus (=Harpocrates), "debased by matter through the bodily element" (*Moralia* 373b3-4), corresponds to the deformed offspring of the Valentinian Sophia, and is described as "substance disorganized and without form"... Just as Isis is called "the seeking of Osiris,"... Sophia is "the seeking of the Father,"...[1]

Concerning Sophia's deformed offspring, professor of Ecclesiastical History at Harvard Divinity School Dr. Karen L. King remarks:

It also reflects parthenogenic activity on the part of the gods and goddesses. Hera's jealousy over Zeus's production of Athena leads to the birth of Hephaesto. According to one version of the myth, she throws him out of heaven because of his deformity.[2]

Hence, again we find a discussion of "parthenogenesis" or *virgin birth*.

As we can see, it is the opinion of Dr. Tardieu that Valentinian Gnosticism was based in significant part on the Egyptian religion and mythology, filtered through the Greek mind via Plutarch. This point is singularly important, as it provides a smooth link between various Egyptian concepts and those found in the later orthodox Christianity.

As a further comparison, in section 27 (361D), Plutarch speaks of Isis's "manifold deeds of wisdom,"[3] the latter term being *sophia* in Greek. Later (41, 367E), Plutarch states, "In fact, the actions of the moon are like actions of reason and perfect wisdom."[4] The word for "reason" is *logos*, while the term for "wisdom," of course, is *sophia*. Plutarch (52, 372D) further relates that "there are those who declare that Isis is none other than the Moon."[5] Hence, it could be said that "Isis's actions are like those of Logos and Sophia," a very Gnostic sounding statement.

Expert on "Gnosticism" Dr. Michael A. Williams, chairman of the Department of Comparative Religion at the University of Washington, likewise analyzes the equation of Sophia with Isis in Plutarch, tracing inferences of the association to Philo:

...Plutarch also equates Isis with the "receptacle" of Plato's *Timaeus* (49A, etc.), that is to say, with matter, and as such she receives the imprints of the Logos, Osiris (372E-373B). Isis seems to bear features similar to those of Wisdom or Sophia as found in Philo's writings, and this results in "an entity which is on the one hand fallen and imperfect, though filled with longing for completion by the

---

[1] Bonnefoy, *REM*, 189.
[2] King, K., 102.
[3] Plutarch/Babbitt, 67.
[4] Plutarch/Babbitt, 101.
[5] Plutarch/Babbitt, 129.

logos of God, while on the other being the cause of our creation and the vehicle by which we can come to know God," which means that for Plutarch Isis plays a role analogous to the gnostic Sophia.[1]

As we shall see, Philo's development of the Word bears a striking resemblance to Jesus as the Logos in the gospel of John, which by all evidence was written long after the Alexandrian Jewish philosopher lived.

Regarding the connection between the Egyptian religion, Gnosticism and Christianity, Dr. Bishai states:

> ...the Copts of Egypt during the early Christian centuries were known for their massive production of Apocrypha and pseudepigrapha. This characteristic of the early Copts should not be surprising to us in light of the evidence of gnostic influence on the early Coptic Christian thought. The gnostics were literate people and well acquainted with ancient religions and mythology. As Christianity was spreading in Egypt, a group of these gnostic Christians apparently made an effort to tie old Egyptian myths to Christian beliefs.[2]

Bishai next reminds us of the assertion by Egyptologist Bleeker that "a number of gnostic conceptions go back to ancient Egyptian religious thought." In this same regard, Witt provides further, *archaeological* evidence:

> The fusion of Horus with Judaeo-Christian features can be exemplified on Gnostic gems from Egypt. On one of these the deity Iao (to be connected no doubt with the Iah of the Pentateuch) is seen standing on a crocodile....
>
> *In the theology and art of Gnosticism Horus and Christ could easily be blended.* One of the Gnostic sects indeed labelled itself "Carpocratian" and in general they propounded cosmologies in terms of "Aeons", the final and perfect Aeon being Jesus Christ. Those who bore the name Peratae in their astrological theories recognized the rule of Isis and Osiris over the hours, which Horus as the God of Time created. The Valentinian Gnostics can plausibly be said to have evolved a doctrine in which Isis fulfils the role of Sophia and Horus/Harpocrates that of Logos. As to the term Aeon, we learn from Epiphanius, who produced his massive anti-heretical treatise at the end of the fourth century, that among the pagans at Alexandria Horus/Harpocrates was the Aeon *par excellence*. Aeon/Horus was born of the Virgin Isis on 6 January. Clearly in the Gnosticism which fringed Christian orthodoxy Horus and Christ could merge.[3]

In this pithy paragraph from a well-respected, modern scholar emerge a number of intriguing assertions that validate previous observations made here. Firstly, we discover there are archaeological artifacts from Egypt that demonstrate the Gnostic merging of Horus with Jesus. Secondly, we read that Sophia is Isis, and Horus is the

[1] Williams, 120.
[2] Bishai, 128.
[3] Witt, 218. (Emph. added.)

Logos/Word, in the Alexandrian Gnostic system. But he could also be *Horos*, in his similar function as concerns *time*. We have already seen how the pertinent part of Epiphanius's work in which he discusses the virgin birth of "Aion" was edited out of the Migne Greek edition—here Witt contends that Epiphanius was referring to *the virgin birth of Horus* and that the Valentinians had incorporated Horus the Egyptian god into their system. We would add to Witt's final assessment that it was not only within the "fringe" Gnostic movement that Horus and Christ could merge but that within Orthodox Christianity as well did Horus serve as a *prototype* for the Jesus character.

The relationship between Isis and *Osiris* is also reflected in the doctrine of the "Gnostics of Irenaeus," who held that Sophia and Christos were *brother* and *sister*.[1] Another occurrence of the incorporation of Egyptian mythology into Gnosticism happened with the god Khnum, Kneph or Kem-atef, who was reworked into the gnostic Chnubis, a serpent with a lion's head surrounded by a halo or "crown of thorns," which surely represents another astrotheological/solar motif.[2] One more analogy may be found in the goddess Nut, whose body arches across the sky and who "prefigures that episode in the Gnostic cosmologies where Sophia, striving to extricate herself from the abyss of matter into which she has fallen, creates the firmament in a similar manner."[3]

One Gnostic group, the Peratae—whom Doresse says were "very specially addicted to astrology"[4]—*overtly* incorporated Osiris, Isis and Horus into their ideology, possibly even as the central focus, although, naturally, they attempted to usurp the Egyptian religion by disparaging its followers, calling them "the ignorant," for example, for deeming the "ruler of the twelve hours of the night" *Osiris*, when in fact his name was *Soclan*.[5] Doresse avers that "Soclan" is in reality the god Sokar, who is identified with Osiris. Doresse likewise recognizes in the Peratae's position an acknowledgement of Isis and Osiris as "rulers of the hours of the day and of the night, represented respectively by the Day Star (Sothis, i.e., Sirius) and by the constellation of Osiris."[6] These Peratae were associated in the *Philosophumena* (V) by Church father Hippolytus with both astrology and the Greek Mysteries, and Doresse finds in their ideology other allusions to classical Greek mythology as well.[7] Concerning the Gnostic reliance on Egyptian mythology as found in the Gnostic texts discovered at Chenoboskion, Egypt, Doresse further remarks:

---

[1] *Enc. Brit.*, XXVII, 854.
[2] See Doresse, 93.
[3] Doresse, 272.
[4] Doresse, 50.
[5] Doresse, 51.
[6] Doresse, 274.
[7] Doresse, 264.

...the hell of our Coptic writings retains not only the Egyptian name of *Amente* (that is, the Occident), but also its population of fantastic demons. Finally, the passwords and the seals that our sectaries thought would give their souls safe conduct through the planetary spaces are much the same in spirit as the formulas by which the deceased Egyptian had always had to protect himself, since the days of the Pyramid texts until the latest of the *Books of the Dead*.[1]

Thus, according to Doresse the Gnostic-Christian Coptic texts are clearly influenced by Egyptian religion, a logical conclusion. The word "Amente" or "Amenta," etc., was "originally the place where the sun set," which was subsequently deemed "Hades" by the Copts.[2]

From the abundant evidence, including texts and archaeological artifacts, it seems obvious that the Alexandrian Gnostic creators of this myth were well aware of what they were doing and that they were intentionally rewriting the Egyptian mythology, attributing Greek meanings to the translated names of the deities. In any event, the ancient 12/30 theme is quite apparent within Gnosticism, as is its relationship to Egyptian mythology, via the Gnostic interpretation. It is further evident the Gnostics were attempting to preserve hidden, esoteric and difficult-to-understand knowledge—*gnosis* meaning "knowledge"—in their bizarre creations, including information regarding the Egyptian god *Horus* that may have been available to initiates but not necessarily to the public at large.

From these Gnostic endeavors and the concerted effort by early Church fathers to debunk them it is obvious that the numbers 12 and 30 were highly significant in rituals and mysteries around the Mediterranean during and preceding the period when Christianity truly began to be formulated. The origin of this reverence for these numbers—and the mystics among us, including such luminaries as Plato and Philo, whose philosophies were unquestionably incorporated into both Gnostic and Orthodox Christianity, have always been fascinated by so-called sacred numbers—likely lies mainly with the 12 months of the year divided into 30 days each, to equal 360 days, as well as the same division concerning the degrees of a circle, especially as regards that of the zodiac.[3] It is further evident that these two numbers were associated with Horus, as ages or periods involved in rites of passage, in festivals, in both, or for some other reason. In any event, it has been proved that Horus was associated with the important "ages" of 12 and 30, like Jesus, but long prior to the Christian era.

---

[1] Doresse, 275.

[2] Budge, *EBD* (1967), cxxxiii

[3] For discussion of Philo's "Gnosticism," see Pearson's *Gnosticism, Judaism and Egyptian Christianity*.

Horus the "Savior" with the Sidelock of Childhood
(Magical Stela, 360–343 BCE)

"Anup the Baptizer"

"For washing is the channel through which [the heathen] are initiated into some sacred rites—of some notorious Isis or Mithras. The gods themselves likewise they honour by washings."

Tertullian, *On Baptism*, V (9)

"How natural and expressive the symbolism of exterior washing to indicate interior purification was recognized to be, is plain from the practice also of the heathen systems of religion. The use of lustral water is found among the Babylonians, Assyrians, Egyptians, Greeks, Romans, Hindus, and others."

Catholic Encyclopedia, "Baptism" (II, 260)

"Baptism is a very ancient rite pertaining to heathen religions, whether of Asia, Africa, Europe or America. It was one of the Egyptian rites in the mysteries."

James Bonwick, *Egyptian Belief and Modern Thought* (416)

"The Egyptian baptismal rite has its origins in the Heliopolitan worship of the sun early in the Pyramid Age. The Egyptians believed that each morning the sun passed through the waters of the ocean before being reborn, emerging purified and revitalized. The ritual baptism of the pharaoh each morning symbolized this event and renewed life and vigor of the recipient."

Dr. Richard A. Gabriel, *Gods of the Fathers* (184)

"...all religious ceremonies of Pharaonic times, whether performed on behalf of a deity, a deceased noble, or the living king, were prefaced by some act of ritual cleansing..."

Sir Dr. Alan H. Gardiner, "The Baptism of Pharaoh," *The Journal of Egyptian Archaeology*, 36 (3)

One parallel between the Horus and Jesus myths which causes much controversy is the contention that Horus was "baptized" by a character named "Anup the Baptizer," corresponding to the baptism of Jesus by "John the Baptist." This comparison between Anup and John has been extrapolated for a variety of reasons, including the many other correlations between the Egyptian and Christian religions, which need to be kept squarely in mind. In this regard, "Christian" terminology has been utilized to describe what was found in the ancient Egyptian texts and monuments, as well as elsewhere around the Roman Empire during the era. Moreover, one must also remember that the Egyptian gods—particularly Isis—were *highly popular* around the Roman Empire by the time Christianity was created. With this famed goddess Isis came her entourage, including one of her most faithful attendants, the mysterious god Anubis, also called "Anup" or "Anpu."

The popularity of Isis and her associates, including Anubis, is highlighted by Dr. Frank Cole Babbitt (1867-1935), a professor of Greek language and literature at Trinity College, and a translator of Plutarch's *Moralia*:

the worship of Isis had been introduced into Greece before 330
is certain from an inscription found in...Peiraeus...in which the
_ _chants from Citium ask permission to found a shrine of
Aphrodite on the same terms as those on which the Egyptians had
founded a shrine of Isis. In Delos there was a shrine of the Egyptian
gods, and in Plutarch's own town they must have been honoured, for
there have been found two dedications to Serapis, Isis, and Anubis,
as well as numerous inscriptions recording the manumission of
slaves, which in Greece was commonly accomplished by dedicating
them to a god, who, in these inscriptions, is Serapis (Sarapis)....[1]

The Greco-Egyptian god Serapis, a combination of Osiris and his
"Apis bull," was especially created to appeal to the Greeks—and the
Jews, with the Jewish patriarch during the reign of Hadrian
compelled to attend a congregation of Serapis-worshipping Jews at
Alexandria, an important fact that will be explored later. Concerning
Serapis, in the *Proceedings of the Ninth International Congress of
Egyptologists*, Serry remarks:

The god Serapis was a fusion of Egyptian and Greek religious
concepts originating in Alexandria, where Ptolemy the First started
his cult and constructed the first known shrine for him called the
Serapeum. Serapis was frequently combined with other deities both
Egyptian and Greek. Such combinations were Serapis-Zeus, Serapis-
Helios and Serapis-Amun. His statues are characterized with the
long face, heavy curled beard, long moustaches with curling ends
and five locks of hair falling over the forehead.[2]

Hence, in Serapis emerges a pre-Christian hybrid god created by
the priesthood specifically to unite factions of the Roman Empire, as
we contend the Jesus figure was designed to do as well. Moreover,
not a few observers have commented on the similarities between the
two gods' appearances, to the point where the commonly imagined
visage of Christ has been claimed to be a copy of Serapis, with his
long, curly hair and beard.

In addition, the god Apis himself likewise represents an important
example of the amalgamation and syncretism of Egyptian gods, as
related by Dr. Dieter Kessler, a professor of Egyptology at the Ludwig-
Maximilians-Universität:

Depending on the text, Apis was Ptah, Ptah-Sokar-Osiris, Geb-Shu,
Osiris, Re, Atum, and/or Horus—or, as later texts say, "all in one."[3]

Regarding Serapis, Hornung relates, "From the very beginning, he
was the personification of Osiris, who was at this time not only ruler
of the underworld and the dead but also the sun god."[4] Thus, Osiris
is the same as Serapis, and Serapis, it turns out, was confounded
with Jesus as early as the true beginning of Christianity, i.e., the

---

[1] Plutarch/Babbitt, 3.
[2] Goyon, 119.
[3] Redford, 31.
[4] Hornung, *SLE*, 64.

second century, demonstrating the firm connection between Osiris and Jesus as well. Concerning the spread of the cult of Anubis, Hornung states, "The worship of Anubis was well established in the sanctuaries of Isis, with the god in third place, ranking behind Isis and Sarapis."[1]

The jackal-headed god Anubis was known well enough to the Greeks by the time of Plato in the fourth century that in his book *Gorgias* (482b) the philosopher depicts his mentor, Socrates, as swearing "by the dog, the God of the Egyptians."[2] Plato also mentions "frequent contacts between Egyptians and Phoenicians" that "point to an even older cultural encounter."[3] As Hornung relates, "Egyptian objects and religious concepts were spread throughout the Mediterranean world by Phoenician traders and colonists."[4]

In his *Antiquities of the Jews* (18.3.4), Josephus also tells a story about Anubis, demonstrating that the god was famous enough in the Roman Empire at the end of the first century to warrant mention by the Jewish historian.[5]

The profound importance of Anubis is further illustrated by his considerable presence in the Egyptian texts and images, such as those depicting him with Horus at the weighing of the deceased's heart.[6] Indeed, Anubis factors significantly in the Pyramid Texts, in which he is the "prince of the court of justice (or, divine court)" (PT 610:1713c/M 375), "chief of the temple" (PT 665A:1909a) and "chief of the house" (PT 694:2150c/N 457).[7] Also in the Pyramid Texts (PT 437:804d/P 31), Anubis is said to preside "over the pure (holy) land."[8] In the Coffin Texts (CT Sp. 55), the deceased says he is "within the arms of Anubis in the Pure Place."[9]

When we are aware of these facts of the importance and pervasiveness of the Egyptian religion around the Mediterranean and elsewhere at the time, knowing how its myths and rituals were usurped in numerous instances, as well as that several of its major players have essentially been morphed into Christian characters, we may logically ask what happened to the others, especially one as important as Anubis? Who replaced Anubis within the Christian mythos and ritual? A scientific analysis reveals John the Baptist to represent the most likely candidate.

---

[1] Hornung, *SLE*, 66.
[2] Plato/Nienkamp, 120; Hornung, *SLE*, 21.
[3] Hornung, *SLE*, 21.
[4] Hornung, *SLE*, 21.
[5] Josephus/Whiston, 393.
[6] Lockyer, *DA*, 30.
[7] Mercer, 805, 283, 313; Faulkner, *AEPT*, 253, 274, 303; Allen, J., *AEPT*, 232, 283.
[8] Mercer, 151; Allen, J., *AEPT*, 105; Faulkner, *AEPT*, 145.
[9] Faulkner, *AECT*, I, 53.

Who is Anubis?

The worship of Anubis/Anup/Anpu, also styled Anep, Anepo or Anebo, as well as Anupu and Inpu, among others, may extend back some 6,000 years, making him one of the older gods.[1] As noted, Anubis is often portrayed with the head of a jackal, while the jackal constellation is also called the "Jackal of Set," the latter god at times being identified with Anubis.[2] Hence, this god of the underworld is sometimes deemed "Set-Anubis" or "Sut-Anup." Furthermore, Anubis is at times also depicted as a human being,[3] an important fact to know when comparing him to John the Baptist. Sired by either Set or Osiris,[4] depending on the myth, Anubis is the son of their sister Nephthys. Thus, like John's mother, Elizabeth, who was the Virgin Mary's cousin, Anubis's mother, Nephthys, was related to Horus's mother, Isis.[5] Hence, as John and Jesus are related to each other,

---

[1] The Greek name for this god is "Anubis," while he is "Anoub" or "Anob" in Coptic, apparently reflecting a later stage in the Egyptian for his name. Earlier transliterations of major Egyptologists such as Drs. Birch, Brugsch and Poole rendered the name "Anup," while there arose a preference in more modern times for "Anpu," going against the Coptic and Greek. While Budge transliterates the name as *Anpu*, James Allen prefers *jnpw*, which would essentially be equivalent to "Anpu" or "Inpu," although the final vowel is uncertain, and the name has been written simply as *jnp* or *Anp*. The transliterations into modern languages also vary from country to country, with a range of suggestions, including "Anapa," "Anaahpa," "Yanapu" or "Yanape," as, again, the vowels are uncertain. We are further told that in Egyptian the reversal, transposition or metathesis of letters is not uncommon, based on aesthetics. (Cowie) In fact, there is an "Egyptian propensity for metathesis" or transposition of letters, and Anubis was also written as *jnwp* or *inwp* ("Inup") on occasion by Egyptian scribes. (Colburn) Citing an ancient text favoring "Anup," Edward Butler remarks, "Witness the fact that in an Old Coptic spell (PGM 94ff, text available in *Coptology Past, Present, and Future: Studies in Honour of Rodolphe Kasser*, ed. Giversen, Krause and Nagel (Orientalia Lovaniensia Analecta 61, 1994)), Anubis is clearly spelled out as ANOUP." ("Ancient Egyptian Language Discussion List.") Since the Greek and Coptic favor Anubis/Anoub/Anoup, here we will utilize at times the older convention of "Anup," as it was originally used by Birch, Brugsch and Poole, as well as, in more modern times, by Hare. (Hare, 127.) The debate as to the proper way to transliterate Anubis is irrelevant to the issue at hand, which is whether or not the god served as an archetype upon which the Christian character John the Baptist was predicated in significant part. This particular debate, however, does illustrate a continuing problem with the pronunciation and transliteration of hieroglyphs in general, but not necessarily the meanings of the words. Demonstrating this convention for transposition of letters in Egyptian, the god Tmu, Atmu or Atum is transliterated as *jtmw*; however, modern scholars such as James Allen continue to maintain the name as "Atum." (Allen, J., *AEPT*, 426.) As Dr. David Lorton states, "English-speaking Egyptologists have no single set of conventions for the rendering of ancient Egyptian and modern Arabic personal and place names." (Assman, *DSAE*, xi.)

[2] Lockyer, *DA*, 145-146.

[3] Lockyer, *DA*, 145.

[4] Anubis is named by Diodorus (1.18), for one, as the *son of Osiris*. (Diodorus/Murphy, 22.)

[5] In Hebrew "Elizabeth" is *Elisheba*, meaning "oath of God," the components of which are *El*, or "God," and *sheba*, "seven." Anubis's mother, Nephthys, is the tutelary deity of the *seventh* nome of Upper Egypt, making her the "god seven," so to speak, as well. Interestingly, both Elizabeth and Nephthys have their celebrations in September, the

Anubis and Horus are also relatives, even sharing the same father, Osiris. While Nephthys was Osiris's protector when he was the moon god,[1] in BD 151, in which Anubis attends to the mummified deceased and makes a speech, the god himself is "the Osiris's" protector.[2] Indeed, Anubis helps Isis and Horus restore Osiris's body after Set kills him. Anubis is also Osiris's embalmer, and, in BD 64, he is the "bearer" of the deceased/Osiris.[3] Moreover, Anubis is depicted as carrying the infant Horus, much like St. Christopher—the "Christ-bearer"—who in the Christian myth conveys the baby Jesus across the Jordan River.[4] Indeed, like Anubis, St. Christopher was depicted on ancient coins with a *dog's head*.[5] As professor of Religion at Southwestern University Dr. Laura Hobgood-Oster says, "...there are probable links between the dog-headed Christopher and Hermanubis, a god of healing whose tradition comes from both Egyptian and Hellenistic sources."[6]

A popular god who was "eventually worshipped throughout Egypt," Anubis was involved in the "purification of the dead" and was also identified with Horus, as Anubis-Horus, as related by Egyptian art curator Dr. Denise M. Doxey of the Boston Museum of Fine Arts.[7] Anubis as the god "cleansing me," as the deceased says in CT Sp. 341, prevents or ceases the putrefaction of the dead,[8] truly representing the "preparer of the way" for the eternal life of the savior. Indeed, Anubis has been described as the "divine physician" who resurrects Osiris.[9] Of course, Christ himself, who resurrects *Lazarus*, was called by Augustine and others the "Divine Physician."[10] Anubis's role as "guardian of the way of life"[11] can be seen further in an image in which the god appears "in his office...of assisting at the renovation and restoration of the dead."[12]

---

former on the 8th and the latter on the 13th. Also, John's father is "Zacharias" (Lk 1:5), while Anubis's father(s) is "Set-Osiris."

[1] Spence, 98.

[2] Allen, T., *BD*, 149; Budge, *BD* (1899), 503-508.

[3] Renouf, *EBD*, 118; Bunsen/Birch, 207; Allen, T., *BD*, 57; Faulkner, *EBD*, 106. It should be noted that there exist short and long versions of this important chapter/spell. (Budge, *BD* (1899), cxxxi.) The short version is missing the part about Anubis. Allen and Faulkner's translations, while containing mention of Anubis, are considerably different from that of Renouf. Birch's rendition essentially agrees with Renouf in meaning.

[4] Bonwick, 121.

[5] Hornung, *SLE*, 104.

[6] Hobgood-Oster, 101.

[7] Redford, 22.

[8] Faulkner, *AECT*, I, 275, 276. See also CT Sp. 335: "...Anubis prepared their seats on that day of 'Come thence!'" (Faulkner, *AECT*, I, 261.)

[9] Budge, *LOLM*, liii; Budge, *DON*, 271.

[10] Augustine, "Letter 219."

[11] Cooper, *AAD*, 68.

[12] Lundy, 405.

As Anubis is thus the "Preparer of the Way of the Other World,"[1] so too is John the Baptist called the "preparer of the way of Christ." John is likewise the "precursor," "forerunner" and "messenger," as found in the "prophetic" Old Testament book of Malachi (3:1), directly preceding the New Testament. In fact, John is considered the link between the two testaments, as the last Jewish prophet and the first Christian saint.[2] Anubis is also the messenger of the gods,[3] equivalent to the Greek god Hermes or Mercury,[4] the counterpart of the Egyptian lunar god Thoth or Djehuty/Tehuti. Moreover, like Thoth, whose emblem is the Tau or T, Anubis is "never without a cross,"[5] specifically the life-giving *ankh*, one of the holiest symbols in Egyptian religion. As related by the ancient writer Iamblichus (c. 245- c. 325 AD/CE), "The cross with a handle which Tot [Thoth] holds in his hand was none other than the monogram of his name."[6] Concerning the cross, in *Travels to Discover the Source of the Nile*, famed adventurer James Bruce remarks:

> Besides many other emblems and figures, the common Tot...has in his hand a cross with a handle, or Crux Ansata, which has occasioned great speculation among the decypherers. This cross, fixed to a circle, is supposed to denote the four elements, and to be the symbol of the influence which the sun has over them. Jamblichus [de Myst. sect. 8. cap. 5] records, that this cross, in the hand of Tot, is the name of the divine Being that travels through the world.[7]

The cross being the name of the "divine being" sounds Gnostic, especially in consideration of the fact that in Gnosticism the cross or *stauros* is identified with the character *Horos*, as we have seen. Like the Egyptian holy precursor Anubis/Thoth, John too was strongly associated with the cross, depicted in images holding one or having one nearby.

Furthermore, it is intriguing that Thoth is the speaker of the "Word of God" or *Logos* uttered to create the universe,[8] while at the beginning of John's gospel, the Baptist is sandwiched into a discussion of the Word/Logos. This association of the magical word and Thoth/Anubis appears in the Pyramid Texts (PT 437:796c/P 31), with the "going forth" by the deceased "at the voice of Anubis, while he has spiritualized thee, like Thot..."[9] Thus, again, Anubis is important in the "*akhifying*" or resurrection and immortalization of the dead.

---

[1] Bonwick, 120.
[2] Boguslawski.
[3] *Enc. Brit.*, II, 157.
[4] Witt, 201.
[5] Bonwick, 122.
[6] Bonwick, 103.
[7] Bruce, J., 341.
[8] Budge, *LOLM*, li.
[9] Mercer, 150; Allen, J., *AEPT*, 105; Faulkner, *AEPT*, 144.

In actuality, the Gospel of John, which opens with a pious discourse regarding John "the Baptist"—*although never using that title*—is without a doubt the most Egyptian of the four canonical gospels, and it appears that some of its lofty spiritual language was designed to convert to Christianity the followers of this highly important god Anubis. Moreover, when "the Baptist" is introduced in John's gospel, he is said not to be "the light" itself but to "bear witness to the light" (Jn 1:8), precisely the same role a *lunar* god such as Anubis/Thoth would serve in regard to the sun.

In keeping with the interchangeability of gods within mythology, Anubis is identified not only with Thoth but also with Osiris, his father, depending on the version of the myth.[1] Osiris and Anubis alike not only were associated with the afterlife but also symbolized both the star Sirius and different aspects of the sun, Osiris frequently representing the sun at night, while, like Horus, Anubis was the sun at the horizon, whether rising or setting.[2] According to Plutarch (44, 368E), Anubis is the horizon itself, representing the line between light and dark.[3] He may thus also be considered "twilight."[4] As the baby whom she suckles with her finger, Anubis (the horizon) is Isis's "attendant," who accompanies her when she seeks her own newborn son (the rising sun).[5] In addition, like Osiris, Anubis is the "god of the dead or the night god."[6]

According to Budge, "An was an old name for the sun-god."[7] Interestingly, the original Greek name for "John" is Io-*An*-nes, while, again, the Egyptian name of Anubis is commonly rendered *An*-up or *An*-pu, while in Coptic, it is Anoub. Another very famous water god from Babylonia is *Oannes*, who likewise shares many characteristics with John the Baptist, as demonstrated in my book *Suns of God: Krishna, Buddha and Christ Unveiled.*

Anubis is further the "'giver of Sirius,' the starry opener of the year,"[8] corresponding to the summer solstice, which just happens to be the traditional nativity and feast day of John the Baptist, as we have seen. Indeed, St. John's Nativity or Feast Day occurs on June 24th, the last of the three days the sun "stands still" during the summer solstice. Like John, who was said to be born six months before Jesus, Anubis was born shortly before Horus. The connection between John the Baptist and Anubis becomes more pointed when it is realized that, while John's feast day is on the summer solstice,

[1] Bruce, J., 337.
[2] Bruce, J., 472.
[3] Plutarch/Babbitt, 107.
[4] Brodrick, 19.
[5] Bruce, J., 472.
[6] Nuttall, 382.
[7] Nuttall, 382. (Emph. added.)
[8] Bonwick, 121.

:tually represents the *personification* of the summer solstice.
  states:

> ...strictly speaking, Anubis was the opener of the roads of the North, and Ap-uat the opener of the roads of the South; in fact, Anubis was the personification of the Summer Solstice, and Ap-uat of the Winter Solstice.[1]

Anubis is sometimes confounded or identified with the god Ap-uat as the "opener of the ways," while, again, Apuat/Wepwawet is also "identical with Osiris."[2] Like Anubis, Osiris too was the opener of the way, being born at the beginning of the Egyptian New Year, when it occurred at the summer solstice with the inundation of the Nile. However, since Wepwawet has been identified with Osiris, who in turn has been identified with Jesus, this comparison between John and Anubis becomes increasingly apparent, as Anubis would represent the summer solstice and Osiris the winter, while John the Baptist was supposedly born at the summer solstice, six months before Jesus, who was purportedly born at the winter solstice, according to popular tradition dating from at least the third century onward and taught to billions of people worldwide since then. This juxtaposition of John and Jesus as the sun at the summer and winter solstice brings vividly to light the meaning of the enigmatic remark made by "the Baptist" at John 3:30, previously mentioned: "He must increase, but I must decrease." As the sun passes through the summer solstice, the days begin to decrease in length, until the winter solstice, when the days increase again. This peculiar remark, which would not seem to be applicable to a *human being*, is all the more interesting in view of the fact that it appears *only* in the gospel of John, again the most Egyptian of the canonical texts, likely written at Alexandria for an Egyptian audience. It may thus serve as evidence that the writer of the gospel was aiming to usurp Anubis with the Jewish "prophet."

In addition, as the jackal-headed god, Anubis ranks as "one crying in the wilderness," as those animals notoriously do, and is likewise considered a guide to those who are lost in the desolation.[3] Indeed, one thesis holds that, in the biblical story, the Israelites wandering in the wilderness worshipped Anubis, the dog-headed guide.[4] In the Bible (Neh 2:13) appears the "jackal's well," which is traditionally placed in the Hinnom Valley[5] and which also demonstrates a relationship between that animal and water, possibly based on the "dog's" ability to find water in the wilderness. This relationship may explain the pervasive aquatic connection to Anubis

---

[1] Budge, *GE*, 264.
[2] Renouf, *EBD*, 99.
[3] "The expression in Jer 10 22, 'to make the cities of Judah a desolation, a dwelling-place of jackals,' seems...esp. appropriate of jackals." (Orr, 1548.)
[4] Faber, 438; Mackey, 140.
[5] Freedman, 666.

and jackals in the Egyptian texts as well. The jackal's cry in the wilderness was unquestionably well known to the nomads of the biblical era. While John the Baptist is depicted as the "one crying in the wilderness" to prepare the way of Lord Jesus, Anubis the jackal would be crying in the wilderness to prepare the way of Lord Osiris.

The Boat of the Dead

Anubis is not only the protector of Osiris but also the conductor or guide of *the* Osiris, or the deceased as he or she passes through the underworld. Indeed, Anubis is "associated with the Eye of Horus," steering the dead to Osiris.[1] In *The Horus Myth in Its Relation to Christianity*, William Cooper describes the function of Anubis as guide or "psychopomp," the traditional role of the god Hermes in Greek myth:

> Having quitted the boat of the river of Hades, the deceased is met by the god Anubis, who conducts him in safety through the devious windings of an intricate labyrinth, and leaves him at the threshold of the judgment-hall of Osiris, the hall of the Two Truths.[2]

In the judgment hall, if the deceased is not sufficiently pure, he is changed into a pig and "reconveyed to earth by Anubis in a boat."[3] The "bark of Anubis" is likewise referred to in the Coffin Texts, as at CT Sp. 344, in which we also find reference to the "celestial ferryman."[4] Moreover, as "the 'opener of the road' it was the duty of Anubis to guide the boat of the Sun through the underworld during the hours of darkness."[5]

Anubis is thus deemed the "ferryman of the dead" or "ferryman of souls."[6] Perhaps not surprisingly, in a similar role we find John the Baptist:

> The idea that the souls of the dead were ferried over to the Land of the Blessed by a righteous ferryman passed from the Books of the Dead into the literature of the Christian Egyptians, or Copts. Thus St. John Chrysostom tells us that our Lord gave to John the Baptist a boat of gold, which he was to use in transporting the souls of the righteous over the river of fire in Amente. This boat was provided with oars, to which lamps were attached. The oars, apparently, worked themselves under the direction of John the Baptist, and when the souls landed from the boat the lamps rekindled themselves and lighted the paths over the roads of darkness until John brought the souls to the Third Heaven.[7]

The Coptic text Budge cites here is called *Encomium on John the Baptist*, which is in reality *pseudonymously* attributed to Church

---

[1] Budge, *GE*, 261.
[2] Cooper, *HM*, 30.
[3] Rawlinson, *HAE*, I, 317-318.
[4] Faulkner, *AECT*, I, 279.
[5] *ROTP*, II, 197.
[6] Hornung, *SLE*, 66; Mojsov, 17.
[7] Budge, *Mummy* (2003), 466.

father John Chrysostom (c. 347-c. 407 AD/CE), but which is nonetheless an ancient work. And who may be the "righteous ferryman" who "passed from the Books of the Dead into the literature of the Christian Egyptians," specifically as John the Baptist? Could it be *Anubis*, the protector, conductor and guide of the dead, who himself was said to possess a "bark" or *boat*? It appears these early Christians recognized the correlation between Anubis and John the Baptist, as others did many centuries later.

In his *Coptic Apocrypha* (xx), Budge further elucidates upon this theme:

> The boat was intended for the use of the souls of those who had loved John upon earth. These souls would, after the death of their bodies, find their way to the boat of gold, and John would ferry them over the Lake of Fire, and land them in the Third Heaven, which was John's peculiar appanage [station]. No soul, good or bad, could enter this Heaven except after baptism in the river of fire...[1]

One of the most important *Egyptian* rituals, in fact, was to conduct the dead through the Lake of Fire, in a form of "baptism by fire." In the Book of the Dead (e.g., BD 98), the deceased is instructed on how to "catch a ferryboat in the sky" or "Sacred Bark," also making reference to the "Great Waterway" and the "Lake of Fire" or "Lake of Burning in the Field of Fire."[2] Assman calls this passage a "spell for fetching the ferry" that arrives "at the place of eternal life."[3] As in the later Christian myth, it is into this Lake of Fire that the "wicked were to be thrown," for purposes of purification.[4] Not only the wicked but also the righteous were purified in this baptism by fire. The baptism by fire also made it into the New Testament, with Jesus said to be its initiator. (Mt 3:11)

The Living Water

As noted, the sacred ritual of baptism by water can be found dating back millennia in many places around the world, including and especially in Egypt. As a source of life, particularly along the Nile, water figured prominently in the spiritual imagery of ancient Egypt. As Renouf remarks, "The water from heaven was supposed in Egypt to be especially refreshing for the dead."[5] This concept may also be found at PT 685:2063a/N 519: "The waters of life which are in the sky, the waters of life which are in the earth come," to purify and cleanse the king, who is afterwards *reborn*.[6] The "water from heaven" and "in the sky" would sensibly refer to rain, of course,

---

[1] Court, 124.
[2] Renouf, *EBD*, 166; Faulkner, *EBD*, 109; Allen, T., *BD*, 78; Bunsen/Birch, 233.
[3] Assman, *DSAE*, 132.
[4] Sharpe, *EABM*, 140; Budge, *BR*, 30.
[5] Renouf, *EBD*, 113.
[6] Mercer, 303; Allen, J., *AEPT*, 291; Faulkner, *AEPT*, 295.

which comes from "the Weeper," who is "primarily Heaven."[1] As Renouf points out, "The Nile god who proceeds from [the Weeper] also bears the same name." [2] The Nile god traditionally is Osiris; hence, it could be said that *Osiris's tears resurrect the dead*. Indeed, one popular theme during the Middle Kingdom in particular was that "mankind was created out of the tears of the creator-god, especially the sun-god."[3] This motif of life-giving tears is reminiscent of the scripture at John 11:35: "Jesus wept," in the pericope of raising Lazarus from the dead. It is interesting that this odd saying too appears *only* in the gospel of John—which is clearly the most *Egyptian* of the canonical texts—again, in the resurrection of *Lazarus*, who is demonstrably *Osiris*.

Regarding this Egyptian "living water," Plutarch (36, 365B) remarks, "Not only the Nile, but every form of moisture they call simply the effusion of Osiris; and in their holy rites the water jar in honour of the god heads the procession."[4] Plutarch (38, 366A) continues:

> "As they regard the Nile as the effusion of Osiris, so they hold and believe the earth to be the body of Isis, not all of it, but so much of it as the Nile covers, fertilizing it and uniting with it. From this union they make Horus to be born."[5]

Thus, Osiris's "effusion" combining with the "virgin matter" of Isis produces the divine son, Horus, another variant of the myth that has nothing to do with a phallus or any other human body part. The effusion of Osiris, also called "effluxes" or "sap," is abundantly discussed in the ancient Egyptian texts. In a note to BD 63a, for example, regarding a sentence about the "effluxes of Osiris," Renouf states:

> *Effluxes*,...the ιχωρ ["ichor"], the vital *sap*, as it were, of the body of Osiris, which is the source of life both to men and the gods, and in default of which his own heart would cease to beat. It is celebrated in all the mythological texts extant from the time of the Pyramids down to the latest inscriptions of Denderah and Edfu, and even in Demotic documents. All moisture was supposed to proceed from it, and the Nile was naturally identified with it.[6]

Regarding the remark that the "sap of Osiris" is the "source of life both to men and the gods," Renouf further notes, "In one of the ancient chapters preserved in the tomb of Horhotep, the deceased, speaking in the person of Horus, talks of quenching his thirst with the [effluxes/sap] of his father Osiris."[7] Thus, like Jesus, who

---

[1] Renouf, *EBD*, 114.
[2] Renouf, *EBD*, 114.
[3] Morenz, 183; Assman, *ESRNK*, 168.
[4] Plutarch/Babbitt, 87.
[5] Plutarch/Babbitt, 93.
[6] Renouf, *EBD*, 117.
[7] Renouf, *EBD*, 117.

presents the woman at the well in John (Jn 4:10-11) with the "living water," Osiris too is the source of the "living water." Once again, it is interesting that it is the most *Egyptian* gospel, John, which contains this concept of living water, so highly emphasized in the Egyptian religion.

The watery language continues in a number of other utterances in the Pyramid Texts, including one (PT 33:25c/N 125) addressing Osiris as "you being young in your name of Fresh Water."[1] The "coolness," "cold water" and youthfulness in Osiris's name of "Fresh water" are also discussed at PT 423:765-767/P 7.[2]

Moreover, "effusion," "purification" and "immersion" are terms used over the centuries in discussions of Christian *baptism* as well.

The Baptism

Along with the concept of holy, living water in Egyptian religion comes its use for purification in actual *baptism*, with immersion into water or sprinkling of water. Concerning Egyptian baptism, Bonwick relates:

> The baptism in Egypt is known by the hieroglyphic terms of "water of purification." In Egypt...the water so used in immersion absolutely cleansed the soul, and the person was said to be *regenerated*. The water itself was holy, and the place was known, as afterwards by the eastern Christians, by the name of *holy bath*. The early Christians called it being "brought anew into the world." The ancients always gave a new name at Baptism, which custom was afterwards followed by moderns. The Mithraic font for the baptism of ancient Persians is regarded as of Egyptian origin.[3]

We have already seen abundantly this ritual of purification in water within the Egyptian religion, in which the deceased becomes revivified, a cleansing equivalent to Christian baptism. Indeed, one definition of "baptism" is a "ceremony, trial, or experience by which one is initiated, *purified*, or given a name."[4] As do Christians during baptism, the deceased/Osiris frequently received a new name, depicted in the texts as speaking from the perspective of many deities, as demonstrated. Since "baptism," which comes from the Greek word *baptizo*, is called "purification by water" in the Egyptian, the word for "baptizer" or "baptist" would be "purifier."

In this regard, concerning the use of the term "baptism" in his article on the purification of the kings called "The Baptism of Pharaoh," Gardiner states:

> The analogy of our rite to that of Christian baptism is close enough to justify the title given to this article. In both cases a symbolic

---

[1] Faulkner, *AEPT*, 7; Mercer, 25; Allen, J., *AEPT*, 255.
[2] Allen, J., *AEPT*, 101; Mercer, 145; Faulkner, *AEPT*, 140.
[3] Bonwick, 416.
[4] *Webster's*, 90. (Emph. added.)

cleansing by means of water serves as initiation into a properly legitimated religious life.[1]

Far from belonging to Christianity, the term "baptizo," its root "bapto," or other derivative thereof, meaning "to dip" or "to baptize," can be found in several pre-Christian and non-Christian texts.[2]

Naturally, the early Church fathers were aware of the baptismal commonality, although, as usual, they worked hard to create distinctions that denigrated the Pagan religion and elevated their own. For example, the ancient "heathen" practice of water purification is discussed by Church father Tertullian in his treatise "On Baptism" (5), in which he attempts to assert Christian superiority:

> Chapter 5. Use Made of Water by the Heathen...
>
> "...the nations, who are strangers to all understanding of spiritual powers, ascribe to their idols the imbuing of waters with the self-same efficacy." (So they do) but they cheat themselves with waters which are widowed. For washing is the channel through which they are initiated into some sacred rites—of some notorious Isis or Mithras. The gods themselves likewise they honour by washings. Moreover, by carrying water around, and sprinkling it, they everywhere expiate country-seats, houses, temples, and whole cities: at all events, at the Apollinarian and Eleusinian games they are baptized; and they presume that the effect of their doing that is their regeneration and the remission of the penalties due to their perjuries. Among the ancients, again, whoever had defiled himself with murder, was wont to go in quest of purifying waters. Therefore, if the mere nature of water, in that it is the appropriate material for washing away, leads men to flatter themselves with a belief in omens of purification, how much more truly will waters render that service through the authority of God, by whom all their nature has been constituted![3]

Tertullian further discusses the "pool of Bethsaida," which appears *only* in the highly Egyptian gospel of John (5:2), as does the "pool of Siloam" (Jn 9:7, 11), with a focus of having the infirm bathe in it to be healed. Naturally, we find the precedent of the "Pool of Truth," "pool of right and truth," "divine pool," "pool of the water of

---

[1] Gardiner, "The Baptism of Pharaoh," 6.

[2] E.g., the works of Homer, Aristophanes, Aristotle, Plato, Euripides, Chariton and Plutarch. See search results in *Thesaurus Linguae Graecae* for "βαπτ*." Per Strong's G907: "The clearest example that shows the meaning of baptizo is a text from the Greek poet and physician Nicander, who lived about 200 B.C. It is a recipe for making pickles and is helpful because it uses both words. Nicander says that in order to make a pickle, the vegetable should first be 'dipped' (*baptō*) into boiling water and then 'baptised' (*baptizō*) in the vinegar solution. Both verbs concern the immersing of vegetables in a solution. But the first is temporary. The second, the act of baptising the vegetable, produces a permanent change."

[3] Roberts, A., *ANF*, III, 671.

life" and the "pool of peace" in the Egyptian religion as well.[1] The Pool of Bethsaida or Bethesda, in should be noted, provides an evidently unambiguous anachronism within John's gospel, in that the building at Jerusalem with the five porches in which the healings took place was apparently not in existence until *after the reign of Emperor Hadrian*, beginning in 135 AD/CE.[2] John's gospel, therefore, could not have been written before that time and indeed does not clearly show up in the historical record until *the end of the second century*.

In addition to these "Pagan" precedents of baptism, the *Catholic Encyclopedia* focuses on pre-Christian *Jewish* "foreshadowings," such as the mythical Great Flood representing a "type of *purification* to be found in the Christian baptism":

> Other forerunners of baptism were the numerous purifications prescribed in the Mosaic dispensation for legal uncleannesses. The symbolism of an outward washing to cleanse an invisible blemish was made very familiar to the Jews by their sacred ceremonies. But in addition to these more direct types, both the New Testament writers and the Fathers of the Church find many mysterious foreshadowings of baptism. Thus St. Paul (1 Corinthians 10) adduces the passage of Israel through the Red Sea, and St. Peter (1 Peter 3) the Deluge, as types of the purification to be found in Christian baptism. Other foreshadowings of the sacrament are found by the Fathers in the bathing of Naaman in the Jordan, in the brooding of the Spirit of God over the waters, in the rivers of Paradise, in the blood of the Paschal Lamb, during Old Testament times, and in the pool of Bethsaida, and in the healing of the dumb and blind in the New Testament.[3]

As can be seen, the "water of purification"—or *baptism*—is an old concept long predating the common era, found not only in Judea but also in Egypt, from which the Jews garnered a number of their rituals and beliefs. As another example, in describing the initiation into the *mysteries of Isis* undergone by the character Lucius in ancient Latin writer Apuleius's *The Golden Ass*, Dr. Assman clarifies that, when Lucius is "first bathed," he is *baptized*. The German scholar then comments, "The bath thus has the sacramental sense of a remission of sins."[4] In this regard, at CT Sp. 761, the deceased is instructed as follows: "...Go up and bathe in the Lake of Life; what is evil on you will be purged in the Lake of the Firmament..."[5]

As we can see, in the Egyptian religion appear "divine pools," the "lake of fire" and other lakes for purification as discovered in the funerary literature. In this same regard, in BD 125 the deceased addresses Osiris, saying:

---

[1] Faulkner, *EBD*, 116; Budge, *EBD* (1967), 207; Renouf, *EBD*, 165; Bunsen/Birch, 233; Massey, *AELW*, II, 236, 450.
[2] See my book, *Who Was Jesus?*, 231-232.
[3] *CE*, "Baptism," II, 260.
[4] Assman, *DSAE*, 205.
[5] Faulkner, *AECT*, II, 293.

...for I have done the right for the Lord of Truth. I have purified myself and my fore parts with holy water, and my hinder parts with the things that make clean, and my inward parts have been [immersed] in the Lake of Truth. There is not one member of mine wherein truth is lacking. I purified myself in the Pool of the South....[1]

The purpose of the purification in the south and north pools is clarified by Massey, who further explains the two different types of Egyptian baptism and their relationship to Christian doctrine:

There was a double baptism in the ancient mysteries: the baptism by water and the baptism by spirit. This may be traced to the two lakes of heaven at the head of the celestial river in the region of the northern pole, which were also repeated as the two lakes of purification in Amenta. The manes [soul/spirit] says, "I purify me in the southern tank, and I rest me at the northern lake" (ch. 125). They will account for the two forms of baptism mentioned in the Gospels. John baptizes with water, Jesus with the Holy Spirit and with fire.[2]

Hence, again we have precise and detailed correspondences between spiritual concepts of the Egyptian and Christian religions, specifically as concerns *baptism*.

In the Pyramid Texts (PT 665b:1919a) as well can be found a divine lake in which the deceased may be purified to attain to everlasting life: "Draw fully from the divine lake, the lake in which [they] purify thee, as a god."[3] At PT 670:1979a/N 348, Osiris comes forth from the "Lake of Life, having been cleansed" in the "Lake of Cool Water," which Breasted calls the "celestial lake."[4] In the Coffin Texts, at CT Sp. 891, the speaker remarks, "I am cleansed in the Lake of the Netherworld..."[5] Concerning the sun god's nightly journey back to life, Egyptologist Dr. Jacobus Van Dijk of the University of Groningen says that "according to the Pyramid Texts, the sun god purifies himself in the morning in the Lake of the Field of Rushes."[6] Thus, the morning sun—or *Horus*—was said to pass through the purifying or baptismal waters to become reborn, revivified or resurrected.

Horus the Baptist

Horus is not only purified or baptized, but, as we have seen from his role as *purifier* in the funerary literature, Horus himself is a *baptizer* as well, as in CT Sp. 74, in which the deceased is told that

[1] Budge, *LAE*, 54: Bunsen/Birch, 256-257; Faulkner, *EBD*, 116; Allen, T., *BD*, 99-100. This section constitutes the ending of BD 125 in the Nebeni papyrus. (See Budge, *EBD* (1967), 351.) Allen's translation omits references to water, while Faulkner's rendition includes being purified in the "Pool of Truth" and bathing in the "Southern Pool."
[2] Massey, *AELW*, II, 795.
[3] Mercer, 285. This passage appears at PT 666, § 1918-19 in Faulkner's *AEPT*, 277.
[4] Faulkner, *AEPT*, 286; Breasted, *DRTAE*, 32; Mercer, 294; Allen, J., *AEPT*, 267.
[5] Faulkner, *AECT*, III, 53.
[6] Redford, 311.

"Horus has purified you."[1] Horus is depicted as the baptist also in CT Sp. 345: "Ho N! Horus himself will cleanse you in that pool of cold water."[2] In a "supplementary ceremony," Horus "hath purified the Osiris in the Lake of the Jackal,"[3] in which the deceased is purified also in CT Sp. 33-35.[4]

Moreover, Horus is the "anointer with water" of the pharaohs: "In scenes from temples, [Thoth] and Horus anoint the king with water."[5] In this regard, Gardiner discusses numerous "Scenes Representing the Baptism of Pharaoh" depicting the purification or baptism by Horus and Thoth of kings/pharaohs such as Sethos I, Ramesses II, III and IV, et al.[6] In this regard, Dr. Gabriel remarks:

> The officiating priests...wore the masks of Thoth and Horus, both of whom had prominent roles in the Osirian myth. It was these gods who performed the ritual of resurrection over the corpse of Osiris. New life was brought to Osiris' limbs and body by washing, clearly linking washing with magic water to rebirth.... So important was the ritual of baptism to the Egyptians that some form of it, purification or offering of a libation, became an essential rite in all important religious and state rituals. It even appeared in the funerary liturgy where the daily ritual was repeated in the washing of the dead.[7]

It is important to note that Gabriel specifically refers to the "ritual of *resurrection*" as concerns Osiris's *body*, which was brought *new life*. Furthermore, Gardiner avers that scenes in which *four* gods are purifying the king represent the four cardinal points,[8] demonstrating another astrotheological motif.

Anubis, the Jackal Lake and House/Tent of Purification

Sharing the same father after a certain point, Horus has been identified with Anubis, as we have seen from the hybrid Anubis-Horus, the god of Cynopolis or "Dog City," for example.[9] As Hornung says of Anubis, "From the New Kingdom on, he was also considered to be son of Osiris and thus often appeared in the role of Horus."[10] Anubis also shares with Horus the role of purifier/baptizer: In addition to previous examples, the purification of Anubis is also referred to in CT Sp. 527.[11]

---

[1] Faulkner, *AECT*, I, 70.
[2] Faulkner, *AECT*, I, 280. See also CT Sp. 346:377: "Ho N! Horus himself will cleanse you in the pool of cold water." (Faulkner, *AECT*, I, 281.)
[3] Budge, *BOM*, 125; Assman, *DSAE*, 156.
[4] Faulkner, *AECT*, I, 22.
[5] Redford, 353.
[6] Gardiner, "The Baptism of Pharaoh," 4-5.
[7] Gabriel, *GOF*, 184.
[8] Gardiner, "The Baptism of Pharaoh," 9-11.
[9] Budge, *FFGAE*, 108. See also Fisher, 18;
[10] Hornung, *SLE*, 66.
[11] Faulkner, *AECT*, II, 152.

In this same regard, in the Pyramid Texts we find much discussion of the "purifying lake," which, as at PT 697:2170a/N 564, is that of the *jackal*: "Thou purifiest thyself in the lake of the jackal; thou cleansest thyself in the lake of the Duat [Netherworld]."[1] In addition, at PT 504:1083b/P 458, the Osiris says, "I have cleansed myself in the lakes of the jackal."[2] At CT Sp. 551, we also discover the Osiris bathing in the "Lakes of the Netherworld" and washing in the "Lakes of the Jackals."[3] The "lake of the jackal" or "jackal lake," in which the deceased or the souls are *purified* in their progress to immortality, as also at PT 697:2170a/N 564,[4] could be understood to be that of *Anubis*. In CT Sp. 61, the deceased is "cleansed in the Lake of Cold Water," while Anubis "burns incense for you...."[5] The Jackal Lake, in fact, features prominently in the purification of the sun during its nightly journey.[6]

Anubis as a jackal purifying the dead is undoubtedly based on that scavenger's role in keeping the land free of putrefaction. This idea is indicated by certain passages in the sacred scriptures, as in CT Sp. 73, discussing the names of Anubis and the "Jackal of Upper Egypt" associated with protection against "rotting" and "putrefaction."[7]

Moreover, as embalmer, Anubis's purifying role in mummification is made clear in the fact that he presides over the "House of Purification"[8] and "Tent of Purification," the latter called *tp-jbw* in Egyptian.[9] In describing the funerary rituals, Dr. Lesko states:

> Pouring of water, for its life-giving as well as purification qualities, was part of every ritual. The corpse, whether first desiccated or not, would have been washed (in the Tent of Purification) and then anointed and wrapped in the embalmer's shop. Seven sacred oils used for anointing the body are known already in the first dynasty....[10]

As we can see, not only was the Osiris *baptized* but he was also anointed or *Christed*, as the word would be in Greek. In the "mortuary workshop," the "rites of embalmming and purification"[11] thus go hand in hand. Hence, the deceased—who is at times Osiris and at others Horus—is purified or *baptized*.

Concerning the cleansing of the deceased in the "Tent of Purification," in *The Apis Embalming Ritual*, Dutch Egyptologist Dr. René L. Vos states:

---

[1] Mercer; 315; Allen, J., *AEPT*, 298; Faulkner, *AEPT*, 304.
[2] Mercer, 187; Allen, J., *AEPT*, 155; Faulkner, *AEPT*, 180.
[3] Faulkner, *AECT*, II, 163.
[4] Faulkner, *AEPT*, 304; Allen, J., *AEPT*, 298; Mercer, 315.
[5] Faulkner, *AECT*, I, 56.
[6] See, e.g., Willems, 297-298.
[7] Faulkner, *AECT*, I, 68.
[8] Hart, 26. See also Vos, R.L., 31-32, 34, 51-52, etc.
[9] Redford, 150.
[10] Redford, 76.
[11] Davis, W.M., 170.

This washing of the corpse with water is an ancient solar rite, the object being the removal of impurity and the bringing about of resurrection, just as the sun rises from the primeval waters or, which amounts to the same thing, from the horizon.[1]

After the corpse is purified, it is moved into the House of Embalming, about which Dr. Vos remarks that it was "above all the house in which the mystery of resurrection was performed, as Osiris had risen from the dead... Purity is a precondition for resurrection... The embalmers enter the House of Embalming after they have met the requirements of purity..."[2]

Dr. Roth also describes the ritual for the deceased, in which the procession "went aboard a special boat," which "carried the procession to the *sh ntr Jnpw*" or the "divine booth of Anubis— probably to be equated with the purification tent..."[3]

Throughout this complex ritual of purification and resurrection, in which **"Osiris is risen from the dead,"** as is Horus as the morning sun rising from the "primeval waters," Anubis is thus the "purifier"[4]— or *baptist*—a role spelled out also in BD 97, as recapped by Massey:

> The scene of the baptism by John can be paralleled in the Ritual (97). Horus claims to be the master of all things, including the water of the Inundation. When he comes to be baptized, it is "*said at the boat,*" called the "staff of Anup," "Look upon me, oh ye great and mighty Gods, who are foremost among the spirits of Annu; let me be exalted in your presence." The plea for baptism is very express. "Lo, I come, that I may *purify this soul of mine in the most high degree*: let not that impediment which cometh from your mouth be issued against me, *let me be purified in the lake of propitiation and of equipoise*: let me plunge into the divine pool *beneath the two divine sycamores* of heaven and after." After the baptism, he says, "*Now let my Fold be fitted for me as one victorious against all adversaries who would not that right should be done to me. I am the only one just and true upon the earth.*"[5]

In this analysis, Massey accurately quotes Renouf's translation of BD 97, concerning a speech made by the deceased, who is essentially identified as *Horus*, as he approaches the "bark" or "boat" of Anubis:

> Said at the Bark: Staff of Anubis, may I propitiate those four Glorified ones who follow after the Master of [all] things. I am the Master of the champaign at their behest, and I am the Father of the Inundation, when he who hath charge of the canals is athirst. Look therefore upon me, oh ye great and mighty gods, who are foremost among the Spirits of Annu [Heliopolis]; *let me be exalted in your presence.* I am a well-doer towards you. Lo I come, that *I may purify this Soul of mine* in the most high degree; let not that impediment

---

[1] Vos, *R.L.*, 31.
[2] Vos, *R.L.*, 34.
[3] Redford, 152.
[4] Renouf, *EBD*, 49; Renouf, *PSBA*, XIV, 390.
[5] Massey, *AELW*, II, 795.

proceeding from your mouth be issued against me which giveth one over to ruin: *let me be purified in the lake of propitiation and of equipoise: let me plunge into the divine pool* beneath the two divine sycamores of Heaven and Earth. Now let my Fold be fitted for me as one victorious against all adversaries who would not that right should be done to me. I am the Only one; just and true upon the Earth. It is I who say it.[1]

In the previous chapter/spell 96, the deceased is identified as "he who dwells in his Eye,"[2] which would basically be Horus, although the deceased is more often Osiris, while the priest plays the role of Horus. In this case, however, *Horus*—evidently called here the "Only One," which Renouf identifies as an appellation of the sun[3]—would be approaching the "staff of Anubis" at the boat, asking for purification and exaltation in the "lake of propitiation" and "divine pool." With such a role for Anubis, it is obvious why the connection has been made between Horus approaching Anubis for "water purification" and Jesus drawing near John for "baptism," both terms, as we have seen, referring to the same sacred ritual. *Thus, it could be said that Horus is baptized by Anup the baptizer!*

In BD 145 (or 146),[4] which Budge calls the "Chapter of the Pylons," and Massey labels the "chapter of the baptisms," the deceased, as *Horus*, must pass through a series of "pylons" or portals in order to become purified.[5] According to T. George Allen, the pertinent BD 145 was composed in the 21st dynasty, and it differs from prior editions in that the "Osiris" or "N." is clearly identified as "Horus."[6] In this chapter/spell, each pylon/portal is dedicated to a different god, and at every one Horus is washed in the name of that god, as well as anointed with unguent, or, again, *Christed*. After each washing—or "baptism"—the deceased/Horus is pronounced "pure." At the fourth pylon, Horus washes himself in the water in which the "Un-nefer"—meaning "Good Being," an epithet of Osiris—also washed himself after his victory over Set (Satan). In the fifth pylon, the deceased washes himself in the water in which Horus was purified "when he made himself the Chief reader and *Sa-mer-f* ["his beloved son"] for his father, Osiris."[7] This passage is reminiscent of the New Testament scripture in which Jesus is baptized by John, and God's voice from heaven booms, "This is my beloved Son, in whom I am well pleased." (Mt 3:17) In the eighth pylon, Horus washes himself in the

---

[1] Renouf, *EBD*, 165. (Emph. added.) See Allen, T., *BD*, 77-78; Faulkner, *EBD*, 109.
[2] Allen, T., *BD*, 77.
[3] Renouf, *EBD*, 11.
[4] Birch numbered this chapter/spell as 146, the title of which he rendered, "The Beginning of the Gates of the Aahlu [Elysium], or the Abode of Osiris." (Bunsen/Birch, 283.) BD 145 is missing in Faulkner.
[5] See, e.g., Budge, *BD* (1899), 453.
[6] Allen, T., *BD*, 129ff. Birch too translates the edition with Horus clearly featured as the speaker. (Bunsen/Birch, 283ff.)
[7] Budge, *BD* (2006), 246; Allen, T., *BD*, 130.

water "wherein the god Anpu washed when he had performed the office of embalmer and bandager," also called the "Chief reader of Osiris."[1] Here too Horus becomes anointed or christed. Massey summarizes the scene:

> Here we find...that Anup was the baptizer in preparing Osiris (or the mortal Horus) to become the Horus in spirit, the anointed and beloved son of the father in the rite of embalmment, or baptism; that Osiris, or Horus, was baptized preparatory to or at the time of his contest with Sut (Satan); and that the baptism of Horus took place when he became chief minister, the beloved son *Su-meri-f* of his father....[2]

It is at this point when Horus becomes the "Chief reader" and the "anointed and beloved son of the father," Massey contends, that he attains to manhood, reaching the *sherau* ("adult son") stage of 30 years old, like his Jewish counterpart Jesus, who is about 30 when he is baptized by John (Lk 3:23).[3] In other words, it is not necessarily that Horus is 30 years old when he is baptized but that through his baptism he becomes a man, traditionally associated with the age of 30. The affect remains the same, however, that *a central mystery in the Egyptian religion is the baptism of the king or godman, evidently in association with the age of 30*—a ritual that makes sense in consideration of the importance given to the 30-year period or "age" celebrated, for example, in the Sed festival of the Horus-kings, at which sacred water was used for purification.

This notion of the baptism at the "age of 30" or a 30-year interval is given validation by Gardiner, who discusses the "baptism of pharaoh" or "*ḥes*-purification":

> It is not often that the legends beside the picture of the *ḥes*-purification allude to its ultimate purpose, but they do so in one Karnak example of the time of Sethos I..., where we read: *I purify thee with life and dominion, that thou mayst grow young...like thy father Re and make* Sed *festival like Atum, being arisen gloriously as prince of joy.*[4]

Here we see in an inscription the purification in association with the Sed festival designed to allow the king to rise "gloriously" as "prince of joy," another "Christian"-sounding attribute.

To summarize, in the ancient Egyptian texts we discover a number of instances in which the deceased, as *Horus*, must be purified by water—or *baptized*—in order to attain to immortality, including one portal or *station* where Anubis or "Anup" himself acts as a purifier or *baptizer*. Of course, every time the king/pharaoh is baptized/purified, so too is Horus, as the royal alter ego.

---

[1] Budge, *BD* (2006), 247. The purification of Anubis occurs in the 9th portal of the rendition from the 21st dynasty translated by Dr. T. George Allen. (Allen, T., *BD*, 131.)
[2] Massey, *AELW*, II, 794.
[3] Massey, *AELW*, II, 794; *ABB*, 246.
[4] Gardiner, "The Baptism of Pharaoh," 7-8.

Significantly, the Christian Baptist too has been called "John the Purifier" over the centuries, during which a controversy erupted regarding this appellation and role, with proponents citing the biblical verse at Malachi 3:3 as referring to John: "...he will sit as a refiner and *purifier* of silver, and he will *purify* the sons of Levi..."[1] (RSV) In actuality, "purifier" may be a more appropriate term, since the word "baptist" or "baptizer" as applied to John "has no precedent in Second Temple Judaism."[2] What this fact means is that such a title did not exist within Judaism at the time John supposedly lived, with this figure then becoming anachronistic and, in reality, likely fictional. Indeed, even though he is highlighted in the Gospel of John, John is never called therein by his epithet of "baptist." Since not even John is to be considered a "baptist," per se, when we apply the term to "Anup," it should not be viewed as the exclusive property of the Jewish character or, therefore, inappropriate to the Egyptian figure. In other words, as Anubis was not necessarily termed "the baptizer," so too was John not called "baptist" during his alleged lifetime. Both of these figures, in fact, are deemed "purifiers," involved in the act of *purification by water*, i.e., baptism.

While John the Baptist is sketchy as a historical character, even in light of his mention in the writings of Josephus, the idea of a god who baptizes or purifies by immersion in water is as old as the hills and highly popular. The Egyptian god Anubis/Anup is evidently just such a god, as is the Babylonian water god Oannes, while the Christian figure Ioannes/John seems to be based on both of these mythical forerunners.[3]

Aquarius the Water-Bearer

Like his popular predecessor the Babylonian water and fish god Oannes, over the centuries the biblical figure of John the Baptist has been associated repeatedly with the zodiacal sign and constellation of Aquarius, the Water Bearer, who "pours down the water on the heads of the people." As Dr. Herbert J. Hardwicke relates of John:

> His nativity is fixed by the Catholic church at June 24th, at the first moment of which day *Aquarius* rose above the horizon, to pursue his course along the ecliptic; and thus is accounted for the passage "he must increase, but I must decrease," which means that John's days become shorter from June 24th to Dec. 25th, when Jesus is born; after which the days grow longer. At midnight on Aug. 28th and 29th *Aquarius* was seen at Alexandria above the southern horizon, travelling along the ecliptic with his head above the equator, as though it had been cut off. (Matt. xiv. 10). On that very day the

---

[1] Emph. added.
[2] Rothschild, 65.
[3] For more information on the mythical nature of John, including a discussion of the Josephus material, which may in fact be based on the very ancient and popular god Oannes, see my books *The Christ Conspiracy* and *Suns of God*.

Church keeps the anniversary of John's death. In the fourth gospel
we find the same personification of Aquarius depicted...[1]

As we can see, the story of John the Baptist's beheading is
written in the stars, like so much else of the gospel story, casting
doubt once more on his place in "history."

Moreover, the overt Christian tradition of identifying John the
Baptist with Aquarius goes back well over a thousand years:

> In England the Venerable Bede, 673-735, substituted the eleven
> apostles for eleven of the early signs, as the Corona seu circulus
> sanctorum Apostolorum, John the Baptist fitly taking the place of
> Aquarius to complete the circle.[2]

We have noted that in the Egyptian sacred rites someone carrying
a water jar leads the procession of Osiris. In the Pyramid Texts (PT
16-18:10a-c/N 95-97), in the "Ritual of Bodily Restoration of the
Deceased," appear invocations by the deceased, who at times says, "I
am Horus," mentioning a "jar of water" and a "pitcher of water."[3]
Could this ritual and these scriptures be a source for the strange
remark by Jesus at Mark 14:13 and Luke 22:10?—

> "Behold, when you have entered the city, a man carrying a jar of
> water will meet you; follow him into the house which he enters..."

More than one commentator over the centuries has observed the
parallel between this peculiar biblical scripture and the figure of
Aquarius, the man carrying a jar of water. As may be expected, we
also find *Anubis* the purifier associated with the constellation of the
Water Bearer, as one of the three "Cynocephali ["doghead" stars] at
the feet of Aquarius."[4]

In addition, in the gospel story John the Baptist is decapitated,
while, as noted, at different times the constellation of Aquarius also
appears to have lost *its* head. Furthermore, Isis is depicted as
decapitated, as the constellation of Virgo at certain times, while
Anubis too is associated with headlessness:

> Anubis has a special emblem symbolizing his role as an embalmer. It
> is a headless animal skin...sometimes dripping blood, tied to a pole.
> This emblem can also be jackal-headed, as in the Litany of Ra
> describing the sun-god's journey through the underworld.[5]

Dr. Doxey also relates Anubis's headless symbol:

> Anubis is represented by the *my-wt* fetish, a headless animal skin
> hanging from a pole.[6]

---

[1] Hardwicke, H.J., 195.
[2] Allen, R., 6.
[3] Mercer, 22; Allen, J., *AEPT*, 252; Faulkner, *AEPT*, 3.
[4] Herbert, 138; Zitman, 199.
[5] Hart, 27.
[6] Redford, 21.

Hence, like John the Baptist, Anubis was symbolized by headlessness. In fact, in the Anubis myth, the god in human form himself is decapitated, with his head replaced by that of the jackal:

> It was the god Anubis, which was formed by striking off the head of a human being and affixing the head of a jackal to the decapitated lump of humanity, thus making a deity of the first order.[1]

Indeed, it is possible that the headless skin constituted the rest of the jackal whose head the decapitated human figure bore.

The god Set/Seth likewise was depicted as headless, constituting "the Akephalos."[2] Regarding the "headless god," in discussing a Gnostic text called, "The stele of Jeou the Painter," Doresse remarks:

> The "headless" god is there referred to as creator of earth and heaven, of the night and the day..., he is identified with Osiris-Onnophris, the Egyptian god of the other world. It is said that he judges the just and the unjust; that he created all that is masculine and all that is feminine. And then the magician, identifying himself with Moses, invokes the god Osoronnophris, saying to him, "This thy true name, which thou hast bequeathed to the prophets of Israel"...
>
> Are we amazed at this admixture of Jewish and Egyptian elements? But did not the Greek historian Manetho say that Moses had been a priest of Osiris in Egypt?—which shows that such a belief was current in fairly early times. And does not the Talmud also suggest that in the second century of our era there were Biblical manuscripts in "demotic" writing—that is, in the latest, most popular form of the old hieroglyphic script? Moreover, one can point to some *Ptolemaic Books* in Greek, which combined the Egyptian theology with the Jewish.[3]

The historian Manetho wrote during the 3rd century BCE, while the term "Ptolemaic books" apparently refers to texts composed during the Ptolemaic period (305-30 BCE). That the Jews of the Diaspora did not live in a hermetically sealed community separate, apart and uninfluenced by their surroundings either in pre-Christian or Christian times is obvious and sensible, as is the conclusion that Egypt influenced much Jewish culture and religion. This contention is evident from numerous examples, as demonstrated throughout this work. Another example of Jewish knowledge of Egyptian culture may be found in the biblical Hebrew word *Shihor* or *Sihor*—שיחור—which means the "waters of Horus," evidently referring at times to a "stream of water associated with northeastern Egypt" that was a branch of the Nile river[4] and that formed the border between Egypt and Israel, the significance of which is that it shows Hebrew

---

[1] Duffield, 218.
[2] Doresse, 104.
[3] Doresse, 105-106.
[4] *ISBE*, 476; *Eerdman's Dictionary of the Bible*, 1210. Strong's (H7883) identifies the word as referring to the waters/river, but traces its root to the Hebrew word for "dark." (See Jos 13:3; Is 23:3; Jer 2:18; 1 Chr 13:5.)

awareness of the god Horus centuries prior to the common era. "Shihor" is the "Waterway of Horus" as in CT Sp. 340,[1] which means that this "place" was a mythical motif before being given location on Earth. Another important apparent etymological connection between Israel and Egypt occurs in the word *shm* or *shem*, which in the languages of both nations is a title of divinity, meaning "mighty one" or "Power" in Egyptian, and "Name" as in the "Name of God" in Hebrew (שם).[2] Indeed, in Egypt the sun is "frequently" deemed *shm* or "power" in the "eulogies of the offering" of the sun hymns,[3] while the Judean tribal god Yahweh—called "Shem"—has likewise been demonstrated to possess solar attributes and to have served as a sun god at various times.[4]

In this regard, scholars over the centuries have found a number of correspondences between the languages of Egypt and the Levant. Regarding the Egyptian language, Gardiner remarks:

> Unfortunately the origin of the EGYPTIAN LANGUAGE lies so far back in the uncharted past that only little that is certain can be said about it. Since it is generally agreed that the oldest population of Egypt was of African race, it might be expected that their language should be African too. And in fact many affinities with Hamitic and in particular with Berber dialects have been found, not only in vocabulary, but also in verbal structure and the like. On the other hand, the relationship with Semitic (Hebrew, Arabic, &tc.) is equally unmistakable, if not greater.[5]

It would appear that not only did the Egyptian language precede Hebrew, but also that, since there is an "unmistakable" relationship, the Egyptian may have influenced the Hebrew, and with language often comes other aspects of culture, including and especially religion. The Talmudic suggestion that by the early period of the Christian effort the Old Testament/Tanakh had been translated into Egyptian adds to this continual relationship between Egypt and Israel. Such a longstanding relationship would also make it easier for the Jewish creators of Christianity to turn once again to the Egyptian religion in their endeavors.

Moreover, not a few writers have suggested that the "Golden Calf" idol smashed down by Moses in the biblical story of Mt. Sinai in fact referred to the Egyptian god Horus. Concerning the presence of Egyptian religion and deities in the Near East, Dr. Tryggve N.D. Mettinger, a professor of Old Testament Studies at the University of Lund, remarks:

---

[1] Faulkner, *AECT*, I, 275.
[2] Hornung, *CGAE*, 63; Faulkner, *CDME*, 241. See Strong's H8034.
[3] Assman, *ESRNK*, 121.
[4] See, e.g., my book *Suns of God*, 116ff. See also Dr. J. Glen Taylor's *Yahweh and the Sun: Biblical and Archaeological Evidence for Sun Worship in Ancient Israel.*
[5] Gardiner, *EP*, 19. See also "Notes on Egypto-Semitic Etymology. II" by W.F. Albright.

Egyptian gods must have been known in the Levant during the Late Bronze Age, the time of the Egyptian empire, and probably already during the latter part of the Early Bronze Age. During later periods, names of Egyptian deities even occur as theophoric ["god-bearing"] elements in Phoenician and Punic personal names. This testifies to the continued importance of cultural contacts between Egypt and the rest of the Mediterranean world. Thus, Isis occurs as an onomastic element from the eighth century and onwards and Osiris as early.[1]

"Onomastic" means that Isis's name was used either as a part or whole of a proper name for mortals, demonstrating knowledge of her in these various areas of the world at that time. In consideration of the popularity of Isis and her entourage, not only in Egypt but also in other locales around the Mediterranean, it would not be unreasonable to suggest that headlessness or decapitation associated with a religious figure was an important motif to usurp in the creation of Christianity. As has been indicated by the many depictions of John as the constellation of Aquarius, this decapitation likely also represents the time of the year when the Water Bearer appears to lose his head.

Etymologically as well there may be a connection between John and Aquarius: In Greek, "Oannes" becomes "I-oannes" (John), which in turn is "Joannes" or "Jonas," which then would become the name of the god Janus, as in "January," the month associated with Aquarius. Anubis may be related to Janus as well. Indeed, Colonel John Garnier, for one, finds them both to be epithets for the one "father of the gods," as well as Anubis and Janus alike representing aspects of the sun, a point confirmed by Macrobius (1.17), who named Janus as yet another solar god.[2] A dual-natured god, the "double-faced Janus" also could be identified with Set-Anubis, for instance.

Moreover, the correspondence of Anubis with *Christian* tradition was so striking to early Christians that they even identified the Egyptian god with *Jesus*, invoking him in their magical spells as "Jesus Anubis"[3]—a critically important fact to note, as it demonstrates the parallels to be real and obvious even or especially to the most pious early Christians. Certainly, the most learned among them, i.e., the priesthood, would have been well aware of all these numerous similarities between the Egyptian religion and the later Jewish rehash of it in Christianity. In consideration of the popularity of Anubis around the Roman Empire beginning centuries before and continuing into the common era, it would not be unreasonable to suggest that the Christ figure was also influenced in part by him as well, as indicated by the association of the two in magical spells.

---

[1] Mettinger, 175.
[2] Garnier, 51, 52, 274.
[3] Hornung, *SLE*, 60.

In any event, when we analyze the facts that Anubis was a popular figure around the Mediterranean, that he was associated with the summer solstice, as was John the Baptist, that he conducted souls through the underworld, as did John in one tradition, and that he purified souls with the water of purification, in a baptismal rite, specifically approached for such baptism by Horus, the equation of "Anup the Baptizer" with John the Baptist is well founded and logical, as well as identifiable as yet another correspondence between the Egyptian religion and the later Christianity.

Priests anointing and purifying the Osiris
(Wilkinson, J., *A Popular Account of the Ancient Egyptians*, II, 360)

Anubis purifying or baptizing the Osiris
(Renouf, *Egyptian Book of the Dead*, 51)

Horus purifying and giving life to Osiris
(Budge, *Osiris and the Egyptian Resurrection*, II, 83)

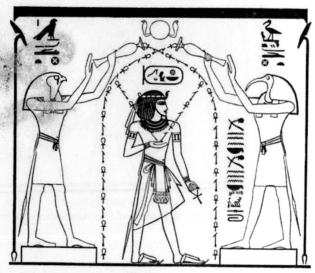

Horus and Thoth of Hat purifying Amenophis II. 'Thou art pure; thou art pure again, again.'

Horus and Thoth purifying the King.
(Wilkinson, *The Manners and Customs of the Ancient Egyptians*, III, 362)

From the Sanctuary of Philip Arrhidaeus at Karnak (Leps., *Denkm.* IV, 2)
THE BAPTISM OF PHARAOH

"The Baptism of Pharaoh,
From the Sanctuary of Philip Archidaueus at Karnak..."
(Gardiner, "The Baptism of Pharaoh," pl. II)

The Twelve Followers

"...The sun of the Lower Hemisphere took more especially the name of Osiris. Its companions and deputies were the twelve hours of the night personified as so many gods, at the head of which was placed Horus, the rising sun itself..."

Francois Lenormant, *Chaldean Magic: Its Origins and Development* (83)

"[Osiris's] twelve companions were supposed to be the signs of the zodiac; like the twelve men who bore his ark, or six twelves who conspired, and the same number who carried his body."

James Bonwick, *Egyptian Belief and Modern Thought* (175)

"The Ritual shows us how the apostles were established on the same foundation, beginning with two brothers, who were followed by the four brethren, the cycle being completed by the twelve in the fields of divine harvest.... The four brothers of Horus=the four brothers of Jesus. Amsta, Hapi, Tuamutef, Kabhsenuf=James, Joseph, Simon, Judas. At a later stage the followers in the train of Horus are the twelve who are his harvesters in the cornfields of Amenta....

"The twelve with Horus in Amenta are they who labour at the harvest and collect the corn (otherwise the souls) for Horus. When the harvest is ready "the bearers of sickles reap the grain in their fields. Ra says to them, on earth as bearers of sickles in the fields of Amenta, "Take your sickles, reap your grain" ("Book of Hades," Records, vol. 10, 119). Here the labourers who reap the harvest in Amenta are the object of propitiatory offerings and of adoration on the earth, as the twelve disciples of Horus, son of Ra, the heavenly father. And this was ages before the story was told of the twelve fictitious harvesters in Galilee."

Gerald Massey, *Ancient Egypt: Light of the World* (I, 864)

As is the case with other major characteristics of the Egyptian gods that have been associated with Jesus, the claim that Horus had 12 "disciples" cannot be found easily in modern encyclopedias or mainstream books. In reality, the association of the sun god with "the Twelve" constitutes a common motif, based on both the months of the year and the 12-hour divisions of day and night. Indeed, we find the theme of "the Twelve" in a number of other cultures, including the 12 Olympian gods of Greece, as well as those of the Romans, along with the 12 adventures of Gilgamesh, the 12 labors of Hercules and the 12 Tribes of Israel, all of which symbolize the months of the year and/or the zodiacal signs.[1] The same can be said of the Christian Twelve, as

---

[1] Jackson, *MGC*, 93; Frazer, *FOTS*, 50. See Exodus 39:9-14: "...they made the breastplate... And they set in it four rows of stones... And the stones were according to the names of the children of Israel, twelve...according to the twelve tribes." As Josephus says (*Antiquities*, 3.8): "And for the twelve stones, whether we understand by them the months, or whether we understand the like number of the signs of that circle which the Greeks call the zodiac, we shall not be mistaken in their meaning." (Josephus/Whiston, 75.) Earlier than Josephus, Philo ("On the Life of Moses," 12) had made the same comments regarding Moses: "Then the twelve stones on the breast,

apostles and disciples of Jesus, who also have been depicted as signs in the circle of the zodiac, including, as we have seen, by the Venerable Bede in the seventh century, with their zodiacal significance extending back much further, to as early as the second century.[1] So too do we find the theme of "the Twelve" in Egypt in a variety of places, including groupings of gods and goddesses. Indeed, in addition to the commonly depicted groups of eight or nine Egyptian gods, the latter being styled "the Ennead," there were other companies of *12*, as we have seen in the nativity scene and as is to be expected from a culture so focused on time and astronomy, since the number 12 generally symbolizes hours and months. The term "Ennead" or "Enneads" does not therefore always refer to a group of *nine* gods. It could be more, as in 12, or fewer as in eight.[2] This fact is exemplified at PT 601:1660-1671/P 582, in which appears reference to the "Big Ennead," followed by invocations of 12 gods. Concerning this text, James Allen notes, "This stanza and those that follow refer to the individual members of the 'Big Ennead.'"[3]

Adding to this fact, in *The Histories* (2.43-44), Herodotus discusses the Egyptian version of "Heracles" or Hercules as "one of the twelve gods." He next states of the Egyptians, "They say that seventeen thousand years before the reign of Amasis the twelve gods

which are not like one another in colour, and which are divided into four rows of three stones in each, what else can they be emblems of, except of the circle of the zodiac?" (Philo/Duke, 99.)

[1] In his *Against Heresies* (2.21), Church father Irenaeus objects to the Gnostic notion that the 12 apostles symbolized the "aeons," which have been asserted to represent the zodiacal signs. (Legge, II, 152.) Apparently, this association occurred fairly early in Christian history, as Church father Clement of Alexandria (c. 150-c. 211) wrote in his work *Excerpta ex Theodota* (1.25.2) that, according to the Valentinian Gnostics, "the apostles replaced the signs of the zodiac, for as birth is governed by them, so rebirth is directed by the apostles." (Grant, *AC*, 62.) Evidently this important passage was considered an interpolation by Rev. William Wilson in his translation of Clement's work, as it is nowhere to be found. (Roberts, A., *ANF*, VIII, 39ff.) McCloskey cites Clement's writings on the subject as appearing on pp. 69-76 of "Clement of Alexandria, *Excerpta ex Theodoto*, Ed. F. Sagnard, Sources Chretiennes, 23, Paris 1948." The original Greek of the pertinent passage is: "Οι Αποστολοι, φησι, μετετεθησαν τοις δεκαδυο ζωδιοις ως γαρ υπ εκεινων η γενεσις διοικειται, ουτως υπο των Αποστολων η αναγεννησις εφοραται." (Clement, 1.25.2.) The apparent dismissal of this quote as an interpolation by Wilson verifies two serious problems with ancient texts: 1. Ancient writers' works frequently have been altered; and 2. Mainstream scholarship is heavily censored, both of which assertions we contend to be true. Thus, the average encyclopedia surfer will not find these important correspondences between Christianity and other religions, and may therefore claim they are untrue, while in fact they are *true*.

[2] See, e.g., Long: "...J.G. Griffiths...suggested that Herodotus' Twelve [Egyptian gods] were an expanded form of the Heliopolitan Ennead." (Long, 147.) See also Horsley: "The Ennead does not necessarily include nine gods, strange as that may seem. We have lists of the gods that include up to twelve." (Horsley, 66.) See also Wiedemann: "...from several texts in which the ennead is specified it is clear that the members of the ennead referred to were eight only." (Wiedemann, 105.)

[3] Mercer, 254-255; Allen, J., *AEPT*, 199-200, 206.

were produced from the eight...".[1] The pharaoh Amasis or Ahmose I (fl. c. 1550-1525 BCE) was the founder of the 18th Dynasty; thus, Egyptian culture conceived a very ancient origin for itself, one not given serious consideration by mainstream scholars today.

Regarding his experiences with Egyptian priests at Heliopolis, Herodotus (2.4) further relates:

> ...They also told me that the Egyptians first brought into use the names of the twelve gods, which the Greeks took over from them, and were the first to assign altars and images and temples to the gods, and to carve figures in stone.[2]

The notion that the Greeks adopted the 12 Egyptian gods is intriguing and not without foundation. The Greek gods, however, possess Indo-European names related to the ancient Indian language of Sanskrit, indicating a common root. The influence of Indian culture, religion and mythology on the Mediterranean in general and on Christianity in specific ranks as another important subject that is addressed in my book *Suns of God* and elsewhere.

Concerning the various groupings of deities, in *The Gods of the Egyptians Or Studies in Egyptian Mythology*, Budge relates that in the Pyramid Text of Pepi II there appear "the Great Company of the gods who are in Annu," numbering nine,[3] again, a group called the Ennead. Later in the same text appears another company—or *paut* in the Egyptian—in which *twelve* gods are named:

> ...Tem, Shu, Tefnut, Seb, Nut, Osiris, Osiris-Khent-Amenti, Set of Ombos, Heru of Edfu, Ra, Khent-Maati, and Uatchet; thus the Great company of the gods of Heliopolis may contain either nine or twelve gods."[4]

As noted, Brunner names the 12 gods at Deir el Bahari as Osiris, Isis, Horus, Nephthys, Seth, Hathor, Montu, Atum, Shu, Tefnut, Geb and Nut.[5] Hence, in the ancient Egyptian writings and images we find both Osiris and Horus with 10 others, totaling 12 gods.

---

[1] Herodotus/de Selincourt, 102. Regarding the value of Herodotus and the dismissal of his work over the centuries by various Egyptologists, Zitman remarks: "The [negative] opinion of the Egyptologist De Meulenaere has caused the loss of important information.... In general [Herotodus's] manuscripts are regarded as 'the source of numerous errors and hackneyed phrases, which quite commonly still receive credit.' This attitude leads unwittingly to the gradual dismissal of fundamental information on astronomical-cum-religious knowledge of the Egyptians and their chronology." (Zitman, 37.) From Herodotus's own remarks about "mysteries," etc., it is evident that he knew more than he was divulging—and possibly more than scholars looking back nearly 2,500 years after Herodotus himself was evidently in the presence of living Egyptian priests.

[2] Herodotus/de Selincourt, 87.

[3] Budge, *GE*, I, 86.

[4] Budge, *GE*, I, 87.

[5] Brunner, 15.

This theme of "Horus and the Twelve" in Egyptian religion also has been demonstrated by a relatively recent discovery of a large Horus temple with 12 rooms in the Sinai desert:

Temple of ancient Egyptian sun god found

CAIRO, May 31 (AFP)—Egyptian archeologists have discovered a 3,000-year-old temple honoring the Pharaonic-era sun God Horus, in the first such find in the northern Sinai, the antiquities authorities said Monday. Black granite and sandstone statuettes of gods and people were found inside the temple which dates from the New Kingdom (1567-1065 BC), the Supreme Council of Antiquities said in a statement. Horus, son of Isis and Osiris, is normally portrayed as a one-eyed falcon or sun-dial, but the council did not disclose which statuettes were found. The temple, whose dry-stone walls are from four meters (13.2 meters) to 10 meters (33 feet) thick, spans a surface area of 2,400 square meters (25,824 square feet) and houses a dozen rooms, they added. The discovery defines the location of Tharo [Tharu], a fortified city built by the ancient Egyptians at the eastern entrance to the route armies took from Egypt to the land of Canaan.[1]

It should be noted that this article, unlike so many other articles and encyclopedia entries, correctly identifies Horus as a *sun god*. Also, this important temple was found in the *Sinai*, along the ancient route from Egypt to Palestine and *Judea* called the "Horus Road"— the *only* established land route connecting these neighboring cultures, which surely enjoyed much cultural exchange. Moreover, the finds at Tharo/Tharu include a massive fort, which was "one of the most important locations in ancient Egypt."[2] In addition, the dozen rooms in this Horus temple may symbolize the 12-hour nightly and daily divisions, as well as the company of 12 Egyptian gods. Further astrotheological meaning may be indicated by the intriguing fact that the square footage of this massive building—equivalent to about 26,000 feet in Egyptian measurements[3]—is essentially the same as the roughly 26,000 years constituting one "Great Year" or precession of the equinoxes. If this correspondence was intended by the original Egyptian architects of the temple layout, it might signify that they possessed a zodiacal circle with 12 divisions, which could represent an added symbolism of the edifice's dozen rooms, fitting in with the common zodiacal significance of "the Twelve" as well.

---

[1] The original article concerning this find appeared on Yahoo News in 1999 but disappeared long ago off the internet and is therefore reproduced here. In 2008, the media reported that the "giant fortress" at Tharo or Tharu had been found dating to the time of Ramses II (1304-1237 BCE). Included in some of those reports was mention of the Horus temple, stating that it was the first temple of the New Kingdom (1570-1070 BCE) ever discovered in the Sinai. ("Prehistoric fortress in Egypt excavated.")

[2] "Giant Fortress's Remains Found in Egypt."

[3] The Egyptian foot is equivalent to 1.013 English feet and 300 mm. (Lockyer, *Nature*, VIII, 148.) The precession of the equinoxes comprises approximately 25,816 years. (Hawking, 147.)

Fast forwarding closer to the common era, once again we find an archaeological site possessing a theme of "Horus and the Twelve," at the Ptolemaic-era Edfu, where the Horus temple was erected with 12 columns.[1] In consideration of the Greek influence at that time, it would not be surprising if this construction represented the signs of the zodiac, along with the 12 monthly divisions, 12 hours of the day and night, and the *paut* or company of 12 gods.

The Egyptian Zodiac

Over the years, it has been claimed that the Egyptians were not in possession of the zodiac until Hellenistic times (323-146 BCE), as suggested by Hornung, for example, when he says, "The zodiac was adopted early in the Ptolemaic Period..."[2] A close investigation of the currently available data, however, may indicate earlier recognition of the zodiac, as it does also with knowledge of the precession of the equinoxes centuries before its purported discovery in the second century BCE by the Greek astronomer Hipparchus.[3] For example, as regards one of the most famous astrotheological Egyptian artifacts, the zodiac of the temple of Dendera, while the construction represents a late *restoration*, in general form the portrayal itself may date back thousands of years earlier.[4] Discussing Dendera, Budge cautions that it should not be concluded that the Egyptians were the "inventors of the zodiac" and asserts that they "borrowed their knowledge of the Signs of the Zodiac, together with much else, from the Greeks, who had derived a great deal of their astronomical lore from the Babylonians," including the zodiac.[5] Budge next claims that "we are fully justified in assuming that the earliest forms of the Zodiac date from an exceedingly primitive time."[6] These contentions are not incorrect, in that the zodiac certainly existed in Mesopotamia millennia ago, worked over by the famed Chaldean astronomers, with

---

[1] Bard, 270.
[2] Hornung, *SLE*, 30.
[3] See Acharya, *SOG*, 39-40.
[4] The claim is that the complex circular Dendera zodiac depicts the configuration of the sky at some point several millennia ago—up to 10,000 years by some "amateur" estimates. (Saint-Hilaire, 203.) Concerning this assertion, Burritt indignantly writes, "On both these Zodiacs the equinoctial points are in Leo, and not in Aries; from which it has been concluded, by those who pertinaciously endeavor to array the arguments of science against the chronology of the Bible and the validity of the Mosaic account, that these Zodiacs were constructed when the sun entered the sign of Leo, which must have been 9720 years ago, or 4000 years before the inspired account of the creation. The infidel writers in France and Germany make it 10,000 years before." (Burritt, 30.) In this instance, the objection to the antiquity of the zodiac is that it contradicts the Bible. Many such discoveries and insights have been subjected to the same form of antiscientific censorship over the centuries. By "infidel writers," the bibliolater Burritt evidently meant Abbé Charles Dupuis, for one. Fortunately, despite Burritt's calumny, German scholarship has frequently been subjected to less censorship in this regard and at times is therefore superior.
[5] Budge, *GE*, II, 312.
[6] Budge, *GE*, II, 314.

...s further polishing it. In this regard, several sources—such ...oyal astronomer Dr. Edward Walter Maunder (1851-1928), the devout Christian author of *The Astronomy of the Bible*—have indicated an origin of the zodiac, including the popular signs, to some 4,000 or more years ago.[1] We also possess the relatively recent find of the "Karanovo Zodiac" from Bulgaria, which has been dated to around 6,000 years ago and which seems to bear rudimentary renditions of the constellations found in the Western zodiac.[2] As concerns Egypt, there nevertheless remain many suggestions that the zodiac in some form or another was utilized there prior to the arrival of the Greeks.

Modern scholarship thus has disassociated the zodiac from Egypt and denied Egyptian influence on the much later Babylonian civilization, to which is credited the origins of the zodiac as we have it.[3] However, the arguments raised here provide a logical basis for the developmental evolution of the zodiac in Egypt as well, a highly advanced culture keenly aware of astronomy and astrology dating back many hundreds of years prior to the maturation of the same sciences in Babylon. A probable Egyptian influence on Babylonian culture becomes more evident when it is considered how close in proximity were the two nations and how much cultural interchange, both hostile and peaceful, occurred between these rivals over the millennia during which civilizations thrived there.

The case for the presence of the zodiacal rudiments in Egypt remains relevant, and over the centuries a number of scholars and writers have averred not only an *Egyptian* origin for the zodiac but a *very old one* at that. For example, in *A Dissertation on the Calendar and Zodiac of Ancient Egypt*, Mure relates that French Egyptologist Remi Raige argued for an Egyptian zodiac originating 15,000 years ago,[4] while the French Count Constantin-François Volney (1757-1820), whose work influenced Napoleon Bonaparte, contended for an origin of the principles of astronomy arising in North Africa around 17,000 years ago.[5] While Mure does not concur with such antiquity, he is certain that the inferences of the Egyptian zodiac are clear long prior to the fanciful attachments thereto supposedly devised by the Greeks.

In this regard, the arguments and evidence regarding the antiquity of the zodiac in Egypt preceding the Greeks are worthwhile exploring, such as are found in Mure's in-depth analysis:

> Each sign of the zodiac...appears to have been a mere hieroglyphic of the season of the year to which it corresponded, or of the deity to whom that season was specially sacred.... The hieroglyphical zodiac,

[1] Maunder, 160.
[2] Flavin, "The Karanovo Zodiac."
[3] See, e.g., Barton, 13.
[4] Mure, 53.
[5] Volney, 204.

therefore, represented the seasons mythologically or figuratively, and had no connexion with imaginary forms or creatures in the heaven itself... Thus Cancer or the Scarabee represented the solstitial month of summer... Libra the month of the autumnal equinox, Aries that of the vernal equinox, and so of the rest; afterwards, when the signs were attached by the Greeks to particular groups of stars, embodied into fantastical forms, the ancient terms became unmeaning, and the origin and history of the whole system was confounded and obscured.

That the twelve divisions of the zodiac, among the ancient nations, (whether Chaldee or Egyptian,) with whom the institution originated, were, from the first, signs or δωδεκατημορια [*dodekatimoria*, i.e., "twelve divisions"], and not constellations—portions of the sun's course in the heavens, corresponding, more or less accurately, to the seasons, not imaginary forms in the celestial sphere—we have strong proof in the tradition preserved of the manner in which the astronomers of those nations subdivided the ecliptic....[1]

Mure goes on to list the descriptions by Macrobius regarding the Egyptian divisions of the year, as well as those of the philosopher Sextus Empiricus (2nd-3rd cents. AD/CE) concerning the Chaldeans. The Scottish scholar continues his analysis with "some close critical and etymological illustrations of the names and characters of the individual months of the calendar, in connexion with the signs of the zodiac, derived from the mythology, language and general antiquities of Egypt."[2] Mure next describes a scene of several figures on a tomb of a Theban king showing a "procession headed by a figure bearing an ear of corn, or some such object, followed at some little distance by the god Thot, with his ibis-head; a scarabee supporting the disc of the sun; another procession, headed by a somewhat similar figure, of whose hieroglyphic title the chief feature is a new-born infant; a lion couchant; a bull standing on another emblem resembling the zodiacal sign Libra; a non-descript animal, on whose back rides a crocodile; a vase, a scorpion, etc."[3] Mure continues: "These figures, several of which are repeated on each side of the tablet or planisphere, are unquestionably, in great part at least, astronomical symbols, and most of them, it can hardly be doubted, signs of the zodiac, although the irregularity of their arrangement bears little or no reference to the corresponding seasons."[4] Mure further remarks, "Other fragments there are, also connected with astrology, and probably of great antiquity, engraved in the same splendid work..."[5] He then proceeds through a long dissertation regarding many more

---

[1] Mure, 52-53
[2] Mure, 61.
[3] Mure, 63. Mure cites the multi-volume French publication on Egypt, "Antiquités, vol. ii, pl. lxxxii," created from the expedition by Napoleon involving some 150 scientists and artists.
[4] Mure, 64.
[5] Mure, 64.

in Egyptian texts, on monuments and other artifacts ...g astronomical or astrological significance that infer the ...iac, moving through each month and its possible symbols.

Regarding the zodiac in Egypt, Schmidt submits similar findings and conclusions:

> The signs of the zodiac, to which we have been accustomed from earliest childhood, were derived from the symbols of the Egyptian months. The science of astronomy, as taught in Egypt, was carried to Babylonia and surrounding countries shortly after the Hyksos Invasion, and, although it was changed in many particulars to confirm to new conditions and local notions, many surviving features enable us to trace it back to its original home on the banks of the Nile.[1]

Schmidt proceeds to list the months along with the corresponding zodiacal signs, going into details of each, with his dates evidently based on the old Egyptian calendar a couple of thousand years before the common era.

Concerning this same line of research on the subject, West notes:

> Though the zodiac as we know it does not seem to have existed in Egypt, Schwaller de Lubicz believed that knowledge of the zodiac and of astrology was what determined the erection and destruction of temples and shifts in emphasis of Egyptian symbolism. In the Temple of Luxor, he found symbols corresponding to zodiacal signs in most of the halls and chambers in which medieval astrology would have assigned them.[2]

The research showing that the "symbols corresponding to zodiacal signs" existed at Luxor indicates they may have constituted *mysteries.*

Massey's suggestions concerning which Egyptian gods might correspond to the zodiacal signs as they eventually became known are as follows:

1. The ram-headed Amun with the constellation of Aries
2. Osiris the "Bull of Eternity," with the sign of Taurus
3. The Twin god of Set-Horus with Gemini
4. The beetleheaded Kheper-Ptah with the sign of the Beetle, which was later the Crab of Cancer
5. The lion-faced Atum with the sign of Leo
6. The Virgin Neith with the constellation of Virgo
7. "Har-Makhu of the Scales" equivalent to the sign of Libra
8. Isis-Serqet, the scorpion goddess, with the sign of Scorpio
9. Shu and Tefnut "figured as the Archer" with the sign of Sagittarius
10. Khnum, the goat-headed, with the sign of Capricorn

---

[1] Schmidt, 48.
[2] West, J.A., *SS*, 90.

11. Menat/Hathor, the "divine wetnurse," with the sign of Aquarius
12. Horus of the two crocodiles with the sign of Pisces[1]

While these associations cannot be presumed to be absolutely correct, they make for an intriguing hypothesis for further study. (We would add that Aquarius could be represented by the god *Anubis*, as previously demonstrated.) Moreover, while the symbols may differ, the identification of certain Egyptian gods with zodiacal signs is evident in later times, as verified by Wiedemann, who remarks that "later texts transfer both Shu and Tefnut to the zodiac as the Twins."[2]

Based on all of the evidence, it is reasonable to suggest that the Egyptians possessed the rudiments of the zodiac, which were later developed elsewhere, including Babylon and Greece, to their present form. India also lays an impressive claim to developing and influencing certain aspects of the zodiac.

In traditional astrological religion, astromythology and astrotheology, the meaning of the Twelve symbolizes the months of the years and/or, usually, their corresponding zodiacal signs or constellations, which begin and end around the third week of the month, and which differ somewhat from era to era and location to location. At some point in Egyptian religious history the symbolism of the Twelve also likely came to represent the 12 constellations of the zodiac as "companions" or "helpers" through whose stations the sun god travels annually, as it did in other cultures. In *Egyptian Belief and Modern Thought*, James Bonwick states, "The twelve gods may be more readily identified with Mazzaroth, or the twelve signs of the Zodiac, through which the sun passed every year."[3] The "Mazzaroth," it should be recalled, is the Hebrew name for the zodiac, as found in the biblical verse at Job 38:32.

Furthermore, within astrology—an ancient practice dating back thousands of years and heavily utilized by priesthoods to influence human culture—there are also the 12 *houses*, which comprise 2-hour divisions of the 24-hour day. Again, the prominent number 12 also stands for the two 12-hour divisions of day and night, as exemplified in a number of ancient Egyptian "books of the netherworld." Therefore, the association of the Egyptian sun god with the number 12 can be demonstrated readily by pre-Christian texts and artifacts.

The Book of Amduat

The configuration of Re, Osiris or Horus with 12 other individuals, whether gods or men, can be found abundantly in Egyptian texts, essentially reflecting the sun god with 12 "companions," "helpers" or "disciples." This theme is repeated

---

[1] Adapted from Massey, *AELW*, I, 302.
[2] Wiedemann, 34.
[3] Bonwick, 99.

numerous times in the nightly passage of the sun: Like Hercules in his 12 labors, when the Egyptian sun god entered into the night sky, he was besieged with trials, as found in some of the Egyptian "Holy Scriptures." One such text is the "Book of the Amtuat/Amduat," which "describes the journey of the sun god through the twelve hours of the night,"[1] the term "Amduat" meaning "underworld" or "netherworld." The Book of Amduat has been known by a number of other names, such as the "Book of what is in the Tuat,"[2] the "Book of What is in the Underworld,"[3] the "Book of That Which Is in the Underworld,"[4] the "Book of Him Who is in the Other World"[5] and the "Book of him who is in the Underworld."[6]

Parts of the Book of Amduat possibly date to as early as the reign of the female pharaoh Hatshepsut, with the bulk of it evidently from the New Kingdom (1570-1070 BCE).[7] The Book of Amduat was among those "underworld texts" used for only the pharaohs and other royalty and nobles for centuries, until the 21st Dynasty (1077-943 BCE), at which point it was included on the coffins and papyri of priests as well.[8] After this point, select hours were utilized in a variety of tombs, while as late as the 30th Dynasty a nearly complete version was created for the pharaoh Wereshnefer (c. 380-300 BCE), with all but the eighth hour inscribed on his impressive diorite sarcophagus now housed at the Metropolitan Museum of Art in New York.[9]

In the seventh hour or division of the Book of the Amduat, as found in the tomb of the pharaoh Tuthmosis/Thutmose III (15th cent. BCE), for example, "Horus of the netherworld" is clearly depicted seated on a throne *as the sun god*, with 12 "star gods" in front of him.[10] Horus's throne surrounded by "his Enneads" is also mentioned at CT Sp. 1099.[11]

Recounting the seventh hour as found in the tomb of Seti/Sety/Sethos I (13th cent. BCE) at Thebes, Budge remarks:

> On the right of the Boat of AFU-RĀ, and facing it, are HORUS, and the twelve gods of the hours, who protect the tombs of Osiris, and assist RĀ in his journey...[12]

Hence, the Twelve are "protectors" and "assistants," essentially "helpers" as well. Adding to the picture of Horus and the Twelve, in his *Egypt* handbook, Baedeker likewise describes images from the

---

[1] Hornung, *AEBA*, 33.
[2] Budge, *EHH*, III, 80.
[3] Myśliwiec, 29.
[4] Redford, 374
[5] Murray, *STWE*, 128.
[6] Baedeker, 295.
[7] Hornung, *AEBA*, 27-28. See Brier, 18, for date.
[8] Hornung, *AEBA*, 30.
[9] Hornung, *AEBA*, 30.
[10] Hornung, *AEBA*, 39, 48.
[11] Faulkner, *AECT*, III, 154.
[12] Budge, *EHH*, III, 85, 153.

tomb of Seti/Sethos I, aka "Belzoni's Tomb," including t
hour:

> Room XIII.... On the Left Entrance Wall and the Left Wall appears the
> sun's journey during the 7th hour of night... Middle Row. The sun
> god once more is shown in his boat, on the prow of which stands
> Isis, to drive away evil spirits with her spells.... Bottom row. Horus,
> before whom are the twelve star-gods who conduct the sun at
> night...[1]

Horus is thus firmly associated with 12 "star-gods," who, in
conducting the sun god through his passage, can be deemed his
"protectors," "assistants" or "helpers," etc. The tomb of Seti I, it
should be noted, is a magnificently decorated structure with a winged
goddess occupying the central place, arms outstretched in a crosslike
or cruciform position. Such *crucial* imagery could not failed to have
impressed any viewers of it, wherever it may be found.

Also, in the tenth hour of the Amduat, Horus the Elder leaning on
his staff is depicted as leading the 12 "drowned" or lost souls to their
salvation in the "Fields of the Blessed."[2] These 12 deceased, Hornung
relates, are "saved from decay and decomposition by Horus, who
leads them to a blessed posthumous existence..."[3] In this manner,
Horus's companions, like the disciples of Jesus, are meant to
"become like gods," so to speak, and to exist forever, reaping eternal
life, as do those who believe in Christ. (Jn 3:15; 1 Tim 1:16) It is
interesting to note that the part where Jesus reminds the Jews of
their scripture, "Ye are gods," can be found in the New Testament
only in the gospel of John (10:34-35). In the end, like the much later
Jesus, Horus is the *savior* and *leader* of the Twelve *followers*.

Even though it represented one of the secret or esoteric texts of
the solar religion,[4] the Book of Amduat was obviously popular
enough among the priesthood, indicating that the motif of "Horus
and the Twelve" might have been known by a significant number of
influential people over a long period preceding the supposed time of
"Jesus and the Twelve." The theme of Horus with his 12 followers/
helpers may not have been well known to the "vulgar masses,"
because the sacred writings within which it can be found may have
constituted some of the "secret texts" discussed by Morenz, for
example.[5] Certainly, however, the motif was, like many others, well
known by the powerful *priesthood*, i.e., those who make religions,
beginning thousands of years ago into the common era.

---

[1] Baedeker, 275.
[2] Hornung, *VK*, 138, 144; Hornung, *AEBA*, 40, 51.
[3] Hornung, *AEBA*, 40.
[4] Assman, *ESRNK*, 25.
[5] Morenz, 225.

The Book of Gates

Another popular text of the netherworld is the "Book of the Pylons," named in Egyptian *Shat En Sbau*[1] and translated also as the "Book of the Portals" or "Book of Gates."[2] This book, found in tombs beginning in the 18th to 19th Dynasties (c. 1500-c. 1200 BCE), recounts the sun's passage through various pylons, portals or gates representing the twelve nighttime hours. Describing scenes from the Book of Gates also in the tomb of Seti/Sethos I, specifically the third hour through which the sun passes in his boat, Budge states:

> On the right hand of the boat of the god are twelve holy gods of the Tuat, each in his shrine, with the doors open, and twelve gods of the lakes of fire...[3]

Thus, in this one passage we possess two instances of the sun god surrounded by the Twelve.

The fourth hour depicts all three gods Re, Horus and Osiris in scenes with the Twelve:

> On the right side of the boat of the god are twelve gods, who are described as the "bringers of their doubles," and twelve jackal-headed figures, who are walking on the Lake of Life... On the left side of the boat of the god is Horus the Aged, who follows eleven human forms as they march behind the uraeus called Flame...to a shrine in which the god Osiris...stands upon a serpent. Behind Osiris are the twelve gods, "who are behind the shrine," and four gods, who preside over the pits in the earth... [4]

In this image, Re is accompanied by two sets of 12, including what seems to be a dozen Anubii on the "Lake of life," possibly reflecting the "baptism" motif previously discussed. Next, we have Horus as part of the company of the Twelve, with the addition of Osiris, making 13, like the 12 apostles and Jesus. Osiris is again associated with the 12 behind him, as well as four "brother" gods, like Jesus with his 12 disciples and four brothers (Mt 13:55).

The Four Brothers

The motif of the "four brothers" is likewise common to both the Egyptian religion and Christianity. Although in various texts they are depicted as his four *sons*, Qebehsenuf/Qebehsenuef, Hapi/Hapy, Duamutef and Imset/Imsety/Amset, Horus's four relatives are at times essentially represented as his *brothers*, because it is also said

---

[1] Mercatante, 25.

[2] In *The Egyptian Heaven and Hell*, Budge critiques the various names by which the Book of Gates has been called, including the Book of the Lower Hemisphere, the Book of Hades and the Book of Hell. (Budge, *EHH*, III, 85.)

[3] Budge, *GE*, I, 182. Hornung uses the tomb of Ramses IV to illustrate his description of the Book of Gates, including for this gate/hour Three. Hence, some of his descriptions are different from Budge. (Hornung, *AEBA*, 59, 61, 68.)

[4] Budge, *GE*, I, 184; Hornung, *AEBA*, 60, 69.

that they were *Osiris's* sons, as at BD 151.[1] In describing the raising of Osiris with the help of the "ministrants of the tomb" combined with the Sem-priest making the fourth, Budge relates that these "represent the four sons of Horus, or according to another legend, the four sons of Osiris."[2] In the magnum opus *The Mythology of All Races*, Dr. Max Müller (1823-1900), a professor of Comparative Theology at Oxford, also refers to the "four sons of Osiris-Horus" or "four sons of Osiris or Horus," whom he also calls the "four genii."[3] Concerning these four, Müller remarks:

> Four genii termed "the sons of Horus" or "of Osiris" often follow Osiris, watching his corpse and assisting him in his judgment; accordingly they become guardians of the embalmment of all dead, whose viscera are placed under their protection in "canopic vases," which are ornamented with their likenesses, i.e., a man, a baboon, a jackal, and a hawk.[4]

Hornung too describes these four, relating that in BD 151 they call themselves "son of Osiris" and stating, "The Egyptian did not concern himself with the genealogy of these four, however, so that either Osiris or Horus can appear as the father of the four, their mother remaining anonymous."[5] It is further clarified in BD 112 and CT Sp. 157 that these are the sons of *Horus the Elder* and Isis,[6] which would still make them the *brothers* of Horus the Child, since they shared the same mother. Also, in CT Sp. 240 is mention of the "four Horuses" as "offspring of Osiris."[7] These four brothers are said to represent the cardinal points, just like the four evangelists, as asserted in *Against Heresies* (3.11.8) by Church father Irenaeus, who was the first to number and name the canonical gospels.

Continuing with the 12 nightly pylons, in the fifth division or hour, Horus—who is the "steersman at the rudder"[8] and whom Hornung calls "the divine pilot-coxswain,"[9] reflecting his leadership role—addresses, among others, a group of 12 men who "bear ladders in Ament,"[10] thus being his "helpers," or "disciples." Twelve gods appear in the sixth hour as well. The same can be said of the seventh hour:

> ...In the centre is the boat of the Sun-god being towed along, presumably by four gods of the Tuat as before. Marching in front of those who tow the boat are twelve gods with sceptres...[11]

---

[1] Allen, T., *BD*, 150; Faulkner, *EBD*, pl. 33;
[2] Budge, *BOM*, I, 76.
[3] Gray, 97, 104, 105, 111, 112.
[4] Gray, 111-112.
[5] Hornung, *VK*, 59.
[6] Faulkner, *EBD*, 114; Allen, T., *BD*, 91; Faulkner, *AECT*, I, 135. See also Redford, 113.
[7] Faulkner, *AECT*, I, 189.
[8] Armour, 60.
[9] Hornung, *VK*, 76.
[10] Budge, *GE*, I, 188. See also Hornung, *AEBA*, 62, 70.
[11] Budge, *GE*, I, 191-192.

The twelve gods who march in front of the boat in these various scenes likewise represent the "deputies," as noted French archaeologist Lenormant deemed these dozen "companions of Osiris," who are essentially *led by* Horus.

Twelve gods also emerge in the tenth hour, along with 12 females or goddesses.[1] Indeed, the 12 hours of the night are frequently personified as goddesses, who help the deceased through his transition, sometimes towing the rope of the sun god's boat.[2] These 12 helpers are depicted often in the 12th or "Last Hour" of the night before the sun god's resurrection, to "fend off Apophis,"[3] much like Jesus with the 12 in his "Last Hour" on the night before his passion (Mt 26:45). In other words, the Twelve help the "Sun of God" make the transition from darkness to light.

In *Records of the Past*, Egyptologist Dr. Eugene Lefébure (1838-1908) describes the same scenes, in what he called the "Book of Hades" (*le Livre de l'Enfer*):

> ...Horus leaning upon a stick, and eleven gods walking towards Osiris, the inhabitant of the Amenti, upright upon a serpent, and shut into a naos [inner sanctuary] with a cover. In the naos a mountain is pictured from which the god's head emerges. Before Osiris, an uraeus, the flame, and behind him twelve gods who are behind the naos...[4]

> ...Horus with a hawk's head, leaning upon a long stick... Twelve personages carrying a long serpent, above which and behind each of them, except the last, is the hieroglyph of the duration, the bearers of the duration in the Amenti. Eight persons, the divine chiefs of Hades.[5]

> ...Five persons who bend towards an enormous ear of corn (those who labour at the harvest in the infernal plains). A bearer of a sickle with this inscription: these (are the reapers). On the tomb of Rameses VI., the first persons are preceded by a god leaning on a staff, the master of joy; they are twelve in number, and there are seven reapers.[6]

This last "god leaning on a staff" is, as in the other scenes, Horus the Elder or "Aged," as Budge deemed him. Regarding these images, Massey remarks:

> The pictures show the children of Ra both as the group of twelve and also as the twelve *with* Horus. In one scene Horus is depicted leaning on a staff, and eleven gods are walking towards Osiris. These are the twelve altogether, of whom Horus is one in presence of the father. But on the tomb of Rameses the Sixth the twelve appear, *preceded*

---

[1] Budge, *GE*, I, 197. Here the scene from Ramses IV's tomb, as illustrated in Hornung, is substantially different. (Hornung, *AEBA*, 75.)
[2] Hornung, *VK*, 77, 85, 93.
[3] Hornung, *VK*, 107; Spence, 118.
[4] *Records of the Past*, X, 101.
[5] *ROTP*, X, 107.
[6] *ROTP*, X, 117.

by Horus, the master of joy, leaning on his staff. These are the harvesters: seven of them are the reapers, the other five are collectors of the corn.[1]

As we can see, once again Gerald Massey's analysis has proved itself to be on solid ground, as he has depicted these scenes accurately. Moreover, in his previously provided quote regarding the reapers of the harvest in Amenta, Massey is likewise accurately reproducing the translation of the Book of Hades/Book of Gates by Lefébure: "Ra says to them: Take your sickles! (Reap your grain...)."[2] Nor are the comparisons inapt to Christian motifs of the 12 disciples and the "reapers" at Matthew 13:30. Indeed, as the head of this procession, Horus is "the chief of the twelve companions of his father,"[3] much like Christ, the head of the Twelve, proceeding in the name of the Father.

Finally, in the Book of Caverns, dating from the 13th century BCE onward, we again encounter the scene of the sun god in his boat being towed out of the underworld by 12 gods.[4] The theme of the god with the 12 is also repeated in the Book of the Earth, found as early as the Ramesside period (1292-1077 BCE) and containing an image of Osiris-Re surrounded by "a wreath of twelve stars and twelve disks."[5] Also, in the funerary rites depicted in the tomb of King Tut appear 12 "royal companions and counselors" who "drag the coffin in a shrine," while the succeeding "loyal son" carries out the actual rites,[6] much like the Horus-priest. The twelve companions of the Osiris are also mentioned in BD 64, representing the hours of daylight, who are "circling round, uniting hands, each of them with another."[7]

In any case, the 12 symbolize the hours not only of the night but also of the day. In this regard, Dr. Maya Muller discusses images in the temple of Horus at Edfu: "On the ceiling of a chapel are depicted the twelve figures of Re as diurnal [daily] sun..."[8] The sun god (Re) is also named in the Coffin Texts as having followers or an "entourage," as at CT Sp. 1146.[9] Moreover, the *Shemsu-Hor* or *šmsw Ḥr*— "Followers of Horus"—are specifically invoked in several ancient texts, referring to the various kings, et al.[10] CT Sp. 157 describes "Horus

---

[1] Massey, *AELW*, II, 650.

[2] *ROTP*, X, 119.

[3] Smith, P., 172.

[4] Hornung, *AEBA*, 83, 90, 91, 95.

[5] Hornung, *AEBA*, 100.

[6] Hornung, *VK*, 136.

[7] Renouf, *EBD*, 119; Allen, T., *BD*, 57; Faulkner, *EBD*, 106. In an instance of where the translation does matter because some renderings are clearly more difficult to understand than others, Faulkner's version of BD 64 is somewhat different than Renouf's, while Allen's is in between, providing clarity and common points to both. From Allen, it is evident that there were 12 "attendants," as he calls them, since he states that each one represents "one-twelfth."

[8] Redford, 328.

[9] Faulkner, *AECT*, III, 179, 180.

[10] Bury, 3.

and His Followers,"[1] while the "followers of Horus" can also be found in CT Sp. 267.[2] Various other gods, including not only Re and Horus but also Osiris, are likewise depicted as having a "following" or "followers," such as in CT Sp. 60 and CT Sp. 237, the latter of which refers to the "Followers of Osiris."[3] In a Coffin Text also appears reference to "the Followers of the Lord of All."[4]

Also in the Coffin Texts, Osiris is repeatedly referred to as "sitting at the head of the Ennead," instantly invoking the image of Christ and his disciples at the Last Supper.[5] In CT Sp. 648 appears a reference to "Horus at the head of the Ennead."[6] Once more, the term "Ennead" could refer not only to nine gods but also, to the *twelve* Egyptian deities, as according to Herodotus (2.4) and as revealed repeatedly here.[7] Hence, in this case Horus would be at the head of the 12 as well. In the final analysis, these various texts reveal an ongoing theme of the god with 12 protectors, assistants, helpers, companions, followers and disciples, etc.

The Fishers of Men

Various of these groupings of a dozen towing the sun boat could be deemed the "Twelve Rowers in the Boat with Horus" or the "Twelve Sailors in the Ship of Ra."[8] It is not much of a leap from these particular aquatic terms to the "Twelve Fishers of Men with Jesus" (Mt 4:18-22; Mk 1:16-20), especially in light of how much of the Egyptian religion evidently became incorporated into Christianity. Indeed, in the Coffin Texts we discover mention of the "fishers of Osiris" (CT Sp. 229),[9] while there are also "Lords of fishing" (CT Sp. 429),[10] as well as references to "fishers of the dead" (CT Sp. 473),[11] fishermen, fish-traps, nets, etc. CT Sp. 474 is a paean to the fishermen, with a detailed description of that occupation, as applied spiritually and to the afterlife journey.[12] CT Sp. 475—the "Spell for the Net for Fishing"—addresses "him who fishes for himself; he is the great and mighty one..."[13] The "fishers who fish...of Abydos" are also mentioned in CT Sp. 477.[14] In CT Sp. 703, the Osiris fishes "in the

---

[1] Faulkner, *AECT*, I, 55, 135.
[2] Faulkner, *AECT*, I, 203.
[3] Faulkner, *AECT*, I, 186.
[4] Faulkner, *AECT*, II, 71.
[5] See, e.g., CT Sp. 317:111. (Faulkner, *AECT*, I, 241.)
[6] Faulkner, *AECT*, II, 224.
[7] Herodotus/de Selincourt, 87. See also Long: "...J.G. Griffiths therefore suggested that Herodotus' Twelve were an expanded form of the Heliopolitan Ennead." (Long, 147.)
[8] Kuhn, 208.
[9] Faulkner, *AECT*, I, 182. These "fishers of Osiris" are disposers of the dead from whom the deceased needed to be saved.
[10] Faulkner, *AECT*, II, 72.
[11] Faulkner, *AECT*, II, 107.
[12] Faulkner, *AECT*, II, 112-114.
[13] Faulkner, *AECT*, II, 116.
[14] Faulkner, *AECT*, II, 119.

waters of the Abyss."[1] In CT Sp. 479, a spell for escaping from fish-nets and traps full of piscatorial references, appears a mention of "fishermen of men," as well as "fishermen of gods."[2] Again, Horus too is a "fisher" when he spears the "serpent of the celestial river."

Speaking of fish, in *The Mythology of All Races*, Gray, et al., remark that the "*uz*- or *woz*-fish, to which a curse is attached, according to the Osiris-myth allude to the sin for which Horus-Osiris had to die,"[3] which brings up yet another correspondence to Christianity: The death of the god as remover of sins.

The Gnostic 12

In tracing the transition of the astrotheological motifs of the Twelve from the Egyptian religion to Christianity, we once again encounter the movement of Gnosticism, with its motif of the Twelve as well. For example, after citing a long portion of the Gnostic/Coptic-Christian work the *Pistis Sophia* (3rd cent. AD/CE) in which are mentioned the "twelve governors...in the serpent of outer darkness," Budge comments:

> It is quite clear that in the above extract from the famous Gnostic work we have a series of chambers in the outer darkness which has been borrowed from the twelve divisions of the Egyptian Tuat already described, and the reader has only to compare the vignettes to Chapters cxliv. [144] and cxlv. [145] of the Book of the Dead with the extract from "Pistis Sophia" to see how close the borrowing has been.[4]

As a devout Christian who knew very well both his own cherished faith and that of the Egyptians, Budge was in an excellent position to recognize the many correspondences between the two quite clearly—and his insight and candor are refreshing in their truthiness.

From his discussion of the Gnostic-*Christian* text *Pistis Sophia* being largely Egyptian in origin, Budge moves onto "Book of Ieu," also known as the Book(s) of Jeu, Jeou or Ieou, likewise a Gnostic-*Christian* text, written *before* the *Pistis Sophia* and mentioned therein:

> An examination of another great Gnostic work, generally known as the "Book of Ieu," proves that the Underworld of the Gnostics was nothing but a modified form of that Amentet or Amenti of the Egyptians, to which were added characteristics derived from the religious systems of the Hebrews and Greeks. The Gnostic rivers and seas of fire are nothing but equivalents of those mentioned in the *Book of the Dead*, and the beings in Amenti, and Chaos, and Outer Darkness are derived, in respect of form, from ancient Egyptian models. The great dragon of Outer Darkness and his twelve halls, and their twelve guardians or governors who change their names and

[1] Faulkner, *AECT*, II, 265.
[2] Faulkner, *AECT*, II, 123.
[3] Gray, 125.
[4] Budge, *GE*, I, 266-267.

forms every hour are, after all, only modifications of the old Egyptian system of the Twelve Pylons or Twelve Hours which formed the Underworld.[1]

Hence, in the Gnostic system we find the Twelve as "guardians" and "governors," also not far from roles of the 12 Christian *apostles*. In addition, it is apparent that this important esoteric teaching found in the Book of Amduat, Book of Gates and elsewhere maintained currency among the Egyptian priesthood that evidently contributed to the Gnostic effort, into the common era, well over a millennium after these texts were composed. It is therefore evident that these texts were well known to the priesthood before and during the formative period of Christianity, which largely took place during the *second century*, with the canonical gospels clearly showing up in the literary record at the end of that period, possibly around the time this Gnostic book—"considered part of the New Testament apocrypha" or hidden texts—was being written. These texts reveal that the theme of the sun god—and *Horus*, as his alter ego—with the Twelve was current from long before the common era until well into it, and that it was of interest to *early Christians*. Also demonstrating the Gnostic adoption of the theme of the Twelve during the precise era when Christianity was largely being formulated are the 12 Aeons, or Duodecad, representing the months of the year, as previously discussed.

Furthermore, in the booklet "Bandlet of Righteousness," Budge identifies "Ieu" as equivalent to "Iao" or "Jah," as in the name of the Jewish tribal god Yahweh.[2] Indeed, in the Egyptian scriptures, we find an entity called "Iaau," as at CT Sp. 170.[3] Thus, we see once more that Gnosticism signifies a synthesis of Egyptian and Jewish religion and mythology, as well as others. Moreover, we assert that Christianity constitutes Gnosticism historicized and Judaized, likewise representing a synthesis of Egyptian, Jewish and Greek religion and mythology, among others from around the "known world."

Serapis and the Twelve

Adding to the theme of the Egyptian god with the Twelve, as well as its relevance to Christianity, during the reign of Emperor Antoninus Pius (c. 138 AD/CE) a series of coins was created that depicted astrological mythology or astrotheological scenes:

> In the eighth year we have the head of Serapis circled by the seven planets, and the whole within the twelve signs of the zodiac; and on

---

[1] Budge, *GE*, 267; Budge, *BR*, 7.
[2] Budge, *BR*, 7.
[3] Faulkner, *AECT*, I, 146.

another coin we have the sun and moon within the signs of the zodiac.[1]

This portrayal of the important Greco-Egyptian hybrid god Serapis surrounded by the 12 is significant, especially in consideration of the facts that Serapis was also created in order to incorporate the Jews of Alexandria into Egyptian worship, as well as that the influence of Christianity upon the Mediterranean world at this point was insignificant. Indeed, there is no clear trace of the canonical gospels by this time, and Christ himself had not yet been portrayed in art surrounded by the Twelve. Thus, it cannot be scientifically concluded that by this point Christianity influenced meaningfully the religion of Serapis, which had existed for at least 400 years by then.

The creation of Serapis was part of a movement during the Hellenistic period to "transform cults," as part of a Roman "religious policy" to "unite Greeks and Egyptians."[2] In this regard, Morenz remarks:

> In saying that the god Sarapis was created, we wish to bring out the conspicuous point that he owes his form and role to the Macedonian ruler's need for a deity who could be worshipped jointly by Greeks and Egyptians...[3]

Of course, the "Macedonian ruler" refers to Alexander the Great.

In addition, over the centuries it has been asserted that the Emperor Hadrian (76-138 AD/CE), ruling just before Antoninus Pius (86-161 AD/CE), had deemed Serapis the "peculiar god of the *Christians.*" Hadrian's remarks purportedly appeared in a letter from him to one Servianus, as reproduced by the Sicilian writer of the third century Vopiscus (*Vita Saturnini* 8), who claimed to have taken it in turn from a writer named Phlegon. Regarding this fascinating situation, in his article with the eye-opening title, "On the Infrequency of the Allusions to Christianity in Greek and Roman Writers," Dr. H.G. Tschirner, a German professor of Theology, writes:

> In this letter the emperor inveighs against the manners of the Egyptians, i.e. of the Alexandrians, pronouncing them a most seditious, false and violent class of men; and on this occasion he speaks of the Christians in language as follows: "Those, who worship Serapis, are Christians; and these are those devoted to the service of Serapis, who call themselves the bishops of Christ. There is no ruler of the Jewish synagogue there, no Samaritan, no presbyter of the Christians, who is not an astrologer, a soothsayer, a diviner. The [Jewish] patriarch himself, when he comes to Egypt, is compelled by some to worship Serapis, by others, Christ."[4]

---

[1] Rappoport, 110-111.
[2] Morenz, 246.
[3] Morenz, 246.
[4] Peters, 210. It is clear from the remark that the *Jewish* patriarch was compelled to worship Serapis that this god was created to unite not only the Egyptians and Greeks

jurported letter from Hadrian has been reported in
s relatively reliable publications as being genuine, and, from
and scientific analysis of the origins of Christianity, the
rema. s would appear to be accurate for the most part. Nevertheless,
many believing scholars and writers have wished to find in this
revealing epistle a "forgery" or "malicious satire." The notable
defender of the faith Bishop Dr. J.B. Lightfoot, however, did not
consider the letter to be spurious but insisted that the emperor was
in reality *ridiculing* the Christians.[1] Be that as it may, it should be not
assumed that by "Christ" in the Hadrian quote is necessarily meant a
man in Judea executed under Pontius Pilate, and the fact will remain
that the word "Christos"—*Christ*—was applied to anyone considered
"anointed," likely including the revered god Serapis; hence, his
followers could also be styled "Christians." Indeed, the word "Christ"
as referring to various ancient Jewish heroes, such as Saul, David
and Solomon, appears 40 times in the Greek Old Testament.[2]
Knowing the fractured state of Christian origins, these followers of
Serapis certainly could have constituted one of the many factions
that were rolled together to create Christianity. In addition, that so
few Greek and Roman writers took notice of Christianity, as reflected
in Dr. Tschirner's thesis, is worthy of note, especially in consideration
of the fallacious notion that Christianity suddenly and under divine
influence sprang up and took the world by storm.[3]

In reality, the cult of Serapis/Asclepius—who was called "Savior"
centuries before the common era[4]—was evidently a major faction in
the very mundane, priestly genesis of Christianity, with the image of
Serapis as a man with a dark beard and long, curly hair wearing a
robe eventually morphed into Jesus. The claim is given further weight
by the fact that the earliest representations of Christ are not of a man
with a beard and long hair at all but of a fair-haired youth with short
locks,[5] much like Apollo, the Greek sun god, indicating not a portrait

but also the Jews. Indeed, the Greeks and Jews both had in common an insistence for
bloody animal sacrifice, satisfied in Serapis by the combination of Osiris with the god
Apis, who became the sacrificial bull. The French philosopher Voltaire (1694-1778)
claimed that, in his *Stromata*, Clement of Alexandria asserted the worshippers of
Serapis were forced to wear on their clothes the name of "God eternal" or "I-ha-ho,"
essentially the moniker of the Hebrew god Yahweh. (Voltaire, 51.) However, this quote
has apparently never been pinned down in the original Greek of Clement. As we have
seen, nevertheless, Clement's works have been tampered with over the centuries, as
have been those of practically every author from antiquity.

[1] Lightfoot, 505.
[2] Murdock, *WWJ*, 92.
[3] For an analysis of the worth or lack thereof concerning the various brief passages in
the works of Jewish, Roman and Greek writers during the first couple of centuries of
the common era, including Josephus, Tacitus, Suetonius and Pliny, among others, see
my books *The Christ Conspiracy, Suns of God* and *Who Was Jesus?*
[4] MacMullen, 48, 84, 167.
[5] See Witt, 217.

of a "real person" but that of a mythical god, whose image was changed at will to suit the priesthood.

Like so many other characteristics common to both Paganism and Christianity, it appears that the sun god with the Twelve may constitute another mystery of the Egyptian religion, not necessarily to be shared among the common people in Egypt but well known at least to the priests who create religions. From its abundance in the Egyptian texts and images, it is also possible, of course, that the motif of the god with the twelve was in the minds of many priests and other religionists in Egypt, including, perhaps, countless thousands of worshippers as well, long before the common era. The motif's reverence continued well into the common era, as evidenced by its inclusion in Gnostic texts and thought as well. Thus, the story of Jesus and the 12 is neither new nor unique, not representing "divine revelation" or even an actual, historical occurrence, as it was quite likely based on this motif found in other cultures around the Mediterranean for hundreds to thousands of years. In the end, the theme of the god or godman with 12 "helpers," "companions," "followers" or "disciples" appears abundantly in religion predating the common era by centuries, including in Egypt concerning the sun gods or solar aspects Re, Osiris, Horus and others.

12 Egyptian Signs of the Zodiac.

Ra in his Boat led by the Twelve Helpers,
Sixth Section, Book of Caverns.
(Hornung, *The Ancient Egyptian Books of the Afterlife*, 95)

Horus enthroned before the Twelve,
Seventh Hour of the Amduat.
(Hornung, *The Ancient Egyptian Books of the Afterlife*, 48)

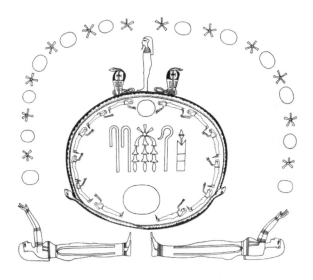

Osiris surrounded by Twelve Circles and Stars
(Hornung, *The Valley of the Kings*, 94)

"Osiris with the Water and Plant of Life, on which Stand His Four
Sons."
(Gray, *Mythology of All Races*, XII, 97)

Serapis and the Twelve Signs of the Zodiac.
(Ebers, *Egypt: Descriptive, Historical, and Picturesque*, I, 30)

Performing Miracles, Walking on Water, Healing the Sick and Raising the Dead

"They say Horus, in the Greek tongue, is Apollo, who was taught both medicine and divination by his mother Isis, and who showers benefits on the race of men through his oracles and his cures."

Diodorus Siculus, *The Antiquities of Egypt* (31-32)

"It is intriguing that the legends of all three deities, Hercules, Isis and Asclepius also feature a story of their raising someone from the dead."

Dr. Wendy Cotter, *Miracles in Greco-Roman Antiquity* (12)

The subject of miracles has been the purview of the priesthood since time immemorial, and no one religion has any corner on the miracle market, despite the beliefs of fervent followers. In reality, practically every religion and cult has made claims to miracles, particularly in appeals to veracity. In other words it is asserted that miracles provide "proof" that the religion/cult is "the one true faith." If that were the case, however, virtually all faiths would be true and, therefore, none of them would be true, since each claims all the rest to be false. Although Christianity, for example, makes much ado of being the "one true faith" full of miracles proving its contentions, the reality will remain that long before Christianity was ever conceived, the Egyptian religion, for one, was chockablock with miracles of every sort, attributed at one point or another to a number of gods and goddesses. The main Egyptian deities, in fact, such as Osiris and Isis, were well known to bestow miraculous favors upon their devout followers. Indeed, one of the reasons there *were* such devoted worshippers is because they *expected* such miracles, which included the standard healing of the sick, casting out of demons and raising of the dead. Apparitions of the gods were another favorite, so much so that banquets were held in which the god or goddess, particularly the great Savior[1] and Healer Isis, was anxiously awaited.[2] Right around the time of Christ's alleged advent, Isis's savior role was reprised in the testimonial to her at Philae by the emperor Tiberius, who called her, "Mighty protectress without her equal, who saves all those she loves on the battlefield..."[3] No less impressive were the miracles of the Goddess's beloved son, Horus.

In *Miracles in Greco-Roman Antiquity: A Sourcebook for the Study of New Testament Miracle Stories*, pre-Christian miracles expert and Loyola University professor of Scripture Dr. Wendy Cotter describes the goddess Isis as "that major deity from Egypt whose devotion around the Mediterranean also included mystery initiations..."[4] Isis

---

[1] Žabkar, 138.
[2] MacMullen, 37-39.
[3] Žabkar, 69.
[4] Cotter, 131.

was one of the healing gods, "worshiped for her beneficence toward humanity" and "approached for healings, especially in her role as loving mother to all her devotees, no matter what their social rank or status."[1] Dr. Cotter further states that "in a broad sense Isis is a healer as part of her larger role as queen of the universe and goddess of cosmic good in every form."[2]

Around 88 BCE, the Greek poet Isidorus wrote a heartfelt prayer and paean to the highly revered Isis, revealing her omnipotence and esteem:

Mighty One, I shall not cease to sing of Your great Power,
Deathless Saviour, many-named, mightiest Isis,
Saving from war, cities and all their citizens;
Men, their wives, possessions, and children.
As many as are bound fast in prison, in the power of death,
As many as are in pain through long, anguished, sleepless nights,
All who are wanderers in a foreign land,
And as many as sail on the Great Sea in winter
When men may be destroyed and their ships wrecked and sunk...
All (these) saved if they pray that you be present to help.
Hear my prayers, O One Whose Name has great Power;
Prove Yourself merciful to me and free me from all distress.[3]

Thus, Isis was not only the Healer but also the Savior long before Christianity usurped these concepts with Jesus.

Also during the first century BCE, Diodorus highlighted the widespread belief in the many miracles of Isis:

The Egyptians credit Isis both with the discovery of many therapeutic drugs and with having skill in understanding the art of healing. Thus, having become immortal, her greatest delight is to bestow cures on mankind, and to give remedies during sleep to those who have implored her aid, openly displaying to men who seek her assistance her beneficence as well as her very apparition. And in proof of these miracles, they claim to adduce not myths, as do the Greeks, but palpable evidence: for nearly all the world bears witness to them, and renders praise to Isis because of her manifestations through healing. For hovering near the sick while they slumber, she grants them succor in their afflictions, and those who have submitted to her are miraculously made well. She even saves many of those for whom, from the stubbornness of their maladies, the doctors have despaired; and many, entirely deprived of sight or some other bodily function, are restored to their former healthy condition when they have recourse to this goddess.[4]

As we can see, Isis's status as divine healer and miraclemaker was very much like that of Jesus, with her followers claiming "palpable evidence" of her reality and divinity, as do Christians

[1] Cotter, 11.
[2] Cotter, 30.
[3] Cotter, 32.
[4] Diodorus/Murphy, 31.

concerning purported proofs of their faith. Isis was, in fact, no less real to her many millions of worshippers—"nearly all the world" becoming witness to her miracles—than Christ is to his devotees today.

As Diodorus also states, the immortal Isis's healing powers were famed throughout the known world, with countless miracles attributed to her for illnesses that appeared irresolvable by ordinary medicinal methods and physicians. Like Jesus, who healed the sightless (Mt 11:5) but who also struck St. Paul blind (Acts 13:11), Isis was known both to cure and to cause blindness.[1] Also like that of Jesus, it was often the *blood* of Isis to which was attributed the power of healing, many centuries before the common era:

> The great Codices of the Book of the Dead written under the XVIIIth [18th] dynasty prove that the blood of Isis was believed to possess great magical protective powers, and models of the internal organs of the goddess which produced this blood were buried with the dead to preserve them from harm.[2]

In discussing a style of ancient Egyptian amulet made of blood-red stone such as carnelian, red jasper, glass or other red substance, Budge remarks:

> It is always associated with the CLVIth [156th] Chapter of the Book of the Dead, which is frequently inscribed upon it, and which reads:—
>
> "The blood of Isis, and the strength of Isis, and the words of power of Isis shall be mighty to act as powers to protect this great and divine being, and to guard him from him that would do unto him anything that he holdeth in abomination."[3]

As we can see, the Egyptian goddess Isis rates as a significant and popular figure who, we maintain, was unquestionably imitated in the creation of the Christ character. Summarizing the competition between Isis and the newcomer Jesus, Witt remarks:

> A bitter struggle had to be waged before the Graeco-Roman world at last accepted Jesus instead of Isis. Among the reasons for the keenness of the conflict none was more important than the claim made by the upholders of the Egyptian faith that their goddess was the wonder-worker with the gift of healing the sick....
>
> The rivalry between the two religions can be detected when we turn to the account of an act of exorcism performed by Cyril, who was Archbishop of Alexandria early in the fifth century. As one of the leading Christians in Egypt Cyril must have been familiar with the Gnostic view, there strongly held, that Isis and the Virgin Mary shared the same characteristic, a view he could not have ignored when he was energetically championing the official adoption of the dogma of Panagia Theotokos—the All-Holy Virgin Mother of God—at

---

[1] Curl, 67.
[2] Budge, *LOLM*, liv.
[3] Budge, *EM*, 43; Allen, T., *BD*, 155; Faulkner, *EBD*, pl. 32; Bunsen/Birch, 315. Birch has this scripture as appearing in chapter 157.

ncil of Ephesus in 431. Cyril was certainly not blind to the
t Isis still maintained over Egypt.[1]

..... not only for raising Osiris and Horus from the dead but
also for these many other healings, Our Lady Isis was thus the great
Savior of the Mediterranean during the period before and well into
the common era, beginning long prior to the creation of Christianity
and the Jewish rendition of the Virgin Mother, Mary.

The Bread of Life

Isis's son, Horus, also was a miracle maker, healer, and raiser of
the dead, like his much later Jewish counterpart, Jesus. For
example, one of the favorite miracles in the gospels is when Jesus
multiplies the loaves of bread. (Mk 6:41; 8:6) Like Jesus, however,
Horus too miraculously brings forth bread, making this johnny-come-
lately Christian miracle mundane and derivative. Bread, in fact, plays
a major part in the Book of the Dead (e.g., BD 53), in which the
Osiris says, among other things, "I eat bread from the house of the
Lord of offerings."[2] Indeed, bread was so sacred to the Egyptians that
at PT 508:1113c-1117, the deceased, essentially as Horus,
"propitiated" the gods with it.[3] Also, at PT 338:551d/T 148, reference
is made to the "bread of Horus" or the "wheat bread of Horus," by
means of which the Osiris will not go hungry.[4] At PT 468:905a-b, the
Osiris receives bread and beer from Horus,[5] like Jesus presenting the
disciples with bread and wine (Mt 26:26-28).

In the gospels of Matthew (15:34, 36; 16:10) and Mark (8:5-6)
much is made about Jesus multiplying the *seven loaves* of bread.
Meanwhile, centuries to millennia earlier, a similar fuss occurred
over the "*seven loaves*" in the Book of the Dead, as in chapter 53b:

---

[1] Witt, 185.

[2] Renouf, *EBD*, 107; Allen, T., *BD*, 52; Faulkner, *EBD*, 105; Bunsen/Birch, 202. While
Allen essentially agrees with Renouf's translation, Faulkner renders it such that there
is no "lord" or "house" but the deceased has eaten bread in "every pleasant room,"
while Birch renders it, "I have eaten in every place of sacrifice." It should be noted that
preceding this passage the Osiris says, "I am Lord of the Bread in Annu."
(Bunsen/Birch, 202.)

[3] Faulkner, *AEPT*, 183; Allen, J., *AEPT*, 140; Mercer, 191. The identification of the
Osiris N. with Horus comes in § 1113c, in which the deceased's sweat and scent are
that of the god. Allen and Mercer's rendering intimates that the Osiris/Horus is asking
the gods for bread, while Faulkner's clearly states that the deceased has come to
propitiate the Ennead "with its bread."

[4] Mercer, 115; Allen, J., *AEPT*, 74; Faulkner, *AEPT*, 109. "Utterance 93...O King, take
this bread of yours which is the Eye of Horus." (Faulkner, *AEPT*, 21) Other utterances
(e.g., PT 197) also address the Eye of Horus as relating to bread, including the
"morning bread," which Faulkner calls "the bread of worship." (Faulkner, *AEPT*, 36.) At
PT 211:132d/W 144, it is the Osiris who brings forth the bread, from "the Abyss."
(Faulkner, *AEPT*, 40; Allen, J., *AEPT*, 30; Mercer, 58.) At PT 223:217a/W 134, the
speaker—who would be the priest, serving as Horus—commands the king to rise and
says, "receive this your bread from my hand..." (Faulkner, *AEPT*, 52; Allen, J., *AEPT*,
28; Mercer, 69.)

[5] Allen, J., *AEPT*, 124; Mercer, 164-165; Faulkner, *AEPT*, 158.

> There are seven loaves in Heaven at Heliopolis with Ra, and there are seven loaves upon earth with Seb [Osiris's father], and there are seven loaves with Osiris.[1]

In BD 52, we find that it is Horus who "makes" these seven loaves:

> Thou hast brought these seven loaves for me to live by, bringing the bread that Horus makes.[2]

The seven loaves are also mentioned in BD 189:

> I live on the 7 loaves brought to me: (4) loaves by Horus, 3 loaves by Thoth.[3]

The Coffin Texts also speak of the seven loaves in various places, such as at CT Sp. 166, which again associates "four loaves on earth" with Horus,[4] while CT Sp. 772 mentions the "seven loaves [which] are with Horus and with Seth."[5]

As we can see, this motif of a savior god with seven loaves of bread is very old and pre-Christian, emphasized in important Egyptian texts, such that a significant number of people undoubtedly had it in mind by the time Christianity was created.

Moreover, the Egyptian gods also *out-miracle* the Christian godman, as in the Pyramid Texts (PT 437:807a/P 31; PT 675:2006b/N 410), in which the god offers the deceased "thy *thousand* (loaves) of bread..."[6]

In BD 18, the deceased pleads his virtues before the Lord and Prince of Amenta, listing his desire for "Bread," an element of truth and righteousness as part of the Netherworld:

> I am not knowingly a speaker of wrong; I am not given to duplicity; grant me Bread, the right of appearance at the tables of the Lords of Maat ["truth"], entering in and going out of the Netherworld, and that my soul may not suffer repulse in its devotion to the orb of the Sun and the vision of the Moon-god for ever.[7]

Bread, in fact, is one of the main symbols of sustenance for the immortality of the deceased in the Egyptian heaven, as in the Pyramid Texts as well:

> Oho! Oho! Raise yourself, O King; receive your head, collect your bones, gather your limbs together, throw off the earth from your

---

[1] Renouf, *EBD*, 107. Faulkner, et al., do not number the loaves as seven in chapter 53. The preceding chapter, 52, however, does number the loaves at seven, as in the translations of Budge, Renouf and Allen, the latter of whom translates this passage as: "I live on these 7 loaves of her whose loaves have been brought by Horus and by Thoth." (Allen, T., *BD*, 52; Budge, *BD* (1899), 194; Renouf, *EBD*, 105.)

[2] Bunsen/Birch, 202. (See note above for other translations.)

[3] Allen, T., *BD*, 211; Faulkner, *EBD*, 135.

[4] Faulkner, *AECT*, I, 143.

[5] Faulkner, *AECT*, II, 302.

[6] Mercer, 151, 297. (Emph. added.) See Faulkner, *AEPT*, 145, 289; Allen, J., *AEPT*, 106, 276.

[7] Renouf, *EBD*, 50; Faulkner, *EBD*, pl. 12. Allen leaves off the "introduction" in which this pertinent part appears in both Renouf and Faulkner. (Allen, T., *BD*, 32.)

ceive your bread which does not grow mouldy and your beer
)es not grow sour... [PT 373:654-655a/T 204][1]

... [Osiris] N. lives on the morning bread, which comes at its
(appointed) time. [PT 339:553b/T 149][2]

...The bread of your father is for you... [W 13/PT 238:242a][3]

...sit down to a thousand of bread... [W 134/PT 223:214b][4]

In the Coffin Texts, we find many references to the same spiritual
bread, including as the "bread of Osiris," also called the "daily bread"
and the "bread of N.,"[5] where "N," of course, is the deceased. The
bread of life may serve as part of the "funerary Meal in On," as at CT
Sp. 237.[6] At CT Sp. 334, the speaker identifies himself as the "first
seed" of Re, begotten "in the womb of my mother Isis..."[7] He is also
the "Lord of bread" and "one in charge of beer..."[8] Moreover, at CT Sp.
767, we hear of Osiris not only receiving but also giving bread daily,[9]
immediately reminding us of the Lord's Prayer, in which the Christian
God is beseeched, "Give us this day our daily bread." (Mt 6:11)

As bread is highly emphasized in the Book of the Dead, as well as
in the Pyramid and Coffin Texts, being mentioned *dozens* of times, it
would not surprise us to learn that the gospel of John is *full* of
references to bread, including and especially as representing Jesus,
who himself is portrayed in John as repeatedly stating that "he is the
bread of life" and assorted other spiritual concepts apparently
straight out of the Egyptian texts:

Jesus then said to them, "...my Father gives you the true bread from
heaven. For the bread of God is that which comes down from heaven,
and gives life to the world." (Jn 6:32-33)

Jesus said to them, "I am the bread of life..." (Jn 6:35)

And the Jews then murmured at him, because he said, "I am the
bread which came down from heaven." (Jn 6:41)

"I am the bread of life.... This it the bread which comes down from
heaven, that a man may eat of it and not die. I am the living bread
which came down from heaven; if anyone eats of this bread, he will
live for ever; and the bread which I shall give for the life of the world
is my flesh." (Jn 6:48-51)

*In no other gospel is this emphasis on the "bread of God," "bread of
"life" and "bread from heaven" so clearly and abundantly made as it is
in the gospel of John.* This fact would make sense, since in the
Egyptian texts and motifs upon which much of John is so evidently

---

[1] Faulkner, *AEPT*, 123; Mercer, 129; Allen, J., *AEPT*, 83.
[2] Mercer, 115; Faulkner, *AEPT*, 109; Allen, J., *AEPT*, 74.
[3] Allen, J., *AEPT*, 18; Mercer, 72; Faulkner, *AEPT*, 56.
[4] Allen, J., *AEPT*, 27; Mercer, 68; Faulkner, *AEPT*, 51.
[5] Faulkner, *AECT*, I, 182.
[6] Faulkner, *AECT*, I, 186.
[7] Faulkner, *AECT*, I, 257.
[8] Faulkner, *AECT*, I, 257.
[9] Faulkner, *AECT*, II, 297.

built, the spiritual and heavenly "bread of Ra" and the "bread of your father" represent major tenets.[1]

The Lord of Wine and the Sacred Meal

As in the gospel story, both wine and figs figure in the Egyptian religion, as in CT Sp. 516, in which the Osiris "shall eat figs and drink wine."[2] Also in the Pyramid Texts (PT 610:1723a-b/M 375) appears a reference to "the great bread and this wine-like water" given to the "chief of Letopolis" (Horus)[3] who was "raised up,"[4] a ritual resembling the Christian communion/eucharist with sacramental bread and wine. (Mt 26:26; Mk 14:22; Lk 22:19) Another such passage—this time involving beer, rather than wine—occurs in BD 30B:

> "Let there be given to him bread and beer which have been issued in the presence of Osiris, and he will be forever like the Followers of Horus."[5]

We find this same sort of eucharistic empowerment in CT Sp. 404:

> Those who rebel will have no power over this flesh of mine, for my bread is in Pe and my beer is in Dep, and this power of mine belongs to me. My power is bread and beer, my power is life, prosperity and health.[6]

The sacred meal is also discussed in CT Sp. 644, where the Osiris—afterward identifying himself as Anubis—remarks, "I have come that I may conduct the funeral meal and propitiate those who are in the upper houses..."[7] The theme crops up again in CT Sp. 1033, when Re/Ra partakes of "the meal as the Lord of Right."[8]

Again in BD 72, the deceased is to receive the "holy sacraments": "Given him are bread and beer and a chunk of meat from the altar of

---

[1] Budge, *EBD* (1967), lxxv; Allen, J., *AEPT*, 18.

[2] Faulkner, *AECT*, II, 146.

[3] See PT 438:810b: "...like Horus lived, who dwelt in Letopolis." Per Faulkner, in BD 18, reference is made to "Horus-Preeminent-of-Letopolis." (Faulkner, *EBD*, pl. 12)

[4] Mercer, 262; Allen, J., *AEPT*, 232; Faulkner, *AEPT*, 254. While Mercer names the place over which the god presides as "Letopolis," Faulkner renders the city by its Egyptian designation, "Khem," also the native name for Egypt. Allen prefers "Akhmim," the modern name for the city of Chemmis. Also, while the others prefer describing the liquid in terms of *wine* Faulkner renders the word "grape-juice."

[5] Faulkner, *EBD*, pl. 4. Birch and Allen are missing this section, which is in the Papyrus of Ani. Budge calls chapter 30, including parts A and B, "one of the most important in the Book of the Dead" as well as "one of the oldest," found in numerous papyri as well as "hundreds of hard green stone scarabs." (Budge, *BD* (1899), cviii.) This situation illustrates the difficulty with producing one unified and sanctioned rendition of the BD.

[6] Faulkner, *AECT*, II, 50.

[7] Faulkner, *AECT*, II, 220.

[8] Faulkner, *AECT*, III, 129.

Osiris."[1] This shared symbolism was apparently not lost on the Gnostic followers of the Egypto-Christian religion:

> Bread and wine have been held to be the body and blood of Bacchus [Dionysus], and Mr. St. Chad Boscawen (1900) announces that he has just received from Egypt some old Gnostic papyri of the 2nd or 3rd century A.D. in which the names of Jesus, John, and Peter are said to be powerful. Over a cup or chalice these words appear in Greek: "This is not wine, this is the blood of Osiris," and over a piece of bread: "This is not bread, this is the very body of Osiris."[2]

A member of the prestigious and influential Society for Biblical Archaeology, the lawyer St. Chad Boscawen worked as an assistant to the great Dr. Samuel Birch in the British Museum's Oriental Department and was considered one of the "principal English Orientalists" of his day.[3] Validating this contention of an ancient papyrus discussing wine and bread as the *blood and body of the Egyptian god*, the "blood of Osiris" is referred to in ancient Egyptian literature, such as the Leyden or Leiden papyrus (or "Demotical Magical Papyrus"), which purportedly dates to around the same era as that in possession of Boscawen and which describes the blood of Osiris as being poured into "this cup, this wine."[4] Indeed, for eons prior to that time, the Nile's reddish water and banks were themselves considered the "blood of Osiris"[5]—a life-replenishing motif difficult to miss. It would also be reasonable and logical, based on all the evidence, to contend that these very words of the Christian eucharist as applied to Osiris existed *first*, long before the common era and the creation of Christianity. The eucharist drink as the blood of the god is also prefigured in an enigmatic Coffin Text (CT Sp. 394): "My blood is drunk..."[6]

Moreover, at PT 442:820a, Osiris—who was the "first to drink wine" and who taught mankind about the vine, according to Plutarch—is referred to as the "Lord of Wine in the...festival,"[7] evoking the wedding feast of Cana in John's gospel. Regarding the water-to-wine miracle at John 2:3-9, Dr. Neumann remarks that Osiris was a wine god and relates that January 6—supposedly both one of Christ's several birthdays and the "Feast of Epiphany,"

---

[1] Allen, T., *BD*, 65; Renouf, *EBD*, 10; Bunsen/Birch, 215.
[2] Yarker, 75.
[3] Blathwayt, 294, 297.
[4] Griffith, 107; Gabriel, *JE*, 115.
[5] Mojsov, 7.
[6] Faulkner, *AECT*, II, 19.
[7] Faulkner, *AEPT*, 147; Mercer, 153. Mercer phrases the pertinent part, "lord of the wine-cellar at the...feast." Allen's translation (P 38) is peculiar: "...the lord wine-colored with supplies..." (Allen, J., *AEPT*, 107.) The "Winepress-god" or "wine-press god" addressed in various scriptures such as the Coffin Texts (CT Sp. 205) is believed to be not Osiris, as some have suggested, but the god Shesmu, who then himself would be "Lord of Wine." See, e.g., CT Sp. 473. (Faulkner, *AECT*, I, 167; II, 108.)

commemorating Jesus turning water into wine—"is also the anniversary of the water-wine transformation performed by Osiris."[1] It should be noted that this miracle occurs *only* in the gospel of John, again indicating an Egyptian origin.

Another relevant utterance occurs in the Pyramid Text of Unas/Unis/Wenis (W 143/PT 210:130c): "...the water of Unis is wine, like the Sun."[2] This last verse indicates the real meaning behind the miracle of turning water into wine, which is also found in the myth of the Greek god Dionysus[3]: To wit, the sun's ripening of the grape on the vine and fermenting of the grape juice. In this regard, the divinities who turn water to wine are traditionally *sun gods*, as we contend is the mythical character of Jesus Christ as well.[4] Having command over water, in fact, ranks as a significant theme in *mythology*, including that of the Egyptians.

Commanding the Waters

The god who controls or commands the water represents part of a mythical category, as laid out by Dr. Wendy Cotter, in a chapter entitled, "Gods and Heroes Who Control Wind and Sea."[5] We have already seen that in the Egyptian religion water was highly revered, with several important rituals, spells and incantations pertaining to it, including baptism, as well as myths and legends, such as Osiris's role as the life-giving Nile and as water in general. In the Book of the Dead emerges a repeated emphasis on *controlling* water. In BD 62, for example, the deceased, who is Re or Osiris, pleads to have "command of the water,"[6] saying, "May I be granted power over the waters..."[7] *Spells* 57, 58 and 59 of the BD are titled chapters for "command of water" or "having power over water," while BD 57 includes the request:

> Oh Hapi, Chief of the heaven! in thy name of Conductor of the Heaven, let the Osiris prevail over the waters...[8]

---

[1] Neumann, E., 239, citing Gressmann's *Tod und Auferstehung des Osiris* for this miracle by Osiris.

[2] Allen, J., *AEPT*, 30; Faulkner, *AEPT*, 39; Mercer, 57.

[3] For more instances of the water-to-wine miracle, see Cotter, 164ff.

[4] See my books *The Christ Conspiracy, Suns of God* and *Who Was Jesus?* for more on this subject. See *WWJ* (142-143) in particular for the illogicalness of the gospel water-to-wine tale, in which Jesus is said to have conjured between 100 and 160 *gallons* of wine for guests who were already half-drunk! (Jn 2:6)

[5] Cotter, 131ff.

[6] Renouf, *EBD*, 114.

[7] Faulkner, *EBD*, 106. Allen's translation has the Osiris timidly asking for the water to be "made available..." (Allen, T., *BD*, 55.) Birch's deceased requests to "prevail over the waters like Stone-Arms," the latter representing the limbs of Set. (Bunsen/Birch, 205.) Renouf relates it as "...grant that I may have command of the water..." (Renouf, *EBD*, 10), while Faulkner also says, "May you grant that I have power over water..." (Faulkner, *EBD*, 105; pl. 16.)

[8] Bunsen/Birch, 203-204.

As Budge says of BD 57, "The recital of this Chapter gave the deceased 'dominion over the water,'" referring to the Nile.[1]

In this chapter/spell 57, in fact, appears an indication that the Egyptians possessed in their mythology the ancient motif of walking on water, after a fashion. In his comparison of the Egyptian and Christian depictions of water walking, Massey writes:

Walking on the Waters.

The scene of the miracles of the loaves and fishes is followed by an attempt to take Jesus by force, but he withdrew himself; and this is succeeded by the miracle of his walking on the waters and conquering the winds and waves. So in the *Ritual.* Chapter 57 is that of the *"Breath prevailing over the Water in Hades."*

The speaker, having to cross over, says; *"—O Hapi! let the Osiris, prevail over the waters, like as the Osiris prevailed against the taking by stealth the night of the great struggle. Let the Osiris pass by the great one who dwells in the place of the inundation."*

The disciples were afraid when they saw Jesus; and they did not recognize him, but he said, *"It is I, be not afraid!"* In the Ritual it says, *"While they conduct that great god they know not his name,"* i.e., in the passage of the waters, *"the Osiris passes through wherever he wishes, and sits there."*[2]

Here Massey is directly quoting Birch's translation of the Book of the Dead (57), also titled "The Funereal Ritual" and found in volume V of Bunsen's *Egypt's Place in Universal History.*[3]

In Faulkner's translation of BD 57, under the title "Chapter for breathing air and having power over water in the God's domain," the Osiris beseeches Hapi—the god of the Nile, "symbolic of abundance"[4]—to give him "power over water like Sekhmet who saved Osiris on that night of the storm."[5] In Faulkner's translation of BD 156, the Osiris Ani addresses the "Mistress of trembling," beseeching "the one who proclaims words which repel storms..."[6] At PT 247:261a-b, according to Faulkner and Mercer, Horus is called "Lord of the Storm" or "Lord of the Tempest."[7] James Allen (W 158) avers that it is *Seth* who is the "storm-lord" in the same utterance/ recitation.[8] Even so, when Horus slays Seth, he could then be said to have "prevailed over the storm-lord"; in other words, *Horus calmed the storm.* Indeed, in one of the Coffin Texts, the "lord of the flame" is said to "destroy the storm."[9] CT Sp. 1069 refers to the god who

[1] Budge, *BD* (1899), cxxxvi.
[2] Massey, *HJMC*, 74-75.
[3] Bunsen/Birch, 203-204.
[4] Faulkner, *EBD*, 173.
[5] Faulkner, *EBD*, 105.
[6] Faulkner, *EBD*, pl. 11; Allen, T., *BD*, 134.
[7] Faulkner, *AEPT*, 60; Mercer, 75.
[8] Allen, J., *AEPT*, 42.
[9] McDermott, 72.

Performing Miracles

"drives away the storm,"[1] while in CT Sp. 1099 the speaker first identifies himself as Horus and then says, "What I detest is storm, and there shall be no heaping up of water in my presence..."[2] Concerning Horus's role in the Pyramid Texts, Dr. Jean Sainte Fare Garnot (1908-1963), a professor of History and Archeology at the University of Paris, concludes, "...Horus, vanquisher of Seth, is henceforth the one who presides over storms, in order to hold them in check."[3] The use of miraculous powers or magic to calm the sea is likewise mentioned at Edfu, as related by Morenz:

> In the Horus myth of Edfu, Thoth utters magical incantations for the ship "in order to calm the sea...in his time...when it rages..."[4]

In CT Sp. 572 we find reference to the "magic of Horus,"[5] while the command of water appears in CT Sp. 353, for example, titled, "SPELL FOR HAVING POWER OVER WATER."[6] In the same spell, the deceased requests that Osiris "grant that I may have power over water just as Seth had power over the water in the eye of Osiris on that night of the great storm."[7] Also in the Coffin Texts (CT Sp. 1015) appears the "GREAT GOD WHO GIVES WATER AND WATCHES OVER WATER."[8]

In any event, the calming of the storm would rate as a typical role for the sun god and solar hero, and in the Egyptian texts we possess command of the water extending to the miracle of "calming the storm," as was said of Jesus (Mt 8:24-26).

Massey continues his analysis of the Egyptian command over water and water walking:

> The Lord appears on the water in the morning watch, the "fourth watch of the night," that is, the πρωι [proï] or dawning (cf. Mark xiii. 35), at which time the Sun-God begins his march or his "walking," as it is termed, upon the waters of the Nun [the primordial abyss]. It is said to the God who walks this water at sunrise, "Thou art the only one since thy coming forth upon the Nun." And here we may discover the prototype of the Gospel version. The deceased addresses Ra at his coming forth to walk the water and pleads, like Peter, that he may do so likewise. "Grant," he says, "that I too may be able to walk (the water) as thou walkest (on the Nun) without making any halt."[9]

In this paragraph, Massey is evidently discussing an Egyptian text called the "Book of Hades," as translated by Dr. Lefébure and as found in *Records of the Past*. In that book, Re appears in his boat/bark, above those who are "submerged." Next, the story goes:

---

[1] Faulkner, *AECT*, III, 143.
[2] Faulkner, *AECT*, III, 154.
[3] Garnot, 101.
[4] Morenz, 77.
[5] Faulkner, *AECT*, II, 174.
[6] See CT Sp. 225, 353, 356, 358, 431 and 820. (Faulkner, *AECT*, I, 177, 284; II, 1, 2, 73; III, 11.)
[7] Faulkner, *AECT*, I, 285.
[8] Faulkner, *AECT*, III, 115.
[9] Massey, *AELW*, II, 830-831.

...ller in Nun says to the submerged who are in (the water), to ...mmers who are in the water: See RA who rises in his boat, the ...st of mysteries!... Oh, arise, manes!... Lift up to your heads, ...ers, movement to your arms, you who float, swiftness to your le...s, swimmers, breath into your nostrils, divers! Be masters of your waters, repose yourselves in your tank, walk into the Nun, move onwards in the water.[1]

The "Nun" or "Nu" (*nwj*) is the primordial, watery abyss: "The universal ocean, existing before the world was created and source of all water."[2] As Dr. Bunsen says, "Water is *Nu*, who is the father of the Gods,"[3] and Budge calls Nu "the great primeval god of the watery abyss..."[4] A related term is Nut (*nwt*), the *Goddess* of the "celestial waters,"[5] which are also "Nu."[6] "*The* Nu" is "the firmament."[7] In BD 64, the speaker says, "'I know the deep waters' is my name.... I travel on high, I tread upon the firmament..."[8] Since the firmament is ostensibly Nu—indeed, T. George Allen notes that the firmament in this scripture is "watery"—it appears appropriate to say that the Osiris was to trod across the celestial waters, as in BD 15: "Osiris N....thou crossest the (watery) firmament."[9] As another example, in BD 145/6, according to Birch, the deceased, as *Horus*, says, "I navigate the water, fording it."[10] The traditional water-control refers not only to treading in it but also to trodding upon it, as well as parting it and moving "dryshod" through it.

Massey further explains walking on water as part of the *solar myth*:

> We are told that his disciples being on board a ship, "when even was come, in the fourth watch of the night, Jesus went unto them walking upon the sea." Now the fourth watch began at three o'clock, and ended at six o'clock. Therefore, this was about the proper time for a solar God to appear walking upon the waters...[11]

This "proper time" of day refers to when the sun's reflection on a body of water may be at its most brilliant or richest.

The command over water includes the crossing of the "celestial river": "Upon reaching the sky, the life-essence of the King approaches the celestial gate and/or the celestial river."[12] When the king reaches the river with his "mentor" Horus, he requests the god

---

[1] *ROTP*, X, 125-126.
[2] Allen, J., *AEPT*, 438.
[3] Bunsen/Birch, 92.
[4] Budge, *GE*, 52.
[5] Bunsen/Birch, 141. See Allen, J., *AEPT*, 438.
[6] Budge, *EHD*, I, 349.
[7] Bunsen/Birch, 169, 174, 219.
[8] Renouf, *EBD*, 119; Bunsen/Birch, 208; Faulkner, *EBD*, 106; Allen, T., *BD*, 57.
[9] Allen, T., *BD*, 13; Faulkner, *EBD*, pl. 21.
[10] Bunsen/Birch, 292.
[11] Massey, *Lectures*, 8-9.
[12] Davis, W.M., 171.

to take him with him: "Since Horus has already crossed the river with his father in mythical times..., he can apparently then cross the river at will."[1]

In any event, the theme of "walking on water" is old and non-Christian, found in Buddhist tales, for example, such as in the legend of Buddha's disciple Savatthi Sariputta,[2] as well as in the stories of Indian yogis. Also, in *The Homeric Epics and the Gospel of Mark*, Claremont Graduate University professor of Theology Dr. Dennis R. MacDonald sees in the story of Hermes and Zeus in *The Iliad* (2.4) a pre-Christian instance of "walking on water."[3] In the end, the supposed miracle of Christ's walking on water would be neither original nor, we maintain, historical, but, rather, reflects the astrotheological motif concerning the sun god, e.g., Re, Osiris and/or Horus.

The Raising of Osiris

As remarked upon by Diodorus before the alleged advent of Jesus Christ, the Egyptian son of God, Horus, was revered as a miracle maker and healer. Like Jesus, who cures the blind man with his spit, Horus heals wounds using his spittle (PT 455:850a/P 50).[4] In CT Sp. 331, the "saliva and spittle" of Horus are also sought out by the deceased as his mother Hathor.[5] Indeed, in CT Sp. 527, the "spittle which issued from the mouth of Rēᶜ-Atum" represents the purification of the Osiris.[6] In CT Sp. 622, we discover that the spit of the Osiris is a "healing operation,"[7] while in CT Sp. 818, the spitting is "prophylactic in purpose."[8] In CT Sp. 1113, the deceased as Horus says, "I am one who spits on wounds which will heal..."[9] In the Pyramid Texts (PT 219:192b/W 152), Horus is depicted as relieving "intestinal pain"[10] as well as assorted other ailments, including the disease of death. Demonstrating the remarkable ancient Horus-Jesus connection, one of the old Coptic spells to remove pains of childbirth and the stomach was "Jesus! Horus" or just simply "Jesus Horus!"[11]

Regarding Horus's role in healing, professor of Egyptology at the University of Chicago Dr. Robert K. Ritner remarks:

> In medical texts, the patient is almost invariably identified with the youthful Horus, whose recovery from assaults by Seth and his confederates serves as the pattern for all healing.... Direct

---

[1] Davis, W.M., 173.
[2] Carus, 212.
[3] MacDonald, 151.
[4] Allen, T., *HPT*, 33; Mercer, 157; Allen, J., *AEPT*, 110; Faulkner, *AEPT*, 151.
[5] Faulkner, *AECT*, I, 256.
[6] Faulkner, *AECT*, II, 152.
[7] Faulkner, *AECT*, II, 206.
[8] Faulkner, *AECT*, III, 9.
[9] Faulkner, *AECT*, III, 162.
[10] Allen, T., *HPT*, 41; Mercer, 165; Allen, J., *AEPT*, 38; Faulkner, *AEPT*, 48.
[11] Meyer, *ACM*, 363.

identification with a deity is integral to Egyptian magical recitations into Coptic times, and it permeates Greco-Egyptian spells by means of the untranslated native phrase *anok* ("I am")....[1]

Dr. Ritner also states, "In most spells, cures are effected by means of direct identification between patient and deity, either completely ("I am Horus; it is not I who recites but the goddess Isis") or in part..."[2] In fact, Horus's healing function is so important that "Horus the good doctor"—a title reminding one of "Jesus the Physician"—was at the center of a "popular cult," as found at the site of Kom Ombo or Ombos, for instance.[3] Moreover, a "popular innovation of the later New Kingdom was the antivenom stela or '*cippus* of Horus,'" used well into Roman times."[4] These small pillars were inscribed with curing spells and were "brought in contact with water subsequently drunk by the patient."[5] Regarding the healing spells, Dr. Ritner remarks:

> ...Many treatments combine "rational" and "magical" strategies "charged" by spell and rite. In most such cases, the patient is equated with the youthful Horus, whose cure is sanctioned by the gods.[6]

Also just like Jesus, Horus was esteemed for resurrecting the dead, especially his father, Osiris, but also others, including Re and the deceased in the mortuary literature, with the priest serving as Horus during the ritual. In CT Sp. 29, it is by a "great word" made by Horus that Osiris is resurrected and akhified,[7] while at PT 301:449b-450a/W 206, Horus is depicted as "he who brings Re to life every day; He refashions the King and brings the King to life every day."[8] The story of Horus resurrecting Osiris strongly resembles the much later biblical tale of Jesus raising the dead man Lazarus, a miracle surprisingly found *only* in the gospel of John, a book we contend is of Egyptian origin and represents Egyptian theology in significant part, designed specifically to appeal to the followers of the Egyptian religion.[9]

The resurrection of Osiris by Horus occurs in many ancient Egyptian texts and is often the primary focus of the deceased's bid for immortality in like kind. At PT 606:1683a-1685b/M 336, for example, Horus is vividly described as raising Osiris from the dead and avenging him:

---

[1] Redford, 198.
[2] Redford, 200.
[3] Redford, 204.
[4] Redford, 208.
[5] Redford, 208.
[6] Redford, 208.
[7] Faulkner, *AECT*, I, 18.
[8] Faulkner, *AEPT*, 90; Allen, J., *AEPT*, 55; Mercer, 100.
[9] For more on the subject, see my books *The Christ Conspiracy, Suns of God* and *Who Was Jesus?*

Stand up for me, father! Stand up for me, Osiris N...! It is I, your son: I am Horus.

I have come for you that I might clean you, cleanse you, revive you, assemble for you your bones, collect for you your swimming parts, and assemble for you your dismembered parts. For I am Horus who saves his father...[1]

The resurrection miracle of Horus is also depicted elsewhere in the Pyramid Texts, the phrase "to stand" meaning to be resurrected, and "upon his side" signifying that the individual is dead. Thus, in the Egyptian texts, the Horus-priest frequently tells the Osiris to "Stand up!" and "Rise up!" as part of his renewal or *resurrection* to life. The deceased/Osiris is also exhorted to "Live!" and "Raise yourself on your side!" or "Lift thyself on thy side," etc.

In *Horus in the Pyramid Texts*, T. George Allen summarizes the resurrection account, rolling into one entry the events as found in separate utterances, demonstrating how composite myths are made:

Horus causes Osiris the king to stand. [PT 364:617a-c/T 196; PT 369:640a/T 200]...

Horus and Thoth raise Osiris (the king) (from) upon his side and cause him to stand among...the two divine enneads. [PT 477:956a-c/P 327]....

Horus bids Osiris the king come forth (from tomb?) and awake. [PT 620:1753a-b/N 11]

Horus comes to king, parts his bandages, and casts off his bonds...[PT 703:2202a/N 615][2]

This description of Osiris the mummy being summoned from the tomb amid his two siblings sounds very much like the episode or pericope in the New Testament of Jesus calling forth the "mummy" Lazarus from the tomb in front of *his* two sisters:

When he had said this, he cried with a loud voice, "Lazarus, come out." The dead man came out, his hands and feet bound with bandages, and his face wrapped with a cloth. Jesus said to them, "Unbind him, and let him go." (Jn 11:43-44)

Like Jesus, at PT 268:372a-d/W 175 Horus also purifies the dead and removes evil:

Horus...purifies...him in the jackal-lake, cleanses his ka in the Dewat-lake, and purifies...the flesh of his bodily ka...[3]

After the purification, it is said (PT 419:746b/T 225) that "Horus has dispelled the evil which was on you for four days."[4]

---

[1] Allen, J., *AEPT*, 226; Mercer, 257; Faulkner, *AEPT*, 250.

[2] Allen, T., *HPT*, 40; Mercer, 124, 127, 171, 266, 318; Allen, J., *AEPT*, 80, 82, 129, 242, 303; Faulkner, *AEPT*, 119, 122, 164, 257, 306.

[3] Allen, T., *HPT*, 43; Mercer, 90; Allen, J., *AEPT*, 49; Faulkner, *AEPT*, 77. Again, the *ka* is the second material body or "double" that must be purified in order to receive the immortal *ba* or soul.

[4] Faulkner, *AEPT*, 38; Allen, T., *HPT*, 43; Mercer, 142; Allen, J., *AEPT*, 86.

Coincidentally, the time of Lazarus's period in the tomb is also *four days*: "Now when Jesus came, he found that Lazarus had already been in the tomb four days." (Jn 11:17; 11:38) As can be seen, there is good reason to assert that the raising of Lazarus represents a rehash of the resurrection of Osiris—and the parallels continue.

In *Monumental Christianity*, devout Christian antiquities expert and presbyter Rev. Dr. John P. Lundy (1823-1892) provides an image of Horus holding an ankh with "the Osiris" reclining on a couch, along with the caption, "Horus, with his Cross, Raising the Dead."[1] Lundy also comments:

> In all the representations of the resurrection of Lazarus on early Christian monuments, some of which are scattered through this volume, Lazarus is seen standing at the door of his tomb, like an Egyptian mummy; and Christ is touching him with a wand... This same wand is also seen in the hand of Christ when he turns the water into wine, and multiplies the bread in the wilderness. It must, therefore, have some significance, especially when applied to the mummy figure of Lazarus. That significance is nothing more or less than that of life-giving power, otherwise symbolized by the cross, which early Christianity did not use on her monuments...[2]

The contention that the cross was not represented in early Christianity may come as a surprise, but the fact remains that the cross held great significance in Pagan religion—including the Egyptian—long before Christ was purportedly crucified upon it. This pre-crucifixion significance of the cross is indicated by the peculiar remarks by Jesus in the gospel story itself: "...and he who does not take his cross and follow me is not worthy of me." (Mt 10:38) The Greek word here for cross is σταυρός or *stauros*, the same term used to describe both Horos the Cross and Christ's cross.

Again Dr. Lundy remarks upon the comparisons between the two scenes of Jesus and Horus raising the dead:

> In Denon's plate above, the dead man is the King, as appears from the pointed cap, crooks, and flagellum; and Horus is raising him up from death by his wand or cross, just as we see Christ doing the same thing in the same way to Lazarus, in our Christian monuments.[3]

As the "dead man" is also the Osiris, even in imagery we find the Christian myth reproducing the Egyptian one, with art depicting Christ raising Lazarus from the dead in the same manner as Horus resurrecting Osiris. The connection between the two could scarcely be clearer, and it would be reasonable and logical to conclude that the entire episode of Lazarus comes straight out of Egyptian mythology, with little change.

Lundy concludes his analysis with more important observations:

[1] Lundy, 403.
[2] Lundy, 402.
[3] Lundy, 405.

Horus is thus represented as a cross-like, young, mummy figure, because he is the life-giving power of the sun, using his cross to produce life and joy; and he is thus a type of Christ, in His greater conflict with sin, Satan, and death, and His triumph through the Cross.[1]

In this pithy paragraph, Lundy has described Horus in *cruciform*, or in the shape of a cross, in other words, "hung on the cross," validating the Horos-as-Cross connection of the Gnostics previously discussed. The Egyptian god is the "life giver," and Lundy further acknowledges that Horus is the *sun*—"using his cross to produce life and joy!" Lundy has no problem identifying Horus as a *"type of Christ,"* in an act seemingly designed to maintain his faith by assuring that, while these obvious parallels are very real and significant, Jesus ranked as "the real thing," fulfilling a sort of "prophecy" in the appearance of Horus in Egyptian mythology. Fortunately, Lundy—an admirable and erudite scholar whose work remains worthy of studying—did not *deny* the blatant correspondences between Christianity and the religion and mythology of other cultures, including Egypt. Nor did he argue that Paganism borrowed these substantially alike motifs *from* Christianity.

Adding to the obvious correlations between the raising of Osiris by Horus and that of Lazarus by Jesus, at the scene of the Egyptian god's resurrection appear his two sisters, deemed *Merta* in the Book of the Dead,[2] precisely as Lazarus's sisters, *Mary* and *Martha*, were present at *his* resurrection. In BD 37, these two sister goddesses are expressed by the hieroglyphs for Isis and Nephthys, with the word "Merta" meaning "two eyes,"[3] as in *eyewitnesses*. As Renouf says, "Merta...is the name given to the goddess pair Isis and Nephthys."[4] In the Pyramid Texts (PT 619:1750c/M 399), the two sisters are depicted thus: "Isis weeps for thee; Nephthys calls thee,"[5] referring to their dead brother Osiris, much like Mary and Martha mourning for their brother, Lazarus. At CT Sp. 345, the Horus-priest says to the deceased, "Those who wept for Osiris will weep for you on that day of the fourth-day festival,"[6] reflecting the sisters' role is an ongoing ritual that must have been fairly commonly known.

In PT 357:584a-c/T 146, Osiris's sisters, Isis and Nephthys protect the king, as Osiris, and give him to Horus to resurrect.[7] In the

---

[1] Lundy, 405.
[2] Renouf, *EBD*, 13, 85.
[3] Renouf, *EBD*, 85. Budge (*BD*, cxiv) transliterates this term as "Merti," while Birch calls them "Asps" (Bunsen/Birch, 192), and Faulkner (104) deems them "Songstress-snakes." In chapter 37, they are considered "terrible sister-serpents" who need to warded off. Dr. Allen calls them "*mrty*-snakes." (Allen, T., *BD*, 45.)
[4] Renouf, *EBD*, 113.
[5] Mercer, 266; Allen, J., *AEPT*, 235; Faulkner, *AEPT*, 257.
[6] Faulkner, *AECT*, I, 280. In this text, the aggrieved also mourn a "six-day festival." (CT Sp. 345.)
[7] Allen, T., *HPT*, 41; Faulkner, *AEPT*, 115; Mercer, 120; Allen, J., *AEPT*, 73.

gospel story, Mary and Martha throw themselves upon Jesus, begging him to raise their brother. After Osiris is risen his two sisters say, "Our brother comes to us" (PT 606:1696a-c/M 336).[1] Of course, Mary and Martha likewise rejoice in their brother coming back to *them* as well.

In PT 676:2008a-2009d/N 411, a "resurrection" text, we find again the deceased/Osiris being called forth by his two sisters:

> Collect thy bones; arrange thy limbs; shake off thy dust; untie thy bandages. The tomb is open for thee; the double doors of the coffin are undone for thee; the double doors of heaven are open for thee. "Hail," says Isis; "(come) in peace," says Nephthys, when they see their brother at the feast of Atum.[2]

While Isis and Nephthys thus partake in a feast associated with the resurrection of Osiris, after Lazarus's resurrection, Jesus goes to the house of Lazarus, Mary and Martha for a feast. (Jn 12:2)

Furthermore, while Lazarus's sister Mary is depicted as wiping Jesus's feet with her hair (Jn 11:2; 12:3; Lk 7:38), in BD 17, the deceased/Osiris is portrayed as "found with [sister Isis's] hair spread over him."[3] BD 164 refers to "the Goddess joined unto life with flowing hair,"[4] while the very bandages with which the deceased is wrapped, the ties binding the deceased to Earth, are termed the "tresses of Nephthys" or "locks of Nephthys" (P 526/PT 553:1363c).[5] The tresses, locks or hair of both Isis and Nephthys are referred to repeatedly in the Coffin Texts, such as in CT Sp. 168.[6] Indeed, in CT Sp. 317, the Osiris mentions "my women with braided hair,"[7] presumably a reference to Isis and Nephthys. We also find reference in CT Sp. 405 to the "Braided tress of Isis."[8] In CT Sp. 562 mention is made of the "hair of Isis" being "knotted to the hair of Nephthys..."[9] Moreover, the goddess Hathor is said to be "the lady of good things, whose tresses are anointed with fragrant myrrh,"[10] while in a hymn at Esne, Neith is depicted with hair that "exudes the fragrance of fresh myrrh."[11] Myrrh is in fact a special substance revered for its mummification properties; it is also a gift traditionally given to

---

[1] Faulkner, *AEPT*, 251; Mercer, 259; Allen, J., *AEPT*, 227.
[2] Mercer, 298; Allen, J., *AEPT*, 276; Faulkner, *AEPT*, 289.
[3] Budge, *TBD*, 54, 290: "The Osiris Ani is safely guarded. He is Isis, and he is found with [her] hair spread over him." Faulkner (pl. 10) translates this passage somewhat differently, with the speaker in the first person—"I am Isis..."—such that it is her hair on *herself*, rather than the hair of Isis on the Osiris. Allen renders it : " '[I] LET MY [HAIR] DOWN OVER MY FACE IN DISORDER SO THAT MY PARTING WAS MUSSED,' means when Isis was hiding; then she wiped [her] hair." (Allen, T., *BD*, 32.)
[4] Budge, *BD* (1898), 430.
[5] Allen, J., *AEPT*, 187; Mercer, 220.
[6] Faulkner, *AECT*, I, 145. See also CT Sp. 219. (Faulkner, *AECT*, I, 174.)
[7] Faulkner, *AECT*, I, 242.
[8] Faulkner, *AECT*, II, 54.
[9] Faulkner, *AECT*, II, 169.
[10] Žabkar, 111.
[11] Žabkar, 113.

the sun. Interestingly, also in the gospel story (Mt 26:7;
find a woman with an "alabaster box" containing
washing Jesus's feet with her tears and wiping them '
Concerning the gospel story, professor of Hebrew and J
at New York University Dr. Lawrence H. Schiffman comments that
such behavior would have been viewed as "bizarre" in the Jewish
world of the time. This oddity may thus be explained not as a
"historical event" but as a *mythical motif* based on Egyptian religion.

In addition, like Jesus, Osiris is also depicted as having his feet
washed with water, with foot-washing considered a sacred rite in
Egypt as well as in Israel, including when done to the disciples by
Jesus himself.[1] (Jn 13:4-14) The fact that this pericope appears only
in John constitutes cause, once again, for us to consider that the
foot-wiping and washing was an important part of the Egyptian ritual
that passed into Christianity.

Moreover, the raising of Lazarus with his sister Mary and Martha
as two witnesses or "two *eyes*" takes place in Beth-any—*Bethania*
(Βηθανία) in the Greek and *Beit-Anyah* in the Aramaic, meaning
"house of dates" or "house of misery"[2]—which appears to be
equivalent to the Egyptian "House of Anu." The Book of the Dead
discusses the "house of the great god in Heliopolis" or *Annu*, as that
city was called in Egyptian.[3] Annu is the "celestial On or Heliopolis,"
the city of the sun, as well as "the capital of the mythological world."[4]
In BD 89, Annu is "the land wherein are thousands of reunions,"[5]
referring to the souls in the afterlife reuniting with their *kas*. In BD
57, the Osiris says, "I rest in Annu,"[6] where he goes to be
resurrected: "Every good Egyptian that died was believed to be
assimilated to Osiris, to go the dark journey, and have his
resurrection in Annu in like manner."[7] In addition to this reunion in
the afterlife comes another with the deceased's loved ones, as
typically perceived within Christianity but which existed within the
Egyptian religion beginning with the introduction of the Coffin Texts
during the third millennium BCE.[8]

In addition, the "great sanctuary" at Annu is called *Het-Saru*—
"House of the Prince."[9] Concerning this motif, Massey remarks:

---

[1] See BD 17: "Thou washest they feet in bowls of silver..." (Allen, T., *BD*, 180.)
[2] Strong's G963.
[3] Renouf, *EBD*, 152.
[4] Budge, *BD* (2003), 25.
[5] Renouf, *EBD*, 158; Faulkner, *EBD*, pl. 17. Faulkner terms it the "land of thousands of abodes," but the "heavenly" context remains apparent, as Faulkner's rendering of the title is "Chapter for letting a soul rejoin its corpse in the God's Domain." Allen calls it "land where<in> are thousands of joined ones." (Allen, T., *BD*, 74.)
[6] See Massey, *AELW*, II, 845; Bunsen/Birch, 204; Faulkner, *EBD*, 105; Allen, T., *BD*, 54.
[7] St. Clair, 202.
[8] Hornung, *AEBA*, 9.
[9] Renouf, *EBD*, 6.

The house of Osiris in Annu was called Hat-Saru, the house of the Prince—that is, the abode of Horus when he came to raise Osiris from the tomb. It was the sanctuary of Osiris who was attended by the two Mertae or Merti, the pair of divine sisters better known by the names of Isis and Nephthys.[1]

Hence, while Lazarus is raised at Bethany, the "house of Anyah," Osiris is resurrected in the "House of Annu."

The correspondences continue, with Lazarus and Osiris even sharing the same name, as explained in my book *Who Was Jesus? Fingerprints of The Christ*:

> The Greek name "Lazarus" or "Lazaros" equals "Eleazar" in Hebrew and, per Strong's [Concordance] (G2976), means "whom God helps." It is a strange coincidence firstly that the person whom Jesus resurrects happens to be named "whom God helps," and secondly that "Eleazar"—or, breaking down its original components in Hebrew, El-Azar—closely resembles a combination of the Semitic word for God, "El," with the Egyptian name for Osiris, "Ausar." Interestingly, there exists an ancient Phoenician inscription called "the Carpentras" that does indeed identify Osiris with the Semitic god "El" or "Elohim," calling him "Osiris-Eloh."[2]

Regarding "El Osiris," Albert Ross Parsons remarks:

> ...El Osiris in another form is L'Azarus, an account of whose death and resurrection occur in the gospel of John, where the Lord Jesus personates the central sun which restored to life El Osiris...[3]

In addition, the word *el* or *al* in Arabic means "the"; hence, "El-Azar-us" would be equivalent to "the Osiris," which is in fact the frequent name of the deceased yearning to be resurrected. Verifying this fact, the village in Judea where the Lazarus miracle supposedly took place, Bethany, today is called in Arabic *"El Azarieh."*[4]

Nor are the funerary texts the only place where we find correspondences between Osiris and Lazarus, as there were other characters by these names in both Egyptian and Christian legend. For example, referring to one of the "magical tales" found in the British Museum Papyrus DCIV, containing "the story of the birth and childhood of Se-Osiris (son of Osiris) the son of Kha-m-muas,"[5] Boscawen comments:

> The part which describes the visit of Se-Osiris and his father to Amenti contains a curious parable resembling that of the "Rich man and Lazarus," again in touch with St. Luke, and also teaching as to the judgment and future life quite different from the ordinary eschatology of the Egyptians.[6]

---

[1] Massey, *AELW*, II, 845.
[2] Murdock, *WWJ*, 234. See Heath, 92; Genesis 3:21, et al.
[3] Parsons, A., 187.
[4] Parsons, A., 190; Rousseau, 15; Davies, W.D., 143.
[5] Davis, 308.
[6] Davis, 311.

Performing Miracles

This comparison refers to the story of the poor man Lazarus in the gospel of Luke (16:20-25), a pericope apparently also taken from Egyptian legend. Concerning this Lukan pericope, Egyptologist Dr. Maspero states:

> We remember in the *Gospel according to St. Luke* the rich man, clothed in purple and fine linen, who feasted sumptuously every day, while at his gate lay Lazarus full of sores and desiring in vain to be fed with the crumbs that fell from the rich man's table. "And it came to pass that the beggar died and was carried by the angels into Abraham's bosom, and the rich man also died and was buried; and in hell he lift up his eyes, being in torments, and seeth Abraham afar off and Lazarus in his bosom." In the second romance of Satni-Khamois, we read an Egyptian version of this parable of the Evangelist, but there it is dramatised and amalgamated with another popular conception, that of the descent of a living man into hell.[1]

As can be seen, the Egyptian influence in the gospels appears to be solid, although Maspero—a sincere Christian—wishes to place the "borrowing" at the foot of the Pagans, falling in with his religious devotion but not the scientific evidence.

Upon scientific scrutiny, it appears that some of the ancient Egyptian texts were directly influential on biblical passages, particularly in John's gospel, such as the following.

Egyptian Texts	Gospel of John (KJV)
[The Osiris]...was born in Heliopolis [Annu]...[2] (PT 307:483a/W 212) [The Osiris is] anointed with the best ointment...[3] (PT 576:1511a/P 518) Behold this King, his feet are kissed by the pure waters...[4] (PT 685: 2065a/N 519)	Now a certain [man] was sick, [named] Lazarus, of Bethany, the town of Mary and her sister Martha. (It was [that] Mary which anointed the Lord with ointment, and wiped his feet with her hair... (Jn 11:2)
Two sisters, Isis and Nephthys, come to thee; they hasten to the place in which thou art.[5] (PT 593:1630a-b/M 206)	Therefore his sisters sent unto him, saying, Lord, behold, he whom thou lovest is sick. (Jn 11:3)

---

[1] Maspero, *PSAE*, xv.
[2] Mercer, 105; Allen, J., *AEPT*, 58; Faulkner, *AEPT*, 95.
[3] Mercer, 238; Allen, J., *AEPT*, 182; Faulkner, *AEPT*, 231.
[4] Mercer, 304; Allen, J., *AEPT*, 291; Faulkner, *AEPT*, 295. The "waters" here are the semen of Shu and the discharge from Tefnut, obviously differing from the gospel story. It should be kept in mind that the contention is not that the Christian copyists reproduced the texts identically but that they borrowed what suited them, according to their more stoic Jewish background.
[5] Mercer, 250-251; Allen, J., *AEPT*, 217; Faulkner, *AEPT*, 244.

an Texts	Gospel of John (KJV)
ris the King, you have gone, but you will return, you have slept, [but you will awake], you have died, but you will live."[1] (PT 670:1975a-b/N 348)	These things said he: and after that he saith unto them, Our friend Lazarus sleepeth; but I go, that I may awake him out of sleep.... Then said Jesus unto them plainly, Lazarus is dead. (Jn 11:11-14)
I am...the Lord of Resurrections, who cometh forth from the dusk and whose birth from the House of Death.[2] (BD 64)	Jesus said unto her, I am the resurrection, and the life: he that believeth in me, though he were dead, yet shall he live... (Jn 11:25)
...as the mourning-women of Osiris call for thee.[3] (PT 667a:1947b/Nt 243) Isis weeps for thee; Nephthys calls thee....[4] (PT 619:1750c-1751a/M 399)	And when she had so said, she went her way, and called Mary her sister secretly, saying, The Master is come, and calleth for thee.... When Jesus therefore saw her weeping... (Jn 11:28, 33)
The tomb is open for thee; the double doors of the coffin are undone for thee...[5] (PT 676:2009a/N 411) Flesh of [the Osiris], rot not, decay not, let not thy smell be bad.[6] (PT 412:722a-b/T 228) Horus has exterminated the evil which was in [the Osiris] in his four day (term)...[7] (PT 419:746b/T 225)	Jesus therefore again groaning in himself cometh to the grave. It was a cave, and a stone lay upon it. Jesus said, Take ye away the stone. Martha, the sister of him that was dead, saith unto him, Lord, by this time he stinketh: for he hath been [dead] four days. (Jn 11:38-39)

---

[1] Faulkner, *AEPT*, 285; Mercer, 294; Allen, J., *AEPT*, 267.
[2] Renouf, *EBD*, 118; Allen, T., *BD*, 56; Faulkner, EBD, 106; Bunsen/Birch, 206.
[3] Mercer, 290; Allen, J., *AEPT*, 325; Faulkner, *AEPT*, 281.
[4] Mercer, 266; Allen, J., *AEPT*, 235; Faulkner, *AEPT*, 257.
[5] Mercer, 298; Allen, J., *AEPT*, 276; Faulkner, *AEPT*, 289.
[6] Mercer, 139; Allen, J., *AEPT*, 86; Faulkner, *AEPT*, 135.
[7] Mercer, 143; Allen, J., *AEPT*, 86; Faulkner, *AEPT*, 138.

Egyptian Texts	Gospel of John (KJV)
I am Horus, Osiris N., I will not let thee sicken. Come forth, awake, I will avenge thee.[1] (PT 620:1753a-b/N 11) Let them who are in their graves, arise; let them undo their bandages.[2] (PT 662:1878a/N 388) O N., live, thou shalt not die. Horus comes to thee; he separates thy bandages; he casts off thy bonds.[3] (PT 703:2201c-2202a/N 615)	And when he thus had spoken, he cried with a loud voice, Lazarus, come forth. And he that was dead came forth, bound hand and foot with graveclothes: and his face was bound about with a napkin. Jesus saith unto them, Loose him, and let him go. (Jn 11:43-44)

In the story of Osiris, Isis and Horus we find a plethora of miracles, including the standard fare as in the New Testament regarding Jesus Christ. These *Egyptian* miracles include commanding water, healing the sick and raising the dead. The raising of Osiris by Horus, in fact, so resembles the tale of Lazarus's resurrection by Jesus that we may logically conclude that the latter was derived from the former. Indeed, the very language of the story of Lazarus appears to have been taken directly from ancient Egyptian writings such as the Pyramid Texts and Book of the Dead.

In the end, there is little unique about Christ's miracles that, even if they could be demonstrated to have happened and did not reside in the realm of myth, would serve to prove Christianity any more "real" than the many other religions both ancient and modern that likewise insist upon multitudes of miracles that "truly happened."

---

[1] Mercer, 266; Allen, J., *AEPT*, 242; Faulkner, *AEPT*, 257.
[2] Mercer, 280; Allen, J., *AEPT*, 272; Faulkner, *AEPT*, 272.
[3] Mercer, 318; Allen, J., *AEPT*, 303; Faulkner, *AEPT*, 306-307.

Horus resurrecting the Deceased/Osiris using the Cross of
Eternal Life.
(Lundy, *Monumental Christianity*, 403)

"The Truth, The Light and The Good Shepherd"

"While we have various representations of Osiris, he mainly comes before us in a celestial and a terrestrial form. He is in heaven, and yet he was on earth.

"In heaven—or, rather, in the spiritual existence—he is the *Absolute*, the *All*. He is styled on monuments, 'Lord of life'; 'Lord of ages'; 'Light of the world'; 'Dispenser of nourishment'; 'King of gods'; 'Creator of gods'; 'Nameless One'; 'Opener of truth'; 'Full of goodness and trust'; 'Eternal One'; 'Supreme Being'; 'Glorified One'; 'Lord of Heaven'; 'Rule of eternity'; 'Beholder of good,' etc."

James Bonwick, *Egyptian Belief and Modern Thought* (153)

"The very first of the chief epithets applied to Horus in...his third great office has a startlingly Christian sound; it is the 'Sole begotten Son of the Father,' to which, in other texts, is added, 'Horus the Holy Child,' the 'Beloved son of his father.' The Lord of Life, the Giver of Life [are also] both very usual epithets...the 'Justifier of the Righteous,' the 'Eternal King' and the 'Word of the Father Osiris.' There were other names which we are expressly told in the sacred texts no man knew but himself, no ear had ever heard, no tongue had ever spoken—names so awful an import that if pronounced they would arrest the sun in his career, control the powers of hell, and threaten the duration of the universe itself....

"The publication of more recently translated texts in the volumes of the 'Records of the Past,' and some yet unpublished texts, which by the courtesy of the editors I am permitted to cite, have proven that very many of the essential names and attributes of Horus were attributed to Ra, Tum, and the other deities also, they were alike 'self-created,' 'born of a Virgin,' 'deliverers of mankind,' 'only begotten sons...'"

W.R. Cooper, *The Horus Myth in Its Relation to Christianity* (22, 76-77)

As is the case with so much of Christian ideology, many sacred epithets attached to Jesus were previously associated with the highly revered Egyptian deities Re, Osiris, Isis and Horus, among others. Since the Egyptian gods and goddesses are frequently interchangeable, a number of writers have taken the liberty to incorporate the epithets as applied to Osiris or Re, for example, into their comparative analysis of Horus with Jesus. Although, again, this type of synopsis may not be not found in this exact manner previously, the bottom line is that these many characteristics *were* in existence for centuries to millennia before the purported advent of Christ. Hence, Jesus Christ is simply not the unique "son of God" and "one true God" whom he is alleged to be. The point of this edification is that many people remain unaware of these facts regarding the worship and religiosity of prior, so-called Pagan cultures, which ignorance creates a needless amount of disparagement and divisiveness. Contrary to what is regularly taught in the name of Jesus Christ, the ancients

possessed many of the germane and significant concepts within
Christianity, and the derision of the cultures and religions of other
places and eras is unnecessary and unwarranted. Indeed, such an
attitude has allowed for the massive and tragic destruction of
cultures around the world for centuries. Regardless of this
disparagement, however, the profound reverence of the Egyptian
religion extended to various sacred epithets, some of which we have
already seen, such as Isis being called "Healer" and "Savior" centuries
before the common era. Other epithets of Isis are recounted by Dr. M.
Eugene Boring, a professor of New Testament at Texas Christian
University:

> The "Hymn to Isis" had a long list of self-affirmations by the goddess:
> "I am the eldest daughter of Time.... I am wife and sister of King
> Osiris.... I am she that riseth in the dog star.... I am the Queen of
> War.... I am the Queen of the Thunderbolt.... I am the Lord of
> rainstorms." People are aware that there is a mysterious power in the
> storm and everywhere in nature; Isis says, "I am," "That's me."[1]

Isis is not only "savior" but also essentially the "alpha and
omega," among many other roles and epithets previously mentioned
such as "Mother of God," "Queen of Heaven," "Star of the Sea," etc.
Naturally, many other gods and goddesses of Egypt were revered in
like manner, including and especially Osiris and his son, Horus.

Lord of Truth and Good Shepherd

As we have previously seen, according to the hymns some 1,400
years before the purported advent of Christ, the sun is the "unique
shepherd, who protects his flock,"[2] also serving as a "savior." In the
Coffin Texts appears another mention of the Egyptian god as "savior,"
as in CT Sp. 155, in which the speaker specifically defines himself as
a god and also says, "Open to me, for I am a saviour..."[3] In CT Sp.
847, the deceased—who at times is Osiris and/or Horus—is the
"Saviour-god."[4] As a protector like both Re and Isis, Osiris too may be
deemed "Savior of mankind," per his role as outlined by Plutarch (13,
356B):

> One of the first acts related of Osiris in his reign was to deliver the
> Egyptians from their destitute and brutish manner of living. This he
> did by showing them the fruits of cultivation, by giving them laws,
> and by teaching them to honour the gods. Later he travelled over the
> whole earth civilizing it without the slightest need of arms, but most
> of the peoples he won over to his way by the charm of his persuasive
> discourse combined with song and all manner of music. Hence the
> Greeks came to identify him with Dionysus.[5]

---

[1] Boring, 309-310.
[2] Assman, *ESRNK*, 86.
[3] Faulkner, *AECT*, I, 133.
[4] Faulkner, *AECT*, III, 32.
[5] Plutarch/Babbitt, 35.

"The Truth, The Light and The Good Shepherd"

Concerning Osiris's savior role, Morenz remarks that the god is "the ideal of salvation, first of the king and then of all the dead..."[1]

Plutarch (54, 373A) also relates that the Egyptians "have a legend that the soul of Osiris is everlasting and imperishable."[2] As noted, Osiris is called the "Lord of Resurrections," among many other divine and kingly epithets, including "Lord of life."[3] BD 17—which Budge labels "one of the most valuable and important Chapters of the Book of the Dead"[4]—opens with "the Osiris" making the statement: "I am He who closeth, and He who openeth, and I am but One. I am Ra at his first appearance."[5] Faulkner translates the same quote by "the Lord of All" as, "I was Atum when I was alone in the Primordial Waters; I was Re in his glorious appearings when he began to rule what he had made."[6] Renouf compares these statements with Revelation 1:8: "I am the Alpha and the Omega."[7] Another noteworthy scripture appears in CT Sp. 98, in which the speaker announces, "I am tomorrow and the Lord of yesterday."[8] Concerning this beginning-end correlation, Anthes raises a certain Pyramid Text:

> "The mother of NN [the deceased] was pregnant with him who was in the Naunet. NN was given birth by his father Atum before heaven came into being, before earth came into being, before mankind (*rmṯ*) came into being, before the gods were born, before death came into being."[9]

This passage is reminiscent of Christ's purported eternal pre-existence.

Also, in the famous chapter 125 of the Book of the Dead the deceased addresses Osiris as the "Lord of Truth," "Lord of the Two Truths," "Great God, the Lord of Right and Truth."[10] Moreover, in hieroglyphs at Thebes, as well as in ancient Greek texts, the father god Ptah, the "demiurgos, or creative power of the Deity," likewise is

---

[1] Morenz, 191.
[2] Plutarch/Babbitt, 131.
[3] Budge, *OER*, II, 16.
[4] Budge, *BD* (1899), xcvii.
[5] Renouf, *EBD*, 35. Birch renders the passage thus: "I AM Tum, the only being in Nu [the firmament]. I am the Sun when he rises. His rule commences when he has done so." (Bunsen/Birch, 172.) Budge's translation is: "I am the god Tmu in [my] rising; I am the Only One. I came into existence in Nu.... I am Ra who rose in the beginning. [He hath rule that which he made.]" (Budge, *EBD* (1967), 281.) Budge also translates it as: "I am Tem in rising. I am the only One. I came into being in Nu. I am Ra who rose in the beginning, the ruler of what he made." (Budge, *BD* (1899), xcvii.). Allen's rendition is: "(All was) mine when (I) existed alone in the Deep; (I was) Re at (his) dawnings when he began his reign." (Allen, T., *BD*, 27.)
[6] Faulkner, *EBD*, pl. 7.
[7] Renouf, *EBD*, 42.
[8] Faulkner, *AECT*, I, 97.
[9] Anthes, 173.
[10] Faulkner, *EBD*, pl. 30; Allen, T., *BD*, 97; Budge, *EBD* (1967), 345, citing Naville's "*Todtenbuch*, Bd., I., Bl. 133." See also Assman, *ESRNK*, 124.

l of Truth,"[1] while in some instances, the Lord of Truth is
oth,[2] as well as Ra/Re, the "lord of maat."[3]

142 appears a long "List of the Forms and Shrines of
Osiris, ith over 140 epithets for the god, including the "Protector"
or "Shepherd"—*Asar-Saa*.[4] The sun god Re too was the "good
shepherd,"[5] and Horus's "Good Shepherd" role is made clear in the
Pyramid Texts as well, for example, at PT 690:2106a-b/N 524: "O
King, stand up for Horus, that he may make you a spirit and guide
you when you ascend to the sky."[6]

"Horus," in other words, the king, is called "the good shepherd"
also in the third inscription at the Temple of "Redesiyeh" or *El-
Radesia* at Wady Abad, near Edfu in Upper Egypt.[7] As Lundy says, "
"The royal Good Shepherd is the antitype of Horus..."[8] The idea of the
Horus-king as the "good shepherd," in fact, was so important that it
constituted a major shift in perception and public policy,
representing the general mentality of the 11th and 12th Dynasties (c.
2050-1800 BCE). As remarked upon by Egyptologist Dr. John A.
Wilson, a director of the Oriental Institute at the University of
Chicago, "The concept of the good shepherd rather than the distant
and lordly owner of the flocks shifted the idea of kingship from
possession as a right to responsibility as a duty."[9]

Sin Bearer and Redeemer

Another title that could be applied to Osiris is "sin bearer,"
because upon his death he "adopted the burden of the sins of the
dead."[10] As McClintock and Strong say:

> Osiris seems to have been finally revived, and to have become the
> judge of...Hades, presiding at the final judgment of souls in the hall
> of the two Truths, with the forty-two demons who presided over the
> capital sins, and awarding to the soul its final destiny.[11]

As also revealed in BD 125, the deceased is to be judged in the
Hall of the Two Truths, by declaring he has avoided various sins.
Regarding BD 125 and the notion of sin in the Egyptian religion,
Morenz remarks:

---

[1] Wilkinson, *MCAE*, III, 15.
[2] Maspero, *PSAE*, 63; Rawlinson, *HAE*, 372.
[3] Morenz, 130.
[4] Budge, *OER*, II, 16; Allen, T., *BD*, 118-119; Bunsen/Birch, 276-279.
[5] Hopkins, 337.
[6] Faulkner, *AEPT*, 299; Mercer, 308; Allen, J., *AEPT*, 295.
[7] Breasted, *ARE*, III, 86.
[8] Lundy, 403.
[9] Wilson, J., 120; see 125ff.
[10] *Iraq*, 207.
[11] McClintock, 469.

"The Truth, The Light and The Good Shepherd"

The statements of innocence in Chapter 125 of the Book of the Dead, which at first sight seem to show that Egyptians had no sense of sin, in fact demonstrate the opposite, if one interprets them correctly.[1]

As we have seen, much else in the Book of the Dead exists in order to purify the Osiris, such as is expressed at BD 30B, which essentially opens the sacred text: "The vindicated Osiris Ani is straightforward, he has no sin, there is no accusation against him before us..."[2] If the deceased were found unworthy, he could be sent back to earth as a pig, whereas those whose sins were redeemable would take part in the Resurrection. Indeed, in the Coffin Texts appears a suggestion of the miracle of Jesus driving the demons into the swine and killing them (Mt 8:32; Mk 5:13; Lk 8:33), in a spell (CT Sp. 440) entitled, "Spell for Driving off Pigs."[3]

These various concepts are not overt in the Jewish religion, but they do thus rank as salient within the Egyptian religion, and it is likely from there that Christianity got them, rather than from Judaism. In the sense that the deceased counted on Osiris's resurrection to produce his own immortality, it could be said that Osiris died for the sins of mankind.

Moreover, it is Horus who introduces the deceased to Osiris in the Judgment Hall or Hall of the Two Truths and who pleads on the Osiris's behalf for atonement of his sins: "Horus further transferred to the benefit of the deceased the various good offices which he had himself performed in behalf of his father, and more especially those ceremonial rites which were called the 'Assistances of Osiris.'"[4] Horus could thus be called "the Redeemer."

Osiris the Christ?

Not only is Osiris the "Lord of Truth," the "good shepherd" and "sin-bearer," but, as the "lord of the tomb," he was essentially also called "Christ," since one Egyptian term for "tomb," "funeral," "dead body" or "mummy" is *krst*, likewise transliterated as *krst, karast, qeres-t, qrs.t* and *qrst.* Concerning this term, Massey comments:

> We now proceed to show that Christ the anointed is none other than the Osiris-karast, and that the karast mummy risen to its feet as Osiris-sahu was the prototypal Christ. Unhappily these demonstrations cannot be made without a wearisome mass of detail.... Dr. Budge, in his book on the mummy, tells his readers that the Egyptian word for mummy is *ges,* which signifies to wrap up in bandages.... [The word] ges or kes, to embalm the corpse or make the mummy, is a reduced or abraded form of an earlier word, karas (whence krst for the mummy). The original word written in hieroglyphics is ⌒⇔⇒⌒ krst, whence kas, to embalm, to bandage, to

[1] Morenz, 133.
[2] Faulkner, *EBD,* pl. 3.
[3] Faulkner, *AECT,* 77.
[4] Cooper, *AD,* 238-239.

make the mummy or karast (Birch, *Dictionary of the* ⟨h⟩ics, pp. 415-416; Champollion, *Gram. Egyptienne*, 86). The ⟨ ⟩ denotes the embalmment of the mummy, and the krst, as the mummy, was made in the process of preparation by purifying, anointing, and embalming. To karas the dead body was to embalm it, to bandage it, to make the mummy. The mummy was the Osirian *Corpus Christi*, prepared for burial as the laid-out dead, the karast by name. When raised to its feet, it was the risen mummy, or sahu. The place of embalmment was likewise the krs. Thus the process of making the mummy was to karas, the place in which it was laid is the karas, and the product was the krst, whose image is the upright mummy=the risen Christ. Hence, the name of the Christ, Christos in Greek, Chrestus in Latin, for the anointed, was derived...from the Egyptian word krst....

Say what you will or believe what you may, there is no other origin for Christ the anointed than for Horus the karast or anointed son of god the father. There is no other origin for a Messiah as the anointed than for the Masu or anointed....[1]

Massey goes on to explain that the "anointed mummy" represents one of the Osirian *mysteries*, as we may have expected, and as we have also seen asserted by Cooper, for one, to incorporate a number of sacred epithets and "awful names." Massey further supplies two quotes from funereal texts provided by Birch, both of which contain the word *krast* in reference to Anubis, the embalmer:

We read in the funeral texts of Anup being "Suten tu hetep, Anup, neb tser khent neter to *krast*-ef em set." (Birch, *Funereal Text*, 4th Dynasty). "Suten hept tu Anup tep-tuf khen neter ha am ut neb tser *krast* ef em as-ef en kar neter em set Amenta" (Birch, *Funereal Stele of Ra-Khepr-Ka*, 12th Dynasty). Anup gives embalmment, krast; he is the lord over the place of embalmment, the kras; the lord of embalming (krast), who, so to say, makes the "krast."[2]

Indeed, in the Coffin Texts, Anubis is called *nb qrs.t* or "lord of the tomb."[3]

Digging into Massey's references for his assertion that Osiris too was essentially deemed "Christ" centuries prior to the purported existence of Jesus, we first find the pertinent *karast* hieroglyph in Champollion's *Grammaire Égyptienne* (IV, A, 80). The first four letters in this hieroglyph spell out ◿� (N29, D21, O34, X1) or *krst*—the transliteration also used by Drs. Collier and Manley[4]—with the last figure, the "determinatif," representing the standing mummy 𓀾 (A53). Champollion identifies this determinative hieroglyph as "Une momie" and gives the meaning of the hieroglyph as "Embaumement, action d'envelopper de bandelettes."[5] In other words, the *krst* hieroglyph,

---

[1] Massey, *AELW*, I, 218-219.
[2] Massey, *AELW*, I, 219.
[3] Loprieno, *AE*, 192.
[4] Collier, 160.
[5] Champollion, 160.

with the *mummy* determinative—a sign indicating the "general idea of the word"[1]—stands for embalmment and the action of wrapping in strips or bandages.

In exploring the works of Birch to find Massey's other reference, we discover an intriguing tale that sheds light on the development of Egyptology vis-à-vis the history of the hieroglyphic decipherment. In the "Introduction" to his *Egyptian Hieroglyphic Dictionary*, which he dedicated to Birch, Budge includes a long and complicated recounting of why Birch's very valuable *Dictionary of Hieroglyphics* was virtually impossible to find in Budge's time, just a couple of decades after it was published with great difficulty.

After the publication of Champollion's *Dictionnaire Égyptien* in 1841, Birch determined to organize and publish in a hieroglyphic dictionary every inscription in the British Museum, which he had previously faithfully recorded. Budge describes the atmosphere of the time:

> In those days no fount [font] of hieroglyphic type existed, and lithography was expensive, and publishers were not eager to spend their money on a dictionary of a language of which scarcely a dozen people in the whole world had any real knowledge. At length Messrs. William Allen & Co., of Leadenhall Street, London, were induced to consider the publication of a hieroglyphic dictionary, but they decided to issue first of all a few specimen pages, with a short Preface by Birch, with the view of finding out how far the work would be supported by the learned and the general public.[2]

The result was Birch's "Sketch of a Hieroglyphical Dictionary, Part I," which was very short and not the work to which Massey refers as a source for his remarks about *krst/karast/krast*.

As of 1847, when Birch informed Budge of his progress in publishing the dictionary, there remained no font for the hieroglyphs. Birch's *Dictionary of Hieroglyphics* was finally published in 1867, buried in the fifth volume of the English translation of Bunsen's Egyptian chronology called *Aegyptens Stelle in der Weltgeschichte*, titled in English, *Egypt's Place in Universal History*. Unfortunately, Bunsen had died seven years earlier, and the interest in his work had waned, to the point where the fifth volume of the English translation garnered little interest, and Birch's Dictionary, published within this volume of Bunsen, basically failed with it. In fact, Budge implies that he never saw a copy of the print edition, and states that the publishers "'disposed' of the sheets of a large number of copies."[3]

Since no one republished Birch's hieroglyphic dictionary, for a long time it survived only in bits and pieces that were copied by other scholars. Although the book became extremely scarce to the point where it was all but lost outside of major collections, we are fortunate

[1] Allen, J., *ME*, 3.
[2] Budge, *EHD*, xvii.
[3] Budge, *EHD*, xxxviii.

that it is available today as a computer file. Having the electronic book now in my possession, I can verify that, once again, Gerald Massey cited his material properly. This text is very important, because it proves that Massey is correct in his contentions and did not innovate his transliteration and definition of the Egyptian words *karas, kras* and *karas-t, kars.t* or *krst*, etc., the latter group meaning, "embalmment" and, importantly, "*mummy*," as found on pp. 415-416 of Birch's dictionary, precisely as Massey stated.

Verifying these assertions, in *The Mummy*, regarding the word *qes*, meaning "to wrap up in bandages," Budge says, "But *qes* may be a shortened form of *qeres*, ◁⟨▭, which generally means the mummy and coffin and all the funerary equipment."[1] According to Budge's *Book of the Dead*, *qeres* may also be translated as "buried,"[2] while in his *Egyptian Hieroglyphic Dictionary*, the British scholar defines *qeres* as "to wrap a dead body in cloth and make it ready for burial"[3] or "to wrap up in bandages," in other words, *to mummify*.[4] Budge transliterates *karast* as *qeres-t*, meaning "funeral, burial, sepulture, funeral bier, a happy burial."[5] Anything that is buried, such as the "funerary equipment" and the mummy, could thus be *qeres-t*. In his book *Middle Egyptian*, James Allen prefers *qrs* as the transliteration of the Egyptian term for "to bury," while the burial or buried object is *qrst*.[6] In the Beinlich Wordlist it is *qrs.t*, while Faulkner chooses *krst*, also defining it as "burial."[7]

As we have seen, the hieroglyph in question, *karast/qeres.t/ qrs.t/ḳrst*, is composed of the signs ◁▭▭, qualified by different signs as "determinatives," including a coffin ▭ (Q6)[8] and a standing mummy ⌐, the latter of which, as James Allen relates, indicates a *mummy*.[9]

Obviously, this situation is complicated, as there are a number of hieroglyphs that represent the same sound and meaning, as well as those that sound alike and seem to be related but that have a slightly to somewhat different meaning. It is also possible that the identification of the *ḳrst* specifically as a mummy/embalmment represented a *mystery*, as indicated by Massey. The fact that the sign ◁ (N29)—the "k," "q" or "ḳ"—is pronounced like a Greek "chi" (x), which is the first letter in "Christos," lends credence to Massey's thesis of *Ḳrst* serving as the origin of *Christ*.

---

[1] Budge, *Mummy* (2003), 203.
[2] Budge, *EBD* (1967), 152.
[3] Budge, *EHD*, 776.
[4] Budge, *Mummy* (2003), 203.
[5] Budge, *EHD*, 777.
[6] Allen, J., *ME*, 358, 443, 491. See Woodard, 205; Loprieno, *AEL*, 44.
[7] Faulkner, *CDME*, 281.
[8] Allen, J., *ME*, 439.
[9] Allen, J., *ME*, 425.

In BD 17, we find the combination *qeres Ausar* meaning the "sarcophagus of Osiris" or "tomb of Osiris,"[1] also transliterated as *qrs.t Wsir.*[2] Also verifying Massey, who says that Osiris is called *neb-karast*, Budge informs us of the phrase *neb qeres*—"the lord of the sarcophagus."[3] In the mortuary literature, including the Coffin Texts, we find reference to *nb qrs.t*, or "lord of the tomb"[4] and, *specifically as concerns Osiris*, "lord of the funeral."[5] In *Lexikon der ägyptischen Götter und Götterbezeichnungen*, Dr. Christian Leitz of the University of Tübingen also lists several instances of *nb ḵrst.*[6] *Ḵrst* or *qrs.t* is therefore an epithet or title of Osiris—a highly important point that cannot be overemphasized.

Adding to this significant development, the *ḵrst/qrst* is that which is buried and, in the case of the dead body/mummy, embalmed. What does it mean to embalm a body? In the ancient Egyptian process of embalming, several different materials were used, including natron, a salt that desiccated the flesh. Other substances such as spices, oils and ointments were also utilized, as we find in the New Testament concerning the burial of Jesus: Just like the Osiris, Jesus's body was wrapped in linen, after which "Mary Magdalene, and Mary the mother of James, and Salome, bought spices, so that they might go and anoint him."[7] (Mk 15:46, 16:1) To cover someone with these substances is thus "to anoint." Hence, it could be said that a human *qeres.t/karast/qrs.t/ḵrst*, i.e., a *mummy*, would be "anointed," as related in the article "Egyptian Mummification":

> Mummification may have included anointing the body with fragrant gum-resins (frankincense and myrrh) and various oils and fats (cedar oil, ox fat and ointments) as a religious ceremony between the end of embalming and the beginning of wrapping. This process is mentioned in several late Egyptian papyri.

This paragraph is noteworthy not only for the *anointing* as part of the mummification process, but also for the use of *frankincense* and *myrrh* as the anointing spices, both of which are named as two of the three gifts presented to the baby Jesus in the gospel of Matthew (2:11). The other gift, gold, is a well-known symbol of the *sun*. In the rubric to BD 125, the deceased—as Osiris—is anointed with myrrh as part of the preparation for his resurrection.[8] Concerning myrrh and other material, Žabkar remarks:

---

[1] Budge, *EBD* (1967), 50; Faulkner, *EBD*, pl. 10; Allen, T., *BD*, 31.
[2] Backes, 284.
[3] Budge, *FSE*, 258.
[4] Loprieno, *AE*, 192.
[5] *Wiener Zeitschrift für die Kunde des Morgenlandes*, 219.
[6] Leitz, 226.
[7] RSV. See also Lk 23:53, 56, 24:1; Jn 19:40.
[8] Faulkner, *EBD*, pl. 32.

The role that myrrh, incense, unguents, and various aromatic substances played in the cult and ritual was of great significance. Much more than just creating a pleasant atmosphere for gods and men, such substances had the effect of propitiating the deities, of purifying them, of repelling evil influences from them, and of bestowing new vitality upon them...[1]

Furthermore, even the process of mummification itself possessed astrotheological meaning, in that the 70 days typically set aside for the procedure represent, per Hornung, "a period not determined by technical necessity, but rather chosen for its cosmic suitability."[2] Hornung explains that the cosmic significance of the 70 "correspond to the period during which each of the decans remains invisible before reappearing above the horizon to be observed again." As concerns the age of Egyptian observation of the decans, Hornung remarks, "They are already mentioned in the Pyramid Texts, but the system of thirty-six decans with which we are familiar was not developed until the First Intermediate Period [2181-2041 BCE] and the Middle Kingdom [2040-1782 BCE]..."[3] Thus, days typically dedicated to royal mummification in the amount of "70" represent the 72 dodecans, which, as we have seen, are also symbolized by the 72 sami of Seth, as well as the amount of Jesus's immediate disciples.

In any event, in the case of the mummy previously noted, the *krst/qrst* was also "the anointed," leading to the suggestion that the Greek and Latin terms Christos and Christus indeed may be related to the Egyptian *KRST*—and that the concept for the anointed and resurrected god called "Christ," so to speak, could be discovered originally in Egypt. Although it is widely perceived as something unique to Jesus, the *title* "Christos" could be found abundantly prior to the Jewish savior's alleged advent, particularly within the Greek Old Testament, as applied to various heroes, such as Samuel, David and Solomon, used some 40 times in fact in the Septuagint. For example, Leviticus 4:16 says: "And the priest that is anointed shall bring of the bullock's blood to the tabernacle of the congregation..." In the Greek, the priest who is anointed is ὁ χριστος—"the Christ." The word *Christos* also appears in several other pre-Christian and non-Jewish Greek texts, such as Euripides (*Hippolytus*, line 516) and Aeschylus (*Prometheus vinctus*, line 480).[4] Any Greek text describing someone or something as "anointed" would likewise use the word "Christos," including those concerning Osiris.

---

[1] Žabkar, 44.
[2] Hornung, *VK*, 136.
[3] Hornung, *SLE*, 28. Dates are from Brier, 12, 13.
[4] Murray, G., *Euripidis fabulae*, vol. 1; *Aeschyli tragoediae*.

Horus the Anointed and Beloved Son of the Father

As we have seen, in the Pyramid Texts (e.g., PT 576:1511a/P 518), the Osiris is anointed with oil,[1] essentially making him a "messiah" or "christ," as those two words both mean "anointed one."[2] We have also seen that in BD 145 it is *Horus* who is anointed, thus rendering him likewise a *Christ*. As the deceased who is Horus becomes anointed on his passage through the gates of heaven, he is thus *Christed*, as in Pyramid text W 51/PT 77:52a-b: "Ointment, ointment, where should you be? You on Horus's forehead, where should you be? You were on Horus's forehead, but I will put you on this Unis's forehead."[3] The anointing is specifically designed to "akhify" the deceased, which means to unite his *ka* (double/life force) with his *ba* (soul). The *Christing* of "Horus" thus makes him immortal.

In addition to *gs*, as in the Beinlich Wordlist, the Egyptian word for "to anoint" is *urh* or *wrh*, meaning "to rub with oil or salve, to anoint, to smear," while, per Budge's transliteration, *urhu* means "anointed ones."[4] Yet another term is *merh*, meaning "to anoint, to rub with oil or fat," with *merh-t*, *merhet* or *mrht*, referring to ointment, "oil, unguent, grease, suet, fat of any kind."[5] Per James Allen's transliteration, "to anoint with oil" is *wrh m mrht*.[6]

While in Greek "anointed" is χριστός, in Hebrew the word is transliterated as *mashiyach*, i.e., messiah. Adding to the previous Egyptian terms for "anointed" and "messiah," *The University Magazine* asserts, like Massey, that the Egyptian terms *mas* or *masu* also connote "anoint" and are linked etymologically to "messiah":

> In Egyptian hieroglyphs may be found *mas*, anoint; *masu*, anoint, dip. In Zend *mashya* is clarified butter. In Hebrew and Syrian *messiah*, *meshihha*, in Arabic *masih*, signify anointed.[7]

Indeed, in Birch's *Dictionary of Hieroglyphics* appears the word *masu*, which is defined as "Anoint, dip."[8] In Budge's *Egyptian Book of the Dead*, his transliteration of the same hieroglyph is *mesu*, the meaning of which he gives as "anointed."[9]

Thus, as anointed ones, it could truly be said that both Osiris and Horus were *Christs* and *Messiahs*, titles that ranked, in fact, as not uncommon in the pre-Christian world, as we have already seen

---

[1] Mercer, 238; Faulkner, *AEPT*, 231; Allen, J., *AEPT*, 182.
[2] Strong's H4899, G5547.
[3] Allen, J., *AEPT*, 22; Faulkner, *AEPT*, 18; Mercer, 35.
[4] Budge, *EHD*, 175; Erman, *EG*, 11.
[5] Budge, *EHD*, 315; Faulkner, *CDME*, 112.
[6] Allen, J., *ME*, 84.
[7] *UM*, 2.
[8] Bunsen/Birch, 428.
[9] Budge, *EBD* (1967), 15.

by the presence of the term "anointed" in the Old Testament.[1] In this regard, if the Egyptian kings were anointed, as were the Israelite kings, they would have been called "Christos" in Greek, especially during the Ptolemaic/Greco-Roman period. If the king of Egypt was called "the Christos," it is possible that thousands of people were quite aware of this term long before the common era—and that, since the pharaoh was considered *Horus* on Earth, they may have been aware of the concept of "Horus the Christ" as well, especially since Horus is called "anointed" in the Book of the Dead centuries before the common era.

In addition to being "the Christ," as we have seen repeatedly Horus is also called "beloved Son" of the father, Osiris,[2] among other epithets reproduced later to describe the Lord Jesus. Concerning Horus, Cooper remarks:

> Such...was the character, the office, and the filiation of the great benevolent deity of the Egyptians—of Horus, Only-begotten son of his Father, the God of God, the Anointed and the Deliverer. All the Egyptian literature bore testimony to him, all Egyptian life and art was moulded by his influence.[3]

In the Pyramid texts appear the following epithets of Horus, among others:

> God, Great God, Great one, Son of a Great One, Heir of the father, Hereditary Prince, First-born god, King of the gods, Lord of the sky, Lord of men, Lord of men and gods, Presider over spirits, Presider of the living, Presider over the imperishable ones, Presider over the mighty, Morning star, God of dawnings, the Gleaming One, Lord of the two lands, Lord of the horizon, Master of the sustenance of truth, Master of his people, Mighty over gods.[4]

Horus is also named as "Ruler of rulers" or "King of kings."[5] In the Coffin Texts, he is "Lord of Justice" (CT Sp. 16/17),[6] "Lord of Life" (CT Sp. 60)[7] and "Lord of the Netherworld" (CT Sp. 458),[8] among many other epithets as already seen applied not only to Horus but

---

[1] As a related aside, there exists a symbol called the "Chi Rho," which consists of the first two Greek letters of the word *Christos* and which is traditionally held to represent Jesus Christ. The chi-rho is pre-Christian, however, and can be found on coins from Egypt commemorating King Ptolemy III (246/222 BCE), indicating its use as an important symbol centuries before Christianity. It would appear, nevertheless, that the chi-rho symbol on coins represented the word *chrysos*, or "gold," and was merely adopted by Christians to indicate Christ. Therefore, chi-rho would not constitute a pre-Christian use of the term "Christos" as applied to Egyptian gods or kings.

[2] Faulkner, *EBD*, pl. 33, 110; Faulkner, *AEPT*, 3, 47, 122; Mercer, 22, 127, 192; Allen, J., *AEPT*, 36. (E.g., PT 20:11a; PT 219:179b; PT 369:644c; PT 510:1130c; PT 540:1331b; W 152) See also Cooper, 28.

[3] Cooper, 41.

[4] This list is compiled from Allen, T., *HPT*, 17ff.

[5] Hornung, *CGAE*, 233.

[6] Faulkner, *AECT*, I, 10.

[7] Faulkner, *AECT*, I, 55.

[8] Faulkner, *AECT*, II, 87.

also to other Egyptian divinities. As can be determined from his epithets, Horus represents no less a towering theological figure than Jesus, long prior to the common era. In addition, Horus is confounded with the Egyptian god "Shed," who is "the savior," representing the "helper of mankind in times of need."[1] The concept of a "savior god," in fact, was quite common in Egyptian religion, as related by Morenz:

> ...apparently during the Eighteenth Dynasty, the ancient idea that every deity provided help in distress gave rise to an independent "savior" god...[2]

Morenz also states that the "youthful saviour" is "intimately connected with Horus..."[3]

Not only is this Savior god "close to Horus in character," as Hornung states, but he is also part of the composite god "Shed-Horus" or "Horus-Shed," who is represented on the Metternich stela, as well as on an ancient amulet.[4] As Hornung further relates, "Here, as Shed ('savior'), the youthful Horus becomes the vanquisher of all dangerous animals..."[5] Thus, like Jesus, Horus *is* the Savior. Indeed, in his savior role, Horus-Shed was further identified by early Christians *with Jesus*, as related by Hornung: "On another amulet, one side depicts the head of Christ and scenes from the New Testament, and the other a winged, youthful god (Horus-Shed) as tamer of crocodiles and scorpions..."[6]

Horus the Word/"Iusa," the Coming Son and Savior

Other epithets for Horus that essentially also emerge in the Christian effort include "the Word" and apparently the term "Iusa," which may be related to "Jesus." In addition to the previous discussion of the Logos, Plutarch equates not only Osiris (49, 371A; 64, 377A) but also Horus with the Word, in discussing Harpocrates (68, 378C), as well as when he says that Horus's defeat of Set was a "victory of reason over disorder and evil" (55, 373D-E).[7] As we have seen, the Valentinian Gnostics likewise identified Horus with the Logos, and, indeed, in Egyptian writings, such as the "Funeral Text of Hertu," Horus, like Thoth, is deemed "the Word."[8] Of course, the equation of Horus with the Logos makes sense considering the solar nature of the Word, previously demonstrated.

---

[1] Hornung, *CGAE*, 282.
[2] Morenz, 109.
[3] Morenz, 269.
[4] Hornung, *SLE*, 75. See also Petrie, *AEE*, 86.
[5] Hornung, *SLE*, 56.
[6] Hornung, *SLE*, 75.
[7] Plutarch/Babbitt, 121, 133, 151, 158-159. See Griffiths, *Plutarch*, 505; Boylan, 12-13.
[8] Budge, *FGAE*, 349.

As concerns the peculiar epithet "Iusa," it should be noted that "Jesus" in the original Greek is *Iesous* or *Iasous*,[1] while in Arabic the name is *Issa*. In Croatian and other Slavic languages "Jesus" takes the forms of *Isus, Isusu* or *Isusa*, while in Irish and Gaelic the name is *Iosa*.[2] Concerning, "Iusa," in *Ancient Egypt, Light of the World*, Gerald Massey remarks:

> The miracles of the virgin birth and physical resurrection of Jesus; the miracles of giving sight to the blind and of raising the dead, the descent into Hades, and the resurrection in three days or on the third day, are all Egyptian, all in the Ritual. They were previously performed by the Christ who was not historical, the Christ of the Egypto-gnostics who is Horus or Jesus, identical with the Osirian Christ who was Horus the lord by name, and who, as the records show, was also extant as a divine type or spiritual impersonation as Iusa or Iu-em-hetep many thousand years ago.[3]

Not surprisingly, this term *Iusa* or *Iu-sa* is not found in encyclopedias or reference books on Egypt, such that it has been claimed to be a "fabrication." As Massey explains it, *Iusa* is a combination of the Egyptian word *iu*, also transliterated as *iy, iw, ii, jj, jw* or *jwj*, correctly stated by him to mean "to come,"[4] and *sa*, likewise transliterated as *za* or *z3*, rightly defined as "son."[5] Hence, *Iu-sa* would be "the coming son," which would refer to Horus on a daily and annual basis, if applied to him.

Massey further identifies *Iusa* as the child of the goddess Hathor-*Iusaas*.[6] Regarding this goddess named "Iusaas," the English scholar states:

> ...She is a form of Isis or Hathor, to judge by her head-dress.... She is the mother of the son whose name is Iu-em-hept. She herself also has

---

[1] The word *Iesous*—"Jesus" in the New Testament—is asserted by Strong's (G2424) to be from the Hebrew term *Yĕhowshuwa* (H309), meaning "Jehovah is salvation." However, St. Cyril (4th cent.), the archbishop of Jerusalem, among others, evinced that *Iesous* meant "the Healer," based on Greek roots. ("Cathechetical Lectures," X; Schaff, VII, 61.) This assertion would mean that Iesous, or *Iasous* in the *Attic* Greek, comes from the Greek verb ιασομαι— "iasomai," meaning "to heal"—and is therefore related to the Greek name *Jason*. It has further been asserted that Jason in turn is related to the name "Iaso," an epithet of a pre-Christian healing goddess. (*POCGD*, 161.) The fact that the disciples (Acts 4:10) and others (Mk 9:38-39) were said to *heal* in Jesus's name is a strong indication that the word *Iesous* was considered in ancient days to be related to, if not derived from, the Greek *iasomai*. As Drews states, "Epiphanius (*Haeres. c, xxix*) clearly perceived this connection when he translated the name Jesus 'healer' or 'physician' (*curator, therapeutes*)." (Drews, 196.)

[2] See, e.g., "The Gaelic Gospel of Mark."

[3] Massey, *AELW*, II, 811.

[4] Budge, *EL*, 227; Allen, J., *ME*, 160, 155; Beinlich's "Ägyptische Wortliste"; Sciortino. In Birch's *Hieroglyphic Dictionary*, the word *iu* means "go out" (Bunsen/Birch, 408), while Faulkner gives the meaning as not only "come" but also "return," among others. (Faulkner, *CDME*, 10.)

[5] Budge, *EL*, 68; Bunsen/Birch, 625, 630; Beinlich; Allen, J., *ME*, 41. One of the god's many names is "Osiris in Sa." (Bunsen/Birch, 278.)

[6] Massey, *AELW*, I, 451.

the title of Neb-hept, the mistress or lady of peace. The accented SA in her name implies the earlier Sif; both Sa and Sif are names of the son who is IU. As is a name of the genitrix, Isis; the As, the seat, chamber, house, bed, resting-place, maternal abode, the secreting part of the body. IU-SĀ-AS is thus the As or womb of IU-SĀ, IU-SIF or IU-SU, the three modes of naming the son IU. IU means he who comes, and Iu-sa, Iu-su or Iu-sif, is the coming son, the messiah of mythology.[1]

In an Egyptian text, the term *iu sa* refers to the evening sun god Tem, Tmu, Atmu or Atum "masturbating" his children Shu and Tefnut into existence, and was posited by Maspero to be related to the name of the solar goddess "Iusaaset,"[2] Atum's eventual consort, who was the same as Iusaas, the goddess popular at Heliopolis, city of the sun.[3] Indeed, this goddess is also deemed "Hathor-Iusas of Heliopolis," as related by German Egyptologist Dr. Johannes Dümichen (1833-1894), a professor at the University of Strasbourg.[4] Iusaset was thus identified with Hathor, who in turn was "the goddess of the sky wherein Horus, the sun-god, rose and set."[5] Since traditionally, the sky goddess is Nut, from whom is born the sun god, it could be said that Hathor is thus also Horus's mother, which in turn would make *Iusaset* his mother as well.

In this regard, in texts Horus is called *sa Aset* or "son of Isis,"[6] while "Iu-sa-Aset" would simply translate as "coming son of Isis," an appropriate designation for her daily-born offspring. "Iusaaset" or "Iusaset" is in fact a "variant spelling" of "Iusaas" or "Iusas."[7] As we have seen, Horus has been said to be identified with Hathor's son *Ihy*, the "first-born of Hathor," who "himself is the Sun, conceived of as a child emerging from his mother every day at dawn..."[8] That it was the morning sun who was the "coming son" is further indicated by the depiction of the "boat of the day" carrying the morning sun god, who, "in the guise of a scabbard," is "the one 'coming into being.'"[9]

According to Dr. Leitz, the goddess is likewise called the "Cobra Iusaas," who protects Atum-Re during a "big fight."[10] Brugsch also discusses the goddess Hathor-*Iusas*, "mistress of heaven," wife of Tum at On/Heliopolis, and mother of Shu and Tefnut.[11] Although she is depicted as Atum's "masturbating hand" that produces the "first

---

[1] Massey, *BB*, 2, 298.
[2] Budge, *GE*, II, 88; Hart, 99, 104.
[3] Hornung, *CGAE*, 71.
[4] Dümichen, 27.
[5] Budge, *GFSER*, 7.
[6] Clarysse, 299.
[7] Mercatante, 77. See also Budge, *SA*, 62; Armour, 31.
[8] Iamblichus/Clarke, xlv.
[9] Morenz, 167.
[10] Leitz, 141.
[11] Brugsch, *RMAA*, 284, 313, 336, 574.

beings,"[1] as an epithet of Hathor, Iusas or Iusaset herself was at times the sole progenitor of the twins Shu and Tefnut,[2] giving further credence to Massey's assessment of *Iusa*. Indeed, Shu and Tefnut are depicted as the eyes of Horus, thus essentially equating them with him. By the Ptolemaic Period, in fact, Horus and Shu are identified with each other, as "Horus-Shu."[3]

In the Coffin Texts, Shu appears in the "trinity of becoming" with Atum-Shu/Tefnut,[4] reflecting his role as the "coming son." Regarding the supposed "masturbation" that produced Shu and Tefnut, Morenz discusses the word *msi*, which means "to bring forth," remarking:

> ...this classical Heliopolitan concept of procreation need not by any means be described in this grossly sensual way, as onanism, but may be referred to simply and briefly as "bringing forth (*msi*)"; it was Atum who "brought forth" Shu and Tefnut.[5]

Moreover, like Shu, Horus is also named in the Egyptian writings (e.g., PT 465:881b/P 316) as Atum's son or *sa*, as is the word in Egyptian.[6] The "come in peace" god Iu-em-hetep/I-em-hetep/Imhotep is the child in a holy trinity, making him equivalent to Horus in the Osiris triad. In addition, Massey suggests that the son of Atum/Ptah, Iu-em-hetep,[7] or just "Iu," is one with the Gnostic figure "Ieou" or "Iao," as in the famous Egypto-Gnostic text the *Pistis Sophia*.[8] The Egyptian god Iao was identified by Diodorus with the Jewish tribal god Yahweh, while "Ieou" is likewise equivalent to Yahweh[9] but could also apply to his son, Jesus, since they are one. (Jn 10:30) Interestingly, the "god of physicians," Iemhetep/Imhotep was equated by the Greeks, who called him "Imouthes," with the healing god Asclepius,[10] who has also been claimed as one of the prototypes for Jesus. Hence, the identification of Iemhetep or "Iu" with both Horus and Jesus is reasonable, as is the determination of Horus as both the Word and Iusa.

The Shu Theology

The significant god Shu "refers to 'luminous air,' light-filled living space," according to Assman.[11] At CT Sp. 78 we discover that "the deceased is Shu (air) between earth and sky."[12] Deemed by some to

---

[1] Leeming, 144.
[2] Mercatante, 76; Armour, 31.
[3] Vassilika, 118.
[4] Morenz, 148.
[5] Morenz, 163.
[6] Faulkner, *AEPT*, 155; Mercer, 162; Allen, J., *AEPT*, 122.
[7] Budge, *GE*, 1, 523; Spence, 150. See Budge, *FSE*, 227.
[8] Massey, *AELW*, I, 499-500.
[9] Meyer, *GGJ*, 307.
[10] Budge, *GE*, 1, 522.
[11] Assman, *ESRNK*, 81.
[12] Faulkner, *AECT*, I, 81.

be "the void,"[1] according to Dr. Jennifer Houser-Wegner, a co-curator at the Penn Museum, "Shu's name (*šw*) meant 'dryness' or 'emptiness,'" the latter definition preferred by Goelet.[2] Yet, Dr. Wegner continues, "This empty space was not considered as a void, but rather an arena for the possibility of activity."[3] In referring to the "theology of Shu," principally laid out in the Coffin Texts (CT Sp. 75-80), Assman also says of its form during the Middle Kingdom: "Shu appears here as a god of the air between heaven and earth and the god of the breath of life 'in the nostrils' of the individual creatures."[4] The German Egyptologist further relates that Shu is the life-giver:

> It is his duty to give life to creatures and provide them with the conditions necessary for life and keep them alive, and he does this on behalf of his father Atum the creator god.[5]

Shu as the air and breath of life constitutes essentially the same role as that of the Holy Spirit, the *pneuma*, or "breath" and "wind" of God in Christian theology. Concerning Shu, Morenz remarks that he is "regarded as god of the air and bearer of heaven, at times also as the sun."[6]

The hieroglyphic word for Shu, transliterated as *šw*,[7] is one of several using the same signs, with the difference of determinatives at the end, in the case of the deity, of course, the god sign 𓀭 (A41). The basic word *šw* 𓈙𓏲 (H6, G43) with other determinatives can also mean "emptiness" "ascend" and, importantly, "sun" and "sunlight."[8] This latter word is determined, of course, by the addition of the determinative representing "sun" and/or "Re/Ra" ⊙ (N5), revealing the intimate connection between Shu and the sun. Indeed, in one hymn the sun is addressed thus: "You have created yourself as the day-time sun (*šw*)..."[9] As concerns *šw* here meaning "sun," Assman notes that in the Late Egyptian the term is equivalent to *jtn* or Aten in the Middle Egyptian.[10]

As the god of air as well as of "the space between earth and sky and of the light that fills that space,"[11] Shu is the sunlight at dawn,[12] while Horus is the sun at dawn. In one of the "sunrise" sun hymns from the New Kingdom, Assman relates that Ra/Re in his rising appears "in the house of Shu,"[13] once again demonstrating a

---

[1] Redford, 155.
[2] Faulkner, *EBD*, 143.
[3] Redford, 335.
[4] Assman, *ESRNK*, 178.
[5] Assman, *ESRNK*, 178.
[6] Morenz, 269.
[7] Collier, 160.
[8] Faulkner, *CDME*, 263.
[9] Assman, *ESRNK*, 181, citing "O. Vienna 6155 and O. Cairo CG 25214 (242)."
[10] Assman, *ESRNK*, 181, fn 169.
[11] Redford, 23.
[12] *Nature*, XLIII, 561.
[13] Assman, *ESRNK*, 13.

connection to Horus, in the role of Horakhty. Another of the sun hymns addressing the God Sun also includes a description that sounds much like Shu—and quite possibly was, having been merged into the divine sun disc Aten during the Amarna period—in his typical *cruciform* posture:

> Your feet are on the earth,
> your head is in the sky.
> You stand up with the strength of your arms,
> but your weight rests upon the secret.
> The sky is over you, the underworld beneath you...
> the wind is the air in your nostrils.[1]

And from another hymn:

> You are the sky, the earth and the underworld,
> you are the water, you are the air between them.[2]

This all-encompassing role reminds us once again of Jesus as the Alpha and Omega.

One of Shu's epithets is "life,"[3] and the god has also been called the "creative life force"[4] as well as "the god of air, light, and life..."[5] Since Horus also is a god of the air, as well as light and the resurrecter to life, it is easy to see why he has been identified with Shu. In this regard, Wegner further remarks that "Shu might also be envisioned as the rays of the sun,"[6] a role likewise similar to that of Horus as the morning sun. In this regard, the texts describe the sun in the east, where "it rises as Shu,"[7] in the same role as Horus of the Horizon, the morning sun.

Furthermore, Shu is again associated with Horus in the cartouche of Amenhotep IV/Akhenaten.[8] Regarding the debate concerning the meaning of this pharaonic name, Morenz relates that most scholars have assumed Shu is "simply...a term for the sun."[9] However, Morenz further remarks, it is more probable that the god's presence represents "an allusion...to Shu as son" of the "primordial god Re." Morenz also calls Shu a "more recent manifestation" of the sun god,[10] in other words reflecting that, although Shu is a very old god, his solar significance is newer than that of Re-Horakhty, for example.

Whereas Shu and others, such as Ptah-Sokar-Osiris, are deemed "the separator," specifically between sky and earth,[11] Horos too is

---

[1] Assman, *ESRNK*, 177.
[2] Assman, *ESRNK*, 177.
[3] Willems, 262.
[4] Redford, 335.
[5] Redford, 229.
[6] Redford, 335.
[7] Morenz, 44.
[8] Morenz, 147.
[9] Morenz, 147.
[10] Morenz, 147.
[11] Morenz, 173.

"the boundary," and it is therefore possible that the same role occupied by Shu—an alter ego of Horus, especially in later times—was rehashed in that of the Gnostic Horos.

The identification of Shu with Horus is also made at CT Sp. 167, in which the deceased says, "May I come and go as Shu, for I am Shu, my face is that of the Great Flood, I am born as Horus of Shesmet..."[1] Not only do we see Shu equated with Horus, but we also discover the "Great Flood" within Egyptian religion, meant both metaphorically and as referring to the Nile.

Commenting upon the identification of Shu with Horus, Maspero relates:

> Thus we find that Horus the son of Isis at Buto...Khnumu the son of Hathor at Esneh, were each in turn identified with Shu the son of Atumu, and lost their individualities in his... Through constant reiteration of the statement that the divine sons of the triads were identical with Shu...[2]

In this same regard, Wiedemann states, in later times Horus the Elder "appears as HER-UR-SHU, the son of Ra..."[3]

The deceased/Osiris too is identified with Shu in the Coffin Texts, as at CT Sp. 725: "O N-Shu, receive this bread of yours which is brought to you. I have placed sky and earth for you under <your> son Horus, your heir..."[4]

Demonstrating the totality of Egyptian deities, in various hymns Osiris is deemed "Lord of fear" and "great of terror," while at the site of Kom Ombo, the combined god Haroeris-Shu—"Haroeris" being Horus the Elder—is called "lord of carnage."[5] Isis too is given "fearsome" attributes in later hymns.

During the Middle Kingdom, the god Shu became popular enough to warrant what is modernly called a "Shu Theology," as exemplified in the Coffin Texts. CT Sp. 75, for instance, is specifically devised "for the soul of Shu and for becoming Shu."[6] In the same spell, Shu is the "one who foretells him when he ascends from the horizon," whom Faulkner suggests is the sun god, while "Shu is the god of air" and the "'foretelling' of the sunrise may refer to the atmospheric hues which announce the coming dawn."[7] Shu is also "he who despatches the word of the Self-created to the multitudes,"[8] like Jesus in his role as the Word of the Creator appearing to the masses. And we also hear that Shu is "one invisible of shape" and is "merged in the Sunshine-

---

[1] Faulkner, *AECT*, I, 146.
[2] Maspero, *DC*, 151.
[3] Wiedemann, 27-28.
[4] Faulkner, *AECT*, II, 276.
[5] Žabkar, 33.
[6] Faulkner, *AECT*, I, 72.
[7] Faulkner, *AECT*, I, 75.
[8] Faulkner, *AECT*, I, 72.

god,"[1] reminding us both of the Ineffable God the Father and his "Sun of Righteousness" Jesus Christ. Also, in CT Sp. 80, Shu is "everlasting," and the speaker invites, "Come joyfully at meeting the god in me, for I am Shu, whom Atum fashioned, and this garment of mine is the air of life."[2] Here may be the forerunner of the sentiment expressed in the New Testament to the effect of Christ saying, "Come unto me, learn of me, for I am Jesus, whom the Father created, and this garment of mine will heal you."[3] As Jesus removes sin and bestows eternal life, so too is Shu the life-giver.

Shu, of course, is the son of Atum, the Primeval One, who was "alone in his existence,"[4] as is said of the monotheistic biblical God. Discussing the "association between father and son" regarding Atum and Shu, Assman states that the relationship approaches a "unity of natures in terms that bring to mind the Christological formulae of the Early Church."[5] Morenz cites the Coffin Texts as discussing Shu as the son of God, again comparable to Christ.[6]

Another connection to Jesus and the "blood of the Lamb" comes with mention of the "blood of Shu" at CT Sp. 464.[7] Also, while Jesus is called the "Lion of Judah" at Revelation 5:5, in CT Sp. 510 appears reference to "Shu the Lion."[8] In CT Sp. 829, the deceased is also "the Lion," as well as Horus and "he who makes calm after storm."[9] Yet another correspondence occurs between the story of Jesus borrowing the ass and her foal to ride into Jerusalem (Mt 21:5), and the "two asses of Shu," as at CT Sp. 662.[10]

While the believer may rely on the Cross of Jesus, so too may the Egyptian deceased count on the "Supports of Shu" (CT Sp. 746).[11] The support of the sky is evidently also considered as such for the various gods and goddesses, giving Shu or other *Himmelsträger* a salvational role as well.[12] The mythological category of *Himmelsträger* or "Sky-maker" includes the Greek god Atlas and the Egyptian god *Ḥeh*.[13]

---

[1] Faulkner, *AECT*, I, 72.

[2] Faulkner, *AECT*, I, 83.

[3] This quote represents a *paraphrase* of biblical scriptures, such as at Mt 11:28, 29 and 9:21, etc.

[4] Faulkner, *AECT*, I, 85.

[5] Assman, *ESRNK*, 178.

[6] Morenz, 257.

[7] Faulkner, *AECT*, II, 90.

[8] Faulkner, *AECT*, II, 144. Faulkner's clarification that "the reference is not to quadrupeds but to ass-headed spirits" is logical, since, like the rest of the Egyptian pantheon, Shu was not a real person. The ass-headed "spirit" reminds one of both Set-Anubis and the crucified ass-headed god found in an early, supposedly anti-Christian rendition.

[9] Faulkner, *AECT*, III, 18.

[10] Faulkner, *AECT*, II, 234.

[11] Faulkner, *AECT*, II, 284.

[12] See Žabkar, 85.

[13] Žabkar, 84.

"The Truth, The Light and The Good Shepherd"

At CT Sp. 990, the speaker says, "I have flown up to the Shu the great,"[1] reminding one of the promised "rapture" of modern times said to be rooted in biblical doctrine. Additionally, like Christ, who is kissed by Judas, Shu too is a recipient of a kiss at CT Sp. 1065.[2] Moreover, like the welcoming Jesus, who invites the little children to "come unto him," at CT Sp. 101, we read, "Shu opens his arms to you..."[3] Also in the Coffin Text (CT Sp. 1145), there is indication that it is Shu who is protector of the deceased's heart: "Your heart has been taken by Shu,"[4] reminding one of the "sacred heart of Jesus." The Shu theology overall thus reflects a similar spirituality found in Christianity wherein the believers "let Jesus into their heart."

The resemblance between Shu and Jesus—called Jo-*SHU*-a or Ye-*SHU*-a in the Hebrew—is clear: The incarnated son of a "virgin" as life-bestower on behalf of the Father. The Shu Theology from its inception thus provides "foreshadowing" of the Christian story, with the only begotten son of God created parthenogenetically to serve essentially as savior of life on earth by supporting the heavens and giving air to all who breathe.

The Lord of Light and Lamb of God

As is obvious, the Horus-Jesus connection is profound and meaningful, not to be dismissed lightly by a quick search of encyclopedia entries. Indeed, when we look closely at translations of Egyptian texts, we can compile a long list of numerous sacred epithets that undoubtedly made their way in some form into Christianity. The following constitutes such a compilation of some of the names applied to various deities in the Book of the Dead, including Osiris, Isis, Horus, Re, Anubis, Thoth and Seb:

> Lord of Lords, King of Kings, Lord of the Universe, Lord of Eternity, Lord of Truth, Savior, the Divine, All-Powerful, the Unknowable, Great God, Lord of All, Inviolate God, God of Justice, Lord of Justice, Lord of Right, Lord of Power, Lord of Might, God of Authority, the Sole and Only One, the Eternal One, Most Glorious One, His Majesty, Mighty One, God of Mighty Names, Mighty Enlightener, Wise One, Potent One, Holy Soul, Good Being, the Great, the Mighty, the Ancient One, Sovereign, Protector, Universal Lord, Author of Eternity, Eternal Lord, Ruler of Eternity, Ruler of Everlasting, Lord of Everlasting, King of Eternity, the Eternal King, King of Everlasting, Prince of Eternity, Prince of the divine Powers, Hereditary Prince of the gods, the Peaceful One, Lord of Resurrections, Lord of Righteousness, Lord of Life, Living Lord, Lord of Time, Lord of Life for All Eternity, Giver of Life from the Beginning, Master of masters, Supreme among gods, Father of the gods, Lord of the Gods, Leader of

[1] Faulkner, *AECT*, III, 99.
[2] Faulkner, *AECT*, III, 142.
[3] Faulkner, *AECT*, I, 99.
[4] Faulkner, *AECT*, III, 178.

the gods, King of the gods, Everlasting King, King of Heaven, Lord of Persons, Lord of the Law, Leader of the Host, Primeval One, Great One, Son of a Great One, United of Good, Lord of mysteries, Lord of the Age, Lord of the Soul, Lord of Strength, Lord of Offerings, Defender in the Netherworld, Lord of the Unseen World, Lord of Oneness, Lord of the Earth, Lord of millions, Lord of Millions of Years, Lord on High, Lord of Light, Radiant One, the Giver of light, Lord of the Horizon, Lord of Daylight, Lord of the Sunbeams, Soul of his Father, Lord of Years, Lord of the Great Mansion, Lord of Grain, etc.[1]

The plethora of sacred titles—*which number some 140 in BD 142 for Osiris alone*—reflects not only the tremendous reverence with which the Egyptian gods were held but also, in the case of Osiris in particular, the spread of his worship as well, as in the epithet "Osiris among the Aegean Islanders" and so on.[2] As the biblical God the Father possesses "many mansions" (Jn 14:2), so too is Horus's father, Osiris, the "Lord of the Mansion," as at CT Sp. 36 as well, in which the god denies transgressors access to his Mansion.[3] In CT Sp. 1119, Osiris is depicted as possessing "mansions,"[4] while in CT Sp. 862, we also find mention of the "Mansion of Ptah,"[5] Ptah being another "father of the gods." As but one of numerous demonstrations of the proximity between Osiris and Jesus, while "the Osiris" is the king/pharaoh, and Osiris is called "King of kings,"[6] Jesus, of course, is considered the heir of King David and likewise the "King of kings." (1 Ti 6:15) The epithet "Lord of lords" also appears in the Coffin Texts, as at CT Sp. 888,[7] while at CT Sp. 1033 appears reference to the "Lord of Wisdom."[8]

The Pyramid Texts likewise demonstrate the correlations between the Egyptian and biblical scriptures, as at PT 364/T 196, in which the Osiris N. is addressed as follows: "You are the god in control, and there is no god like you."[9] Compare this scripture with that at Exodus 20:2-3: "I am the Lord your god... You shall have no other gods before me." Considering how much of the Egyptian religion and culture the Israelites/Hebrews appear to have copied it is not unreasonable to suggest that the biblical scribes obtained this concept from the Egyptians. Of course, in this specific case copying may not necessarily be so, as this monotheistic concept could naturally occur

---

[1] This list represents a compilation of epithets from the translations of the Book of the Dead by Allen, Birch, Budge, Faulkner and Renouf. See also the Coffin Texts for many of the same sacred names.

[2] Hare, 14; Allen, T., *BD*, 119.

[3] Faulkner, *AECT*, I, 26. See also CT Sp. 280; CT Sp. 306. (Faulkner, *AECT*, I, 211, 225.)

[4] Faulkner, *AECT*, III, 164.

[5] Faulkner, *AECT*, III, 41.

[6] See, e.g., the Book of the Dead, "Introductory Hymn to Osiris," plate 2 of Faulkner.

[7] Faulkner, *AECT*, III, 52.

[8] Faulkner, *AECT*, III, 129.

[9] Allen, J., *AEPT*, 80.

to the human mind contemplating the cosmos. The parallel does, however, reveal that the Egyptians were not "spiritually deficient heathens," as has been suggested by religious rivals over the centuries.

In the long list of divine roles and titles applied to the gods in Egyptian texts there also appear a number of solar epithets, of course, such as the "Lord of Daylight," "Lord of Light," "Lord on High," "Lord of the Horizon" and "Lord of the Sunbeams." As another example of the astrotheological nature of the various sacred titles, again, regarding the epithet "Sole and Only One" used in BD 2, Renouf remarks that it is "one of the many appellatives of the Sun." He further states, "He is here represented as shining *in* or *from* the Moon."[1]

In the same vein, one of the Coffin Texts says: "I am lord of the flame who lives on truth; lord of eternity maker of joy, against whom that worm shall not rebel. I am he who is in his shrine, master of action who destroys the storm; who drives off the serpents of many names when he goes from his shrine."[2] The same text continues, "Lord of lightland, maker of light, who lights the sky with his beauty."[3] This scripture is clearly about the sun, with the appropriate solar epithets. Note again the destruction or "calming" of the storm, as was said of Christ as well, as does Jesus also possess the power to "tread on serpents." (Lk 10:19)

Another divine epithet that possesses astrotheological connotations is the "lamb of God," which at times refers to the sun in the Age of Aries and which may be applicable to Horus "the golden calf" after the end of the precessional Age of Taurus, when his power is transferred to the god Sobek.[4] Says Massey, "As Egyptian, the lamb, 'son of a sheep,' had been a type of Horus who was called the child."[5] Massey further remarks:

> In the text Horus is addressed as the *"Sheep, son of a sheep; Lamb, son of a lamb,"* and invoked in this character as the protector and saviour of souls.... Horus is the Lamb of God the father, and is addressed by the name of the lamb who is the protector or saviour of the dead in the earth and Amenti.[6]

Verifying these contentions, in *The Manners and Customs of the Ancient Egyptians*, Wilkinson notes that the "mystical inscription,

---

[1] Renouf, *EBD*, 11; Allen, T., *BD*, 8. Faulkner translates the same passage thus: "O you Sole One who shine in the moon, O you Sole One who glow in the sun..." (Faulkner, *EBD*, pl. 18.)

[2] McDermott, 72.

[3] McDermott, 72.

[4] Massey, *AELW*, II, 718, 722.

[5] Massey, *AELW*, II, 723.

[6] Massey, *NG*, 471. Massey cites "Chabas, *Bulletin Archéologique*, p. 44, Juin, 1855. Sharpe, *Eg. Inscrip.* pls. 9-12, fol. 1837. Wilkinson, pl. 83." This latter refers to the volume of plates from Sir John Gardner Wilkinson's *Manners and Customs of the Ancient Egyptians*, printed during the 1840s.

stating Horus to be the god, son of a god, sheep, son of a sheep...is given by Messrs. Chabas and Pierret, in 'Zeitsch. f. aegypt. Spr.,' 1868, pp. 99-136."[1] In *Chaldean Magic*, Lenormant relates Chabas's translation thus: "O sheep, son of a sheep! lamb son of a sheep..."[2] In any event, it is apparent that Horus was essentially deemed the "lamb of God."

In light of these facts regarding so many divine epithets long prior to the Christian era, including the Egyptian deities as saviors, messiahs and christs, it seems unscientific and dishonest to conclude that the Jewish Christ figure constitutes a unique "divine revelation." Indeed, it could be asserted that, as Re, Osiris and Horus, et al., symbolized important astrotheological concepts, so too does Christ represent the personification of the sun, the real "way, life and truth," as well as "good shepherd," among many other divine epithets applied to the solar orb and its numerous adjuncts.

---

[2] Lenormant, 92, citing Chabas, *Bulletin Archéologique*, Juin, 1855, p. 44.

Enthroned Osiris judging the Dead. The Wicked are sent back to
Earth as Swine.
From the Sarcophagus of Seti I.
(Budge, *Egyptian Heaven and Hell*, 161; Renouf, *Egyptian Book of
the Dead*, 62, pl. XI)

кλc.т,   Une momie, (de la racine Embaume -
                          кuλ,)   ment, action
                                     d'envelopper
                                     de bandelettes.

Hieroglyph signifying *KRST* or Mummy.
(Champollion, *Grammaire Égyptienne*, 80)

kårs . t.   Embalmment,
mummy. G. 86.

(Birch, *Dictionary of Hieroglyphics*, 416)

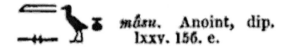

mâsu. Anoint, dip.
lxxv. 156. e.

Hieroglyph for "Anoint," pronounced *Masu*, like "Messiah."
(Bunsen, *Egypt's Place in Universal History*, 428)

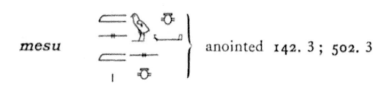

mesu   anointed 142. 3 ; 502. 3

Hieroglyph for "Anointed," pronounced *Mesu*, as in "Messiah."
(Budge, *BD* (1898), 149)

Crosslike image showing Horus as Shed, the Savior
(Hornung, *The Secret Lore of Egypt*, 57)

Was Horus "Crucified?"

"Osiris and Horus were crucified as 'saviors' and 'redeemers'; the sufferings, death, and resurrection of Osiris forming the great mystery of the Egyptian religion. Prometheus, of Greece, was with chains nailed to the rocks on Mount Caucasus, 'with arms extended,' as a saviour; and the tragedy of the crucifixion was acted in Athens 500 years before the Christian era...."

William W. Hardwicke, *The Evolution of Man* (218)

"*Osiris*, the Egyptian Saviour, was crucified in the heavens. To the Egyptian the cross was the symbol of immortality, an emblem of the *Sun*, and the god himself was crucified to the tree, which denoted his fructifying power.

"*Horus* was also crucified in the heavens. He was represented, like...Christ Jesus, with *outstretched arms in the vault of heaven*."

Thomas W. Doane, *Bible Myths and Their Parallels in Other Religions* (484)

"...[Horus] came from the...sacred birthplace... With outstretched arms he is the vault of heaven."

James Bonwick, *Egyptian Belief and Modern Thought* (157)

"Horus shows himself in the image of the hawk whose wings span the sky..."

Dr. Eric Hornung, *Conceptions of God in Ancient Egypt* (124)

In ancient mythology, in which immortal gods can die, the death of a deity is very significant and is often attended by a sentiment of redemption and salvation, such as the ultimate sacrifice of God's son in Jesus Christ. We have already seen how Osiris and Horus both were betrayed and murdered by their brother/uncle Typhon/Set, with Osiris's death plotted during a sort of "Last Supper" gathering.[1] But were either Osiris or Horus "crucified," as has been claimed by a number of writers? Firstly, when it is asserted that Horus (or Osiris) was "crucified," it should be kept in mind that it was not part of the Osiris/Horus myth that the murdered god was held down and nailed to a cross, as we perceive the meaning of "crucified" to be, based on the drama we believe allegedly took place during Christ's purported passion. Rather, in one myth Osiris is *torn to pieces* before being raised from the dead, while Horus is *stung by a scorpion* prior to his resurrection. However, Egyptian deities, including Horus, *were* depicted in *cruciform*, with arms extended or outstretched, as in various images that are comparable to *crucifixes*, such as was discussed previously by Lundy, describing Horus as "cross-like" and a "type of Christ in...His triumph through the Cross." In addition, we find the peculiar Gnostic identification of Horus/Horos with the Cross, which may reflect a possible Egyptian mystery revolving

---

[1] See Plutarch, "Isis and Osiris," *Moralia*, V, (13, 356 B-C); Babbitt, 35, 37.

around Horus as the sun god perhaps at the equinoxes, when day and night are the same length, and *the sun is "hung on a cross."*

The verb "to crucify" comes from the Latin *crucifigere*, which simply means "to fix to a cross" and does not necessarily signify to throw down to the ground and nail a living person to a cross. To be "crucified," therefore, could refer to *an image of a god or man simply fixed to a cross*, as in a *crucifix*. In discussing "crucifixion," then, the point to keep in mind is the contention that various mythical motifs such as the god with outstretched arms or the sun on the cross were already in existence and revered long prior to the common era, likely utilized in the weaving of the Christ myth. Again, we are not asserting that the creators of Christianity took an already fully formed myth and simply scratched out Osiris's or Horus's name and wrote in Jesus, but we *are* averring that there is little doubt existing themes were combined with Jewish scriptures, rendering a unique telling in the gospel story which is nonetheless based on Pagan precedents. These pre-Christian motifs include the cross as a religious object, as well as venerated images of gods in the shape of a cross or crosses with men on them.

The Pre-Christian Cross and Crucifix

Although many people may not realize it, the cross is a very ancient sacred symbol long predating the Christian era, when it is pretended to have gained significance. In "Archaeology of the Cross and Crucifix," the *Catholic Encyclopedia* discusses the history of the cross, its use as a punishment, its appearance in pre-Christian art with *a god upon it*, and the Egyptian origin of one form:

> The sign of the cross, represented in its simplest form by a crossing of two lines at right angles, greatly antedates, in both the East and the West, the introduction of Christianity. It goes back to a very remote period of human civilization....

> The penalty of the cross goes back probably to the *arbor infelix, or unhappy tree*, spoken of by Cicero...and by Livy.... According to Hüschke...the magistrates known as *duoviri perduellionis* pronounced this penalty...styled also *infelix lignum*.... This primitive form of crucifixion on trees was long in use, as Justus Lipsius notes.... Such a tree was known as a cross (*crux*). *On an ancient vase we see Prometheus bound to a beam which serves the purpose of a cross*.... [Emph. added.]

> In Greek it is called σταυρος [stauros], which Burnoff would derive from the Sanskrit *stavora*. The word was, however, frequently used in a broad sense. Speaking of Prometheus nailed to Mount Caucasus, Lucian uses the substantive σταυρός and the verbs ανασταυρόω [anastauróo] and ανασκολοπίζω [anaskolopizo], the latter being derived from σκόλοψ [skolops], which also signifies a cross....

> ...The Christian apologists, such as Tertullian (Apol., xvi; Ad. Nationes, xii) and Minucius Felix (Octavius, lx, xii, xxviii), felicitously

replied to the pagan taunt by showing that their persecutors themselves adored cruciform objects....

...It would seem that St. Anthony bore a cross in the form of tau on his cloak, and that it was Egyptian in origin....[1]

Thus, the *CE* states that the sign of the cross is very ancient and that the Greek god Prometheus was portrayed as having been bound to a "cross-beam" both on an ancient pot and in the writing of Lucian (c. 125-180 AD/CE), who used *two* Greek words for "cross": *stauros* and *skolops*. Both of these terms mean "stake," with *stauros* specified as an "upright cross" and serving as the same word used in the New Testament concerning Jesus's death. Indeed, the original term in the New Testament Greek is σταυρόω or stauróo, which means "to stake" as well as "to crucify." It is also important to keep in mind that the "unhappy tree" upon which one may be hung is, according to the *Catholic Encyclopedia,* likewise "known as a *cross.*" In the biblical book of Acts (10:39, 13:29), in fact, Christ is depicted as having been *hung on a tree.*[2] Again, that the cross possessed significance before Christ allegedly died upon it is indicated in the gospel story itself, when Christ tells his followers to "take up their crosses" in order to follow him. (Mt 16:24; Mk 10:21; Lk 14:27)

As regards pre-Christian images of gods on crosses or in the shape of a cross ("cruciform"), in his *Apology* (16) Church father Tertullian remarks:

> We have shown before that *your deities are derived from shapes modelled from the cross.* But you also worship victories, for in *your trophies the cross is the heart of the trophy.* The camp religion of the Romans is all through a worship of the standards, a setting the standards above all gods. Well, as *those images decking out the standards are ornaments of crosses.* All those hangings of *your standards and banners are robes of crosses.*[3]

The place where Tertullian has "shown before" that the Pagan gods were cross-shaped was in his treatise *Ad Nationes,* in which he remarks:

---

[1] *CE*, IV, 517-519. (Emph. added.)

[2] The word used in Acts is ξύλον—"xylon"—which is defined in Strong's (G3586) as "wood," including "1a) that which is made of wood 1) as a beam from which any one is suspended, a gibbet, a cross..." However, the second definition given is "tree," and, in the New Testament, *xylon* is never translated as "cross" or "gibbet" but mostly as "tree," with other translations being "staff," "staves," "wood" and "stocks," the latter of which occurs only once in reference to prisoners at Acts 16:24. The instances in the New Testament that refer to the *cross* upon which Christ is crucified use the word *stauros.* At Luke 23:31 and Revelation 2:7, 22:2 and 22:14, *xylon* clearly means "tree," as it does also at Genesis 1:11, 1:12, 1:29, 2:9—referring to the tree of life and tree of knowledge of good and evil, and so on. There are, in fact, 62 uses of the word *xylon* in the Greek Old Testament/Septuagint, the majority of which refer to a *tree* (or, as in Leviticus and Numbers, "cedar wood," which is nonetheless a tree). This exercise demonstrates that the "cross" and "unhappy tree" are essentially interchangeable, such that a god "hanging on a tree" could also be said to have been "crucified."

[3] Roberts, A., *ANCL*, XI, 85. (Emph. added.)

Chapter 12.—The Charge of Worshipping a Cross. The Heathens Themselves Made Much of Crosses in Sacred Things; Nay, Their Very Idols Were Formed on a Crucial [Crosslike] Frame.

As for him who affirms that we are "the priesthood of a cross," we shall claim him as our co-religionist. A cross is, in its material, a sign of wood; amongst yourselves also the object of worship is a wooden figure. Only, while with you the figure is a human one, with us the wood is its own figure. Never mind for the present what is the shape, provided the material is the same: the form, too, is of no importance, if so be it be the actual body of a god. If, however, there arises a question of difference on this point what, (let me ask,) is the difference between the Athenian Pallas, or the Pharian Ceres, and wood formed into a cross, when each is represented by a rough stock, without form, and by the merest rudiment of a statue of unformed wood? Every piece of timber which is fixed in the ground in an erect position is a part of a cross, and indeed the greater portion of its mass. But an entire cross is attributed to us, with its transverse beam, of course, and its projecting seat. Now you have the less to excuse you, for you dedicate to religion only a mutilated imperfect piece of wood, while others consecrate to the sacred purpose a complete structure. The truth, however, after all is, that *your religion is all cross*, as I shall show. You are indeed unaware that *your gods in their origin have proceeded from this hated cross*. Now, every image, whether carved out of wood or stone, or molten in metal, or produced out of any other richer material, must needs have had plastic hands engaged in its formation. Well, then, this modeller, before he did anything else, hit upon the form of a wooden cross, because even our own body assumes as its natural position the latent and concealed outline of a cross. Since the head rises upwards, and the back takes a straight direction, and the shoulders project laterally, *if you simply place a man with his arms and hands outstretched, you will make the general outline of a cross*. Starting, then, from this rudimental form and prop, as it were, he applies a covering of clay, and so gradually completes the limbs, and forms the body, and covers the cross within with the shape which he meant to impress upon the clay; then from this design, with the help of compasses and leaden moulds, he has got all ready for his image which is to be brought out into marble, or clay, or whatever the material be of which he has determined to make his god. (This, then, is the process:) after the cross-shaped frame, the clay; after the clay, the god. In a well-understood routine, the cross passes into a god through the clayey medium. The cross then you consecrate, and from it the consecrated (deity) begins to derive his origin.[1]

In these two passages we find some startling contentions about which many people may not be aware: To wit, the non-Christians possessed crosslike sacred objects and revered their idols of gods in the shape of a cross or in *cruciform*. In fact, Tertullian is very insistent on this point, stating of the Pagans: "*your religion is all cross*" and "*your gods in their origin have proceeded from this hated*

---

[1] Roberts, A., *ANF*, III, 122. (Emphasis added.)

cross." The Church father then proceeds to describe the human body with its arms outstretched as a model of the cross, a description that invokes the Egyptian cross—the crux ansata, or *ankh*, which represents *eternal life*, precisely as Jesus's cross is symbolic of everlasting life. In consideration of the fact that the ankh does indeed resemble a human being in cruciform, or on a *crucifix*, it is possible that Jesus's purported crucifixion was a *contrivance* based in part at least on this pervasive and highly important Egyptian image that had been significant for thousands of years by the time of Christ's alleged existence. This suggestion becomes even more likely when one considers how widely used was the ankh or crux ansata in early Egypto-*Christian* art. Indeed, the Copts themselves consistently used ankhs as symbols of the cross within their own brand of Christianity. As related by Rev. James Leslie Houlden, a professor of Theology at King's College, London: "...the Copts claim that the early Church of Alexandria had long used the ancient *Ankh* symbol as Egypt's cross."[1]

While Osiris is commonly associated with the ankh, so thorough has Horus's relationship been with it as well that one speaks of the "Horus cross" and "cross of Horus," which again lends credence to the idea that the Horos-Stauros was in reality based on the Egyptian god Horus.

Moreover, certain ankhs are depicted with arms and hands bearing objects, such as at Philae, where two ankhs are portrayed holding "was-scepters," the head of which has been speculated to represent either a type of animal or the god Set. In this case, the image resembles either Osiris or Horus throttling Set. The point here, however, is that these crosses are clearly anthropomorphized, representing *humans* to some extent—and that they resemble stylized *crucifixes*. Furthermore, in early Egyptian art we find primitive human images in the shape of the "crooked cross" or *swastika*; thus, again we possess anthropomorphized crosses or *crucifixes*, long pre-dating Christianity.

In addition, contrary to the impression given by the gospel story and Christian tradition, in addressing the Romans in his *Octavius* (29), Church father and Christian apologist Minucius Felix (fl. between 150 and 300?) *denied* that the Christians worshipped either the cross or a "criminal" upon it, remarking:

CHAP. XXIX.—ARGUMENT: NOR IS IT MORE TRUE THAT A MAN FASTENED TO A CROSS ON ACCOUNT OF HIS CRIMES IS WORSHIPPED BY CHRISTIANS...

For in that you attribute to our religion the worship of a criminal and his cross, you wander far from the neighbourhood of the truth, in thinking either that a criminal deserved, or that an earthly being was able, to be believed God. Miserable indeed is that man whose whole

---

[1] Houlden, 188.

hope is dependent on mortal man, for all his help is put an end to with the extinction of the man. The Egyptians certainly choose out a man for themselves whom they may worship... *Crosses, moreover, we neither worship nor wish for.* You, indeed, who consecrate gods of wood, adore wooden crosses perhaps as parts of your gods. For your very standards, as well as your banners, and flags of your camp, what else are they but crosses gilded and adorned? *Your victorious trophies not only imitate the appearance of a simple cross, but also that of a man affixed to it.*[1]

In *The Non-Christian Cross* (ch. II), John Denham Parsons calls these statements a "remarkable denunciation of the Cross as a Pagan symbol by a Christian Father who lived as late as the third century after Christ..." Moreover, while thus denying that Christians worship the cross, Felix contended that the Romans themselves possessed *crucifixes.* The assertion is all the more peculiar in consideration of the fact that Christ himself was never represented in art on a cross or as a crucifix, until the late fifth to sixth centuries.[2] Furthermore, Minucius says that the *Christians also do not worship an "earthly being,"* giving the impression that Christ was never a mortal man on Earth. Regarding this apparent contention, Felix translator and professor of Classical Studies at the University of Melbourne, Dr. G.W. Clarke, comments, "A remarkable avoidance of any mention of the Incarnation.... Indeed, so anxious is [Minucius Felix] to avoid admitting such a difficult doctrine that he gives the appearance of denying it..."[3] In fact, Minucius seems to be toeing the party line of the Docetists, a group of Gnostics who did not believe in the Incarnation. Regarding the Gnostic distaste for *matter* and *flesh,* as well as the Docetic denial of Christ's incarnation, theologian Rev. Dr. Cyril Richardson states:

> Other serious consequences followed from the Gnostic disparagement of the body. The doctrine of the incarnation was denied. Jesus only "appeared": he did not genuinely take on human flesh. Hence these Gnostics came to be known as "Docetics" (from *dokeo*, appear)... [4]

This denial of Christ come in the flesh—recorded in the canonical epistles of John (1 Jn 4:3; 2 Jn 1:7)—would constitute an admission that the gospel story is essentially *mythical* and therefore no more historical than the myths of other cultures. Adding to this air of mythicalness, in his *First Apology,* early Church father Justin Martyr discusses a number of important correspondences between Christianity and Pagan mythology:

Chapter 21. Analogies to the history of Christ.

---

[1] Roberts, A., *ANF*, IV, 191. (Emph. added.)
[2] *CE*, "Archaeology of the Cross and Crucifix," IV.
[3] Clarke, 327.
[4] Richardson, C., 25.

Was Horus "Crucified?"

And when we say also that the Word, who is the first-birth
was produced without sexual union, and that He, Jesus Ch
Teacher, was crucified and died, and rose again, and ascended into
heaven, we propound nothing different from what you believe
regarding those whom you esteem sons of Jupiter. For you know how
many sons your esteemed writers ascribed to Jupiter: Mercury, the
interpreting word and teacher of all; Æsculapius, who, though he
was a great physician, was struck by a thunderbolt, and so ascended
to heaven; and Bacchus too, after he had been torn limb from limb;
and Hercules, when he had committed himself to the flames to
escape his toils; and the sons of Leda, and Dioscuri; and Perseus,
son of Danae; and Bellerophon, who, though sprung from mortals,
rose to heaven on the horse Pegasus.[1]

Surprisingly, Martyr insists that, in contending Jesus Christ to
have been "produced without sexual union," crucified and
resurrected, Christians are "propounding *nothing different*" from what
the Pagans believed regarding the "sons of Jupiter"—a fact that most
people may be amazed to hear! How many have been taught that the
"sons of Jupiter"—*ancient Greek and Roman gods*—were "born of a
virgin" and crucified, rose from the dead and ascended into heaven,
like Jesus?

In addition, we must wonder precisely who in this list fits with
which characteristic. As previously noted, we know that, according to
Justin, it was *Perseus* who was born of the virgin Danae. We also
know that, among others—including Osiris and Horus—it is
Bacchus, or *Dionysus*, who was resurrected,[2] but who was *crucified*?
Martyr's contention that Christians propound nothing new leads us
to investigate very seriously the claims regarding various pagan gods
having been "shaped like crosses" or *on crosses*, as Tertullian and
Minucius Felix assert, as well as "crucified," as Justin himself notes.
We must further recall the words of the *Catholic Encyclopedia*
regarding the Greek god Prometheus as having been depicted on a
cross. And we need to be mindful of the definition of *crucifigere*,
whence comes "crucify," meaning "to fix on a cross," but not
necessarily to toss a human being to the ground and nail him to a
piece of wood. The cross to which one may be fixed, of course, could
be *any* substance, including "space" or the "vault of heaven," as we
shall see. The motifs of both the cross and the god on the cross or in
cruciform were thus popular long before the common era—and these
revered pre-Christian motifs are evidently direct lifts into the
Christian religion.

With these facts at hand, could there be any truth to the
assertion that any *Egyptian* gods were "crucified?" Firstly, we have
seen that the crux ansata or ankh represented a highly popular
sacred object for thousands of years prior to the common era. We

---

[1] Roberts, A., *ANF*, I, 170. (Emph. added.)
[2] Johnston, 487.

have also noted that the ankh resembles a human being with arms outstretched in the shape of a cross or in cruciform. Moreover, in very archaic times in Egypt humans were likewise depicted in the shape of the swastika or crooked cross, likewise appearing in cruciform.

In addition, over the millennia—*greatly antedating Christianity*—the cross has been a symbol of the sun,[1] for a variety of reasons, including the sun's crossing the sky, as well as it being "hung on a cross" during the equinoxes and a predominant image created when the solar orb is on the horizon. In this regard, in numerous Egyptian scriptures, the sun is depicted as "crossing over" the sky, by its movement essentially making the sign of the cross.[2] In reality, sunrise is the time of "Horus who crosses the sky," as in a sunrise hymn.[3] One sun hymn addressing Horus says:

How "passing over" you are, Harakhty
completing your task of yesterday every day
The one who creates the years and joins together the days and months
days and nights
the hours correspond to his stride....[4]

This paean is astrotheological and is also reminiscent of the Judeo-Christian interpretation of the Creator. The God Sun is likewise addressed as the one who "crosses the heavens and passes through the underworld." Self-renewing, he is ever watchful and awake. He is omnipresent, as the "light on every way."[5]

This idea of the sun god "passing over" or "crossing over" is thus repeated many times in the ancient texts, his movements representing a sort of "crossification."[6] Indeed, in the Coffin Texts appear many references to the "crossing over" of the sky by the sun.[7] Along the same lines, the deceased at CT Sp. 357 possesses the epithet of "he who crosses the sky."[8] The sign of the cross is also formed as the sun god "crosses the Two Lands night and day..."[9]

The significance of saying that the sun god was "crucified" is not that his myth follows the gospel story exactly but that he was a revered pre-Christian god "on a cross" and that this particular motif was adopted by those who created the Christian myth specifically for the reason that it *was* a popular and revered theme.

---

[1] See, e.g, Lockyer, *Nature*, XXXV, 346.
[2] See, e.g., CT 307; Faulkner, *AECT*, I, 226.
[3] Assman, *ESRNK*, 15.
[4] Assman, *ESRNK*, 97.
[5] Assman, *ESRNK*, 97.
[6] See, e.g., Assman, *ESRNK*, 51, 97.
[7] See e.g., CT Sp. 57:246; CT Sp. 184:83. (Faulkner, *AECT*, I, 54, 154.)
[8] Faulkner, *AECT*, II, 2.
[9] Assman, *ESRNK*, 119.

It is fitting, therefore, for any number of "suns gods" or solar aspects and epithets to be associated with the cross. In this regard, the Egyptian Primeval or "First Cause" God Atum is likewise depicted with arms outstretched, as at CT Sp. 136: "...I have extended my arms, I have ruled the sky..."[1] In reality, Atum in cruciform is not alone, as there were several others in the Egyptian religion in a similar position.

Shu in Cruciform

Another of these crucial gods is Atum's son, Shu, who in the later periods, a few centuries before the common era, became combined with Horus. Shu is thus shown in images in cruciform, separating the earth from the sky, at times holding numerous ankhs or crosses of eternal life.[2] The identification of the crosslike Shu "the uplifter" who separates heaven from earth with Horus seems much like the predecessor of the Gnostic Horos as Stauros, the Cross. Interestingly, while "Shu" thus appears in the shape of a cross, the word in Sahidic Coptic for "cross," as in the wooden stave, is *she, shay* or *shi*.[3]

According to Massey, Shu is the "uplifter of the heavens," "establisher of the equinox,"[4] "raiser of the four pillars of the four quarters."[5] In *Ancient Egypt, Light of the World*, Massey says of Shu, "He is a pillar of support to the firmament as founder of the double equinox.... It was at the equinoctial level that the quarrel of Sut and Horus was settled for the time being by Shu. Shu thus stands for equinox as the link of connection betwixt Sut and Horus in the north and south."[6]

In this regard, Richard Darlow writes: "The Egyptians referred to the four bright stars that formed a great cross in their sky as '*the Pillars of Shu*,' or '*the Four Supports of the Heavens*,' these stars occupying the constellations of Leo, Scorpio, Aquarius and Taurus."[7]

Horus of the Cross

We have previously reviewed the contention that the Valentinian Gnostics of Alexandria utilized Egyptian mythology in their creation and that the god Horus was associated with the Gnostic Horos, who was in turn identified with the *Cross*. Indeed, it is possible that the "confusion" of *Horus* with "the Cross" was likewise a deliberate contrivance based on Egyptian mythological motifs and imagery. This development is intimated in the *Encyclopedia Britannica's* entry concerning "Valentinus":

---

[1] Faulkner, *AECT*, I, 117.
[2] Lockyer, *Nature*, XLIII, 562.
[3] Lambdin, 307.
[4] Massey, *AELW*, I, 325.
[5] Massey, *AELW*, I, 502.
[6] Massey, *AELW*, I, 325.
[7] Darlow, 144.

ntirely peculiar to Valentinian Gnosticism is that of Horos (Jupiter). *The name is perhaps an echo of the Egyptian Horus.* The peculiar task of Horos is to separate the fallen aeons from the upper world of aeons. At the same time he became (first, perhaps, in the later Valentinian systems) a kind of world-creative power, who in this capacity helps to construct an ordered world out of Sophia and her passion. He is also called, curiously enough, Stauros (cross), and we frequently meet with references to the figure of Stauros. But we must not be in too great a hurry to conjecture that this is a Christian figure. *Speculations about the Stauros are older than Christianity,* and a Platonic conception may have been at work here. Plato had already stated that the world-soul revealed itself in the form of the letter Chi (X); by which he meant that the figure described in the heavens by the intersecting orbits of the sun and the planetary ecliptic. Since through this double orbit all the movements of the heavenly powers are determined, so all "becoming" and all life depended on it, and thus we can understand the statement that the world-soul appears in the form of an X, or a cross. The cross can also stand for the wondrous aeon on whom depends the ordering and life of the world, and thus Horos-Stauros appears here as the first redeemer of Sophia from her passions, and as the orderer of the creation of the world which now begins. This explanation of Horos, moreover, is not a mere conjecture, but one branch of the Valentinian school, the Marcosians, have expressly so explained this figure. Naturally, then, the figure of Horos-Stauros was often in later days assimilated to that of the Christian Redeemer.[1]

As is clear here and elsewhere, the identification of Horos with Horus is not unreasonable or unwarranted, especially since it has been asserted by Witt, for one, that Epiphanius's virgin-born Aion or *Aeon* is *Horus.* Serving as further comparison, Horos the Cross constitutes a "world-creative power," indicative of the overarching role of the *Egyptian sun god.* The Horos-Cross helps to order the world after Sophia suffers a passion, resembling the myth of Horus assisting Isis in restoring Osiris after *his* passion. Indeed, both Horos and Horus play the role of *Redeemer.* Moreover, the *EB* says that speculations concerning "Stauros"—a personified cross of theological significance—are "older than Christianity."

Indeed, the "world-soul" can be found as a *cross* in Plato's writings four centuries before the common era. Regarding the influence of Platonic thinking upon Christianity, Princeton University professor of History Dr. Peter Brown (b. 1935) remarks:

> ...pagan Platonists regarded the Christian myth of redemption—an Incarnation, a Crucifixion and a Resurrection of the body—as a barbarous innovation on the authentic teachings of their master. To them, it was as if some vandal had set up a vulgar and histrionic piece of Baroque sculpture beneath the ethereal dome of a Byzantine church. The more "liberal" pagan Platonists had hoped to "civilize" the Christian churches by writing *"In the beginning was the Word"* in

---

[1] *Enc. Brit.,* XXVII, 854. (Emph. added.)

golden letters on their walls; but they would not tolerate even S. John when he said that *"The Word was made flesh."*[1]

In other words, the Platonists assumed that the Christians had essentially plagiarized Plato's doctrines and had historicized and carnalized them, to which they strenuously objected. Such contentions would indicate these Platonists did not consider "Jesus Christ" to have been a historical character but, rather, a vulgar anthropomorphization and historicization of Platonic ideals.

In any event, the Platonic solar cross in the sky, the *EB* clarifies, was *astronomical*, representing the sun's orbit intersecting the earth's ecliptic. This Platonic cross in the vault of heaven becomes *astrotheologically* Horos, another reason to suspect the Gnostic Limit to be one with the god Horus, since, as we have seen and will continue to see, Horus the sun god was depicted with outstretched arms in the vault of heaven.

Regarding Horos the Stauros and "his" relationship to the sun and to Horus, Massey states:

> This stave, stake, prop, or stay of the suffering sun was the Stauros, which was primarily a stake for supporting, shaped as a cross. Thus Horus the crosser was called Stauros by the Gnostics.[2]

Moreover, Horos-Stauros "was often assimilated" to Christ[3]—yet, Stauros came first. Indeed, within Valentinianism, the Soter or Savior is sometimes the Christos and at other times Horos-Stauros. Horos's savior role is explained by *EB*:

> This name pronounced at baptism over the faithful has above all the significance that the name will protect the soul in its ascent through the heavens, conduct it safely through all hostile powers to the lower heavens, and procure it access to Horos, who frightens back the lower souls by his magic word...[4]

From such salvational doctrines—including the "magic word" to scare off "lower souls," like the use of Jesus's name as a spell to cast out demons[5]—it may be obvious why Horos was often assimilated to Christ. The same may be said of the sun god Horus as well, for a variety of reasons we have already investigated that demonstrate the solid Horus-Jesus connection.

In Tertullian's *Against the Valentinians*, in which he discusses "Horus" as the "great foundation of the universe," as well as the Cross, Redeemer and Emancipator, we find reference to Horus/Horos

---

[1] Brown, P., 94.

[2] Massey, *NG*, 433.

[3] *Enc. Brit.*, XXVII, 854. (Emph. added.)

[4] *Enc. Brit.*, XXVII, 856.

[5] Mt 7:22; Lk 10:17: "The seventy returned with joy, saying, 'Lord, even the demons are subject to us in your name!'" (RSV) Here is a good place to interject a reminder of the comparison between the 70 or *72* disciples of Christ with the 72 companions of Set, both numbers apparently referring to the dodecans.

being involved in a *crucifixion*. Concerning this Gnostic story of Sophia, Tertullian relates (X):

> ...she indeed remained within the bounds of the Pleroma, but that her Enthymesis, with the accruing Passion, was banished by Horos, and crucified and cast out from the Pleroma.

While the Pleroma represents the "totality of the heavenly divine," the "Enthymesis" of Sophia is defined as "desire" and "inclination," as well as "a spirit-like substance," which, Tertullian claims, was *crucified*—*crucifixam*, in the original Latin—here surely not signifying "she" was a human being tossed to the ground and nailed to a piece of wood but likely reflecting a metaphysical agency impressed upon a "cosmic cross," so to speak, and/or forced into the shape of a cross. In using the term *crucifixam*, Tertullian must have understood this different, more cosmic meaning, since he certainly knew that the Pleroma in which the Gnostic fantasy took place was *not* on Earth.

We have encountered the evidence that the story of Sophia and Horos constitutes a Gnostic remake of Egyptian myth. These Gnosticizing efforts may reflect Egyptian *mysteries*, including the equation of the god *Horus* with Stauros, the personified Cross. Gnosticism is a complex system that did not arise in a vacuum but took into itself the major religious ideas and terminology of the Mediterranean area in which it flourished, including and especially those of the Egyptian religion. In Egypt, Gnosticism eventually emerges as a concerted effort to usurp the Egyptian religion by subordinating its gods to Christ. In this regard, Isis becomes Sophia, Horus is Horos, Set/Typhon becomes "the vicious Passion," Osiris (and Horus) is Christ, and so on. In this convoluted mess of Gnosticism, we seem to be peering into the murky conglomeration of all the mystery schools and religions of the Roman Empire. Indeed, in his refutation, Tertullian specifically compares the Valentinian "heresy" with the *Eleusinian mysteries.* Moreover, mysteries texts such as the so-called "Hermetic writings" absolutely make this connection between these Gnostic concepts and the Egyptian religion. These Hermetic texts were composed by a number of hands over a period of centuries and attributed to "Hermes Trismegistus" or "Thrice-Blessed," the magical scribe of Egypt also called Thoth or Tehuti.

In studying the development of early Christianity, one thing is clear: The Valentinians with their bizarre Egypto-Greco-Syro-Judeo-Gnosticism, were a force strong enough to be reckoned with that Tertullian felt the need to learn this complex and tedious cosmology in his attempt to refute it.

Outstretched Arms as the Sign of the Cross

In addition to its presence in the Gnostic-Egyptian mythology, as we sift through Egyptian imagery, we find this concept associating

Horus with a cross to possess merit, serving as the possible prototype of the Gnostic Horos-Cross. As we have seen, Horus is depicted as the "sun of righteousness" with wings outstretched to cover the world. Again, as Hornung relates, "Horus shows himself in the image of the hawk whose wings span the sky..."[1] Indeed, demonstrating this visual of Horus, combined with that of the biblical "Sun of Righteousness" arising with "healing in his wings" as found at Malachi 4:2, just a few verses before the gospel of Matthew—and referring to Jesus, according to Christian doctrine—Hornung relates that Horus the Elder was "the ancient god of the heavens, whose wings spread over the whole earth."[2]

A number of Egyptian goddesses are likewise depicted in cruciform, with arms and wings outstretched, found in tombs and commonly on coffins. One place for the goddess Nut's loving protection was on coffins, such as that of Henettawy (c. 1040-992 BCE).[3] This magnificent image of a Nut in cruciform, along with its central position, demonstrates the importance of this crosslike symbol. A protective winged Isis also appears on the end of the third anthropoid coffin of King Tut,[4] while goddesses in cruciform were also placed on the four corners of his sarcophagus. This motif of the four "guardian goddesses" with the outstretched *arms* can likewise be found "on the corners of royal sarcophagi of the Eighteenth Dynasty or as freestanding images..."[5]

The coffin of Neskhonsu-pakhered is "replete with images of protective winged deities: three falcons and a winged ram-headed deity, together with Isis and Nephthys..."[6] The theme, of course, reminds one of Jesus as the "Sun of Righteousness rising with healing on his wings..." Also, in Christian times coffins have been adorned in essentially the same spot with *crosses*.

Adding to this picture, in his *Egyptian Antiquities in the British Museum*, Dr. Samuel Sharpe describes various papyri with images of Horus in the "vault of heaven" with "outstretched arms."[7] In this iconography described by Sharpe, Isis too is depicted several times with "outstretched arms," as are other deities, including the Egyptian sun in the vault of heaven with four apes underneath worshipping it.[8] This depiction sounds much like that of Aan in the corners of the Lake in the afterlife, possibly with Re or Osiris in the center.

In another place, Sharpe describes one of these *crucial* images of Horus thus:

---

[1] Hornung, *CGAE*, 124.
[2] Hornung, *VK*, 59.
[3] "Coffin set of Henettawy."
[4] Carter no. 255; Egyptian Museum JE60671, www.griffith.ox.ac.uk/gri/4rostut.html
[5] Lesko, 51.
[6] Capel, 168.
[7] Sharpe, *EA*, 143, 144.
[8] Sharpe, *EA*, 149.

...we find the vault of heaven represented not by the outstretched wings of either that god of Thebes [Amen/Amun], or of Neith the queen of Sais, but by the two arms of Horus, with the head hanging downwards, *as the Almighty is painted by some of the early Italian masters.*[1]

Here Sharpe is obviously struck by the similarity of the Egyptian image of Horus to that of Christ on the cross. In other words, *Horus appeared to be crucified*, which would be logical also in his identity as Shu, previously discussed.

Regarding the cross and the image of a god in cruciform—or the *crucifix*—William Williamson states:

The cross...is a symbol of the highest antiquity, but the representation of a figure with the hands and feet pierced with nails belongs to a later period. The most ancient delineation of the cruciform attitude is the figure of the god in the vault of heaven, with outstretched arms, blessing the universe.[2]

The very ancient god in the "vault of heaven" would naturally be the sun, whose position on the cross evidently evolved into the figure of a man with nails in his hands and feet.[3] That the god in the vault of heaven with outstretched arms has been deemed a "cross" is apparent from these themes, fitting in not only with the assertions by Tertullian and Minucius that the Roman gods in cruciform represented *crosses* but also with those by Justin Martyr and the writer of the apocryphal Christian text the Epistle of Barnabas (12), which relates: "So Moses...spread his two arms out wide, and Israel thereupon began to regain the victory."[4] It is important to note that the provenance for the Epistle of Barnabas is placed by many scholars as *Alexandria, Egypt.* Justin Martyr in *Dialogue with Trypho* (90) based one of his major arguments about the "prefiguring" of Christ's cross upon Moses's gesture: "The Stretched Out Hands of Moses Signified Beforehand the Cross...."[5] Martyr thus contended that, in "outstretching his hands" at Exodus 17:11, the biblical prophet Moses was making "the sign of the cross."[6] Continuing this tradition is a Christian compilation perhaps originally Coptic[7] and possibly begun in the sixth century AD/CE called *The Kebra Nagast*, which purports to contain the history of the Queen of Sheba, and which remarks:

[1] Sharpe, *EMEC*, 83-84. (Emph. added.)
[2] Williamson, 52.
[3] For more on non-Christian gods in cruciform, including those nailed to crosses, see my book *Suns of God.*
[4] Staniforth, 173.
[5] Roberts, A., *ANF*, I, 244.
[6] Although modern translations of Exodus 17:11 do not give this impression that Moses was making the "sign of the cross," such a concept was very much believed by early Christian writers.
[7] Budge, *KN*, xxxi.

And the rod of Moses by means of which he performed the miracle is to be interpreted as the wood of the Cross, whereby He delivered Adam and his children from the punishment of devils...

...And as Moses smote the mountains by stretching out his hands with his rod, and brought forth punishments by the command of God, even so Christ, by stretching out His hands upon the wood of the Cross, drove out the demons from men by the might of His Cross. When God said to Moses, "Smite with thy rod," He meant, "Make the Sign of the Cross of Christ," and when God said unto Moses, "Stretch out thy hand," He meant that by the spreading out of His hand Christ hath redeemed us from the servitude of the enemy, and hath given us life by the stretching out of His hand upon the wood of the Cross....

...The stretching out of the hand of Moses indicateth the Cross of Christ...[1]

In addition to establishing Moses with the outstretched arms or hands making the sign of the cross, one of the main purposes of the *Kebra Nagast*, it would seem, is to provide an account of the conversion of the Ethiopian people away from their ancient astrotheological worship, which much resembled that of Egypt, to the god of Israel.[2]

Another god depicted in cruciform with outstretched arms in the "vault of heaven" would be Osiris, about whom John M. Robertson remarks:

The ritual lamentation of the divine sisters, Isis and Nephthys, for Osiris...is found in the temple remains of the island of Philae expressly connected with the representation of Osiris in the form of a crucifix, the God's head standing on the top of a four-barred Nilometer, faced by the mourning female figures. Here, too, he represents the Trinity, combining the attributes of Phtah-Sokari-Osiris...."[3]

On the Egyptian island of Philae, where Osiris's heart was said to be buried by Isis, exists a Ptolemaic-era temple enclosure full of imagery, apparently including Osiris's head on top of a cross representing a "Nilometer," an architectural device used to measure the Nile—an appropriate depiction in consideration of the fact that Osiris symbolized the Nile itself. Per Robertson's description, this image of "Osiris on the cross" is "faced" by his two mourning sisters,

---

[1] Budge, *KN*, 180-182.

[2] Budge epitomizes the *Kebra Nagast*: "The queen and her people were idolaters and worshipped the sun, and they were under the influence of Satan, who had turned them from the right way." (Budge, *KN*, lvii.) And again: "During her stay in Jerusalem Makeda [the Queen of Sheba] conversed daily with Solomon, and she learned from him about the God of the Hebrews, the Creator of the heavens and the earth. She herself worshipped the sun, moon and stars, and trees, and idols of gold and silver, but under the influence of Solomon's beautiful voice and eloquent words she renounced Sabaism, and worshipped not the sun but the sun's Creator, the God of Israel." (Budge, *KN*, lxix.)

[3] Robertson, 410-411.

the *Merta*, like the sisters of Lazarus as well as the two Marys at the foot of Christ's cross. This scene is also confirmed by other images elsewhere of Osiris as his cross-like *djed* (Tat or Tau) pillar, or as Osiris-Re, with the cross-like horns of a ram, surrounded by Isis and Nephthys.[1] Naturally, it is only in the gospel of John (19:25) that the two Marys are close to Christ in the scene; in Matthew and Mark, they are present but "beholding from afar." (Mt 27:55-56; Mk 15:40) In considering such a scenario, we need to keep in mind again that, when it is said that Osiris or Horus was "crucified," it is not meant that either was thrown to the ground and nailed to a wooden cross but that one or the other was depicted in cruciform or as a *crucifix*, i.e., in "crucial frame," as styled by Tertullian. In this case, however, the comparison to the Christian *crucifixion scene* seems warranted.

In his remarks regarding Osiris being crucified previously provided, Doane cites Sir Rev. George William Cox (1827-1902), an Oxford University scholar, who first speaks of the Egyptian cross or *stauros* of Osiris and then states the god was crucified on a tree.[2] Cox later mentions "the crucifixion and resurrection of Osiris."[3] As we have seen, the "unhappy tree" of execution is deemed a *cross*. Since in one version of the myth Osiris is encased in a tree, it may be possible to say he was "placed on a cross," although Rev. Cox may have had something else in mind in his assessment, including Osiris as, in or on the treelike djed pillar. In any event, this notion of "Osiris crucified" may have been one of the reasons behind the ubiquitous symbol of eternal life, the ankh or *crux ansata*, which resembles a person "crucified in the heavens" or the image of Osiris's head on the "four-barred Nilometer."

Osiris and Djed Pillar

In discussing the meaning of Osiris's djed pillar from the perspective of a neurosurgeon and anthropologist, Dr. Aaron G. Filler addresses the tradition that the djed represents the human spine, as a symbol of resurrection, remarking:

> When an Egyptian was buried, symbols of the spine of Osiris were considered crucial to the opportunity for resurrection in the afterlife. The resurrection of Osiris through the assembly of his vertebrae by Isis was described in the funerary texts placed alongside most major Egyptian burials for thousands of years. The raising of the djed column commemorates this, and, as many religious authorities have pointed out, Christ's resurrection and the Roman Cross make much more sense when it is appreciated that for thousands of years in the Middle East, erection of the djed cross was the symbol of resurrection of Osiris, king of the afterlife.[4]

[1] Hornung, *VK*, 120, 121, 124.
[2] Cox, 115 (Kessinger); 352 (Kegan Paul).
[3] Cox, 125.
[4] Filler, 73.

Was Horus "Crucified?"

As a symbol of Osiris's backbone, the djed stands for
and "strength."[1] A "roughly cruciform" object, the djed is the
"principal symbol" of Osiris, no mere token but quite popular around
Egypt for thousands of years. In this same regard, Dr. Knapp states:

> Parallels have been made between the raising of the *Djed Column* on
> which Osiris's body rested, the chaining of Prometheus to a pillar in
> the Caucasus, and Christ's crucifixion on the wooden cross.[2]

The erection of the djed cross at the 30-year Sed festival is also
noteworthy, in that the latter represents the renewal of the Horus-
king, indicating the cross's role in "eternal life." The "age" at which
the life-giving cross is erected is significant in that Jesus's cross was
also erected when he was about 30. In addition, the erection of the
djed cross during the celebration also apparently took the place of
human sacrifice, which was designed to propitiate the god or God in
order to remove sins and bring about continuity of the community as
a whole.[3] Hence, Osiris's djed cross was essentially erected for "our
sins," much like the Christian cross, with Christ's *sacrifice* upon it.

Regarding Osiris and the djed pillar, in *The Riddle of Resurrection:
"Dying and Rising Gods" in the Ancient Near East*, Dr. Mettinger
remarks:

> ...The Osiris celebrations took place during the month of Khoiak,
> more precisely Khoiak 18-30 (New Kingdom) or Khoiak 12-30 (Late
> Period). After various preparations, the funeral took place during
> Khoiak 24-30 and ended with the erection of the Djed pillar on the
> 30th of the month as an emblem of Osiris' resurrection....

> Two important features of the Khoiak festivals should be noted here:
> (a) The central role of so-called Osiris gardens or Osiris effigies, with
> sprouting corn that symbolized the resurrection of the god...(b)...
> About a hundred occurrences of the expression..."raise
> yourself"...are known already in the *Pyramid Texts*... The dead
> Osiris...is summoned to rise again.[4]

As we can see, the "erection of the Djed pillar" constitutes an
"emblem of Osiris's resurrection," while "sprouting corn...symbolized
the resurrection of the god." Moreover, the *dead* Osiris is "summoned
to rise again," with 100 or so invocations of resurrection in the
Pyramid Texts alone. Again, concerning the Khoiak/Koiak
celebration, Mettinger remarks, "The death and resurrection of Osiris
are the most central features of this festival."[5] Osiris is thus a *dying
and rising god*, erected as and on a crosslike pillar.

---

[1] Ruiz, 142.
[2] Knapp, 375.
[3] Neumann, E., 92.
[4] Mettinger, 169.
[5] Mettinger, 182.

Set "Crucified"

Even Osiris and Horus's enemy Set/Seth was deemed by mythologist Joseph Campbell to have been "crucified." In referring to an ancient depiction of a crucifixion found at Rome, in which the figure is portrayed with an ass's head and which is supposed to be "Christian," Campbell remarks:

> From exactly the same period we have, from Egypt, a depiction of Set, crucified. Set slew Osiris. Osiris's son, Horus, then had a great battle with Set. Set is not depicted exactly crucified. He is tied, hands behind his back, to the slave post, down on his knees, and knives are in him.... And Set is represented as having an ass's head...[1]

In *The Mythic Image*, Campbell also states, "The figure with the head of an ass, stuck with knives and bound by his arms to a forked slave-stick, is Seth, conquered."[2] A "forked slave-stick" could be considered a stake or *stauros*, to which Christ too was said to have been bound. Regarding the ass-headed god, Doresse notes:

> The god with the head of an ass is the image of the Demiurge Ialdabaoth, the "god of the Jews"... It is upon certain monuments of Egypt that we find the most ancient proofs of the attribution of a donkey's head to a god, who was to become progressively identified with the god of the Jews. This originated from the Asiatic god Sutekh, whom the Egyptians assimilated to one of their own greatest gods: Seth, the adversary of Osiris. They represented Seth also, after the period of the Persian invasions, with a human body and an ass's head. Afterwards, this god Seth was definitely regarded by the Egyptians—in accordance with a late myth mentioned by Plutarch in his *De Iside*, § 31—as the father of the legendary heroes Hierosolymus and Judaeus—that is, as the ancestor of the Jews!...[3]

From these remarks as well as the early "Christian" image of an ass-headed god being crucified that may in fact represent Set/Seth, we may suggest again that the Egyptians themselves possessed traditions of a "crucified god." Since Horus is also portrayed as Set's brother as well as being identified with or as Set himself, it could be claimed that "Horus" likewise was "crucified." Indeed, regarding a stela from the period of the pharaoh Shabataka/Shebitku (fl. 702-690 BCE) now in Turin and described by Dr. William Pleyte, a director of the Museum of Antiquities at Leyden, Budge remarks:

> On this stele is a figure of the double god Horus-Set with outstretched arms, which seems to indicate that one arm specially protects the two royal personages who were connected with the South, and the other the two who were connected with the North.[4]

As we have seen, early Christians considered a god with outstretched arms to be a form of the *cross*, as they did likewise with

---

[1] Campbell, *TAT*, 66.
[2] Campbell, *MI*, 29.
[3] Doresse, 42.
[4] Budge, *ESHM*, 33. Budge cites the reference to Pleyte's "*Aeg. Zeit.*, 1876, p. 51."

Was Horus "Crucified?"

Moses purportedly making the sign of the cross by raising i.. or hands. Thus, the figure of Horus with outstretched arms co. also by deemed a god in the shape of a cross or crucified in the vault of heaven/space.

The "Divine Man" Crucified in Space

Regarding Egyptian human figures in cruciform, or in the shape of a cross with outstretched arms, Massey remarks upon one found in Nubia in lower Egypt and then comments:

> Osiris has been found in this attitude. Also [the Indian god] Vishnu as Witoba is presented as the crucified in what has been termed the crucifixion in space; the crucifixion without a cross, in which the god himself *is the cross* in a male form, just as the genitrix is the crossed one in a female form, and as Horus was Stauros.

> It is true that the sun of the western crossing was considered to be the suffering, dying sun. As Atum he was said to set from the land of life. As Horus the elder we see the god on the cross, at the crossing which is represented by the cross-beam of the scales. This is Horus the Child, and Horus "the Lamb," who was described as the divine victim that died to save....

> The crossing of the west was on the dark side where Typhon triumphed over the lord of light, and in a sense here was the cross of death, the opposite to the cross of Easter and the resurrection.[1]

The "crucifixion in space" usually refers to that of Plato's "second God, who impressed himself on the universe in the form of the cross,"[2] constituting the Greek philosopher's "world-soul" on an X, which, as we have seen, represents the sun crossing the ecliptic. This "second god" is not only the "Demiurge," or "artificer of this world," but also the Logos/Word itself. Another Platonic concept is the crucified "divine man"[3] or "just man," found in Plato's *Republic* (II, 361A-362B), concerning whom Cardinal Ratzinger (Pope Benedict XVI) states:

> ...according to Plato the truly just man must be misunderstood and persecuted in this world; indeed, Plato goes so far as to write: "They will say that our just man will be scourged, racked, fettered, will have his eyes burned out, and at last, after all manner of suffering will be crucified." This passage, written four hundred years before Christ, is always bound to move a Christian deeply.[4]

---

[1] Massey, *NG*, 441.
[2] Lundy, 173; Bradshaw, 52; Roberts, A., *ANF*, VII, 238. See Philo for this "second God" as well: "On Dreams," 1, xxxix (227); Philo/Yonge, 385.
[3] "...the divine man described by Plato, who bicussated and was stamped upon the universe *in the likeness of a cross*." (Massey, *AELW*, II, 724.)
[4] Ratzinger, 292. The Pope uses Lindsay's translation, which renders the pertinent Greek term "crucified," whereas Jowlett translates *anaschinduleuthêsetai* (analogous to *anaskolopizo*) as "impaled," demonstrating the different meanings of the word derived from *skolops* or "stake."

Although this passage may be "bound to move a Christian deeply," what is not discussed is that this Platonic concept constitutes one possible *blueprint* for the Christian crucifixion motif, particularly in consideration of the popularity of Plato's writings, especially among philosophers and religionists. Another significant blueprint in the creation of Christ's passion narrative, of course, would be the Jewish scriptures in the Old Testament, especially the "Suffering Servant" at Isaiah 53:4-12 (RSV):

> Surely he has borne our griefs and carried our sorrows; yet we esteemed him stricken, smitten by God, and afflicted.
>
> But he was wounded for our transgressions, he was bruised for our iniquities; upon him was the chastisement that made us whole, and with his stripes we are healed....
>
> He was oppressed, and he was afflicted, yet he opened not his mouth; like a lamb that is led to the slaughter, and like a sheep that before its shearers is dumb, so he opened not his mouth.
>
> By oppression and judgment he was taken away; and as for his generation, who considered that he was cut off out of the land of the living, stricken for the transgression of my people?...
>
> Therefore I will divide him a portion with the great, and he shall divide the spoil with the strong; because he poured out his soul to death, and was numbered with the transgressors; yet he bore the sin of many, and made intercession for the transgressors.

Other scriptures serving as a blueprint for Christ's passion may be found in Psalms (69:22; 22:18; 109:25; 22:1) as well.[1] It is apparent that this passage in Isaiah 53 was used as a *blueprint* for the creation of the New Testament passion narrative. There are a couple of other clues here that indicate why the gospel story was created like it was: 1. The Suffering Servant is "stricken for the transgressions of my people," which would explain why "the Jews" are blamed for Christ's death; and 2. "number with the trangressors" may explain the inclusion of the "two thieves" theme in Christ's passion narrative. (Mt 27:38; Mk 15:27)

The combination of the theme of the god on a cross or in cruciform with the Jewish "messianic" scriptures—which represent in large part a description of human sacrifice or, specifically, the sacred-king ritual sacrifice[2]— rates as the reason the Christian crucifixion motif focuses more on the suffering part of the passion, although even this aspect is not unique, as we can see from both the Just Man of Plato and the story of Osiris's passion. The god crucified in space may not be considered to be "suffering," although in the solar myth the sun is said very much to be afflicted as it moves towards the

---

[1] For other scriptural precedents apparently used in the creation of the Christ character, see my book *Who Was Jesus?*, 124-137.

[2] For more on the subject of ritualistic human and "sacred king" sacrifice, see my book *Suns of God.*

death of winter. Nevertheless, although human sacrifice was not unknown in Egypt, the sacred-king sacrifice element of the "god on a cross" motif is not emphasized in Egyptian religion, as the "crucifixion" in Egypt is perceived as symbolic rather than actual—a fact we opine is likewise applicable to Christianity as well.

Concerning the "divine man" crucified in space, Massey finds another precedent in Egypt:

> Thus the divine man, as the cruciform support of all in Ptah-Sekeri or Osiris, was the prototype of the Crucified. This god of the four quarters is portrayed as Atum-Ra in the Ritual (ch. 82). It is he who says (by proxy) "My head is that of Ra and I am summed up as Atum, four times the arm's length of Ra, four times the width of the world." Thus Atum, the divine man, was a quadrangular figure of the four quarters in the heaven founded according to "the measure of a man" which is reproduced in Revelation. [Rev. 21:17][1]

Indeed, this passage is reminiscent of Atum's posture in CT Sp. 136, previously noted, with his arms extended.[2] The pertinent part of BD 82 is titled "Chapter whereby one assumeth the form of Ptah" per Renouf's translation, which was used by Massey above. Budge renders the title, "The Chapter of changing into Ptah," while Faulkner translates it as "Chapter for becoming Ptah," with the pertinent passage as follows: "My head is that of Re who is united with Atum, the four suns of the length of the land..."[3] Budge translates part of the relevant text as, "The four regions of Ra are the limits of the earth."[4] This passage does sound much like a description of the ancient solar symbol of a *cross*, as well as the equally solar images of a "crooked cross" or *swastika* found in early Egyptian cylinder-seals, some of which reflect *humans* in this cross shape. The creator god Ptah is one of the oldest and most important, deemed to be the "father of the gods," while Atum is also a highly ancient and revered deity, likewise the "father of the gods."

Further elucidating upon the divine man, Albert Parsons remarks:

> Plato spoke of a crucified divine man floating in space. Light is thrown upon his meaning by an ancient figure of the Galaxy in the form of a man, with the axis of the poles represented by a perpendicular spear resting on the feet and issuing forth from the top of the head, while the equator is represented by another spear run horizontally through the body. This is only extending the axial and equatorial lines of the earth from our position at the centre of the Galaxy to its limits in both directions. Thus is the divine man crossified in space. The obliquity of the ecliptic, as the result of the disaster which titled the earth's axis, is indicated in this ancient

[1] Massey, *AELW*, II, 724.
[2] Faulkner, *AECT*, I, 117.
[3] Faulkner, *EBD*, pl. 27.
[4] Budge, *EBD* (1967), 338.

..gure by a spear thrust diagonally upward through the side of the divine man.[1]

This figure is called by Parsons the "Medieval Macrocosmic Crucifixion," an interesting image worthy of further study, particularly in consideration of its apparent connection to Plato, Christ and Christianity.

This "divine man crucified in space" may be related to the many instances of Horus and other Egyptian deities with outstretched arms in the vault of heaven and may be at the basis of the Horos-Stauros figure in Alexandrian Gnosticism. This popular form of Gnosticism doubtlessly was influenced by Plato, a copy of whose *Republic* was found in the library at Nag Hammadi in Egypt,[2] a collection that likewise contained numerous Egypto-Gnostic compositions. Moreover, it is possible that the explanation behind this cruciform imagery of Egyptian gods constituted a *mystery* not readily shared with non-initiates but known to the priestly faction, including both Pagan and Jewish.[3]

Astrotheology of the Cross

We have noted that the sign of the cross is a solar symbol, dating to millennia ago. The astrotheological aspect of the Cross "in space" or "in the heavens" is further indicated in the apocryphal Christian book the *Acts of John*, a relatively early text dated to around 150-200 AD/CE. As Doresse remarks:

> Later on in this apocryphon, the Christ reveals to the same Apostle [John] that it was only in appearance that he had undergone the Crucifixion; and directs his gaze to the true Cross, shining in the heavens, which is not the wooden one of Golgotha but the wonderful "cross of light."[4]

Thus, in an early Christian text we have a crucifixion *in the heavens* that is patently *solar* in nature, very much resembling the "divine man" crucified in space.

Concerning the Christ of the Gnostics, Doresse also states:

---

[1] Parsons, A., 219.
[2] Robinson, J., 290ff. Although the Nag Hammadi collection has been dated to the 4th cent. AD/CE, there is good reason to suppose that the works of both Plato and *Philo* were well known to the religious communities and mystery schools of Egypt long prior to that period. The fact that Plato's *Republic* was still valued at that time is a testimony to its popularity and influence, obviously, as it was among the prized texts repeatedly copied with tremendous effort and expense over the centuries.
[3] It is noteworthy that, by Philo's estimate, some 50 percent of the population of Alexandria at his time was "Jewish," i.e., Judean, Hebrew, Samaritan or Israelitish in some manner. As stated in the *Cyclopaedia of Biblical, Theological and Ecclesiastical Literature* (II, 822), "Two of the five quarters of the city were occupied almost exclusively by Jews (Philo, *Opp.* ii, 525), and these made up well-nigh one half the population (*ib.* p. 523.)"
[4] Doresse, 95.

...a flood of light is thrown upon the strange figure that the Gnostics made of Jesus.... For them, his incarnation was fictitious, and so was his crucifixion.[1]

This assertion cannot be overemphasized, as it contends essentially that the Gnostic figure of Christ is a *mythical being*—one that in fact has precedent in pre-Christian religion, mythology and philosophy.

As evidence of the astrotheological nature of the "cross in space," the "cross-beam of the scales" in Massey's analysis above refers to the zodiacal sign of Libra. Hence, Horus the Elder represents the sun at the cross of the autumnal equinox, which is also the "cross of death," as Massey describes it, leading to the darkness of winter. This balance is the reason behind the scales of the constellation of Libra and the cross of Easter.

Further explaining the theme of the Egyptian sun god Horus on a cross, Massey states:

...The dual nature of the Osirian son was as old as the myth itself. The two Horuses were the suffering Messiah, the Mother's Child, and Horus the Son of the Father. Their astronomical stations are at the place of the two equinoxes. These two Horuses as the biune one were blended in Hor-Makhu, the deity of both horizons or equinoxes, the symbol of which was the cross because the equinoxes were the crossings....

...Horus was the one God of the two horizons, and the cross was the sign of him who "decussated in the form of the letter X," in the two characters of the child and the Virile God; the sun that descended crossed the waters and rose again on the horizon of the resurrection.[2]

We have seen that Plato's "crucifixion in space" represents the sun on the cross of the ecliptic. "Horus on the cross" would thus likewise be the sun as depicted on the cross of the equinoxes and solstices, an astrotheological motif that constitutes yet another link to the Christ myth, with *its* god upon the cross in crucifixion scenes that differ from gospel to gospel. Moreover, in this crucial mystery we find the constant focus in the Egyptian texts on the "crossing" or "crossing over" previously demonstrated.

The Two Thieves?

In the gospel story and in Christian art occurs a striking emphasis on "two thieves" who appear on either side of Christ as he is hanging on the cross. Knowing what we do—what has become obvious throughout this present work—about the many germane aspects of the gospel tale evidently constituting rehashes of earlier motifs found within Pagan religion and mythology, we may logically ask whether or not the "two thieves" tale is yet another mythical

[1] Doresse, 305.
[2] Massey, *NG*, 442.

remake, since it apparently does not represent part of a "true story" and would seem not to be "just made up" for no good reason. Indeed, as we have seen, according to Jewish "messianic prophecies" that were evidently used in the creation of the Christ character, the "suffering servant" needed to be "numbered among the transgressors," such that a precedent apparently had to be found for this theme. With these facts in mind, we may search out any possible connections to other mythologies, including but not limited to the Egyptian. As it turns out, there was another instance of a god surrounded by two "companions," in the imagery of the highly popular Perso-Roman religion of Mithraism. There is additionally a "two thieves" motif in the myth of the Mexican god Quetzalcoatl,[1] and the theme may be found in other mythologies as well, including the Egyptian, particularly as an *astrotheological* motif.

The comparison between Mithraism and Christianity is appropriate, in consideration of how widespread was the former within the Roman Empire *before* Christianity took serious root. This relationship between the Mithraic and Christian "two thieves" imagery was not lost on Joseph Campbell and famed psychologist Dr. Carl Jung (1875-1961), as two examples of commentators upon it.[2] To begin with, of the two thieves on either side of Christ *the Lamb*, one is destined for heaven, the other hell; while the two "torchbearers" or *Dadophores* on either side of Mithra *the Bull* carry torches, one pointing up, the other down:

> Christ was crucified between two thieves. It was thus a triple crucifixion. Similarly, Mithra was commonly represented between two dadophori or torch bearers, one with torch raised, the other with torch lowered.[3]

Dr. Jung recounts that Mithraic expert Dr. Franz V.M. Cumont (1868-1947) viewed the torchbearers as "offshoots" from Mithra himself and also found in this "trinity" part of a sun myth,[4] as explained by Plutarch (46-47, 369D-370B) regarding the Zoroastrian god Oromazes, Ormuzd or Ahura-Mazda.[5] Cumont also saw in these torchbearers representations of the zodiacal signs of Scorpio and Taurus, as they are depicted carrying a scorpion and a bull's head. Concerning this theme, Jung states, "Taurus and Scorpio are equinoctial signs, which clearly indicate that the sacrificial scene refers primarily to the Sun cycle..."[6] Foremost Mithraic expert Dr. Roger Beck, a professor emeritus at the University of Toronto, concurs with the thesis associating the two torchbearers with Taurus and Scorpio, evincing that these two represent the signs into which

---

[1] Acharya, *SOG*, 270.
[2] Campbell, *MG*, 260; Jung, 225.
[3] *Journal for Analytical Psychology*, 108.
[4] Cumont, *MM*, 129.
[5] Plutarch/Babbitt, 112-115; Plutarch/Griffiths, 477.
[6] Jung, 226.

the sun passes immediately *following* the equinoxes.[1] The "sun cycle" would refer to the sun not only as it rises and sets daily,[2] then, but also as it appears on the *cross of the equinoxes*, surrounded by the "transgressors" or "thieves" of the signs into which the sun passes *after* the equinoxes, with Taurus at the vernal equinox and Scorpio at the autumnal. The torchbearer on the left with the torch pointing up is named Cauti or Cautes, representing the vernal equinox ("heaven"); while Cautopati or Cautopates is the name of the one on the right with the downward-pointing torch, symbolizing the autumnal equinox ("hell"). In this regard, we have seen how Massey discussed the two Horuses on the horizon, as well as at the equinoxes—he too considered the autumnal equinox to be the "cross of death," for the same reason as it may be deemed "hell," while at the vernal equinox or "Easter" exists the "cross of life" representing "heaven."[3]

According to Christian tradition, the thief going to heaven is named Dysmas/Dismas/Desmas/ Demas/Dimas/Dymas, while the one destined for hell is Ctegas/Cystas/Cesmas/Gestas/Gistas, the names being introduced in several texts, including the apocryphal *Acts of Pilate* or *Acta Pilati*.[4] In most manuscripts, Demas appears on the right of Jesus, while Gestas is on the *left*. In one manuscript of the Acts, however, and in several other texts, these positions are reversed.[5] It is interesting that the manuscript of the *Acta Pilati* in which the positions are reversed, with Demas on the left and Gestas on the right—the same as their counterparts in Mithraism—is *Armenian*,[6] since Mithraism thrived in that land long before Christianity usurped it. The fact that the names of the thieves are "widely divergent," as are their roles, indicates a *mythological construct*, not a true story. This suspicion of myth is borne out by the apocryphal tale found in the *Arabic Gospel of the Saviour's Infancy* (23), in which appears a story of two robbers—held to be the same as the "two thieves"—assaulting the Holy Family in *Egypt*, by the names of *Titus* and *Dumachus*, the former of whom discouraged the latter from carrying out the crimes. For this act, according to the Infancy Gospel, "Titus" was promised by "the Lord"—a 2-year-old child!—to

---

[1] Beck, 136-137.

[2] Beck, 33.

[3] The ancient Egyptian awareness of both equinoxes is also revealed in the alignment of the Sphinx Temple at Giza, which was "oriented so that on the spring and autumn equinox, the rays of the rising sun would illuminate its inner sanctum." (Davies, V., 82.)

[4] See Nicoll, 165ff., for a discussion of the name variants. It is therein posited that "Dymas" is an abbreviation for Dymachus or Dumachus, which in turn is a form of *Theomachos*, meaning "God fighter." (Nicoll, 170.) Hence, Demas would be the *non-penitent* malefactor, although he is traditionally but not always held to be the "good thief." With a small change in the Coptic-Greek letters Γ to Π, Gestas could be equivalent to *Pistos*—"faith." (Nicoll, 170)

[5] Merback, 24.

[6] Nicoll, 166.

sit at his right hand in heaven.[1] This tale is patently fictional, as well as illogical, as the omnipotent God/Jesus could surely have prevented himself from being robbed, as he could have thwarted Herod from assailing him and from heartlessly massacring a bunch of infants.[2] Rather than representing "history," in the end it seems that, to those who were initiated into the Mithraic mysteries, with the important imagery of Mithra surrounded by the two torchbearers, the depiction of Christ in between the two "thieves" would have been instantly recognizable as part of a pre-existing religious and *mythological* construct.

Another apparent parallel to the "two thieves" motif occurs in other Persian mythology as well, as stated by Dr. Edward J. Wheeler (1859-1922) in an entry on "Babylonian Influence in the New Testament":

> The mocking of Christ before his death is a third event that has special significance. A parallel to this is to be found in a peculiar rite of the Persian Saccian festival, during which the God of that year, in the semblance of a slave, is mocked at. The two thieves on the cross also have their counterparts in the two high court officials who constantly deride the King of the Year.[3]

This correspondence is intriguing in consideration of the fact that Mithra was originally an Indo-*Persian* god who became somewhat popular in Babylon.[4] To this observation, Dr. Wheeler adds, "The healing miracles of Jesus can be paralleled to a phenomenal extent in Babylonian literature, more particularly in the accounts of Marduk, the Sun-God of the Babylonians."[5]

We also find a parallel in the Old Testament story of Joseph, who shares many characteristics with Jesus and who is depicted as being imprisoned with two criminals.[6] (Gen 40:1-3) Moreover, it is asserted that the Jewish law did not condemn thieves to death but the Egyptian law did, so "crucifying" or putting to death thieves in *Egypt* would make more sense than this tale taking place historically in Judea.[7] It is odd that the author of Mark's gospel—in which this pericope of the thieves being crucified first appears, according to the Markan priority hypothesis—supposedly lived in *Egypt* and apparently did not know that thieves were not put to death in Judea.[8]

It is further intriguing that the apocryphal Christian tales place the two thieves as first encountering the Holy Family in *Egypt*, the

[1] Metzger, *NTS*, 36.
[2] For more on the illogicality and other problems with the gospels, see my book *Who Was Jesus?*
[3] Wheeler, 646.
[4] Cumont, *MM*, 20, etc.
[5] Wheeler, 646.
[6] For more comparisons between Joseph and Jesus, see *Who Was Jesus?*, 119-121.
[7] Vetterling, 1073.
[8] Vetterling, 1073.

"good thief" convincing Gestas to leave them alone. Placing this "two thieves" mythical motif in Egypt may have been deliberate, based also partly on a popular "two thieves" tale revolving around the king "Rhampsinitus" (Ramses III?), according to Herodotus (2.120).[1]

With these facts in mind, let us recount the intriguing insights by Massey as concerns the subject of the "two thieves" in Egyptian mythology. Regarding Horus on the cross, the English scholar says:

> And in the zodiac of Denderah, just where Horus is on the cross, or at the crossing of the vernal equinox, these two thieves, Sut-Anup and Aan, are depicted one on either side of the luni-solar god. These two mythical originals have, I think, been continued and humanised as the two thieves in the Gospel version of the crucifixion.[2]

Interestingly, Anup or Anubis is identified with the lunar god Thoth or Tehuti, who represents Hermes, the notorious *thief* of Greek mythology who steals from Apollo, the *sun god*. The association of Anubis, the jackal, with a thief is appropriate, since jackals are known for their thieving ways. Aan, the "dog-headed ape" or baboon, also appears at the corners of the Lake of Fire through which the deceased must pass while being judged by Anubis/Anup.[3] Both gods thus possess functions in the "afterlife" like the heaven/hell roles of the Christian "two thieves." Moreover, baboons are likewise infamous thieves, and we learn from the writer of the fifth century AD/CE Horapollo (1.14) that in Egypt the baboon was a sacred animal which symbolized the moon.[4] Unsurprisingly, then, Aan too was associated with Thoth, who was equivalent to the lunar god Hermes and who was also represented as a baboon.[5] As we know, the moon receives or "steals" the sun's rays, making it one of the "thieves" at the side of the sun, e.g., Horus.

One of the sun hymns of the New Kingdom analyzed by Assman reveals a similar theme, with baboons that announce the rising sun appearing "on both sides of the god."[6] Their number is not mentioned; nevertheless, in this hymn we have the rising sun on the cross of the horizon surrounded by "thieves." In another of the sun hymns, the "western ba's are the jackals that belong to sunset, just as the eastern ba's (baboons) belong to sunrise."[7] Again, we have the sun between the "thieves," with the role of these attendants to tow the solar bark through the underworld: Jackals are thus the "thieves"

---

[1] Herodotus/de Selincourt, 128-131.
[2] Massey, "Luniolatry: Ancient and Modern."
[3] Budge, *EIA*, 140; Faulkner, *EBD*, 116. As a side note, the baboon was considered by the Egyptians to be the ultimate sun worshipper because it "warms its belly by facing the rising sun while placing its forepaws on its knees," which the Egyptians believed was a sign of "'greeting Re as he rises,' in a solemn gesture of obeisance..." (Singh, 332.)
[4] Horapollo/Boas, 52-53.
[5] Hornung, *SLE*, 6; *CGAE*, 126.
[6] Assman, *ESRNK*, 24.
[7] Assman, *ESRNK*, 60.

at sunset who tow the boat through the night hours, while the "thieves" on the other side, the baboons, tow the boat through sunrise. Hence, depending on the hours, both Osiris and Horus would be the "crucified" sun—as the sun crossing the sky—between the two thieves of sunset and sunrise.

Concerning these various figures, Massey further states:

> ...Two other lunar types were Anup, the jackal, and Aan, the dog-headed ape. These two may be seen figured back to back at the place of the Vernal equinox in the zodiac of Denderah. Each of the two had represented the dark half of the lunation (the one with Horus, the other with That [Thoth]) in two different stages of the mythos; each had been the thief of the light; the Mercury who was the thief personified. In these two thieves at the crossing we may perhaps identify the two thieves at the cross, as Horus, the solar lord of light in the moon—in the form of his hawk—is placed between or just over these two thieves at the crossing, the station of the cross! The birthplace of the god who was reborn or who rose again at the Vernal equinox is shown by the constellation of the Thigh or Uterus. Anup on one side of Horus, and Aan on the other, are the two thieves on either hand of the Kamite [Egyptian] Christ upon the cross at Easter.[1]

The figures Massey is describing in both paragraphs as being Anup and Aan "back to back" with Horus as the hawk or falcon between or directly above them are indeed positioned on the line of the vernal equinox of around 100 BCE, as determined by René A. Schwaller de Lubicz (1887-1961) in his analysis of the circular zodiac of Dendera.[2] The cluster of the three pertinent figures falling directly on the equinoctial line is numbered 24 in the drawing of the Dendera zodiac by British astronomer and member of the Asiatic Society John Bentley (c. 1750-1824).[3] The equinoctial line drawn by Schwaller de Lubicz is precisely on the perpendicular of the temple axis in his rendition of the circular zodiac,[4] and the Horus-Anup-Aan image described by Massey is exactly on that "cross," the vernal equinox, of course, being "Easter," when Christ was purportedly hung on the cross. Once again, Massey is thus proved correct in his description of an Egyptian artifact, as he has also been with citations of texts and translations as well.

It is important to note that in his depiction of "Horus on the cross," Massey did not say that Horus was thrown to the ground and nailed to a piece of wood. Dr. Alvin Boyd Kuhn (1880-1963) further summarizes this motif of Horus on the cross surrounded by two thieves:

---

[1] Massey, *HJMC*, 116-117.
[2] Pratt, citing Schwaller de Lubicz, R.A., *Sacred Science: the king of Pharaonic theocracy*, Inner Traditions, 1982, pp. 283-6.
[3] Bentley, pl. VIII. (Simpson)
[4] Different drawings of this complex zodiac render the individual images and their locations variously.

The jackal of Anup and the cynocephalus of Taht-Aan, which figured as types of the dark lunation, were conceived as having stolen the light from the bright moon. As the dark period before and after the illumination, they stood on either side of the Christ light on the moon. They were dubbed "thieves of the light," in contrast to the twelve solar characters who were guardians of the treasure of light. Hermes, cognate with Anup, was in Greek mythology the thief. In the zodiac of Denderah just where Horus is shown on the cross or at the crossing of the vernal equinox, these two thieves Anup and Aan are drawn on either side of the sun-god. Here would appear to be the authentic pre-Christian prototype of the Gospel crucifixion between two thieves.[1]

To reiterate, Anubis is identified with Thoth, Taht or Tehuti, equivalent to the Greco-Roman god Hermes/Mercury, who in Greek mythology steals from the sun god—evidently symbolizing the "theft" of the sun's light by the moon. Again, Aan too is a sort of lunar "thief," as he likewise signifies Thoth: "Another of the commonest symbolic forms of Thoth is the dog-headed ape."[2] Regarding this imagery, George Robert Stowe ("G.R.S.") Mead (1863-1933) relates that Aan is not only Thoth but also representative of the equinoxes, once again adding to the indication of "Horus on the cross" at "Easter":

> Brugsch has suggested that this ape is a form of Thoth as God of "equilibrium," and that it elsewhere symbolises the equinoxes...[3]

In consideration of all these facts, Horus on the cross surrounded by two thieves would appear to be the most logical interpretation of this composite figure in the zodiac of Dendera, a clearly astrotheological monument predating the common era by a century or more. In addition, this image of Horus "on the cross" with the two "companions" could likewise represent the same theme as the Mithraic torchbearers, especially since Anubis and Aan are also associated with the afterlife.

Regarding the solar motifs of the "crucifixion" and "two thieves," in *Suns of God*, I write:

> In the solar mythology, the sun god is regularly "crucified" as he crosses over the equinoxes and when he wanes towards the end of the year. The "thieves" denote stars, or constellations/signs of the zodiac, in particular Sagittarius and Capricorn, which, as the winter descends, steal the sun's strength.[4]

Again, the cross has long been a symbol of the *sun*, representing significantly the crux of the equinoxes, upon which the sun is "crossified." Hence, it can truly be said that the *sun* of God was

---

[1] Kuhn, *LL*, 528.
[2] Mead, *TGH*, 55.
[3] Mead, *TGH*, 55-56.
[4] Acharya, *SOG*, 272.

"crucified" at the vernal equinox—and this motif, we contend, is at the basis of the gospel "crucifixion" at "Easter."

The Mystery of the Cross

Christian literature over the centuries has discussed the "mystery of the cross"—we know, therefore, that the cross was a *mystery*, at least during Christian times. The question is, was it also a mystery prior to the Christian era? In consideration of its religious significance and prominence, the cross could be deemed a "mystery" in the most ancient times as well. Regarding this subject, Massey remarks:

> We have evidence from the pyramid of Medum [Meidoun] that from 6,000 to 7,000 years ago the dead in Egypt were buried in a faith which was founded on the mystery of the cross, and rationally founded too, because that cross was a figure of the fourfold foundation on which heaven itself was built.[1]

In fact, the image of Moses with outstretched arms, claimed by early Church fathers to be making the "sign of the cross," accordingly represents the "mystery of the cross" as well. As related by Dr. Cornelia B. Horn of St. Louis University's Theology Department:

> In early Christian texts it is not uncommon that elements from the life of Moses are seen as clear prefigurations of the mystery of the Cross of Christ. In John 3:14-15, the evangelist compared the Cross to the serpent made of brass. Early Christian catechesis associated the image of the Cross with the memory of Moses preaching with outstretched arms while Joshua was fighting (Exodus 17:8-13).[2]

If Moses was a "clear prefiguration" of the mystery of the cross, then said mystery must have existed at a minimum by the purported time of Moses. And the Hebrew patriarch has a long relationship with Egypt, with some speculation that a "historical" Moses was an Egyptian priest, who would then have brought the mystery of the cross with him out of Egypt. As we know, Egypt very much possessed its own mystery of the cross with its life-giving ankh, resembling a man on a cross or crucifix, as well as with the Tat or djed pillar. Concerning the ankh, Major Edward Moor (1771-1848) remarks:

> It is well known that the supposed mystery of the Cross is not merely modern. Its frequent recurrence among the hieroglyphics of *Egypt* excited the early curiosity of Christians. Converted heathens explained...that it signified "the Life to come."[3]

Indeed, we hear implication that the ancient mystery of the cross is a brotherhood secret:

---

[1] Massey, *AELW*, II, 749-750.
[2] Horn, 367.
[3] Moor, 292.

> There seems even no doubt that the pre-Christian Rites had a
> Mystery of the Cross, and there is said to be an ancient painting in
> Egypt of a candidate laid upon a cruci-form bier.[1]

In fact, the mystery of the cross is deemed one of the "greater
mysteries."[2] It is also the "axis mundi" or "axis of the world"
according to Christian mystics, attributing an obvious astrotheological
meaning to the cross.

Although some of the mysteries, such as the virgin-mother motif,
appear to have enjoyed more or less wide dissemination and were
thus known to the public at large, despite evidently not being written
about extensively or openly, other ancient religious aspects such as
"Horus the Cross" may have been true mysteries in the sense that
they were not widely understood by the "vulgar masses." Yet,
certainly the association of both Osiris and/or Horus with the
cross/ankh and the djed/Tau symbolizing eternal life and
resurrection *was* widely known.

In addition to pre-Christian texts depicting the "crucified man in
space," we possess various ancient Egypto-Christian artifacts
identifying Jesus with Horus and Osiris, including Gnostic gems. In
Ancient Christian Mage: Coptic Texts of Ritual Power, by Dr. Marvin W.
Meyer, a professor of Religious Studies at Chapman College, and Dr.
Richard Smith, a professor at Claremont Graduate School, the
authors report on a *crucifix* in the Coptic Museum in Old Cairo "with
the crucified figure of Jesus together with a falcon (Horus)."[3] This
artifact demonstrates that identifying Horus with the crucified Jesus
occurred even in antiquity.

While Osiris, Horus, Set or other Egyptian deities were not
"crucified" in the sense of being "real people" thrown to the ground
and nailed to a cross, if we go by the terms used in the New
Testament to describe how Jesus was allegedly executed, either by
being impaled on a *stauros* (Mt 27:40) or hung on a tree (Acts 5:30;
10:39; 13:29), it may be misleading to say that even *Christ* was
"crucified" in the manner commonly believed. If, however, we may in
fact depict Jesus as having been "crucified," we may likewise be
accurate in portraying Osiris and Horus—who were essentially
represented in the shape of a cross prior to the common era—as
having been "crucified," particularly in light of the definition of "to
crucify" as meaning "to fix upon a cross." In fact, as we can tell from
the admissions by Church fathers Tertullian and Minucius Felix,
there *were* depictions of *other* gods on the cross or in cruciform,
while, again, Christ was never portrayed in Christian art on the cross
until well into the fifth century at the earliest.

---

[1] Yarker, 98.
[2] Bolton, xli.
[3] Meyer, *ACM*, 363.

In our analysis of ancient mythology, including the Egyptian, we discover ancient depictions of a god in *cruciform*, with arms outstretched such that his body forms a cross, precisely as early Christians described the posture of Moses as making the "sign of the cross." Indeed, the fact that this motif of a god on a cross was important long prior to when Jesus Christ supposedly gave significance to the cross can be proved by the words of the Church fathers. In any event, in non-Christian eras and areas there existed a reverence for the image of a god or goddess in the form of a cross— and that is the main point of this discussion.

The images and descriptions of deities in cruciform we possess include Osiris, Isis and Horus, and the answer to the question of whether or not Horus was ever associated with the cross and ever depicted on a cross or in cruciform appears to be *yes*. We must therefore conclude that the figure of Christ on a cross or in the shape of a cross is a johnny-come-lately in the world of religious iconography, and the story of the crucifixion appears more likely a contrivance based on this important iconography, as well as on Jewish "messianic prophecies" or *blueprints*, rather than an implausible "historical" tale.

Cross hieroglyph (Gardiner's F35)—a symbol of "Goodness."
(Wilkinson, *The Manners and Customs of the Ancient Egyptians*, III, 352)

Ankh/Crux Ansata with Arms upholding the Sun Disk, representing a Human in Cruciform.

Ankhs holding *Was*-Scepters

Bird-headed Woman in Cruciform,
Hierakonpolis, Egypt, c. 4,000 BCE.
(Ruffle, *The Egyptians: An Introduction to Egyptian Archaeology*,
21)

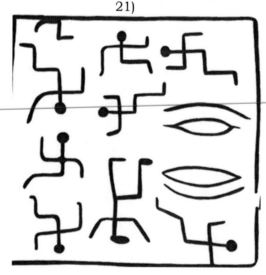

Humans in Crooked Cross/Swastika Shape,
Early Egyptian Cylinder Seal from Negada.
(*Proceedings of the Society for Biblical Archaeology*, XXII, 278, 280)

Cross statuette from Lemba-Lakkous, Cyprus, c. 2500 BCE.
(Biedermann, 82)

Anubis in Cruciform as "Guardian of the Dead"
(Lundy, *Monumental Christianity*, 60)

Shu in Cruciform holding up the Sky
(Hornung, *The Ancient Egyptian Books of the Afterlife*, 115)

Horus in Cruciform in the Sky
"The eternal God is your dwelling place, and underneath are the
everlasting arms."
Deut. 33:27
(Sharpe, *Egyptian Antiquities in the British Museum*, 143)

Winged Goddess Maat in Cruciform protecting the Deceased.
(Hornung, *The Valley of the Kings*, 193)

The Winged Goddess Nut in Cruciform, from Tutankhamun's
Tomb.
(Armour, *Gods and Myths of Ancient Egypt* (2002), 23)

Protective Winged Goddess in Cruciform on the Sarcophagus of
King Tut.

Coffin with Protective Goddess in Cruciform
Coffin of Khnum-nakht, c. 1900–1800 BCE.
(The Metropolitan Museum of Art)

Resurrected Osiris as the crosslike Djed Pillar, surrounded by the
Two Merti.
(Hornung, *The Valley of the Kings*, 121)

Egyptian Coffin with Cruciform and Christian Coffin with Cross.

Light and Reflection of the Sun forming Crosses.

Round Zodiac at the Temple of Dendera
A perpendicular Line to Temple Axis Runs through "Horus between
the Two Thieves" (Anubis and Aan) and Represents the Vernal
Equinox around 100 BCE.
(Schwaller de Lubicz, *Sacred Science: the King of Pharaonic
Theocracy*, 178)

Close-up of Horus between Anubis and Aan at the Vernal
Equinox on Dendera Zodiac.

Burial for Three Days, Resurrection and Ascension

"The myth of Osiris involves his own death and resurrection, a theme that echoes the daily cycle of the sun's death and its rebirth at dawn."

Dr. Edwin C. Krupp, *Echoes of the Ancient Skies* (16)

"According to the faith of later times, Osiris was three days and three nights in the waters before he was restored to life again."

The American Journal of Theology (XX, 5)

"The Isia, the solemn mourning for the god Osiris, 'the Lord of Tombs,' lasted for three days, and began at sunset..."

R.G. Halliburton, *Journal of the Royal Astronomical Society of Canada* (14, 66)

"...the image of Osiris was consigned to a sepulcher for three days; and...on the fourth, the priests opened it and brought forth a heifer to the people, as the deity restored to life."

The Classical Journal (XXIX, 92)

"...Osiris rose to new life in his son, Horus..."

Dr. Tryggve N.D. Mettinger, *The Riddle of the Resurrection* (172)

"Isis also discovered the elixir of immortality, and when her son Horus fell victim to the plots of the Titans and was found dead beneath the waves, she not only raised him from the dead and restored his soul, but also gave him eternal life."

Diodorus Siculus, *The Antiquities of Egypt* (31)

"The *Book of the Dead* promised resurrection to all mankind, as a reward for righteous living, long before Judaism and Christianity embraced that concept."[1]

Dr. Ogden Goelet, *The Egyptian Book of the Dead* (18)

We have already seen that numerous aspects of the Christian ritual and mythos can be found in the earlier Egyptian religion. As may be evident from the constant focus on an afterlife and everlasting life, with extensive funerary or mortuary literature and rituals, including expensive burial procedures such as mummification and entombment, the Egyptians were very interested in the *resurrection of the dead* in one form or another, eons before Christianity was created. This important theme of resurrection in Egypt is emphasized in spells in the Pyramid Texts, including those specifically titled for this transition,[2] while the entire Book of the Dead was concerned with this very premise, as were the Coffin Texts, of course. In addition to these are many other Egyptian texts that deal with the

---

[1] Faulkner, *EBD*, 18.
[2] Allen, J., *AEPT*, 76ff.

afterlife,[1] while the massive structures throughout Egypt in the shape of pyramids have been deemed by Egyptologists to be "resurrection machines," likewise designed for the express purposed of restoring their royal builders to life.[2] In reality, in the very prominent Egyptian resurrection, combined with the burial in the tomb for three days and the ascension—all of which can be found in the stories of gods besides Jesus Christ—we possess important archetypes upon which the Christ myth was evidently founded.

In addition to all the instances already provided, the salient subject of death and resurrection in the Egyptian religion is exemplified also in BD 3, in which the deceased is identified with the sun god, in a prayer to allow him to "live after death, like Ra daily."[3] Moreover, the title of BD 2 can be translated as the "chapter of Coming forth as the Sun, and Living after Death," while BD 3 is "Another chapter like it."[4] Thus, in very ancient times in Egypt the sun was associated with resurrection and the afterlife, as we have seen abundantly. Concerning Re and Osiris, along with death and resurrection, Dr. Herman te Velde, a chairman of the Department of Egyptology at the University of Groningen, states:

> As Re [Ra] who manifests himself in the sun goes to rest in the evening and awakes from the sleep of death in the morning, so do the death and resurrection of Osiris seem to be equally inevitable and natural.[5]

Adding to the hundreds of Egyptian texts, the resurrection and immortality of the deceased are expressed on many Egyptian coffins, in images of the sky goddess, Nut, giving birth to the sun. Concerning the sun's role in resurrection, Dr. Goelet states:

> This theme of rebirth is one of the reasons for the frequent identification of the deceased with Re. Here lay the hope not for mere rebirth but for a *daily* rebirth in the manner of the sun.[6]

As we can see, the resurrection of the deceased in the Egyptian funerary literature was tied into the rebirth of the sun out of the death of night, a point that needs to be emphasized because there is much debate, denial and ignorance of these simple and basic facts concerning the Egyptian religion.

---

[1] In his book *The Ancient Egyptian Books of the Afterlife*, Hornung refers to the following in addition to the Pyramid Texts, Book of the Dead and Coffin Texts: The Amduat, the Spell of the Twelve Caves, the Book of Gates, the Enigmatic Book of the Underworld, the Book of Caverns, the Book of the Earth, the Book of Nut, the Book of Day, the Book of the Night, the Litany of Re and the Book of the Heavenly Cow. (Hornung, *AEBA*, xiii-xv.)

[2] See Davies, V., 53ff.

[3] Renouf, *EBD*, 12; Allen, T., *BD*, 8; Faulkner, *EBD*, 101.

[4] Bunsen/Birch, 164.

[5] te Velde, 81.

[6] Faulkner, *EBD*, 153.

The Resurrection Machine

In Egyptian architecture as well we find the prominent theme of resurrection. The concept of pyramids as virtual "resurrection machines" is expressed in *Egypt Uncovered* by Drs. Davies and Friedman, in an entire chapter entitled, "Resurrection Machine":

> It was the hope of every Egyptian to be reborn after death, to attain an afterlife with the sun-god Ra and be resurrected with each sunrise, and to join with Osiris in the cyclical regeneration of nature and plant life with the receding Nile flood....

> The three pyramids at Giza are the most visited attraction in Egypt, if not the world. The Great Pyramid of the Fourth Dynasty king Khufu, the ultimate "resurrection machine," is the largest pyramid ever built.[1]

In this regard, Davies and Friedman also remark:

> The pyramid was essentially this mound of creation, a cocoon in which the king underwent the transformation or recreation into an eternal transfigured spirit called an *akh*. Journeying to the sky, he was united with the gods and resurrected each morning.[2]

While discussing the Giza complex, Davies and Friedman also refer to the pyramids as "this new type of solar resurrection machine..."[3]

Lord of Eternity

With the conspicuousness of resurrection in the Egyptian funerary literature, the god Osiris has come under great scrutiny as to the precise nature of his revivification. Regarding Osiris, Bonwick remarks, "His birth, death, burial, resurrection and ascension embraced the leading points of Egyptian theology."[4] Likewise, Frazer writes:

> And from the death and resurrection of their great god the Egyptians drew not only their support and sustenance in this life, but also their hope of a life eternal beyond the grave. This hope is indicated in the clearest manner by the very remarkable effigies of Osiris which have come to light in Egyptian cemeteries.[5]

In reality and as we have seen, numerous of the spells in the Book of the Dead and various of the old Pyramid Texts upon which much of the BD is based, along with the 1000+ Coffin Texts, are specifically designed to allow the deceased to be resurrected not only along *with* Osiris, after the "dark night of the soul" or nightly journey, but also *as* Osiris himself. Frazer thus has accurately represented the Egyptian religion as it would have been perceived by the *average*

---

[1] Davies, V., 53.
[2] Davies, V., 56.
[3] Davies, V., 78.
[4] Bonwick, 150.
[5] Frazer, *AAO*, 262.

Egyptian worshipper. To wit, the promise of eternal lif
death, based on the death and resurrection of Osiris.
subject is that simple: Few truly wish to die, and most w___
back to life. This factor is what the Egyptian believer commonly found
in his religion: Death followed by resurrection to life.

This desire is readily exemplified yet again in the important
chapter 64 of the Book of the Dead, in which the deceased/Osiris
states, "I am Yesterday, Today and Tomorrow, for I am born again
and again,"[1] as well as referring to himself as the "Lord of
Resurrections."[2] Birch's translation is as follows: "I AM the Yesterday,
the Morning, the Light at its birth the second time; the Mystery of the
Soul made by the Gods... Lord of mankind seen in all his rays, the
Conductor coming forth from the darkness... I am the Lord of Life."[3]
Budge translates the pertinent passage in BD 64 as, "I am the Lord of
those who are raised up from the dead, who cometh forth from out of
the darkness."[4] Faulkner's rendition of this sentence is: "I have risen
as a possessor of life..."[5] T. George Allen renders this scripture as:
"Mine are yesterday and each morrow, (for I am) in charge of (its)
successive births. (I am) the Hidden of Soul who made the gods..."[6] In
reality, BD 64—a chapter called by Renouf "one of the most
important as it is one of the most ancient"[7]—is full of spiritual
concepts found in the later Judeo-Christian bible, Elsewhere, Osiris
is called the "Lord of Eternity" and "Maker of Everlastingness,"[8] and
Budge deems Osiris's alter ego, Ptah-Sokar-Osiris, the "triune god of
the resurrection."[9]

Osiris was not only the night sun resurrected on a daily basis but
also, as the light when the moon wanes, he died *monthly,* to be
restored to life with the lunar waxing. Osiris likewise died and was
resurrected annually in his role as the Nile, and he was reborn in the
vegetation such as corn as well.[10] We have already seen that the
Egyptians celebrated the Festival of the Seeking of Osiris at various
times in different eras. During this period when Isis was said to be in
search of Osiris, the god was claimed to be dead and buried for *three
days*—the same amount of time during which Christ was said to be
dead—and, on the fourth, he is called out by his son, Horus. As Sir
Rev. Dr. W. Robertson Nicoll relates, "The death and resurrection of

---

[1] Renouf, *EBD*, 117.
[2] Renouf, *EBD*, 118.
[3] Bunsen/Birch, 206-209.
[4] Budge, *BD* (1899), 218.
[5] Faulkner, *EBD*, 106.
[6] Allen, T., *BD*, 56.
[7] Renouf, *EBD*, 121.
[8] Budge, *OER*, I, 43.
[9] Budge, *AGFSER*, 123.
[10] See, e.g., Mettinger, 169.

Osiris embraced three days from Nov. 12-14."[1] Concerning the festival of Osiris, Dr. G.A. Wells comments:

> ...according to Plutarch...the festival of Osiris was spread over three days, his death being mourned on the first and his resurrection celebrated on the night of the third with the joyful shout "Osiris has been found."[2]

Regarding the death of Osiris, Plutarch (39, 366D-E) relates:

> Consequently they say that the disappearance of Osiris occurred in the month of Athyr, at the time when, owing to the complete cessation of the Etesian winds, the Nile recedes to its low level and the land becomes denuded. As the nights grow longer, the darkness increases, and the potency of the light is abated and subdued. Then among the gloomy rites which the priests perform, they shroud the gilded image of a cow with a black linen vestment, and display her as a sign of mourning for the goddess, inasmuch as they regard both the cow and the earth as the image of Isis; and this is kept up for four days consecutively, beginning with the seventeenth of the month. *The things mourned for are four in number*: first, the departure and recession of the Nile; second, the complete extinction of the north winds, as the south winds gain the upper hand; *third, the day's growing shorter than the night*; and, to crown all, the denudation of the earth together with the defoliation of the trees and shrubs at this time. On the nineteenth day they go down to the sea at night-time; and the keepers of the robes and the priests bring forth the sacred chest containing a small golden coffer, into which they pour some potable water which they have taken up, and a great shout arises from the company for joy that Osiris is found.[3]

In his description of Osiris's death, while Plutarch claims four days for the "gloomy rites," he likewise gives a three-day period, the 17th, 18th and 19th of the month Athyr (Hathor), until "Osiris is found." In another reference, previously cited, Plutarch discusses the month of Athyr as occurring during the passing of the sun through Scorpio. Indeed, in the Alexandrian calendar, Athyr ran from October 28th to November 26th. Hence, using the Alexandrian calendar, Plutarch evidently places the three-day period around November 12-14. Moreover, part of the mourning for Osiris emanates from "the day's growing shorter than the night," confirming that the winter solstice represented a time of death for the god as well, as we would expect of a deity with solar attributes. Therefore, the winter solstice or "December 25th" would constitute the annual resurrection from death or rebirth of Osiris as the baby sun Horus, as demonstrated and as occurred every other day of the year as well.

[1] Nicoll, 344.
[2] Wells, 18.
[3] Plutarch/Babbitt, 95-97. (Emph. added.)

The Passion Play of Osiris

As seen throughout this present work, the god a[...] death and resurrection the Egyptian mortuary literature came [...] revolve was the great soli-lunar Osiris, whose passion we have previously explored as being astrotheological. Osiris's death and resurrection were so important that the "seeking of Osiris" constituted a yearly festival. We have also already discussed the Koiak festival during the month of December, in which the raising of the djed pillar or Tat cross/Tau symbolized *Osiris's resurrection*, specifically named as such by Mettinger, for one.[1] Concerning the yearly festival commemorating the Passion of Osiris, Mojsov recounts:

> Every year in the town of Abydos his death and resurrection after three days were celebrated in a publicly enacted passion play called the Mysteries of Osiris. In the New Kingdom (1550-1069 BC), after the rise of the sun cult and the monotheistic religion introduced by King Akhenaton, the cult of Osiris clasped hands with the cult of Ra and Osiris became an enlightened savior-god, shepherd to immortality for ordinary people. By the Late Period (1069-332 BC), his cult had spread around the Mediterranean. As the redemptive figure of the Egyptian god loomed large over the ancient world, Isis came to be worshipped as the Primordial Virgin and their child as the Savior of the World.[2]

Budge too depicts the ritual reenactment of the "Miracle Play" of Osiris at his cult's major center:

> ...The spread of their cult [Osiris and Isis] was largely caused by the annual performance of the great Miracle Play at Abydos, in which the principal events of the life, death, funeral ceremonies, and resurrection of Osiris were represented. The Play was based on Legends which had been current in Egypt for untold centuries...[3]

Part of the mystery play was the "Great Coming Forth":

> This act was the greatest in the Osiris play, for it represented the "coming forth" of Osiris from the temple after his death, and the departure of his body to his tomb....[4]

In this annual play, after a ritual in the temple, the body was carried away, surrounded by the wailing and mourning crowd. A reenactment of the fight with Seth and his followers ensued, and Osiris's body disappeared. After three days, he was found again.

Nan M. Holley of Bedford College, London, summarizes the Osirian Passion Play thus:

> The celebration of his death and resurrection took place, in historical times, in the fourth month of the inundation, just before the first ploughing. The ritual is known to us from documents of the Ptolemaic and Roman periods; but the celebration goes back to the

---

[1] Mettinger, 169.
[2] Mojsov, xii. See also Frazer, *AAO*, 211.
[3] Budge, *LOLM*, lii.
[4] Budge, *OER*, II, 6.

Old Kingdom... The body of Osiris was "found" in the Nile and brought to the shrine.... Human actors probably carried out an equivalent rite. Elaborate ceremonies were then performed to revive the dead Osiris...[1]

Rev. Dr. George Hodges, a dean of the Episcopal Theological School of Cambridge, also describes the passion of Osiris, giving a different date for its beginning, equivalent to the 1st of Athyr according to the Alexandrian calendar:

On the 28th of October was enacted in a kind of passion play the death of Osiris, killed by Set the god of evil, with weeping and mourning. Three days after, the lamentation was changed to cries of joy: "We have found him, let us rejoice together!" Osiris had risen from the dead.[2]

The passion play of Osiris is in fact very ancient, which would explain the roving date, as it passed through centuries of the Egyptian wandering calendar:

Since the time of the twelfth dynasty, and probably much earlier, there had been held at Abydos and elsewhere a sacred performance similar to the mysteries of our Middle Ages, in which the events of Osiris's passion and resurrection were reproduced.[3]

The 12th Dynasty ranged from around 1991 to 1802 BCE, demonstrating the great antiquity of the "sacred performance." Another such celebration involved the god Min, who was likewise identified with Osiris[4] and who, Morenz relates, was "a god in mummy form, around whose death and resurrection the important festivals revolved."[5] As we can see, the death and resurrection of Osiris were central to the Egyptian religion and were enacted in a *Passion Play* many ages before the common era. Therefore, the claim for uniqueness of Christ's passion, which has also been acted out as a *play* many times over the centuries, and which we aver is not "historical," becomes questionable.

Three Days in the Tomb

In Christian tradition, Jesus's passion includes a three-day period of "death" in a "tomb" or "cave," essentially representing the "underworld." We have seen this theme of the three-day disappearance or "burial" abundantly in the Egyptian religion as well, as related by Plutarch, among others, and as in the ancient Egyptian texts. As we have also noted, in the case of Egyptian gods, this "tomb" is likewise a boat or *ark*, as in the "ark of Noah," which constitutes a motif found in the mythos and ritual of Osiris and Horus. Concerning the god of the underworld, Judge Thomas L.

---

[1] Holley, 43-44.
[2] Hodges, G., 22.
[3] Cumont, 98.
[4] Goyon, 1069.
[5] Morenz, 25.

Burial for Three Days

Strange comments, "Osiris was shut up in his ark for three days,"[1] precisely in the same month, in fact, as the biblical Noah, another mythical character symbolizing astrotheological phenomena.[2] Meanwhile, Horus, like other gods, including Sokar, was carried about ritually on a boat or ark, as in the "Ark of the Covenant."[3] Like other sun gods as well, Horus ended up in the underworld, with the epithet in CT Sp. 74 of "Horus of the Netherworld,"[4] a title of Osiris as well.[5] Of course, Osiris resurrecting from his "sleep" and rising out of his "tomb" is thus a very common motif that occurs on a nightly basis and can likewise be found in the sacred scriptures. As Faulkner notes of CT Sp. 74, "The deceased, identified with Osiris, is summoned to wake from his sleep in the tomb."[6] In CT Sp. 66, the speaker says "the earth has been removed for you," about which Faulkner also notes: "An allusion to the resurrection from the tomb."[7] The resurrection could also be deemed a "daily rejuvenation," as rendered by Faulkner in CT Sp. 238.[8] As we can see, *resurrection out of the tomb was a common motif long before the common era.*

The theme of resurrection from the dead and "raising up" in three days is present in the Old Testament as well, at Hosea 6:2: "After two days he will revive us; on the third day he will raise us up, that we may live before him." (RSV) It should be noted that the verb "to raise up" in the Septuagint, *anistemi* (Strong's G450), is essentially the same as the noun used in the New Testament for "resurrection," *anastasis* (G386). Concerning the three-day period before resurrection, Mettinger remarks:

> The idea of a three-days span of time between death and return, a *triduum*, seems to be at hand in Hosea 6:2 in a context where the imagery ultimately draws upon Canaanite ideas of resurrection... Apart from Hosea 6:2 one should remember also Jonah 2:1...where Jonah is in the belly of the fish three days and three nights. I understand the belly of the fish as a metaphor for the Netherworld.[9]

From this illuminating paragraph we discover a number of facts: 1. The three-day period is a motif recognized by scholars and given the Latin name of *triduum*; 2. There were "Canaanite ideas of resurrection," preceding the common era by centuries; and 3. Jonah's interment in the "whale" constitutes a *triduum* in the *netherworld*, the

---

[1] Strange, 242.
[2] See Acharya, *CC*, 237ff; Acharya, *SOG*, 44-45.
[3] See Acharya, *SOG*, 123.
[4] Faulkner, *AECT*, I, 69.
[5] At CT Sp. 74:310, Faulkner notes that "Horus of the Netherworlds" is used here "as an epithet of Osiris." (Faulkner, *AECT*, I, 71.)
[6] Faulkner, *AECT*, I, 70.
[7] Faulkner, *AECT*, I, 61, 62.
[8] Faulkner, *AECT*, I, 187.
[9] Mettinger, 214.

where Osiris was said to reside.[1] Furthermore, reflecting
~~~e-day sojourn in the underworld in the gospel story,
~~~ made to raise the tale of Jonah, saying: "For as Jonah was
three days and three nights in the belly of the whale, so will the Son
of man be three days and three nights in the heart of the earth." (Mt
12:40)

The archetypal precedent of this *triduum* theme would also be
demonstrated by an apparent pre-Christian ancient Hebrew tablet
evidently discovered near the Dead Sea in Israel that purportedly
relates this motif of a messiah dying and resurrecting after a three-
day period.[2] If this tablet is authentically from the period claimed and
truly says what is alleged, it would provide proof that shortly before
the creation of Christianity, this messianic theme of death and
resurrection after three days was important in pre-Christian Jewish
tradition, such that it could have been used as a *blueprint* in the
creation of the Christ character.

The legends of Re, Osiris, Horus and others revolve largely around
solar mythology, in which traditionally the three days in the tomb or
cave constitute the period during the solstices and equinoxes
required for the sun to change perceivably its direction and/or
status. Thus, in the minds of the ancient mythographers and time-
keepers, the three days during the solstices constituted the period
when the sun was "battling" with the night, as did the time of the
equinoxes, such that the vernal equinox began around March 21st-
22nd and ended with the sun's triumph, resurrection or rebirth
around March 24th-25th. In this regard, even within early Christianity
Jesus was said to have been resurrected or "reborn" on March 24th or
25th, this date, of course, claimed to be "Easter." Indeed, Church
father Tertullian (*Adversus Iudaeos*, 8.18) averred that Christ had
been crucified on March 25th,[3] while Lactantius (*De Mortibus
Persecutorum*, ii) placed it on the 23rd.[4]

As further evidence of its astrotheological meaning, mythologist
Joseph Campbell also explores the identification of the three-day
period and resurrection as a lunar phase as well:

> The Moon remains the high symbol of the dead and resurrecting god.
> Even the Christian image of the Resurrection has elements of this
> symbolism inherent in it: Christ spends three days in the tomb, just
> as the Moon is three days dark; and the dating of Easter is always
> made in relation to the full Moon.[5]

---

[1] The term *triduum* refers to any period of three days and is not limited to the time
spent in a "tomb."
[2] Bronner, "Tablet ignites debate on messiah and resurrection."
[3] Dunn, G., 84.
[4] Christensen, 70. For a fuller discussion of the traditional dates for Christ's
crucifixion, see Hastings, 414ff.
[5] Campbell, *ML*, 16.

In any event, the effect is the same: The soli-lunar hero lies in the "tomb" or "cave" for three days until he wins the battle over death/darkness and is "resurrected" to life and/or "adulthood."

The Descent into the Underworld

Along with the "entombment" motif come stories of gods, goddesses, godmen and heroes who thus descend into the underworld, including Adonis, Aeneas, Empedocles, Hercules, Kore, Odysseus, Orpheus, Pythagoras and Tammuz. In the scholarly survey *Resurrection*, Dr. Stanley E. Porter, president and dean of MacMaster Divinity College, discusses the many myths of the descent into the underworld, some of which long predate Christianity, including that of the goddess Persephone or Kore, recorded in the *Homeric Hymn to Demeter* six to eight centuries before the common era, as well as that of Orpheus, who descended into the underworld (Hades) to bring back his wife, Eurydice.[1] The descent or journey into the underworld is related in the Greek poet Homer's *The Odyssey* (11) as well, dating to at least eight centuries BCE.

Like these figures, Jesus too is depicted as descending into the underworld, a common Pagan motif that was evidently attached to the Christ myth in order to explain where the godman had gone during the three days when he was supposedly dead in the tomb. There are inferences of the descent at Matthew 12:40, in the reference to Jonah previously mentioned, and at Romans 10:7, along with a couple of oblique references in other epistles. The descent into "hell" is also part of the "Apostles' Creed," which in fact sounds much like an encapsulation of the mythological motifs found here.[2] Certain apocryphal texts, including and especially the "Gospel of Nicodemus" (3rd-6th cents. AD/CE), contain this legend as well.[3] The Christians added a new twist to the tale, however, by having the Greek god of the underworld, Hades, chatting it up with Satan! Christ himself is depicted as rescuing from Hades/Hell certain "righteous ones," including the biblical figures Adam and King David. The scenes portrayed in the Gospel of Nicodemus are patently fictional and mythological, seemingly straight out of Greek myth, for one. In this regard, Hornung is certain that these "Christian" underworld scenes are adapted from Egyptian mythology as well:

> There was also an association of the passion of Jesus with traditions regarding Osiris, especially in the apocryphal Gospel of Nicodemus, with its detailed description of a descent into Hades.[4]

---

[1] Porter, *Res.*, 77.
[2] *CE*, "Apostles' Creed," I, 631. There are different editions of the Apostles' Creed, with the descent into hell apparently a later addition, likely based on the motif's presence in Pagan religion.
[3] See Trumbower, 106.
[4] Hornung, *SLE*, 75.

Hence, this respected Egyptologist recounts the evidently ancient tradition of associating Jesus's passion with that of Osiris, including the god's descent into the underworld or netherworld, as it is commonly rendered in the Egyptian religion. We ourselves are therefore not remiss in identifying the two gods and their adventures.

Moreover, the followers of the Greek demigod Orpheus were quite convinced of *their* godman's powers over Hades as well:

> The secrets of Hades were in his possession. He could tell his followers what the fate of their souls would be, and how they should behave to make it the best possible. He had shown himself capable of melting the hearts of the powers below, and might be expected to intercede again on their own behalf if they lived the pure life according to his precepts....[1]

As does Christ, Orpheus descends into the underworld to rescue souls, such as his beloved wife, and, like Jesus, the Greek hero ascends once again out of the underworld. Interestingly, devout followers of Orpheus comprised proselytizers and missionaries who traveled around the Mediterranean to bring the "good news" of their godman in much the same way and in the same places where Paul and the later Christians preached.[2]

Like the Gospel of Nicodemus, some of the Church fathers, such as Clement of Alexandria and Origen, likewise discussed the descent of Jesus into the underworld—the period later deemed the "Harrowing of Hell," Christ's arising from which is called the *Anastasis* or "standing up," the same word used to describe the resurrection of both Jesus and Horus, the latter at least one century before Christ's alleged revivification, as we shall see. This fact of Jesus's ascension out of the underworld being deemed his "resurrection" would suggest that, despite any theological bickering, the others in the same underworldly position could likewise be said to have been *resurrected*. It is significant that Clement of Alexandria—in the heart of Egypt and "infected with Gnosticism," per the Catholic Encyclopedia[3]—would be interested in the descent into the underworld, in consideration of the fact that this theme was prominent also in Egyptian religion. It would be logical to assert that this motif in the Christ myth ranks as yet another rehash from the earlier Egyptian religion and others of the Roman Empire at the time.

Another instance of the descent theme in Egyptian mythology appears in the Book of the Dead: "The descent into the under-world is spoken of by Horus in the Ritual (ch. 38). He goes to visit the spirits in prison or in their cells and sepulchres."[4] In BD 38, the deceased is to be given air in the "Other World" or "Netherworld,"[5] as

---

[1] Guthrie, W.K.C., 29.
[2] See Acharya, *SOG*, 97.
[3] *CE*, "Marcus," IX, 650.
[4] Massey, *AELW*, II, 772.
[5] Budge, *EBD* (1967), xxxv; *IAEL*, 43; Renouf, *EBD*, 86.

the Egyptian term *Dewat, Duat* or *Tuat* is often translated. "Horus"—the "heir of Ra and Tmu [Atum] in Chemmis"—is accompanied by "those who are in their cells" as his guides, and attempting to assist the breathless in the underworld.[1] In Birch's translation of BD 38, the "chapter of Life and Breath in Hades," the deceased speaks as the "second of the Sun, Tum in the Lower Country." As the sun in the underworld, the deceased passes "those in their halls" and traverses "by those in their caves." Standing "in the course of the boat of the sun," the deceased proposes "his words to the living Souls." Indicating his nature as Horus, he says, "I have sought after my father at dawn."[2]

Faulkner calls the place in BD 38 "God's Domain" and the beings there "spirits whose seats are hidden," as well as "those who are in their booths" and "those who are in their holes," the former of whom "serve me," while the latter "guide me." According to Faulkner, the speaker is "Atum" himself, who is "associated with Horus and Seth."[3] The deceased's association also with Chemmis/Khemmis, the place where Isis gave birth to Horus, indicates identification with Horus as well, as does the fact that he is also "heir" to Atum, since, in the Pyramid Texts, for example, Horus is represented as the "son of Atum."[4] Regarding Horus in the underworld rescuing souls from the dungeons, CT Sp. 491 refers to "you who watch over all souls and constrain the souls of all who are dead,"[5] who in CT Sp. 494, are called "shades," and about whom Faulkner notes that one rendition appends they were "imprisoned in caverns."[6] Thus, in Egyptian mythology as well we possess a discussion of souls imprisoned in caverns or caves in the underworld. The opening by "Horus" of caverns also appears in the Coffin Texts, as at CT Sp. 875: "I open the caverns,"[7] while in CT Sp. 891, the speaker says, "Raise yourselves, O you who are in your caverns..."[8]

Additionally, the sun hymns of the New Kingdom likewise address the sun "leading" its disk into the caves, where his "light irradiates the corpses,"[9] in effect purifying them and restoring them to life. Hence, the sun and/or Horus is responsible for rescuing souls from the underworld, as was said of the much later Jesus.

In any event, the Egyptian sun god—and the deceased—appears in the underworld on a daily basis, to be resurrected in the morning, as stated in BD 38 as well: "I daily live after death... I live again after

---

[1] Renouf, *EBD*, 86.
[2] Bunsen/Birch, 193.
[3] Faulkner, *EBD*, 104.
[4] See, e.g., PT 461:874b/M 284 and PT 465:881b/P 316. (Allen, T., *HPT*, 22; Mercer, 161, 162; Allen, J., *AEPT*, 224, 122; Faulkner, *AEPT*, 154, 155.)
[5] Faulkner, *AECT*, II, 133.
[6] Faulkner, *AECT*, II, 135.
[7] Faulkner, *AECT*, III, 44.
[8] Faulkner, *AECT*, III, 53.
[9] Assman, *ESRNK*, 61.

death like Re every day."[1] To live again after death can only be identified as being raised from the dead, revivified or *resurrected*.

The emergence of Horus himself from the underworld—his own *anastasis* or resurrection—can likewise be found in the Book of the Dead, called *Pert em Heru* in the Egyptian, which is translated also as "The Day of Manifestation" or "*The Coming Forth by Day*," reflecting the coming forth from the dark underworld into the light.[2] As Goelet states:

> The very title of the *BD* in Egyptian, "The Chapters of Going Forth by Day," evokes an image of the soul emerging into the restorative rays of the sun's light after revival during the nighttime in the underworld.[3]

The resurrection of Horus/Re/Osiris in large part represents the return of the sun from both its nightly and its annual descent into darkness, as well as, in the case of Osiris, the light waxing in the moon and the restoration of the Nile to its height among other life-renewing aspects, previously discussed. As stated, the death and resurrection of Horus likewise demonstrates another astrotheological meaning: While in the funerary texts Horus is basically resurrected as the morning sun on a daily basis, in a later myth he is killed by the scorpion of Set, to be raised from the dead by his mother, Isis, as related by Diodorus in *The Antiquities of Egypt* (1.25.6), worthwhile reiterating here:

> Isis also discovered the elixir of immortality, and when her son Horus fell victim to the plots of the Titans and was found dead beneath the waves, she not only raised him from the dead and restored his soul, but also gave him eternal life.[4]

The term used here by Diodorus for *Isis raising Horus from the dead* is from the verb αναστησαι, the noun for which is *anastasis*, the very word utilized in the description of the later Jesus's resurrection.[5] Obviously, in this *resurrection* account of Horus we discover a pre-Christian *dying and rising god* strangely overlooked in the debate on the subject over the past decades.

In any event, Set as the "scorpion" likely symbolizes in part the constellation of Scorpio, the "backbiter," the time of the year when the sun begins to "die" at the winter solstice, to be "born again" on December 25th. It is also interesting to note that Plutarch (13, 356C) said Osiris was likewise dead and sought during the time when the sun passed into Scorpio.[6] Osiris and Horus are thus interchangeable based once again on their solar roles.

---

[1] Faulkner, *EBD*, 104.
[2] Kuhn, *Easter*, 15-16.
[3] Faulkner, *EBD*, 149.
[4] Murphy, 31.
[5] Porter, *Res.*, 76. See also Diodorus/Murphy, 31.
[6] Plutarch/Babbitt, 37.

"Easter"—The Resurrection of Spring

Although it is believed to represent the time of Jesus Christ's resurrection, the festival of Easter existed in pre-Christian times and, according to the famous Christian saint Venerable Bede (672/672-735 AD/CE), was named for the Teutonic or German goddess Eôstre, who was the "goddess of dawn" and who symbolized the fertility found abundantly during the springtime of the year.[1] Regarding the ancient fertility goddess, in *How the Easter Story Grew from Gospel to Gospel*, Dr. Rolland E. Wolfe, a professor of Biblical Literature at Case Western Reserve University, relates:

> In the polytheistic pantheons of antiquity there usually was a king or chief of the gods, and also a female counterpart who was regarded as his wife. This mother goddess was one of the most important deities in the ancient Near East. She was called by the various names of Ishtar, Athtar [sic], Astarte, Ashtoreth, Antit, and Anat. This mother goddess always was associated with human fertility. In the course of time Mary was to become identified with this ancient mother goddess, or perhaps it should be said that Mary was about to supplant her in certain Christian circles.[2]

The comparison between the Babylonian goddess Ishtar and the Jewish maiden Mary becomes even more evident when it is factored in that in an ancient Akkadian hymn Ishtar is called "Virgin."[3] Yet, like Mary, Ishtar too was the "Mother of God," in this case Tammuz, the *dying and rising god* mourned by the Israelite women at Ezekiel 8:14.[4] Indeed, Old Testament scholar Rev. Dr. W. Robertson Smith identifies Ishtar as the *virgin-mother* goddess worshipped at Petra who was mentioned by Church father Epiphanius. In a footnote, Smith remarks, "The identification of the mother of the gods with the heavenly virgin, *in other words*, the unmarried goddess, is confirmed if not absolutely demanded by Aug. *Civ. Dei*, ii. 4."[5] The reference is to St. Augustine's *The City of God* (2.4), in which the Church father discusses with undisguised contempt the Pagan rites surrounding "the virgin Caelestis" and "Berecynthia the mother of them all."[6] From these remarks and many others over the past centuries it is clear that the educated elite have been well aware of the unoriginality of

---

[1] See *CE*, V, 224; Weekley, 491. The name "Eostre" is evidently related to the Greek word for "dawn," *eos*.

[2] Wolfe, 234.

[3] Sayce, *Lectures*, 268.

[4] See Mettinger's exhaustive analysis on the subject of Tammuz-Dumuzi, in which he concludes: "From the end of the third millennium B.C.E. there is thus narrative, mythological evidence for Dumuzi as a god who dies and returns." (Mettinger, 213.) Although his studies assure us that there *are* several important "dying-and-rising gods," Mettinger at times appears reluctant to use the term "resurrection," likely for the reasons given here as concerns what he also sees as a "Christian bias." (Mettinger, 43fn.)

[5] Smith, W.R., 56

[6] Augustine/Dyson, 54.

the virgin-mother motif within Christianity. Yet, to this day the public remains uninformed and/or in fervent denial about such facts.

As may be evident, variants of the goddess's name from which the term "Easter" appears to be derived include Ishtar and Astarte, among others such as Ostara and Ostern. As Rev. Dr. William Howard Van Doren remarks:

> The festival called Easter from the heathen goddess Astarte, called in Nineveh, as read on the Assyrian monuments, Ishtar, and by our Saxon ancestors Easter, Œster, or Oster, the same with the Latin Venus, whose festival was observed by the Pagans at the same time.[1]

We have already seen that this springtime/Easter resurrection myth occurred in Greek mythology with the tale of Kore/Persephone descending into the underworld to reside with Hades, leading to the death of winter. Her reemergence out of the underworld represented the springtime renewal of life on Earth—thus, *Persephone's resurrection symbolized eternal life*, precisely as did that of Jesus *and Osiris*.

Comprising the entombment for three days, the descent into the underworld, and the resurrection, the spring celebration of "Easter" represents the period of the vernal equinox, when the sun is "hung on a cross" composed of the days and nights of equal length. After a touch-and-go battle for supremacy with the night or darkness, the sun emerges triumphant, being "born again" or "resurrected" as a "man," moving towards "his" full strength at the summer solstice:

> Great are the storms and tribulations of winter, but the Sun-God survives them all, and His strength is steadily growing as the days lengthen towards the vernal equinox. At that equinox, as the name implies, day and night are exactly equal...; and after it the sun crosses the line, so that in the northern hemisphere the days grow steadily longer, and the victory of the Sun-God over night is assured. He rises triumphantly over the line and ascends in the heavens, ripening the corn and the grape, pouring His life into them to make their substance, and through them giving Himself to His worshippers.[2]

It is noteworthy that even older scholarship reflects the knowledge of the strengthening of the *sun* at Easter, as exemplified by Rev. George W. Lemon, who in his *English Etymology*, published in 1783, gives the meaning of "Easter" as:

> ...at that time or on that day, the Sun of Righteousness arose with healing in his wings, like the sun all glorious in the east...

The "Sun of Righteousness" refers to Jesus Christ, as purportedly prophesied in the last book before the New Testament, Malachi (4:2). Christ's identification as the "Sun of Righteousness," the placement of his "resurrection" at Easter, and his association with the "sun all

[1] Van Doren, 238. See Kearney, 106.
[2] Leadbetter, 183.

glorious in the east," all reflect his *solar* role, serving as e╌
Jesus himself being a sun god. Indeed, "Easter" or the verr╌
truly represents the resurrection of the "Light of the Woィ╌ ╌ぃ╌
sun—bringing with it the fertility of spring.

That Easter constituted a pre-Christian festival concerning
resurrection is apparent from the discussion in the *New International
Encyclopaedia* regarding Easter customs:

> The use of eggs in this connection is of the highest antiquity, the egg
> having been considered in widely separated pre-Christian
> mythologies as a symbol of resurrection...[1]

The *NIE* thus specifically states that *the notion of resurrection
existed in pre-Christian mythologies.* The *NIE* also relates that in its
use of Easter eggs the Church likely "adopted and consecrated an
earlier custom," adding that this development is "almost certainly
true of the Easter fires which formerly celebrated the triumph of
spring over winter (See BELTANE)..." Beltane is the name of the Celtic
celebration of the triumph of spring's life over the death of winter. In
other words, Easter represents the *"triumph of spring over winter,"
light over dark,* or *day over night,* a point that cannot be emphasized
enough.

In his extensive analysis of the "dying and rising gods," Frazer
concluded that the story of Easter as a time of rebirth, renewal and
resurrection of life in general could be found in the myths of non-
Christian deities such as the Greco-Phrygian god Attis and the Greco-
Syrian god Adonis, among others.[2] While various of Frazer's
contentions have come under fire, frequently from Christian
apologists, Mettinger's research demonstrates the dying-and-rising
theme overall to be sound.[3] As concerns the correspondences
between Christ and the god Attis, Dr. Gary Taylor, a professor at the
University of Alabama, states:

> Similarities between Attis and Christ had become increasingly
> prominent in the ritual celebrations of Attis in Rome and elsewhere:
> The "Hilaria" turned his humiliated suffering into an occasion of joy,
> celebrants were "redeemed by the blood" of a sacrificial victim, and
> the promise of resurrection was held out to believers.[4]

Discussing Attis along with his consort/mother Cybele (the
"Metroac" cult/mysteries), Dr. Andrew T. Fear, a professor of Classics
and Ancient History at the University of Manchester, remarks:

[1] Gilman, VI, 492.
[2] See Frazer, *GB*, II, 116-117, etc.
[3] As but one pertinent example, after discussing Origen's remarks about Adonis being
called Tammuz, Mettinger says: "The name Tammuz in Ezek. 8:14 is here understood
to refer to Adonis. We note that the annual celebration of Adonis as described by
Origen had two subsequent steps: (1) Adonis is bewailed as though he were dead. (2)
Then there was a celebration of joy on his behalf 'as if he had risen from the dead.'"
(Mettinger, 129.)
[4] Taylor, G., 72.

The youthful Attis after his murder was miraculously brought to life again three days after his demise. The celebration of this cycle of death and renewal was one of the major festivals of the metroaccult. Attis therefore represented a promise of reborn life and as such it is not surprising that we find representations of the so-called mourning Attis as a common tomb motif in the ancient world.

The parallel, albeit at a superficial level, between this myth and the account of the resurrection of Christ is clear. Moreover Attis as a shepherd occupies a favourite Christian image of Christ as the good shepherd. Further parallels also seem to have existed: the pine tree of Attis, for example, was seen as a parallel to the cross of Christ.

Beyond Attis himself, Cybele too offered a challenge to Christian divine nomenclature. Cybele was regarded as a virgin goddess and as such could be seen as a rival to the Virgin Mary... Cybele as the mother of the Gods, *mater Deum*, here again presented a starkly pagan parallel to the Christian Mother of God.

There was rivalry too in ritual. The climax of the celebration of Attis' resurrection, the *Hilaria*, fell on the 25th of March, the date that the early church had settled on as the day of Christ's death....[1]

The festival associated with Cybele and Attis, called the "Megalensia," was celebrated specifically in the spring, with a *passion play* commemorating Attis's death and resurrection.[2] Dr. Fear thus asserts this mourning period of the god Attis to have comprised *three days*. In reality, this pre-Christian cult remained popular well into the common era, and its similarities to Christianity were not considered "superficial" by the Church fathers such as Augustine who wrote about them. The parallels between the Attis myth and the gospel story are in fact startling and highly noteworthy, and in reality represent an archetypal myth that was evidently changed to revolve around a Jewish messiah, with numerous details added for a wide variety of purposes. Fear's analysis includes the debate as to *when* this prototypical springtime death-and-resurrection motif was associated with the pre-Christian god Attis, with various scholars averring its components to have been added *in response to Christianity.*

Contrary to the current fad of dismissing all correspondences between Christianity and Paganism, the fact that Attis *was* at some point a "dying and rising god" is concluded by Mettinger who relates: "Since the time of Damascius (6th cent. AD/CE), Attis seems to have

---

[1] Lane, 39-40.

[2] Salzman, 87. The "Preface" for Prof. Michelle Renee Salzman's study of the Roman calendar of 354 AD/CE states: "Her work reveals the continuing importance of pagan festivals and cults in the Christian era and highlights the rise of a respectable aristocratic Christianity that combined pagan and Christian practices. Salzman stresses the key role of the Christian emperors and imperial institutions in supporting pagan rituals. Such policies of accommodation and assimilation resulted in a gradual and relatively peaceful transformation of Rome from a pagan to a Christian capital."

been believed to die and return."[1] By that point, we possess clear discussion in *writing* of Attis having been resurrected, but when exactly were these rites first celebrated and where? Again, Attis worship is centuries older than Jesus worship and was popular in some parts of the Roman Empire before and well into the "Christian era."

In addition, it is useful here to reiterate that simply because something occurred after the year 1 AD/CE does not mean that it was influenced by Christianity, as it may have happened where Christianity had never been heard of. In actuality, not much about Christianity emerges until the second century, and there remain to this day places where Christianity is unknown; hence, these locations can still be considered *pre-Christian.*

It is probable that the Attis rites were celebrated long before Christianity was recognized to any meaningful extent. Certainly, since they are mysteries, they could have been celebrated but not recorded previously, especially in pre-Christian times, when the capital punishment for revealing such mysteries was actually carried out. We have seen cautious reticence expressed on the part of Herodotus, for example, who declined to reveal the mysteries of Osiris he had witnessed. Herodotus's concerns would not be misplaced, as evidenced by the "witchhunt" that ensued within his lifetime concerning the Athenian politician Alcibiades (c. 450–404 BCE), who was accused of "profaning the Mysteries" and was sentenced to death for his alleged transgressions.[2] Under such circumstances, it is understandable that the mysteries were never recorded overtly such that we now have them readily at our disposal.

Moreover, frequently lacking in critical analyses from extant ancient texts is any acknowledgement of the massive destruction of culture waged by Christians for many centuries, undoubtedly designed in significant part to obliterate any record of correspondences between Paganism and Christianity. In the case of Attis, for example, we possess a significant account in Diodorus (3.58.7) of his death and mourning, including the evidently annual ritual creation of his image by priests.[3] Hence, these significant aspects of the Attis myth are clearly pre-Christian. But what about the resurrection itself? In consideration of all the forgery and fraud committed by religious fanatics over the centuries, we would not be remiss in suggesting that it would be a simple matter of merely editing Diodorus, for one, to make it appear as if the resurrection motif were never in his works. In the final analysis, there currently exists only a relative handful of writings from the pertinent eras, out of a mass of literature and other artifacts—who can conclude with

---

[1] Mettinger, 159.
[2] Bauman, 62-64.
[3] Diodorus/Oldfather, 277.

100% certainty that amidst all of these destroyed writings appeared
no Pagan parallels to Christianity? Indeed, as we have seen from the
Egyptian data alone, such a conclusion is entirely untenable. In this
regard, we need not rely on the Attis myth to demonstrate that
Christianity is not original or unique in most of its salient concepts.

In reality, the theme of life renewal was based largely on natural
phenomena that were unquestionably observed long before the
Christian era, with its similar drama surrounding a Jewish godman.
It is therefore reasonable to ask whether or not these other gods
already symbolized these motifs long prior to the era in which they
are clearly recorded as such. Also, let us not forget that a number of
these highly significant motifs constituted *mysteries* that were not
readily and easily recorded anywhere, but that may have been known
more or less widely through oral tradition, especially among the elite
who create religions. That festivals celebrating the end of winter's
death and the resurrection of life in spring long predate Christianity
in numerous parts of the world is a fact, as we know from the
Persephone story, for one, and there is little reason to suppose that
such "Easter" commemorations were not prevalent in other places
also centuries prior to the common era. Moreover, we possess
testimony from early Christian fathers such as Justin Martyr that
appears to prove the existence of these various motifs *preceding*
Christ's purported advent.

Concerning the pre-Christian resurrection theme, Dr. Porter
remarks:

> During the Graeco-Roman period, there were numerous cults that
> had their basis in earlier thought and relied to varying degrees on
> some form of a resurrection story. Three of them can be mentioned
> here, although it is not clear that these are different myths. They
> may be simply the same myth many times retold....[1]

In his discussion of this retelling of myths, Porter recounts the
comments by Diodorus that the Egyptian gods are called by many
names, such as various Greek counterparts. He then addresses the
Orphic myths, which include that of Dionysus, "first developed
around the sixth century BC in the east."[2] Porter subsequently says:

> The cycle of nature, reflected in the myth of Dionysius's [sic] death
> and rebirth, tied to the harvest, emphasized the promise of new life
> to those who followed the cult....

> A second cult worth recounting is that of Isis. This cult was arguably
> the most important of the mystery religions of the Roman Empire.
> The figure of Isis was identified with Demeter...but developed her
> own cult, well-reflected in evidence from Egypt during the Roman
> period, especially in terms of health and overcoming of disease.[3]

---

[1] Porter, *Res.*, 74-75.
[2] Porter, *Res.*, 75.
[3] Porter, *Res.*, 76.

Next Porter relates the story of Horus's resurrection from death as recounted by Diodorus (1.25.6), adding:

> The word used for raised from the dead is αναστησαι [anastesai], widely used in the New Testament for "resurrection" as well. This same power, evidenced also in Isis's husband/brother Osiris, was then in some sense transferred to all later initiates, who went through a process of initiation into the cult of Isis.[1]

Again, in Horus's myth emerges a resurrection or *anastasis*, using the precise term found in the later New Testament, in the century *before* Christ's purported revivification. This fact is highly significant in that it demonstrates yet another solid link between the Egyptian and Christian religions.

Horus and Osiris at the Vernal Equinox

As concerns "Easter" in Egypt, we have already discussed the festival known as "Shamo," which dates to at least 4,500 years ago and which is celebrated to this day. Regarding Easter and Horus, Massey states:

> ...the place of rebirth for Horus the eternal Son was celebrated in the vernal equinox... The double birth of Horus at the two times, or the birth of the babe in the winter solstice and the rebirth as the adult in the Easter equinox is acknowledged in the Egyptian Book of the Divine Birth.... it was commanded in the calendar of Esné that the precepts of the Book on the Second Divine Birth of the child Kahi "were to be performed on the first of the month Epiphi" (cited by Lockyer, *Dawn of Astronomy*, pp. 284-6). The child Kahi is a pseudonym for the child-Horus.... Now the first and second "divine births" (or the birth and rebirth) of Horus were celebrated at the festivals of the winter solstice and the Easter equinox, and these are the two times of the two Horuses identified by Plutarch, the first as manifester for Isis, the Virgin Mother, the second as Horus, the Son of God the Father, when he tells us that "Harpocrates (Har the Khart, or child) is born about the winter solstice, immature and infant-like in the plants that flower and spring up early, for which reason they offer to him the first-fruits of growing lentils; and they celebrate her (Isis) being brought to bed after the vernal equinox" (of Is. and Os., ch. 65)... Two different birthdays were likewise assigned to the Greek Apollo. One of these was commemorated by the Delians at the time of the winter solstices; the other by the Delphians in the vernal equinox.[2]

In the Greek myth, Apollo was born on the island of Delos and was said to journey to the mainland village of Delphi, where he had a temple and a famed oracle. The ancient writer Macrobius (1.18.7-10) names Apollo as a sun god—albeit as the "summer sun"—and then discusses the sun god being born at the winter solstice, which is

---

[1] Porter, *Res.*, 76. See also Diodorus/Murphy, 31.
[2] Massey, *AELW*, II, 739.

a solar hero.[1] As was the case with Dionysus, likewise the ... born at the winter solstice, that time of the year was celebrated in the name of Apollo with "orgies."[2] The festival of Apollo called the Delphinia was held "at the vernal equinox, during the month of Monouchion," or March.[3] Apollo and his sister Artemis are called the "vernal deities,"[4] while Apollo is likewise the "vernal Sun."[5] It is easy to understand why Apollo was said to have been born at both the winter solstice *and* the vernal equinox. Since Horus was repeatedly identified with Apollo in ancient times, one can see why the same might be asserted about the Egyptian god as well.

Concerning the solar nature of Osiris and the birth of Horus at the vernal equinox, Bunsen remarks:

> The myth of Osiris typifies the solar year—the power of Osiris is the sun in the lower hemisphere, the winter solstices. The birth of Horus typifies the vernal equinox—the victory of Horus, the summer equinox—the inundation of the Nile. Typhon is the autumnal equinox.[6]

Indeed, the double birth of Horus is described without explanation by Plutarch (65, 377C), who, in addition to his discussion of Harpocrates being "brought forth" by Isis at the winter solstice next comments that "the days of his birth they celebrate after the spring equinox."[7]

As previously noted, an inscription found at both Edfu and Esne discusses the festival of the "suspension of the sky by Ptah," as well as that of the entrance of Osiris into the moon, which festivities are "connected with the celebration of the Winter Solstice...."[8] These festivals are mentioned by Lockyer along with the book "on the Divine Birth" as part of a discussion of the "reconstruction of the calendar."[9] The royal astronomer next discusses the date of "1 Epiphi" in the Esne calendar, the entry for which he quotes as: "1 Epiphi. To perform the precepts of the book on the second divine birth of the child Kahi."[10] Lockyer subsequently remarks that the 26th of the Egyptian month of Payni, which is the "New Year's Day," is "associated with "the second divine birth" and "may have some dim reference to the feast."[11] Lockyer finally demurs from discussing the subject further, much to our loss about this important issue. The

---

[1] Macrobius/Davies, 129.
[2] Sophocles/D'Ooge, 136fn.
[3] Lennard, 171.
[4] Müller, 27.
[5] Forlong, 82.
[6] Bunsen/Birch, 451.
[7] Plutarch/Babbitt, 153.
[8] Lockyer, *DA*, 284.
[9] Lockyer, *DA*, 285.
[10] Lockyer, *DA*, 286.
[11] Lockyer, *DA*, 286.

26th of Payni in the Alexandrian calendar is equivalent to J┊
which would indeed represent the summer-solstice, new ┊
observance with the rising of Sirius and the pending birth of Osiris.

In the Alexandrian calendar, the first of Epiphi or Epeiph is
equivalent to June 25th,[2] reflecting the end of the summer solstice
and the birth of Osiris. In the roving or "vague" Egyptian calendar the
1st of Epiphi fell on the vernal equinox in the years 1142-1139 BCE,
which date during those years would translate as April 1 in the
Julian calendar.[3] It is possible that at that time 1 Epiphi was
designated the "second divine birth of the child Kahi." In this regard,
the Egyptian word *kahi* means "soil," "earth," "land" and "region,"
and, while *kahi* is typically represented as a goddess, it was also an
epithet of *Horus*, as in "Horus of the Two Lands" in the Book of the
Dead, or "Horus of the land,"[4] as at the temple of Edfu, where Horus
is likewise deemed *Hor-hat-kah*: "Horus of the land of Hat."[5]

In addition to connecting it with the winter solstice, Plutarch (43,
368C) also places Osiris's "Coming to the Moon" as a festival marking
the *vernal equinox*:

> Moreover, at the time of the new moon in the month of Phamenoth
> they celebrate a festival to which they give the name of "Osiris's
> coming to the Moon," and this marks the beginning of the spring.
> Thus they make the power of Osiris to be fixed in the Moon, and say
> that Isis, since she is generation, is associated with him. For this
> reason they also call the Moon the mother of the world, and they
> think that she has a nature both male and female, as she is receptive
> and made pregnant by the Sun, but she herself in turn emits and
> disseminates into the air generative principles.[6]

Concerning Osiris and his "discovery" or *rebirth* at the winter
solstice, as well as his entrance into the moon during the vernal
equinox, the *Encyclopedia Britannica* states:

> Among the most characteristic celebrations of the Egyptians were
> those which took place at the αφανισμός [aphanismos] or
> disappearance of Osiris in October or November, at the search for his
> remains, and their discovery about the winter solstice, and at the
> date of his supposed entrance into the moon at the beginning of
> spring.[7]

Regarding Osiris's "entrance into the moon," by the time of the
Decree of Canopus (238 BCE), the wandering year had placed the
lunar event on the 29th of Koiak, which in the Alexandrian calendar
was equivalent to December 26th.[8] Thus, like Horus, we possess in

---

[1] Jones, 317.
[2] Jones, 319.
[3] *PSBA*, XXVII, 257.
[4] Duncker, 189.
[5] Kenrick, 392.
[6] Plutarch/Babbitt, 106.
[7] *Enc. Brit.*, X, 221.
[8] Massey, *AELW*, II, 739.

the myth of Osiris another kind of "dual birth" with his rediscovery or "rebirth" at the winter solstice and his renewal or "rebirth" as the light in the moon at the vernal equinox. If Osiris's "real" birth at the summer solstice is factored in, we possess *three* annual, astrotheological times of renewal for the god, as well as his purported birth on January 6th, making him equivalent to "Aion."[1]

The Christian celebration of "Easter," the supposed time of Christ's death and resurrection, also follows a roving date traditionally placed on the first full moon following the vernal equinox, which has occurred occasionally during the equinoctial three-day period, as it did in 2008.[2] This wandering date indicates that Christ's passion and resurrection are not "historical," with their placement at the full moon after or at the vernal equinox, demonstrating their astrotheological nature instead. Indeed, if, as according to certain Gnostics, Jesus's incarnation and crucifixion were "fictitious," then so too would be his resurrection, obviously taking place in the "Pleroma," quite similar to that of Osiris.

The "Christos" is not only the sun triumphing over the darkness as the day becomes longer than the night, but it is also the sun's light in the moon, as the moon waxes and wanes monthly. Hence, the full moon likewise represents the sun's "resurrection," and the theme within Christianity also appears to have been influenced by Osiris's entrance into the moon at the vernal equinox as well. That the date of Christ's death and resurrection is based on astrotheology is thoroughly demonstrated in the subject's discussion by ancient Church fathers, including the writers of the Alexandria or Paschal Chronicle, also called the "Easter Chronicle." In that text, the authors spend significant time calculating the proper dates for Easter, based on *astrotheological considerations*. In any event, the deity reborn or raised up at the vernal equinox or springtime is a recurring theme not representing a "historical" personage but, rather, a natural phenomenon, i.e., *Spring*.

The "Ascension into Heaven"

In the Christian tale, Jesus's miraculous ascension into heaven is appended as an afterthought in the Gospel of Luke and as a footnote in Mark, not appearing at all in Matthew or John—who were nevertheless supposed to have been eyewitnesses to the astounding

---

[1] Kelly, 59; van der Toorn, 14.
[2] The establishment of the Christian "Easter" as transpiring on the first full moon after the vernal equinox occurred at the First Council of Nicea (325 AD/CE), in an attempt both to usurp the non-Christian festivals and to unify them on one set day, since they varied in diverse places. The full moon date was also established in order to prevent the Pagan-Christian celebration from coinciding with the Jewish Passover. (Gilman, VI, 493.)

event![1] After studying the precedents for the ascension in the myths of other cultures, it becomes obvious that the motif was added to the Christ myth in order to compete with these others. As one of these mythical precedents, the god's ascension to heaven is repeatedly referred to in the very ancient Egyptian texts as well. In the *Journal of Near Eastern Studies*, in an article entitled, "The Ascension-Myth in the Pyramid Texts," Berkeley professor of History Dr. Whitney M. Davis states that the "myth of the ascension of the King" represents "one of the principal myths of the ancient Egyptian Pyramid Texts."[2] The ascension of both Osiris and Horus may be found at PT 303:464a-467a/W 208, for example:

> "O you western gods, eastern gods, southern gods, and northern gods! These four pure reed-floats which you set down for Osiris when he ascended to the sky, so that he might ferry over to the firmament with his son Horus beside him so that he might bring him up and cause him to appear as a great god in the firmament—set them down for me!"

> "Are you Horus, son of Osiris? Are you the god, the eldest one, the son of Hathor? Are you the seed of Geb?"

> "Osiris has commanded me to appear as the counterpart of Horus...[3]

The word Faulkner translates here as "firmament"—*kbhw* or *qbhw*—represents the hieroglyph for "cool water," "libation" or "celestial lake." Mercer calls the act in question an "ascension to heaven," while Allen prefers the rendering of "going forth to the sky." In addition, Faulkner labels 29 utterances in the Pyramid Texts as "An 'ascension' text,"[4] demonstrating the prominence of this theme.

Osiris and Horus's ascension in PT 303 is summarized by Griffiths thus:

> He (Osiris) voyages to heaven with his son Horus at his side, that he may nurture him and cause him to appear in glory as a great god in heaven.[5]

As we can see, the deceased is to "appear" or "dawn" as a "counterpart of Horus," or a "second Horus," after Horus ascends to the sky in the company of his father, Osiris.

T. George Allen also summarizes a pyramid text (PT 537:1301a-b/P 281) in which the deceased, as *Horus*, ascends:

> King ascends as...Horus of Dewat, presider over the Imperishable Stars, and sits upon his marvelous throne at the head of his celestial lake...[1]

---

[1] For more on this subject, including a discussion of the illogicality of the ascension not appearing in Matthew and John, as well as other non-Christian precedents for the ascension, see my book *Who Was Jesus?*
[2] Davis, W.M., 161.
[3] Faulkner, *AEPT*, 92; Mercer, 102; Allen, J., *AEPT*, 57.
[4] See, e.g., PT 271, 306, 321, 326, 330, 332, 335, 337, 421, 467, 471, 484, 485, 488, 503, 505, 507, 525, 539, 566, 572, 582, 624, 667A, 669, 673, 684, 688, 699.
[5] Griffiths, *OOHC*, 14.

As another example, PT 670/N 348, which Mercer calls, "The Death, Resurrection, and Spiritualization of the King," and which James Allen deems, "Commending the Spirit to Isis and Nephthys," describes the mourning, resurrection and ascension of the deceased/Osiris.[2] In this spell, Horus calls forth Osiris after his "fourth day," as in the parallel story of Jesus and Lazarus. The last line depicts the Osiris as "coming from" or *ascending up from* Geb/Seb, the earth.

In PT 684:2051a-b/N 514, which Mercer titles, "THE DECEASED KING ASCENDS TO HEAVEN," the departed rises up with Osiris:

> To say: N. ascended at thy ascension, Osiris; N. has spoken (with) his ka in heaven.[3]

Faulkner renders this "ascension text" as: "This King ascended when you ascended, O Osiris; his word and his double are bound for the sky..."[4] Allen calls this spell simply, "Meeting the Gods,"[5] translating it as: "Pepi Neferkare ["N" or the deceased] has emerged in your emergence, Osiris; Pepi Neferkare has claimed his ka for the sky."[6] Allen's translation reflects his preference for the rendition of the pertinent hieroglyph as "sky," rather than "heaven," in order to avoid "the use of words that may connote concepts not present in Egyptian."[7] As concerns the rendering of "sky" as "heaven," however, it should be noted that in his analysis of the abundant sun hymns from the New Kingdom, Assman employs the terms "heaven" and "heavens" on numerous occasions.[8]

In any event, unless we know what we are looking at in Allen's rendering, we might have a difficult time seeing that the basic concept is the "ascension into heaven," as the deceased becomes "spiritualized" or "akhified." That the deceased is rising into the sky becomes clear from the next utterance, per Allen: "...the (grand)mother of Pepi Neferkare, Tefnut, will take Pepi Neferkare to the sky, to the sky on the smoke of incense."[9] Again, the deceased— in this case, Pepi II—is "the Osiris," rising into the sky. Tefnut, we have seen, is the daughter created by Atmu/Atum from himself, and

---

[1] Allen, T., *HPT*, 27; Mercer, 213; Allen, J., *AEPT*, 117; Faulkner, *AEPT*, 206. Allen prefers the phrase "emerge as Horus of the Duat," rather than "ascendest like Horus," as in Mercer. Regarding the epithet "Imperishable Ones," Hare states: "In Egypt, the etiology of the death of god is complex. In the stellar religion of early Egypt, the stars were thought to represent deities, and those which never sank below the horizon were called the imperishable ones. The corollary would assign to those stars which did fall below the horizon a kind of perishing, or death." (Hare, 15.)

[2] Mercer, 294; Allen, J., *AEPT*, 266.

[3] Mercer, 302.

[4] Faulkner, *AEPT*, 294.

[5] Allen, J., *AEPT*, 290.

[6] Allen, J., *AEPT*, 290.

[7] Allen, J., *AEPT*, 13.

[8] See, e.g., Assman, *ESRNK*, 12.

[9] Allen, J., *AEPT*, 13.

her status as Pepi's "grandmother" once again displays the divinity of the king and his identification as a god, in this case Osiris, grandson of Tefnut. From this lofty position, it is said later in this spell, "Pepi Neferkare will not fall to the ground from the sky."[1] In order to attain to the sky, the deceased must use the "Winding Canal," which is the 12° ecliptic or path the sun traverses during the year.[2] In addition, the Osiris will put himself on the path of "Horus of Shezmet," the sun at dawn, the route upon which Horus "leads the gods to the perfect paths of the sky..."[3] The ascension into the sky is also repeatedly referred to in the Coffin Texts,[4] including in a passage (CT Sp. 74) discussing Horus of the Netherworld rising up and ascending into the "Celestial waters."[5]

Also in the Pyramid Texts, Osiris is depicted as ascending into heaven via the *ladder* of Horus and Set,[6] which could likewise be deemed the "stairway to paradise." As Dr. W.M. Davis says, "The King may use a ladder...to reach the Hereafter," as at PT 568:1431c/P 507, which states that "a ladder is set up for him that he may ascend on it..."[7] CT Sp. 550 concerns this same "ladder to heaven," used by the Osiris to reach the sky.[8] Meanwhile, in CT Sp. 76 the "air god" Shu, who supports the heavens while standing on the earth, also possesses a ladder.[9] The ascension by ladder of the god into the sky likewise occurs at PT 688/N 522: "Pepi Neferkare ["The Osiris"] shall go thereby to his mother Nut and Pepi Neferkare shall go ascend on her in her identity of the ladder."[10] Once more, the deceased is identified with Osiris, son of Nut, the sky, to whom the son/sun ascends. Interestingly, while Set *supplants* Osiris, the biblical character who also possesses a ladder to heaven is named "Jacob," which likewise means "supplanter." (Gen 28:10-12) In discussing the ascension of Osiris by ladder, Griffiths remarks, "One recalls the celestial ladder in Jacob's dream at Bethel."[11] In light of the obvious cultural exchange between Egypt and the Levant, it is logical to suggest that, rather than representing a "true story" of a "historical Jacob," the biblical tale is likewise a *myth*, emanating out of Egypt and not the other way around.[12]

As is evident, however it is translated, Osiris and Horus are described as *ascending into the sky*, which, again, is sensible for solar

---

[1] Allen, J., *AEPT*, 291.
[2] Allen, J., *AEPT*, 9, 244.
[3] Allen, J., *AEPT*, 441, 291.
[4] See, e.g., CT Sp. 21, et al. (Faulkner, *AECT*, I, 12.)
[5] Faulkner, *AECT*, I, 70.
[6] Griffiths, *OOHC*, 11.
[7] Davis, W.M., 169. See Mercer, 228; Allen, J., *AEPT*, 176.
[8] Faulkner, *AECT*, II, 163.
[9] Faulkner, *AECT*, I, 77.
[10] Allen, J., *AEPT*, 279; Faulkner, *AEPT*, 297.
[11] Griffiths, *OOHC*, 2.
[12] See, e.g., Greenberg, 142.

deities, describing the sun's daily and annual transits. As the ascension is "generally associated with the daylight rather than with the nighttime,"[1] it would therefore be out of the netherworld, precisely as was said of Jesus's anastasis out of the underworld. Another instance of this rebirth/resurrection is termed the "Emergence from the Duat," which is the title of a Pyramid Text spell (W 158).[2] As we can see, like the resurrection, the "ascension to heaven," "going forth to the sky" or "voyage to heaven" is a common occurrence with Egyptian gods, as is appropriate for *the sun*.

Spiritual or Bodily Resurrection?

In an attempt to establish any difference, however slight, between the Egyptian and Christian religions, the argument has been put forth that, while it may be true that Osiris had something to do with resurrection, it was a completely different concept than the physical or bodily resurrection of Jesus and the promise the latter held for all mankind. For example, Dr. Robert M. Grant, a professor of New Testament at the University of Chicago, avers, "Other gods died and rose; only Jesus rose in the flesh."[3] This notion is a step up from the denial that there was *any* kind of resurrection within pre-Christian religion, which, astonishingly, certain individuals have tried to argue along the way in order to prove Christianity a "unique divine revelation," separate and apart from, as well as superior to, "diabolical Paganism." Contrary to such a fallacy, the idea of resurrection was not only abundant but an almost constant focus of Egyptian religion, for one, with the mortuary texts designed specifically for this transition, as we have already seen many times.

The dilemma of the Christian perspective is evident in such remarks as the following by apologists who endeavor to differentiate between the resurrections of Osiris and Jesus, first asserting that "there is no account that claims Osiris rose from the dead." In the next paragraph, however, the authors relate the story of Osiris being killed, with Isis reassembling his body, after which she "brought him back to life!"[4] Surely this death and revivification constitutes a *resurrection* in which *the god rises from the dead*. The next distinction is attempted by dismissing Osiris's resurrection as a "zombification." From such comments, however, it would appear that said apologists have not read a single scripture from the enormous body of writings and are therefore not expert on the Egyptian religion. On the contrary, a professional Egyptologist who was one of the most respected authorities of his day, sincere Christian Budge was so struck by the profound similarities that he believed Christ was the

---

[1] Davis, W.M., 171.
[2] Allen, *AEPT*, 41.
[3] *The Journal of Religion*, 126-127.
[4] Habermas/Licona, 91.

fulfillment of the Egyptian religion. Other Egyptologists, including Morenz, Hornung and Mojsov, have recognized and commented upon some of the more germane correspondences between the Egyptian and Christian religions as well, as we have seen throughout this present work.

Another apologist book asserts:

> Part of the uniqueness of Christianity is its insistence on the bodily resurrection of Jesus Christ and on the future bodily resurrection of believers in Christ. The reuniting of the soul with the body—a new, permanent body—is unheard of in the ancient mystery religions.[1]

In reality, this "uniqueness" is revealed to be an illusion. In the first place, do Christians really believe that their old rotting bodies will be restored for them? The author clarifies it will be a *new* body that believers inherit by their mere faith in Christ. In that regard, this belief is *virtually identical* to that of the Egyptians, although lacking in the finer spiritual nuances of the Egyptian religion. Moreover, if the Osirian cultus is to be considered a "mystery religion," as demonstrated here repeatedly to be, then the last contention is certainly false.

The Word "Resurrection"

In an effort to create any possible distinction between the Egyptian and Christian religions, the Egyptian resurrection is denied to the point where even the word "resurrection" is avoided in designating it, as if the term belongs solely to the much later Christian religion and should not be used when describing the revivification of other gods, heroes and legends in the ancient world. This argument is spurious and is rejected here because, firstly, the concept of a resurrection to life, after a period of death, is very much prevalent in ancient religion long prior to the common era. Secondly, the term translated as "resurrection" in the New Testament— αναστασις or *anastasis* (Strong's G386), which means "standing up" or "rising up," the same translated phrase as used in the Egyptian texts to describe the deceased's resurrection—can be found dozens of times in the Greek Old Testament, such as at Lamentations 3:63 and elsewhere. *Anastasis* and other derivatives also appear in the works of the pre-Christian Greek writers Aeschylus (c. 525-456 BCE), Sophocles (c. 496 BCE-406 BCE), Euripides (c. 480-406 BCE), Thucydides (c. 460-c. 395 BCE) and Demosthenes (384–322 BCE), with a variety of meanings, and in no way represent the sole possession of the Christian effort.[2] Indeed, the same word *anastasis* is used in the first century *before the common era* by Diodorus Siculus to describe

---

[1] Komoszewski, 259.

[2] See, e.g., Aeschylus, *Agamemnon*, line 589 and *Eumenides*, line 648 in Murray, G.; Sophocles, *Philoctetes*, line 276 in Dain, A.; Euripides, *Troiades*, line 364 in Murray, G.; Thucydides, *Historiae*, 2.15.1.1 in Jones, H.S., I, and 7.75.1.2 in Jones, H.S., II, 193; Demosthenes, *Olynthiaca* 2, sect. 1, line 8 in Butcher, S.H.

the *resurrection* of Horus after he is stung by a scorpion and dies. It is quite obvious that anastasis is not the exclusive territory of the Christian doctrine—indeed, Christianity evidently borrowed the phrase with the precise same meaning in order to apply it to *their own* created godman, in a competitive move.

While the apologists and theologians thus try to create such differences, their views are not in accordance with experts on the Egyptian religion, e.g., various Egyptologists who consistently use the word "resurrection" when referring to the transition proposed in both the myth of Osiris and the ongoing ritual of the mortuary literature. In her book on Osiris, for instance, Mojsov uses the term "resurrection" or variant thereof some 24 times, while Frankfort employs the term "resurrection," etc., some 50 times, including an entire section entitled "Resurrection," in his seminal work *Kingship and the Gods*. Therefore, the word "resurrection" has been used here freely in reference to a *return to life* or *revivification*, as appropriate.

The Dying and Rising Debate

The modern dismissal of the Egyptian resurrection revolves largely around the debate of the past several decades concerning the mythical genre entitled "dying and rising gods," scholarship originally developed significantly by Frazer in his voluminous *The Golden Bough* series. The dying-and-rising category appreciably watered down the uniqueness of the entire Christian premise and led to much speculation that Christ himself was one of the same *mythical* type. Hence, the concept came under intense scrutiny, particularly by Christian apologists attempting to create a distinction between these pre-Christian gods and Jesus. After some back and forth, the flawed blanket dismissal of the Pagan dying-and-rising-god motif[1] was effectively dismantled in the scholarly and well-documented monograph *The Riddle of the Resurrection* by Mettinger, who not only noted the Christian bias in the debate but also concluded:

> From the 1930s through the rest of the century, a consensus has developed to the effect that the "dying and rising gods" died but did not return or rise to live again. The present work—which is the first monograph on the whole issue subsequent to the studies by Frazer and Baudissin—is a detailed critique of that position. It is based on a

---

[1] While some of the critical scholarship may be sound, the conclusion that there were *no* gods in ancient times who essentially died and were resurrected appears to be based solely on this ongoing thrust to differentiate Christianity from Paganism. The notorious article by historian Dr. Jonathan Z. Smith, "Dying and Rising Gods," which appeared in *The Encyclopedia of Religion* (4:526), is fraught with special pleading and seems to contain biased and erroneous remarks indicating that the author was neither an Egyptologist nor particularly knowledgeable about the Egyptian religion, including the long history of early Egyptian Christians themselves identifying Osiris with Jesus, especially in consideration of both these gods' deaths and resurrections. The quality of this article seems out of line with that of others in this series, such as the well-done treatment of the "Virgin Birth" by Dr. David Adams Leeming in volume 15, 272ff.

fresh perusal of all the relevant source material from the ancient Near East, Egypt, and the Graeco-Roman world and profits from new finds of great importance.... **The author concludes that Dumuzi, Baal, and Melqart were dying and rising gods already in pre-Christian times and that Adonis and Esmun may well have been so too. Osiris dies and rises but remains all the time in the Netherworld.** The deities that die and rise do not represent one specific type of god (e.g. the Baal-Hadad type) but are deities of widely divergent origin and character....[1]

In the end, Mettinger remarks:

Finally, there is the resurrection of Jesus in the New Testament. Dying and rising gods were known in Palestine in New Testament times.[2]

This last statement cannot be overemphasized:

> **Dying and rising gods were known in Palestine in New Testament times.**

As opposed to those who contend that "Osiris is in no sense a resurrected god," Mettinger says of Osiris, "He died and rose." However, this biblical scholar follows with the obligatory disclaimer that the god "rose to continued life in the Netherworld."[3] The distinction is therefore made that the resurrected Osiris supposedly stays in the netherworld or underworld and does not return to *this* world. In this regard, Goelet states:

Once revitalized, he usually appears as Wennefer, an epithet which perhaps means "he who is always perfect." When Osiris comes back to life, however, he never returns to the land of the living, but remains in the Underworld, the Duat, where he rules as King of Eternity and supreme judge of the dead. His resurrection was limited to the next world and so he passed on the rights of kingship to his son and avenger, Horus....[4]

Often in an effort to differentiate him from Jesus, a number of Egyptologists and other scholars thus emphasize that Osiris's resurrection was in the netherworld, not the material world. Nonetheless, regardless of where he ends up and when he arrives there, Osiris was clearly *resurrected* to life after having been killed, in the same sense as was believed of Christ millennia later.

Indeed, Osiris's netherworldly status is not unlike that of the *Gnostic* Christ, which is to be expected, since so much of Gnostic Christianity is demonstrably based on the Egyptian religion. As the *Encyclopedia Britannica* notes, according to the "Gnostics of

---

[1] Mettinger, 4. (Emph. added.) See also Mettinger, 43fn.
[2] Mettinger, 220. Mettinger insists on making a hasty disclaimer at the end of his book attempting to disassociate Jesus from these gods, possibly fearful of stepping on Christian toes, but he nevertheless concludes that the category of the "dying and rising god" is soundly based.
[3] Mettinger, 175.
[4] Faulkner, *EBD*, 149.

Irenaeus," the Christos essentially "dies and resurrects" as he "sinks down into matter but rises again."[1] The Gnostic resurrection was therefore also "spiritual," taking place outside of the material world.

Moreover, in the standardized myth it is implicit that Osiris returns to life in *this* world, as Isis puts his body back together and then hovers above it to impregnate herself. If Osiris wasn't resurrected first in the "real world," why were his body parts needed to raise him? And why is he depicted as "resuscitated" so that he can impregnate Isis as a bird hovering over his body? Surely he is not dead, and Isis is not in the netherworld, in this instance of fecundation.

In addition, after discussing various Pyramid Texts in which appears the phrase "in the arms of the divine offspring," Dr. Garnot remarks, "It is very probable that the resurrection of Osiris was considered to take place 'in the arms' of Horus, who held the body of the god in his embrace."[2] If Horus is in *this* world, and he is holding his father in his arms when the latter revives, then Osiris must have been said to resurrect into the material world as well.

In this case, then, the difference between Osiris's resurrection into this world and that of Jesus would be the amount of time each god spends on Earth before ascending to heaven or returning to the netherworld. As biblical scholar and mythicist Dr. Robert M. Price says in regard to the apology denying Osiris's resurrection because the god "reigned henceforth in the realm of the dead":

> But then we might as well deny that Jesus is depicted as dying and rising since he reigns henceforth at the right hand of God in Paradise as judge of the dead, like Osiris.[3]

Furthermore, Plutarch (19, 358B) specifically states that after Isis puts Osiris's body parts back together, "Osiris came to Horus from the other world and exercised and trained him for the battle."[4] Osiris has a detailed discussion with Horus, implying that he spent a significant amount of time in *this* world, unless this conversation takes place on a different plane, with Osiris appearing either as a vision or only audibly. Plutarch's original Greek reads, "Επειτα τω Ώρω τον Οσιριν εξ Ἀιδου παραγενόμενον διαπονειν επι την μάχην και ασκειν."[5] The pertinent words here are "εξ Ἀιδου," which means "out of Hades," and παραγενόμενον, from the verb παραγίγνομαι, meaning "be present *or* at hand; arrive at, happen; assist, help."[6] While εξ or "ex" can also mean "from," judging by the terms Plutarch uses, it appears that he believed this resurrection to be a true physical one along the lines of the return of Persephone or Orpheus from *Hades*,

---

[1] *Enc. Brit.*, XXVII, 854.
[2] Garnot, 100.
[3] Price, R., "Jonathan Z. Smith: *Drudgery Divine*."
[4] Plutarch/Babbitt, 46.
[5] Plutarch/Babbitt, 46.
[6] *OCGD*, 242.

as in the Greek mythology with which this Greek scholar was surely familiar. Indeed, the same phrase "ε§ Άιδου" is used by Euripides in his play *Alcestis* (line 359), in reference to the character Ademetus "snatching back" his deceased wife, Alcestis, from Hades.[1] In this story predating the common era by almost four and a half centuries, the Greek son of God Heracles/Hercules succeeds in rescuing Alcestis, who is thus resurrected out of the underworld, on the third day, no less![2] In any event, even if Horus's instruction by the resurrected Osiris were "merely" a vision, it would be akin to St. Paul's vision of Christ, the latter likewise empowering the former to do battle against his enemies. Of course, the whole drama takes place on a different plane in any event, representing *mythology*—as, we aver, does the gospel story.

Osiris as the Life Force in the Material World

In addition, if Osiris resides in the netherworld for all eternity—a *heavenly* realm much the same as where Jesus is said to be—he nevertheless is resurrected again into the material world both as his own son on a daily basis and as the gift of life in several ways during the months and years, including as the light waxing in the moon and the inundating Nile. As such, Osiris is clearly a "dying and rising god," despite the magical waving away of the hand in certain circles.

In this regard, while Frankfort makes the distinction about Osiris obtaining renewed life in the *netherworld*, saying, "Osiris was resurrected, but he did not resume his former existence, i.e., he did not reascend the throne" and "Osiris was resurrected to a life in the Beyond,"[3] he nonetheless states:

> His resurrection meant his entry upon life in the Beyond, and it was one of the inspiring truths of Egyptian religion that, notwithstanding his death, Osiris became manifest as life in the world of men. From his grave in the earth or in the depleted Nile, from the world of the dead, his power emanated, mysteriously transmuted into a variety of natural phenomena which had one common feature: they waxed and waned.[4]

Frankfort further remarks:

> If many natural phenomena can be interpreted as resurrections, the power of resurrection is peculiarly Osiris' own. The divine figure of the dead king personified the resurgence of vitality which becomes manifest in the growing corn, the waxing flood, the increasing moon.[5]

The Dutch Egyptologist concludes, "Hence, Osiris was the god of resurrection."[6]

---

[1] Euripides/Hadley, 15; Euripides/Aldington, 22.
[2] Euripides/Aldington, 71; Gayley, 133-136.
[3] Frankfort, *KG*, 197.
[4] Frankfort, *KG*, 185.
[5] Frankfort, *KG*, 197.
[6] Frankfort, *KG*, 185.

In addition, according to Mojsov:

> The western mountain of Thebes became the new residence of Osiris.
> In tomb decorations he was often represented rising out from the
> mountain's edge at dawn, his arms risen and his manhood ready to
> inseminate the new day.[1]

From these decorations, the thousands of chapters, spells, hymns
and prayers, and the annual ritual raising of Osiris that may have
been celebrated thousands of times, it is apparent that the average
Egyptian must have viewed Osiris as being renewed *in this world*, as
well as the next. In addition, it should be recalled that, just as
Christians believe Jesus to have been an actual, historical figure, so
too did millions of Egyptians believe that Osiris had truly walked the
earth, that he was verily and indeed killed, and that he was also
verily raised from the dead. Hence, in this belief system, not a few
adherents probably understood Osiris to have undergone a real,
physical resurrection, especially after watching the annual Osirian
"passion play," in which his body was displayed.

Another apology designed to differentiate between Osiris and
Jesus claims that Osiris was not really dead, despite the fact that his
body was ripped to pieces. As we have already seen abundantly,
Osiris's resurrection was celebrated annually in "a rite symbolizing
Osiris's revivification after death,"[2] as asserted by respected
Egyptologist Dr. James P. Allen. Osiris, having been *murdered* by Set,
is clearly *dead*. Even so, as an immortal god, was Jesus himself ever
really dead?

Yet another argument to distinguish between the resurrections of
Osiris and Christ is that Osiris did not raise himself "on his own
power." The reality is, of course, that neither did Christ, as he first
pathetically begged God the Father in the garden of Gethsemane not
to make him suffer his Passion (Mt 26:39, 42, 44; Mk 14:36, 39; Lk
22:42), and then cried out from the cross, "My God, my God, why
have you forsaken me?" (Mt 27:46), finally commending himself into
his father's hands. (Lk 24:36) In Christian mythology, it is clearly the
power of *God* that resurrects Christ.

Moreover, the sun/Re and/or the king/deceased were viewed as
self-renewing, representing *their own fathers*.[3] Hence, they are in
effect *self*-empowering. Demonstrating the self-empowerment
maintained in the deceased's resurrection, in the Coffin Texts, the
Osiris says, "I died yesterday, I raised myself today..."[4] Furthermore,
apart from the annual resurrection in which Isis is involved, when
the sun dies on a nightly basis, *it is Osiris's power itself that
resurrects*, as he is the Lord of Resurrections, as well as the Lord of

---

[1] Mojsov, 61.
[2] Allen, J., *AEPT*, 428.
[3] Allen, J., *AEPT*, 427.
[4] Faulkner, *AECT*, II, 145.

Eternity and the Lord of Life. Like Jesus (Jn 11:25), therefore, Osiris himself in effect *is* the resurrection. It is once again interesting to note that this comment of Jesus—"I am the resurrection"—occurs only in the gospel of John, the most Egyptian of the canonical texts. Its presence there indicates that the Christian resurrection was indeed based significantly upon that of Osiris.

Bodily Necessity

When perceiving Egyptian resurrection as it applied to the *human* deceased, it is not sufficient to deem it "merely" a spiritual matter, as, according to important Egyptian doctrines, while the resurrection could be viewed as "spiritual," in its totality it included and necessitated the *physical* and *material*. Concerning Osiris's resurrection and its meaning to the faithful, for example, Budge states:

> He became the type of eternal existence, and symbol of immortality; and as judge of the dead he was believed to exercise functions similar to those attributed to God. *Through the sufferings and death of Osiris, the Egyptian hoped that his body might rise again in a transformed, glorified, and incorruptible shape,* and the devotee appealed in prayer for eternal life to him who had conquered death and had become the king of the underworld through his victory and prayer.[1]

Hence, in Osiris was the anticipation of the deceased also to be resurrected, and it is noteworthy that, through the god's resurrection, "the Egyptian hoped that his *body* might *rise again*," uncorrupted and glorified. This paragraph, of course, sounds very much like the doctrine of Christ's death and resurrection, as well as its promise to humanity.

Budge further clarifies the Egyptian concept of resurrection:

> The religious texts show that many different views were current about the **resurrection of the body**. The material body was called *khat*...a word meaning "something that decays," "corruption," etc., and Osiris had a material body of this kind. One view was that the very substance of this corruptible body was re-made and re-born by means of mummification, and by the magical and religious spells that were recited by properly qualified priests whilst the various processes were being carried out, and that the body of every man who appeared before Osiris was the actual body in which he lived upon earth. Another view was that the mummification and spells made to spring from the natural body another body which was identical with it in shape and form, but was so immaterial in character that it might be called a "spirit body."[2]

In discussing BD 1, in reference to "Words which bring about Resurrection and Glory," as rendered in the rubric of the chapter,

---

[1] Budge, *AGFSER*, 4-5. (Emph. added.)
[2] Budge, *DON*, 271-272. (Emph. added.)

Renouf remarks, "The 'raising up' or 'resurrection' here spoken of is said not only of the soul but of the body of the deceased person."[1] Adding to this contention, Budge states that "the belief...in the resurrection of the body and of everlasting life, is coeval with the beginnings of history in Egypt."[2] Moreover, at PT 12:19-c/N 95-97 appear utterances for the "Ritual of Bodily Restoration of the Deceased" or "Restoration of the corpse..."[3]

That there is more to the Egyptian religious doctrine than "just" a spiritual resurrection is obvious from the focus on the physical remains of the deceased:

> To ancient Egyptians, life's fulfillment was the journey into death. To enjoy an afterlife, two conditions rigid and unchanging need be met: The body must be intact—*intact*—hence, mummification. Secondly, the spiritual double of the deceased—called "ka"—must be provided.[4]

Adding to this observation, Brier says, "To gain a perfect eternal life required an intact body,"[5] and W.M. Davis notes, "If the body decayed..., it could not reach the Hereafter."[6] Morenz remarks that "the purpose of mummification was to keep the body intact..."[7] Morenz further states, "Who can say whether Egyptian mummies may not have had something to do with the Christian concept of 'resurrection of the flesh,' which belongs neither to the Old Testament religion nor to that of the earliest Christians, let alone to that of the Greeks?"[8] Obviously, if the Egyptian and Christian ideas of resurrection were so disparate and exclusive, this respected Egyptologist would not have made this connection between them; nor would he specifically have mentioned that the resurrection was "of the flesh," unless the notion within the Egyptian religion also considered *bodily* resurrection.

The complex notion of resurrection within the Egyptian religion is explained by James Allen:

> The ancient Egyptians believed that each human being consists of three basic parts: the physical body and two nonmaterial elements known as the ka and the ba. The ka is an individual's life force, the element that makes the difference between a living body and a dead one; each person's ka ultimately came from the creator and returned to the gods at death. The ba is comparable to the Western notion of the soul or personality, the feature that makes each person a unique individual, apart from the physical element of the body.
>
> At death, the ka separated from the body. In order for an individual to survive as a spirit in the afterlife, the ba had to be reunited with

---

[1] Renouf, *EBD*, 3.
[2] Budge, *GE*, II, 220.
[3] Mercer, 22; Faulkner, *AEPT*, 2; Allen, J., *AEPT*, 252.
[4] "The Pyramids and the Cities of the Pharaohs."
[5] Brier, 42.
[6] Davis, W.M., 164. See, e.g., PT 412:722b/T 228. (Mercer, 139; Allen, J., *AEPT*, 86.)
[7] Morenz, 200.
[8] Morenz, 212-213.

its ka, its life force: in the Pyramid Texts and elsewhere, the d/ are called "those who have gone to their kas." The resultant sp... entity was known as an akh: literally, an "effective" being. No longer subject to the entropy of a physical body or the limitations of physical existence, the akh was capable of living eternally, not merely on earth but also in the larger cosmic plane inhabited by the gods. If the ba could not reunite with its ka, it continued to exist but was no longer "alive"; in contrast to the akhs, such beings were regarded as "the dead."

The function of the Pyramid Texts, in common with all ancient Egyptian funerary literature, was to enable the deceased to become an akh... Two forces played a key role in this transition, incorporated by the Egyptians in two gods, the Sun and Osiris....[1]

The "ka" is thus the life force, similar to that called "chi" in the Eastern mystical system of Taoism, while the "ba" may be considered the soul or individual personality.[2] The two together, "ka-ba," so to speak, constitute the "akh," which might be conceived as a "ghost" or "spirit," also representing the *spiritual body.*

Continuing the discussion of the Egyptian resurrection, Allen clarifies that by the word "Sun" with the capital "S" he is referring to the god Ra/Re, and he further elucidates that Re *merges* with Osiris to produce the reborn sun at dawn in Horus. Hence, all three are essentially "sun gods." Allen also explains here that in the spells of the Pyramid Texts there exist a "subset" designed to keep worms and snakes away from the deceased's body. There are also a number of such spells against snakes in the Coffin Texts.[3]

The Canaanite Connection

Interestingly, spells that fend off snakes provide an important connection between Egypt and Canaan, land where the later Israelites emerged and the language of which represents proto-Hebrew. In an underground room in a pyramid near Cairo, writing in Egyptian characters was discovered that constituted magic spells in the Canaanite language of some 5,000 years ago. This find represents the oldest Semitic writing ever uncovered and comprises a "magic spell to keep snakes away from the tombs of Egyptian kings." This discovery ranks as a demonstration of the "close relations" of the Egyptians with the Canaanites of the era:

---

[1] Allen, J., *AEPT*, 7.

[2] In his *Concise Dictionary of Middle Egyptian*, Faulkner defines ka also as "soul, spirit; essence of a being; personality; fortune," while ba signifies "soul" only. (Faulkner, *CDME*, 283, 77.) Nevertheless, other authorities such as Allen intently distinguish between these ideas, reflecting that certain concepts within Egyptology are not necessarily set in stone and accepted by all experts. Hornung likewise calls the ka "soul" but clarifies that it is a "kind of double" and represents "restless power rather than a tranquil soul." (Hornung, *VK*, 135, 206.)

[3] See, e.g., CT Sp. 885. (Faulkner, *AECT*, III, 47ff.)

While Egyptians considered their own culture and religion superior to that of their neighbors to the northeast, they were willing to do anything to protect the mummies of their kings from the poisonous snakes.

Believing that some snakes spoke the Semitic language of the Canaanites, Egyptians included the magic spells in inscriptions on two sides of the sarcophagus in an effort to ward them off.

"Come, come to my house," reads one section in the Semitic language that is supposed to be the snake's mother speaking, trying to lure him out of the tomb.

In another passage, the snake is addressed as if he is a lover with "Turn aside, O my beloved."

The Egyptian and Semitic sections are each an integral part of the magic spell and neither can stand alone...[1]

This archaic Canaanite language later evolved into both Phoenician and Hebrew, the language of the biblical tribes.

In consideration of the proximity of Canaan to Egypt, of the fact of Egyptian colonization of Canaan, and of the obvious cultural exchange between the two, including religious concepts passing from Canaan to Egypt, it is more than reasonable to suggest that a significant amount of the highly developed Egyptian spirituality migrated in the other direction as well over the centuries, including certain aspects of religion as found not only in the Old Testament but also in the New. The awareness among scholars of Egyptian influence upon the Old Testament is evidenced by studies such as those done comparing the biblical Psalm 104 with the "Great Hymn of Amarna," as mentioned by Assman, for example.[2] The Egyptian influence in Canaan/Palestine is also described by Morenz:

> During the Middle Kingdom the native princes of the port of Byblos (Gebal), which had always had close links with Egypt, even bore Egyptian titles which only the pharaohs were able to confer; finally, extensive areas of Palestine and Phoenicia are identified as belonging to the Egyptian sphere...[3] During the New Kingdom, Egyptian had a continual presence in Israel/Phoenicia area, while "Syrian places were required to pay tribute to the respective sanctuaries of the great Egyptian deities..."[4]

Morenz also recounts the Egyptian adoption of a Syrian god named "Hurun," in epithets applied to the pharaoh, such as "beloved of Hurun,"[5] evidently the same as the Canaanite god Horon or Hauron. As Meltzer says, "In the person of the Sphinx and elsewhere, Horus was identified in the New Kingdom with the Syrian-Canaanite

---

[1] "Egyptian Tomb Inscriptions May Bear Oldest Proto-Hebrew Text Yet."
[2] Assman, *ESRNK*, 85, 99.
[3] Morenz, 235.
[4] Morenz, 236.
[5] Morenz, 239.

deity Hauron [Horon]..."[1] In this same regard, Gabriel adds that "the Osiran theology of Egypt was well-known and commonly practiced both in Palestine and throughout the Roman world."[2]

In any event, along with the obsessive and expensive mummification process, the rituals to protect the body clearly demonstrate that the Egyptians were keen on preserving the *physical* body, as part of the promised resurrection.

In fact, the physical body was so important in the resurrection process that if it were cremated and the ashes scattered about, the deceased stood no chance of becoming "akhified." Indeed, cremation was considered to be the ultimate penalty for crimes and transgressions—and was greatly feared by the average Egyptian. Also, since the dawn of humanity, placing items of the deceased and others into the grave or tomb, such as food, along with other belongings and sacred objects—as was done in Egypt, where the elaborate burial rites included "all the comforts of home"—has been indicative of the belief in a *physical* afterlife. It is quite probable that when the Egyptians originated their complex rituals, including mummification, they believed or hoped that the resurrection would include the *physical* body, which is why they put so much effort into the resurrection rituals.

In the end, the material body ranked as the "jumping off point" for the spiritual body:

> The Egyptians believed in a life after death, for which the body was as important as the spirit. This was why the pharaohs, nobles and humble citizens went to great trouble to have themselves preserved when they died. It has been calculated that during the reigns of the pharaohs more than half a billion people lived on Egyptian soil, and most them were mummified after death.[3]

The assertion that some 500 *million* people were mummified during the time of the Egyptian pharaohs may come as a shock to most—and it is highly significant to consider, especially in regard to whether or not the numerous important concepts from Egyptian religion and mythology discussed here were prominent in the minds of the masses. Needless to say also that the embalmers/morticians made up a very sizeable, powerful and wealthy class, which would explain the importance and popularity of the god Anubis, among others. In light of the astonishing amount of people involved—one half a billion!—it is logical to assert that these prominent spiritual concepts within the Egyptian religion were well known for millennia by enough people to have significantly influenced and been passed along into many other religions, cults and ideologies around the Mediterranean, including Judaism and especially Christianity. This

---

[1] Redford, 167.
[2] Gabriel, *JE*, 3.
[3] "The Pyramids and the Cities of the Pharaohs."

contention becomes especially reasonable when one factors in the popularity of Egyptian mummification and burial during the Greco-Roman period (c. 332 BCE-3rd cent. AD/CE), during which increasing numbers of upper to middle class citizens, including many Romans, took advantage of these methods of interment.[1]

Jewish or Greek?

In his book *Paul: Apostle of the Heart Set Free* renowned Christian scholar F.F. Bruce (1910-1990), a professor of Bible Criticism at the University of Manchester, sought to show that resurrection was originally a *Jewish* concept, not appearing in the pre-Christian Greek world.[2] In his essay responding to Bruce entitled, "Resurrection, the Greeks and the New Testament," Porter sets out to demonstrate that the concept of resurrection was indeed a theme in the *Greek* world. While Bruce apparently interpreted the Pharisaic belief in the resurrection as recounted by Josephus (*War* 2.163) to indicate a "physical or bodily resurrection akin to Christian resurrection," Porter avers that it could refer to the "Greek belief in reincarnation or metempsychosis."[3] Porter concludes that the Jewish notion of resurrection, according to Josephus, does not support the idea of a bodily resurrection but, in fact, relates the *Greek* concept of an afterlife, as found in the *Works and Days* of Greek poet Hesiod (c. 700 BCE), for example.[4]

Porter analyzes the Jewish literature that might concern resurrection, such as Isaiah 26:19: "Thy dead shall live, their bodies shall rise."[5] (RSV) He finally remarks:

> To this point, there is very little evidence for sustained Jewish development of the concept of resurrection, and certainly very little regarding a physical or bodily resurrection. The same cannot be said for what is found in Greek and Roman religion. In fact, there is a shockingly strong tradition of contemplation of the soul's destiny in the afterlife, along with examples of bodily resurrection.[6]

Porter then goes on to give several "examples of *bodily* resurrection" from Greek religion, including in the underworld accounts from *The Odyssey*, with Odysseus proceeding to Hades to speak to "spirits."[7] This text was well known to the "Alexandrian scholars," as were other Greco-Roman stories of descent into the underworld, along with the ascension out of it serving as a *bodily*

---

[1] Redford, 233.
[2] See, e.g., Bruce, F., 47.
[3] Porter, *Res.*, 55. This situation, of course, demonstrates how scholars are not necessarily in agreement about important facts and how *scholarship changes over time.* See Maier, 739.
[4] Porter, *Res.*, 57.
[5] Porter, *Res.*, 48ff.
[6] Porter, *Res.*, 68.
[7] Porter, *Res.*, 68ff.

resurrection—in a manner similar to Christ's resurre
anastasis out of the underworld.

Porter concludes that Greek thought influenced both Jewish and Christian ideology:

> The inevitable question to be asked is the source of influence upon Christianity. It appears that both Jewish thought and then, inevitably, Christian thought came under the influence of Greek and then Graeco-Roman assumptions regarding resurrection. The conclusion that there was significant antecedent Greek thought regarding resurrection does not, however, lead to the inevitable conclusion that, for example, Paul simply adopted this conception, since, as has been noted, the concept of resurrection is variously and often inadequately developed in various antecedent thinkers. The history of discussion of the influence of Graeco-Roman religious thought on that of Paul indicates that he was not blindly derivative in developing his conceptual framework. Nevertheless, one must not overlook the fact that he lived in a world in which such ideas were present, discussed and, apparently, even believed.[1]

We may ask, naturally, if the gospel story of the resurrection is "true" and "historical," why would the Christian concept need to be influenced by anything at all? Also, if there were no concrete notions of *physical* resurrection within Judaism, by the same argument used by apologists to dismiss Egyptian influence on Christianity, it could be contended that Christianity had nothing to do with Judaism, based on this difference.

The presence of resurrection stories in the Greco-Roman world further resolves the issue of the "dying-and-rising-god" debate, previously discussed. The nature of these gods and their resurrections varies, but the important notion to keep in mind is that the concept of resurrection, whether spiritual or physical, most assuredly existed in the pre-Christian world.

In the end, it would be a simple matter for the creators of Christianity to change the popular story of Osiris and his death and resurrection in order to fit more with Jewish doctrine. As it was obviously the intention of these creators to place a patently mythical tale into "history," naturally they would include elements that would make it appear more historical, such as an emphasis of the god's resurrection into *this* world, to be seen by others here as "proof" of the reality of both him and his anastasis. However, the deliberate placing of a mythical tale into history does not make it any less fictional.

The Glorified Body

As noted, even if—against the bulk of the evidence—we consider that the average Egyptians did not conceive of a physical resurrection, we would still remain with little difference between the

---

[1] Porter, *Res.*, 80-81.

Egyptian and Christian beliefs held by their many followers. In reality, over the centuries hundreds of millions of sincerely believing Christians have perished, and all their bodies have rotted away, never to be seen again on Earth. In this regard, it is evident that the vast majority of Christians believe that their afterlife inheritance represents a *spiritual* rather than physical promise. Indeed, orthodox Christian doctrine clearly emphasizes a spiritual or *glorified* body in many ways the same as the Egyptian akhified or spiritualized body.

For example, at 1 Corinthians 15:35-42 appears a discussion of the nature of the resurrected body in which Paul says:

> There are celestial bodies and there are terrestrial bodies; but the glory of the celestial is one, and the glory of the terrestrial is another.... (RSV)

Regarding this teaching of Paul's, Dr. Andrew T. Lincoln, a professor of New Testament at the University of Gloucestershire, remarks:

> He asserts that not only do different kinds of earthly life have their own distinctive physical manifestation but further distinction can be made between earthly bodies as one class and heavenly bodies as another and that each category has its own type of glory. Even the heavenly category admits of further differentiations, for there is a difference in glory not only between the sun, the moon and the stars, but also between the various stars. The whole point in developing the analogy in this way is to indicate the immense variety in God's creation and that there is no type of life for which God has not found appropriate glory or an appropriate body.[1]

Paul continues, "So is it with the resurrection of the dead. What is sown is perishable, what is raised is imperishable." Again, do Christians believe that their bodies are imperishable, or is it their imperishable *souls* that attain the resurrection? Are not sincere Christians promised a glorious transfiguration essentially the same as that which was assured the Egyptians?

Summing up the main reality of the Egyptian religion, Budge states:

> ...we find that the doctrine of eternal life and of the resurrection of a glorified or transformed body, based upon the ancient story of the resurrection of Osiris after a cruel death and horrible mutilation, inflicted by the powers of evil, was the same in all periods, and that the legends of the most ancient times were accepted without material alteration or addition in the texts of the later dynasties.

> The story of Osiris is nowhere found in a connected form in Egyptian literature, but everywhere, and in texts of all periods, the life, sufferings, death and resurrection of Osiris are accepted as facts universally admitted.[2]

---

[1] Lincoln, 38-39.
[2] Budge, *EBD* (1967), xlviii-xlix.

From the funerary literature to mummification to the pyramidal "resurrection machines," the Egyptian resurrection was an all-encompassing pursuit and the most important promise of the gods.

While Christian followers may hear about a *physical* resurrection, they too are promised a *spiritual* afterlife for all eternity in heaven, as was conceived also within the Egyptian religion. The distinction between the two ideas is therefore slight and irrelevant, not providing evidence that Christianity had nothing to do with the Egyptian religion but readily accounted for by other influences upon the Jewish factions who were in large part responsible for the creation of Christianity, influences including the Greco-Roman traditions and myths.

Horus as the Resurrection

In the final analysis, the fact will remain that Osiris in his role as the life force in natural phenomena very much came back to Earth as, among others, the Nile overflowing its banks, the efflux or sap livening the foliage, the corn growing out of the ground, the light in the waxing moon, and the glorious risen sun—physical, life-bestowing events that were as sacred and real to the devout Egyptian believer as Christ's resurrection is to a Christian. In reality, while the dismembered and revivified Osiris serves as the resurrected Lord of the underworld, he also resurrects daily and annually as his son, Horus, who, as demonstrated throughout this work, shares much in common with Jesus. The resurrection of Horus, the "Son of the Father," is not confined to heaven, however, but represents a true emergence into *this* world as both the sun and the all-important divine king. In this regard, in the works of Egyptologists we read statements concerning "the resurrection of Osiris in his son Horus" and "the resurrection of Osiris in the form of his son Horus..."[1] Thus, like Jesus, Horus *is* the Resurrection.

Moreover, the contention that in the myth Horus is clearly part of the material world, as indicated by his "demarcation" from Osiris, is related by Griffiths:

> ...we constantly confront the demarcation between the world of the living and that of the dead, between the living Pharaoh who is divine as Horus and as the son of Re and the dead Pharaoh who is glorified through his identification with Osiris; in short, between Horus and Osiris.[2]

Since Horus—the resurrected Osiris—is the living pharaoh, it can be argued again that Osiris is indeed resurrected into this world, *as Horus*. The same can be said of Horus as the physical morning sun. Regarding Horus, Bonwick remarks:

---

[1] Griffiths, *OOHC*, 104, 169.
[2] Griffiths, *OOHC*, 6.

ɜ *Generator* is a type of the glorious resurrection. The disk-
headed god reappears as Horus in the horizon, the sphinx deity, to
notify the new birth of the soul. The "Divine child" is the risen sun.[1]

Osiris is thus *risen* with Horus, and Horus is the *risen* Osiris.
This occurrence happens every day, as well as annually. The *risen*
Osiris is a recurring theme throughout the funerary/mortuary ritual,
resurrected as Horus, who is born into *this* world as a brilliant light—
the light of the world, who comes with clouds, and every eye will see
him. (Jn 8:12, 9:5; Rev 1:7) It is interesting that the only canonical
gospel in which Jesus is called the "light of the world" is the highly
Egyptian gospel of John. It is further intriguing to note the "piercing"
of the savior in the pertinent scripture in Revelation (1:7):

> Behold, he is coming with the clouds, and every eye will see him,
> every one who pierced him; and all tribes of the earth will wail on
> account of him. Even so. Amen. (RSV)

The "every one" who pierced him would be Set in the Egyptian
mythos, who gouges out or penetrates Horus's eye.[2]

As stated, Horus himself is a dying and rising god *prior to the
common era*, as made clear by the writings of Diodorus, who
"recorded that Isis found Horus dead in the water as a result of an
attack by the Titans, restored him to life and at the same time gave
him immortality."[3] In this myth, Horus did not reside in the
netherworld like some "zombie" but was stated specifically over a
century before Christ's alleged passion to have been raised from the
dead using the precise Greek term as found in the New Testament
concerning Jesus's resurrection.

As Jesus was the son of the Father on Earth, so too was Horus,
who himself *is* the resurrection, the morning sun rising gloriously
upon the horizon for all the world to see. This Egyptian resurrection
into the *physical world* was so patently obvious that it could not have
been missed by even the most insensate.

Despite the debate by professional theologians and apologists,
what remains important is what the average Egyptian would have
perceived in his own religion. In this regard, it seems certain that the
average Egyptian would have understood the death and resurrection
of Horus in much the same way as that reported of the later Jesus—
and this fact would surely explain why early Christians identified the
two gods with each other, in spells invoked as "Jesus Horus."[4]

In their attempts at creating distinctions and denying the dying-
and-rising-god motif, "skeptical" scholars and apologists generally
ignore the resurrection of *Horus*, also diligently excluding the fact
that Horus *is* Osiris's resurrection *into this world*, as the morning sun

---

[1] Bonwick, 159.
[2] See, e.g., Pinch, 131.
[3] Holley, 44.
[4] Meyer, *ACM*, 363.

on a daily basis. Also ignored is Osiris's role as impregnator of Isis *in this world* after he is resurrected. Osiris thus is certainly resurrected into the material world for at least a short period of time. Hence, to reiterate, the only difference between the Osirian and Christian resurrections into the material world is a question of time. Christ stays just a bit longer, relatively speaking, before he too ends up in the "netherworld" or "heaven" for all eternity.

The Egyptian Heaven and Hell

The ancient Egyptian religion was almost singularly focused on eternal life and the resurrection of a spiritualized or glorified body that would take the deceased to heaven. As in other cultures, the Egyptian "heaven" differs from the "sky"; however, there nonetheless existed in the Egyptian religion a pronounced concept of heaven to which the deceased aspired to attain in his resurrected state and akhified body:

> In heaven the beatified eat bread which never grows stale, and drink wine which grows not musty; they wear white apparel, and sit upon thrones among the gods who cluster round the tree of life near the lake in the Field of Peace; they wear the crowns which the gods give unto them, and no evil being or thing has any power to harm them in their new abode, where they will live with Ra for ever.[1]

Even in this description of heaven we can perceive the later Christian doctrine. The Egyptian heaven, it should be noted, included the reunion of the deceased with their families, as exemplified in the mortuary literature, including a number of Coffin Texts specifically created to "assemble a man's family in the realm of the dead."[2]

As in Christianity, the Egyptian religion also conceived of a hellish afterlife, complete with fire and torture.[3] After describing the Egyptian afterlife trial that led to either "heaven" or "hell," Dr. Donald B. Redford, a professor of Egyptology at Pennsylvania State University, remarks:

> The damned...were consigned to punishment in the Underworld which now undergoes a bifurcation into a realm of the Blessed and a place of torment, a veritable *Paradise* and *Hell*. This concept, providing a fertile field for the imagination, experienced strong growth in detail and was inherited by Christianity which transformed the whole into a Heaven set over against a Dante-esque inferno.[4]

Indeed, virtually all of the spiritual concepts in the Christian religion appear in much the same form centuries to millennia earlier in Egypt, the differences emerging within Christianity attributable to

---

[1] Higgins, II, 102. The word for "field" in Egyptian is *iaru* or *i3rw*. (Faulkner, *AECT*, III, 108.)

[2] *Oxford History of Ancient Egypt*, 115.

[3] See Faulkner, *EBD*, 154. For a lengthy description of the Egyptian hell, see Redford, 161ff.

[4] Redford, xvi.

Jewish and Greek influence, among others. These parallels would include the burial for three days, the resurrection and the ascension, all appearing in the Egyptian religion centuries to millennia before the common era and possessing astrotheological significance, as largely revolving around the sun.

"The House of a Thousand Years"

Another controversial aspect of the Horus-Jesus connection is the suggestion that, like his Jewish counterpart, the Egyptian savior would rule on Earth for 1,000 years. Over the centuries, millions of Christians worldwide have relied on promises based on the supposed "Second Coming," as found at Revelation 20:2-7, in which it is said that Satan will be bound, and Christ and his saints will reign, for a millennium. Regarding this theme, Massey says:

> The Christian opinion most prevalent for many centuries was that the Messiah would come again, like Arthur and other Æonian heroes of the astronomical mythology, and that his kingdom was to last one thousand years. After that the deluge, or the dragon. Christian Chiliasim [sic] was unwittingly founded on the periodic return of the ever-coming one who had been Horus or Iu the prince of peace in the "house of a thousand years"...[1]

This theme of the great god or holy one's return to reign for a thousand years can be found not only in Christianity but also in Islam, and is called "millenarianism."[2] As we can see, there is good reason to believe that this motif is rooted in mythology and represents an ongoing natural cycle, not the coming or second coming of a god or prophet. In this regard, to follow blindly mummified mythology without understanding it could be quite perilous, as these eschatological concepts lead to horrific "End Times" and apocalyptic scenarios.

Like millenarianism, Christian chiliasm is the doctrine that Jesus Christ will reign upon the Earth for 1,000 years. As might be expected, we can find a parallel to this notion within the Egyptian religion as well. The "House of a Thousand Years" is mentioned on a stela that the Nubian king Harsiyotef/Harsiotef/Har-si-atef/Heru-Sa-Atef (404-369 BC) dedicated to Amun at Napata (modern Jebel/Gebel Barkal), dating to the 26th Egyptian Dynasty.[3] On this stela created by Harsiotef/Heru-Sa-Atef—a name meaning "Horus, son of his father"[4]—the inscription relates: "And on another occasion, when the House of a Thousand Years began to fall into ruin, I rebuilt it for thee."[5] As Budge says, "Heru-sa-atef then directed his energies and

---

[1] Massey, *AELW*, I, 541-542.
[2] See Hassan, 45ff.
[3] The Harsiyotef stela is housed in the Egyptian Museum at Cairo (Cairo JE 48864).
[4] Török, *KK*, 203.
[5] Budge, *ES*, 80; Maspero, *Études*, 235. Budge dated the stela of Heru-Sa-Atef to around 560 BCE.

money to the restoration of the House of a Thousand Years."[1] In this regard, in Budge's *Hieroglyphic Dictionary* we find under the entry of *per-kha-renput*, "house of a thousand years," as on the Harsiotef Stela.[2]

Confirming Budge, archaeologist Dr. Timothy Kendall, excavator of the Napatan capital of Jebel Barkal, remarks that Harsiotef "mentions in his stele that he rebuilt for Amun his *Pr-p3-h3-rnpt* ('House of the Thousand Years')." Massey renders this phrase, *pa-pe kha renpat*, as meaning "Celestial House of the Thousand Years."[3] In addition to being an actual temple and hoped-for reign on Earth, the "house of a thousand years" evidently symbolizes a solar cycle, like the precession of the equinoxes,[4] which would be appropriately applied to gods such as Re, Osiris or Horus.

The Phoenix/Benu Bird

In ancient times, the thousand-year cycle appeared within the famous myth concerning the resurrection from ashes of the phoenix, called a "sun bird."[5] Although many writers discuss a 500-year-life cycle, the phoenix was said by the ancient Latin writer Martial (40-102 AD/CE) to have been renewed every "ten centuries,"[6] making a millennium. In this regard, Rutgers University professor Dr. Carol Salvo Heffernan says that "the phoenix will achieve a qualified immortality—post-mortem, through its offspring, every thousand years."[7] In *The Myth of the Phoenix, According to Classical and Early Christian Traditions*, Dr. R. van den Broek describes the celebrated bird's legend:

> In all the variations of the phoenix myth several constant elements are to be found: a) the bird has a long life and shortly before or directly after its death makes an appearance in the world of man; b) by dying it obtains new life; and c) it is pre-eminently the bird of the sun.[8]

As concerns the earliest written mention of the phoenix, Dr. van der Toorn relates that several writers, including various Talmudic rabbis, claim the Hebrew word at Job 29:18—*chowl* or *ḥôl*—normally translated as "sand," is in fact "phoenix,"[9] which indeed makes more sense with the rest of the scripture: "Then I thought, 'I shall die in my nest, and I shall multiply my days as the sand [phoenix]...'" (RSV) The first mention of the phoenix in the Greek tradition occurs in the

---

[1] Budge, *EL*, cxiii.
[2] Budge, *EHD*, I, 239.
[3] Massey, *NG*, II, 324.
[4] Kuhn, *LL*, 547.
[5] Lactantius, "The Phoenix."
[6] *Epig.* Lib. V, VII; Martial/Bohn, 223.
[7] Heffernan, 62.
[8] van den Broek, 10.
[9] van der Toorn, 655, 656; Shuchat, 345.

writings of Hesiod (c. 700 BCE), and a more developed myth was recounted by Herodotus (2.73) that intimates a rebirth of sorts, relating that the bird "is very rare and visits the country [Egypt] (so they say at Heliopolis) only at intervals of 500 years, on the occasion of the death of the parent-bird."[1] In this same regard, we discover that the Greek "comic-poet Antiphanes (fourth century B.C.) also...connected the phoenix with Heliopolis,"[2] i.e., the City of the Sun, called "On" in Egyptian. The correlation of the phoenix with Egypt is so strong, it has been averred that knowledge of the bird by Hesiod "could have come to him only from Egypt."[3]

The phoenix's rise from death was discussed by several other writers in antiquity, such as "the tragedian Ezekiel," Ovid, Seneca, Pliny, Tacitus, Celsus, Clement of Alexandria and Claudius Aelianus or Aelian. Regarding the first of these writers, van der Toorn remarks, "The hellenistic Jewish writer Ezekiel the Tragedian, who most probably lived in Alexandria in the 2nd cent. BCE, is the first Jew known to have introduced the phoenix into his work."[4] Celsus also mentions the bird as being "Arabian" and visiting Egypt, where it "brings its dead father...and puts him in the shrine of the sun,"[5] sounding much like the Horus-Osiris myth. Clement of Alexandria raises the phoenix "only as an Egyptian astronomical symbol."[6] Aelian or Claudius Aelianus (c. 175–c. 235 AD/CE) tells us that the Egyptian priests argued over whether or not the phoenix rose every 500 years,[7] possibly including the thousand-year cycle as an alternative period.

Continuing into the pertinent era of the first and early second centuries, the Roman writer Tacitus contended that "there is no question that the bird is occasionally seen in Egypt."[8] Since antiquity as well, the phoenix has been identified as the Egyptian bird called the *bennu* or *benu*, which was "a sun bird associated with Ra." Concerning the phoenix/benu in Egypt, Heffernan remarks:

> Death and resurrection are at the core of the two principal versions of the phoenix myth; although it cannot be established conclusively that the European phoenix myth developed from the Egyptian *benu* myth, the connection seems sound.
>
> We may infer that the *benu* and phoenix myths are at the least analogous....[9]

---

[1] Herodotus/de Selincourt, 112.
[2] van den Broek, 395.
[3] Greswell, I, 231.
[4] van der Toorn, 656.
[5] Grant, *ECA*, 41.
[6] Grant, *ECA*, 41.
[7] Grant, *ECA*, 40.
[8] Tacitus/Church, 168.
[9] Heffernan, 22.

References to the benu and its role in Egyptian religion appear in the ancient writings, such as the Coffin Texts, in which the bird is presented as the "son of Re" who brings forth the "breath of life."[1] At BD 17, the speaker discusses both Osiris and the "soul of Re" as the "great Benu-bird, which is in Heliopolis, the supervisor of what exists."[2] Again, at BD 29B the deceased says, "I am the Benu-bird, the soul of Re..."[3] The benu is thus the "incarnation of the Soul of the Sun-god..."[4] Budge relates that the "Bennu not only typified the new birth of the sun each morning, but in the earliest period of dynastic history it became the symbol of the resurrection of mankind..."[5] The benu as a symbol of resurrection was likely well known, in consideration of the fact that the bird is often portrayed on coffin lids.[6] As we can see, in the phoenix/benu we possess a popular pre-Christian symbol of divinity who dies and is resurrected, in essence representing a *dying and rising god.*

While the phoenix and the bennu/benu are alike in the acts of dying and resurrecting, Goelet raises the distinction that the latter does not perish in a fiery display and rise out of ashes. Rather, "the Benu made his appearance on the primordial mound when the land emerged from the water, bringing the light with him..."[7] However, the phoenix-benu identification, asserted by ancient testimony, remains appropriate, when one factors in the contention that the benu was resurrected from the "Island of Fire in the Underworld."[8] This association with fire may be indicated by the three zigzag lines in hieroglyphs representing the benu, symbolizing lightning, while other fabulous birds are likewise associated with lightning.[9]

Regarding the phoenix in Egypt, Dr. Howard Schwartz, a professor at the University of Saint Louis, concludes:

...The legend of the Phoenix has been taken from Egyptian mythology.... The myth of the Phoenix moved beyond its Egyptian origins to enter Greek, Jewish, and Christian literature.[10]

This development may well represent the root of the Christian millenarianism, once more connecting Osiris, Horus and Jesus, with the latter figure an apparent remake of the former two.

---

[1] David, 247.
[2] Faulkner, *EBD*, pl. 7.
[3] Faulkner, *EBD*, pl. 32.
[4] Budge, *BD* (2003), 287.
[5] Budge, *GE*, II, 371.
[6] Goyon, 297.
[7] Faulkner, *EBD*, 159.
[8] Drury, 38.
[9] Golan, 254.
[10] Schwartz, 149.

Osiris, Horus and the Benu

The benu bird, identified with the phoenix, was "a symbol both of the rising sun and of the dead Sun-god Osiris, from whom it sprang and to whom it was sacred."[1] Concerning the phoenix/benu, Curl says, "It was perceived as the *ba* of *Re* and as a manifestation of *Osiris*,"[2] while Goelet relates that "the Benu is said to be Osiris in one explanation and Osiris's corpse in another..."[3] Moreover, as Erman says, "The soul of Osiris...dwells in the bird Benu, the phoenix of the Greeks..."[4] Indeed, as Osiris-Neb-Heu/Asar-Neb-Heh—the "lord of eternity"—the god was symbolized by a mummy with a benu bird's head.[5] As "a symbol of the rising and setting sun, the Benu was considered a manifestation of the resurrected Osiris,"[6] while, as we also know, so too is Horus the manifestation of the sun at the horizons, as well as the resurrected Osiris. Indeed, the benu was the *ab* or "heart" of Osiris, while, of course, Horus is his father's "beloved" and, in fact, also the heart of the god Ptah, per the "Memphite Theology."

The bennu/benu is thus associated not only with Re and Osiris but also with Horus, as the sun at the two horizons, sunrise and sunset. Indeed, "it is said that Bennu-Ra (also identified with Horus) as the Morning Sun will enlighten the world from the top of Turquoise Sycamore Tree, where it renovates itself."[7] In this regard, Sayce states that on "an early seal-cylinder of Babylonian type the *bennu* or *khu* is termed 'the double of Horus'" and that the "phoenix was allied to the hawk of Horus."[8] Thus, "Bennu is sometimes identified with the Golden Hawk,"[9] which is, of course, representative of Horus. In BD 13, we discover that "the deceased identifies himself with the hawk of Horus and the *Bennu* bird, which later Greek tradition pronounced to be the fabulous bird the Phoenix."[10] In this spell, the speaker says, "I go in like the Hawk, and I come forth like the Bennu, the Morning Star...of Ra."[11] BD 83 allows for the deceased to become the bennu bird and to identify himself with Horus, Khephri and Khonsu.[12] In line 77 of the Metternich Stela (380-342 BCE), Horus is addressed as, "You are the mighty Phoenix,"[13] while the stela also relates that Horus was "under protection" as the "Divine

[1] Budge, *GE*, II, 371.
[2] Curl, 455.
[3] Faulkner, *EBD*, 159.
[4] Erman, *LAE*, 271.
[5] Budge, *FGAE*, 192; Mercatante, 115.
[6] Lett, vi.
[7] *Occasional Publications in Classical Studies*, 80.
[8] Sayce, *RAE*, 121.
[9] Spears, 6.
[10] Budge, *BD* (1899), xcv; Faulkner, *EBD*, 101.
[11] Budge, *GE*, II, 97; Faulkner, *EBD*, 101.
[12] Budge, *GE*, II, 97; Faulkner, *EBD*, pl. 27. (Budge cites BD 82 here.)
[13] Michel, 65.

Bennu."[1] As Budge says, "Horus is protected as the Divine Bennu..."[2] Moreover, the "Benu was called 'the august falcon,' and this connection between Benu and the falcon of Horus is really significant."[3] The proximity of the two is striking enough to prompt Dr. Walter Beltz (1935-2006), a professor of Religious Studies at Berlin's Humboldt University, to remark, "Some...have said that Horus too appeared in the Benu bird."[4] This conclusion is sensible in that Horus is the resurrected manifestation of Osiris as well as the sun of the two horizons, the same as the benu.

As some might expect from the god's identification with the benu, who in turn is deemed to be the phoenix, a millennium-bringer, Horus is associated with a thousand-year reign on Earth. In "The Dirge of Seti-Menephtah" appears the following, as related by Dr. John A. Paine (fl. 1889-1906), an archaeologist and curator at the New York's Metropolitan Museum of Art:

> O Horus, friend of things that are just!
> Thou shalt dwell a thousand years on the earth...[5]

The same passage is rendered by Charles Reginald Haines as, "O Horus, lover of just, Thy years on earth a thousand be!"[6] In his commentary on this eulogy to the pharaoh Seti-Meneptah/Sethos-Merneptah, Dr. Paine also remarks, "They assure him of a thousand years on earth by embalmment, which insured against a second death."[7] One could say therefore that the "Horus-Bennu" reigned a thousand years before dying and resurrecting to bring a new millennium.

Horus as a sun god, naturally, is part of a solar cycle, in this case evidently reigning in a "house" for a millennium. As Massey says, "Horus or Iusa in the 'house of a thousand years' was the bringer of the millennium, which was renewed in the following cycle."[8] He also explains that Set is bound by chains, while "Horus took possession of the house once more on a lease of a thousand years to establish his reign of peace, plenty and good luck in the domain of time and law, justice and right by the inauguration of another millennium."[9]

Jesus and the Phoenix

In consideration of these facts, it is interesting that not only are Re, Osiris and Horus identified with the benu, but since ancient times as well Jesus has been identified with the phoenix. In reality,

---

[1] Budge, *LG*, lxxvii.
[2] Budge, *LG*, 157.
[3] Maravelia, *EHE*, 96.
[4] Beltz, 193: "Einige aber erzählten, daß Horus auch im Benu-Vogel erschienen sei."
[5] *The Century*, XXXVIII, 728.
[6] Haines, 66.
[7] *The Century*, XXXVIII, 728.
[8] Massey, *AELW*, II, 733.
[9] Massey, *AELW*, II, 733.

Jesus is equated with the phoenix in some of the oldest Christian
literature, since the early Church fathers such as Clement of Rome
(d. c. 99 AD/CE), the phoenix was very much representative of Christ's
resurrection: "The phoenix is a still more marvellous symbol of the
resurrection."[1] Prior to Clement, the bird was also mentioned by the
famous Roman historian Seneca (c. 4 BCE-65 AD/CE), whose writings
were evidently used in the creation of Christianity.

In his epistle to the Corinthians (25-26), Clement clearly relates
that the bird is reborn, renewed or resurrected from the ashes of his
former self. In the 26th chapter in this letter, the Church father asks
whether or not it is a "great and wonderful thing" that God will "raise
up all who have served Him in holiness and in the confidence of a
good faith, seeing that even a bird is made to show the mightiness of
His promise?"[2] Clement then cites various Old Testament scriptures
as promises of the resurrection, passages using terminology that
sounds very Egyptian, as at Psalms 28:7, 3:5 and Job 19:26 in the
Septuagint. The story of the phoenix rising from the dead is deemed a
"widespread myth" by Clement's time, and it is apparent that this
rebirth or resurrection theme existed for centuries before the
common era.

In a Christian text from the second century called *The
Physiologus* we read, "The phoenix assumes the role of our Savior, for
when he came from heaven, spreading his two wings, he carried them
full of sweet scent..."[3] Interestingly, the Physiologus author adds a
"three-day waiting period between the phoenix's death and its
resurrection, further likening the bird to Christ."[4] As we have seen,
this three-day period before resurrection was evidently a theme
known by Jewish scribes hundreds of years prior to Christ's
purported entombment.

In addition to the comparisons by several other Christian writers,
such as Lactantius, who wrote an entire treatise on the phoenix, we
also discover an ancient Coptic text according to which "the last
known appearance of the phoenix marked the birth of Jesus in
Bethlehem."[5]

Again, the identification of the phoenix with Jesus lasted for
centuries, as evidenced by a poem in Old English called "the
Phoenix," in which "Jesus and the phoenix are made explicitly
parallel."[6] Jesus has been called the "true phoenix," which suggests
that the pertinent parts of the phoenix myth, including not only its
death but also its resurrection—essentially of a solar hero—clearly
preceded Christ's purported advent.

[1] Lightfoot, 83.
[2] Clement/Gregg, 23-24.
[3] Grant, *ECA*, 55.
[4] Hassig, 104.
[5] Heffernan, 38.
[6] Carter, 102.

The Astrotheological Millennium

In an article in the *Transactions of the Society of Biblical Archaeology*, biblical scholar Ernest de Bunsen (1819-1903) discusses various astronomical and astrotheological concepts, such as the "fortnightly period of the Hebrews, from the new moon to the full moon, in connection with the precessional cycle of 72 years...." de Bunsen continues:

> The fourteen divisions of the litanies of Thot, the god riding on the moon, and whose secret number was 72, are explained by reference to 14 moon-stations of the lunar zodiac, the hidden Mazzaroth or mansions of the moon in the book of Job, and to the precessional cycle of 72 years, with which can be connected the solar year and the Phoenix-period of the Egyptians, the Saros of the Babylonians, and the Mosaic period of one day like a thousands years....[1]

The Mosaic thousand-year period apparently refers to Psalm 90:4, which has been interpreted to mean that "with the Lord one day is as a thousand years, and a thousand years as one day." (2 Pet 3:8) Here we can see the contention that the 1,000-year cycle comprises an astrotheological development based on the 14-day lunar period multiplied by either 71 or 72, the number of the dodecans, as well as the time it takes for the precession of the equinoxes to move one degree, to equal some 994 to 1008 years.[2]

We further discover that astronomical studies have been done recently on the actual existence of a 1,000-year solar cycle. As related in the journal *Solar Physics*, the results of a study by L.H. Ma published in 2007 and entitled, "Thousand-Year Cycle Signals in Solar Activity," regarding "long-term fluctuations of solar variation," demonstrate "a thousand-year cycle in solar activity."[3]

In light of these facts of the ancients possessing a tradition of a thousand-year-old solar cycle symbolized by various myths, it is highly plausible that this 1,000-year period—whether simply "mythical" as in the ancient phoenix tales, or factual in that these myths truly represented ancient knowledge of such a solar cycle—rates as what is being reflected in the stories of a god or solar hero "returning" to rule for a millennium. In this regard, we should hardly base our futures on an ongoing cycle of the sun that is being erroneously taken as "prophecy," as we find in various Armageddon and "End Times" apocalyptic scenarios, based on millenarianism.

Conclusion

When examining the "true meaning" of Egyptian resurrection and afterlife, one is struck by the complexity of the concept, which needs

---

[1] *TSBA*, VI, 586.
[2] See also Kuhn, *LL*, 547.
[3] *Solar Physics*, v. 245, n. 2 (10/07).

to be and has been addressed thoroughly in entire volumes.[1] In consideration of the importance of the subject, it will not suffice simply to dismiss the Egyptian resurrection and afterlife by claiming some distinction between these concepts and their Christian equivalents, for instance, since the Egyptians arguably possessed every significant spiritual concept found within Christian theology. Regardless of various divergences of meaning and belief, the fact will remain that the Egyptian and Christian religions are very much alike in their ideation of, and focus on, death, resurrection and the afterlife. In the end, there is not only little dissimilarity between the Egyptian resurrection and that of Christianity, but also the Egyptian notions of afterlife and immortality are in fact more complex and all encompassing than the Christian tradition, which indeed appears to be an impoverished and corrupt rendering of the former.

In any event, merely because there are differences between myths does not mean that one was not copied from the other. In fact, there are *always* variations when one culture or group adopts the myths of another. It is a simple matter of picking and choosing what one wishes to include when one is creating a myth. In the current study, the Jewish creators of Christianity could simply change the popular and well-known story of Osiris's resurrection to suit themselves and their scriptures, adding further details from the Greek and other mythologies, as they surely did with other aspects of Christ's purported life.

Regardless of any discrepancies, the following description in *Osiris and the Egyptian Resurrection* by Budge concerning what Osiris meant to his many millions of followers demonstrates a significant connection to Jesus Christ:

> In the divinity and immortality of the god-man Osiris lay the strength of the power with which he appealed to the minds and hopes of the Egyptians for thousands of years...[2]

The resurrection of Osiris represents a triumph over death every bit as significant as that of Jesus. Indeed, in describing afterlife images in the tombs of the pharaohs Ramesses VI and IX, Hornung relates that they "show various stages of the process, adumbrating Christian scenes of the resurrection."[3] Hence, this learned Egyptologist viewed the Christian resurrection scenes to have been "foreshadowed" by the pre-Christian mythological Egyptian resurrection process. Hornung further summarizes the Egyptian influence on Christianity:

---

[1] See, e.g., Budge's *Osiris and the Egyptian Resurrection,* a two-volume study. In addition, in his book *Legends of the Egyptian Gods: Hieroglyphic Texts and Translations,* Budge includes an entire chapter entitled, "The Legend of the Death and Resurrection," revealing resurrection to constitute a central focus of Egyptian religion and mythology. See also Mojsov's *Osiris and the Afterlife.*

[2] Budge, *OER,* I, 17.

[3] Hornung, *VK,* 137.

Notwithstanding its superficial rejection of everything pagan, early Christianity was deeply indebted to ancient Egypt. In particular, the lively picture of the ancient Egyptian afterlife left traces in Christian texts; thus, among the Copts, and later in Islam, we encounter a fiery hell quite like that of the Egyptians... The *descensus* [descent] of Jesus, which played no role in the early church, was adopted into the official Credo after 359, thanks to apocryphal legends that again involved Egypt. Christ became the sun in the realm of the dead, for his descent into the netherworld had its ultimate precursor in the nightly journey of the ancient Egyptian sun god Re...[1]

In addition to these astute observations, we would aver that Christ did not just become the sun at a later point, but that he was always the "Sun of Righteousness," as mythical an entity as were Re, Osiris and Horus.

While the professional theologians and scholars may quibble about the "true meaning of resurrection," or whether or not it is permissible to use the term "resurrection" in a non-Christian context, what the *average Egyptian* perceived remains of interest here, because it is to this audience that the priesthood played. From what we can see here, it is apparent that the average ancient Egyptian worshipper would have viewed the death and resurrection of Osiris, as well as the event's promise of resurrection and eternal life for everyone else, in much the same manner that the average Christian over the centuries has perceived the death and resurrection of Christ.

Despite all the straw men, red herrings and other fallacies, the Egyptian worshipper expected that, after he was at one point *dead*, he would *live again*—and there is no rational and scientific argument which can change that fact or which would honestly allow us to dismiss the term *resurrection* in describing this life-renewing event.

In the final analysis, the fact remains that we know what "resurrection from the dead" means, and we also know that millions of people were introduced to the concept through the *Egyptian religion*, beginning thousands of years before Jesus allegedly existed. The bottom line is that the concept of coming back from the dead certainly does not originate with Christianity, whether applied to mortals or deities. Moreover, the notion that the implausible gospel story of Christ represents a *myth* predicated upon other similar myths found around the Mediterranean remains the most credible, scientific conclusion, regardless of any perceived differences between these stories.

---

[1] Hornung, *SLE*, 73.

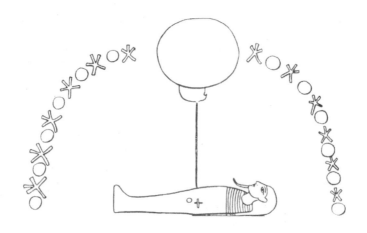

"The Resurrection of Osiris"
Surrounded by Twelve Circles and Stars.
(Hornung, *The Valley of the Kings*, 120)

The Alexandrian Roots of Christianity

"The Christian religion, it might be proposed, owes as much to the Nile as it does to the Jordan, and for the Church Alexandria should be at least as important as Jerusalem (whereas Rome absorbed influences from both cities). In both Western and Eastern iconography the attributes of Isis survived. Coptic *stelai* show the Mother and Child, identified as Christian by the Greek crosses on either side of the head, but the basic iconography of the image is that of Isis and Horus, translated into Mary and Jesus...."

Dr. James S. Curl, *The Egyptian Revival* (66)

"It has been well said that the Egyptians were better prepared to receive and accept Christianity than any of the nations round about them. For thousands of years before St. Mark came to Alexandria to preach the Gospel of his Master Christ, the Egyptians believed in Osiris the Man-god who raised himself from the dead. He was held to possess the power of bestowing immortality upon his followers because he had triumphed over Death, and had vanquished the Powers of Darkness. He was the Judge of souls and the supreme lord of the Judgment of the Dead; he was all-wise, all-knowing, all-just, and his decrees were final and absolute. No man could hope to dwell with him in his kingdom unless he had lived a life of moral excellence upon earth, and the only passports to his favour were truth-speaking, honest intent, and the observation of the commands of the Law (Maat), coupled with charity, alms-giving and humane actions...."

Dr. E.A. Wallis Budge, "The Cult of Isis and the Worship of the Virgin Mary compared," *Legends of Our Lady Mary* (1)

"When the Greeks established themselves as rulers in Alexandria (332-30 BC), they continued to worship Osiris as Sarapis and passed his cult on to the Romans. Through the Greeks the Hellenized version of the Osiris myth endured in Western culture. The rise of science and philosophy in Alexandria paved the way for the rich spiritual legacy of late antiquity. It was in Roman Alexandria (30 BC-AD 394) that the new Christian religion blossomed, inspired by the writings of the Egyptian, Greek, and Jewish philosophers."

Dr. Bojana Mojsov, *Osiris: Death and Afterlife of a God* (xii)

We have seen page after page of evidence that much of Christianity amounts to a remake of Egyptian religion and mythology. We have also noted the extensive spread of Egyptian culture around the Mediterranean centuries prior to the common era, with Egyptian art, architecture and other artifacts including religion enjoying a fascination among both the royalty and the common people, and with travel to Egypt itself popular as well.[1] It is obvious that Christianity constitutes a concerted effort to combine Paganism and Judaism, and the significant presence of Jews in Egypt dating back to the time of Alexander the Great will point us in the right direction as to how

---

[1] See, e.g., Hornung, *SLE*, 68.

this development came about and who was responsible for it. Indeed, Jews were among the earliest occupants of the newly founded city of Alexandria, beginning in the fourth century BCE[1] with further influxes later at the invitation of the Ptolemies,[2] the Greek leaders who ruled Egypt from 325 to 30 BCE. As revealed by the ancient historian Strabo (63/64 BCE-24 AD/CE), Alexandria represented by his time the "greatest commercial centre in the world."[3] Alexandria during the first century of the common era was thus a thriving metropolis that extended out in all directions and that influenced people around the Mediterranean, including in the important field of religion.

The milieu of the time is described by Dr. Dorothy I. Sly, a religious studies scholar at the University of Windsor, Ontario:

> First-century Alexandria vied with Rome to be the greatest city of the Roman empire. More than half a million people lived in its cosmopolitan four square miles. It was a major centre for international trade and shipping.[4]

Historian and religious studies scholar at University College London and Waikato University in New Zealand, Dr. Joan E. Taylor, elucidates further upon the Alexandrian environment of the day:

> It was a large city, with a population of around 500,000. From a variety of sources, literary, papyrological, and epigraphic, we know that this population of Alexandria comprised a large melting-pot of different ethnic groups which were broadly divided—for the purpose of administration—into the categories of "Greek" (Hellene) and Egyptian....
>
> It seems clear that the Jewish population of the city was large and spread out in all of the five areas...[5]

So sizable was the Jewish population at Alexandria that Philo, a member of one of the wealthiest Jewish families in that metropolis,[6] estimated that by his era Jews constituted some 50 percent of the city, [7] while Hornung puts the number of Jews there at that time at 40 percent.[8] Moreover, the Jewish population at Alexandria was so large and powerful that the Jews possessed "their own treasury and court of justice."[9]

By the time of the true formation of Christianity during the second century, after the destruction of Judea, there was likely an even larger number of Jews, Israelites, Samaritans and Hebrews at Alexandria. While some of this Israelitish population remained

---

[1] Taylor, J.E., 27.
[2] Reber, 21.
[3] Tozer, 345. See Strabo's *The Geography*, book 17.
[4] Sly, back cover.
[5] Taylor, J.E., 24-25.
[6] Horbury, 878.
[7] McClintock, II, 822.
[8] Hornung, *SLE*, 45.
[9] Isichei, 16.

isolated sectarians, many in that city were "Hellenizing," in that, as Jews do today, they accepted and lived within the culture or cultures around them, in this case the Greek, which was dominant during the era in question. As *The International Standard Bible Encyclopedia* states:

> It was in Alexandria that the Jews first came so powerfully under the influence of Hellenism, and here that the peculiar Graeco-Jewish philosophy sprang up of which Philo was the most notable representative.[1]

Indeed, Hellenistic Judaism had its "chief seat" at Alexandria, where also the Jewish Bible was translated into Greek and called the Septuagint. In describing the translation at Alexandria of the Septuagint some two to three centuries prior to the common era, Morenz states, "It can be demonstrated that the place of translation left its mark on many passages."[2] One of these marks included the invocation, "Lord, lord, king of the gods," which would be a strange statement for a monotheistic people. However, the Hebrews and Israelites were not always strict monotheists but continually "whored after other gods."[3] The Jews who translated the Septuagint were likely Egyptians, rather than Palestinians, as their knowledge of Hebrew was very poor.[4] At the disposal of Jewish Hellenizing efforts were the University and Library of Alexandria, presenting potential edification from around the known world.

As concerns the Egyptian religion, Alexandria and Christianity, Morenz remarks:

> Without abandoning our principle that Egyptian influence made itself felt as an undercurrent throughout Hellenism, we may nevertheless claim pride of place for Alexandria and so consider Alexandrian theology as the intermediary between the Egyptian religious heritage and Christianity.[5]

As we can see, this respected Egyptologist is not timid in his declaration as to the influence of Egyptian religion upon Christianity, or about Alexandria as being the "crucible" for this new creation.

The Therapeuts

One group of Hellenizing Egyptian Jews, or, rather, "Hebrews of a fashion," was deemed the "Therapeuts," a type of monastic community centered at Alexandria, with similar groups elsewhere around the Mediterranean. The Therapeuts at Alexandria were first mentioned by this name, meaning "healer," "physician" or "servant," by Philo in his work *De Vita Contemplativa* ("On the Contemplative

---

[1] *ISBE*, 857.
[2] Morenz, 253.
[3] See Ps 106:28-39; Judg 2:17, 8:27-33; 1 Chron 5:25; 21:13, Ezek 6:9, 8:14, 23:30, etc. See also "The Myth of Hebrew Monotheism" in my book *The Christ Conspiracy*.
[4] Gundry, xxiv.
[5] Morenz, 257.

Life"), probably composed between 20 and 30 AD/CE.[1] During the 19th century, a debate briefly raged that Philo did not in fact write the book;[2] some of the reasons for dismissing this work, however, seem founded upon the conclusion that the received history of Christianity is accurate and factual. It has also been questioned whether or not "the Therapeuts" really existed, since to our knowledge no one else had discussed any group at Alexandria by that name. However, the *Encyclopedia Britannica* sees the fact that the origin of the Therapeutan name was not known in Philo's time to serve as proof of the sect's antiquity:

> Philo himself was uncertain as to the meaning of the name, whether it was given to them because they were "physicians" of souls or because they were "servants" of the One God.... That the origin of the name of these ascetics was unknown in Philo's time goes to prove their antiquity.[3]

Moreover, we do in fact encounter *therapeutae* elsewhere, including as related to Egypt, as we shall see. In fact, Plato uses the term θεραπευται in his *Phaedrus* (252.c.5), translated by Dr. Benjamin Jowett as "attendants,"[4] and in *Gorgias* (518, b, 5, 8), where the term is accompanied by the word for "body" and which Jowett renders "trainers."[5] In actuality, there is little reason to suspect that this "class of persons," as Philo describes the Therapeuts and their spiritual relatives, did not exist both at Alexandria and elsewhere under a variety of names and forms, especially in consideration of the existence of the Jewish sect called Essenes, for one, as well as the many important mystery schools and religious associations throughout the Mediterranean. As Philo scholar, headmaster of Plymouth College and fellow of St. John's College at Cambridge University, Francis Henry Colson, states:

> That this type of character existed in Philo's time we might take for granted even if we did not have abundant evidence in his own writings, and it would not be surprising to find them occasionally organizing themselves into communities which would not necessarily attract much attention.[6]

---

[1] Mead, *DJL*, 337.

[2] See, e.g, theologian F. Lucius, who believed the work to have been written by an unknown hand sometime around 300 AD/CE. Lucius's thesis was refuted by Drs. Frederick C. Conybeare and Paul Wendland by analyzing the language and style of the lengthy treatise, finding it to be wholly in line with Philo. (Colson, 108.) Wendland's argument viewed the texts as "genuinely Philonic because it has better testimony than any other of the undisputed works; it also has inner support from Philonic and Jewish literature. The words, grammar and style are also Philonic. There are Jewish and Egyptian formative conditions for such a society." (Guthrie, K., 85.)

[3] *Enc. Brit*, XXVI, 793.

[4] Plato/Jowett, *Dialogues*, 557.

[5] Plato/Jowett, *Gorgias*, 99.

[6] Philo/Colson, 105.

After analyzing the situation, Colson concludes that the debate has been put to rest and that the ascription of authorship of that particular book to Philo remains proper. We will therefore continue to call the author "Philo" and to proceed with the description of the contemplative community and its apparent relationship to the Jewish, Egyptian and Christian religions.

Regarding the Therapeuts, in "On the Contemplative Life" (III, 21), Philo remarks:

> Now this class of persons may be met with in many places, for it was fitting that both Greece and the country of the barbarians should partake of whatever is perfectly good; and there is the greatest number of such men in Egypt, in every one of the districts, or nomi as they are called, and especially around Alexandria; and from all quarters those who are the best of these therapeutae proceed on their pilgrimage to some most suitable place as if it were their country, which is beyond the Mareotic lake, lying in a somewhat level plain a little raised above the rest, being suitable for their purpose by reason of its safety and also of the fine temperature of the air.[1]

In this work, Philo provides a long and detailed description that does not seem to be fictional in the least, but that, on the contrary, is highly believable and appears to be completely legitimate. Philo does not claim that one particular group maintained monastic communities all around the Roman Empire, but he does assert that this "class of persons" who constituted a "great number of such men in Egypt" could be found in many places, including in an organized spiritual community located on the shores of Lake Mareotis at Alexandria. Again, there were many such organized spiritual communities, "mystic schools" and "voluntary associations" elsewhere, such as the more famous ascetics, the Essenes, considered to be the "spiritual cousins" of the Therapeuts.

Despite their differences, the Therapeuts resembled the better known Essenes in several important aspects, including their renunciation of personal wealth and their abolition of slavery. Like the Essenes, they also wore white robes, maintained the Sabbath, and deemed God to be all good. The Therapeuts differed from the Essenes, however, in their incorporation of females into their sect. As did the rites of the Essenes, a number of the Therapeutan rituals also resembled those of the later Christians, such as gathering together for group prayers, "in which they stood and stretched their eyes and hands to heaven." As one of their rituals, the Therapeuts held the Pentecost as the most important religious festival, decades to centuries prior to the alleged advent of Christ.[2]

As monastics, the Therapeuts spent much time in solitude, residing in separate cells, and their private houses contained a room

---

[1] Philo/Yonge, 700.
[2] *MNQ*, XIII, 151.

...ther a *semneion* or *monasterion*, used for prayer and study of the Jewish scriptures and other piety-inducing texts. Regarding the Therapeutan studies, Philo states (X, 28-29):

> They read the Holy Scriptures and apply themselves to their ancestral philosophy by means of allegory, since they believe that the words of the literal text are symbols of a hidden nature, revealed through its underlying meanings.

> They have also writings of men of old, who were the founders of their sect and had left behind many memorials of the type of treatment employed in allegory, and taking these as a sort of archetype they imitate the method of this principle of interpretation....[1]

Since the Therapeuts were essentially Jews, Hebrews, Israelites or Samaritans who lived in the Diaspora, their scriptures constituted the Hebrew Bible, while their own writings may have comprised some of the Jewish apocrypha and pseudepigrapha, among others.

In *The Alexandrian Philo Judaeus*, Rev. Dr. Kenneth S. Guthrie (1871-1940) surmises that the Therapeuts "were probably no more than refugees of the more intellectual classes from persecution in Alexandria and that it was inevitable they should form temporary groups."[2] Guthrie also points out that, with the Greek penchant for allegorization all around them, "these same intellectual refugees would inevitably have spent their time allegorizing their own scriptures...."[3] In other words, the Therapeuts interpreted biblical scriptures and their own writings *allegorically*, which means that they did not necessarily perceive them as "history."

In *Buddhism in Christendom*, Arthur Lillie opined that the Therapeuts were part of a mystical Jewish community that existed at least two centuries before the common era.[4] In *The Gnostic Heresies of the First and Second Centuries*, Dr. Henry Longueville Mansel (1820-1871), a dean of St. Paul's and professor of Philosophy at Oxford, follows Rev. Dr. Henry Hart Milman (1791-1868), the previous dean of St. Paul's, in averring that the Therapeuts were the result of Buddhist missionaries sent forth by the Indian Emperor Asoka during the third century:

> The Indian influence in a modified form may chiefly be traced in those forms of Gnosticism which sprang up in Egypt, which appears to have been visited by Buddhist missionaries from India within two generations from the time of Alexander the Great, and where we may find permanent traces of Buddhist influence, established at all events before the Christian era. The Therapeutae or contemplative monks of Egypt, described by Philo, whom Eusebius by an anachronism confounds with the early Christians, appear to have

---

[1] Winston, D., 46.
[2] Guthrie, K., 86.
[3] Guthrie, K., 86.
[4] Lillie, 2.

sprung from an union of the Alexandrian Judaism with the precepts and modes of life of the Buddhist devotees....[1]

We concur with the Indian influence, as there was plenty of cultural exchange between the major Mediterranean cities and India by this time. As Hornung remarks in *The Secret Lore of Egypt*, "To be sure, even in antiquity, India also served as a model of the esoteric..."[2] However, we also evince that Church historian Eusebius is in fact correct and that his equation of the Therapeuts with the early Christians does not constitute an "anachronism," because Christianity was not founded by a divine Son of God in Judea during the first century of the common era.

In addition to their Judaic and Buddhist inclinations, the Therapeuts could be viewed as "sun worshippers" in the broadest and most spiritual sense as found throughout Egypt, per Philo, who said of them (III, 26):

> And they are accustomed to pray twice every day, at morning and at evening; when the sun is rising entreating God that the happiness of the coming day may be real happiness, so that their minds may be filled with heavenly light, and when the sun is setting they pray that their soul, being entirely lightened and relieved of the burden of the outward senses, may be able to trace out truth existing in its own consistory and council chamber.[3]

This ritual sounds very much like Egyptian solar mythology and is part of what may be styled the "lost religion" of antiquity. Furthermore, the *Encyclopedia Britannica* states that the sophisticated priesthood at Heliopolis described by Strabo (11.29), which was "skilled in philosophy and astronomy," possessed "curious resemblances" to the Therapeutic system and profession. As we have seen abundantly, the Egyptian priesthood was very much engaged in *sun worship* at Heliopolis—the *city of the sun*—and elsewhere. On a more earthly level, in discussing the nightly Therapeutan habit of relieving themselves, Conybeare remarked that the Therapeuts' spiritual cousins, the Essenes, were themselves very conscientious to cover their bodily wastes in order not to offend the sun god![4] As is evident, the line between religious ideologies is not always well and absolutely drawn, such that distinctly Jewish groups also engaged in what may be deemed "Paganism." Again, despite their overtly monotheistic devotion to an impersonal God, the Israelitish peoples were known throughout their early history to worship in the same manner and the same or similar gods as their Gentile neighbors.[5]

---

[1] Mansel, 31-32.
[2] Hornung, *SLE*, 3.
[3] Philo/Yonge, 700.
[4] Conybeare, 199, 216.
[5] Again, see Ps 106:28-39; Judg 2:17, 8:27-33; 1 Chron 5:25; 21:13, Ezek 6:9, 8:14, 23:30, etc.

ᵢne Ancient Lowly: A History of the Ancient Working People, C. ᵤsborne Ward, a political economist at the U.S. Department of Labor, provided an interesting and practical take on the Therapeuts and others around the Mediterranean, evincing that they were members of very powerful "business guilds" and "unions" of working class people.[1] Citing various inscriptions, Ward sought to demonstrate a "Solonic dispensation," which constituted a "vast organization" that served as a "veritable vehicle of emancipation of slaves and of equalization of mankind."[2] This overlooked thesis involves economic considerations along with trade unions, and political implications with voting unions, based on "jus coeundi," which is a "right of combination" legal privilege for the poor instituted by the Athenian lawmaker Solon in the 6th century BCE. Regarding this popular social movement, Ward states:

> A thousand proofs, archaeological and written, now attest that the strange moving power which long afterward became known as Christianity was no other than the plant or the inherent existence of that phenomenal force which swept the world and built up a new era of human civilization. It was that organization of brotherhoods under the enormous scope and influence of the Solonic dispensation.[3]

This "Solonic dispensation" that Ward suggests became Christianity represented a "vast system of trade unions over the world."[4] Greek names for these trade unions and "labor organizations" included "eranoi, thiasoi, orgeones, hetaire" and so on, while in Rome they were termed "collegia, sodalicia, conlegia," etc.[5] The brotherhood unions—or *collegia*, as they are best known—were also religious, and, according to Ward, the "hetaire" or *hetaerae* represented "religious beggars."[6] Concerning the religious environment during the era of Solon and for a century afterwards, George Grote comments:

> The century between 620 and 500 B.C. appears to have been remarkable for the diffusion and potent influence of distinct religious brotherhoods, mystic rites, and expiatory ceremonies...[7]

Describing these labor/political/religious brotherhoods as found in Egypt and elsewhere, Ward further remarks:

> The principal name by which they were known, not Coptic but Greek, was Therapeutae, an association closely allied to the Essenes. Later, the Egyptians had similar organizations, which under Christianity assumed a certain monastic and painfully degenerate

---

[1] Ward, 101, 175.
[2] Ward, 62.
[3] Ward, 100.
[4] Ward, 99.
[5] Ward, 101. The collegia are well known and widely believed to have been instituted by the Roman king Numa Pompilius sometime during the 7th century BCE.
[6] Ward, 218.
[7] Grote, 84.

form. They were all derived from the original jus coeundi, long existing but first promulgated through inscriptions upon the celebrated Prytaneum at Athens, and a few years later translated into Latin and honored by being engraved upon one of the Twelve Tables of Roman law.

In Palestine, including old Phoenicia, the same establishments are known as essenes, ossennae, sometimes therapeutae, Nazaraenai, Cainites and synodoi.

Throughout Gaul, Spain and Africa, and so far to the northwestward as the British Islands, and as far northeastward as Germany they generally assumed the Latin names of collegia and sodalicia ["guild corporations"], although traces are found of the German half-civilized Lupercalia.

All these various confraternities, no matter what the name or race, possessed the same tenets and quite frequently they are found to have been linked internationally together. There are inscriptions and other records which show that in times of famine, pestilence, or war, when certain districts flourished while their distant neighbors and brothers were suffering, convoys were sent with provisions, money, medicines and social comforts for their rescue. This was done as late as the apostolic age; for several times provisions, money and comforts were conveyed from Asia Minor to the brotherhood at Jerusalem, and from Ephesus and Corinth to groups in Macedonia, showing the value of Mutual help among the poor and struggling people.[1]

In our present analysis showing extensive comparisons between the religions of the cultures around the Mediterranean and beyond, it bears repeating that the "various confraternities"—the religious associations, which included the Therapeuts, Essenes and Nazarenes—"possessed the same tenets" and were frequently linked together, fashioning a formidable network of religious brotherhoods, long prior to the common era.

This fascinating information provides more flesh on the bones of the era's milieu, painting a fuller picture of life in the Roman Empire at the time. Adding to this picture, except for the Jewish groups these collegia or "voluntary associations" were banned by Julius Caesar (100-44 BCE) because of their political aspirations, before being reinstituted by Augustus (63 BCE-14 AD/CE). The collegia became increasingly restricted and legislated under Nero (37-68 AD/CE), and

---

[1] Ward, 101-102. The Prytaneum or Prytaneion ("town hall") at Athens was a large building that served as the "seat of the chief archon." A number of the inscriptions there concerned the legal reforms instituted by the lawmaker Solon (638-558 BCE), who succeeded the author of the infamous "Draconian laws." Regarding the Solonic legislation, Grote remarks: "The Solonian laws seem to have borne more or less upon all the great departments of human interest and duty. We find regulations political and religious, public and private, civil and criminal, commercial, agricultural, sumptuary, and disciplinarian...." (Grote, 153.) The Twelve Tables recorded Roman law as determined in the fifth century BCE, and were placed in the Roman Forum.

were later bolstered again by Marcus Aurelius (121-180 AD/CE).[1] It
was into this environment that Christianity was born, which may well
explain many of its characteristics and emphases.

Concerning these organizations in Egypt, Harry L. Haywood
(1886-1956) writes:

> Collegia became more or less common in Egypt in the first century
> B.C., especially among the worshippers of Isis. Apuleius
> [*Metamorphosis* 11.17] mentions one such organization under date of
> 79 B.C., and there is reason to believe that they had existed much
> earlier.[2]

In this regard, Ward asserts that the Therapeuts were also
followers of the goddess Isis, who served as their "mother
protectress,"[3] which would make sense for a group of *healers*, since,
as we have seen, Isis was considered the "Great Healer" at that time.
Ward further writes:

> The therapeutae are found in the inscriptions in close relation to the
> eranoi and hetaerae, first worshipping the Isis [sic], and then among
> the oldest christian inscriptions. There is a passage to this effect in
> Eusebius. The important question which we are now endeavoring to
> solve is, if the therapeutae were the very early christians, whether
> they were among the trade and labor unions of the Solonic
> dispensation...[4]

The reference to inscriptions by Ward doubtlessly includes some
of the 2,500 that deal with collegia from hundreds of towns around
the Roman Empire.[5] Oddly enough, Ward also cites research
revealing some "recklessness" and "extravagances in things
disreputable" on the part of the Therapeutae.[6]

Regarding Philo's Therapeuts and the worship of Egyptian deities,
Dr. Stephen G. Wilson, a professor of Religion at Carleton University,
states:

> The Therapeutae are a particularly interesting example: a monastic
> community of both men and women who seem to have been equally
> involved in the most important aspects of communal life, a feature

---

[1] Haywood, II.

[2] Haywood, I. According to Apuleius ("*pastophorum—quod sacrosancti collegii nomen est*"), et al., one Egyptian religious association was composed of the *pastophori* or Egyptian priests, who carried "small shrines" or *arks* of their deities and who were "introduced into Italy along with the worship of Isis, and formed into collegia in various towns." This name *pastophori* was also found in the Septuagint (e.g., 1 Chr. 9:26) and in Josephus to describe "the priests' apartments attached to the Jewish temple." (Smith, W., 349.)

[3] Ward, 182.

[4] Ward, 438.

[5] Haywood, II.

[6] Ward, 438fn. Many of the texts Ward cites in his scholarly analysis are in German and other languages, indicating research and evidence that might not be found in English.

that V. Heuchan (chapter 12) suggests may have derived in part from the influence of the Isis cult...[1]

Again, we find an association of the Therapeuts with the Egyptian goddess Isis, which is fitting in consideration of her prominence and of her obvious metamorphosis into the Jewish Mother of God, the Virgin Mary. Moreover, in the Jewish "wisdom literature," which personifies Wisdom as a feminine entity, can be found traces of Isis worship "taken up into the complex picture of Wisdom to enrich it and make it more attractive and satisfying to a hellenized Jewish readership."[2]

In his "Excursus" on Philo, Conybeare examines indications of the Therapeuts in Philo's other texts, such as *De Decem Oraculis* and *De Profugis*. Like Ward, Conybeare concludes that the Therapeutae "formed a collegium or sodalitas and had legal recognition and status." He also discusses the "analogous guilds elsewhere of Cultores Deorum"—the term "cultores deum" or "cultores deorum" meaning "worshippers of the gods"—as well as "points of resemblances between the Therapeutic colony and that of the Egyptian priests described by Chaeremon the Stoic and by Strabo."[3]

During the first century AD/CE, an Egyptian priest who was also the "head of the Alexandrian school of grammarians," Chaeremon or Chairemon by name, was the teacher of the emperor-to-be Nero.[4] It is speculated that Chaeremon was also a "keeper of the famous Museum in Alexandria."[5] The Alexandrian influence on Rome could hardly be more evident. It is also presumed that Chaeremon was among the ambassadors from Alexandria who met with Emperor Claudius in 40 AD/CE.

Concerning Chaeremon's take on the Egyptian religion, Dr. van der Horst relates:

> ...he explains in a typically Stoic way the tales about these gods and goddesses as referring to the sun, moon, planets, and other heavenly bodies, to the Nile, καὶ ὅλως πάντα εἰς τα φυσικά, "and in general everything referring to physical things."...[6]

Chaeremon wrote an influential book about Egyptian hieroglyphs that, naturally, has not survived—yet another instance of an important primary source to which we can no longer look for proof. In any event, the Alexandrian Therapeuts thus resembled in some respects the priesthood of the astrotheological Egyptian religion.

---

[1] Kloppenborg, 12. "V. Heuchan" refers to Valerie Heuchan, who, with Peter Richardson, wrote an article published in Kloppenborg entitled "Jewish Voluntary Associations in Egypt and the Roles of Women."
[2] Collins, J., 203-204.
[3] Conybeare, xiii-xiv.
[4] van der Horst, ix.
[5] van der Horst, ix.
[6] van der Horst, ix.

In reality, Philo's Therapeuts evidently constituted one of the many collegia around the Roman Empire, some of which were known by the designation of "healers." Concerning this development, Dr. Joseph H. Hellerman, a professor of New Testament at Biola University, remarks:

> *Therapeutae*, Philo's term for a celibate monastic group of Egyptian Judeans, is elsewhere used to describe members of certain Graeco-Roman associations on Delos.[1]

In this regard, professor of Archaeology and Architecture at the University of Toronto Dr. Peter Richardson states that the "Delos inscriptions (third to second century B.C.E.) refer to worshipers as Therapeutae..."[2] Hence, we find in *Greece* collegia by the name of "Therapeutae," and it is further noteworthy that there were also *Jews* and *Samaritans* on the island of Delos during this time when *therapeutan collegia* could be found there.[3] As theologian Dr. John Dominic Crossan states, "We know from 1 Maccabees 15:17-23 that there was a Jewish community on Delos as early as 139 B.C.E...."[4] The island of Delos was a major Greek seat for the worship of Isis and Serapis, and it is possible that Philo's Therapeuts constituted members of the Alexandrian temple of Serapis/Sarapis, who dominated the city's spiritual landscape, as related by Strabo (17.1.17).[5] In consideration of these facts, it is possible that by "class of persons" Philo was referring to these religious associations and collegia by the name of *therapeutae*, as located at not only at Alexandria but also at Delos and elsewhere.

As further evidence of the Therapeutan network, concerning the followers of Serapis, Dr. Joan Taylor states:

> In Magnesia ad Sipylum, the devotees of Serapis and Isis are termed θεραπευταί [therapeutai], as they are also in inscriptions from Demetrias and Cyzicus. The term θεραπευταί appears numerous times in inscriptions from Delos, relating to [the] Egyptian cult.[6]

Taylor further relates that "the Suidas [Greek lexicon] has, under the entry for θεραπευτηρες [therapeutires]...'those who manage the holy places/temples, devotees of Isis of the Egyptians.'"[7] Moreover, in speaking of the servants in the temple of the popular savior god Asclepius—the Greek counterpart of Serapis and Jesus—Latin writer Aelius Aristides (117-180 AD/CE) refers to them and himself as *therapeutae*, while famed physician Galen (129-200/216 AD/CE) likewise mentions the "Asclepius *therapeutae*."[8]

---

[1] Hellerman, 233.
[2] Richardson, P., 364.
[3] Crossan, 52ff.
[4] Crossan, 55.
[5] Strabo/Hamilton, 238.
[6] Taylor, J.E., 58.
[7] Taylor, J.E., 58.
[8] Kloppenborg, 152.

The fact that collegia of Alexandria could be found in o
of the Roman Empire is further proved by an inscription
ancient city of Tomi in Bulgaria dated to March 29, 160 ʌ.., ᴏᴇ ɑɴᴅ
dedicated to the syncretistic god Zeus-Helios-Serapis, as well as to
the emperors Antoninus Pius (86-161 AD/CE) and Marcus Aurelius.
The inscription came from the "house of the Alexandrians," the word
"house" evidently referring to "a religious and an ethnic society whose
members were Alexandrian merchants and seamen temporarily
residing at Tomi."[1] Of course, the fact of the widespread worship of
Isis and other Egyptian gods outside of Egypt itself provides
testimony that the Egyptian priesthood traveled around the
Mediterranean.

Considering all these factors, it appears that in the Egyptian
Therapeuts we possess a Jewish religious community that was
evidently part of a massive brotherhood and that was "Hellenizing,"
bringing into its doctrines the beliefs of Pagan religions as well,
including and especially the Egyptian. The reverence for Isis and
Serapis by the Jewish Therapeuts is not difficult to believe in
consideration of the fact that the Madonna and Child iconography
was taken over wholesale from images of Isis and Horus, as well as
the many other parallels between Judeo-Christianity and Egyptian
religion demonstrated here.

Indeed, it is apparent from the purported remarks of the emperor
Hadrian in a letter to his brother-in-law Servianus around 134
AD/CE, as related by the Pagan writer Vopiscus circa 300, that the
Jews at Alexandria were very involved in the worship of Serapis, as
were the Christians. Over the centuries that this letter has been
translated, scholars of certain sensibilities have found it expedient
either to expunge various parts of it or to denounce it as a forgery,
because of the uncomfortable conclusions the epistle affords by a
respected authority, i.e., the Roman emperor himself. A faithful and
literal translation of this letter with the controversial parts included
is provided by Dr. Benjamin H. Isaac, a professor of Ancient History
at the University of Tel Aviv:

> Those who worship Serapis there, are [in fact] Christians, and those
> who call themselves bishops of Christ are [in fact] devotees of
> Serapis. There is no Jewish *archisynagogus* ["synagogue ruler"], no
> Samaritan, no Christian presbyter, who is not an astrologer, a
> soothsayer, or a master of wrestlers. When the Patriarch himself
> visits Egypt, he is forced by some to worship Serapis, by others to
> worship Christ. They are a most seditious sort of people, most
> deceptive, most injurious; their city is wealthy, rich, and [their land]
> fertile and no one is idle.... Their only god is money, and this the
> Christians, the Jews, and all people adore.[2]

---

[1] Tacheva, 12-13.

[2] Isaac, 368. While various apologists today cast doubt upon this letter for obvious
reasons, fervent Christian Bishop Lightfoot was among the many who have not

It may be easy to understand why some authorities have been squeamish about divulging the full contents of Hadrian's letter concerning the Christians and Jews as followers of Serapis—and of money! Indeed, some translators censor the words about Christians and Jews representing astrologers and "quacks," as the term Isaac deems "master of wrestlers" has been rendered previously, as well as the calumny about them being "seditious," "deceptive" and "most injurious." Others remove the part about "their only god is money," which, like the rest, is in reality present in the original Latin of Vopiscus (*Scriptores Historiae Augustae*, 8.6): "*Unus illis deus nummus est.*"[1] In actuality, investigating the role of Serapis worship in the formation of Christianity would require another volume, as it ranks as extremely significant.[2] From all the evidence, it seems clear that the Jewish branch of the Therapeutae, not being satisfied with worshipping Greek and Egyptian deities, contrived to create an equivalent mythical godman of their own in Jesus Christ.

Regarding the Therapeuts, Christianity and Hadrian, noted historian Edward Gibbon (1737-1794) states:

> The extensive commerce of Alexandria, and its proximity to Palestine, gave an easy entrance to the new religion [of Christianity]. It was first embraced by great numbers of Therapeutae, or Essenians, of the Lake Mareotis, a Jewish sect which had abated much of its reverence for the Mosaic ceremonies.... It was in the school of Alexandria that the Christian theology appears to have assumed a regular and scientific form; and when Hadrian visited Egypt, he found a church composed of Jews and of Greeks, sufficiently important to attract the notice of that inquisitive prince.[3]

It is quite likely these Hellenizing Jews—those who "had abated much of [their] reverence for the Mosaic ceremonies"—and Christians at Alexandria who were worshippers of Serapis represented in significant part descendants of Philo's Therapeuts. In addition to those other points of commonality that lead to this conclusion, the Therapeuts incorporated a hierarchy similar to that of the later Christian religion, including a title for individuals involved in certain sacred rituals called *Ephemereutae* (VIII, 66).[4] Regarding the term

---

doubted it to be genuine. These facts should be kept in mind when assessing the task of the researcher interested in Christian origins and ancient religion.

[1] Isaac provides the original Latin in a footnote on page 368. See also Griggs, 40.

[2] See Charles W. King: "In the second century the syncretistic sects that had sprung up in Alexandria, the very hot-bed of Gnosticism, found out in Serapis a prophetic type of Christ as the Lord and Creator of all, and Judge of the living and the dead.... Thus at length Serapis had become merely the idea of the Supreme Being, whose manifestation upon Earth was the Christ." King next discusses Hadrian's letter equating the worshippers of Serapis with Christians, remarking: "There can be no doubt that the head of Serapis, marked as the face is by a grave and pensive majesty, supplied the first idea for the conventional portrait of the Saviour." (King, C.W., *TGR*, 68)

[3] Gibbon, 59-60.

[4] Philo/Yonge, 704.

ephemereutai, Conybeare remarks that it is a "fairly old word in Egypt, indicating one who in daily rotation takes the service in a temple."[1] Philo gives other functions and roles much like those we find in the Christian church as well. In fact, the Greek word for "church" itself—*ekklesia* or *ecclesia*—was in common usage centuries prior to the advent of Christianity.[2] In ancient Athens, the *ecclesia* represented gatherings of citizens on the hill of the Pnyx, where much policy was made over the centuries. In Strong's (G1577), *ecclesia* has several meanings, including the first one of "a gathering of citizens called out from their homes into some public place, an assembly..." Other definitions include "the assembly of the Israelites" and "an assembly of Christians gathered for worship in a religious meeting." Although it is most often translated in the King James Version of the New Testament as "church," in Acts (19:32, 39, 41) the older meaning of "assembly" is preferred. The word *ecclesia* or a related term is also found over 75 times in the Greek Old Testament or Septuagint and is translated as "assembly" and "gathering." While the Pagan use of the word *ecclesia* is not necessarily religious, the Jewish use *is* religious, leading to the conclusion that the pre-Christian Jewish assembly could be translated as the "Church of God."[3] Moreover, the *ecclesia* could be considered yet another one of the "voluntary associations" that included not only *collegia* but also *systema,*[4] the term used by Philo to describe the Therapeutan "order." Other translations for *systema* are "guild," "college" and "association."

Regarding the roles in the Therapeutan order, Lillie remarks:

> That the Christians should have taken over this ephemereut and these presbyters, or priests, and deacons, as their three chief officers, is perhaps the greatest stumbling-block in the way of those writers, chiefly English and clerical, who maintain there was no connection between Christianity and mystic Judaism.[5]

The term "deacon" generally refers to the Greek word *diakonos,* which is also translated as "servant" or "minister," and which was also in usage long prior to the common era.[6] In his treatise (IX, 70-72; X, 75), Philo refers to those within the Therapeutan community who minister to the guests at the sacred community meal, including "servants":

> And they do not use the ministrations of slaves, looking upon the possession of servants or slaves to be a thing absolutely and wholly contrary to nature, for nature has created all men free... Accordingly in this sacred entertainment there is, as I have said, no slave, but

---

[1] Conybeare, 238.
[2] See, e.g., Thucydides, *Historiae*; Aristophanes, *Ecclesiazusae*; and Xenophon, *Hellenica.*
[3] See Ellegård.
[4] Aune, 114.
[5] Lillie, 78.
[6] See, e.g., Euripides, *Cyclops*; Aristophanes, *Ecclesiazusae*; and Plato, *Respublica.*

ıen minister to the guests, performing the offices of servants,
ɔnder compulsion, nor in obedience to any imperious
commands, but of their own voluntary free will, with all eagerness
and promptitude anticipating all orders, for they are not any chance
free men who are appointed to perform these duties, but young men
who are selected from their order...[1]

The original Greek terms for "ministrations" and "minister" are
related to the word *diakonos*, meaning "servant," "attendant" or
"deacon." This same sense of service is found in the usage of the
word *diakonos* in the New Testament, particularly at John 2:5 and
2:9, as well as at Romans 13:4. The word for "order" from which the
young ministers or *deacons* are selected is *systema*.

At VIII (67) and IX (73), Philo discusses the "old men" or *elders*,[2]
which is *presbyteroi* in Greek, another term that can be found in
texts long predating the common era.[3] Regarding this Therapeutan
hierarchy, Conybeare states:

> ...there was a severe novitiate to be gone through before an aspirant
> was admitted to be one of the πρεσβύτεροι [presbyteroi] in the σύστημα
> [systema] of the Therapeutae... [The Contemplative Life] implies as
> much, for it says that [the young men were selected from their order
> or guild] (to wait on the πρεσβύτεροι) with the most careful regard to
> their excellence. And the elders themselves had to *be elected* into the
> σύστημα, their order of dignity being that in which they had been
> elected.[4]

In Conybeare's analysis, rather than just being "old men," these
Therapeutan elders or *presbyters* clearly represented a "higher grade"
to which those of the lower orders aspired.

Furthermore, in Philo (X, 83) we find a Therapeutan *precentor*, or
"ecclesiastical dignitary, sometimes an administrative or ceremonial
officer," existing also within Judaism and passing over into
Christianity.[5]

Concerning the Therapeutan order as presented by Philo not only
in "On the Contemplative Life" but also in other treatises, Conybeare
comments:

> Are we to suppose that συστήματα [systemata] of the same type as
> that which Philo proceeds to describe, were found all over the
> inhabited world? or was the one settled on the Lake Mareotis, to
> which the best persons resorted from all quarters, the only one? I
> think the truth may lie between the two suppositions. There may
> have been such societies in several of the great Jewish communities
> scattered round the Mediterranean, e.g. in Cyprus, Corinth, Tarsus,
> Colossae, Antioch, Rome, Smyrna and elsewhere. But in the

---

[1] Philo/Yonge, 704.
[2] Philo/Yonge, 704; Winston, 54.
[3] Strong's G4245. See, e.g., Thucydides, *Historiae*; Aristophanes, *Fragmenta*;
Xenophon, *Memorabilia*, *Anabasis* and *Cyropedia*; and Plato, *Apologia Socratis*.
[4] Conybeare, 273.
[5] Winston, 56; *CE*, "Precentor," XII, 372.

Alexandrian centre of which they were all offshoots, the members may have been more strict in their discipline, more severe in their asceticism.... That there were many such societies elsewhere, is quite credible, if we bear in mind the wide dissemination all around the Mediterranean of Greek Judaism, and the widespread propaganda of the religion which, in Philo's day, had been in progress for at least two centuries.[1]

Thus, we see that Conybeare was of the educated opinion that the Therapeutan *systemata* or guilds, as he translates the term, *were* spread around the Mediterranean, emanating out of headquarters at Lake Mareotis. Moreover, these guilds or religious brotherhoods are found previously in the same places where Paul supposedly set up "churches"—a term, as we have seen, already in use prior to the supposed founding of Christianity. In this regard, Curl states:

Paul's journeyings took him to places where Isiac cults were well-established: Isis-Artemis rules in the great Ionic temple at Ephesus (one of the Wonders of the Ancient World), and devotion to her was intense; Antioch had thriving Hellenistic religions; and Philippi was not guiltless of a devotion to Isis the Great Queen. Clearly the worship of Isis (by what ever name) was widespread, and, as the goddess of a Myriad Names, Isis was dangerous to Christianity by her oecumenical and catholic nature....[2]

As noted, the Therapeuts around the Mediterranean were associated with Isis worship, which in turn can be found at the sites in the Pauline epistles.

Concerning the various religious groups, Conybeare further notes:

The name therapeutai was no doubt the official name under which such guilds or collegia would be known to the government, which gave them legal recognition. As such we meet with inscriptions (C.I. 2293, 2295) as the official title of certain pagan guilds. So the Latin title Cultores deum often occurs in inscriptions in the same sense.[3]

Following this fascinating key to the Therapeutan mystery, Conybeare also states:

[Theologian] Prof. Massebieau truly says that the Therapeutae or cultores of Lake Mareotis would have seemed to a Greek reader to be one of those associations called θίασοι [thiasoi], σύνοδοι [synodoi], or collegia, which were common in Alexandria and all over the Roman Empire.... The ascetic societies which Philo describes, must have gained legal recognition and sanction from the governments of Augustus and Tiberius... In using the word σύστημα [systema] of the Therapeutic society, Philo distinctly assimilates it to the religious corporations which were then very common, especially as burial societies. Many pagan deities towards the end of the first century had their guilds or συστήματα [systemata]; and the members of these

---

[1] Conybeare, 292.
[2] Curl, 67.
[3] Conybeare, 293fn.

like the Therapeutae, were called...cultores deorum, had
n burial-places, common meals, and a priest to preside over
them. The members were also, like the Freemasons of today, bound
by mutual oaths to help each other, and were pledged not to go to
law with one another, but to arrange their disputes outside the law
court. They called each other brethren...[1]

As we can see, at the time of the alleged founding of Christianity,
there existed all around the Mediterranean—at the very places where
Christianity took root, in fact—religious brotherhoods with very much
the same tenets, doctrines, hierarchy and structure of the later
Christian effort. These widespread brotherhoods included those by
the title of "Therapeuts" or "healers," which possessed a distinctly
"Christian" feel about them—such as was noticed even in ancient
times.

In addition, we discover from Philo that the proto-Christian
Therapeuts engaged in *mysteries*. As Conybeare further relates:

In 475. 16 we are told that the Suppliants abiding alone in their
private sanctuaries are *initiated* in the *mysteries* of the holy life....
The language also in which the conversion...of these recluses is
described in 473. 15 foll., is borrowed from the heathen mysteries.
The characterization of the end or supreme good as a vision of the
truth Being no less reminds one of the ancient mysteries. From many
hints up and down the works of Philo it is certain that among the
Alexandrian Jews there existed a system of mysteries, perhaps in
imitation of their Greek mysteries of Demeter which were celebrated
year by year on the hill of Eleusis close to Alexandria.[2]

Conybeare next discusses how serious a transgression was the
divulgence of these mysteries. Nevertheless, in "On the Cherubim" (2,
XIII, 43), Philo himself does divulge them, first warning the reader:

But that we may describe the conception and the parturition of
virtues, let the superstitious either stop their ears, or else let them
depart; for we are about to teach those initiated persons who are
worthy of the knowledge of the most sacred mysteries, the whole
nature of such divine and secret ordinances.[3]

One of the mysteries was God as a "Trinity in Unity,"[4] a doctrine
predating the founding of Christianity, despite that religion's claim of
being "unique, divine revelation." Another of the mysteries, as we
have seen, was the supposed ability of a virgin to "bring forth" as well
as that of a woman becoming a "born-again virgin" by virtue of the
grace of God. Again, in this regard we possess ancient testimony from
Christian writers, e.g., Epiphanius and the Chronicle author, that
there was at *Alexandria* a temple to the maiden goddess Kore in
which a virgin brought forth a newborn baby at the winter solstice.

[1] Conybeare, 297.
[2] Conybeare, 303.
[3] Philo/Yonge, 84.
[4] Conybeare, 304.

The evidence points to the Egyptian Therapeuts constituting a powerful group of paganizing Jews "of a fashion" whose affiliation extended around the Mediterranean and included non-Jewish religious groups and organizations as well. These organizations, as evidenced by the Egyptian Therapeuts, possessed a structure very similar to the later Christian religion. Indeed, there are a number of important and profound similarities between the Therapeuts and the later Christians, again, a comparison noted in antiquity as well.

The Proto-Christians?

While some scholars have denied that there is a connection between the Therapeuts and the Christians, "Catholic writers maintain that it is quite impossible to make any historical gap or line of severance between the Therapeuts...and the Christian monks of Alexandria."[1] One Catholic writer who insisted upon the connection between Philo's Therapeuts and the Christians was Eusebius during the fourth century. In *The History of the Church* (2.17), in speaking of "Philo's account of the Egyptian ascetics," Eusebius remarks:

> Whether he invented this designation [Therapeutae] and applied it to them, fitting a suitable name to their mode of life, or whether they were actually called this from the very start, because the title Christian was not yet in general use, need not be discussed here.[2]

As demonstrated previously, Philo did not invent the designation of "therapeutae," as it was connected to religious associations or collegia centuries prior to the common era.

Eusebius goes on to compare Philo's description of the Therapeuts with Christian monastic life, as found especially in the Acts of the Apostles. Although Eusebius asserts that the Therapeuts were the "original Christian community converted by St. Mark,"[3] the case could be made that this rare moment of candor from an early Church father will prove deleterious to the implausible claim of Christianity's supernatural genesis, since Philo's account preceded the creation of that faith. In actuality, Eusebius's claim of Mark founding the Church in Alexandria is anachronistic, as according to Jerome (*On the Illustrious Men*, 8),[4] the evangelist died there in the eighth year of Nero's reign, which would be 62 AD/CE, when, according to Paul, Mark was with *him*, very much alive, in 65 AD/CE. Moreover, Eusebius contends that Mark was at Alexandria from around 41-44 to 61-62; yet, Acts depicts him at Jerusalem and Antioch in 46, as well as in Salamis around 47, and then back at Antioch in 49 or 50.[5] In addition, neither Clement of Alexandria nor Church father Origen, an Egyptian who taught at the Alexandrian

---

[1] Lillie, 241.
[2] Eusebius/Williamson, 50.
[3] Guthrie, K., 8.
[4] Schaff, III, 364.
[5] Acts 12:25; 13:5; 15:37-39.

school, make any mention of this story connecting Mark to the Therapeuts or of his presence in their city at any point,[1] which they surely would have done to increase their own credibility as spokesmen for a "sanctioned" church. The reason Eusebius wanted Mark to be in Alexandria, of course, was to explain why there were "Christians" there at so early a time. The reality, however, may be that the Therapeuts morphed into Christians because it was *they* who essentially created much of Christianity, with no "historical Jesus" in fact founding the faith in Judea.

In his commentary, Eusebius springs another surprise on us with his assessment that the Therapeuts' "allegorical writings" represented the basis of the canonical gospels! After quoting Philo's discussion of the Therapeuts' "short works by early writers, the founders of their sect, who left many specimens of the allegorical method," Eusebius (2.17) remarks:

> It seems like that Philo wrote this after listening to their exposition of the Holy Scriptures, and it is very probable that what he calls short works by their early writers were the gospels, the apostolic writings, and in all probability passages interpreting the old prophets, such as are contained in the Epistle to the Hebrews and several others of Paul's epistles.[2]

A more blatant identification of the Egypto-Jewish origins of Christianity we could not hope to find. Yet, scholars who hold onto the received Christian history have assiduously ignored or dismissed this "smoking gun."

Despite the dismissal of them by modern scholars, Eusebius's remarks regarding the Therapeuts being "proto-Christians" are quite pointed, as summarized by de Bunsen, who was the son of Baron C.C.J. Bunsen and a member of the Society of Biblical Archaeology:

> ...Eusebius...declares it "highly probable" that the ancestral commentaries of the Alexandrian Essenes were made use of in the Gospels as well as in the Epistles of Paul, especially in the "Epistle of the Hebrews." The words of Eusebius clearly assert even, that these Essenic commentaries "are the very gospels and writings of the Apostles," that is, that they formed the foundations of Apostolic writings. Eusebius insists upon it that the religious rites of the Therapeuts, which Philo "has accurately described and stated in his writings, are the same customs that are observed by us alone at the present day, particularly the vigils of the great festival," which precedes the feast of Easter, and the Greek Fathers call "the great week."[3]

As can be seen, Eusebius declared the Therapeuts to be Christians, their writings to be the basis of the New Testament texts, and their customs to be the same as those of the Christians. The

---

[1] *CE*, "Mark," IX, 673.
[2] Eusebius/Williamson, 52.
[3] *Miscellaneous Notes and Queries*, XIII, 19.

question remains, was the Church historian just grasping at straws in order to find an early path for Alexandrian Christianity, or did he know more, unwittingly admitting, perhaps, that this Therapeutan network, by whatever name, was the real source of the Christian religion?

Discussing the same material in Philo, although under a different title ("On the Iessaioi"), Church father Epiphanius—who was very keen to denounce as heretical any type of sect outside of the realm of orthodox Christianity—concurred with Eusebius's declarations regarding the Therapeuts being Christians (*Panarion* 1.29.5.1-3):

> If you are a lover of learning and read the writings of Philo, you would find an account of these people in the book entitled *on the Iessaioi*. He describes their way of life and their praiseworthy customs and recounts their monasteries in the vicinity of the Marean marsh, speaking about none other than the Christians. For he himself was present in the area (the place is called Mareotis) and spent some time with them, receiving hospitality in the monasteries in this locality. Since he was there during the time of Pascha [Easter], he observed their practices, how some of them prolonged their fast for the entire holy week of the Pascha, others ate every second day, while yet others broke their fast every evening. All these matters are dealt with by the man in his account of the faith and practices of the Christians.[1]

Epiphanius thus was quite sure Philo was describing Christians—"Christians," in fact, who lived at Alexandria before Christianity was created in Judea!

Describing these circumstances, the *Encyclopedia Britannica* comments:

> To the modern reader the importance of the Therapeutae, as of the Essenes, lies in the evidence they afford of the existence of the monastic system long before the Christian era. We have no clue to the origin of the Therapeutae, but it is plain that they were already ancient when Philo described them. Eusebius was so much struck by the likeness of the Therapeutae to the Christian monks of his own day as to claim that they were Christians converted by the preaching of St. Mark. He goes so far as to say that "the writings of ancient men, who were the founders of the sect" referred to by Philo, may very well have been the Gospels and Epistles....
>
> Nothing is more likely than that Christianity gained adherents among the Therapeutae, and that their institutions were adapted to the new religion, just as they seem to have been borrowed by the Jews from the Egyptians.[2]

Hence, we discover again that the Therapeuts were "already ancient," that they were quite well suited to be Christians, and that they had already borrowed their institutions from Egypt. How much

---

[1] Runia, 228.
[2] *Enc. Brit.*, XXVI, 793.

more did the Therapeuts borrow from Egypt? As demonstrated here, the answer would appear to be many major aspects of the gospel story.

In the New Testament itself emerge a few inferences of possible Therapeuts, including Apollos of Alexandria (Acts 18:24), who purportedly met up with Paul at the Greek city of Corinth, a site where many Alexandrian Jews engaged in commerce. Regarding Apollos and Christianity, Dr. Birger A. Pearson, a professor emeritus of Religious Studies at the University of California at Santa Barbara, remarks:

> If we recall that Apollos was an Alexandrian Jew and a learned and eloquent teacher of scripture (Acts 18:24-26), we have a plausible link between the religiosity of the Corinthians and that of Alexandrian Judaism as represented by Philo.[1]

In Acts, Paul is depicted as teaching Apollos about Jesus, but it remains peculiar, in consideration of the miracle-making Christ's purported fame as outlined in numerous scriptures,[2] that Apollos, a member of the large Jewish community in a major city not far from Judea, had never heard of Christ, as if he never existed!

Another possible connection exists with Paul's Ananias (Acts 22:12), who may represent a student of the Therapeuts at Alexandria, as may also the famous disciple Stephen. As concerns this development, de Bunsen remarks:

> ...Stephen, Paul, and Apollos we regard as promulgators of the universalist Alexandrian Gnosis of the Essenic Therapeuts, as applied to Christianity.[3]

The disciple Stephen, who is made to give a long speech that is in reality obvious propaganda by the author of Acts, and who is portrayed as murdered in front of Paul, is also depicted at Acts 6:9 as debating with some Alexandrian Jews, demonstrating their importance in the religious scene of the time.

Could it be that Paul's own Syro-Gnostic Christ was syncretized with the Alexandrian-Philonic Logos at Corinth, and then spread by Apollos throughout the *therapeutan* collegia network? If the theory about Apollos is correct, then the Therapeutae branches would be the same as the Christian churches in Paul's letters. Since we know that there existed mystery schools and religious brotherhoods in these very cities addressed in the Pauline epistles, it would not be surprising to find *them* both representative of the Therapeuts and engaged in the creation of Christianity.

Regarding the Therapeuts and early Christians, Lillie concludes:

---

[1] Pearson, *GJEC*, 171.
[2] See Mt 4:23-25, 5:1, 8:1, 8:18, 9:8, 9:31, 9:33, 9:36, 11:7, 12:15, 13:2, 14:1, 14:13, 14:22, 15:30, 19:2, 21:9, 26:55; Mk 1:28, 10:1; Lk 4:14, 4:37, 5:15, 14:25, etc.
[3] *MNQ*, XIII, 145

Eusebius, St. Jerome, Sozomenes, and Cassien, all maintained that monasteries in Christendom were due to the Therapeut converts of St. Mark, the first Bishop of Alexandria.... It is important that no writer in the early Christian Church could see any difference between a Therapeut and a Christian monastery. Without a doubt the three grades of Christian ecclesiastics—the ephemereut or bishop, the presbyter, and the diakonos [deacon], were derived from the three grades of Therapeut monks.[1]

From another early Church father we learn one more intriguing fact: "In the *Ecclesiastical Hierarchy*...Dionysius the Areopagite regularly uses the term 'therapeut'...in referring to monks."[2] In his *Ecclesiastical Hierarchy* (6.1), "Dionysius," supposedly writing to the disciple of Paul named Timothy, speaks about the "sacred Order of the Monks"—indeed the highest initiates—who are deemed by "our Divine Leaders" either "Therapeutae" or "Monks."[3] In fact, Dionysius claims that the term *therapeut* was the designation of the "third and highest grade of Christian initiation, the perfected adept," within the early church.[4] In addition, some of Dionysius's letters are addressed to one "Gaius Therapeutes," and in another epistle (8), the Church father again refers to the Christian rank of "Therapeutae." While these texts are considered forgeries from the fourth to fifth centuries in the name of one of Paul's disciples at Athens, they do reflect a fairly early instance of associating the term "Therapeuts" with Christianity, with the intent of making the association appear to be much earlier, reflecting also the ancient Church "forgery mill" that shamelessly cranked out pious propaganda for centuries.

Concerning the identification of the Therapeuts with early Christians, Mead summarizes the issue thus:

> The question, then, naturally arises: At such a date can the Therapeuts of Philo be identified with the earliest Christian Church at Alexandria? If the accepted dates of the origins are correct, the answer must be emphatically, No. If, on the contrary, the accepted dates are incorrect, and Philo's Therapeuts were "Christians," then we shall be compelled to change the values of many things.

> ...The Therapeuts, however, were clearly not Christians in any sense in which the term has been used by dogmatic Christianity; Philo knows absolutely nothing of Christianity in any sense in which the word is used to-day. Who, then, were those Christian non-Christian Essene Therapeuts? The answer to this question demands, in our

---

[1] Lillie, 241.
[2] von Balthasar, 300. The author is often called "Pseudo-Dionysius" or the "Pseudo-Areopagite" because he appears to be writing in the name of the disciple of St. Paul as found in Acts of the Apostles. (For information regarding the identify of Paul, see my books *The Christ Conspiracy* and *Suns of God*.) The works of Dionysius the Areopagite are considered to be fourth to fifth-century forgeries, as they do not appear in any writings prior to the sixth century. (See von Mosheim, 184-185.)
[3] Dionysius/Parker, 85-86.
[4] Lillie, 242.

opinion, an entire reformulation of the accepted history of the origins.

The dilemma is one that cannot be avoided. It is chief of all problems which confront the student of Christian origins. The Therapeuts have been recognized throughout the centuries as identical with the earliest Christian Church of Egypt. They were known to Philo at the very latest as early as 25 A.D., and they must have existed long before. If the canonical dates are correct, they could not have been Christians, in the sense of being followers of Jesus; and yet they were so like the Christians, that the Church Fathers regarded them as the model of a Christian Church. We are, therefore, confronted with this dilemma; either Christianity existed before Christ, or the canonical dates are wrong. From this dilemma there seems to me to be no escape.[1]

Hence, Mead understood this problem as acute to the study of Christian origins, possibly reflecting, in fact, that "Christianity existed before Christ." Mead is not alone in his queries, as others in modern times averred that the Therapeuts comprised the earliest Christian church at Alexandria. For example, Dr. Grant states:

The best precedent for the Christian schools of Alexandria seems to lie...among the Therapeutae by the Mareotic lake, described in Philo's work *On the Contemplative Life.*... Such Therapeutae would be ready for Alexandrian Christianity.[2]

As concerns this situation, Philo scholar Dr. David T. Runia, a master of Queen's College at the University of Melbourne, asks:

How could Philo's description of his Therapeutae so closely resemble what we know about early Christian monasticism, although this movement does not appear to commence until some 3 centuries later?[3]

And George Reber also raises pertinent questions:

If Christian churches are not indebted to the Therapeutae for their form of church government, from what source do they derive it? *Not* from the Jews; not from Paul; not from the Apostles.[4]

Conybeare likewise relates the problem with equating the Therapeuts with the Christians:

But, asked Bolingbroke and Voltaire, if the Therapeutae and the Palestinian Essenes were so similar to Christians in their lives and self-discipline, as to have been actually considered to be Christians by the fathers of the fourth century, what became of the claims of that religion to be an entirely new revelation? If men had already by their unaided efforts made themselves so like the primitive Christians, that the fathers themselves could not distinguish them therefrom, and if they had already reached this pitch of saintliness

---

[1] Mead, *DJL*, 337-338.
[2] Runia, 134.
[3] Runia, 32.
[4] Reber, 256.

before ever Christ was born into the world, what becam
supposed necessity for an incarnation of God, and for the g
Holy Spirit?[1]

The solution to these various problems with identifying the Therapeuts and the first Christians in Egypt, as well as their texts as the basis of the canonical gospels and epistles, lies in a "radical" analysis of the data concerning Christian origins along *strictly scientific lines*, without fervent faith or blind belief in the gospel story preventing us from seeing the facts. What we discover when we look closely at the evidence is that the gospel story represents a largely *fictional* account begun towards the end of the first century, and reworked and reformatted until the end of the *second* century, at which point it was solidly written into history and backdated to the beginning of the first century.[2] With these facts in mind, especially that there is no credible scientific evidence for the existence of Jesus Christ at any point, or for the existence of the four canonical gospels as we have them before the end of the second century, the pieces of the puzzle begin to fall neatly into place.

One of the pieces would be the allegorizing "short works" of the Therapeuts depicted by Philo around 20 to 30 AD/CE that possibly discussed the coming messiah or a spiritual savior not yet incarnate, Hellenized texts that were later Gnosticized and historicized in several different directions until they eventually ended up codified in the four canonical gospels at the end of the second century. Another, of course, would be the pre-existing Church structure complete with hierarchy and holidays that existed in Egypt and elsewhere, known by the name of "Therapeuts" and other designations.

Viewing this situation scientifically and logically, factoring in all the correspondences between the Egyptian and Christian religions, could we not reasonably conclude that, rather than having been instituted by a supernatural Jewish son of God, a significant part of Christianity constitutes the natural outcome of a Hellenizing and

---

[1] Conybeare, 325-326. Like other devout Christians, Conybeare believes that Eusebius, Jerome and Epiphanius were in error when they equated the Therapeuts with the early Christians, but this perspective is obviously influenced by the scholar's devotion to Christianity tradition, including accepting *a priori* that "Jesus of Nazareth" was a historical personage who was truly the founder of the Christian religion. In fact, Conybeare wrote a book attempting to refute the Jesus-mythicist position as outlined by J.M. Robertson, Arthur Drews and W.B. Smith. Conybeare's apparent reason, however, for dismissing what appear to be truthful admissions on the part of the Church fathers is that these would be fatal to the received Christian history. Thus, it was evidently Conybeare's belief in the faith in which he was raised, rather than a scientific analysis of all the data that led to his conclusions regarding the Therapeuts and Christians.

[2] This dating, of course, utilizes a convention, as there was no such BC/AD line drawn at the time, existing not until centuries later with the work of Dionysius Exiguus in the sixth century. Also, again, what is considered "pre-Christian" in some areas is much later than in others, the former of which not having been exposed to or affected by Christianity until centuries after Christ was supposedly born.

allegorizing Jewish sect living outside of Alexandria, home of the famed library possessing half a million texts from around the known world, including many discussing religion and mythology?

Lake Mareotis

As another piece of the puzzle of Christian origins, according to Philo the monastic class of persons existed around the Mediterranean, while "the" Therapeuts themselves specifically were headquartered at Lake Mareotis, a large and bustling waterway on the southern border of the city of Alexandria.

As we have seen, the existence of the Alexandrian Therapeuts has been questioned because they were evidently not named as such by anyone else, although in fact the term "therapeutae" *was* utilized to designate religious associations elsewhere, including on the small but important Greek island of Delos where Jews and Samaritans had a noticeable presence. Indeed, these systemata, synodoi, collegia or ecclesiae were found in numerous places, including the very sites where Paul allegedly founded "churches."

The reality of the Therapeuts has also been under suspicion because, if, as Philo states, they remanded all of their assets to their families and friends, they could not maintain themselves. Regarding the Therapeuts and their financial considerations, Conybeare remarks:

> The statement of Philo that the Therapeutae divested themselves of their property before joining the ascetic community, must not be taken too literally. Their houses, however humble...must have cost something. So must their common sanctuary, and even their diet of bread and salt and hyssop, though it was the everyday diet of the humbler inhabitants of Egypt. And if the statement at 483. 4, 5, that wine was not taken by them at their banquets on the Day of Pentecost and on its eve, be taken to mean that on other occasions they did allow themselves the use of wine, this would involve some further expense; even though the neighbourhood in which they lived was noted for the excellence and plenty of its wine. It is possible, however, that their co-religionists who remained in the world contributed to the support of so holy a confraternity. We can infer from Philo's references in the De Profugis that it was the rich in particular who joined the brotherhood. Probably they gave up the bulk of their fortunes, retaining just enough for their necessary wants.[1]

A feasible solution to the Therapeutan financial needs lies in the fact that Lake Mareotis was famous in ancient times for its wine production and the quality of its grapes, constituting a huge wine-making area full of grapevines and large grape-growing estates. Concerning Lake Mareotis, Strabo (17.1.14) reported that "the vintages in this region are so good that the Mareotic wine is racked

---

[1] Conybeare, 294.

off with a view to ageing it."[1] It is possible, therefore, that this Therapeutan community comprised *vintners* who made their living growing grapes and making wine.

With this fact of Alexandrian wine-making, we are reminded instantly of the New Testament tale of the wedding feast at Cana, which—not surprisingly—appears *only* in the (Egyptian) Gospel of John (Jn 2:1-11). The amphorae that would have held those 130+ gallons Jesus purportedly miraculously conjured up for the already half-drunk guests could also have been manufactured at Lake Mareotis, since there was an amphora-making industry there as well.

Naturally, *fishing* was likewise a big enterprise at the lake, which may explain in part the central focus in the gospels on fish. Indeed, Jesus himself was called *ichthys*, Greek for "fish," deemed by Tertullian the "Great Fish."[2] Interestingly, the speaker in a number of Coffin Texts is likewise the "Great Fish,"[3] and, as we may have expected, there were sacred fish in the Egyptian religion, such as the oxyrhynchus.[4] The fishy theme in the gospels also evidently has to do with the precessional Age of Pisces, into which we just happened to enter around the era when Christ allegedly walked the Earth. Indeed, not a few people have suggested that, rather than being a real person, Jesus Christ symbolizes the mythological "avatar" of the Piscean Age.

In any event, the finances of the Therapeuts could easily have been handled by commerce in local products, as well as donations from the Jewish population at Alexandria, including the wealthy Philo and his family, especially his brother Gaius Julius Alexander the "alabarch" or governor of Jews in that city, said to be the "richest man in the world" at the time.[5]

The Hybridizing Emperor?

During the centuries surrounding the era when Philo wrote about the Therapeuts, Greeks and Jews engaged in "extensive rioting" at Alexandria, which likely explains the push for their unification through the worship of hybrid gods such as Serapis. It is in this fractured environment that the idea for Christianity likewise evidently began to become formulated. Of course, various religious movements in Judea and Syria, as well as at Rome, also constituted factors in what eventually became Christianity. Indeed, Antioch and Jerusalem may be considered the "birthplace" of certain Christian ideas, while Alexandria served as the crucible of the Christian religion.

In 37 AD/CE, Emperor Caligula appointed as king of Judea the hated Herod Agrippa I—who owed a great deal of money to Philo's

---

[1] Strabo/Jones, 59.
[2] Tertullian, *On Baptism*, 1.
[3] See, e.g., CT Sp. 969 and 991. (Faulkner, *AECT*, III, 93, 100.)
[4] Wilkinson, *MCAE*, III, 341.
[5] Atwill, 343. See Josephus, *Antiquities*, 20.5.2.; Josephus/Whitson, 418.

wealthy brother in *Alexandria*[1]—an act that was the source of much Jewish unrest. This selection probably served as the seed of the anti-Herodianism that eventually made its way into Christianity, a new religion specifically created to remove these thorny issues from the Empire. After Judea broke out into troubles during the last half of the first century, Vespasian was appointed governor of Palestine by Emperor Nero (37-68 AD/CE). Once in Palestine, Vespasian was "surrounded by flatterers" and those who freely applied to him "the omens which were supposed to popularly point to a Jewish deliverer and Messiah."[2] Jewish general and historian Josephus, who knew Vespasian personally, having essentially surrendered to him, evidently found it expedient to spread the rumor that the future emperor was the "fulfillment of prophecy and the world's savior."[3] An apparently fictional account of the time depicts a Jewish faction led by Rabbi Yohanan ben Zakkai determining that Vespasian was the "king" predicted at Isaiah 10:34.[4]

Moreover, rumor has it that when future emperor Vespasian went to Mt. Carmel in Judea to visit priests in 69 AD/CE, he specifically discussed creating a hybrid religion that would unite Judaism and Paganism. The site of Mt. Carmel had been used for religious purposes as far back as 3,500 years ago, if not much earlier. By the time Vespasian visited Mt. Carmel, the altar to the Jewish tribal god Yahweh was being shared by the Greek god Zeus, among others. As stated by van der Toorn:

> In the fifth or fourth century BCE, Pseudo-Scylax described Mount Carmel as "the holy mountain of Zeus"...

> In 1952 Avi-Yonah published a late second- or early third-century CE inscription on a big marble votive foot, found in the monastery of Elijah (on the north-west side of mount Carmel), with a dedication to the "Heliopolitan Zeus of the Carmel."..[5]

Vespasian's "all-important meeting" on Mt. Carmel included the governor of Syria, Mucianus, as well as Basilides, a priest who was possibly a representative of the very wealthy nephew of Philo of Alexandria,[6] Tiberius Julius Alexander, the procurator of Judea under Claudius who later became prefect/governor of Egypt and Alexandria, eventually electing Vespasian emperor.[7] Tiberius's father was one of the only Alexandrian Jews granted Roman citizenship,

---

[1] Horbury, 878.
[2] Merivale, 114.
[3] Porter, *HOTNT*, 93.
[4] Porter, *HOTNT*, 89.
[5] van der Toorn, 183, citing Periplus, 104.
[6] Horbury, 878. Not only was Tiberius Julius Alexander the right hand man of Titus, Vespasian's son, but he was evidently responsible for the deaths of as many as 50,000 Jews, even though he himself was originally Jewish. (Horbury, 878.)
[7] See Scott, "The Role of Basilides in the Events of A.D. 69." See also Josephus, *Wars*, 4.10.6. (Josephus/Whitson,

which made Tiberius a citizen as well.[1] According to Josephus (*War*, 6.236), in what would seem a blasphemous act of betrayal, Tiberius became commander under Vespasian's son Titus and helped destroy Jerusalem, including the very temple his Jewish father had assisted in building.[2]

According to the Roman historian Tacitus (c. 56-c. 117 AD/CE), during this auspicious occasion on Mt. Carmel the priest Basilides sacrificed an animal and, after examining its entrails, told Vespasian: "Whatever are your designs, whether to build a house, to enlarge the boundaries of your lands, or increase your slaves, a mighty seat, immense borders, a multitude of men, are given to you."[3] This prophecy of good fortune and abundance was spread far and wide by Vespasian's underlings, to the effect that the Roman politician gained great esteem and confidence.

After this famed episode, Vespasian journeyed to Alexandria, where he entered the Serapeum alone, when suddenly Basilides appeared miraculously in front of him, along with "sacred leaves, chaplets, and cakes."[4] After this apparition, says the Latin historian Suetonius (69/75-c. 130 AD/CE) in "The Deified Vespasian" (*The Live of the Caesars*, 8.7.2), Vespasian performed the miracles of healing a blind man and a lame man in the name of Serapis.[5] Regarding Basilides, who was depicted by Suetonius as Vespasian's "freedman," Suetonius editor Forester notes:

> Tacitus describes Basilides as a man of rank among the Egyptians, and he appears also to have been a priest, as we find him officiating at Mount Carmel... This is so incompatible with his being a Roman freedman, that commentators concur in supposing that the word "libertus," although found in all copies now extant, has crept into the text by some inadvertence of an early transcriber. Basilides appears, like Philo Judaeus, who lived about the same period, to have been half-Greek, half-Jew, and to have belonged to the celebrated Platonic school of Alexandria.[6]

The fact of a half-Greek, half-Jew member of the Alexandrian Platonic school influencing the Roman Emperor is significant in our quest to determine how the Egyptian religion came to be rehashed in Christianity, since the latter faith largely constitutes a combination of Greek, Jewish and Egypto-Alexandrian ideology and mythology.

---

[1] Modrzejewski, 163, 185.
[2] Josephus, *War*, 5.1.6; 5.5.3 (Josephus/Whitson, 549, 555.)
[3] *The Works of Tacitus*, II (2.78); Tacitus/Oxford, 119. See Suetonius, II (8.5.5); Suetonius/Rolfe, 293.
[4] Suetonius/Thomson, 449; Suetonius/Rolfe, 297.
[5] Suetonius/Rolfe, 298-299; Suetonius/Thomson, 450.
[6] Suetonius/Thomson, 449. Some scholars, like Murphy, have believed that the two Basilides were separate individuals, the priest actually being a resident of Mount Carmel—a strange coincidence, unless it was a very common name. Scott is quite sure they are one and the same, i.e., the important Egyptian representative of Tiberius Julius Alexander, prefect of Egypt and nephew of Philo.

Also included in this analysis is a comparison of Vespasian's use of spittle to heal a blind man with the same miracle as Christ was said to have done at John 9:6, in a text that *post-dates* this episode with Vespasian. It is interesting to note that this *spittle* incident of curing a *blind* man occurs in the (Egyptian) gospel of John[1]—as if to compete with this famous miracle at Alexandria by Vespasian—the canonical text of which was nowhere to be found until the end of the first century, by conservative estimates. In reality, there is no hint of the existence of the canonical gospel of John as we have it until the end of the *second* century, so this famed spittle healing of Vespasian's was known to Alexandrians for over a century before hearing about the same miracle of Jesus Christ via John's gospel. Once more, it must be remarked that the gospel of John appears to have been written specifically to win over the Alexandrian followers of Egypto-Greco-Jewish-Gnostic religion by usurping their myths and legends and reworking them to revolve around a *fictional* Jewish messiah.

In actuality, it is quite evident from the blithe ignorance of all those involved in this story, including Vespasian and other emperors of the first century, that no such miracle-making godman as portrayed in the gospel tales had made any impact upon anyone, *as if he never existed.*[2] For example, when Vespasian was in Judea making pretenses to messiahship, one might imagine he would be besieged with agitators who believed that the messiah had already come, especially if Christ had not only existed but had done all the astounding miracles said of him, including healing the sick, multiplying fishes and loaves, raising other people and himself from the dead, with the bodies of "saints" pouring out of their graves and wandering the streets of Jerusalem, as well Christ ascending to heaven! Yet, there is no mention in any history of the era of any such agitation—which might have originated in the Jerusalem church, one might think, if *it* had really existed as such at the time. The gospel depiction of the Jewish and Roman milieus of the time of Jesus's purported advent becomes absurd and naïve when the true history and politics of the region are understood.

In any event, even after Vespasian's time, the unrest accelerated, with the destruction of the Jewish temple and Jerusalem in 70 AD/CE under Vespasian's son, Titus, and lasting well into the second century in Palestine and at Alexandria. During the reign of Trajan, the Jews continued to rabblerouse, seriously rebelling in 115 and then battling with Christians, even participating in the death of the

---

[1] At Mark 8:23, Jesus is also depicted as healing a blind man with spit.

[2] For further arguments on the mythical nature of Jesus Christ, including the utter dearth of evidence for his existence as a "real person," whether the son of God, a "political rebel," or "spiritual master," see my books *The Christ Conspiracy, Suns of God* and *Who Was Jesus?*

bishop of Jerusalem in 117.[1] Regarding the Jewish population at Alexandria, Dr. Runia remarks:

> There is...general agreement...that the dramatic events of 115-117 must have formed a watershed in the relations between Jews and Christians in the city. The Jewish community was pulverized to such a degree that all intellectual vitality was lost, and Hellenistic Judaism as it had developed in Alexandria appears virtually to have died out.[2]

In *The Jews of Egypt*, papyrologist Dr. Joseph Mélèze Modrzejewski, a professor of Ancient History at the Sorbonne, proposed that "if primitive Christianity had not left any marks on Egyptian soil until the end of the second century, it was because it had been annihilated along with the entire body in which it was immersed—the Jewish community of Alexandria."[3] At this point, Jewish Egyptian Christianity ceased and was replaced by Pagan Egyptian Christianity. Dr. Pearson does not find this perspective of "total rupture" to be convincing, however. In reality, the promulgation of this hybrid religion became even more urgent in Alexandria after the revolt against Trajan in 116. By this time, the rudiments of the messianic faith of Judea had been grafted onto Philo's Logos, and numerous elements of Paganism began to be incorporated into the tale. It is only in the early part of the second century that the major aspects of the Christian myth find their way into literature. Previously, we see only the Jewish Gnostic efforts by Paul and others, whose works do not reflect the gospel story as historical.[4] The Gnostic synthesizing efforts, in fact, are far more abundant at this time than are the Judaizing and historicizing endeavors found in later Christianity.

As demonstrated throughout the present work, much of Christianity can be shown to have its origin in Egypt, including and especially during this time. Regarding this troubled period, Ellen Brundige remarks:

> Christian thought was both refined and bizarrely altered during this turbulent era in Alexandria. Introduced by the Alexandrian St. Mark according to tradition, it was initially mistaken by the Emperor Hadrian as a troublesome offshoot of the cult of Serapis. Indeed, the Eucharist, resurrection, and reverence to the Mother were developed in Alexandria during this period, and seem to have echoes in the cult of Serapis, with its Dionysian-style feasting and resurrection, and his consort Isis/Cybele/Demeter.

As can be seen, rather than representing parts of a "true story," the "Eucharist, resurrection, and reverence to the Mother" are

---

[1] Flannery, 21, 36.
[2] Runia, 120.
[3] Modrzejewski/Cornman, 228.
[4] See Doherty's *The Jesus Puzzle* for an analysis of the value of the Pauline literature in demonstrating a "historical Jesus."

considered to have been "developed" at Alexandria, based on the cult of Serapis. Indeed, Christianity was perceived by Hadrian as an *offshoot* of that cult, an observation we believe was *not* mistaken.

While there may have been Christians at Alexandria during this period, those at Rome were so few that Hadrian's predecessor Trajan apparently had not even heard of them, if we accept as genuine the letter to him by the Roman historian Pliny the Younger (61/63-c. 113), who felt the need to explain to the emperor what Christians were.[1]

During Hadrian's time some 20 years later, in 135 AD/CE, the Jewish homeland was nearly completely destroyed, with the resultant end of Israel as a nation. It was at this point that Christianity as we know it truly began to be formulated, with various factions jockeying for position until the end of the second century when Catholic efforts essentially began to dominate within the Roman Empire, culminating with the officialization of the religion in the fourth century by Emperor Constantine. During this time—in particular in the critical second century—the religious concepts of Egypt, especially at Alexandria, exercised a great deal of influence on the organized Christian effort.

In actuality, the influence of the Egyptian religion upon the Roman *rulers* of the era was profound, beginning before the common era and, as noted, into the first century with Chaeremon and continuing. As historian and archaeologist Dr. Margarita Tacheva remarks:

> There is no room for doubt that the presence of many learned men from Egypt who maintained close contact with the emperors (e.g. Chaeremon of Naucratis or Dionysos of Alexandria in the period between the mid-1st and mid-2nd century AD) contributed to the popularity of the Egyptian cults at the Imperial court.[2]

Tacheva further states that the peak of this popularity of Egyptian religion among Romans occurred during the time of the emperors Antoninus Pius (reigned 138-161 AD/CE) and Marcus Aurelius (reigned 161-180 AD/CE)—precisely when the Alexandrian Gnostic-Christian efforts evidently bore the fruits of the canonical gospels, among other texts. Again, the fascination with all things Egyptian began much earlier, including among the elite, such as Augustus's daughter, Julia (39 BCE-14 AD/CE), who was "wild about Egyptian motifs, which she used in the decoration of her villa at Boscotrecase."[3]

The emperor Tiberius (42 BCE-37 AD/CE) was a follower of the Egyptian religion to such an extent that at Philae he created

---

[1] This letter is widely touted as evidence that Christ existed. However, its value as such as is nil, as explained in my books *The Christ Conspiracy, Suns of God* and *Who Was Jesus?*

[2] Tacheva, iii.

[3] Hornung, *SLE*, 69.

depictions of himself "smiting the enemies" in the sight of Isis, Horus, Hathor and a god named *Ha*.[1] Tiberius's reign occurred precisely during the purported advent of Christ, whose alleged miraculous endeavors, had they really occurred, would hardly have failed to impress the followers of the highly metaphysical and supernatural Egyptian religion. Yet, from all evidence, Tiberius was completely oblivious to Christ's alleged existence.

So fascinated was the infamous emperor Caligula with Egypt that he enjoyed imitating the pharaohs "(to the point of marrying his sister Drusilla!) and even considering making Alexandria his new capital."[2] Regarding other imperial influences, Hornung states:

> Claudius was also positively disposed toward Egyptian religion, and Nero expressed interest in the sources of the Nile. Nero also had an Egyptian teacher, Chaeromon, who saw to the dissemination of Egyptian knowledge at Rome. According to Suetonius, Otho (69 C.E.) was the first Roman emperor to participate publicly in the cult of Isis. Notwithstanding his well-known stinginess, Vespasian dedicated a large statue of the Nile to Rome, after a Nile miracle occurred during his visit to Alexandria in the year 69. Together with his son Titus, he spent the night before their triumph over Judea (71 C.E.) in the temple of the Roman Isis, which was first depicted on Roman coins that year. Titus is probably the anonymous "pharaoh" depicted in front of the Apis bull in the catacombs of Kom el-Shuqafa in Alexandria. From the reign of Domitian on, Apis was represented on imperial coins.[3]

To reiterate an important fact, according to Josephus (*Wars*, 7.123) our hybridizing emperor Vespasian and his son Titus spent the night before their victory over the Jews in a temple to Isis.[4]

Hornung continues with the list of emperors involved in some manner with Egypt and Egyptian religion, such as Trajan and Hadrian, the latter of whom actually "promoted Alexandrian religion" in a variety of ways including building Egyptian temples, while his young lover, Antinous, was sacrificed in the Nile and later depicted as a pharaoh.[5] As we have seen, the Egyptomania did not end there, as the two next emperors, Antoninus Pius and Commodus, were very fond of Egypt, the latter giving the Isis cult "considerable state support."[6] The last emperor to visit Thebes was the inquisitive Septimus Severus (145-211 AD/CE), in 199 AD/CE, when, according to the account (76, 13) of contemporary Roman historian Cassius Dio (c. 155 or 163/164-c. 229 AD/CE), Severus "took away from practically all the sanctuaries all the books that he could find containing any secret lore" and evidently enclosed them in the tomb

---

[1] Žabkar, 67.
[2] Hornung, *SLE*, 69.
[3] Hornung, *SLE*, 70.
[4] Josephus/Whitson (*Wars*, 7.5.4), 594; Maier, 916.
[5] Hornung, *SLE*, 70-71.
[6] Hornung, *SLE*, 71.

er the Great, "in order that no one in future should either
_____ander's body or read what was written in the above-
mentioned books."[1] This activity was followed sometime later by
emperor Diocletian (244-311 AD/CE) burning whatever may have been
left of Egypt's "secret lore."[2] Also according to Dio, just prior to
arriving in Egypt, Septimus had sojourned in Palestine, "where he
sacrificed to the spirit of Pompey," leaving us to wonder whom he
visited and what was discussed there.

In consideration of all that we have learned here, from the
blatantly obvious influence of the Egyptian religion on Christianity to
the fact of the canonical gospels not concretely appearing in the
historical record until the end of the second century, could it be that
what was contained in these "secret books" of Egypt would further
prove the Christian religion to be the remake of the Egyptian?

Under such circumstances as described here, it is obvious why
an emperor or emperors would make efforts to synthesize the many
faiths of Rome to unify the empire under one state religion, as we
contend happened with Christianity.[3]

The Library of Alexandria

The city of Alexandria where so much religion making occurred
represented one of the greatest seats of learning in the ancient world.
The renowned Library of Alexandria comprised several buildings
evidently spread out over a large area of the city, including the
smaller collections in the Serapeum and in the Caesareum. There
was also apparently a massive study hall near what is called the
Bruchium or Bruchion that may likewise have been part of the
University of Alexandria, which included the older Mouseion or
Museum as well. Although according to Plutarch (*Caesar* 43.6) the
library was destroyed in 48 BCE during a battle with Julius Caesar,[4] it
appears enough of it remained, or was replenished by the plundering
by Marc Anthony of the Pergamum library, to retain its significance
in the ancient world, since a few decades later the historian Strabo
conducted his own research in the Museum, which he deemed the
"finest library known in antiquity."[5] The collection remained intact
until the destruction by Emperor Aurelian in the last quarter of the
3rd century AD/CE. A portion of the library was said to have been
preserved in the Serapeum until its devastation by Christians under

---

[1] Dio/Cary, 225. See also Hornung, *SLE*, 71. Hornung cites this passage as being at "75, 13," whereas it actually appears at book *76*, section 13.
[2] Hornung, *SLE*, 71.
[3] For more on how this development was accomplished, see *The Christ Conspiracy*. Adding to the intrigue surrounding the founding of Christianity is the claim that early Church father Pope Clement I of Rome was married to Vespasian's granddaughter. (CE, *IV*, 14.)
[4] Plutarch/Perrin, 560.
[5] Tozer, 345.

Emperor Theodosius (347-395 AD/CE), although historian Marcellinus (325/330-c. 391 AD/CE) claimed it too had been destroyed by Caesar in 48 BCE.

Regarding the extensive Alexandrian library system, beginning with the Museum, which evidently housed the bulk of the library, Brundige states:

> Here 100 scholars lived, carried out new scientific research, published, lectured, performed the first systematic study of Greek literature (inventing the notions of accents and of grammar, a mixed blessing to some), edited, critiqued, and collected all Greek classics, and also gathered translations of Assyrian, Persian, Egyptian, Jewish, Indian, and other nations' literature, having nearly a million works in its holdings during the late Ptolemaic period. A second "daughter" library, the Serapeion, was soon established in the temple of Serapis, a popular god invented by the Ptolemies as a synthesis of Zeus, Pluto, Osiris, and the Apis bull. This library, found in the Rhakotis or Egyptian sector, was open to all, not just to royally pensioned scholars, and had copies of many of the Museum's scrolls.

Contrary to popular belief that depicts the origins of Christianity as having sprung up in a primitive vacuum of ignorance of the outside world, it was in *this* environment of monumental scholarly efforts involving hundreds of thousands of texts from as far east as India, at least, and encompassing practically all known literate cultures that Christianity truly was born. Knowing these facts, the popular picture of Christian origins with a babe in the manger in the little town of Bethlehem becomes erroneous at best and delusional at worst.

As concerns the cosmopolitan learning environment represented by the Alexandrian Library, Brundige also remarks:

> An intriguing dialogue between Pagan, Jewish, and, later, Christian thought developed among the scholars of Alexandria, as religious thought was refined and ideas adapted not only from the other theologies common in Alexandria, but from the Zoroasterism of Iran, and even through the founder of Neoplatonism, Ammonius, Buddhism and Hinduism from India.

In such an atmosphere, populated by various cultures and ethnicities, it would be highly logical to suggest that the many educated Jews, Hebrews, Israelites and Samaritans were likewise engaged in endeavors to refine and adapt religious thought from around the known world. Within the walls of the Library of Alexandria, therefore, existed numerous texts that quite possibly would have been used in the creation of Christianity, particularly vis-à-vis the Hellenized Egypto-Jewish community thriving there despite all odds and motivated by adversity to renew and reestablish itself. Indeed, we maintain that just such activity of refinement and adaptation, as evident from the writings of Philo and others, produced Christianity.

Philo of Alexandria

One of the writers whose works undoubtedly existed in the Library of Alexandria was Philo Judaeus, who repeatedly wrote about spiritual doctrines that would be familiar to followers and students of the Christian religion. Yet, Philo wrote before Christianity was created and was most definitely an influence on the Jewish religious thought that likewise preceded the true genesis of Christian religion. Although Philo was an Alexandrian native, his writings were widely disseminated and esteemed within both the Jewish and Gentile spiritual communities in Egypt and elsewhere—likely because of his own and his family's personal wealth, which would make such a costly endeavor possible. That Philo was influential within both Judaism and Christianity has been a source of great study over the centuries, and for the most part has been proved satisfactorily, although there remain those apologists who in spite of all evidence continue to deny the many obvious correspondences between Philonic ideology and Christianity.

Concerning the clear connection between Philo and the Christian religion, Dr. Pearson relates:

> [Theologian Dr.] Attila Jakab argues that it is among the Jews of education and Hellenistic culture—the spiritual heirs of Philo—where the first Christians must be sought. People of education and means, they probably included proselytes and God-fearers. They were the inheritors and transmitters of the works of Philo and of the Septuagint Bible. Their openness to Hellenistic culture also provided an environment in which Christian Gnosticism could thrive.[1]

Thus, Philo is indicated as a link between Judaism and Christianity—rather than the latter constituting a stunning, new "divine revelation" from God. Regarding the relationship of both religions to Philo, Runia states:

> Various scholars have pointed to the undeniable continuity between Judaism and early Christianity in Alexandria. In Philo a number of varieties of Judaism (even including an apocalyptic strain) are visible, and these may have exerted various kinds of influence on nascent Alexandrian Christianity.[2]

When we look closely, the facts reveal that Philo's writings unquestionably preceded the publication of *any* Christian work, that he possessed no apparent knowledge whatsoever of Christ, Christians or Christianity, that his work was popular in some of the very places where Christianity gained its greatest momentum, and that he was wealthy enough to be influential in his lifetime and long after. Knowing the fact that his writings bear an astounding amount of serious correspondences to Christianity, we can hardly go wrong

---

[1] Pearson, *GCRCE*, 16.
[2] Runia, 120.

by asserting that Christianity is founded in significant p
writings of Philo.

Space here will only permit us to explore a few more instances o
the concepts in the massive works of Philo that evidently found their
way into Christianity—or that served as a basis for that faith in
considerable part. As one example of Philo's pre-Christian
"Christianity," in "On the Confusion of Tongues" (*De Confusione
Linguarum*, XXVII, 146), the philosopher describes a "son of God":

> ...And even if there be not as yet any one who is worthy to be called a
> son of God, nevertheless let him labour earnestly to be adorned
> according to his first-born word, the eldest of his angels, as the great
> archangel of many names; for he is called, the authority, and the
> name of God, and the Word, and man according to God's image, and
> he who sees Israel.[1]

As we can see from this one paragraph—and there are many
other pertinent passages in his lengthy writings—Philo possessed the
seed of Christianity without having any inkling whatsoever that
anything or anyone remotely resembling his ideology had ever
existed. It is doubtless that Philo's son of God and Logos philosophy
existed *before* Christianity was ever heard of, serving, we contend, as
a major foundation for the creation of that religion, which truly took
place during the *second* century, based upon not only Philo but also
Gnosticism and the Egyptian religion, among other mythologies and
ideologies around the Mediterranean.

This Philonic portrayal thus represents a close description of the
character called Jesus Christ, whom we find in the later Christian
writings. Even though it was his passion to study and write about his
beloved Israel and Judaism, and he was in position to be well
connected and informed about the goings on within the Jewish
community around the Mediterranean, Philo was completely oblivious
to the claims that, precisely when he was writing these words, the
son of God and "first-born word" was allegedly walking the Earth,
causing great tumult and uproar with his miracles, manifestations
and troubles for the orthodox Jewish priesthood! Philo's homebase of
Alexandria was a mere 300 miles from Jerusalem as the crow flies,
and, at some point, Philo made a "pilgrimage" to "temple of his native
land" at Jerusalem ("On Providence," II, 64).[2] Yet, there exists nary a
word from him about Christ, Christians or Christianity.

In "On the Migration of Abraham" (*De Migratione Abrahami*, I, 6),
Philo describes the Word in greater detail:

> ...What, then, can it be except the Word, which is more ancient than
> all the things which were the objects of creation, and by means of
> which it is that the Ruler of the universe, taking hold of it as a
> rudder, governs all things. And when he fashioned the world, he

---

[1] Philo/Yonge, 247.
[2] Philo/Yonge, 755.

used this as his instrument for the blameless arrangements of all the things which he was completing.[1]

Once again, Philo portrays "the Word" or *Logos* in a very similar manner as applied to Jesus Christ. Nevertheless, when the Word purportedly became incarnate a few hundred miles away in Philo's ancestral homeland, he was completely unknown to the Jewish philosopher!

In "Who Is the Heir of Divine Things" (XXXIV, 165), Philo speaks of God thus: "And he apportioned cold and heat, and summer and spring, the different seasons of the year, divided by the same dividing Word."[2] In the same treatise (XLII, 205), Philo remarks:

> And the Father who created the universe has given to his archangelic and most ancient Word a pre-eminent gift... And this same Word is continually a suppliant to the immortal God on behalf of the mortal race...and is also the ambassador, sent by the Ruler of all, to the subject race. And the Word rejoices in the gift, and, exulting in it, announces it and boasts of it, saying, "And I stood in the midst, between the Lord and you..."

The Word as depicted basically represents the mediator between God and man, precisely as was said of Jesus (1 Ti 2:5). Yet, again, there is no acknowledgement from Philo that his alleged contemporary, Jesus of Nazareth, fulfilled this very role.

Philo continues to speak of the "divine word" and the "sacred word," which is responsible for many things in the cosmos, both the divisions and the bindings, sounding much like the Gnostic *Horos*. Even the "manna from heaven," so important for the survival of the Israelites in the small stretch of desert during the 40 years Moses allegedly led them around in circles, constitutes the "word of God."[3]

In "On Dreams That They Are God-Sent" (*De Somniis*, XV, 85), in reference to the biblical patriarch Joseph's supposedly "symbolical language," the Alexandrian sage states:

> But according to the third signification, when he speaks of the sun, he means the divine word, the model of that sun which moves about through the heaven...[4]

Thus, according to Philo, per Plato as well, the Word is the *sun*, just as we claim Christ—the remake in large part of the Egyptian *sun gods* Osiris and Horus—to have symbolized.

Even the virgin birth may have been incorporated into the gospel story not only because of the miraculous births of so many other gods and legendary men but also because of Philo's influence. As we have seen, the miraculous birth was a part of the mysteries, as

---

[1] Philo/Yonge, 253.
[2] Philo/Yonge, 290.
[3] "On Flight and Finding"/*De Fuga Et Inventione*, XXV-XXVI, 137, 139. Philo/Yonge, 333.
[4] Philo/Yonge, 372.

explained by the Jewish writer. Philo also focused heavily itself, including the God-bestowed "born-again" virginity many other instances, as described by Conybeare:

> The Words virgin, virginity, ever-virginal, occur on every other page of Philo... It is indeed Philo who first formulated the idea of the Word or ideal ordering principle of the Cosmos being born of an ever-virgin soul, which conceives, because God the Father sows into her his intelligible rays and Divine see, so begetting His only well-loved Son the Cosmos. [1]

The writings of the Church fathers themselves demonstrate familiarity with Philo's writings, including and especially the influential Clement of Alexandria, who was quite aware of the Jewish philosopher's works and found them to be useful to Christian doctrine, as can be readily seen in the extensive study done by Dr. Annewies van den Hoek, Lecturer in Greek at Harvard Divinity School, entitled *Clement of Alexandria and His Use of Philo in the Stromateis* and published in 1988 by E.J. Brill.

Concerning the correspondences between Christ's purported teachings and the doctrines of Philo, Dr. Alvar Ellegård, a historian at the University of Goteburg, remarks:

> ...Why should Jesus, as a Jew from Galilee, who according to the myth had never set foot outside Palestine, exhibit so many points of agreement with the learned hellenised Egyptian Jew? Again, the problem disappears if the Gospel story is rejected as history, and the Diaspora matrix of Christianity is admitted.[2]

In the end, Philo's very Christian-sounding theology *preceded* the formation of Christianity and quite likely contributed to it in major ways, as one part of the patchwork of religious, mythological and mystical concepts evidently rolled into one state religion.

The Hermetic Writings

Other texts that appear to have influenced Christianity can be found in the Hermetic or Trismegistic writings, also known as the Corpus Hermeticum, among others, attributed to the legendary Greco-Egyptian godman Hermes Trismegistus or "Thrice-Blessed."[3] Past scholarship has averred that the Corpus Hermeticum represents a third-century product featuring Neoplatonism, Kabbalism, and

---

[1] Conybeare, 302-303.

[2] Ellegård, 5.

[3] These Hermetic or Trismegistic texts are to be distinguished from the "the Egyptian 'Books of Thoth' and the Hermes Prayers of the popular Egyptian cult, as found in the Greek Magic Papyri, and also from the later Hermetic Alchemical literature..." (Mead, *TGH*, 3.) However, Corpus Hermeticum ("CH") expert Dr. William C. Grese avers that there is in fact more of a connection between the CH and the Hermetic magical literature than previously believed. (Grese, 1988, 49) The Trismegistic writings include other texts besides the CH, such as "The Perfect Sermon," also known as "The Asclepius," "Excerpts by Stobaeus"; and fragments of texts found in the early Church fathers and non-Christian philosophers. (Mead, *TGH*, 3.)

"plagiarism" from Christianity. However, the entire body of work cannot be considered to have emanated from one person but represents a *tradition* over a period of centuries in the name of Hermes Trismegistus as well as his counterpart in older Egyptian mythology, Thoth or Tehuti. Concerning the god Thoth/Hermes, Mead remarks:

> In the mystic sense Thoth or the Egyptian Hermes was the symbol of the Divine Mind; he was the incarnated Thought, the living Word— the primitive type of the Logos of Plato and the Word of the Christians...[1]

In the Hermetic mythology, it was said that Hermes/Thoth—the *Divine Word*—taught the sacred arts and mysteries to humanity. According to Dr. Richard Reitzenstein, a professor of Classical Philology at the University of Göttingen, this mythology dates back centuries before the common era:

> Reitzenstein...proceeds to show that in the oldest Egyptian cosmogony the cosmos is brought into being through the Divine Word, which Thoth, who seems to have originally been equated with the Sun-god, speaks forth.[2]

Thus, in the Hermetic writings, as in Plato and Philo, we possess the Divine Word/Logos, who is also the sun. In consideration of these facts, Mead appropriately calls this corpus "Archaic Gnosis,"[3] since the term *gnosis*, meaning "knowledge," is commonly reserved for esoteric philosophy and religion. Indeed, the concept of the Word and its relationship to the sun constitute one of the elements of a Gnosticism that long predates the common era, as well as serving as one of the mysteries. In this regard, Hornung relates that certain scholarship has traced the Hermetic tradition to "the priests of the temple of Thoth in Hermopolis of Dynasty 12 (c. 1938-1759 B.C.E.) who conceived of the Book of Two Ways, which can be called the first hermetic work..."[4]

The story of the Hermetic literature's survival presents a significant example of the peril in preserving texts that might possess knowledge unfavorable or challenging to the dogma and received history of the Catholic Church. Indeed, to circulate such texts when the Catholic Church was at its height of power could cause one to forfeit one's life; hence, those interested in such preservation were keenly aware that they must *denounce* the contents of the writings, regardless of whether or not they agreed with them. One possible example of this "duplicity" in the name of safeguarding life and liberty evidently occurred in the case of Michael Psellus of Byzantium, who was singlehandedly responsible for circulating anew the Trismegistic

---

[1] Mead, *TGH*, 27.
[2] Mead, *TGH*, 52.
[3] Mead, *TGH*, vi.
[4] Hornung, *SLE*, 5.

or Hermetic writings during the 11th century.[1] It is fortunate for us that Psellus, who appears to be criticizing these "heretical" texts, had the foresight to make the publication palatable enough for the Inquisitors that it *was* preserved. Yet, this example goes to show what scholars of the ancient world, in particular of the origins of Christianity, are up against in trying to find appropriate and reliable data. In addition, the Trismegistic literature in particular was "largely reserved and kept secret,"[2] as the public was "catered for" by omitting or denigrating anything that might affect popular faith.[3] What remains is, like so many other bodies of literature, merely a fraction of what was, much of it lost even in ancient times, as stated in the literature itself. If so much censorship had not occurred, in fact, we would have a much easier time demonstrating the thesis that Christianity in large part constitutes a rehash of Pagan and Jewish religious, spiritual and mythological concepts, using ancient texts such as the Hermetic or Trismegistic writings.

The age and origin of the Trismegistic writings are the subject of much debate, particularly because a significant amount of Christianity may have been founded upon this literature. Regarding their age, Mead says:

> The early Church Fathers in general accepted the Trismegistic writings as exceedingly ancient and authoritative, and in their apologetic writings quote them in support of the main general positions of Christianity.[4]

Because of their evident connection to Christianity, the Trismegistic writings were eventually rejected as "forgeries," such as by Edward Gibbon, who dismissed the entire class of literature along with the Orphic and Sibylline texts as a "cloak for Christian forgery."[5] After recounting that for over 200 years prior to his era these writings thus fell into disrepute as "Neoplatonic forgeries and plagiarisms of Christianity," Mead remarks:

> Finally, with the dawn of the twentieth century, the subject has been rescued from the hands of opinion, and has begun to be established on the firm ground of historical and critical research, opening up problems of the greatest interest and importance for the history of Christian origins and their connection to Hellenistic theology and theosophy, and throwing a brilliant light on the development of Gnosticism.[6]

---

[1] Mead, *TGH*, 7.
[2] Mead, *TGH*, 4.
[3] Mead, *TGH*, 24.
[4] Mead, *TGH*, 17.
[5] Mead, *TGH*, 23-24.
[6] Mead, *TGH*, 17-18.

lso concludes:

> lore attention is bestowed upon the Trismegistic writings, the
> is apparent that they cannot be ascribed to Neoplatonism...[1]

Although certain older scholars have dated the literature much earlier, such as Flinders-Petrie's range of 500-200 BCE, the extensive survey by more modern scholar Dr. William C. Grese reveals the widely accepted dates for the Hermetic texts to range from 200 BCE to 300 AD/CE.[2]

As concerns the origin of these texts, Champollion averred that the Trismegistic literature preserved ancient Egyptian religion, as well as the doctrines in Plato's Timaeus.[3] The French Egyptologist Théodule Devéria (1831-1871) proclaimed the Trismegistic literature as "an almost complete exposition of the esoteric philosophy of ancient Egypt."[4] The value of such an insight, of course, is twofold, as not only are these texts declared absolutely to be of Egyptian origin but the statement also serves as an acknowledgement that there existed an *esoteric philosophy in ancient Egypt*: That is, hidden doctrines or *mysteries*, which, we contend, constituted several of the most pertinent parallels between the Egyptian and Christian religions.

Explicating upon the origins of the Trismegistic literature, Mead comments:

> The fragments of the Trismegistic literature which have reached us are the sole surviving remains of that "Egyptian philosophy" which arose from the congress of the religious doctrines of Egypt with the philosophical doctrines of Greece. In other words, what the works of Philo were to the sacred literature of the Jews, the Hermaica were to the Egyptian sacred writings. Legend and myth were allegorised and philosophised and replaced by vision and instruction. But who were the authors of this theosophic method? This question is of the greatest interest to us, for it is one of the factors in the solution of the problem of the literary evolution of Christianity, seeing that there are intimate points of contact of ideas between several of the Hermetic documents and certain Jewish and Christian writings, especially the opening verses of Genesis, the treatises of Philo, the fourth Gospel (especially the Prologue), and beyond all the writings of the great Gnostic doctors Basilides and Valentinus.[5]

The clarification of the Hermetica being to Egyptian religion what Philo is to Judaism ranks as very helpful, as does emphasizing that the Trismegistic literature shows "points of contact" with Judaism and Christianity. These facts lead us to wonder precisely who *were* the authors of this syncretistic effort.

[1] Mead, *TGH*, 26.
[2] Grese, 35.
[3] Mead, *TGH*, 27.
[4] Mead, *TGH*, 28.
[5] Mead, *TGH*, 28.

In *Hermes Trismégiste*, Dr. Louis-Nicolas Ménard (1822-1901) discussed the Trismegistic literature as a combination of the efforts of the Jewish, Greek and Egyptian populaces specifically at *Alexandria*, representing the "missing link" between Philo and Gnosticism:

> Between the first Gnostic sects and the Hellenic Jews represented by Philo, there was missing a link: One can find it in some Hermetic books, particularly in the *Poimandres* and the *Sermon on the Mountain*; perhaps one may also find there the reason for the oft-noted differences between the first three gospels and the fourth.[1]

The Hermetic texts are thus intricately linked to the efforts of Gnosticism, especially in that both systems thrived at Alexandria, seat where so much of the creation of Christianity evidently took place. As Dr. Redford states:

> The only conduit, both geographical and spiritual, through which something of Ancient Egypt survived to enter the world of the European West, was Alexandria, that great intellectual and mystical hub of the world, wherein all beliefs, cults and philosophical systems thrived, often in a syncretistic amalgam. It is to Alexandria that we must look for the origins of two great systems of thought, Gnosticism and Hermeticism, in which a modicum of the Ancient Egyptian belief system survived the Middle Ages to re-emerge in the Renaissance.[2]

In "The Poemandres of Hermes Trismegistus," Dr. Frank Granger (1864-1936), a professor of Philosophy at University College in Nottingham, finds in Plutarch's writings about Osiris and Isis intimations of familiarity with the Hermetic literature,[3] which would mean, of course, that the pertinent concepts predated the time of Plutarch, who died around 120 AD/CE—*before* the canonical gospels as we have them clearly emerged in the historical record. Following Mead, the *Catholic Encyclopedia* ("Gnosticism") states that "Alexandrian non-Christian Gnosticism is perceptible in Trismegistic literature,"[4] likewise giving the literature a possible pre-Christian origin as well.

Also following these scholars, Reitzenstein argued that the provenance of the Hermetic literature was Egypt, eventually modifying his opinion to include Iranian influence. For some time after Reitzenstein, scholarly consensus took the origins of the Hermetic literature away from Egypt, agreeing, however, that there is no Christianity in the writings. After a long back and forth about whether or not there was Egyptian influence in the Hermetic literature, Doresse's publication of the Chenoboskion Gnostic texts, as well as the Nag Hammadi discovery, which included Hermetic writings, helped to reestablish a partial Egyptian origin for some of the Corpus Hermeticum (particularly as found in the text called "the

[1] Menard, xliv-xlv.
[2] Redford, xvii.
[3] Granger, 400.
[4] *CE*, VI, 600.

Asclepius").[1] In more modern times, Dr. Jean-Pierre Mahé (b. 1944), a member of the Institute of France, contended that "Hermetic sentences derived from similar elements in ancient Egyptian wisdom literature, especially the genre called 'Instructions' that reached back to the Old Kingdom..."[2] Regarding Mahé's conclusion, in *Hermetica: The Greek Corpus Hermeticum and the Latin Asclepius*, Dr. Brian P. Copenhaver, a professor of History at the University of California at Los Angeles, states:

> Mahé decided that the Gnostic content of the *Hermetica* is a secondary feature associated with commentary, a later overgrowth distinguishable from a primary core of Greco-Egyptian sentences formulated before Gnostic ideas had developed.[3]

Summarizing Mahé's work, Dr. Copenhaver asserts that "the greatest impact of his two volumes on *Hermes in Upper Egypt* is to re-establish an Egyptian ancestry for the *Hermetica*, three quarters of a century after Reitzenstein's 'Egyptomania.'"[4]

Copenhaver is convinced enough by the abundant evidence to pronounce in his "Introduction":

> It was in ancient Egypt that the *Hermetica* emerged, evolved and reached the state now visible in the individual treatises.[5]

Discussing a bias that has prevented the most scientific analysis of the situation, Copenhaver further addresses the efforts of scholars during the 20th century to show biblical inferences in the Hermetica, after which he remarks that "the possibility of influence running *from* Hermetic texts *to* Christian scripture has seldom tempted students of the New Testament."[6] In this regard, Morenz remarks:

> Egypt's links with the religion of the Old Testament have been known and studied for a long time. But hardly any consideration has been given to the fact that the religious forms of the land of the Nile also had an effect upon the New Testament and so upon early Christianity. Such a lack of interest can scarcely be due to dogmatic reservations, for if this were so such a ban would also have affected investigations into the contributions of Greek philosophy and the Hellenistic mystery religions, which have long since been recognized. It is rather the case that scholars have failed to appreciate the influence which Egypt had exerted upon the entire Hellenistic world in which Christianity was destined to take shape.[7]

In consideration of various notorious episodes suffered by those who have in fact endeavored to outline comparisons between the Egyptian and Christian religions, Morenz may be too optimistic in his

---

[1] Copenhaver, lvi.
[2] Copenhaver, lvii.
[3] Copenhaver, lvii.
[4] Copenhaver, 95.
[5] Copenhaver, xvi.
[6] Copenhaver, lviii.
[7] Morenz, 253.

assessment. In any event, although we possess no such bias as Copenhaver discusses that prevents us from looking for influence *from* the Hermetica *upon* Christianity, an exhaustive study of the issue would require significant time and space. Hence, we will rely here on the insights of certain other scholars, such as Mead, who did not shrink from conclusions that contradicted received Christian history. In any event, the final word on the subject of the provenance of Trismegistic literature, as stated by Dr. Garth Fowden of the National Hellenic Research Foundation in Athens, is that "Hermetism was a characteristic product of the Greek-speaking milieu in Egypt"[1]—in other words, the Hermetica constitute a Greco-Egyptian product, precisely as Mead and others had evinced over a century ago.

The Poimandres

One of the most prominent Hermetic or Trismegistic texts is called the "Poimandres" or "Poemandres," widely interpreted to mean "Shepherd of Man," but also perhaps more fittingly as "the knowledge of the Sun-God (*Ra*)."[2] The *Poimandres* is known in scholarly circles as "Corpus Hermeticum I" ("CH I"), concerning which Spence comments:

> The "Poimandres," on which all later Trismegistic literature is based, must, at least in its original form, be placed not later than the first century. The charge of plagiarism from Christian writings, therefore, falls to the ground. If it can be proved that the "Poimandres" belongs to the first century, we have in it a valuable document in determining the environment and development of Christian origins.[3]

Prior to Spence, Mead had reached the same conclusion as concerns the *Poimandres*:

> The theory of plagiarism from Christianity must for ever be abandoned. The whole literature is based on the "Poemandres" as its original gospel, and the original form of this scripture must be placed at least prior to the second century A.D.[4]

When these scholars say that the *Trismegistic* literature is based on the *Poimandres*, they are addressing a narrow genre that does not include all the Hermetic texts, a number of which predate the common era.

Mead places the *terminus ad quem* or latest possible date of composition of the *Poimandres* at the beginning of the second century. Copenhaver provides the argument that the *Poimandres* is apparently related to the work of Valentinus, but that it likely

---

[1] Fowden, 213.
[2] Cartlidge, 239.
[3] Spence, *AEO*, 209.
[4] Mead, *TGH*, 43.

predates his era, with the best evidence of an early second-century or possible late first-century date.[1]

In reality, the cosmology behind the *Poimandres* is ancient, dating to at least 700 BCE, as found on an Egyptian inscription that itself claimed to be reproducing an older text.[2] It is intriguing that in this "Prayer to Ptah," reproduced in the "Memphite Theology," the "heart" and "tongue" of Ptah—"God the Father"—are Horus and Thoth,[3] the latter being the "Word" or Logos, long prior to the common era. Horus as the Heart of "God the Father," of course, reminds us of the "Sacred Heart of Christ."

Demonstrating both its Platonic and Gnostic relevance, in the *Poimandres* we find the Archons as the seven planets, while in Plato the "subaltern demiurgic gods, among whom are the heavenly bodies," are likewise called Archons (αρχοντες).[4] In this regard, it is interesting to note that in Coffin Text spells 550 and 1026 appear references to "seven gods."[5] The *Poimandres* as we have it seems to have been Judaized and, if not Christianized, certainly would represent a link between the Egypto-Jewish "Gnostic" or Platonic/Philonic efforts and Christianity.

The Egyptian origin of the *Poimandres* has also led to the opinion that the author was a *Therapeut*.[6] Dr. Ménard, for example, specifically names the *Poimandres* as constituting a text out of the Therapeutan sect.[7] Ménard places the *Poimandres* significantly earlier than the formation of the Gnostic sects by Basilides and Valentinus, which occurred shortly after the composition of the Hermetic text called "The Sermon on the Mountain."[8] Ménard also avers that the Therapeuts eventually disappeared into Christianity, Gnosticism and Paganism, a sensible assessment, although some of them, of course, could likewise have joined the mainstream Jewish community as well.

Reflecting the Greco-Jewish coloring of the text, Dr. Granger relates that the third chapter of the *Poimandres* bears a Platonic origin, styled after Philo, "as a commentary upon *Genesis* i-iii."[9] While the *Poimandres* therefore possesses both Greek and Jewish character, as well as Egyptian, since it is clearly about Egyptian mythology, there is nary a trace of the Christian scriptures or any aspect of a life of Christ—in fact, no mention whatsoever of Christ,

---

[1] Copenhaver, 95.
[2] Mead, *TGH*, 130.
[3] Mead, *TGH*, 131-133.
[4] van den Broek, 271.
[5] Faulkner, *AECT*, II, 138; III, 125.
[6] Mead, *TGH*, 26.
[7] Ménard, lvi.
[8] Ménard, lix, lxv. Other than the title, this text bears little resemblance to the famous biblical "Sermon on the Mount," although it is a highly spiritual and lofty tractate worthy of reading.
[9] Granger, 403.

Christians or Christianity. Indeed, demonstrating that the borrowing occurred in the opposite direction, Granger —an apparently devout Christian—remarks upon "how the Greek representations of Hermes furnished Christian art with one of its earliest motives."[1] Granger also states:

> The functions of Hermes in Greek religion, and of Thoth in Egyptian religion, offered a sufficiently close analogy to the mission of Jesus, and Christian writers hastened to make use of this analogy.... Now since the *Poemandres* belongs to the same school of thought, we need not be surprised to find that Jesus is represented under the figure of the Egyptian Hermes.

> Since then, the identification of Jesus with Hermes took place in circles which formed part of the Christian community, we shall not be surprised to find that one of the leading types of Christian art, the Good Shepherd, was immediately adapted from a current representation of the Greek Hermes...[2]

Thus, we find in the *Poimandres*, or the "Shepherd cycle"—which predates the clear emergence of the canonical gospels—indications for the identification of Christ with Hermes, the pre-Christian Greco-Egyptian Divine Word and Good Shepherd.

Granger's insights further lead us to a connection between the *Poimandres*—which, again, Ménard identified as *Therapeutan*—and Gnostic Christianity:

> We now approach what is perhaps the most important contribution which the *Poemandres* makes to our knowledge: namely the light which it throws upon the *Gospel according to the Egyptians* and the *Logia Jesu*.[3]

Granger goes on to demonstrate how widely known was the Gospel of the Egyptians, which was used by the Gnostic Valentinians, for one. He also avers that the author of the *Poimandres* used the Gospel of the Egyptians, from which he further suggests were taken the *Logia Iesu*, or "Sayings of Jesus."[4] We would submit that the evidence, however, may allow for the opposite to be the case, the *Poimandres* preceding the Gospel of the Egyptians and serving as a basis thereof.

The connection between the *Poimandres* and Christianity has been remarked upon many times and is so evident that, as we have seen, the Hermetic text has been considered a "Christian forgery" or, at least, a plagiarism from Christianity. However, as we have also seen, concepts in the *Poimandres* are very old, dating to several centuries before the Christian era in Egypt. Moreover, there is no scientific evidence to show specific Christian influence upon the *Poimandres* and, incorporating the rest of the facts, we may logically

---

[1] Granger, 395.
[2] Granger, 407-408.
[3] Granger, 409.
[4] Granger, 410.

conclude that Christianity was built upon such texts as the *Poimandres*, rather than the other way around.

When faced with the parallels between Christianity and the Trismegistic literature as a whole, it is noticeable that the latter, while possessing what appear to be "Christian" concepts, contains nothing of the gospel story, "not a single word breathed of the historical Jesus,"[1] and so on. Hence, with all factors, logic suggests that if there be any borrowing, it is *from* the Hermetic tradition *by* the Christian effort—and we would evince that rather than simply "borrowing" the two endeavors were intertwined, with one leading into the other.

The Gnostics

From the Therapeuts, Philo and the Hermetic literature, we move on to the organized movement of Gnosticism, which developed alongside Christianity, as both a sibling and a competitor. Over the centuries, many writers have speculated upon a pre-Christian Gnosticism of sorts, because several of Gnosticism's defining characteristics have their roots in the hoary mists of time, in writings such as those of Plato, as well as in Egyptian mythology, among others. As Hornung says, "Gnosis, one of the chief forms of syncretism in late classical antiquity, drew on every area of culture in its day, including the *Iliad* and the *Odyssey*."[2] Concerning the origins of formalized Gnosticism, Gnostic text expert Doresse remarks, "Gnosticism appeared originally in Syria. It is in Samaria and the valley of the Lycos that we trace it for the first time."[3] Doresse next names the first Gnostics as Simon, Menander, Satornil, Cerdon and Cerinthus—all from the Syro-Samaria/Palestine area. One individual who evidently brought Gnostic ideas into the early Church at the Syrian city of Antioch was Nicolas, founder of the dreaded Nicolaitans, as discussed at Acts 6:5, as well as at Revelation 2:6 and 2:15-16.

Regarding Gnosticism and Simon in particular, Hornung relates:

With its origins at least in part on Egyptian soil—Simon Magus, one of its founding fathers, was supposed to have acquired his learning in Egypt—and with Alexandria as one of its most important centers, it also incorporated concepts from pharaonic Egypt.[4]

As examples of these pharaonic concepts, in discussing the nature of Divinity within Egyptian religion, Griffiths first notes that one of the oldest forms of God in Egypt was Atum, who brought forth offspring without a female consort, asking whether or not he should

---

[1] Mead, *TGH*, 35.
[2] Hornung, *SLE*, 43.
[3] Doresse, 13.
[4] Hornung, *SLE*, 43.

"therefore be regarded as an androgynous deity in the strictest sense..."[1] Griffiths continues:

> [Dutch Egyptologist Dr. Jan] Zandee's admirable study (1988) posits this view forcefully, and he adduces many Gnostic points. God as mother-father or father-mother is often present in varied periods of Egypt's literature... It was especially evident in Amarna and pre-Amarna hymns... In Elaine Pagels' *The Gnostic Gospels...*, there is an eloquent chapter on "God the Father/God the mother," but with no mention of the strong Egyptian background.[2]

Griffiths's remarks reveal some important notions, for example that Egyptian religion contained sophisticated ideas later found in Gnosticism, as we have also already seen abundantly in this present work.

In *Two Powers in Heaven*, Dr. Alan F. Segal, a professor of Religion at Columbia University, cites the work of Dr. Moritz Friedlander, who "put forth the thesis that gnosticism is a pre-Christian phenomenon which originated in antinomian circles in the Jewish community of Alexandria."[3] Citing the conclusion of various scholars that Gnosticism "grew out of Jewish thought that had absorbed Indo-Iranian themes," Segal remarks: "Based on this consensus, many New Testament scholars feel that Christianity actually adapted a pre-existent gnostic savior myth to the facts of Jesus' life."[4] As we can see from the abundant evidence presented here, there is very good reason to believe that Christianity is in significant part an adaptation of pre-Christian myths.

Pearson also explores this thesis of pre-Christian Gnosticism:

> This Gnosticism, against which Philo polemicizes, came early to Palestine; and the rabbinic polemics against the Minim [outsiders] are directed specifically at such Gnostics. Christian Gnosticism is simply a secondary version of the older Gnosticism, which attached itself to the emergent Christian sect and appropriated for itself the figure of Jesus Christ.[5]

Dr. Friedlander's timeline puts "heretical" Jewish Gnosticism in Palestine by at least the early first century AD/CE.[6] Several pre-Christian Jewish texts demonstrate this development, including, Pearson asserts, the "tractate *Eugnostos the Blessed*," which "reflects the existence in the first century of a Jewish Gnosticism..."[7] In any event, the Gnostics preceded the Christians.

Moreover, we would submit that, as Jews who followed the Old Testament scriptures, these particular Gnostics already possessed

---

[1] Redford, 252.
[2] Redford, 252.
[3] Segal, 15. The "antinomian circles" were those who opposed the Mosaic law.
[4] Segal, 15.
[5] Pearson, *GJEC*, 11.
[6] Pearson, *GJEC*, 16.
[7] Pearson, *GJEC*, 18.

1 or allegorical "Anointed Savior"—as is the meaning of the
Jesus Christ"—decades before "Jesus of Nazareth" was
created. The words "Jesus" and "Christ," in fact, would have been
very familiar to the Greek-speaking Jewish population at least two
centuries before the common era, after the Old Testament/Tanakh
was translated into Greek. In the Septuagint, the word "Jesus"—
meaning "God is salvation"—appears wherever the name "Joshua" is
used, while, again, "Christos" can be found at least 40 times in
relation to God's anointed priests and kings. The Hebrew word for
"salvation" in the OT, as used in regard to God (2 Sam 22:3), for
example, is *yesha*, while "savior" is *yasha*—both terms essentially the
same as *Jesus*, which in the OT is *Yeshua* or *Yehoshua*, etc.[1]
Salvation is a repeated theme throughout the OT, with the word
yasha used over 200 times. Thus, the concepts of anointing and
salvation were highly significant to religious Jews in the pre-
Christian era, and are to be found in the intertestamental literature
that undoubtedly influenced Christianity.

Regarding the origins of Gnosticism, Pearson concludes: "The
evidence continues to mount that Gnosticism is not, in its origins, a
Christian heresy, but that it is, in fact, a Jewish heresy."[2] He further
remarks, "There is a strong case to be made for the view that ancient
Gnosticism developed, in large part, from a disappointed messianism,
or rather as a transmuted messianism."[3] So, too, we aver, did
Christianity develop in precisely the same way—as an offshoot of this
Jewish mysticism, combined with Pagan philosophy, religion and
mythology, increasingly historicized and Judaized to the point where
what was a mythical messiah was claimed to be "historical."

At the time when Christianity began to be formulated, there had
been a long trend within Judaism to allegorize the scriptures and to
integrate Hellenistic philosophy into the faith. This effort, it is evinced
by Drs. Friedlander, Pearson, et al., produced Judaic Gnosticism.[4] As
one example, the Gnostic figure of Sophia or personified "Wisdom" is
pre-Christian, appearing in the works of the Alexandrian Jew Philo,
as we have seen.[5] Philo was building upon concepts in the Old
Testament, in which Wisdom is called *Hokmah* or *Chokmowth*—
"Sophia" in the Septuagint, personified in various scriptures, such as
at Proverbs 9 and elsewhere. Presenting a brand of Gnosticism that
was the self-deprecating sort or "mortification of the flesh" which
later dominated both Gnostic and Orthodox Christianity, Philo
attempted to distinguish between true and false *gnosis*, and was
already aware of at least one "Gnostic" sect, i.e., that of the Cainites,[6]

[1] Strong's H3091.
[2] Pearson *GJEC*, 26.
[3] Pearson, *GJEC*, 28.
[4] Pearson, *GJEC*, 12ff.
[5] Pearson, *GJEC*, 13.
[6] Pearson, *GJEC*, 13.

against whom he wrote, as did the Church fathers following h...
a century later. As Pearson says: "There can be no doubt that the
heretics combated by Philo are the forerunners of the Christian
Gnostics later combated by the church fathers..."[1]

Named among these pre-Christian Gnostic sects that came out of
the Diasporic Jewish community are not only the Cainites but also
the Ophites and Sethians, listed by Christian Bishop Filastrius or
Philastrius (d. 397 AD/CE) "among the sects that flourished in
Judaism 'before the advent of Jesus.'"[2] Ophitism was the most
important Jewish Gnostic heresy to arrive in Palestine prior to
Christ's purported existence.[3] Friedlander suggests that the pre-
Christian Jewish-Gnostic cult of Melchizedek was the starting point
for Christian Gnosticism, and he opines that the author of the
canonical Epistle to the Hebrews was Alexandrian and involved in
Melchizedekiniasm.[4] The "various Jewish or Baptist sects, such as
the Essenes, Galileans, Ebionites, Samaritans, Nazarenes," are also
the forerunners of the main Gnostic sects, including that of the
Egyptians Basilides and Valentinus, according to Church father
Hegesippus.[5] It is interesting to note that some of the sects involved
in or contributing to early Christianity, such as the Pythagoreans,
Essenes, Ebionites and Nazarenes, evidently possessed a peculiar
revered symbol in common: The *ascia*, or mason's trowel,[6] indicating
an intriguing *masonic* connection among the brotherhoods.[7]

The movement of Syro-Palestinian Gnosticism into Egypt
occurred during the reign of Emperor Hadrian (117-138 AD/CE),
which makes sense in that it was also during this period that much
of Palestine and Judea were destroyed, forcing another Hebrew
diaspora. At this point, Gnosticism began to thrive at Alexandria
under Basilides, Carpocrates and Valentinus, before migrating to
Rome, where it threatened the budding orthodox Christian effort.

During this second century, Gnosticism in Egypt depended
significantly upon not only Philo but also Plato, as well as traditional
Egyptian religion and Greek philosophy. Indeed, the Gnostic
Valentinus was accused by his detractors of "having stolen doctrines
from Pythagoras and still more from Plato,"[8] and the "general
consensus of opinion is that Valentinus must have known Philo's
writings."[9] Valentinus, of course, was Alexandrian, as was Basilides,
both of whom were responsible for much of the predominant Gnostic

---

[1] Pearson, *GJEC*, 14.
[2] Pearson, *GJEC*, 14.
[3] Pearson, *GJEC*, 17.
[4] Pearson, *GJEC*, 15.
[5] Doresse, 7.
[6] Doresse, 91.
[7] See "The Mysterious Brotherhood" in my book *Suns of God*.
[8] Doresse, 26.
[9] Runia, 125.

thought. As Eusebius says, "Basilides the heresiarch was living in Alexandria; from him derive the Gnostics."[1] Basilides is also named in a Christian polemic, *The Acts of Archelaus*, as having been influenced by Persian doctrines.[2]

Despite the claims of Church fathers, as well as their uncritical acceptance by modern scholars, there is no scientific evidence that Basilides's "Commentary on the Gospels" utilized any of the four canonical gospels, which, in fact, seem not to have been in existence by his time.[3] What is interesting, however, is that Basilides evidently discussed the "parable of Lazarus and the rich man," which is of apparent Egyptian origin, based on the myth of Osiris. If Basilides did indeed discuss this myth, and we have no reason to believe he did not, it may have been *his* text used by Luke (Lk 16:19-31), rather than the other way around.

In his analysis, Morenz likewise cites the story of Lazarus in Luke as being accepted by the mainstream as originally from the Egyptian religion, explaining that in this case the Egyptian ideation had gone through Judaism first.[4] Naturally, that fact is precisely the point, that Christianity is largely the product of Egyptian religion being Judaized and historicized. Morenz also describes the Epistle of James as "originally Egyptian," demonstrated through a word analysis. In addition, Morenz includes in this process that produced the New Testament and Christianity "Greek elements (Stoic diatribes)..."[5] He also definitively states that the clear way in which the Egyptian religion influenced Christianity was through its previous impact on the Jewish scriptures and apocrypha. Morenz further says, "Finally, the path taken by Egyptian influence can also be followed where the Christian form can be traced back first to an Egypto-Hellenistic one, and this in turn traced back to Egypt itself."[6] The German Egyptologist then provides several examples of these Egypto-Hellenistic precedents to Christian concepts, before progressing to a section entitled, "Egypt's significance for early Christian theology."[7]

Regarding the influence of *Alexandrian* religion in particular on Christianity, Morenz remarks:

> Without abandoning our principle that the Egyptian influence made itself felt as an undercurrent throughout Hellenism, we may nevertheless claim price of place for Alexandria and so consider

---

[1] Pearson, *GCRCE*, 22-23.
[2] Doresse, 7.
[3] For a thorough and scientific analysis of whether or not Basilides's "Commentary" was on the *canonical* gospels, see Cassels, 322-330.
[4] Morenz, 254.
[5] Morenz, 254.
[6] Morenz, 254.
[7] Morenz, 255.

Alexandrian theology as the intermediary between the Egy, religious heritage and Christianity.[1]

As concerns possible influence of Egyptian Gnosticism on the canonical gospels, in discussing the "more ordinary" of the Christian apocrypha found in the Gnostic cache at Chenoboskion, Doresse remarks:

> ...certain elements in them may have come from a fund of traditions that were current before the compilation of the Synoptics, all the more probably because of the fact that our Gnosticism came into being in a period when the canonical Gospels were not yet in general circulation.[2]

The "Synoptics" refers to the first three canonical gospels, Matthew, Mark and Luke, styled as such because they "see together," containing much of the same material, while the gospel of John is the odd-man out.

In regard to Gnosticism preceding orthodox Christianity in Egypt, theologian and scholar of Christian origins Dr. Walter Bauer (1877-1960), a professor at the Universities of Breslau and Göttingen, evinced that that the "earliest form of Christianity in Egypt was heretical, specifically Gnostic, a fact that later ecclesiastical leaders repressed."[3] Pearson pronounces this conclusion as possessing a "certain plausibility in that the earliest Christian teachers active in second-century Alexandria of whom we have any information were the archheretics Valentinus, Basilides and his son Isidore, and Carpocrates and his son Epiphanes..."[4] Bauer's theory, however, remains problematic in consideration of the existence of the "earliest attested Alexandrian Christian literature": For example, the Epistle of Barnabas, written sometime between 70 and 135 AD/CE, and the Gospel of the Hebrews, composed during the second century. However, if we consider the Therapeuts as "original Christians" and their *allegorical* short works as the basis for the gospels, then certainly we would say that a sort of Gnosticism preceded the orthodoxy, if by "orthodoxy" is meant the historicizing, as opposed to allegorizing, Christianity.

Concerning the Gospel of the Hebrews and that of the Egyptians, Pearson states:

> The *Gospel of the Hebrews* was used by the Alexandrian Jewish Christians and reflects not only a special allegiance to James, but also the influence of Alexandrian Jewish wisdom theology.... The *Gospel of the Egyptians* was used by a group of Greek-speaking Egyptian Christians, probably residents of Rhakotis, the native Egyptian section of Alexandria. This group, as seen in its gospel, was oriented to asceticism and may indeed have been influenced by the

---

[1] Morenz, 357.
[2] Doresse, 304.
[3] Pearson, *GCRCE*, 13.
[4] Pearson, *GCRCE*, 13.

Jewish Therapeutae who lived west of Alexandria and whose communal life is described by Philo in *On the Contemplative Life.*[1]

As can be seen, this conservative Christian scholar makes an association between the Therapeuts and those Christians who used (and possibly wrote) the Gospel of the Egyptians. As noted, the Gospel of the Egyptians was utilized by the Valentinians; hence, it would represent a link between the Gnostics, the orthodox Christians and the Therapeuts.

Like the Therapeuts, apparently, the Gnostics recognized not only the personified Wisdom or Sophia but also the Goddess in general: "The Gnostics were *par excellence* worshippers of the supreme Mother-goddess, the Μητηρ [Meter], in whom we have no difficulty recognizing the characteristics of the goddess of heaven of anterior Asia."[2]

The Pistis Sophia

Speaking of Sophia, another possible connection between the Therapeuts, Gnostics and Christians occurs with the famous Gnostic-Christian text the *Pistis Sophia*, extant in the Egyptian Sahidic dialect but, Mead evinces, originally written in Greek.[3] The *Pistis Sophia* has been variously dated across several centuries, from the late second century to the 10th century AD/CE, while current mainstream scholarship places it in the beginning to middle of the third century. The text possesses "some of the mystic dreamy opinions of the Gnostic Christians,"[4] while the "strict fidelity to the biblical text" of Psalms in the *Pistis Sophia* reveals the Jewishness of the authors of that part of the text, which otherwise represents a "free invention."[5]

The Egyptian origins of the *Pistis Sophia* are described in great detail by Massey in *Ancient Egypt: Light of the World* (597-604), in which he subscribes to the older thesis that the *Pistis Sophia* was composed by Valentinus, preceding the clear emergence of the canonical gospels into the historical record. As can be seen from Massey's analysis, the *Pistis Sophia* plainly incorporates Egyptian mythology into a Christian framework:

> *Pistis Sophia*, like the Ritual [Book of the Dead], is mainly *post-resurrectional*, with the briefest allusion to the earth-life. It begins with the after-life in which Jesus has risen from the dead, like Amsu the good shepherd. It opens with the resurrection on the Mount of Glory, the same as the Ritual. The localities, like those in the Egyptian book, are not of this world. They are in the earth of eternity, not in the earth of time. *Pistis Sophia* begins where the Gospel story

[1] Pearson, *GCRCE*, 17.
[2] *Enc. Brit.*, 853.
[3] Mead, *PS*, xvi.
[4] Sharpe, *HE*, 316.
[5] Cheyne, 5008.

comes to an end. Jesus rises in the Mount of Olives, but not on the mount that was localized to the east of Jerusalem. The Mount of Olives, as Egyptian, was the mountain of Amenta. It is termed Mount Bakhu, the Mount of the Olive-tree, when the green dawn was represented by this tree instead of by the sycamore. Mount Bakhu, the Mount of the Olive-tree, was the way of ascent to the risen Saviour as he issued forth from Amenta to the land of spirits in heaven. (Rit., ch. 17). So when the Egypto-gnostic Jesus takes his seat upon the Mount of Olives or the Olive tree, he is said to have "ascended into the heavens." Jesus "descended into hell," according to the Christian creed. This forms no part of the Gospel-legend, but we find it in the Book of the Dead; also in *Pistis Sophia*. Hell or Hades in Greek is the Amenta, as Egyptian. Horus descends into Amenta, or rather *rises* there from the tomb, as the teacher of the mysteries concerning the father, who is Ra the father in spirit and in truth. This descent into the under-world is spoken of by Horus in the Ritual (Ch. 38). He goes to visit the spirits in prison or in their cells and sepulchres. Those "who are in their cells," the manes, "accompany him as his guides." His object in making this descent is to utter the words of the father in heaven to the breathless ones, or the spirits in prison. The passage shows the speaker as the divine teacher in two characters on earth and in Amenta. Speaking of Ra, his father in the spirit, Horus says, "I utter his words to the Men of the present generation," or to the living. He also utters them to those who have been deprived of breath, or the dead in Amenta. So in the *Pistis Sophia* the gnostic Jesus passes into Amenta as the teacher of the greater mysteries. As it is said of his teaching in this spirit-world, "Jesus spake these words unto his disciples in the midst of Amenta." Moreover, a special title is assigned to him in Amenta. He is called Aber-Amentho. "Jesus, that is to say Aber-Amentho," is a formula several times repeated in *Pistis Sophia*.[1]

Thus, in this Gnostic-Christian text we find several correlations between the Egyptian and Christian religions, including and especially the connection between the otherworld realm of Amenta, Amente and Amentho, as well as Jesus in the role of Horus.

Regarding the purpose of Jewish Gnosticism, Pearson remarks, "Gnosticism served as the medium by which Judaism should become a world religion."[2] This world religion, as we know well, turned out to be Christianity, which has spread the Jewish tribal writings across the globe, representing them as "God's Word." We evince that Christianity was always planned as such, not truly representing "divine revelation" through the only begotten Son of God, but constituting a deliberate contrivance by members of a widespread brotherhood, designed to unify the Roman Empire under one state religion. In this regard, "Jesus Christ" is not a real person who walked the earth but an allegorical and mythical character based on Jewish and Gentile philosophy, religion and mythology.

---

[1] Massey, *AELW*, II, 772.
[2] Pearson, *GJEC*, 15.

Christian Texts

examples of early "orthodox" Christian writings that connect Egypt to the Christian effort, two "Petrine" texts—in other words, those attributed to the apostle Peter—may be submitted, including the *Kerygma Petri* or "Preaching of Peter," an early Egyptian Christian work dating to the second century and found as fragments in the works of Clement of Alexandria and Origen. Regarding this text, Pearson says, "It certainly reflects a Logos Christology,"[1] linking it to Gnosticism as well. Considered very orthodox, however, the "Peter, Preaching of" seeks out "prophecies" from the OT of Christ's advent, and represents "the first Alexandrian writing to use the term Christian..."[2]

The Gospel of Peter is another Christian apocryphal text found in Egypt, perhaps written in Syria during the first quarter of the second century. It was known to Origen, but nothing was ever quoted from it. Peter's Gospel depicts Christ's passion, death, burial and resurrection, and was evidently considered by Eusebius to be Docetic, in other words, representing a non-material or "unhistorical" Jesus, which is in fact a prominent form of Gnosticism. Demonstrating the theory that the gospel story largely follows the Old Testament "messianic scriptures" as a *blueprint*, rather than constituting history, in the Gospel of Peter "it appears that almost every sentence of the passion narrative was composed on the basis of Scriptural references in the Old Testament, particularly in Isaiah and the Psalms."[3]

Both of these Petrine texts appear to have been constructed from the Old Testament and may have been used by the compilers of the canonical gospels, who clearly utilized prior texts in their construction, rather than writing accounts from the memory of eyewitnesses.[4] The fact that these texts possess Gnostic elements further demonstrates the difficulty in disentangling the two efforts, which are in fact ultimately inseparable.

Marcion and the Gospel of the Lord

In our quest, we must also turn an eye towards the Christian "heretic" Marcion (c. 110-160 AD/CE), considered a "Gnostic" by some, who was responsible for compiling the first New Testament, composed of Paul's "Gospel of the Lord" and 10 Pauline epistles, omitting the three Pastorals (Titus, 1 Timothy and 2 Timothy), which likely did not exist at the time. As is to be expected, Marcion has an Egyptian connection as well. As Pearson says:

---

[1] Pearson, *GCRCE*, 16.
[2] Pearson, *GCRCE*, 16.
[3] Metzger, *CNT*, 172.
[4] For more on the purported reliability of the canonical gospels as "eyewitness accounts," see my book *Who Was Jesus?*

Yet another group can be identified as a probable part of Alexandrian Christianity: the Marcionites. Gilles Dorival argues that Marcion's New Testament arrived in Egypt sometime around 150 or perhaps a little later... Marcionites were certainly known to Clement, who polemicizes against them...[1]

It was claimed by various Church fathers that Marcion took the Gospel of Luke and expurgated parts of it; whereas, scientific analysis leads to the opposite conclusion, with the author of Luke taking Marcion's gospel and editing it.[2] Since Marcion's gospel was known in Egypt, it is possible that the author of Luke utilized it at Alexandria to compose his own gospel,[3] using other texts as well, some 33 by the count of Dr. Frederick Schleiermacher, considered "the most influential theologian of Protestant Germany" during the 19th Century.[4]

Involved in the later orthodox Christian efforts at Alexandria, following the publication of Marcion's New Testament, were the Church fathers Pantaenus, Clement and Origen, the founders of the "School of Alexandria." Origen's "master," it is claimed, was the Gnostic Heracleon (fl. c. 175 AD/CE),[5] a follower of Valentinus, providing a smooth link between Alexandrian Gnosticism and orthodox Christianity.

Adding to the fact that a number of important texts have Egyptian origins, the provenance of the two earliest complete Greek Bible *manuscripts*, the Vaticanus and Sinaiticus, has likewise been suggested as, among other places, Alexandria or elsewhere in Egypt.[6] Moreover, it is intriguing that the earliest known New Testament in an *Egyptian* dialect is the Bohairic, which comes from the "district near Alexandria between Lake Mareotis and the W. arm of the Nile."[7] The Bohairic edition of the Bible is therefore "almost certainly Alexandrian."

According to Dr. Bart Ehrman, a professor of Religious Studies at the University of North Carolina, the monks of Alexandria who copied the Christian texts were "scrupulous" and "relatively skilled," making fewer mistakes than copyists elsewhere,[8] which would provide a major reason why so much Christian literature came from Egypt—a connection that cannot be overemphasized.

---

[1] Pearson, *GCRCE*, 18.
[2] See Waite's *The History of the Christian Religion to the Year Two Hundred*.
[3] See my book *Who Was Jesus?* for a discussion of the "many" in the Lukan Prologue, as well as an argument for the late dating of Luke.
[4] Waite, 150, 379.
[5] Granger, 411.
[6] See, e.g., *CE*, "Codex Vaticanus," I, 86.
[7] *Enc. Bibl.*, 5012.
[8] Ehrman, 72.

...＿ have seen that the Gospel of John occupies a unique position in Christian literature in terms of its usage in Egypt, its apparent provenance in Egypt, its abundance of Egyptian themes, and its evident borrowing of Egyptian scriptures.

We have also noted that the other canonical gospels display Egyptian or Alexandrian influence, including Luke with its tale regarding Lazarus, among other details. As another example, Reber sees Matthew's gospel as possessing an "Alexandrian look not easily to be mistaken," remarking:

> In what quarter of the globe were the Synoptics written, and by whom? All that can be said on this subject with certainty is, that the Greek version of Matthew...was not written in Judea, or by one who knew anything of the geography of the country, or the history of the Jews. He was ignorant of both.[1]

Citing the healing miracles in Matthew, Reber further states: "Whoever the writer may have been, it is evident he received his education at the college at Alexandria, where Medicine and Divinity were taught, and regarded as inseparable."[2]

Not a few scholars have noticed a distinct connection between the "Last Judgment" scene of BD 125 and that of the gospel of Matthew, chapter 25. Concerning this situation, Bonwick remarks:

> Chapter 125 describes the "Last Judgment."... Mr. Birch supposes the chapter to have connection with "masonic mysteries." No one can doubt that Free-masonry, *Phré* or Sun masonry, existed B.C. 4000, if not much earlier; but the chapter admits certainly other interpretations, as its narrative runs pretty parallel with the 25th of Matthew.[3]

Concerning the scene in the judgment hall and its relationship to Christianity, Griffiths states:

> The judgment before Osiris had a strong impact on other religions, particularly on the eschatology of Judaism and then Christianity— with the development of Judgment Day and the Last Judgment.[4]

The judgment of the dead has traditionally been a function of the sun god, as exemplified in Egypt, where the solar judge is not only Osiris but also Ra/Re.[5]

BD 125 is compared not only to Matthew 25 but also to the biblical 10 Commandments, as a possible source of both. In Matthew 25, after the parable of the talents, Jesus is depicted as describing the "Last Judgment" thus:

---

[1] Reber, 81. Reber subscribes to, and gives good reasons for, the long-held notion that Matthew was composed first, an opinion adhered to by a number of early Church fathers, which is why it is placed first in the canon.

[2] Reber, 82.

[3] Bonwick, 198.

[4] Redford, 307.

[5] Morenz, 128-129.

"When the Son of man comes in his glory, and all the angels are with him, then he will sit on his glorious throne. Before him will be gathered all the nations, and he will separate them one from another as a shepherd separates the sheep from the goats at the left. Then the King will say to those at his right hand, 'Come, O blessed of my Father, inherit the kingdom prepared for you from the foundation of the world; for I was hungry and you gave me food, I was thirsty and you gave me drink, I was a stranger and you welcomed me, I was naked and you clothed me, I was sick and you visited me, I was in prison and you came to me.'..." (Mt 25:31-36)

Speaking of the Egyptian "sayings of the Lord," Massey avers that these were utilized in the creation of Christianity, put into the mouth of Lord Jesus, and remarks:

...a few most significant ones may be found in the Book of the Dead. In one particular passage the speaker says he has given food to the hungry, drink to the thirsty, clothes to the naked, and a boat to the shipwrecked; and, as the Osirified [the Osiris] has done these things, the Judges say to him, "*Come, come in peace,*" and he is welcomed to the festival which is called "*Come thou to me.*" Those who have done these things on earth are held to have done them to Horus, the Lord; and they are invited to come to him as the blessed ones of his father Osiris. In this passage we have not only the sayings reproduced by Matthew, but also the drama and the scenes of the Last Judgment represented in the Great Hall of Justice, where a person is separated from his sins, and those who have sided with Sut against Horus are transformed into goats.[1]

Just as Massey relates, in Birch's translation of BD 125 may be found the following:

The God has welcomed him as he has wished. He has given food to [my] the hungry, drink to [my] the thirsty, clothes to [my] the naked [ness], he has made a boat for me to go by.... Therefore do not accuse him before the Lord of the Mummies; because his mouth is pure, his hands are pure. Come, come in peace...[2]

Dr. Richard Hooker of Washington State University translates the pertinent parts of BD 125 thus:

I have given bread to the hungry man, and water to the thirsty man, And clothes to the naked man, and a boat to the boatless.

Moreover, it is an interesting "coincidence" that the divine scribe Taht-An (Thoth) in the Book of the Dead is styled by Birch as "Mati," while, of course, Jesus's holy scribe is "Mathias" or "Matthew." When we go to Budge's synopsis of BD 125, we see the following:

The words which are to be uttered by the deceased when he cometh to the hall of Maati, which separeth him from his sins, and which maketh him to see God, the Lord of mankind.[3]

---

[1] Massey, *GML*, 59.
[2] Bunsen/Birch, 256.
[3] Budge, *BD* (2003), 42.

The word *mati* or *maati*, in fact, is the plural for "truth," meaning "double right and truth" or symbolizing "the two goddesses of Truth, who probably represent Isis and Nephthys."[1] As we can see, the similarities between Matthew's gospel and the *BD* are striking and important.

Concerning the synoptic gospels, in *History of Early Christian Literature in the First Three Centuries*, Dr. Gustav Krüger, a professor of Church History at the University of Giessen, states, "All three Gospels were written after the destruction of Jerusalem, and their text can hardly have received its present shape before the second half of the second century."[2] As stated, the canonical gospels as we have them do not clearly appear in the historical record until the end of the second century, and there is not even a hint of them earlier than that. What we discover, therefore, is that these texts were created during the second century, with the input of Alexandrian scholarship. Indeed, regarding the Gospel of John, Dr. Krüger asserts, "The author was a Jew, trained in the ideas of Alexandrian religious philosophy."[3] As shown, beginning with Eusebius, not a few people have averred that the canonical gospels originated with the allegorical works of the Alexandrian Therapeuts, so this Alexandrian attribution of John would be sensible as well.

Regarding the Gospel of John and its Egyptian origins, in *The Journal of Theological Studies*, Granger remarks:

> Now it is instructive to note that Salome, who plays so prominent a part in the *Gospel according to the Egyptians*, is the mother of St John, and that the same Gnostic circles in which this Gospel was current, were also those in which we hear for the first time of the Fourth Gospel. That is to say, the Fourth Gospel comes to us from the hands of the Alexandrine Gnostics. The system of Valentinus is really a somewhat fanciful commentary upon the opening chapters of *St John's Gospel*. Heracleon, the first great commentator upon St John, was both a Gnostic and at the same time was really the master of Origen. Now the key to the interpretation of the Fourth Gospel is to be found in the Gnostic ideas which underlie the *Poimandres*, ideas to which Heracleon furnishes a clue...[4]

As demonstrated, the *Poimandres* may have been one of the Therapeutan texts at the basis of Christian writings. In the *Poimandres*, then, we have a connection to John, as well as to Church father Origen, who, again, was influenced by the Valentinian Gnostic Heracleon. Although Origen appears to have been at odds with Heracleon, rather than a willing disciple, his mentor Clement

---

[1] Budge, *BD* (2003), 313, 315, 528.
[2] Krüger, 49.
[3] Krüger, 50.
[4] Granger, 411. In his discussion of Granger's article, Mead notes that he knows of no proof that the Salome of the Gospel of the Egyptians is in fact the same as John's mother. Nevertheless, the point is well taken that John's gospel is "from the hands of Alexandrine Gnostics."

Alexandrinus (*Stromata*, 4.9) called Heracleon "the most distinguished of the school of Valentinians"[1] and appears to have admired the Gnostic. Coptic expert Dr. Aziz S. Atiya (1898-1988), a professor at the University of Utah, remarks that Heracleon "seems to have made a large contribution to Origen's great *Commentary on John* (started c. 227), which sought to explain the Fourth Gospel within the framework of orthodox teaching."[2] Dr. Atiya concludes, "Clement and Origen may both be seen in this respect as the theological descendants of Heracleon." It is interesting to note that Heracleon was the "first great commentator upon St. John," in consideration of the fact that the gospel ascribed to John as we have it did not clearly emerge in the historical record until around 176/8 AD/CE, precisely when Heracleon flourished.

Regarding the relationship between the Gnostic "heretic" Valentinus and the gospel of John, the *Encyclopedia Britannica* remarks:

> ...we cannot be far wrong in suspecting that here already we find Valentinus to have been influenced by the prologue of the fourth Gospel (we also find the probably Johannine names Monogenes and Parakletos in the series of aeons)....

> It has already been seen clearly that Valentinian Gnosticism affected the nearest approach of all the Gnostic sects to the Catholic Church. Valentinus's own life indicates that he for a long time sought to remain within the official Church, and had at first no idea of founding a community of his own. Many compromises of his theories point the same way. The Johannine tendencies of his doctrine of the aeons (Logos, Zoe, Aletheia, Parakletos)...the adoption of the Christian baptism—all this, and perhaps more, indicates a definite and deliberate approach towards the doctrine of the Church.

> These Gnostics, as in the case of most of the other Gnostic sects, possessed their own peculiar holy writings and books, but they also made a great use in their own circle of the canon of the Christian Church, especially the canon of the New Testament and—though with a few reservations—of the Old Testament.... Later Valentinian Gnosticism delighted in making use of the Johannine Gospel as a crowning testimony... the later Valentinian Herakleon wrote a detailed exposition of the whole Gospel [of John].[3]

It is noteworthy that the *EB* asserts Valentinus to have been an *orthodox* Christian and his Gnosticism to be considered the closest to Catholicism. Although it is commonly believed that Valentinus must have been influenced by the gospel of John, if we analyze the situation scientifically, we find that Valentinus appears in the historical record *before* John's gospel, and logic would dictate that if there was any borrowing, it occurred in the opposite direction of what

[1] Roberts, A., *ANF*, II, 422.
[2] Atiya, "Heracleon," *Dictionary of African Christian Biography*.
[3] *Enc. Brit.*, XXVII, 854-856.

has been suggested by the EB and elsewhere. In fact, Church fathers Irenaeus and Jerome stated that John was written *in refutation of Gnostics*, particularly Cerinthus, who, contrary to popular belief, likely lived well into the second century. Again, the connection between the Valentinian Heracleon and Origen, who lived at Alexandria, provides a smooth transition between Gnostic and Orthodox Christianity.

We have already seen many elements in the gospel of John that find their parallels in the Egyptian religion, including: the Logos doctrine; John the Baptist; the god as the "living water"; the numerous references to the "bread of life"; the feast with the wine; the raising of Lazarus; the two Marys; the many scriptural similarities; and the healing of the blind with spittle. Another parallel occurs with Mary Magdalene seeking Jesus's body (Jn 20:13-17), which corresponds to Isis's search for Osiris's body. John's gospel in particular also makes much of the various cosmic epithets of Christ, as we might expect of a gospel with Egyptian connections, as these same concepts flourished in Egyptian religion, especially as concerns Osiris and Horus. Moreover, like Horus and Osiris, at John 10:30 Christ and the Father are one. While Osiris is the "Lord of Resurrections," Jesus himself is the resurrection, as found only in John. Also in the gospel of John (Jn 21:2-3) appears a post-resurrection scene with seven of the disciples in a boat, while in CT Sps. 400 and 401, we find the deceased invoking, "O you seven spirits, the ferrymen of the sky."[1] Moreover, in *De Corona* ("The Chaplet"), chapter 8, Tertullian discusses Christ "girt about with a linen towel" as at John 12:1-5, remarking that the towel is "a garment specially sacred to Osiris."[2] In addition, the use of the word *diakonos* or "deacon" is the same in both Philo and the gospel of John.

Furthermore, it is also interesting that, per Conybeare's analysis of a phrase used by Philo to describe the manner in which the Therapeuts reclined near each other during a banquet, "the phrase has only this formal and technical sense in John 13. 23."[3] Conybeare continues by stating that the term "only means that John as the beloved disciple reclined next to Jesus." This phrase would thus indicate a connection between the gospel and the Therapeuts, if the meaning by Conybeare is understood that it only appears in this manner in antiquity in Philo and John's gospel. Since Conybeare's "Excursus" is meant to be an exhaustive survey of the word and phrase usages in the Alexandrian Jewish philosopher Philo, such exclusivity would indeed appear to be the meaning of his remarks.

---

[1] Faulkner, *AECT*, II, 43, 45.
[2] Roberts, A., *ANF*, III, 98.
[3] Conybeare, 243.

The Alexandrian Roots of Christianity

Concerning the various themes within John that appear to be straight out of Egyptian religion, Tim Callahan notes:

> That the Egyptian motifs in both Luke and John are all from the cycle of Osiris, Isis and Horus would seem to indicate that the reason for incorporating them could either be the result of the influence of the already flourishing Hellenized cult of Isis or part of a deliberate attempt to co-opt this rival's powerful imagery.[1]

From all the evidence, it appears that the gospel of John is an Egyptian composition created at Alexandria and largely based on Egyptian religion and Alexandrian philosophy.

The Memphite Theology

The Egyptian precedent for parts of the gospel of John may also be found in a text called "the Memphite Theology," which, Hare states, "clearly ascribes a intellectual and volitional motive to creation, with a focus on the heart or mind of the creator and the manifestation of thought in language and material reality."[2] Hare continues:

> For this reason the [Memphite] theology has been cited as an antecedent to the first verses of both the Book of Genesis and the Gospel of John...[3]

The Memphite Theology is based on the text found on the "Shabaka Stone" or "Shabaqo Stela," which was created around 710 BCE but preserves a much older tradition. This text contains an account of the father god Ptah creating humans "through the power of his heart and speech." Regarding the Memphite Theology, Dr. Tobin remarks:

> ...The highly abstract nature of the text gives distinct evidence that the Egyptian intellect was capable of dealing with material that would later form the subject of philosophical and theological speculation in the Jewish and Christian worlds.[4]

Even if the Memphite Theology dates to no earlier than the eight century BCE, it would nevertheless demonstrate an early Egyptian conceptualization of "the word," providing a possible precedent for the idea as found in later Jewish, Gnostic, Stoic and Christian ideology.

In any event, the gospel of John was apparently composed also to incorporate the popular doctrines of both Plato and Philo, such that their followers would be more inclined toward the new faith. In consideration of the emphasis by Philo on the Word or Logos, we may suppose that the Gospel of John with its Logos-heavy prologue was devised in significant part not only to counter Gnostics but also to

---

[1] Callahan, 401.
[2] Hare, 179.
[3] Hare, 179.
[4] Redford, 249.

followers, including, apparently, those within the
̣exandria.

John?

It the ̣spel of John is an Egyptian text composed at Alexandria
in the late second century in response to Gnostics, then St. John the
apostle could not have been its author. Indeed, as we have seen, even
in ancient times the apostolic attribution of the gospel of John was
denied. Regarding the "first serious and able criticism" in modern
times of the received view that the Gospel of John was written by the
apostle John at Ephesus, in *An Inquiry into the Character and
Authorship of the Fourth Gospel*, Dr. James Drummond relates that it
was Rev. Dr. Karl Gottlieb Bretschneider's "*Probabilia de Evangelii et
Epistolarum Joannis Apostoli Indole et Origine*, published in 1820, and
written in Latin, as the author assures us, that he might not give any
offence to the 'unlearned plebs,' and that his book might be read by
foreign theologians."[1] From these remarks, it is clear that much
important information concerning Christianity has been suppressed
and hidden from the masses, and that such information would be
considered harmful to the faith, even though it may be factual and
truthful. Continuing his discussion of Rev. Bretschneider's thesis, Dr.
Drummond relates:

> ...the conclusion is reached that the Gospel was fraudulently written
> by a Gentile in the name of John in the beginning or middle of the
> second century, and that the author most probably lived in Egypt,
> whence the Gospel was brought to Rome by Gnostics.[2]

Although his argument was "formidable enough," the
traditionalists essentially forced Bretschneider (1776-1848) to retract
"his objections," leaving the issue as it was previously. Moreover,
Bretschneider's retraction was evidently the result of him being
forced from his job for the mere publishing of this position contrary
to the received Christian history. Bretschneider's haranguement was
followed by the disgraceful treatment of Dr. David Friedrich Strauss
(1808-1874), who lost his occupation because in his book *The Life of
Jesus Critically Examined* he dared to interpret the gospel story as
myth, averring that John's was the most mythical of the gospels.[3]

Renowned theologian and New Testament scholar Dr. F.C. Baur
(1792-1860) likewise did not ascribe to John an apostolic authorship,
dating the gospel to the latter half of the second century. In *History of
the Christian Religion to the Year Two Hundred*, Judge Charles B.
Waite (d. 1909) provided an in-depth analysis demonstrating the
same conclusions, including showing the date of 178 AD/CE for the
gospel's unmistakable appearance in the literary record.

---

[1] Drummond, 67-68.
[2] Drummond, 68.
[3] Culpepper, 281.

The Alexandrian Roots of Christianity

Concerning the case for John having been written at Alexandria, New Testament scholar and professor of Divinity Rev. Dr. Charles Kingsley Barrett (b. 1917) states:

> ...Undoubtedly there is evidence pointing in that direction. The earliest certain use of the gospel is found in Egypt (the Rylands and Egerton papyri, and the Valentinians). Internal evidence (it has been held) confirms the external. Alexandria, "the home of Philo and the authors of the *Corpus Hermeticum*,...was a likely place for the development of a Christian Logos-doctrine" (Sanders, *Early Church*, 40). The hypothesis that John was written in Alexandria, the home both of gnostics and of a large Jewish population, would account for the twofold polemic of the gospel against both docetic and Judaizing tendencies, and perhaps also for the polemic against the followers of John the Baptist. Finally, since it seems that the church of Alexandria was not in its earliest days strictly orthodox, it is easy to understand that a gospel proceeding from such a source should at first be looked upon with suspicion by orthodox Christians.[1]

Indeed, this perspective has not been isolated, with Cambridge professor Rev. Joseph Newbould Sanders also concluding that the "copious evidence for gnostic, particularly Valentinian, use" constituted an indication of "an Alexandrian origin for the Fourth Gospel itself."[2]

Regarding this subject, Dr. Charles E. Hill, a professor of New Testament at Reformed Theological Seminary, likewise says:

> ...The Gospel appears to have been used first of all by the Gnostics, and particularly by the Alexandrians... It was the Valentinians who first ascribed it to "John."[3]

Despite the inference that "Valentinus" commented on John, Drummond admits that, in reality, "Irenaeus...in the last quarter of the second century, is our first witness [to John]."[4] In fact, it was not Valentinus but his later disciples, such as Heracleon, apparently, who "first ascribed it to John," while the first language that seems to come from John's gospel can be found in the *Ad Autoclytum* (2.22) of Bishop Theophilus (c. 176). Either Irenaeus could not have been the "first witness," or he did not ascribe the gospel to John. Oddly enough, even though it was said to have been written *against* the Gnostic "heretic" Cerinthus, there have been those, such as Gaius of Rome around 200 AD/CE, who have claimed that John was in fact written *by* Cerinthus.[5] The impression given is that the gospel emerged not long before Gaius's era and that Cerinthus too flourished near that time. Other individuals who ascribed the Johannine gospel to Cerinthus were the "Alogi" mentioned by

---

[1] Barrett, 129.
[2] Hill, 16.
[3] Hill, 16.
[4] Drummond, 73.
[5] Hill, 14.

s. While the Alogi are treated as a sect, their name may
ean "against Logos," symbolized by their rejection of the
ap᷈ authorship of the Gospel of John.

Since the Old Testament was translated into Greek at Alexandria,
producing the Septuagint, and since it was the Septuagint, not the
Hebrew bible, that was mainly used by the New Testament writers, it
would make further sense to connect the New Testament to
Alexandria. Moreover, at a certain point Jews stopped using the
Septuagint, which was maintained by Christians and attached to the
New Testament as part of their "Holy Bible." With all the factors
combined, the importance of Alexandria on the Christian effort is
obvious and critical to a scientific analysis of the origins of
Christianity.

The destruction of Alexandria as a great seat of intellectualism
can be squarely blamed upon the Christian mob, who rampaged
through the streets, devastating marvelous Pagan sacred sites,
burning the Serapeum and other sources of learning and culture,
and killing all those who stood in their way. Such depravity included
the hideous murder of the last outstanding example of Alexandrian
erudition, the female sage Hypatia (d. 415), who was torn from her
vehicle, stripped, flayed and burned alive by Christians. A viler act
one could hardly imagine, representing the defining moment of the
Death of Paganism and signaling the beginning of the Dark Ages
under Christian dominance. This disgraceful, violent and
heinous oppression lasted until a mere century and a half or so ago,
with people in England, for instance, still being put in prison for
"blasphemy." In some ways, we remain in this violent state of
oppression, with hostile people viciously attacking others over
Christian doctrine, as well as over such facts as popularized here. For
those who may tend to forget what we have endured and made
through in our movement toward greater enlightenment, we
need only remember Hypatia, the great symbol of Alexandrian
sagacity and the longstanding legacy of Egypt.

A white-robed heavenly Egyptian "Brotherhood" with Cross
Hieroglyph
(Hornung, *The Valley of the Kings*, 160)

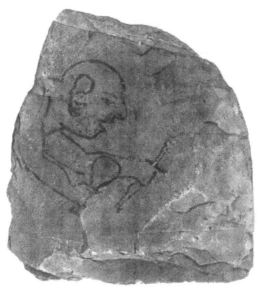

"Stonemason at his work."
(Hornung, *The Valley of the Kings*, 42)

Conclusion

"...the study of Egyptian mythology will throw more light upon the restrictive customs of the Jews, the allusions of the prophets, and the early history of the Christian church than that of any other country."

William R. Cooper, *The Serpent Myths of Ancient Egypt* (73)

"...it would seem that in Egypt we had the first truly Christian people, without record of an initial struggle between heathenry and the Gospel. The blessed Mary had replaced Isis, the little babe Jesus had replaced Horus, the passion of Christ had superseded the suffering and dying of Osiris, the Christian cross had been set up instead of the 'Tet' or fourfold cross with flail and crook in right and left..."

Rev. Dr. William Norman Guthrie, *The Gospel of Osiris* (II)

"...the principles and precepts of the Osiran theology of Egypt are virtually identical in *content* and *application* to the principles and precepts of Christianity as they present themselves in the Jesus saga."

Dr. Richard A. Gabriel, *Jesus the Egyptian* (2)

When analyzing the Egyptian religion and its evident influence upon Christianity, it is necessary to recall a number of important facts, including that the Egyptians practiced a sort of "polytheistic monotheism" or "monotheistic polytheism," rather than just polytheism, as is widely perceived. In reality, Egyptian religion appears to have incorporated every major theology, such as monotheism, polytheism, pantheism, panentheism, monism and henotheism. Reflecting the complex nature of the Egyptian religion, over 100 years ago Swiss Egyptologist Dr. Edouard Naville remarked, "Let us remember that we have not yet unravelled all the intricacies of the Egyptian mythology..."[1] The study of Egyptian religion and mythology, in fact, has only been in full swing for a couple of centuries. Prior to that time, not enough was known to make the correspondences found in this book, although the works of Diodorus, Plutarch and others from the ancient world did allow for some Egyptian mythology to be factored into the comparative-religion studies of scholars such as Charles Dupuis and Count Volney beginning at the end of the 18th century. In fact, it was largely because of Dupuis's fascinating research and conclusions that French Emperor Napoleon Bonaparte (1769-1821) descended upon Egypt with not only his troops but also his team of Europe's most skilled scholars and scientists.[2] The subsequent discovery of the Rosetta Stone by Napoleon's team unlocked an entire new world that has since been mined to reveal gold nuggets which have only come to light in time and with increasing scientific exploration. Hence, we are

---

[1] Renouf, *EBD*, xx.
[2] *Enc. Brit.*, VIII, 690.

just now starting to see the implications of these finds, although certain courageous scholars of earlier eras deserve immense credit for discerning widespread parallels between the Egyptian and Christian religions without benefit of modern scientific methods, discoveries and breakthroughs. In the end, the Egyptian religion rates as highly symbolic and extraordinarily vast, and it may not be unreasonable to assert that, in general, virtually every religious or spiritual idea may be found in some form or another within this ideology, including those appearing in the later Christianity.

A "Unique Divine Revelation?"

Although portrayed as "unique divine revelation," Christianity was neither "new nor strange" but had existed "from the beginning," as declared by Church fathers Eusebius and Augustine in a moment of inspired candor that likely revealed more than they intended. These comments by the Church fathers were apparently meant to demonstrate the eternal nature of the Christian faith but, in actuality, explained why, if Christianity constituted "unique revelation," so many of its tenets could already be found around the known world for centuries to millennia. Indeed, as we can see from the numerous correspondences, if Christianity is to be considered "divine revelation," then so too must be the important Egyptian religion upon which much of the Christian effort was palpably founded. In reality, since it preceded Christianity by millennia, the Egyptian religion could lay claim to being the *original* "divine revelation," closer to the truth and less corrupted. As demonstrated in this present work, there exists good reason to assert that, rather than representing a new disclosure from God, Christianity is in actuality a rehash of older religions, including and especially the Egyptian. In this regard, we have thus far explored numerous significant instances where the Egyptian and Christian religions converge.

Nevertheless, the task of outlining all of the correlations between the two faiths has proved itself so overwhelming that few people have been willing or able to undertake it. Even the great Sir Dr. E.A. Wallis Budge demurred on this exceptional effort, declaring:

> Interesting, however, as such an investigation would be, no attempt has been made in this work to trace out the influence of ancient Egyptian religious beliefs and mythology on Christianity, for *such an undertaking would fill a comparatively large volume*.[1]

Such statements should have spurred a whole field of study, but, as we know too well, vested interests clamped down and rendered this worthy endeavor nearly impossible. We are finally at a time, however, when implausible pabulum will be scrutinized

---

[1] Budge, *GE*, I, xvi. (Emph. added.)

scientifically and revealed as such, so that we may remove the delusion preventing further evolution.

Gods Truly Walked the Earth?

Although Christianity attempts to set itself apart by claiming its story to have truly taken place in history, the Egyptian religion too was supposedly rooted in history, which would make it true as well, by this same reasoning. As we know from ancient writers, the important Egyptian god Osiris was also believed to have been a real man who walked the earth and who was responsible for the civilizing and salvation of mankind. In fact, Osiris is depicted as traveling far and wide in his quest to bring goodness and light to humanity, making him one of the best-known gods of all time. Not only were the deities Osiris, Isis and Horus highly popular, but their sacred sites and relics, including numerous temples and tombs, could be found throughout Egypt and elsewhere, wherever there was a priesthood. Thus, again, to insist that *only* the Christian drama and its characters are "true" and represent "divine revelation" can been viewed as a manifestation of cultural bias, rather than reality.

In this regard, to question the reality of Osiris and Isis as *people*, as well as gods, might constitute a sin as egregious to Egyptians as doubting the historical veracity of Jesus Christ is to many Christians today. Indeed, it should be kept in mind that the Egyptians took their religion very seriously and did not readily accept blasphemy against it, being every bit as pious about their faith as Christians are now. In describing this Egyptian piety, James Bonwick recounts the observations of the French Catholic priest Abbé Noël Antoine Pluche (1688-1761), who wrote *The History of the Heavens*:

> Abbé Pluche has no manner of doubt about the honest belief of the Egyptians in the simple story of Osiris, their individual as well as national benefactor.... He thinks that even supposing the leaders knew something beyond the popular conceptions, "it would have been dangerous for the Egyptian priests to attempt undeceiving the people, and to divert them from the pleasing thought that Osiris and Isis were two real persons."
>
> He adduces a proof of this danger. "The actions of Osiris and Isis," says he, "were incessantly mentioned. The people believed what they saw and what they heard. The perpetual recitals of as many historical facts, as there were figures and ceremonies exhibited, completed their error, and rendered them invincible." His conclusion was: "The people in their frantic enthusiasm would have *torn in pieces* any that should dare to deny the history of Osiris and Isis."....[1]

The fervor with which the Osirian religion was held may have also occurred at certain times as a result of scriptures such as the following

---

[1] Bonwick, 173.

in CT Sp. 317, where the speaker as Osiris, expressing a sentiment similar to that found in the Bible and Koran, states:

> ...As for anyone who is (due) to be decapitated who shall oppose himself to me; as for anyone who cries aloud who shall come opposing me; as for any god or any rebel who shall oppose me or whom I shall find on my path, the *ȝkdw*-spirits who are before me shall seize him, the *ꜥšmw*-spirits who are behind me shall devour him...[1]

Like the Abrahamic religions, it would appear that terrorizing believers into submission was not unknown within the Osirian religion as well.

Obviously, the fervent belief in a god who allegedly "walked the earth" is dependent not on absolute truth or reality but often upon the fashion of the day. The Egyptian gods are now taken to be mythical, despite the ardent beliefs of their hundreds of millions of worshippers over a period of several thousand years. The same may be said in the future concerning Jesus Christ—in fact, the precise machination of demotion under another religion and god is already happening with Jesus, as he is depicted within the fast-growing Islam as a mere mortal prophet, rather than the omnipotent, omniscient and omnipresent Son of God.

In any event, with such fervent belief the Egyptian religion is not to be taken lightly, with culturally biased dismissals disparaging the Egyptians as mere "heathens" and "pagans," while Christians hold up their own religion as sacrosanct "truth" and "divine revelation."

The "Horus Christian Class" Dismissed?

The ancient Egyptian Christians themselves apparently possessed no such prejudices, as they readily identified Horus and Osiris with Jesus, and Isis with Mary, important and fascinating facts that one would think would garner far more attention than they do. This fact of the identification of Jesus with Osiris and Horus *in ancient times* is evidenced by customs, rituals, myths, texts, images and other artifacts. Some of these Egypto-Christian artifacts are quite impressive, as reported by the amateur Egyptologist and devout Christian William R. Cooper, who provided examples of what he called the "Horus Christian class."

As part of this "Horus Christian class," Dr. Meltzer names the following:

> The iconography of Horus either influenced or was appropriated in early Christian art. Isis and the baby Horus may often be seen as the precursor for Mary and the infant Jesus; Horus dominating the beasts may have a counterpart in Christ Pantokrator doing the same;

---

[1] Faulkner, *AECT*, I, 242.

and Horus spearing a serpent may survive in the iconography of Saint George defeating the dragon.[1]

After compiling his own list of artifacts demonstrating Egypto-Christian themes, the pious Cooper concludes:

> These illustrations will now, I think, suffice for the purpose that I have in view—the purpose of proving that **the works of art, the ideas, the expressions, and the heresies of the first four centuries of the Christian era cannot be well studied without a right comprehension of the nature and influence of the Horus myth**; and that it becomes every student, or at all events every expositor of the Book of books, to examine this myth, and work out its operations for himself. Of its immense antiquity there can be no reasonable doubt; equally so can there be none of the extent to which the myth has been modified by the Classic, Jewish, and Christian theologies, although we are not yet in a position to separate the true from the false, and to assign to each interpolation or interpretation its proper place in the chronology of mythology. We cannot, I repeat, ignore these facts. We have, as Christians, no reason to be afraid of them. As philosophical scholars we are bound to make use of the materials brought ready to our hands in the records of the past, and as true believers in the co-eternal divinity and redeemership of our blessed Lord, we should be impelled by our responsibilities to be the first in the field...[2]

The young lawyer Cooper truly believed that by bringing forth these proofs of the merging of the Egyptian and Christian religions he was somehow presenting a defense of the Christian faith, and he was extremely disappointed by the weak reaction he received from the elite scholars and clergy to whom he circulated his ground-breaking work. Again, responding at last to his call to study these intriguing connections, respected modern Egyptologist Dr. Witt remarked that Cooper's "words are still true."[3]

Unfortunately, Cooper passed away "in exile," as he put it, at the age of 35, shortly after presenting his startling findings to England's finest, with flaccid results. Thus, he did not live to see his work attain to fruition, and these significant correlations continued to be suppressed and ignored by the mainstream, although gaining momentum with such diligent and daring individuals as Gerald Massey, whose massive works nevertheless remain mostly unknown in the field of Egyptology today. From the present in-depth, scientific analysis, however, we have discovered that Massey was substantially correct in both his facts and his conclusions, once again vindicating a much-maligned scholar whose works have therefore largely proved themselves to be accurate, as we have seen abundantly.

Before and since Massey's time, those who have ventured into the field of comparative religion and mythology, and who have dared to

---

[1] Redford, 167.
[2] Cooper, *HM*, 49-50. (Emph. added.)
[3] Witt, 279.

include Christianity in their analysis, have frequently been subjected to ridicule or worse. The illogical implication of such abuse heaped upon those who discuss Christianity as *mythology* is that the Jewish culture from which the Christian religion largely sprang, according to believers, possessed *no mythology whatsoever*, as virtually the only culture of significance to make such an unlikely claim. Yet, from the experiences of Cooper and many others, it is obvious that society's elite—including *numerous* churchmen—have known about the research demonstrating elements of *Egyptian* mythology within Christianity, but that this information has been rigorously *censored*. Otherwise, in an open environment it would be inexplicable why Cooper's brilliant insights were ignored and his fascinating lead left unfollowed, particularly in light of what Budge later stated about such Egyptian-Christian comparisons filling a "large volume."

Dangerous Endeavors and Occupational Hazards

In consideration of the very real danger involved in exposing information against the mainstream that has dominated over the past many centuries, previous reticence concerning the Egyptian origins of Christianity may in actuality be understandable. In the history of promoting Christianity, while suppressing information and acts perceived as deleterious to the faith, there have appeared numerous bogus artifacts and forged texts, along with all manner of deceit, calumny, slander and violence, including beatings, torture, slavery, murders, wars and wholesale slaughter. For centuries, hundreds of thousands were brutally tortured and murdered because of their alleged "unbelief" in biblical doctrine. Even in more modern times prominent dissenters have suffered for purported "heresy" and "blasphemy." When they challenged the status quo, people like Dr. David Strauss and Dr. Karl Bretschneider lost their occupations, while others such as Rev. Robert Taylor were imprisoned for questioning Holy Writ. Today, those who try to expose information as found here are labeled every sort of vitriolic and libelous epithet imaginable, while in fact they too are risking their own life and limb. In such an environment, it is no wonder that the information contained in this book has been suppressed and has not made it into popular literature and the minds of the public. Also, without the support of mainstream academia and media, any such endeavor could turn out to be a financially challenging "labor of love," and not a few maverick thinkers have died impoverished for their efforts. In any event, the odds have been clearly against those who step outside the box and extend above the curve.

In the past centuries to the present in some circles, scientific theories have thus been dismissed and censored purely because they contradict the Bible and/or Judeo-Christian tradition. Biblical prejudice and irrational devotion—that which upholds the Bible for no rational reason and which is called "Bibliolatry"—has allowed for credible scientific ideas and theories to be roundly dismissed. As Massey stated, many individuals of the past have been bibliolaters first and scholars second. The toning down or omission of anything that might offend Judeo-Christian sensibilities, has clearly led to censorship of important information—and this censorial pressure has often created a pronounced divide between religious scholars and others such as, in this case, Egyptologists, with the result that the twain has rarely met, leaving us to make the connections ourselves in what at times amount to Herculean efforts.

As yet another example of such censorship, regarding the Philonic text "On the Embassy to Gaius" (*De Legatione Ad Gaium*) Conybeare remarks:

> Thus time and Christian editors have truncated the De Legatione in a threefold way. Firstly, a good part of the second book has been removed because it ran counter to Christian traditions regarding Pontius Pilate....[1]

Hence, again, censors have removed material threatening to the faith—a common occurrence that reduced much of the ancient world to rubble, the wrecked pieces of which we are only now putting back together.

The inability to think outside of the biblical box, even by the most erudite and renowned scholars, is further displayed in the musings of Sir Wilkinson, one of the greatest Egyptologists of all time. In contemplating the nature of Egyptian religion, beginning with the possible "Sabean worship"—in other words, astrotheology, especially *star worship*—Wilkinson wondered if the Egyptians were not first sun worshippers who eventually "learnt to consider the divine mind of the Creator superior to the work He had created." Wilkinson goes on to state that it is not possible to "settle this question," with it remaining "uncertain if that was the primitive mode of worship in Egypt, or if their religion was corrupted from the originally pure idea communicated to them by the early descendants of Noah, who established themselves in the valley of the Nile."[2] According to Wilkinson and many others, therefore, the Israelite religion was superior to that of the Egyptians, who could only attain to true knowledge of God through following the "chosen people." However, if the mind is so clouded by fabulous tales such as Noah's Ark, how can it be clear enough to interpret data properly? Moreover, in more modern times we know that the biblical Jews borrowed much of their religion and mythology *from* Egypt; therefore, it could only constitute bias and ignorance to suggest that the Egyptians were "impure" or "corrupted" from the "purity" of "Noah's descendants," thereby believing the hegemony of the Bible for no sound scientific reason.

---

[1] Conybeare, 284.
[2] Wilkinson, *MCAE*, III, 48.

Conclusion

Such was the reigning atmosphere even among intellectual
and academics prior to the past century or so.

Scholars in general can also be notoriously cautious, particularly
when it comes to stepping on the toes of mainstream institutions,
especially those of a religious bent—and there have been many such
establishments, including major universities like Yale and Harvard,
both of which started as Christian divinity schools.[1] Numerous other
institutions in the Christian world were either founded specifically as
Christian universities and colleges or had seminaries attached to
them. As stated on the Princeton Theological Seminary website,
regarding early American education:

> Within the last quarter of the eighteenth century, all learning...could
> be adequately taught and studied in the schools and colleges, nearly
> all of which were church initiated.[2]

As yet another example of scholarly timidity in the face of
Bibliolatry, while discussing the similarities between Egypt and
Israel, Dr. Beyerlin, in collaboration with Dr. Brunner, remarks that
Egypt and Israel share some striking similarities—indeed, his book
on the Near Eastern religious texts and the Old Testament is
designed to show various correlations—to the point where he states,
"Egypt and Israel became great in the same area of the ancient Near
East, with similar conceptions and similar thought-forms."[3] Yet, he
feels the need to refrain from making any firm conclusions as
concerns "real or apparent consonances." Beyerlin even goes so far as
to say, "Is it not important to realize that each of the two religions
inhabits a self-contained world of its own?" Nevertheless, he also
states, parenthetically, "In any case, for many centuries Egypt ruled
Palestine or influenced it culturally—with interruptions, over a period
lasting for two millennia." At the same, time, we are told that, other
than one text, the "Teaching of Amenemope," there is no real evidence
showing "a work from Egyptian being taken over in Palestine." While
it may be so that we do not necessarily possess other texts identical
to both nations in different languages, nonetheless we find, as
Beyerlin earlier says, "similar conceptions and similar thought-
forms," which, when combined with the fact that Egypt influenced
culture in Palestine for almost 2,000 years, we can be fairly certain
that *there was a substantial amount of exchange in religious ideology.*
It is this unfortunate type of obfuscation that has prevented any
meaningful movement in the field of comparative religion when it

---

[1] See the Yale Divinity School website: "Training for the Christian Ministry was a main
purpose in the founding of Yale College in 1701." ("History of Yale Divinity School.")
See also the Harvard Divinity School website: "The origins of Harvard Divinity School
and the study of theology at Harvard can be traced back to the very beginning of
Harvard College." ("Harvard Divinity School–History and Mission.")
[2] "About Princeton Theological Seminary–History of the Seminary."
[3] Beyerlin, 1.

includes ideologies currently held to be "true" by significant numbers of people.

At the same time, we have also seen that, in order for individual texts and even entire genres of literature to survive they needed to be treated with disdain and to be denounced, such as the Hermetic literature. Certain detractors, in fact, were instrumental in preserving the arguments of their opponents, which would have otherwise been "lost," as a result of deliberate destruction. Because of cherished beliefs and biases, entire premises have either been overlooked or routinely rejected, such as, for instance, trying to find influences *from* the Hermetic literature *on* Christianity. Because of entrenched institutions, there has often been neither the will nor the financial incentive to encourage such studies. On the contrary, ensconced academicians have been discouraged in such endeavors because of this lack of support and turning of a blind eye. This neglected research has then been left to "outsiders" who enjoy no such support or imprimatur stamped upon their work by mainstream authorities, making it much easier for them to be dismissed, ridiculed and ignored.

Modern scholars, in fact, appear to go out of their way to avoid comparison to Christianity or the use of Christian terminology, although on occasion they drop hints of related subjects in need of further study, as demonstrated here. Exhibiting the wariness applied to scholarship involving religion, which has certainly crossed the line into censorship on numerous occasions, in "Christ versus Apollo in Early Byzantine Kourion?," Dr. Hans Hauben, a professor of Ancient History at Katholieke Universiteit Leuven, cautions:

> The preceding study reminds us of the necessity to handle matters of religious history with extreme care, especially when confronted with at first glance unexpected or strange developments. More than in other circumstances, fantasy should be firmly restrained to avoid that early believed and increasingly repeated misunderstandings go their own way before ending up as a quasi historical facts.[1]

While they themselves may not wish to go out on limbs, professional scholars sometimes leave breadcrumb trails to follow, often as the last sentence in their books, as if the subject of comparing the Egyptian and Christian religions were on their minds the whole time. As one exception to the rule, Egyptologist Dr. Morenz is somewhat more forthcoming, including, for example, in his opus *Egyptian Religion* a section entitled, "Contribution to Old and New Testaments," in which he says, "The influence of Egyptian religion on posterity is mainly felt through Christianity and its antecedents."[2] In his exploration of the influence on the Old Testament, Morenz describes a sentence appearing in a document called the "Instruction

---

[1] Janssens, 281-282.
[2] Morenz, 251.

of Ptah-hotep" regarding not altering sacred texts: "Take no word away, and add nothing thereto, and put not one thing in the place of another..."[1] Morenz follows this discussion by saying that "this sentence found its way to Palestine together with Egyptian wisdom literature." Indeed, the sentence sounds very much like the warning at the end of the New Testament Book of Revelation (22:18-19). Morenz further remarks that the "similarity of genres... is also found in the familiar parallels between Egyptian and Israelite wisdom literature, which in general may be regarded as a gift of Egypt."[2] With such hints, would not a person passionate about these parallels between Egyptian and Israelite literature go on a quest to discover them?

Morenz concludes his work with a telling paragraph that once again summarizes the influence of the Egyptian religion on Christianity, mentioning the Isis-Mary parallels as well as the similarity between Egyptian monkishness and Christian monasticism. He ends by saying, "All this entitles us to the opinion that Egypt played its part in the efforts of Christians to achieve an understanding of God and his works, which are eternal."[3] This last part appears to be an appeasement for any readers who might by this time be questioning Morenz's Christian piety based on his previous remarks definitively stating that the Egyptian religion influenced the New Testament and early Christian theology. In view of what had happened previously to scholars who spoke out in a manner too frank, it is possible that Morenz's concern was not simply paranoia. Yet, later, in a note this German scholar cautions against "exaggerations" in seeing survivals of the Egyptian religion in Christianity, of which he too was guilty, remarking:

> This admission does not imply that one cannot reckon with such survivals, but one should not seek them out.[4]

With this seemingly fearful warning we are left with the paradox that, while many aspects of Egyptian religion are in need of further study vis-à-vis their relationship to Christianity, we should not seek out any parallels that may be revealed by such scholarship! Again, we find this sort of tiptoeing and timidity in numerous books on the subject.

---

[1] Morenz, 251.
[2] Morenz, 252.
[3] Morenz, 257.
[4] Morenz, 350.

"Nolo Comprehendere"[1]

It is noteworthy that much of the important research regarding comparative religion and mythology has been done in French, German and other languages, and is thus not easily accessible to the English-speaking public. Significant sources may be difficult or impossible to obtain, as well as in foreign languages, and the expense and complication of finding and translating these may be prohibitive for the individual. In this regard, it is stunning to discover very little information in English on the highly important Egyptian winter solstice, for example, when in Dr. Brugsch's German notebooks there are multiple pages concerning the *Winterwende*. Indeed, in this example of pertinent information not being readily available in English, from Brugsch's work with the original Egyptian images and hieroglyphs, combined with many other essentials, such as the words of Plutarch and Macrobius, we know that the Egyptian sun god was brought out as a "babe" in a "manger" or "ark" on the winter solstice. Yet, these salient facts are not extensively understood or are purposely ignored and forgotten by mainstream writers in English.

As another, more modern example of important contentions in another language that may not be easily found in English, turning to the *Proceedings of the Ninth International Congress of Egyptologists*, which took place in September 2004, we find a discussion in French by Egyptologist Dr. Omaïma M. El-Shal of the Institut de Papyrologie et d'Egyptologie and Fayoum University, regarding the correlation between Osiris and "Le Christ," as well as "Isis et Horus—la Vierge et l'enfant" or "Isis and Horus—the Virgin and the Infant." Under these two categories, Dr. El-Shal remarks:

> There might be a symbolic relationship between the god Osiris and (the) Christ. It would have been achieved through five common factors based on the topology, theology, history, idealism and finally the significance of the two "myths."...
>
> The iconography of the goddess Isis breastfeeding her son the god Horus is reminiscent of the Virgin and Child.[2]

El-Shal also summarizes, among other motifs, the adoption by the Christian Copts of the "afterlife" boat and ladder of the Book of the Dead and elsewhere, as previously discussed here. In addressing the ancient Egyptian tradition of the ladder, she says that "it could also symbolize the sacred mound emerging from the primordial waters where the solar boat arose each morning." She also remarks that the Christians may have brought together this sacred mound and solar boat as a reflection of the biblical story of the ark "stranded

---

[1] This subtitle is a *play on words* based on the legal plea *nolo contendere*, which literally means, "I am unwilling to contend." *Comprehendere* in Latin, of course, means "to understand." I explain myself here lest I be accused of ignorantly mangling the phrase.
[2] Goyon, 634. (English translation mine.)

on the hill" after the flood had subsided. El-Shal further states, "We can therefore conclude that the [Christian] 'Mount of the Cross' derives from the solar tradition of ancient Egypt." As we can see, some significant comparisons between the Egyptian and Christian traditions appear in this scholarly essay in French.[1]

We also discover that where matters were "too delicate" they were either never translated from the original language or were rendered in Latin so they would remain above the heads of the public. Furthermore, we have seen that pertinent material has either disappeared or become difficult to find, such as in the case of Dr. Birch's hieroglyphic dictionary and many other texts over the centuries, as well as censored or edited out of ancient works or left out of translations, preventing it from becoming widely known.

In this regard, we have noted that pertinent comments purportedly from ancient times, such as by Clement of Alexandria concerning the apostles replacing the 12 signs of the zodiac, are deemed "interpolations" and are omitted from analyses. To repeat, the dismissal of various writings as interpolations verifies two serious problems with ancient texts: 1. Ancient writers' works frequently have been altered; and 2. Mainstream scholarship is heavily censored. Hence, a scan of encyclopedias and textbooks will not necessarily reveal germane correlations between Christianity and other religions.

Moreover, one would think the fact that the passage in Epiphanius about the Egyptians worshipping a virgin-mother goddess and her babe in a manger would have been of immense interest to scholars of comparative religion, along with its history of having been edited out of at least one Greek edition. Yet, there remains not only blatant censorship with material being removed from ancient texts but also a sort of embarrassed or fearful silence to recount *anything* that in the slightest way might be deleterious to the Christian faith. This latter development is comprehensible considering the climate of the day, following on the heels of the Inquisition and with an atmosphere that encouraged the firing and blacklisting of anyone who dared challenge the status quo. In view of the volatility of the subject matter and the obvious investment of interest for a large segment of the population, it would not be unreasonable to suggest that a significant portion of the data found in this present work has been deliberately suppressed as well.

Blotting Out the Sun

In addition to avoiding or ignoring the subject have emerged efforts to create as much wriggle room as possible to deny any relationship between the Egyptian and Christian religions, including obliterating the real meaning behind parallels between Christ and

---

[1] Goyon, 634.

other gods. For example, while writing a book on Osiris—thus, professing himself to be an expert on that god—Sir Frazer was so intent on amputating the obvious astrotheological meaning behind numerous myths that, astoundingly, he created an entire chapter entitled "Osiris and the Sun" in order to debunk the notion that the Egyptian god had anything to do with solar mythology! As we have seen plentifully throughout this work, however, Osiris's—and Horus's—solar role in the ancient texts, myths and rituals is evident, although it must be kept in mind that Osiris also served as the "life force," so to speak, in many aspects of Egyptian life, including as the Nile, water in general, the light in the moon, fertility and so on. Yet, this salvational function too is traditionally that of the sun, and Osiris's solar role is made obvious by the mere fact that he was identified repeatedly with Ra, even given the epithet "Osiris-Re."[1] Based on all the facts, it seems unquestionable that in the minds of many millions of worshippers, Osiris was identified with and as the sun.

One of the arguments used by Frazer in his assiduous attempts to downplay the solar aspects of Osiris is a contention by Renouf that the god was never depicted as "dead in the winter"—an odd assertion, considering what we have discovered in this present work regarding the Egyptian perception of the winter solstice! In this regard, Frazer remarks:

> Thus Renouf, who identified Osiris with the sun, admitted that the Egyptian sun could not with any show of reason be described as dead in winter. But if his daily death was the theme of the legend, why was it celebrated by an annual ceremony? This fact alone seems fatal to the interpretation of the myth as descriptive of sunset and sunrise. Again, though the sun may be said to die daily, in what sense can he be said to be torn in pieces?[2]

Frazer evidently believed this question concerning Osiris's rent body to be a fatal flaw in the thesis that the god was largely a solar entity. However, even in ancient times Plutarch (42, 368A), provided the simple answer to this quandary: *Osiris is the sun's light in the moon*, which is rent into 14 pieces/days as it is waxing. Also, if Osiris is the sun dying on a daily basis, as Frazer discusses here, he would likewise die on the day of the winter solstice, just as the daily-born Horus must have been born on that day as well! Indeed, we have seen from Plutarch (39, 366D-E) that the Egyptians very much did celebrate an annual "Seeking of Osiris" that clearly had to do in part with the shortest day of the year.

Frazer followed these remarks by more astonishing and exasperating commentary regarding various authorities who "abandoned" the association of Osiris with the sun. The British

[1] Faulkner, *EBD*, 150.
[2] Frazer, *OAA*, 292.

scholar's intent in amputating astrotheology from ancient
made clear also in his opus *The Golden Bough.* Althou~~~
work was thus deficient in this particular important aspect, the
severe criticism and wave-of-the-hand dismissal of his voluminous
efforts as concerns the "dying-and-rising-god" theme overall has been
demonstrated by Mettinger, et al., as largely unwarranted.
Concerning the fervent and irrational anti-dying-and-rising stance
held by various scholars and apologists, Dr. Bob Price remarks:

> But we lack any reason to give the benefit of the doubt to a
> reconstruction whose only merit would seem to be its function of
> overthrowing Frazer's hypothesis and allowing Christian apologetics
> to breathe a little easier. In other words, it is special pleading.

As we have seen abundantly here, despite the nitpicking and
hairsplitting, the correspondences are not only real but also
significant. Their dismissal and denial, in fact, can only occur if their
roots are yanked out of their milieu not only around the
Mediterranean but also on planet Earth! These contrived "differences"
appear to presuppose that no ancient peoples in any part of the world
could possibly have conceived religious and spiritual reality in the
same general manner as that found within Christianity. Such a
notion would, of course, represent a truly supernatural genesis for
Christianity, out of the blue, untouched by human hands or minds.
Indeed, the very suggestion makes of one a fundamentalist Christian;
henceforth, per typical apologist tactics, no one proposing the "anti-
dying-and-rising god" position could possibly be considered a "real
scholar," because he is too biased.

In any event, with this one fell swoop, Frazer managed almost
single-handedly to put an end to research into the fascinating and
incredibly important field of solar mythology and astrotheology. So
effective has been this eclipsing of the sun that many encyclopedias
and textbooks still do not even include the solar roles of either Osiris
or Horus.

In this endeavor, Frazer was merely reproducing the same actions
of the creators of Christianity in blotting out the sun. As famed
philosopher Thomas Paine (1737-1809) remarked:

> ...the christian religion is a parody on the worship of the Sun, in
> which they put a man whom they call Christ, in the place of the Sun,
> and pay him the same adoration which was originally paid to the
> Sun...[1]

As we have seen throughout this work the severing and darkening
of the sun in Egyptian mythology and religion are utterly
unsustainable notions—indeed, completely contrary to the true
meaning of Egyptian religion. Moreover, this type of sanitization has
led to the virtual ignorance of the very matter that lies at the root of

---

[1] Paine, 293.

our major religions and a number of our minor ones dating back many thousands of years.

The solar foundations of the Egyptian religion have thus been eclipsed by the Abrahamic soli-lunar cults, which fallaciously deny any such astrotheological underpinnings. This eclipse, as well as the resultant silence and avoidance of the subject of astrotheology, is so thorough that it testifies to enduring trauma, created long ago with Christian censorship efforts, including a virulent dislike of astronomy/astrology, as well as the terrorization of farmers, sailors and anyone else who needed to look up at the sky in order to practice their livelihood. This enduring trauma is so complete, it is only recently that people have begun to learn that "December 25th" in reality represents the end of the three-day period of the *winter solstice.* Much other knowledge of the natural world has been omitted from our standard education for the same reasons and much to our detriment as a species.

In the end, the solar and astrotheological origins of much religious and spiritual thought represents one of the most overlooked studies, as revealed by a number of germane examples in this present work. Indeed, *much information challenging the mainstream religions has been willfully suppressed*—and this fact needs to be kept in mind at all times when investigating comparative religion and mythology.

Mysterious Omissions

It is obvious from comments by ancient and modern writers alike that various of the correspondences between the Egyptian and Christian religions constituted what are known as "the mysteries," such as the perpetual virginity of the goddess and the birth of her son at the winter solstice, indicated in a number of places and brought to light here. Exploring the numerous other parallels between the Christian and Egyptian religions using the same "forensic" methodology, we find much of the same veracity behind them as well. Searching across the scope of books available today is quite eye opening, in fact, when it comes to various concepts that are considered mysteries. As *mysteries,* these characteristics and themes were not necessarily spelled out explicitly in texts or inscriptions— although, as we have seen, they are certainly strongly implied in a number of places, as well as overtly disclosed enough to prove themselves real ideas and motifs belonging to the ancient world. Other correlations, however, have been right before our eyes, covered over by delusion and mendacity, to be exposed here and now through great struggle and the passage of thousands of years. We are, in fact, privileged to exist at a time when these mysteries are at last revealed, and humanity can progress to a greater level of edification and enlightenment.

Conclusion

To reiterate, as evidence of the seriousness with which mysteries were held, the ancient Greek writer Herodotus remarked that he was reluctant to speak about what was taught him concerning the Egyptian religion, indicating as well that he knew some of its mysteries. As illustrated by the case of the Greek statesman Alcibiades, capital punishment was often the result for divulging the mysteries—and the penalty was certainly carried out at various times. That there have existed mysteries is an undisputable fact, and the contention that they were real and important within Egyptian religion in specific is likewise doubtlessly true.

Summarizing the mysteries in Egypt, Massey remarks:

> The mystery of an ever-virgin mother; the mystery of a boy at twelve years of age transforming suddenly into an adult of thirty years, and then becoming one with the father, as it had been earlier in the mysteries of totemism; the mystery in which the dead body of Osiris is transubstantiated into the living Horus by descent of the bird-headed holy spirit; the mystery of a divine being in three persons, one of which takes flesh on earth as the human Horus, to become a mummy as Osiris in Amenta, and to rise up from the dead in spirit as Ra in heaven. These and other miracles of the Christian faith were already extant among the mysteries of Amenta.[1]

Furthermore, because of the scarcity of writing materials and the widespread illiteracy, much knowledge was passed along verbally, many times with great emphasis taken in order to ensure accurate transmissions. In reality, it was—and still is in some places—a matter of pride at how well a person could be trained to memorize sacred scriptures. We can rest assured that there was much of the same oral tradition practice in the Egyptian religion. In our quest to know everything about Egypt, we cannot afford to ignore a major form of communication simply because today's standards do not live up to those set within the long history of oral tradition. In this regard, we can also be certain that much important information was transmitted orally, in likelihood a significant amount of it never being written down. In some instances, then, we must examine whether or not hidden knowledge has been transformed in order to continue to disguise it, such as happened with Gnosticism and, we maintain, Christianity, which was in fact an ideology that turned the mysteries inside out and broadcast them to the world. Indeed, it has been posited that it was because of *this transgression* of the mysteries oath—a capital offense—that early Christians were "martyred." This sort of clandestine priestcraft has been common throughout the past several millennia, if not long before, serving as a well-developed science designed to cloak powerful truths in allegory and mysticism, so that the average person will not recognize them. Here we are

---

[1] Massey, *AELW*, I, 226.

interested in peeling back the shrouds of long-hidden secrets and mysteries.

Mutable Mythology

The many correlations presented here between the Egyptian and Christian religions are also not widely known because since ancient times they have not been neatly laid out in sanctioned encyclopedias and textbooks. In actuality, such sources often include only one version of a myth, when there may well be more than one, as is often the case with myths, which are not static but change to suit the time and location. As stated by Dr. Assman regarding the Egyptian religion, "...it is only natural that far-reaching changes occurred during a span of more than three millennia."[1] Illustrating effectively how religion is tailored and changed to suit cultural fancies, Dr. Žabkar includes a significant discussion of the "Isiac aretalogies," from the Greek ἀρετή, meaning "goodness," "excellence" or "merit," etc. Aretalogies are essentially recitations of virtues and characteristics, such as "I am Isis, ruler of every land."[2] Concerning the creator of one basic Isis aretalogy, Žabkar says:

> Its author—either an Egyptian educated in Greek culture and language or a Greek well informed about Egyptian religion—wishing to propagate the cult of Isis among the Greeks, borrowed from the Egyptian Isiac and other texts the ideas and phrases acceptable to the Greeks, eliminated those that may have appeared alien or incomprehensible to them, and added to his text a considerable number of typically Greek features. The result of all this was a strongly hellenized composition: Isis appeared to her Greek devotees as a Greek, not an Egyptian, goddess.[3]

Žabkar also remarks:

> Intent on composing a truly Greek aretalogy and writing for the Greek devotees of Isis far away from her homeland, he, too, suppressed all that might have appeared alien to his contemporaries and presented to the worshipers of the goddess a thoroughly hellenized Isis.[4]

Revisiting this subject of the Greek scribe reworking the Egyptian hymns in order to appeal to Greek followers, Žabkar again comments:

> Inspired by these, he translated some of the Egyptian phrases into Greek and paraphrased and grecized others; for the benefit of the Greek devotees of the goddess, he added to his composition a substantial number of typically Greek statements; all these he blended into a harmonious unit—his work appeared as something new.[5]

---

[1] Assman, *SGAE*, 18.
[2] Žabkar, 147.
[3] Žabkar, 136.
[4] Žabkar, 136.
[5] Žabkar, 159.

This process precisely describes how myths are changed and altered to suit the audience, and we maintain that the same development occurred with Christianity, which was an attempt to blend harmoniously Judaism with the many Pagan religious concepts of the Roman Empire and beyond.

In this regard, the history of religion shows a continual wave of ideas that mutate as they pass from region to region, as well as when they are subjected to domination based on invasion, warfare and other cultural usurpation. In polytheistic societies, deities of various cultures may co-exist, but in monotheistic cultures, the gods of the dominated cultures must be demoted, demonized or destroyed. Hence, in terms of peaceful coexistence, monotheism is an inferior and intolerant method of governance. The domination of one deity or religious concept over another often is based on physical strength and brutality—"might being right"—rather than philosophical and theological correctness. Instead of representing truth, a religious ideology may be mainly propaganda. In extrapolating the true meaning of myths and why they have been changed over the eras, therefore, we must factor into our analyses the principle of *cui bono*—who benefits?

Well Known in Egypt?

In the final analysis, the questions come down to these: Were the various important mythical motifs explored here part of Egyptian religion, and, despite their apparent status as mysteries, were they known to those who created Christianity? We have already seen abundantly throughout this work that numerous of these concepts *were* found in one form or another in the Egyptian writings and other artifacts, predating the common era by centuries to millennia. Regarding the Egyptian sacred texts, for example, which contain many of these concepts, Budge remarks:

> The *Scriptures must have been well known,* as copies of chapters are found by the thousands on the persons of mummies themselves, and on the walls of the thousands of tombs, which would not have been the case were the living majority unable to read.[1]

We have also seen that there were evidently possibly a *half a billion* followers of the Egyptian religion over the thousands of years. In *The Ancient Egyptian Books of the Afterlife*, after discussing the "whole libraries of ancient writings" that were "collected on tomb walls and sarcophagi," Hornung remarks, "All the conditions were thus at hand for an influence that continued beyond the pharaonic period and into the new spiritual currents of Hellenism and early Christianity."[2] As we can see, this erudite Egyptologist is certain that the Egyptian religion was available to and influential upon early

[1] Bonwick, 188.
[2] Hornung, *AEBA*, xix.

Christianity, a fact thoroughly demonstrated herein. By their presence also in the Coffin Texts, by which "every deceased person was an Osiris NN," these myriad concepts must have been well known to the *average people* as well.

In these well-known scriptures appeared basics of the myths of the Egyptian gods, such as Osiris, Isis and Horus, that must have been of interest to tens if not hundreds of millions of people throughout the ages. These concepts included elements of Osiris's story that may be encapsulated as follows: Osiris was called "Father." He once walked the earth. He was the savior and deliverer of mankind. He was killed, buried in a tomb and resurrected, before ascending to heaven.[1] Adding to this familiar story—which so closely parallels the Christ myth—are the numerous aspects and characteristics of other Egyptian gods and goddesses explored here, such as:

- The divine son of God battling the Evil One
- The son being born on December 25th of a virgin named "Mery"
- Three "wise men" following a star in the east
- The divine son at the ages of 12 and 30
- The holy baptizer of souls
- The god having 12 followers
- The deity performing miracles such as healing the sick, walking on water, raising the dead
- The god being called "Anointed," "Lord of Truth," "Lord of Light," "Lord of Resurrections" and so on
- The god associated with the cross, which symbolizes eternal life
- The god being buried for three days, resurrecting and ascending into heaven, etc.

In the end, the correspondences between these religions are real, so we must ask again why they are being censored out of the historical record, as well as merely overlooked. Rather than simply denying these many correlations between the Egyptian and Christian religions, the truthseeker may be struck that they did in fact exist, that they were revered in the ancient world, particularly by the priesthoods who created such myths, and that anyone wishing to enter the profitable religion business would need to incorporate them into their myths, as we contend was done with the gospel story. The bulk of the correspondences between the Egyptian and Christian religions do not rank as inconsequential details but constitute prominent motifs within Egyptian religious life. The point is that these very important spiritual and religious concepts—a number of which represented *mysteries* but which were nonetheless known to the educated elite—were themselves evidently taken one by one by the creators of Christianity and rolled into a fictional story. In light of

---

[1] See Bonwick, 154-156.

these facts, carefully hidden from the masses, it is objectionable to insist that the Egyptian and Christian religions are entirely unrelated, especially when ancient Egyptian Christians themselves readily and often made the "Horus-Jesus connection," so to speak.

Which Came First?

In analyzing this situation of influence, Christian apologists may grudgingly agree that there are instances where borrowing may or must have occurred, but they frequently claim there is no solid evidence that such borrowing was *by* Christianity *from* Paganism. Of the pre-Christian primary sources presented here and available elsewhere, there is no doubt, obviously, which came first and likely influenced the other. Sources that do not clearly predate the purported time of Christ, in other words, beginning around the first quarter of the first century AD/CE and continuing, are automatically suspected of being influenced *by* Christianity. Yet, in such cases as the writings of Philo and Plutarch, for example, who most assuredly described concepts that found their way into Christianity, there is absolutely no evidence of either writer having the slightest awareness of the existence of Christ, Christianity or Christians. The same can be said for a number of other writers during the so-called first century of the "Christian era," as there exists in reality no credible, scientific evidence for a significant "Christian" presence involving a "historical" Jesus Christ during that time. In addition, major contentions of Plutarch, for instance, can be backed up in the ancient pre-Christian Egyptian writings and other artifacts, as established here. Indeed, in the world of Egyptology we possess a massive amount of pre-Christian data previously unavailable that appears to verify the assertion that virtually nothing within Christianity is new or original and that a significant portion of it emanated out of Egypt. Hence, in many instances the argument of precedence is settled.

Regarding this matter of precedence for parallels, Witt advocated proceeding with caution, but was also certain that the Egyptian religion influenced Christianity, remarking:

> Historians, generally, and specifically those who trace the development of religious ideas, need to avoid the trap of confusing the chronological order with cause and effect: *post hoc ergo propter hoc.* On the other hand, the veneration (*hyperdulia*) of the Blessed Virgin Mary was certainly introduced at about the same time as Theodosius ordered the destruction of the pagan temples, including the Sarapeum and other shrines of the Egyptian gods. Here, we may think, lies a reason for the absorption of elements, ideas and usages from the old religion into the new.[1]

As can be seen, the evident borrowing *by* Christianity continued well into the common era, during Theodosius's time in the fourth

---

[1] Witt, 273-274.

century. Thus, simply because borrowing occurred during the "Christian era" does not mean it was by Paganism from Christianity. Again, what is designated as the "Christian era" did not descend suddenly upon the entire world after the year 1 AD/CE but is relative, and to this day there remain places that are still *pre-Christian*, showing no knowledge of or influence by Christianity.

In capitulating to the fact that there are indeed very serious correspondences between the Egyptian and Christian religions, apologists insist that these motifs can only be found dating to the middle of the second century at the earliest, when Justin Martyr discussed them in detail, thereby supposedly showing that Paganism must have borrowed them *from* Christianity. In the first place, this present work reveals otherwise, as practically everything significant within Christianity existed in one form or another in the Egyptian religion long before the common era, much of it revolving around the characters of Osiris, Isis and Horus.

Moreover, in his *First Apology* (54) Justin specifically claims these parallels, including the Greek god Bacchus/Dionysus's ascension into heaven, as well as the virgin birth and ascension of Perseus, were the result of "the devil" *anticipating* Christ's story:

> For having heard it proclaimed through the prophets that Christ was to come...[the wicked demons] put forward many to be called sons of Jupiter, under the impression that they would be able to produce in men the idea that the things which were said with regard to Christ were mere marvelous tales, like the things which were said by the poets.[1]

In chapter 56 of his *Apology*, Justin pointedly states that the "evil spirits" were making their mischief *"before Christ's appearance."*[2] In other words, Justin—and others using the same "devil did it" excuse, such as Tertullian and Lactantius—did not dishonestly deny the parallels, as have many modern apologists. Indeed, these early Church fathers happily used these correspondences in their polemics and apologies to make Christianity appear less ridiculous—and ridiculous it evidently was perceived to be by the educated Greeks and Romans of the time. To these latter groups, the gospel story could not have been any more "real" or "historical" than that of Apollo or Neptune, and they surely doubted Christ's existence as a "historical" figure in ancient times. Moreover, nowhere does Justin Martyr claim that the Pagans *copied* Christianity *after* Christ's alleged advent, which he certainly would have done, had the copying occurred in that direction.

It is obvious from Justin's "devil got there first" excuse that these mythical motifs existed *before* Christ's purported manifestation on Earth and that there were those in his time who sensibly questioned

---

[1] Roberts, A., *ANCL*, II, 53-54.
[2] Roberts, A., *ANCL*, II, 55.

the historical veracity of the gospel story, essentially calling it "mere marvellous tales"—in other words, a *myth*. In *Dialogue with Trypho* (69), in fact, Justin again invokes the "devil got there first" argument, specifically stating that these Pagan "counterfeits" were likewise "wrought by the Magi in Egypt."[1] Now, which "counterfeits" and "Magi" would these be? The "Magi" must be the Egyptian priests, apparently called as such by people of Justin's era, while the "counterfeits" must refer to at least some of the Egyptian gods. Justin also specifically names the Greek gods Dionysus, Hercules and Asclepius as those whose "fables" were emulated by the devil in *anticipating* Christ. As we have seen, these gods have their counterparts in Egyptian mythology as well, in Osiris and Horus, as prime examples.

The idea that the Pagan world just suddenly switched to themes stolen *from* Christianity merely a few decades after the latter had been conceived ranks as a false scenario, as demonstrated copiously throughout this present work, in which it has been shown that these numerous motifs in one form or another had been in the minds of enough people—especially those who actually create religions, i.e., priests—by the time Christianity was formulated. When we read what Justin said about the Pagan myths in existence prior Jesus's purported time—and there is no evidence of the existence of the gospel *story* until the *end* of the first century at the earliest, nor does Justin himself ever mention the canonical gospels themselves by name, as if he never heard of them[2]—we know him to be speaking truthfully in significant part, as we possess sufficient evidence to demonstrate his accuracy, albeit a vast amount has been destroyed, hidden and covered up.

Despite all of the destruction and censorship, enough telltale signs remain for us to piece together the puzzle that reveals an image of religious and mythological motifs stretching back into the hoary mists of time and paralleling concepts found in the much later Christianity. As yet another example, the idea of a divine savior and son of God whose birth was "good news for the world" and who was a god himself existed already in the minds of many within the Roman Empire years *before the purported advent of Jesus Christ*. This fact can be easily proved by the testimony concerning Caesar Augustus (63 BCE-14 AD/CE), including the so-called Priene calendar inscription and "many other inscriptions and papyri" in which Augustus is deemed "son of God."[3] In fact, this one inscription, the Priene, possesses several words used in later Christian doctrine, such as god (*theos*), savior (*soter*), appearance (*epiphanein*) and good news

---

[1] Roberts, A., *ANCL*, II, 184.
[2] See Cassels's exhaustive *Supernatural Religion* for a survey of the earliest Christian literature, including whether or not Justin reveals any awareness of the canonical gospels as we have them.
[3] Porter, *HOTNT*, 93.

(*evangelion*). Scholars such as Drs. Porter and Helmut Koester believe the evangelist Mark, in using the term *evangelion*, was copying this imperial decree and other such usages. Speaking of *evangelion*, when Vespasian arrived at Alexandria, he too was "greeted with this good news (ευαγγέλια)."[1] This Greek word, of course, serves as the root for "evangelism." As we can see from this one example, there was nothing new under the sun when the solar mythos of Christianity was created.

Part of the difficulty in understanding what transpired in the creation of Christianity lies in the erroneous impression regarding the milieu of the Mediterranean at that time. Contrary to popular belief, much of the area was highly populated, with sophisticated culture dating back hundreds to thousands of years, including bustling trade routes that extended to India and beyond. Millions of people passed through the major cities of the Roman Empire, and it is evident that the Christian effort was not confined to the tiny outback of Judea. Indeed, as revealed here, much of Christianity was undoubtedly created in the large and important city of Alexandria with its substantial and wealthy Jewish population, and with its massive library filled with hundreds of thousands of manuscripts from around the known world, which undoubtedly contained treatises on every major religion of the time and many minor ones as well.

Reading the scholarly analyses of Egyptian religion today often gives the impression that principal concepts found therein reside beyond the grasp of the average mind, as if only the most erudite among us can fathom their profundity. While it is possible that some of the priests who fabricated these religious notions over the millennia did intend a mysticism that remains above the average person's head, it is necessary to recognize that *in reality it is the common people who determine a religion*. The average taste dictates the marketplace, and this case is proved handily within religion. If our finest theologians and scholars of religion were given free rein in creating faith anew, it is possible that they would never fill a single pew!

Perhaps the greatest value of the Egyptian religion—which may have led to it being one of the longest lasting spiritual traditions in human history—is that it focused on solving the problems associated with death, for both the deceased and the bereaved, thus appealing to all people. As Egyptologist Assman says, "A comprehensive treatment of the theme of death can thus constitute an introduction to the essence of all of ancient Egyptian culture."[2] The understanding and explanation of the daily death-and-rebirth myth associated with the sun, as well as the spiritual relationship with other natural phenomena, serving as a transition for people dying every day,

---

[1] Stanton, 29.
[2] Assman, *DSAE*, 2.

provided a real and meaningful role for the religion and its priesthood. In this regard, instead of the constant violence and intolerance of the megalomaniacal and culturally bigoted monotheistic religions, we are currently in a position to recognize fully our natural surroundings, based not on blind belief but, rather, on scientific observation as well as aesthetic appreciation. Regardless of religious beliefs or nonbeliefs, as human beings we can all relish the splendor of the natural world, with most people able to cherish an exquisite sunset or full moon, for example.

To defend an intangible concept such as God by killing a living, breathing human being constitutes one of the greatest evils in the world, and it simply must stop, or humankind has no right to call itself "civilized." Nor do we need to perceive the material world as something "inherently evil," as the Abrahamic religions would lead us to believe. The comprehension of the astrotheological and nature-worshipping perception behind the world's religious ideologies greatly benefits humanity in a number of ways, revealing not only the imaginative and creative capacity of the human mind but also the beauty and awe of creation that inspire and unite mankind beyond its divisive and destructive beliefs. In the end, we are free to develop true human community based not on neurotic and psychotic "religious" pathologies that see "other" and "infidel" but on shared, common experiences and reference points, such as the mysterious and marvelous planet upon which we all live.

Bibliography

"About Princeton Theological Seminary–History of the Seminary,"
http://www.ptsem.edu/About/mission.php

"Abu Simbel," www.touregypt.net/abusimbel.htm

"Ancient Egyptian Calendar,"
www.kingtutshop.com/freeinfo/Ancient-Egyptian-Calendar.htm

"Ancient Egyptian Language Discussion List,"
www.rostau.org.uk/AEgyptian-L/archives/week226.txt

"Block statue and stela of Sahathor,"
www.britishmuseum.org/explore/highlights/highlight_objects/ae
s/b/statue_and_stela_of_sahathor.aspx

"Brunner Collection," www.lib.mq.edu.au/collections/brunner.html

"Coffin set of Henettawy,"
www.metmuseum.org/toah/hd/tipd/ho_25.3.182-184.htm

"Decree of Canopus," en.wikipedia.org/wiki/Decree_of_Canopus

"Egyptian Mummification," Spurlock Museum,
www.spurlock.uiuc.edu/explorations/online/mummification/
Pages/materials1.html

"Egyptian Tomb Inscriptions May Bear Oldest Proto-Hebrew Text
Yet," www.foxnews.com/story/0,2933,246379,00.html

"Egyptologists," *International Directory of Egyptology*,
www.iae.lmu.de/iae/ide/ide.htm

"A Festival Calendar of the Ancient Egyptians,"
howcase.netins.net/web/ankh/calendar1.html

"Giant Fortress's Remains Found in Egypt," *National Geographic
News*, news.nationalgeographic.com/news/2008/06/080602-
egypt-fort.html

"H. Res. 847: Recognizing the importance of Christmas and the
Christian faith,"
www.govtrack.us/congress/billtext.xpd?bill=hr110-847

"Harvard Divinity School-History and Mission,"
www.hds.harvard.edu/history.html

"Historical Images of Surgery,"
www.imageofsurgery.com/Surgery_history_art.htm

"Historical Maps,"
www.specialtyinterests.net/map_abydos_to_edfu.JPG

"History of Yale Divinity School,"
www.yale.edu/divinity/abt/Abt.HistMish.shtml

"Horus Map," www.geocities.com/zurdig/images/HorusMap.jpeg

"Library of Alexandria," en.wikipedia.org/wiki/Library_of_Alexandria

"Luxor—Temple of Luxor—Birth Room,"
www.planetware.com/luxor/temple-of-birth-room-egy-qena-
brtrm.htm

"Map of Ancient Egypt," id-
  archserve.ucsb.edu/Anth3/Courseware/Egypt/sims/HorusMap/
  Horus_Map.html
"Map of Egypt as it Appears Today,"
  oncampus.richmond.edu/academics/education/projects/webunit
  s/egypt/Map.html
"Memphite Theology," *Encyclopedia Britannica,*
  www.britannica.com/EBchecked/topic/374563/Memphite-
  Theology
"Precentor," en.wikipedia.org/wiki/Precentor
"Prehistoric fortress in Egypt excavated," *Thaindian News,*
  www.thaindian.com/newsportal/uncategorized/prehistoric-
  fortress-in-egypt-excavated_10054288.html
"Prytaneum," *Encyclopedia Britannica,*
  www.britannica.com/eb/article-9061671/prytaneum
"Rulers of Egypt's 25th Dynasty & Ancient Nubia,"
  wysinger.homestead.com/mapofnubia.html
"Sothiac year," www.thefreedictionary.com
"The Gaelic Gospel of Mark,"
  www.bibledbdata.org/onlinebibles/gaelic_mark/41_001.htm
"The Mummy Who Would Be King," NOVA,
  www.pbs.org/wgbh/nova/mummy/ikra-01.html
"The Pyramids and the Cities of the Pharaohs," Questar Video,
  Chicago, 1995.
"The Seven Wonders of the Ancient World," Questar Video, Chicago,
  1990.
Acharya S, *Suns of God: Krishna, Buddha and Christ Unveiled,*
  Adventures Unlimited Press, IL, 2004.
  —*The Christ Conspiracy: The Greatest Story Ever Sold,* AUP, IL,
  1999.
  (See also "D.M. Murdock.")
A Guide to the Egyptian Galleries (Sculpture) at the British Museum,
  British Museum, London, 1909.
Allbright, W.F., "Notes on Egypto-Semitic Etymology. II," *The
  American Journal of Semitic Languages and Literature,* vol. 34, no.
  4, July 1918.
Allen, James P., *Middle Egyptian: An Introduction to the Language and
  Culture of Hieroglyphs,* Cambridge University Press, 2000.
  —*The Ancient Egyptian Pyramid Texts,* Society of Biblical
  Literature, Atlanta, 2005.
Allen, Richard Hinckley, *Star-names and Their Meanings,* G.E.
  Stechert, NY, 1899.
Allen, Thomas George, *Horus in the Pyramid Texts,* University of
  Chicago Press, 1916.
  —*The Book of the Dead, or Going Forth by Day,* University of
  Chicago Press, 1974.

The American Journal of Theology, vol. 20, University of Chicago
    Divinity School, 1916.
Anderson, Karl, *Astrology of the Old Testament or the Lost World
    Regained*, Kessinger, 1996.
Anderson, William, *The Scottish Nation*, III, A. Fullarton & Co.,
    Edinburgh, 1863.
Anthes, Rudolf, "Egyptian Theology in the Third Millennium B.C.,"
    Journal of Near Eastern Studies, vol. 18, no. 3, University of
    Chicago Press, 1959.
Apuleius, *Metamorphoseon*, XI,
    www.thelatinlibrary.com/apuleius/apuleius11.shtml#17
    —*The Golden Ass of Lucius Apuleius*, tr. William Adlington,
    Navarre Society, 1924.
    —*The Metamorphosis, or Golden Ass*, tr. Thomas Taylor, London,
    1822.
Aristides, "Apology," www.newadvent.org/fathers/1012.htm
Armour, Robert, A., *Gods and Myths of Ancient Egypt*, The American
    University in Cairo Press, Cairo/NY, 1989
    —*Gods and Myths of Ancient Egypt*, The American University in
    Cairo Press, Cairo/NY, 2002.
Armstrong, A.H., ed., *The Cambridge History of Later Greek and Early
    Medieval Philosophy*, Cambridge University Press, 1967.
Arnold, Dieter, *The Encyclopaedia of Ancient Egyptian Architecture*,
    I.B. Tauris, 2003.
Artemidorus, *Oneirocritica*, Lipsiae, 1805.
Assman, Jan, *Death and Salvation in Ancient Egypt*, tr. David Lorton,
    Cornell University Press, Ithaca/London, 2005.
    —*Egyptian Solar Religion in the New Kingdom: Re, Amun and the
    Crisis of Polytheism*, Kegan Paul International, London/NY, 1995.
    —*Thebanische Beamtennekropolen: Neue Perspektiven
    archäologischer Forschung*, Heidelberger Orientverlag, 1995.
    —*The Search for God in Ancient Egypt*, tr. David Lorton, Cornell
    University Press, Ithaca/London, 2001.
Atiya, Aziz S., "Heracleon," *Dictionary of African Christian Biography*,
    www.dacb.org/stories/egypt/heracleon.html
Atwill, Joseph, *Caesar's Messiah: The Roman Conspiracy to Invent
    Jesus*, Ulysses Press, Berkeley, 2005.
Aufrecht, Th., *A Catalogue of Sanskrit Manuscripts*, Deighton, Bell &
    Co., Cambridge, 1869.
Augustine, *Concerning the City of God against the Pagans*, tr. Henry
    Bettenson, Penguin Books, 2003.
    —*Retractiones*, ed. and tr. J.H.S. Burleigh, Westminster John
    Knox Press, London, 1953.
    —*The City of God against the Pagans*, ed. R.W. Dyson, Cambridge
    University Press, UK, 1998.
    —*The Works of Aurelius Augustine*, X, ed. Marcus Dods, T&T
    Clark, Edinburgh, 1873.

—"Letter 219," www.newadvent.org/fathers/1102219.htm

—"Tractates on the Gospel of John," 19,
www.newadvent.org/fathers/1701019.htm

—"Tractates on the Gospel of John," 34,
www.newadvent.org/fathers/1701034.htm

Aune, David, ed., *The Gospel of Matthew in Current Study*, William B. Eerdmans, MI, 2001.

Backes, Burkhard, *Das altägyptische "zweiwegebuch": Studien zu den Sargtext-sprüchen 1029-1130*, Harrassowitz, 2005.

Baedeker, Karl, *Egypt: A Handbook for Travelers*, Karl Baedeker, Leipsic, 1902.

Bagnall, Roger S. and Derow, Peter, eds., *The Hellenistic Period: Historical Sources in Translation*, Blackwell Publishing, 2004.

Baikie, James, *Egyptian Antiquities in the Nile Valley*, Methuen & Co., London, 1932.

Bakke, Odd Magne, *"Concord and Peace": A Rhetorical Analysis of the First Letter of Clement*, Mohr Siebeck, 2001.

Balfour, Edward, *Cyclopaedia of India, and Southern and Eastern Asia*, Scottish, Lawrence and Foster Presses, Madras, India, 1873.

Bard, Kathryn A., ed., Encyclopedia of the Archaeology of Ancient Egypt, Routledge, 1999.

Barrett, C.K., *The Gospel According to St. John*, The Westminster Press, Philadelphia, 1978.

Basil, "Hexaemeron (Homily 6),"
www.newadvent.org/fathers/32016.htm

Baton, Tamsyn, *Ancient Astrology*, Routledge, 1994.

Bauman, Richard A., *Political Trials in Ancient Greece*, Routledge, London/NY, 1990.

Beal, Samuel, *The Romantic Legend of Sakya Buddha*, Trubner & Co., London, 1875.

Beauregard, Ollivier, *Les Divinités Égyptiennes*, A. LaCroix, Paris, 1866.

Beck, Roger, *Beck on Mithraism: Collected Works With New Essays*, Ashgate Publishing, 2004.

—*A Brief History of Ancient Astrology*, Blackwell Publishing, 2007.

Beinlich, Horst, "Ägyptische Wortliste,"
www.geocities.com/cgbusch/egyptology/beinlich-english4.txt,
www.newton.ac.uk/egypt/beinlich/beinlich.html

Bell, John, *Bell's New Pantheon Or Historical Dictionary of the Gods, Demi Gods, Heroes and Fabulous Personages of Antiquity*, I, Kessinger, 2003.

Beltz, Walter, *Die Mythen der Ägypter*, Claassen, 1982.

Benko, Stephen, *The Virgin Goddess: Studies in the Pagan and Christian Roots of Mariology*, E.J. Brill, Leiden, 1993.

Berkowitz, Luci, et al., *Thesaurus Linguae Graecae Canon of Greek Authors and Works*, Oxford University Press, Oxford, 1986.

Bernand, André, *Pan du Désert*, E.J. Brill, Leiden, 1977.
Betz, Hans Dieter, *The Greek Magical Papyri in Translation*, University of Chicago Press, 1997.
Beyerlin, Walter and Brunner, Hellmut, et al., *Near Eastern Religious Texts Relating to the Old Testament*, The Westminster Press, Philadelphia, 1978.
—*Religionsgeschichtliches Textbuch zum Alten Testament*, Vandenhoeck & Ruprecht, Göttingen, 1985.
Biedermann, Hans, *Dictionary of Symbolism*, tr. James Hulbert, Facts on File, NY/Oxford. 1992.
Bishai, Wilson B., "A Possible Coptic Source for a Qur'anic Text," *Journal of the American Oriental Society*, vol. 91, no. 1, Jan-Mar 1971.
The Bizarre. Notes and Queries, V, S.C. & L.M. Gould, NH, 1888.
Blathwayt, Raymond, *Interviews*, A.W. Hall, London, 1893.
Bleeker, Claas Jouco, *Hathor and Thoth: Two Key Figures of the Ancient Egyptian Religion*, E.J. Brill, Leiden, 1973.
Blue Letter Bible, www.blueletterbible.org
Blunt, John Henry, ed., *Dictionary of Sects, Heresies, Ecclesiastical Parties, and Schools of Religious Thought*, Rivingtons, London, 1874.
Boas, George, tr., *The Hieroglyphics of Horapollo*, Princeton University Press, NJ, 1993.
Bogusławski, Alexander, "John the Baptist," www.rollins.edu/Foreign_Lang/Russian/baptist.html
Bohn, Henry George, *The Epigrams of Martial*, George Bell and Sons, London, 1890.
Bolton, Kingsley, ed., et al., *Triad Societies: Western Accounts of the History, Sociology and Linguistics of Chinese Secret Societies*, Taylor & Francis, 2000.
Bonnefoy, Yves, *Roman and European Mythologies*, tr. Wendy Doniger, University of Chicago Press, 1992.
Bonwick, James, *Egyptian Belief and Modern Thought*, The Falcon's Wing Press, Colorado, 1956.
Boring, M. Eugene and Craddock, Fred B., *The People's New Testament Commentary*, Westminster John Knox, 2004.
Botterweck, G. Johannes, ed., *Theological Dictionary of the Old Testament*, I, Wm. B. Eerdmans Publishing, MI, 1974.
Botterweck, G. Johannes and Ringgren, Helmer, eds., *Theological Dictionary of the Old Testament*, II, Wm. B. Eerdmans Publishing Co., MI, 1999.
Boyd, Kelly, ed., *Encyclopedia of Historians and Historical Writing*, I, Fitzroy Dearborn Publishers, London/Chicago, 1999.
Boylan, Patrick, *Thoth or the Hermes of Egypt*, Kessinger, 2003.
Bradshaw, David, *Aristotle East and West*, Cambridge University Press, 2004.
Brand, Peter J., *The Monuments of Seti I*, E.J. Brill, Leiden, 2000.

Breasted, James Henry, *Ancient Records of Egypt,* II & III, University of Illinois Press, 2001.
—*Development of Religion and Thought in Ancient Egypt,* Charles Scribner's Sons, NY, 1912.
Brenk, Frederick E., *Relighting the Souls: Studies in Plutarch, in Greek Literature, Religion and Philosophy and in the New Testament Background,* Franz Steiner Verlag, 1998.
Brier, Bob and Hobbs, Hoyt, *Daily Life of the Ancient Egyptians,* Greenwood Press, Westport/London, 1999.
Brodrick, Mary, *A Concise Dictionary of Egyptian Archaeology,* Methuen & Co., London, 1902.
Bromiley, Geoffrey W., ed., et al., *The International Standard Bible Encyclopedia,* 3, William B. Eerdmans Publishing Company, MI, 1986.
Bronner, Ethan, "Tablet ignites debate on messiah and resurrection," *International Herald Tribune,*
www.iht.com/articles/2008/07/05/africa/06stone.php?page=1
Brown, Brian, *The Wisdom of the Egyptians,* Bretano's, NY, 1923.
Brown, Peter, *Augustine of Hippo,* University of California Press, Berkeley/LA, 2000.
Bruce, Frederick Fyvie, *Paul: Apostle of the Heart Set Free,* Wm. B. Eerdmans Publishing, 2000.
Bruce, James, *Travels to Discover the Source of the Nile,* James Ballantyne, Edinburgh, 1804.
Brugsch-Bey, Karl Heinrich/Henry, *A History of Egypt Under the Pharaohs,* I, John Murray, London, 1881.
—*Die Aegyptologie,* Elibron Classics/Adamant Media Corporation, London.
—*Egypt Under the Pharaohs: A History Derived Entirely From the Monuments,* John Murray, London, 1891.
—*Hieroglyphisch-demotisches Wörterbuch,* IV, Georg Olms, 1868/2004.
—*Religion und Mythologie der alten Aegypter,* J.C. Hinrichs'sche Buchhandlung, Leipzig, 1891.
—*Thesaurus Inscriptionum Aegyptiacarum,* J.C. Hinrichs'sche Buchhandlung, Leipzig, 1883.
—*Thesaurus Inscriptionum Aegyptiacarum,* Akademische Druck, Austria, 1968.
Brundige, Elle, "The Decline of the Library and Museum of Alexandria," www.digital-brilliance.com/kab/alex.htm
Brunner, Hellmut, *Die Geburt Des Gottkönigs,* Otto Harrassowitz, Wiesbaden, 1964.
—*Die Geburt Des Gottkönigs,* Otto Harrassowitz, Wiesbaden, 1986.
Bryant, Edwin, ed., *Krishna: A Sourcebook,* Oxford University Press, Oxford/NY, 2007.
—*Krishna: The Beautiful Legend of God,* Penguin Classics, 2003.

Budge, E.A. Wallis, *Amulets and Superstitions*, Dover, 1978.
—*The Book of the Dead: The Chapters of Coming Forth by Day*, Kegan Paul, Trench, Trubner & Co., London, 1898.
—*The Book of The Dead: The Chapters of Coming Forth by Day*, Kessinger, 2006.
—*The Book of the Dead: An English Translation of the Chapters, Hymns, Etc, of the Theban Recension*, Routledge & Kegan Paul, London, 1899.
—*The Book of the Dead: The Hieroglyphic Transcript of the Papyrus of Ani*, Kessinger, 2003.
—*The Book of the Kings of Egypt*, I & II, Kegan Paul, Trench, Trübner & Co., 1908.
—*The Book of Opening the Mouth*, Ayer Company, NH, 1984.
—*A Catalogue of the Egyptian Collection in the Fitzwilliam Museum Cambridge*, Kessinger Publishing, 2004.
—*Cook's Handbook for Egypt and the Sudan*, Part 2, Kessinger, 2003.
—*The Decrees of Memphis and Canopus*, III, Kegan Paul, Trench, Trubner & Co., 1904.
—*The Dwellers on the Nile*, Kessinger, 2003.
—*The Egyptian Book of the Dead*, Dover, New York, 1967.
—*The Egyptian Book of the Dead*, Routledge, 1984.
—*The Egyptian Heaven and Hell*, III, Kessinger, 2004.
—*An Egyptian Hieroglyphic Reading Book*, Courier Dover, 1993.
—*Egyptian Ideas of the Future Life*, Kessinger, 2004.
—*Egyptian Literature*, II, Kegan Paul, 1912.
—*An Egyptian Reading Book for Beginners*, Kegan Paul, Trench, Trubner & Co, London, 1896.
—*Egyptian Religion*, Citadel Press, 1991.
—*The Egyptian Sudan, Its History and Monuments*, II, Kegan Paul, Trench, Trubner & Co., London, 1907.
—*Egyptian Tales and Romances*, Kessinger, 2003.
—*Egypt Under the Great Pyramid Builders*, Kessinger, 2004.
—*First Steps in Egyptian: A Book for Beginners*, Health Research, 1996.
—*From Fetish to God in Ancient Egypt*, Dover, 1988.
—*The Gods of the Egyptians or Studies in Egyptian Mythology*, vol. 2, Adamant Media, 2001.
—*A Guide to the First and Second Egyptian Rooms*, British Museum, 1904.
—*A Guide to the Egyptian Galleries*, British Museum, 1909.
—*A Hieroglyphic Vocabulary to the Book of the Dead*, Dover, NY, 1991.
—*A History of Egypt from the End of the Neolithic Period*, Henry Frowde, NY, 1902.
—*An Egyptian Hieroglyphic Dictionary*, Dover, NY, 1978.
—*An Introduction to Ancient Egyptian Literature*, Courier Dover,

1997.
— *The Kebra Nagast*, Cosimo Classics, NY, 2004.
—*Legends of the Egyptian Gods: Hieroglyphic Texts and Translations*, Courier Dover, 1994.
—*Legends of the Gods*, Kegan, Paul, London, 1912.
—*Legends of Our Lady Mary the Perpetual Virgin and Her Mother Hanna*, The Medici Society, 1922.
—*Literature of the Ancient Egyptians*, Kessinger, 2003.
—*The Mummy: Chapters on Egyptian Funereal Archaeology*, Cambridge University Press, 1894.
—*The Mummy: Chapters on Egyptian Funereal Archaeology*, Biblo & Tannen, 1994
—*The Mummy: A Handbook of Egyptian Funerary Archaeology*, Biblo & Tannen, 1964.
—*The Mummy: A Handbook of Egyptian Funerary Archaeology*, Kessinger, 2003.
—*The Nile: Notes for Travellers in Egypt*, T. Cook & Son, 1907.
—*The Papyrus of Ani*, G.P. Putnam's Sons, London, 1913.
—*Of the Future Life: Egyptian Religion*, Kessinger, 2005.
—*On the Hieratic Papyrus of Nesi-Amsu*, Kessinger, 2006.
—*Osiris and the Egyptian Resurrection*, I, Courier Dover, 1973.
—*Osiris and the Egyptian Resurrection*, II, Kessinger, 2003.
—*Osiris and the Egyptian Resurrection*, University Books, NY, 1961.
—*Papyrus of Ani: Egyptian Book of the Dead*, NuVision Publications, 2007.
—*The Sarcophagus of Ānchnesrāneferab, Queen of Ahmes II*, Whiting & Co., London, 1885.
—*A Short History of the Egyptian People*, Kessinger, 2003.
Bullinger, Ethelbert W., *The Witness of the Stars*, Kessinger Publishing, 2006.
Bunsen, C.C.J. and Birch, Samuel, *Egypt's Place in Universal History*, V, tr. Charles H. Cottrell, Longmans, Green, and Co., London, 1867.
Burkert, Walter, *Savage Energies: Lessons of Myth and Ritual in Ancient Greece*, tr. Peter Bing, University of Chicago Press, Chicago, 2001.
Burleigh, J.H.S., ed., *Augustine: Earlier Writings*, WestMinster John Knox Press, 1953.
Burnet, John, *Platonis opera*, vol. 1, Clarendon Press, Oxford, 1900/1967.
Burritt, Elijah H., *The Geography of the Heavens, and Class-Book of Astronomy*, Mason Brothers, NY, 1860.
Bury, John Bagnell, et al., eds., *The Cambridge Ancient History*, vol. 1, part 2, Cambridge University Press, 1971.
Busenbark, Ernest, *Symbols, Sex, and the Stars*, Book Tree, 1997.

Butcher, Samuel Henry, *Demosthenis orationes*, vol. 1, Clarendon Press, Oxford, 1903.

Caillois, Roger and Lambert, Jean-Clarence, *Tresor de la poesie universelle*, Gallimard, 1958.

Callahan, Tim, *Secret Origins of the Bible*, Millennium Press, Altadena, 2002.

Campbell, Joseph, *In All Her Names*, HarperSanFrancisco, 1991.
—*The Masks of God*, Viking Press, 1959.
—*The Mythic Image*, Princeton University Press, 1974.
—*The Mythic Image*, Princeton University Press, 1981.
—*Myths of Light: Eastern Metaphors of the Eternal*, New World Library, 2003.
—*Thou Art That: Transforming Religious Metaphor*, New World Library, 2001.

Campbell, Joseph and Toms, Michael, et al., *An Open Life*, HarperCollins, 1990.

Capel, Anne K., *Mistress of the House, Mistress of Heaven: Women in Ancient Egypt*, Hudson Hills Press, 1996.

Capuani, Massimo, et al., *Christian Egypt: Coptic Art and Monuments Through Two Millennia*, Liturgical Press, 2002.

Carlile, Richard, *The Lion*, IV, London, 1829.

Carpenter, Edward, *Pagan and Christian Creeds: Their Origin and Meaning*, Harcourt, Brace & Co., 1921.

Carrier, Richard C., "Brunner's Gottkoenigs & the Nativity of Jesus: A Brief Communication," www.frontline-apologetics.com/Luxor_Inscription.html

Carson, Alexander, *Baptism in Its Mode and Subjects*, American Baptist Publication Society, 1850.

Carter, Albert Howard, *Rising from the Flames: The Experience of the Severely Burned*, University of Pennsylvania Press, 1998.

Cartlidge, David R. and Dungan, David L., eds., *Documents for the Study of the Gospels*, Fortress Press, 1994.

Carus, Paul, *The Gospel of Buddha*, Open Court, Chicago, 1917.

Cassels, Walter Richard, *Supernatural Religion: An Inquiry into the Reality of Divine Revelation*, Watts & Co., London, 1902.

Cassius Dio, *Dio's Roman History*, tr. Earnest Cary, Harvard University Press, 1961.
—*Roman History*, penelope.uchicago.edu/Thayer/E/Roman/Texts/Cassius_Dio/76*.html

Catholic Encyclopedia, II, ed. Charles G. Herbermann, The Encyclopedia Press, NY, 1907/1913.
—III, ed. Charles G. Herbermann, Universal Knowledge Foundation, NY, 1908/1913.
—IV, ed. Charles G. Herbermann, Universal Knowledge Foundation, NY, 1913.
—IX, ed. Charles G. Herbermann, The Encyclopedia Press, NY,

1910.
—XV, ed. Charles G. Herbermann, The Encyclopedia Press, NY, 1912.
—"Archaeology of the Cross and Crucifix," www.newadvent.org/cathen/04517a.htm
—"Baptism," www.newadvent.org/cathen/02258b.htm
—"Christmas," www.newadvent.org/cathen/03724b.htm
—"Marcus," www.newadvent.org/cathen/09650b.htm
—"Precentor," www.newadvent.org/cathen/12372a.htm
—"St. Hippolytus of Rome," www.newadvent.org/cathen/07360c.htm
Cauville, Sylvie, *Dendara III: Traduction*, David Brown, 2000.
The Century, XXXVIII, T. Fisher Unwin, London, 1889.
Champollion le Jeune, *Grammaire Égyptienne*, Typographie de Firmin Didot Freres, Paris, 1836; www.lib.uchicago.edu/cgi-bin/eos/eos_title.pl?callnum=PJ1135.C45
Chandler, Richard, *Travel in Asia Minor and Greece*, II, Clarendon Press, Oxford, 1825.
Cheyne, T.K. and Black, J. Sutherland, eds., *Encyclopaedia Biblica*, IV, Adam and Charles Black, London, 1907.
Christensen, Arne Soby, *Lactantius the Historian*, Museum Tusculanum Press, 1978.
Chronicon Paschale, Migne PG 92, "Documenta Catholica Omnia," www.documentacatholicaomnia.eu/02g/0600-0700,_Anonymous,_Chronicon_Paschale_%5BPG_092%5D,_MGR.pdf
—ed. J.P. Migne, *Patrologia Graeca*, vol. 92, Paris, 1860.
Cicero, Marcus Tullius, *De Natura Deorum*, III, ed. Joseph B. Major, Cambridge University Press, Cambridge, 1885.
—*De Natura Deorum*, tr. Francis Brooks, Methuen & Co., London, 1896.
Clagett, Marshall, *Ancient Egyptian Science: A Source Book*, II, American Philosophical Society, Philadelphia, 1995.
Clark, Rosemary, *The Sacred Tradition in Ancient Egypt*, Llewellyn, 2004.
Clarke, G.W., tr., *The Octavius of Marcus Minucius Felix*, Newman Press, NY/NJ, 1974.
Clarysse, Willy, *Egyptian Religion: The Last Thousand Years*, Part 1, Peeters Publishers, 1998.
The Classical Journal, XXIX, Longman, Hurst, et al., 1824.
Clayden, P.W., *Samuel Sharpe: Egyptologist and Translator of the Bible*, Kegan Paul, Trench & Co., London, 1883.
Clement Alexandrinus, *Excerpta ex Theodoto*, patrologia.ct.aegean.gr/PG_Migne/Clement%20of%20Alexandria_PG%2008-09/
Clifton, Chas S. and Harvey, Graham, eds., *The Paganism Reader*, Routledge, NY, 2004.

Cline, Eric H. and O'Connor, David, eds., *Thutmose III: A New Biography*, University of Michigan Press, 2006.

Colburn, Jerome, "Ancient Egyptian Language Discussion List," www.rostau.org.uk/AEgyptian-L/archives/week246.txt

Collier, Mark and Manley, Bill, *How to Read Egyptian Hieroglyphs*, University of California Press, Berkeley/LA, 1998/2003.

Collins, Adela Yarbro, *Cosmology and Eschatology in Jewish and Christian Apocalypticism*, Brill's Scholars' List, 2000.

Collins Contemporary Greek Dictionary, Wm. Collins Sons & Co., Glasgow, 1978.

Collins, John J., *Jewish Wisdom in the Hellenistic Age*, T&T Clark, Edinburgh, 1998.

Colson, F.H., *Philo*, IX, Harvard University, 1956.

Columella, *De Re Rustica*, XI, www.thelatinlibrary.com/columella/columella.rr11.shtml

The Concise Sanskrit-English Dictionary, ed., Vasudeo Govind Apte, Motilal Banarsidass Publishers, Bombay, 2002.

Condos, Theony, *Star Myths of the Greeks and Romans*, Phanes Press, 1997.

The Contemporary Review, LII, Isbister and Company, London, July-December 1887.

Conway, D.J., *Magick of the Gods and Goddesses*, The Crossing Press, 2003.

Conybeare, Frederick C., *Philo about the Contemplative Life*, Clarendon Press, Oxford, 1895.

Cooper, William R., *An Archaic Dictionary*, Samuel Bagster & Sons, London, 1876.

—*The Horus Myth in Its Relation to Christianity*, Hardwicke & Bogue, London, 1877.

—*The Serpent Myths of Ancient Egypt*, Robert Hardwicke, London, 1873.

Copenhaver, Brian P., *Hermetica: The Greek Corpus Hermeticum and the Latin Asclepius*, Cambridge University Press, 1992.

Cory, Alexander Turner, *The Hieroglyphics of Horapollo Nilous*, William Pickering, London, 1840.

Cotter, Wendy, *Miracles in Greco-Roman Antiquity: A Sourcebook for the Study of New Testament Miracle Stories*, Routledge, 1999

Court, John, *The Book of Revelation and the Johannine Apocalyptic Tradition*, Continuum International, 2000.

Cowie, Paul James, "Ancient Egyptian Language Discussion List," www.rostau.org.uk/AEgyptian-L/archives/week244.txt

Cox, George W., *The Mythology of the Aryan Nations*, Kegan Paul, Trench & Co., London, 1887.

—*The Mythology of the Aryan Nations*, II, Kessinger, 2004.

Crossan, John Dominic, *In Search of Paul*, HarperCollins, 2004.

Culpepper, R. Alan, *John: The Son of Zebee, The Life of a Legend*, Continuum International, 2000.

Cumont, Franz, *The Mysteries of Mithra*, Dover, NY, 1956.
—*The Oriental Religions in Roman Paganism*, The Open Court
Publishing Co., Chicago, 1911.

Curl, James Stevens, *The Egyptian Revival: Ancient Egypt as the
Inspiration for Design Motifs in the West*, Routledge, 2005.

Cyril of Jerusalem, "Catechetical Lecture 6,"
www.newadvent.org/fathers/310106.htm

Dahl, Jeff, "Ancient Egypt Map,"
en.wikipedia.org/wiki/File:Ancient_Egypt_map.svg

Dain, Alphonse and Mazon, Paul, *Sophocles*, vol. 3, Les Belles
Lettres, Paris, 1960.

Darlow, Richard, *Moses in Ancient Egypt & the Hidden Story of the
Bible*, Lulu, 2006.

David, Gary A., *The Orion Zone: Ancient Star Cities of the American
Southwest*, Adventures Unlimited Press, 2007.

Davies, John Llewelyn and Vaughan, David James, tr., *The Republic
of Plato*, MacMillan and Co., London, 1908.

Davies, Vivian and Friedman, Renée, *Egypt Uncovered*, Stewart
Tabori & Change, NY, 1998.

Davies, W.D. and Allison, D.C., *The International Critical Commentary:
Matthew 19-28*, III, Continuum International, 2004.

Davis, Chas. H.S., *Biblia: Devoted to Biblical Archaeology and Oriental
Research*, XV, Biblia Publishing Company, CT, 1903.

Davis, Whitney M., "The Ascension-Myth in the Pyramid Texts,"
Journal of Near Eastern Studies, vol. 36, no. 3, Jul. 1997.

De Boer, *Etudes Preliminaires aux Religions Orientales dans L'Empire
Romain*, E.J. Brill, Leiden, 1978.

de Bunsen, Ernst, *Die Plejaden und der Thierkreis, oder, das
Geheimniss der Symbole*, Verlag von Mitscher & Rostell, Berlin,
1879.

de Genoude, E.A., "Tertullian: Contre Les Valentiniens,"
www.tertullian.org/french/g3_04_adversus_valentinianos.htm

de Lesseps, Ferdinand, *The Suez Canal: Letters and Documents
Descriptive of Its Rise*, Henry S. King, Beccles, 1876.

DeMeo, James, *Saharasia: The 4,000 BCE Origins of Child Abuse, Sex-
Repression, Warfare and Social Violence in the Deserts of the Old
World*, Natural Energy Works, OR, 2006.

Denon, Dominique Vivant, *Voyage dans la Basse et la Haute Égypte*,
H. Gaugain, Paris, 1829.
—*Voyage dans la Basse et la Haute Égypte*, Le Promeneur, 1998.

Depuydt, Leo, *Civil Calendar and Lunar Calendar in Ancient Egypt*,
Peeters Publications, Leuven, 1997.

Dershowitz, Nachum and Reingold, Edward, *Calendrical Calculations*,
Cambridge University Press, London, 2007.

Dieterich, Albrecht, ed., *Archiv für Religionswissenschaft*, vol. 8,
Druck und Verlag von B.G. Teubner, Leipzig, 1905.

Diodorus Siculus, *The Antiquities of Egypt*, tr. Edwin Murphy, Transaction, 1990.
—Library *of History*, III, penelope.uchicago.edu/Thayer/E/Roman/Texts/Diodorus_Siculus/3D*.html
Dionysius Areopagitus, *The Celestial and Ecclesiastical Hierarchy*, tr. John Parker, Skeffington & Son, London, 1894.
—"Letter VIII. To Demophilus, Therapeutes," tr. John Parker, www.sacred-texts.com/chr/dio/dio32.htm
Doane, Thomas, *Bible Myths and Their Parallels in Other Religions*, The Truth Seeker, 1882.
Doherty, Earl, *The Jesus Puzzle*, Canadian Humanist Publications, Ottawa, 1999.
—"A Conjunction of Nativity Stories: Massey, Acharya, and Carrier," home.ca.inter.net/~oblio/supp13D.htm
Donehoo, James deQuincey, *The Apocryphal and Legendary Life of Christ*, The MacMillan Company, NY, 1903.
Doresse, Jean, *The Secret Books of the Egyptian Gnostics*, Inner Traditions International, Vermont, 1986.
Doxey, Denise M., *Egyptian Non-Royal Epithets in the Middle Kingdom*, E.J. Brill, Leiden, 1998.
Dowson, John, *Classical Dictionary of Hindu Mythology and Religion*, Kessinger, 2003.
Drews, Arthur, *The Witnesses to the Historicity of Jesus*, tr. Joseph McCabe, Watts, London, 1912.
Drummond, James, *An Inquiry into the Character and Authorship of the Fourth Gospel*, Williams & Norgate, London, 1903.
Drury, Nevill, *The Watkins Dictionary of Magic: Over 3,000 Entries on the World of Magical Formulas, Secret Symbols, and the Occult*, Sterling Publishing Company, 2006.
Duchane, Sangeet, *Beyond the Da Vinci Code: From the Rose Line to the Bloodline*, Sterling Publishing Company, 2005.
Duffield, Geo, *Magazine of Travels: Notes of Foreign Travel*, ed. Warren Isham, Detroit, 1857.
Dümichen, Johannes, *Bauurkunde der Tempelanlagen von Dendera*, J.C. Hinrichs'sche Buchhandlung, Leipzig, 1865.
Dunand, Françoise, *Le culte d'Isis dans le bassin oriental de la Méditerranée*, E.J. Brill, Leiden, 1973.
Dunand, Françoise and Zivie-Coche, Christiane, *Gods and Men in Egypt: 3000 BCE to 395 CE*, tr. David Lorton, Cornell University Press, 2005.
Duncker, Max, *The History of Antiquity*, I, tr. Evelyn Abbott, Richard Bentley & Son, London, 1877.
Dunlap, S.F., *Vestiges of the Spirit-History of Man*, D. Appleton and Company, NY, 1858.
Dunn, Geoffrey D., *Tertullian*, Routledge, London/NY, 2004.

Dunn, Jimmy, "Amenemhet I, 1st King of the 12th Dynasty,"
www.touregypt.net/featurestories/amenemhet1.htm
— "Lake Mariut (Mareotis), a Landlocked Sea South of
Alexandria," touregypt.net/featurestories/lakemariut.htm
—"Sokar, an Egyptian God of the Underworld,"
www.touregypt.net/featurestories/sokar.htm
—"The Djed Pillar,"
www.touregypt.net/featurestories/djedpillar.htm
Dupuis, Charles, François, *The Origin of All Religious Worship*,
Garland Publishing, NY/London, 1984.
Ebers, Georg, *Egypt: Descriptive, Historical, and Picturesque*, I, Cassell
& Company, New York, 1878.
Edinburgh Encyclopedia, Routledge, London/NY, 1999.
Ehrman, Bart, *Misquoting Jesus*, Harper Collins, 2005.
Eliade, Mircea, ed., The Encyclopedia of Religion, MacMillan
Publishing Co., NY, 1987.
Ellegård, Alvar, Jesus: One Hundred Years Before Christ, The
Overlook Press, NY, 1999.
Ellis, Normandi, *Feasts of Light: Celebrations for the Seasons of Life
Based on the Egyptian Goddess Mysteries*, Quest Books, 1999.
Ellison, Taylor Ray, "Anat, Mother of Gods,"
touregypt.net/featurestories/anat.htm
Encyclopedia Biblica, IV, ed. T.K Cheyne, Adam and Charles Black,
1903.
Encyclopedia Britannica, IX, X, XIII, XXVI, XXVII, The Encyclopedia
Britannica Company, NY, 1910.
—VIII, Cambridge University Press, Cambridge, 1910.
—Supplement to the Fourth, Fifth and Sixth Editions, IV,
Archibald Constable and Company, Edinburgh, 1824.
Epiphanius, *Panarion*, ed. J.P. Migne,
www.christianhospitality.org/texts/epiph-pan-08-pg41-0873-
0972.pdf
— www.christianhospitality.org/ref-index.htm, 873-972 (Haer.
XLVIIIb-LVa)
—*The Panarion of Epiphanius of Salamis*, II & III, tr. Frank
Williams, Brill, 1987.
Eratosthenes, et al., Mythographoi Scriptores poeticae historiae
graeci, Westermann, 1843.
Erman, Adolf, *Ancient Egyptian Poetry and Prose*, tr. Aylwar M.
Blackman, Dover, NY, 1995.
—*Egyptian Grammar*, tr. James Henry Breasted, Williams and
Norgate, London, 1894.
—*Life in Ancient Egypt*, tr. H.M. Tirard, Dover, Toronto, 1971.
Euripides, *Alcestis*, tr. Richard Aldington, Chatto & Windus, London,
1930.
Eusebius, *The History of the Church*, tr. G.A. Williamson, Penguin
Books, London, 1989.

Evans, James and Berggren, J. Lennart, *Gemino's Introduction to the Phenomena: A Translation and Study of a Hellenistic Survey of Astronomy*, press.princeton.edu/chapters/i8330.html

Evans, Katherine G., *Alexander the Alabarch: Roman and Jew*, kassevans.com/Alexander/AlexanderTheAlabarch_RomanAndJew-Summary.html

Faber, George Stanley, *The Origin of Pagan Idolatry*, I, 1816.

Fagan, Garrett G., *Archaeological Fantasies: How Pseudoarchaeology Misrepresents the Past and Misleads the Public*, Routledge, 2006.

Fairservis, Walter Ashlin, *The Ancient Kingdoms of the Nile and the Doomed Monuments of Nubia*, Crowell, 1962.

Faith and Thought, vol. 60, Victoria Institute, 1928.

Farrar, Frederic W., *The Life of Christ*, I, E.P. Dutton & Company, NY, 1877.

Fazzini, Richard A., *Egypt Dynasty XXII-XXV*. (Iconography of religions XVI, 10), E.J. Brill, Leiden, 1988.

Faulkner, Raymond O., *The Ancient Egyptian Coffin Texts*, Aris & Phillips, Oxford, 1973.
—*The Ancient Egyptian Pyramid Texts*, Clarendon Press, Oxford, 1969.
—*A Concise Dictionary of Middle Egyptian*, Oxford University Press, Oxford, 1962.
—*The Egyptian Book of the Dead*, Chronicle Books, San Francisco, 1998.

Fellows, John, *An Exposition of the Mysteries, or Religious Dogmas and Customs of the Ancient Egyptians, Pythagoreans, and the Druids*, Gould, Banks & Co., NY, 1835.

Filler, Aaron G., *The Upright Ape: A New Origin of the Species*, Career Press, NJ, 2007.

Firmicus Maternus, *The Error of the Pagan Religions*, tr. Clarence A. Forbes, Newman Press, NY/NJ, 1970.

Fisher, Sydney Nettleton, *The Middle East: A History*, Knopf, NY, 1969.

Fitzgerald, Allan D., et al., eds., *Augustine through the Ages: An Encyclopedia*, William B. Eerdmans Publishing Company, MI, 1999.

Flannery, Edward H., *The Anguish of the Jews*, Paulist Press, 2004.

Flavin, Richard D., "The Karanovo Zodiac," www.flavinscorner.com/karanovo.htm

Folk-Lore: A Quarterly Review of the Myth, Tradition, Institution, & Custom, David Nutt, London, 1901.

Forlong, J.G.R., *Faiths of Man: A Cyclopaedia of Religions*, II, Bernard Quaritch, London, 1906.

Foster, Theodore, *The Quarterly Review*, XXXIII, John Murray, London, 1817.

Fowden, Garth, *The Egyptian Hermes A Historical Approach to the Late Pagan Mind*, Princeton University Press, 1993.

Frankfort, Henri, *Kingship and the Gods*, University of Chicago Press, 1978.

Frankfurter, David, ed., *Pilgrimage & Holy Space in Late Antique Egypt*, E.J. Brill, Leiden, 1998.

Frazer, James G., *Adonis, Attis, Osiris: Studies in the History of Oriental Religion*, MacMillan and Co., London, 1906.

— *Folklore in the Old Testament Studies in Comparative Religion Legend and Law*, Kessinger, 2003.

— *The Golden Bough: A Study in Magic and Religion*, II, MacMillan and Company, London, 1900.

—*The Golden Bough: A Study in Magic and Religion*, part IV, volume II, MacMillan and Company, London, 1922.

Freedman, David Noel, et al., eds., *Eerdmans Dictionary of the Bible*, Wm. B. Eerdmans Publishing Co., MI, 2000.

Freeman, James M., *Hand-book of Bible Manners and Customs*, Nelson & Phillips, NY, 1874.

The Freethinker, vol. 85, no. 19, 1965.

Freke, Timothy and Gandy, Peter, *The Jesus Mysteries: Was the "Original Jesus" a Pagan God?*, Three Rivers Press, NY, 1999.

Froude, James Anthony, *Caesar: A Sketch*, Longsman, Green, & Co., London, 1879.

Gabriel, Richard A., *Gods of Our Fathers: The Memory of Egypt in Judaism and Christianity*, Greenwood Publishing Group, 2002.

—*Jesus the Egyptian: The Origins of Christianity and the Psychology of Christ*, iUniverse, 2005.

Gadalla, Moustafa, *The Ancient Egyptian Roots of Christianity*, Tehuti Research Foundation, NC, 2007.

Gardiner, Alan H., *Egypt of the Pharaohs*, Oxford University Press, London, 1964.

—"The Baptism of Pharaoh," *The Journal of Egyptian Archaeology*, vol. 36, The Egypt Exploration Society, 1950.

—"The Egyptian Origin of Some English Personal Names," *Journal of the American Oriental Society*, vol. 56, no. 2, 1936.

Garnett, Richard, et al., eds., *The Universal Anthology*, I, The Clarke Company, London, 1899.

Garnier, John, *The Worship of the Dead: Or, The Origin and Nature of Pagan Idolatry*, Chapman & Hall, London, 1904.

Garnot, Jean Sainte Fare, "A Hymn to Osiris in the Pyramid Texts," *Journal of Near Eastern Studies*, vol. 8, no. 2, Apr 1949.

Gatty, Charles T., *Catalogue of the Mayer Collection: The Egyptian Antiquities*, Liverpool, 1877.

Gayley, Charles Mills, *The Classic Myths in English Literature*, Ginn & Company, Boston, 1898.

Gazetteer of the Bombay Presidency, XV, I, Government Central Press, Bombay, 1883.

Gibbon, Edward, *The History of the Decline and Fall of the Roman Empire*, II, Metheun & Co., London, 1901.

Gilman, Daniel C., Peck, Harry T. and Colby, Frank M., eds., *The New International Encyclopaedia*, VI, Dodd, Mead & Co., 1903.

Gimbutas, Marija, *The Living Goddess*, University of California Press, Berkeley/LA, 2001.

Gliddon, George, *Otia Aegyptica: Discourses on Egyptian Archaeology and Hieroglyphical Discoveries*, James Madden, London, 1849.

Golan, Ariel, *Prehistoric Religion: Mythology, Symbolism*, Ariel Golan, 2003.

Good, Deirdre, *Mariam, the Magdalen, and the Mother*, Indiana University Press, 2005.

Gordon, Cyrus H., *The Common Background of Greek and Hebrew Civilizations*, W.W. Norton & Co., NY, 1965.

Gordon Cyrus H. and Rendsburg, Gary A., *The Bible and the Ancient Near East*, W.W Norton, 1997.

Gordon, Lewis Ricardo and Gordon, Jane Anna, *A Companion to African-American Studies*, Blackwell Publishing, 2006.

Goyon, Jean-Claude and Cardin, Christine, eds., *Proceedings of the Ninth International Congress of Egyptologists*, I, Peeters, 2007.

Granger, Frank, "The Poemandres of Hermes Trismegistus," *The Journal of Theological Studies*, V, MacMillan and Co., NY, 1904.

Grant, Robert M., *Augustus to Constantine: The Rise and Triumph of Christianity in the Roman World*, Westminster John Knox Press, 2004

—*Early Christians and Animals*, Routledge, 1999.

Graves, Robert, *The White Goddess*, Farrar, Straus, Giroux, 1966.

Gray, Louis Herbert, ed., *The Mythology of All Races*, XII, Marshall Jones Company, Boston, 1918.

Greenberg, Gary, *101 Myths of the Bible: How Ancient Scribes Invented Biblical History*, Sourcebooks, 2002.

Greer, John Michael, "The Corpus Hermeticum," www.webcom.com/~gnosis/library/hermes1.html

Gregg, John A.F., *The Epistle of St. Clement, Bishop of Rome*, Society for Promoting Christian Knowledge, E. & J.B. Young & Co., 1899.

Gregory Thaumaturgus, "Oration and Panegyric Addressed to Origen," www.newadvent.org/fathers/0604.htm

Grenfell, Bernard P. and Hunt, Arthur S., *The Hibeh Papyri, Part I*, Kegan Paul, Trench, Trubner & Co., London, 1906.

Grese, William C., *Corpus Hermeticum XIII and Early Christian Literature*, E.J. Brill, Leiden, 1979.

Greswell, Edward, *Origines Kalendariae Italicae*, I, Oxford University Press, 1862.

—*Origines Kalendariae Italicae*, II, Oxford University Press, 1854.

Griffith, Francis L. and Thompson, Herbert, eds., *The Leyden Papyrus: An Egyptian Magical Book*, Courier Dover, 1974.

Griffiths, John Gwyn, *The Divine Verdict*, E.J. Brill, Leiden, 1991.

—ed., *The Isis-Book (Metamorphoses, Book XI)*, E.J. Brill, Leiden,

1975.
—*The Origins of Osiris and His Cult*, E.J. Brill, Leiden, 1980.
Griggs, C. Wilfred, *Early Egyptian Christianity From Its Origins to 451 C.E.*, E.J. Brill, Leiden, 1990.
Grote, George, *Greece*, III, Peter Fenelon Collier, NY, 1899.
Gundry, Robert H., *A Survey of the New Testament*, Zondervan, 2003.
Guthrie, Kenneth S., *The Alexandrian Philo Judaeus: The Platonizing Hebraist's Complete Message 1909*, Kessinger, 2004.
Guthrie, W.K.C., *Orpheus and Greek Religion: a Study of the Orphic Movement*, Princeton University Press, 1993.
Guthrie, William Norman, *The Gospel of Osiris*, Brentano's, NY, 1916.
Haanen, Paul, "Ask the Archaeologist," library.thinkquest.org/C0118421/mesoreply2.html
Haase, Wolfgang and Temporini, Hildegard, *Aufstieg und Niedergang der romischen Welt*, II, Walter de Gruyter, Berlin/NY, 1995.
Habermas, Gary R. and Licona, Michael R., *The Case for the Resurrection of Jesus*, Kregel Publications, 2004.
Hadley, W.S., ed., *The Alcestis of Euripides*, Cambridge University Press, 1896.
Haines, Charles Reginald, *Verses and Versions in English, Greek and Latin*, Bushnell Press, 2008.
Hall, Manly P., *The Secret Teachings of All Ages*, H.S. Crocker Company, San Francisco, 1928.
Halsberghe, Gaston H., "The Cult of Sol Invictus," *Etudes preliminaires aux religions orientales dans l'Empire romain*, vol. 23, E.J. Brill, Leiden, 1972.
The Hamilton Literary Monthly, XXIV, Beers & Kessinger, NY, 1889-1990.
Hancock, Graham and Faiia, Santha, *Heaven's Mirror: Quest for the Lost Civilization*, Three Rivers, NY, 1998.
Hardwicke, Herbert Junius, *The Popular Faith Unveiled*, London, 1884.
Hardwicke, William Wright, *The Evolution of Man: His Religious Systems, and Social Ethics*, Watts & Co., London, 1899.
Hare, Tom, *ReMembering Osiris: Number, Gender, and the Word in Ancient Egyptian Representational Systems*, Stanford University Press, Stanford, 1999.
Harris, Roberta L., *The World of the Bible*, Thames and Hudson, London/NY, 1995.
Hart, George, *The Routledge Dictionary of Egyptian Gods and Goddesses*, Routledge, London/NY, 2005.
Hassan, Farzana, *Prophecy and the Fundamentalist Quest*, McFarland & Co., NC, 2008.
Hassig, Debra, ed., *The Mark of the Beast: The Medieval Bestiary in Art, Life, and Literature*, Routledge, 1998.
Hastings, James, ed., et al., *A Dictionary of the Bible*, I, T. & T. Clark, Edinburgh, 1901.

Haywood, H.L., "Freemasonry and the Roman Collegia," www.freemasons-freemasonry.com/collegia.html

Hawking, Stephen W., *On the Shoulders of Giants: The Great Works of Physics and Astronomy*, Running Press, 2002.

Hawkins, Gerald, *Beyond Stonehenge*, Harper & Row, 1973.

Heath, Dunbar Isadore, *Phoenician Inscriptions*, Oxford University, 1873.

Heffernan, Carol Falvo, *The Phoenix at the Fountain: Images of Woman and Eternity in Lactantius's Carmen De Ave Phoenice and the Old English Phoenix*, University of Delaware Press, 1988.

Hellerman, Joseph H., *The Ancient Church As Family*, Fortress Press, 2001.

Herbert, Lee, *Origins of Architectural Design or the Archaeology of Astronomy*, The Antiquarian Publishing Company, MI, 1912.

Herodotus, *The Histories*, tr. Aubrey de Selincourt, Penguin Books, London, 1996.

—*The Histories*, tr. Robin Waterfield, Oxford University Press, 1998.

Hewitt, J.F., *Story and Chronology of the Myth-Making Age*, James Parker and Co., London, 1901.

Heyob, Sharon Kelly, *The Cult of Isis among Women in the Graeco-Roman World*, E.J. Brill, Leiden, 1975.

Higginbotham, Carolyn R., *Egyptianization and Elite Emulation in Ramesside Palestine*, E.J. Brill, Leiden, 2000.

Higgins, Godfrey, *Anacalypsis: An Attempt to Draw Aside the Veil*, II, J. Burns, London, 1878.

Hill, Charles E., *The Johannine Corpus in the Early Church*, Oxford University Press, 2004.

Hippolytus, Φιλοσοφουμενα/*Philosophumena*, Patricius Cruice, Paris, 1860.

—*Philosophumena, Or the Refutation of All Heresies*, I, tr. F. Legge, The MacMillan Company, London, 1921.

Hobgood-Oster, Laura, *Holy Dogs & Asses*, University of Illinois Press, Chicago, 2008.

Hodges, Henry Clay, *Science and Key of Life*, vols. 5, 6, 7, Kessinger, 2004.

Hodges, George, *The Early Church from Ignatius to Augustine*, Houghton Mifflin, 1915.

Hoffman, R. Joseph, tr., *Celsus on the True Doctrine*, Oxford University Press, Oxford/NY, 1987.

Hoffmeier, James K., *Ancient Israel in Sinai: The Evidence for the Authenticity of the Wilderness Tradition*, Oxford University Press, 2005.

Hölbl, Günther and Saavedra, Tina, *A History of the Ptolemaic Empire*, Routledge, 2001.

Holding, James Patrick, ed., *Shattering the Christ Myth: Did Jesus Not Exist?*, Xulon Press, 2008.

Holley, Nan M., "The Floating Chest," *The Journal of Hellenistic Studies*, vol. 69, 1949.

Homer, *Odyssey*, Books XIII-XXIV, ed. W.W. Merry, Clarendon Press, Oxford, 1878.

Hooker, Richard, "The Coming into Day (Book of the Dead)," www.wsu.edu/~dee/EGYPT/BOD125.HTM

Hopkins, Edward Washburn, *The History of Religions*, The MacMillan Company, NY, 1918.

Horbury, William and Sturdy, John, eds., *The Cambridge History of Judaism* III, Cambridge University Press, 2006.

Horn, Cornelia B., *Asceticism and Christological Controversy in Fifth-Century Palestine: The Career of Peter the Iberian*, Oxford University Press, 2006.

Hornblower, G.D., "Osiris and His Rites," *Man*, vol. 37, Oct 1937.

—"Osiris and the Fertility-Rite," *Man*, vol. 41, Sep-Oct 1941.

Horner, George William, *The Coptic version of the New Testament in the Northern Dialect*, II, Clarendon Press, Oxford, 1898.

Hornung, Erik, *The Ancient Egyptian Books of the Afterlife*, tr. David Lorton, Cornell University Press, NY, 1999.

—*Conceptions of God in Ancient Egypt*, tr. John Baine, Cornell University Press, NY, 1982.

—*The Secret Lore of Egypt: Its Impact on the West*, tr. David Lorton, Cornell University Press, NY, 2001.

—*The Valley of the Kings: Horizon of Eternity*, tr. David Warburton, Timken Publishers, NY, 1990.

Horsley, G. H. R., *Hellenika: Essays on Greek Politics and History*, Macquarie Ancient History Association, 1982.

Houlden, James Leslie, *Jesus in History, Thought, and Culture: An Encyclopedia*, ABC-CLIO, 2003.

Howe, Winifred, E., *A History of the Metropolitan Museum of Art*, NY, 1913.

Humphreys, Andrew, *Egypt*, Lonely Planet, 2004.

Iamblichus *On the Mysteries/De mysteriis*, trs. Emma C. Clarke, John M. Dillon and Jackson P. Hershbell, Society of Biblical Literature, Atlanta, 2003.

Iraq, IX, British School of Archaeology in Iraq, 1934.

Irenaeus, *Against Heresies*, II, www.newadvent.org/fathers/0103221.htm

Isaac, Benjamin H., *The Invention of Racism in Classical Antiquity*, Princeton University Press, 2004.

Isichei, Elizabeth, *A History of Christianity in Africa*, William B. Eerdmans Publishing Company, MI, 1995.

Jackson, John G., *Christianity Before Christ*, American Atheists, 1985.

—*Man, God, and Civilization*, Citadel, 1983.

Janssens, B., et al., eds., *Philomathestatos: Studies in Greek Patristic and Byzantine Texts*, Peeters Publishers, 2005.

Jarrett, Colonel H.S. tr., *Ain-I-Akbari of Abul Fazl-I-Allami*, vol. III, Royal Asiatic Society of Bengal, India 1948.

Johnson, Buffie, *Lady of the Beasts*, Inner Traditions, Vermont, 1994.

Johnson, Paul, *The Civilization of Ancient Egypt*, HarperCollins, 1999.

Johnston, Sarah Iles, ed., *Religions of the Ancient World: A Guide*, Harvard University Press, 2004.

Jokilehto, Jukka, *A History of Architectural Conservation*, Butterworth-Heinemann, 2002.

Jones, Alexander, *Astronomical Papyri from Oxyrhynchus*, I & II, American Philosophical Society, Philadelphia, 1999.

Jones, Henry Stuart and Powell, Johannes Enoch, *Thucydidis historiae*, I & II, Clarendon Press, Oxford, 1942.

Joseph, Peter, "ZEITGEIST: The Movie," www.zeitgeistmovie.com

Josephus, *The Works of Flavius Josephus*, tr. William Whiston, Milner & Sowerby, Halifax, 1864.

—*The Complete Works of Josephus*, tr. William Whitson, Kregel Publications, MI, 1981.

Hopkins, E. Washburn and Torrey, Charles C., *Journal of the American Oriental Society*, vol. 26, The American Oriental Society, New Haven, 1905.

Journal of Analytical Psychology, vol. 9, no. 1, Society of Analytical Psychology, London, 1964.

Journal of Near Eastern Studies, 36:3, 1977; links.jstor.org/sici?sici=0022-2968(197707)36%3A3%3C161%3ATAITPT%3E2.0.CO%3B2-X

Journal of the Royal Astronomical Society of Canada, vol. 9, Royal Astronomical Society of Canada, 1919.

—vol. 14, Royal Astronomical Society of Canada, 1920.

The Journal of Theological Studies, V, Macmillan and Co., London, 1904.

Journal of the Transactions of the Victoria Institute, XVI, Wyman and Sons, London, 1883.

Jung, Carl, *Psychology of the Unconscious*, Moffat, Yard and Company, NY, 1916.

Justin Martyr, *Dialogue with Trypho*, www.newadvent.org/fathers/01283.htm

—*First Apology*, www.newadvent.org/fathers/0126.htm

Kamil, Jill, *Christianity in the Land of the Pharaohs: The Coptic Orthodox Church*, Routledge, 2002.

Kazlev, M. Alan, "The Memphite Theology," www.kheper.net/topics/Egypt/Memphis.html

Kelley, David H. and Milone, Eugene F., *Exploring Ancient Skies: An Encyclopedic Survey of Archaeoastronomy*, Springer, NY, 2005.

Kellner, Heinrich, "Gegen die Valentinianer," www.tertullian.org/articles/kempten_bkv/extra_06_adversus_valentinianos.htm

Kelly, Joseph F., *The Origins of Christmas*, Liturgical Press, MN, 2004.

Kemp, Barry J., *Ancient Egypt: Anatomy of a Civilization*, Routledge, London, 1991.

Kendall, Timothy, "Napatan Temples: A Case Study from Gebel Barkal," rmcisadu.let.uniroma1.it/nubiaconference/kendall.doc

Kenrick, John, *Ancient Egypt Under the Pharaohs*, Redfield, NY, 1852.

King, Charles W., *The Gnostics and Their Remains, Ancient and Mediaeval*, Bell and Daldy, London, 1864.

—*Plutarch's Morals: Theosophical Essays*, Kessinger, 2006.

King, Karen L., ed., *Images of the Feminine in Gnosticism*, Trinity Press International, Harrisburg, 1988.

King, Leonard W., *Legends of Babylon and Egypt in Relation to Hebrew Tradition*, Cosimo, Inc., NY, 2005.

Kingsford, Anna and Maitland, Edward, trs., *The Virgin of the World of Hermes Mercurius Trismegistus*, Health Research, 1968.

Kirby, Peter, "Acts of John,"
www.earlychristianwritings.com/actsjohn.html
—"On the Contemplative Life,"
www.earlyjewishwritings.com/text/philo/book34.html

Kitchen, Kenneth A., *Ramesside Inscriptions*, II, Blackwell Publishers, Oxford, 1999.

Kloppenborg, John S. and Wilson, Stephen G., eds., *Voluntary Associations in the Graeco-Roman World*, Routledge, London/NY, 1996.

Knapp, Bettina L., *French Fairytales: A Jungian Approach*, State University of New York Press, 2003.

Komoszewski, J. Ed., et al., *Reinventing Jesus: How Contemporary Skeptics Miss the Real Jesus and Mislead Popular Culture*, Kregel Publications, 2006.

Krause, Martin, *Gnosis and Gnosticism*, E.J. Brill, Leiden, 1981.

Krupp, Edwin C., *Echoes of the Ancient Skies: The Astronomy of Lost Civilizations*, Courier Dover, 2003.

Kuhn, Alvin Boyd, *Easter: The Birthday of the Gods*, Kessinger, 1993.

—*Lost Light: An Interpretation of Ancient Scriptures*, Kessinger, 1992.

—*Who is This King of Glory?*, Academy Press, NJ, 1944.

Kurger, Gustav, *History of Early Christian Literature in the First Three Centuries*, tr. Charles R. Gillett, Burt Franklin, NY, 1969.

Labrique, Françoise, *Stylistique et théologie à Edfou*, Peeters Publishers, 1992.

Lactantius, "The Phoenix," www.newadvent.org/fathers/0707.htm

Lambdin, Thomas O., *Introduction to Sahidic Coptic* Mercer University Press, GA, 1983.

Lane, Eugene N., *Cybele, Attis and Related Cults: Essays in Memory of M.J. Vermaseren*, E.J. Brill, Leiden, 1996.

Lange, Jon, "A Bibliography to the Masseian Corpus,"
    www.masseiana.org/bib.htm
Leadbetter, Charles W., *The Hidden Side of Christian Festivals*, St.
    Alban Press, Los Angeles, 1920.
Leclant, Jean and Clerc, Giselle, *Inventaire Bibliographique Des
    Isiaca*, E.J. Brill, Leiden, 1997.
Leeming, David Adams, "Virgin Birth," *The Encyclopedia of Religion*,
    vol. 15, MacMillan Publishing, 1987.
Leeming, David and Page, Jake, *God: Myths of the Male Divine*,
    Oxford University Press, Oxford/NY, 1996.
*The Legends of the Old Testament, Traced to Their Apparent Primitive
    Sources*, Trubner & Co., London, 1874.
Legge, Francis, *Forerunners and Rivals of Christianity*, University
    Books, NY, 1964.
Leipoldt, Johannes, *Religionsgeschichte des Orients in der Zeit der
    Weltreligionen*, E.J. Brill, Leiden, 1961.
Leitz, Christian, *Lexikon der Ägyptischen Götter und
    Götterbezeichnungen*, 1, Uitgeverij Peeters, Leuven, 2002.
Lemon, George William, *English Etymology or, a Derivative Dictionary
    of the English Language in Two Alphabets*, G. Robinson, London,
    1783.
Lempriere, J., *A Classical Dictionary*, James Crissy, Philadelphia,
    1822.
Lennard, H.B., tr., *The Ion of Euripides*, Williams and Norgate,
    London, 1889.
Le Noir, Abbé, *Dictionnaire des Harmonies*, Oxford University, 1856.
Lenormant, François, *Chaldean Magic: Its Origins and Development*,
    Kessinger, 1994.
Lepsius, Carl Richard, *Zeitschrift für Ägyptische Sprache und
    Alterthumskunde*, J.C. Hinrichs'sche Buchhandlung, Leipzig,
    1868.
Lesko, Barbara S., *The Great Goddesses of Egypt*, University of
    Oklahoma Press, 1999.
Lett, Donald G., *Phoenix Rising: The Rise and Fall of the American
    Republic*, Phoenix Rising, 2008.
Levillain, Phillipe, ed., *The Papacy: An Encyclopedia*, I, Routledge,
    NY/London, 2002.
Levine, Amy-Jill, ed., *A Feminist Companion to Mariology*, T&T Clark
    International, London/NY, 2005.
Lewis, Charlton T., *An Elementary Latin Dictionary*, American Book
    Co., 1918.
Lichtheim, Miriam, *Ancient Egyptian Literature: A Book of Readings*, I,
    University of California Press, 2006.
Lightfoot, J.B., *The Apostolic Fathers: Part 1, S. Clement of Rome*,
    MacMillan and Co., London, 1890.
Lillie, Arthur, *Buddhism in Christendom: Or Jesus, the Essene*, Kegan
    Paul, Trench & Co., London, 1887.

Lincoln, Andrew T., *Paradise Now and Not Yet: Studies in the Role of the Heavenly Dimension in Paul's Thought with Special Reference to his Eschatology*, Cambridge University Press, 2004.

Lind, G. Dallas, *The Teachers' and Students' Library*, T.S. Dennison, Chicago, 1882.

Livo, Norma J., *Storytelling Folklore Sourcebook*, Libraries Unlimited, 1991.

Lloyd, Alan B., *Herodotus Book II: Commentary 1-98*, E.J. Brill, 1998.

Lloyd, J.Y.W., *The History of The Princes, the Lords Marcher, and the Ancient Nobility of Powys Fadog*, II, T. Richards, London, 1882.

Lockyer, J. Norman, *The Dawn of Astronomy: A Study of the Temple-Worship and Mythology of the Ancient Egyptians*, Cassel and Company, London, 1894.

Long, Charlotte R., *The Twelve Gods of Greece and Rome*, E.J. Brill, Leiden, 1987.

Loprieno, Antonio, *Ancient Egyptian: A Linguistic Introduction*, Cambridge University Press, 1995.

—ed., *Ancient Egyptian Literature: Problem der Ägyptologie*, vol. 10, E.J. Brill, Leiden, 1996.

The Lost Books of the Bible, Bell Publishing Company, NY, 1979.

Luckert, Karl W., *Egyptian Light and Hebrew Fire*, State University of New York Press, Albany, 1991.

Luiselli, Maria Michela, *Der Amun-Re Hymnus des P. Boulaq 17 (P. Kairo CG 58038)*, Otto Harrassowitz, Wiesbaden, 2004.

Lundy, John P., *Monumental Christianity: Or, The Art and Symbolism of the Primitive Church*, J.W. Bouton, NY, 1876.

MacDonald, Dennis R., *The Homeric Epics and the Gospel of Mark*, Yale University, 2000.

Machen, John Gresham, *The Virgin Birth of Christ*, James Clarke & Co., Cambridge, 1958.

Mackey, Albert G., *Encyclopedia of Freemasonry*, The Masonic History Company, Chicago, Kessinger, 2003.

MacMullen, Ramsay, *Paganism in the Roman Empire*, Yale University Press, NY/London, 1981.

Macnaughton, Duncan, *A Scheme of Egyptian Chronology*, Luzac & Co., London, 1932.

Macrobius, *The Saturnalia*, tr. Percival Vaughan Davies, Columbia University Press, NY, 1969.

Macrobii, *Saturnalia*, Liber I, penelope.uchicago.edu/Thayer/L/Roman/Texts/Macrobius/Saturnalia/1*.html

Madden, Patrick J., *Jesus' Walking on the Sea*, Walter De Gruyter, Berlin/NY, 1997.

Mahaffy, John P., *A History of Egypt Under The Ptolemaic Dynasty (IV)*, Metheun & Co., London, 1899.

Maier, Paul L., ed., *The New Complete Works of Josephus*, tr. William Whitson, Kregel Academic & Professional, 1999.

Mangasarian, M.M., *The Truth About Jesus, Is He A Myth?*, Kessinger, 2004.

Mansel, Henry Longueville, *The Gnostic Heresies of the First and Second Centuries*, John Murray, London, 1875.

Maravelia, Amanda-Alice, ed., *Europe, Hellas and Egypt: Complementary Antipodes During Late Antiquity*, Archaeopress, 2004.

—"Ancient Egyptian Inscribed Faience Objects from the Benaki Museum in Athens," *Journal of Near Eastern Studies*, vol. 61, no. 2, Apr. 2002.

Maspero, Gaston, *Études de mythologie et d'archéologie égyptiennes*, Paris, 1898.

—*Guide to the Cairo Museum*, tr. J.E. & A.A. Quibell, French Institute of Oriental Archaeology, Cairo, 1908.

—*History of Egypt*, I, ed. A.H. Sayce, tr. M.L. McClure, The Grolier Society Publishers, London.

—*Popular Stories of Ancient Egypt*, Kessinger, 2003.

—*The Dawn of Civilization*, ed. A.H. Sayce D. Appleton and Company, NY, 1894.

Massey, Gerald, *Ancient Egypt: Light of the World*, I & II, Kessinger, 2002.

—*A Book of the Beginnings*, II, Kessinger, 2002.

—*Gerald Massey's Lectures*, A&B Books, NY.

—*The Historical Jesus and the Mythical Christ*, The Book Tree, 2000.

—*The Natural Genesis*, I, Williams and Norgate, London, 1883.

—*The Natural Genesis*, vol. 2, Cosimo Press, 2007.

—"Luniolatry: Ancient and Modern," www.theosophical.ca/Luniolatry.htm

Matthews, Caitlin, *Sophia: Goddess of Wisdom Bride of God*, Quest Books, 2001.

Matthews, John and Matthews, Caitlin, *The Winter Solstice: The Sacred Traditions of Christmas*, Quest Books, 1998.

Matthews, Victor H., *Old Testament Parallels: Laws and Stories from the Ancient Near East*, Paulist Press, NY, 1997.

Maunder, E. Walter, *The Astronomy of the Bible*, T. Sealey Clark & Co., London, 1908.

McCabe, Joseph, *The Story of Religious Controversy*, The Stratford Company, 1929.

McClintock, John and Strong, James, *Cyclopaedia of Biblical, Theological, and Ecclesiastical Literature*, Harper and Brothers, 1890.

—*Cyclopaedia of Biblical, Theological, and Ecclesiastical Literature*, II, Harper & Brothers, NY, 1891.

—*Cyclopaedia of Biblical, Theological, and Ecclesiastical Literature*, V, Harper & Brothers, NY, 1883.

—*Cyclopaedia of Biblical, Theological, and Ecclesiastical Literature*, VII, Harper & Brothers, NY, 1877.

McDermott, Bridget, *Decoding Egyptian Hieroglyphs*, Chronicle Books, San Francisco, 2001.

Mead, G.R.S., *Did Jesus Live 100 B.C.?*, Kessinger, 1992.

—*Fragments of a Faith Forgotten*, Kessinger, 1992.

—tr., *Pistis Sophia*, www.sacred-texts.com/chr/ps/index.htm

—*Thrice Greatest Hermes*, I, The Theosophical Publishing Society, London, 1906.

Ménard, Louis, *Hermès Trismégiste*, Didier et Cᶜ, Paris, 1867.

Menzies, Allan, ed., *The Ante-Nicene Fathers*, IX, Supplement, Charles Scribner's Sons, NY, 1903.

Merback, Mitchell, *The Thief, the Cross and the Wheel*, University of Chicago Press, 1999.

Mercatante, Anthony S., *Who's Who in Egyptian Mythology*, Barnes & Noble, 1998.

Mercer, Samuel, *The Pyramid Texts*, Longmans, Green & Co., London, 1952; www.sacred-texts.com/egy/pyt/index.htm

Merivale, Charles, *A History of the Romans Under the Empire*, VII, Longmans, Green, and Co., London, 1865.

Meyboom, P.G.P., *The Nile Mosaic of Palestrina: Early Evidence of Egyptian Religion in Italy*, E.J. Brill, Leiden, 1995.

Meyer, Marvin W. and Smith, Richard, *Ancient Christian Magic: Coptic Texts of Ritual Power*, Princeton University Press, 1999.

—*The Gnostic Gospels of Jesus*, HarperCollins, NY, 2005.

Metzger, Bruce M., *The Canon of the New Testament*, Clarendon Press, Oxford, 1997.

—*List of Words Occuring [sic] Frequently in The Coptic New Testament*, E.J. Brill, Leiden, 1961.

—*New Testament Studies: Philological, Versional, and Patristic*, E.J. Brill, Leiden, 1980.

Michel, Simone, *Die Magischen Gemmen*, Akademie Verlag, 2004.

Minucius Felix, *Octavius*, www.earlychristianwritings.com/text/octavius.html

Miscellaneous Notes and Queries, X, S.C. & L.M. Gould, London, 1892.

—XIII, S.C. & L.M. Gould, NH, 1895.

Modrzejewski, Joseph Meleze, *The Jews of Egypt: From Ramses II to Emperor Hadrian*, tr. Robert Cornman, Jewish Publication Society, 1995.

Mojsov, Bojana, *Osiris: Death and Afterlife of a God*, Blackwell, 2005.

Mommsen, Theodor, *The History of Rome: The Provinces of the Roman Empire from Caesar to Diocletian, Part II*, tr. William P. Dickson, Charles Scribner's Sons, NY, 1887.

Monderson, Frederick, *Hatshepsut's Temple at Deir el Bahari*, Author House, 2007.

Monet, Jefferson, "The Coffins of Ancient Egypt,"
     www.touregypt.net/featurestories/coffins.htm.
Moor, Edward, *Oriental Fragments*, Smith, Elder, and Co., London,
     1834.
Morenz, Siegfried, *Egyptian Religion*, tr. Ann E. Keep, Cornell
     University Press, Ithaca, 1992.
Morris, John, *The New Nation*, I, London, 1880.
Müller, W. Max, *Egyptian Mythology*, Marshall Jones Company,
     Boston, 1923/Kessinger, 2005.
     —*Lectures on the Science of Religion*, Scribner, Armstrong, and
     Co., NY, 1874.
Murdock, D.M., *Who Was Jesus? Fingerprints of The Christ*, Stellar
     House Publishing, Seattle, 2007. (See also "Acharya S.")
Mure, William, *A Dissertation on the Calendar and Zodiac of Ancient
     Egypt*, Bell & Bradfute, London, 1832.
Murnane, William J., *Texts from the Amarna Period in Egypt*, Scholars
     Press, Atlanta, 1995.
Murphy, Arthur, *The Works of Cornelius Tacitus*, Thomas Wardle,
     Philadelphia, 1836.
Murray, Gilbert, *Aeschyli tragoediae*, Clarendon Press, Oxford, 1955.
     —*Euripidis fabulae*, vol. 1. Clarendon Press, Oxford, 1902/1966.
     —*Euripidis fabulae*, vol. 2, Clarendon Press, Oxford, 1913.
Murray, Margaret A., *Egyptian Temples*, Dover, NY, 2002.
     —*Legends of Ancient Egypt*, Courier Dover, 2000.
     —*The Splendor That Was Egypt*, Courier Dover, 2004.
Muskett, Georgina M., et al., eds., *Soma 2001: Symposium on
     Mediterranean Archaeology: Proceedings of the Fifth Annual
     Meeting of Postgraduate Researchers, the University of Liverpool,
     23-25 February 2001*, Archaeopress, Oxford, 2002.
Myers, Philip Van Ness, *Ancient History*, Ginn and Company, 1916.
Myśliwiec, Karol, *Eighteenth Dynasty Before the Amarna Period*, E.J.
     Brill, Leiden, 1985.
Nabarz, Payam, *The Mysteries of Mithras: The Pagan Belief That
     Shaped the Christian World*, Inner Traditions, 2005.
Nash, Ronald H., *The Gospel and the Greeks: Did the New Testament
     Borrow from Pagan Thought?*, P&R Publishing, 2003.
Naville, Edouard, Newberry, Percy E. and Fraser, George Willoughby,
     The Season's Work at Ahnas and Beni Hasan, Gilbert & Rivington,
     London, 1891.
Nature, XXXV, MacMillan and Co., London/NY, 1887.
     —XLIII, MacMillan and Co., London/NY, 1891.
     —XLIV, MacMillan and Co., London/NY, 1891.
     —Supplement, MacMillan and Co., London/NY, 1891.
Neumann, Charles William, *The Virgin Mary in the Works of Saint
     Ambrose*, University Press, 1962.
Neumann, Erich, *The Origins and History of Consciousness*,
     Routledge, 1999.

The New Englander, XXXIX, W.L. Kingsley, New Haven, 1880.
The New Schaff-Herzog Encyclopedia of Religious Knowledge, Funk & Wagnalls Company, London, 1912.
—VIII, Funk & Wagnalls Company, NY/London, 1910.
Nibley, Hugh, "All the Court's a Stage," *Abraham in Egypt*, farms.byu.edu/publications/bookschapter.php?chapid=294
—"A Pioneer Mother," *Abraham in Egypt*, farms.byu.edu/publications/bookschapter.php?bookid=&chapid= 295
Nicoll, W. Robertson, *The Expositor*, I, Hodder and Stoughton, London, 1885.
Nienkamp, Jean, *Plato on Rhetoric and Language: Four Key Dialogues*, Hermagoras Press, 1999.
Nissenbaum, Stephen, *The Battle for Christmas: A Cultural History of America's Most Cherished Holiday*, First Vintage Books, 1996.
Nuttall, Zelia, *The Fundamental Principles of Old and New World Civilizations*, Peabody Museum, 1901.
Occasional Publications in Classical Studies: OPCS, University of Northern Colorado Museum of Anthropology, 1978.
O'Connor, David and Silverman, David P., eds., *Ancient Egyptian Kingship*, E.J. Brill, Leiden, 1995.
Olcott, William Tyler, *Star Lore of All Ages*, G.P. Putnam's Sons, New York/London, 1911.
Oldfather, Charles Henry, *Diodorus of Sicily*, vol. 2, Harvard University Press, 1967.
O'Meara, Stephen James, *Hidden Treasures*, Cambridge University Press, Cambridge, 2007.
Origen, *Contra Celsum*, tr. Henry Chadwick, Cambridge University Press, Cambridge, 1980.
Orr, James, ed., et al., *The International Standard Bible Encyclopedia*, II & III, The Howard-Severance Company, Chicago, 1915.
The Oxford Classical Greek Dictionary, Oxford University Press, Oxford/NY, 2002.
The Oxford Dictionary of Modern Greek, Clarendon, Oxford, 1975.
The Oxford History of Ancient Egypt, ed. Ian Shaw, Oxford University Press, Oxford, 2003.
Paine, Thomas, *The Writings of Thomas Paine*, G.P. Putnam's Sons, London, 1896.
Park, David Allen, *The How and the Why: An Essay on the Origins and Development of Physical Theory*, Princeton University Press, 1990.
Parker, Janet, et al., *Mythology: Myths, Legends & Fantasies*, Struik Publishers, 2006.
Parker, John, tr., *The Celestial and Ecclesiastical Hierarchy of Dionysius the Areopagite*, Skeffington & Son, London, 1894.
Parker, Neil, "The Papyrus of Ani," www.bardo.org/ani/

Parsons, Albert R., *New Light from the Great Pyramid*, Metaphysical
    Publishing Company, NY, 1893.
Parsons, John Denham, *The Non-Christian Cross*, London, 1896.
Paschal Chronicle see *Chronicon Paschale*.
Pearson, Birger A., *Gnosticism and Christianity in Roman and Coptic
    Egypt*, T&T International, NY, 2004.
—*Gnosticism, Judaism and Egyptian Christianity*, Fortress Press,
    2005.
Peden, Alexander J., *The Graffiti of Pharaonic Egypt*, E.J. Brill,
    Leiden, 2001.
The Penny Cyclopaedia, XVIII, Charles Knight and Co., London, 1840.
Pérez-Gómez, Alberto and Parcell, Stephen, eds., *Chora Three:
    Intervals in the Philosophy of Architecture*, McGill-Queen's
    University Press, 1999.
Peters, Absalom, *The American Biblical Repository*, XI, Gould &
    Newman, NY, 1838.
Petrie, W.M. Flinders, *Ancient Egypt and the East*, MacMillan & Co.,
    1914.
—*A History of Egypt*, Methuen & Co., London, 1905.
Philo, *The Works of Philo*, tr. C.D. Yonge, Hendrikson Publishers,
    2000.
—"De Vita Contemplativa" (Greek),
    patrologia.ct.aegean.gr/downloads/vivlia/Philo Judaeus/
Pinch, Geraldine, *Egyptian Mythology: A Guide to the Gods,
    Goddesses and Traditions of Ancient Egypt*, Oxford University
    Press, 2004.
Plato, *Gorgias and Timaeus*, tr. Benjamin Jowett, Courier Dover
    Publications, 2003.
—*The Dialogues of Plato*, tr. Benjamin Jowett, Charles Scribner's
    Sons, 1902
—*The Republic*, tr. Benjamin Jowett,
    classics.mit.edu/Plato/republic.3.ii.html
Pluche, Noël Antoine, *Histoire du Ciel, Où l'on recherche l'origine de
    l'idolatrie*, II, la Veuve Estienne & Fils, Paris, 1748.
Plumley, John Martin, *An Introductory Coptic Grammar*,
    www.metalog.org/files/Plumley.pdf
Plutarch, *De Iside Et Osiride*, tr. John Gwyn Griffiths, University of
    Wales, Cardiff, 1970.
—*The Moralia*, tr. Frank Cole Babbitt, Kessinger, 2005.
—*Plutarch's Lives*, VII, tr. Bernadotte Perrin, Loeb Classical
    Library, 1919,
    penelope.uchicago.edu/Thayer/E/Roman/Texts/Plutarch/Lives/
    Caesar*.html
—"Isis and Osiris," tr. Frank Cole Babbitt,
    penelope.uchicago.edu/Thayer/E/Roman/Texts/Plutarch/
    Moralia/Isis_and_Osiris*/A.html

Poole, Reginald Stuart, *Horae Aegyptiacae: Or, the Chronology of Ancient Egypt, Discovered from Astronomical and Hieroglyphic Records Upon Its Monuments*, John Murray, London, 1851.
Porter, Stanley E., *Hearing the Old Testament in the New Testament*, Wm. B. Eerdmans, 2006.
Porter, Stanley E., Hayes, Michael A. and Tombs, David, *Resurrection*, *Journal for the Study of the New Testament*, Supp. 186, Roehampton Institute London Papers, 1999.
Pratt, David, "Poleshifts," ourworld.compuserve.com/homepages/dp5/pole5.htm#re4
Price, Robert M., "Jonathan Z. Smith: *Drudgery Divine*," *Journal for Higher Criticism*, depts.drew.edu/jhc/jzsmith.html
Price, Theodora Hadzisteliou, *Kourotrophos: Cults and Representations of the Greek Nursing Deities*, E.J. Brill, Leiden, 1978.
Proceedings of the Society for Biblical Archaeology, XI, London, 1889.
—XVIII, London, 1896.
—XXIII, London, 1901.
—XXVII, London, 1905.
Proclus, *Commentary on Plato's Timaeus*, tr. Harold Tarrant, Cambridge University Press, 2007.
—*Procli Diadochi in Platonis Timaeum commentaria*, ed. Ernst Diehl, Lipsiae, In Aedibus B.G. Tevbneri, 1903.
Rahner, Hugo, *Greek Myths and Christian Mystery*, Biblo and Tanner, 1971.
Ranchan, Som P. and Jasta, Hariram, *Folk Tales of Himachal Pradesh*, Bharatiya Vidya Bhavan, 1981.
Raphals, Lisa, *Knowing Words: Wisdom and Cunning in the Classical Traditions of China and Greece*, Cornell University Press, 1992.
Rappoport, S., *History of Egypt: From 330 B.C. to the Present Time*, The Grolier Society Publishers, London, 1904.
Ratzinger, Joseph Cardinal/Pope Benedict XVI, *Introduction to Christianity*, Ignatius Press, 2004.
Rawlinson, George, *History of Ancient Egypt*, I, Longmans, Green, and Co., London, 1881.
—*History of Herodotus*, John Murray, London, 1862.
Ray, John, D., *Reflections of Osiris: Lives from Ancient Egypt*, Oxford University Press, 2002.
Reber, George, *Therapeutae: St. John Never in Asia Minor* (1872), Kessinger, 2003.
Records of the Past, II, ed. Henry Mason Baum and Frederick Bennett Wright, Records of the Past Exploration Society, Washington, 1903.
—VIII, Adamant Media Corporation, London, 2005.
—X, Society of Biblical Archaeology, London, 1874.
—X, Adamant Media Corporation, London, 2001.

Redford, Donald B., ed., *The Ancient Gods Speak: A Guide to Egyptian Religion*, Oxford University Press, Oxford/NY, 2002.

Reed, Joseph D., "Arsinoe's Adonis and the Poetics of Ptolemaic Inscriptions," *Transactions of the American Philological Association*, vol. 130, 2000.

Religious Systems of the World, Swan Sonnenschein & Co., London, 1904.

Renouf, Peter Le Page, *The Egyptian Book of the Dead*, Society of Biblical Archaeology, 1904.

—*The Life-Work of Sir Peter Le Page Renouf*, I, Adamant Media Corporation, 2001.

—"Book of the Dead," *Proceedings of the Society of Biblical Archaeology*, XIV, 1891-1892.

Richardson, Cyril C., tr. & ed., *Early Christian Fathers*, I, Westminster John Knox Press, Philadelphia, 1953.

Richardson, Lawrence, *A New Topographical Dictionary of Ancient Rome*, Johns Hopkins University Press, 1992.

Richardson, Peter, *Building Jewish in the Roman East*, Baylor University Press, TX, 2004.

Rice, Michael, *Who's Who in Ancient Egypt*, Routledge, 2001.

Riel, Carl, *Das Sonnen- Und Siriusjahr der Ramessiden*, F.A. Brockhaus, Leipzig, 1875.

Riley, Mark, "Q.S. Fl. Tertulliani Adversus Valentinianos Text, Translation, and Commentary," www.tertullian.org/articles/riley_adv_val/riley_00_index.htm

Roberts, Alexander and Donaldson, James, eds., *Ante-Nicene Christian Library: Translations of the Writings of the Fathers Down to A.D. 325*, II, T and T Clark, Edinburgh, 1867.

—*Ante-Nicene Christian Library*, XI, T&T Clark, Edinburgh, 1869.

—*Ante-Nicene Christian Library*, XII, T&T Clark, Edinburgh, 1869.

—*Ante-Nicene Fathers: Translations of the Writings of the Fathers down to A.D. 325*, I, The Christian Literature Publishing Company, Buffalo, 1885.

—*Ante-Nicene Fathers*, III, Charles Scribner's Sons, NY, 1903.

—*Ante-Nicene Fathers*, IV, Charles Scribner's Sons, NY, 1926.

—*Ante-Nicene Fathers*, VII, The Christian Literature Company, NY, 1890.

—*Ante-Nicene Fathers*, VIII, Charles Scribner's Sons, NY, 1903.

Robertson, John M., *Christianity and Mythology*, Watts & Co., London, 1900.

Robinson, James M., *The Nag Hammadi Library in English*, E.J. Brill, Leiden, 1984.

Rosmorduc, Serge, "Late Egyptian: The Writing System," webperso.iut.univ-paris8.fr/~rosmord/Qenherkhepeshef/intro2.html

Rothschild, Clare K., *Baptist Traditions and Q*, Mohr Siebeck, 2005.

Roukema, Riemer, *The Interpretation of Exodus*, Peeters, Leuven, 2006.

Rousseau, John J. and Arav, Rami, *Jesus and His World*, Fortress Press, 1995.

Ruffle, John, *The Egyptians: An Introduction to Egyptian Archaeology*, Cornell University Press, NY, 1977.

Ruggles, Clive, *Ancient Astronomy: An Encyclopedia of Cosmologies and Myth*, ABC-CLIO, 2005.

—*Astronomy in Prehistoric Britain and Ireland*, Yale University Press, 1999.

—ed., *Records in Stone: Papers in Memory of Alexander Thom*, Cambridge University Press, 2003.

Ruiz, Ana, *The Spirit of Ancient Egypt*, Algora Publishing, 2001.

Runia, David T., *Philo in Early Christian Literature: A Survey*, Van Gorcum Fortress Press, Amsterdam, 1993.

Russell, Jeffrey Burton, *The Prince of Darkness: Radical Evil and the Power of Good in History*, Cornell University Press, 1988.

Saint-Hilaire, J. Barthélemy, *Egypt and the Great Suez Canal: A Narrative of Travels*, Richard Bentley, London, 1857.

Salmond, S.D.F., ed., *The Critical Review of Theological & Philosophical Literature*, VI, T. & T. Clark, Edinburgh, 1896.

Salzman, Michelle Renee, *The Codex-Calendar of 354 and the Rhythms of Urban Life in Late Antiquity*, University of California Press, 1990.

Sayce, A.H., *Lectures on the Origin and Growth of Religion (The Hibbert Lectures, 1887)*, Williams and Norgate, London, 1897.

—*The Religion of Ancient Egypt*, Kessinger, 2004.

Schäfer, Peter and Kippenberg, Hans G., *Envisioning Magic: A Princeton Seminar & Symposium*, E.J. Brill, 1997.

Schaff, Phillip and Wace Henry, *A Select Library of Nicene and Post-Nicene Fathers of the Christian Church*, I, Parker & Company, 1890.

— *A Select Library of Nicene and Post-Nicene Fathers of the Christian Church*, III, Parker & Company, London/NY, 1892.

— *A Select Library of Nicene and Post-Nicene Fathers of the Christian Church*, VI, Parker & Company, London/NY, 1893.

— *A Select Library of Nicene and Post-Nicene Fathers of the Christian Church*, VII, Parker & Company, 1893.

Schemann, Hans and Knight, Paul, *English-German Dictionary of Idioms*, Routledge, 1997

Schmidt, Carl and MacDermot, Violet, *The Books of Jeu and the Untitled Text in the Bruce Codex*, E.J. Brill, Leiden, 1978.

Schmidt, Orlando P., *A Self-verifying Chronological History of Ancient Egypt*, George C. Shaw, OH, 1900.

Schure, Edouard, *The Great Initiates*, Kessinger, 2003.

Schwartz, Howard, *The Tree of Souls: The Mythology of Judaism*, Oxford University Press, 2004.

Sciortino, Paul, "Hieroglyphs.net," www.hieroglyphs.net
Scott, Kenneth, "The Role of Basilides in the Events of A.D. 69," *The Journal of Roman Studies*, vol. 24, 1934.
Scouteris, Constantine, "The Therapeutae of Philo and the Monks as Therapeutae according to Pseudo-Dionysius," www.orthodoxresearchinstitute.org/articles/patrology/scouteris_theraputae.htm
Seawright, Caroline, "Nit (Neith], Goddess of Weaving, War, Hunting, etc.," www.touregypt.net/featurestories/nit.htm
—"Satet, Archer-Goddess of the Inundation and the Nile Cataracts," www.touregypt.net/featurestories/satet.htm
Seeberg, Reinhold, *Der Apologet Aristides: Der Text seiner uns erhalten Schriften, Erlangen und Leipzig*, 1894.
Segal, Alan, F., *Two Powers in Heaven: Early Rabbinic Reports about Christianity and Gnosticism*, E.J. Brill, Leiden, 1977.
Sellers, Jane, *The Death of Gods in Ancient Egypt*, Lulu, 2003.
Senn, Frank C., *Christian Liturgy: Catholic and Evangelical*, Fortress Press, MN, 1997.
The Septuagint, septuagint.org/LXX/search_lxx.pl
Sharpe, Samuel, *Egyptian Antiquities in the British Museum*, John Russell Smith, London, 1862.
—*Egyptian Hieroglyphics: An Attempt to Explain Their Nature, Origin and Meaning*, London, Edward Moxon and Co., 1861.
—*Egyptian Mythology and Egyptian Christianity: With Their Influence on the Opinions of Modern Christendom*, John Russell Smith, London, 1863.
—*Historic Notes on the Books of the Old and New Testaments*, Smith, Elder and Co., London, 1858.
Shaw, David, "Gerald Massey: A Biography," www.gerald-massey.org.uk/massey/index.htm
—"Gerald Massey: Chartist, Poet, Radical and Freethinker," gerald-massey.org.uk/Massey/biog_contents.htm
Shuchat, Wilfred, *The Garden of Eden & the Struggle to be Human: According to the Midrash Rabbah*, Devora Publishing, 2006.
Silver, Morris, *Taking Ancient Mythology Economically*, E.J. Brill, 1992.
Silverman, David P., Wegner, Josef W. and Wegner, Jennifer Houser, *Akhenaten & Tutankhamun: Revolution and Restoration*, University of Pennsylvania, 2006.
Simpson, Shepherd, "Dendera Zodiacs," www.geocities.com/astrologysources/classicalegypt/dendera/
Singh, Madanjeet, *The Sun: Symbol of Power and Life*, Harry N. Abrams, NY, 1993.
Sly, Dorothy, *Philo's Alexandria*, Routledge, 1996.
Smith, Jonathan Z., "Dying and Rising Gods," *The Encyclopedia of Religion*, vol. 4, MacMillan Publishing Company, 1987.

Smith, Philip, *The Ancient History of the East*, John Murray, London, 1876.

Smith, R. Scott and Trzaskoma, Stephen M., trs., *Apollodorus' Library and Hyginus' Fabulae: Two Handbooks of Greek Mythology*, Hackett Publishing Company, Inc., Indianapolis/Cambridge, 2007.

Smith, William Robertson, *Lectures on the Religion of the Semites*, Adam and Charles Black, London, 1907.

Smith, William and Wace, Henry, eds., *A Dictionary of Christian Biography, Literature, Sects and Doctrines*, III, John Murray, London, 1882.

Solar Physics, vol. 245, no. 2 (10/07), Springer Netherlands, 2007.

Sophocles, *Antigone*, ed. Martin L. D'Ooge, Ginn & Company, Boston, 1890.

Southern, Pat, *The Roman Empire from Severus to Constantine*, Routledge, London/NY, 2001

Spear, Athena T., *Brancusi's Birds*, New York University Press for the College Art Association of America, 1969.

Spence, Lewis, *Ancient Egyptian Myths and Legends*, Dover, NY, 1990.

—*An Encyclopedia of Occultism*, Courier Dover, 2003.

Staniforth, Maxwell, tr., Early Christian Writings, Penguin Books, 1988.

Stanton, Graham N., *Jesus and Gospel*, Cambridge University Press, 2004.

Stathis, Stephen W., "CRS Report for Congress: Federal Holidays: Evolution and Application," www.senate.gov/reference/resources/pdf/Federal_Holidays.pdf

St. Clair, George, "Early Background of Scripture Thought," *The Homiletic Review*, L, Funk and Wagnalls Company, NY/London, 1905.

Steinmetz, George, *The Lost Word: Its Hidden Meaning*, Kessinger, 2006.

Stone, Merlin, *When God Was a Woman*, Barnes & Noble, NY, 1976.

Strabo, *The Geography of Strabo*, III, tr. H.C. Hamilton, George Bell & Sons, London, 1889.

—*The Geography*, VIII, G.P. Putnam's Sons, NY, 1923.

—*The Geography*, Loeb Classical Library, penelope.uchicago.edu/Thayer/E/Roman/Texts/Strabo/home.html

Strange, Thomas Lumisden, *The Legends of the Old Testament*, Trubner & Co., London, 1874.

Strauss, David Friedrich, *The Life of Jesus, Critically Examined*, tr. George Eliot, Swan Sonnenschein & Co., London, 1892.

Strobel, Lee, *The Case for the Real Jesus*, Zondervan, 2007.

Strong, James H., *Strong's Exhaustive Concordance*, Baker Book House, 1985; www.blueletterbible.org.

Stuart, H. Villiers, *Egypt After the War*, John Murray, London, 1883.

Suetonius, *Suetonius*, II, tr. J.C. Rolfe, Putnam's Sons, 1920.
—*The Lives of the Twelve Caesars*, tr. Alexander Thomson, ed. T.
    Forester, George Bell & Sons, London, 1893.
Tacitus, The Works of, II, Oxford Translation, Henry G. Bohn, London,
    1854.
Tacheva-Hitova, Margarita, *Eastern Cults in Moesia Inferior and
    Thracia*, E.J. Brill, Leiden, 1983.
Talley, Thomas J., *The Origins of the Liturgical Year*, Liturgical Press,
    1991.
Taylor, Gary, *Castration: An Abbreviated History of Western Manhood*,
    Routledge, 2002.
Taylor, J. Glen, *Yahweh and the Sun: Biblical and Archaeological
    Evidence for Sun Worship in Ancient Israel*, Sheffield Academic
    Press, 1994.
Taylor, Joan E., *Jewish Women Philosophers of First-Century
    Alexandria: Philo's 'Therapeutae Reconsidered,'* Oxford University
    Press, 2003.
Taylor, John H., *Death and the Afterlife in Ancient Egypt*, University of
    Chicago Press, 2001.
Temporini, Hildegard, ed., *Aufstieg und Niedergang der römischen
    Welt*, Walter de Gruyter, Berlin, 1973.
—*Aufstieg und Niedergang der römischen Welt*, II, Walter de
    Gruyter, Berlin/NY, 1984.
Tertullian, *Ad Nationes*, I, www.newadvent.org/fathers/03061.htm
—*Adversus Valentinianos*,
    www.tertullian.org/articles/riley_adv_val/riley_02_text.htm
—*Against the Valentinians*, tr. Dr. Roberts,
    www.newadvent.org/fathers/0314.htm
—*Apology*, www.newadvent.org/fathers/0301.htm
—*On Baptism*, Kessinger, 2004.
—"On Baptism," www.newadvent.org/fathers/0321.htm
—"The Chaplet," www.newadvent.org/fathers/0304.htm
te Velde, Herman, *Seth, God of Confusion: A Study of His Role in
    Egyptian Mythology and Religion*, E.J. Brill, 1977.
Theissen, Gerd and Merz, Annette, *The Historical Jesus: A
    Comprehensive Guide*, Fortress Press, Minneapolis, 1998.
Thesaurus Linguae Graecae: A Digital Library of Greek Literature,
    www.tlg.uci.edu
Thomson, Arthur Dyot, *On Mankind: Their Origin and Destiny*,
    Longmans Green, 1872.
Thorburn, Thomas James, *The Mythical Interpretation of the Gospels*,
    Charles Scribner's Sons, NY, 1916.
Tiele, Cornelius P., *History of the Egyptian Religion*, tr. James
    Ballingal, Trubner & Co., London, 1882.
—*Outlines of the History of Religion to the Spread of the Universal
    Religions*, tr. J. Estlin Carpenter, Kegan Paul, Trench, Trubner &
    Co., London, 1905.

Titcomb, Sarah, *Aryan Sun Myths*, Kessinger, 2005.
Török, Laszlo, *The Image of the Ordered World in Ancient Nubian Art*, E.J. Brill, Leiden, 2002.
—*The Kingdom of Kush*, E.J. Brill, Leiden/NY/Koln, 1997.
Tozer, H.F., *Selections from Strabo*, Clarendon Press, Oxford, 1893.
Transactions of the Society of Biblical Archaeology, II, Longmans, Green, Reader, and Dyer, London, 1873.
—V, Longmans, Green, Reader, and Dyer, London, 1877.
—VI, Harrison & Sons, London, 1878.
Traunecker, Claude, *The Gods of Egypt*, tr. David Lorton, Cornell University Press, NY, 2001.
Tronzo, William, *St. Peter's in the Vatican*, Cambridge University Press, 2005.
Trumbower, Jeffrey A., *Rescue for the Dead: The Posthumous Salvation of Non-Christians in Early Christianity*, Oxford University Press, 2001.
Tsetskhladze, G.R., ed., *Ancient West & East*, vol. 3, no. 2, E.J. Brill, Leiden/Boston, 2004.
Turcan, Robert, *The Cults of the Roman Empire*, Blackwell Publishers, Oxford, 2000.
Tvedtnes, John A., "John the Baptist," www.meridianmagazine.com/gospeldoctrine/nt/070119nt4sf.html
Ulansey, David, *The Origins of the Mithraic Mysteries: Cosmology & Salvation in the Ancient World*, Oxford University Press, 1989.
The University Magazine: A Literary and Philosophic Review, II, Hurst & Blackett, London, 1878.
Unwin, Tim, *Wine and the Vine: An Historical Geography of Viticulture and the Wine Trade*, Routledge, 1996.
Uphill, Eric, "The Egyptian Sed-Festival Rites," *Journal of Near Eastern Studies*, vol. 24, no. 4, 1965.
Urban, Sylvanus, ed., *The Gentleman's Magazine and Historical Review,* John Henry and James Parker, London, 1865.
van Binsbergen, Wim M.J., "Skulls and tears: Identifying and analysing an African fantasy space extending over 5000 kilometres and across 5000 years" (1998), www.shikanda.net/ancient_models/fantasy_space_2006_expanded.pdf
van den Broek, R., *The Myth of the Phoenix, According to Classical and Early Christian Traditions*, E. J. Brill, Leiden, 1972.
van den Broek, R. and Vermaseren, M.J., *Studies in Gnosticism and Hellenistic Religions*, E.J. Brill, Leiden, 1981.
van den Hoek, Annewies, *Clement of Alexandria and His Use of Philo in the Stromateis*, E.J. Brill, Leiden, 1988.
van der Horst, Pieter Willem, *Chaeremon, Egyptian Priest and Stoic Philosopher: The Fragments Collected*, E.J. Brill, Leiden, 1984.

van der Toorn, Karel, Becking, Bob and van der Horst, Pieter W., eds., *Dictionary of Deities and Demons in the Bible*, Wm. B. Eerdmans, 1999.

van Dijk, Jacobus, *Essays on Ancient Egypt in Honour of Herman te Velde*, Styx Publications/Brill, 1997.

Van Doren, W.H., *A Suggestive Commentary on the New Testament*, R.D. Dickinson, London, 1871.

Van Zyl, J.E., *Unveiling the Universe*, Springer, 1996.

Vassilika, Eleni, *Ptolemaic Philae*, Uitgeverij Peeters, Leuven, 1989.

Verbrugghe, Gerald and Wickersham, John Moore, *Berossos and Manetho, Introduced and Translated: Native Traditions in Ancient Mesopotamia and Egypt*, University of Michigan Press, 1996.

Vervloesem, Filip, "Egyptologie," www.filipvervloesem.be/egyptologie.html

Vetterling, Herman, *Illuminate of Gorlitz Or Jakob Bohme's Life and Philosophy*, Part 3, Kessinger, 2003.

Villien, Al and Edwards, H.W., *History and Liturgy of the Sacraments*, Kessinger, 2003.

Volney, C.F., *The Ruins or a Survey of the Revolutions of Empires*, S. Shaw, Albany, 1822.

Voltaire, *Oeuvres Completes de Voltaire*, 7, Librairie de L. Hachette, Paris, 1859.

von Balthasar, Hans Urs, *The Christian State of Life*, tr. Mary F. McCarthy, Ignatius Press, 1983.

von Mosheim, John Lawrence, *Institutes of Ecclesiastical History, Ancient and Modern*, I, Harper & Brothers, NY, 1847.

Vos, Mariette and Arnold de, *L'Egittomania in Pitture E Mosaici Romano-Campani Della Prima Eta Imperiale*, E.J. Brill, Leiden, 1980.

Vos, R.L., *The Apis Embalming Ritual*, Peeters Publishers, Leuven, 1993.

Waite, Charles, *History of the Christian Religion to the Year Two Hundred*, C.V. Waite & Co., 1900.

Walker, Barbara, *The Woman's Encyclopedia of Myths and Secrets*, Harper San Francisco, 1983.

Walsh, William S., *Heroes and Heroines of Fiction*, J.B. Lippincott Company, Philadelphia, 1915.

Ward, C. Osborne, *The Ancient Lowly: A History of the Ancient Working People*, Charles H. Kerr & Company, Chicago, 1900.

Webster's II New College Dictionary, Third Edition, Houghton Mifflin, Boston/NY, 2005.

Weekley, Ernest, *An Etymological Dictionary of Modern English*, vol. 1, Dover, Toronto, 1967.

Weigall, Arthur E.P., *A Guide to the Antiquities of Upper Egypt*, The MacMillan Company, NY, 1910.

—*Paganism in Our Christianity*, Kessinger, 2003.

Weil, Simone, *The Notebooks of Simone Weil*, Routledge, 2004.

Weinstock, Stefan, "A New Greek Calendar and Festivals of the Sun," *The Journal of Roman Studies*, vol. 38, Parts 1 & 2, 1948.

Wells, G.A., *Can We Trust the New Testament?*, Open Court, 2004.

—"Stages of New Testament Criticism," *Journal of the History of Ideas*, vol. 30, no. 2, Apr-Jun 1969.

West, John Anthony, *Serpent in the Sky*, Quest, 1993.

—*The Traveler's Key to Ancient Egypt*, Quest Books, 1995.

West, M.L., *The East Face of Helicon: West Asiatic Elements in Greek Poetry and Myth*, Oxford University Press, 1999.

Wheeler, Edward J., ed., *Index of Current Literature*, XL, The Current Literature Publishing Company, NY, 1906.

White, L. Michael, *From Jesus to Christianity*, Harper Collins, 2004.

White, T.H., ed., *The Book of Beasts*, Courier Dover Publications, 1984.

Whitehouse, David, "Library of Alexandria Discovered," news.bbc.co.uk/2/hi/science/nature/3707641.stm

Whitney, Annie Weston, "Del los' ell an' Yard," *The Journal of American Folklore*, vol. 10, no. 39, Oct-Dec 1897.

Wiedemann, Alfred, *Religion of the Ancient Egyptians*, H. Grevel & Co., London, 1897.

Wiener Zeitschrift für die Kunde des Morgenlandes, Lemck & Buechner, 1982.

Wilkinson, John Gardner, *Hand-book for Travellers in Egypt*, John Murray, London, 1847.

—*The Manners and Customs of the Ancient Egyptians*, III, ed. Samuel Birch, John Murray, London, 1878.

— *The Manners and Customs of the Ancient Egyptians*, V, John Murray, London, 1847.

—*A Popular Account of the Ancient Egyptians*, II, John Murray, London, 1878.

—*A Second Series of the Manners and Customs of the Ancient Egyptians*, John Murray, London, 1841.

Wilkinson, Toby A. H., *Early Dynastic Egypt*, Routledge, 1999.

Willems, Harco, ed., *The Coffin of Heqata (Cairo Jde 36418). A Case Study of Egyptian Funerary Culture of the Early Middle Kingdom*, Peters Publishing, 1995.

—*Social Aspects of Funerary Culture in the Egyptian Old and Middle Kingdoms*, Peters, Leuven, 2001.

Williams, Michael Allen, *The Immovable Race: A Gnostic Designation and the Theme of Stability in Late Antiquity*, E.J. Brill, Leiden, 1985.

Williamson, William, *The Great Law: A Study of Religious Origins and of the Unity Underlying Them*, Longmans, Green & Co., New York, 1899.

Wilshire, Donna, *Virgin Mother Crone: Myths & Mysteries of the Triple Goddess*, Inner Traditions, Vermont, 1993.

Wilson, Epiphanius, *Egyptian Literature: Comprising Egyptian Tales, Hymns, Litanies, Invocations*, The Colonial Press, 1901.

Wilson, John A., *The Culture of Ancient Egypt*, University of Chicago Press, 1956.

Wilson, Robert, *Astronomy Through the Ages*, Taylor & Francis, 1997.

Winston, David, *Philo of Alexandria: The Contemplative Life, The Giants, And Selections*, Paulist Press, 1981.

Witt, Reginald E., *Isis in the Ancient World*, Johns Hopkins University Press, 1997.

Wolfe, Rolland E., *How the Easter Story Grew from Gospel to Gospel*, Edwin Mellen Press, NY, 1989.

Woodard, Roger D., *The Ancient Languages of Mesopotamia, Egypt, and Aksum*, Cambridge University Press, 2008.

Woodbridge, Sally Byrne, *Details: The Architect's Art*, Chronicle Books, 1991.

The World Book Encyclopedia, World Book, Inc., 1993.

Wren, Linnea H. and Wren, David J., *Perspectives on Western Art*, Westview Press, 1987.

Yarker, John, *The Arcane Schools*, Triad Press, 2006.

Žabkar, Louis V., *Hymns to Isis in Her Temple at Philae*, Brandeis University Press, 1988.

Zitman, Willem H., *Egypt: "Image of Heaven,"* Adventures Unlimited Press, IL, 2006.

Index

Every effort has been taken to make this index as useful and complete as possible. In consideration of space, however, included references with over 50 entries are indicated with the notation *"See throughout book."*

D.M. Murdock, also known as "Acharya S," majored in Classics, Greek Civilization, at Franklin & Marshal College in Lancaster, PA. She is also a Member of the American School of Classical Studies at Athens, Greece. Ms. Murdock is the author of the controversial books *The Christ Conspiracy: The Greatest Story Ever Sold*; *Suns of God: Krishna, Buddha and Christ Unveiled*; and *Who Was Jesus? Fingerprints of The Christ*. Murdock's books and many of her articles on the subjects of comparative religion, mythology and astrotheology can be found on her websites TruthBeKnown.com, StellarHousePublishing.com and FreethoughtNation.com.

Breinigsville, PA USA
18 November 2010
249524BV00003B/79/P

9 780979 963117